Master the™ Catholic High School Exams 2021

PETERSON'S®

About Peterson's®

Peterson's has been your trusted educational publisher for over 50 years. It's a milestone we're quite proud of, as we continue to offer the most accurate, dependable, high-quality educational content in the field, providing you with everything you need to succeed. No matter where you are on your academic or professional path, you can rely on Peterson's for its books, online information, expert test-prep tools, the most up-to-date education exploration data, and the highest quality career success resources—everything you need to achieve your education goals. For our complete line of products, visit **www.petersons.com.**

For more information, contact Peterson's, 8740 Lucent Blvd., Suite 400, Highlands Ranch, CO 80129; 800-338-3282 Ext. 54229; or visit us online at **www.petersons.com.**

Peterson's Updates and Corrections

Check out our website at **https://petersonsbooks.com/updates-and-corrections/** to see if there is any new information regarding the test and any revisions or corrections to the content of this book. You should also carefully read the material you receive from the Archdiocese when you register for the test. We've made sure the information in this book is accurate and up to date; however, the test format or content may have changed since the time of publication.

Contents

PART III: VERBAL SKILLS

PART IV: QUANTITATIVE AND NONVERBAL SKILLS

PART V: SIX PRACTICE TESTS

PART VI: APPENDIXES

Credits

Excerpt from *A Christmas Carol,* by Charles Dickens

Excerpt from *Rip Van Winkle,* by Washington Irving

Excerpt from *The Nightingale,* by Hans Christian Andersen

The Rhodora, by Ralph Waldo Emerson

Anne of Green Gables, by Lucy Maud Montgomery

"The Moon," by Emily Dickinson

Around the World in Eighty Days, by Jules Verne

The Adventures of Tom Sawyer, by Mark Twain

Excerpt from *Mysterious Island,* by Jules Verne

"April's Charms," by William H. Davies

Excerpt from *Pennsylvania Dutch Cooking,* by Unknown

Excerpt from *The Outline of Science,* Vol. 1, by J. Arthur Thomson

Excerpt from *White Fang,* by Jack London

Excerpt from *The Colors of Animals,* by Sir John Lubbock

Excerpt from *American Leaders and Heroes: A preliminary text-book in United States History,* by Wilbur F. Gordy

Excerpt adapted from *The Book of Tea,* by Kakuzo Okakura

Excerpt from *Mountaineering in the Sierra Nevada,* by Clarence King

Excerpt from *The Story of Napoleon,* by Harold F. B. Wheeler

Before You Begin

WHY YOU SHOULD USE THIS BOOK

If you're graduating from junior high or middle school and exploring your options for high school, it's an exciting time in your life. This may be your first opportunity to make a big decision about your education—and if you're reading this book, you're taking that responsibility seriously.

You may have a few target schools in mind and, because you have this book in your hands, it's likely that you're considering continuing your education at a Catholic high school. If that's true, then you also know that an essential part of getting into the Catholic high school of your choice is taking and passing an entrance exam.

While some students have no fear of important, high-stakes exams like the TACHS (Test for Admission into Catholic High Schools) and the HSPT® (High School Placement Test)—the two most commonly used Catholic high school entrance exams—other students can use a confidence boost and a bit more help to make sure they are a step ahead of the competition on test day.

If this sounds like you, then fear not—you've come to the right place and are using the right book!

Peterson's *Master the™ Catholic High School Entrance Exams* is designed by test experts and educators to fully prepare you for test-day success, regardless of which entrance exam you're preparing to take. This helpful guide includes the following:

- **Essential test information:** We take the stress out of planning for your entrance exam by providing all the information you'll need to know before the big day in one place—including how to decide which test is right for you, to how to register, where to go, and even what to bring on the day of the exam. We've got you covered!

- **Comprehensive coverage of the TACHS and HSPT® test formats:** After using this book, you'll know the structure and format of your exam from start to finish and have all the information you'll need for success on test day.

- **Thorough test topic review:** You'll get a thorough review of *every topic* tested on the TACHS and HSPT and help creating an effective study plan for reaching your goal score. So not only will there be *no surprises* on test day, you'll have the confidence of knowing that you're thoroughly prepared to tackle the exam.

- **Plenty of realistic test question practice:** Every topic chapter in this book contains realistic practice with questions just like those you'll encounter during the actual exam. In addition, you can customize your preparation based on your target test. Take a full-length diagnostic exam for either the TACHS or the HSPT to help you determine your strengths and weaknesses and target your study time effectively, then build your confidence with 4 (3 in the book and 1 online) full-length practice exams for each test that you can use to strengthen your test skills and get comfortable with the timing and pace of the actual exams. There's no better way to practice for the big day!

- **Expert tips, advice, and strategies:** We *know* what it takes to get a top score on the TACHS and HSPT—you'll get the expert tools that have proven to be effective on exam day, putting you a step ahead of the test-taking competition. Consider this your *inside edge* as you prepare to conquer your entrance exam!

We *know* that doing well on your Catholic high school entrance exam is important, both to you and your family—and we're here to help you through *every step* of your journey. Consider this book your all-in-one test preparation package, to get you through the exam and on your way to the Catholic high school of your choice.

HOW THIS BOOK IS ORGANIZED

This book is divided into six parts that can help you with your preparation. Use **Part I** to learn more about each exam type and how it's scored. You'll find examples of typical questions from each exam. Take the diagnostic test for the TACHS or HSPT in **Part II** to determine your strengths and weaknesses so you can best plan your test preparation. Use **Part III** to review the verbal skills sections of the TACHS and HSPT exams, such as analogies, verbal logic, reading, and composition. Use **Part IV** to review quantitative and nonverbal skills, such as mathematics and ability questions. **Part V** includes practice exams for the TACHS and the HSPT. The **Appendix** section includes a word list and a useful synonyms/antonyms list to help boost your test-prep confidence on the Language Arts sections of the admissions tests. It also includes a useful summary sheet of math formulas that you can tear out and review throughout your day.

HOW TO USE THIS BOOK

Diagnostic Test Method

One way to use this book is to start with a diagnostic test for the TACHS or HSPT. A diagnostic test is a test that helps you understand your strengths and weaknesses on the exam. It "diagnoses" the skills that need the most improvement.

In this method, you take a diagnostic test first, and then you use the results of your test to develop a study plan. Use one of the diagnostic tests in Part II, Chapter 4. This test will give you a sampling of the kinds of questions you are likely to see on your test, and it will show you where you might need to focus your test-prep efforts.

Once you've taken your diagnostic test, score yourself to see your strengths and weaknesses. How did you do? Make a list of your strong and weak areas. If you scored well on math but poorly on verbal skills, then you can count math as a strength. Your verbal skills, on the other hand, will need some work. Rank the different sections in terms of your strongest and weakest skills.

Use your ranking list to develop your study plan. Your plan should prioritize boosting your weaker skills. You don't need to spend as much time brushing up on your strengths. However, you should plan to spend *some* time on "strong skills" exercises—just to stay in shape.

Once you've got a study plan, put it to work. Read the introduction to your test in Part I. Then, focus on improving your weak skills by studying the sections in Parts III and IV. After you've reviewed the content sections, take a practice test in Part V. This test should show an improvement in your score!

Front-to-Back Method

Another way to use this book is the front-to-back method. In this method, you work through the book the way it is organized.

Start at Part I of the book and carefully read through the introductory section on your exam. This will help you understand the exam and how it's scored. Next, study the content sections in Parts III and IV. Focus on the sections that relate to your exam. If you know your strong and weak skills, you might devote extra time to sections where you need the most improvement.

After you've reviewed the content, take a practice test or two in Part V. Even taking one test will help you be more prepared for exam day. Sometimes, the process of taking the test itself can help increase your score. This is because you become more familiar with the test, which increases your confidence.

After you complete each test, review your answers with the explanations provided. If you still don't understand how to answer a certain question, you might ask a teacher for help. A review session with a friend might prove helpful, too.

The expert subject review and skill-specific exercises in Peterson's *Master the™ Catholic High School Exams* can help familiarize you with the unique content, structure, and format of the test. Test-taking tips and advice guide you smoothly from your first day of test preparation to test day.

In addition, taking online practice tests is desirable because you get immediate feedback and automated scoring. *Peterson's Master the™ Catholic High School Exams* gives you access to not only the tests in this book, but access to additional practice tests online, with detailed feedback to help you understand the concepts presented. The content in these practice tests was created by the test-prep experts at Peterson's to help you boost your test-prep confidence. You can access the TACHS and HSPT practice tests at www.petersons.com/testprep/product/master-the-catholic-high-school-entrance-exams-online-book-component. Use coupon code MTC2021 for complimentary access with the purchase of this book.

NOTE

You have the option to take the practice tests either in the book or online. For more information, go to **www.petersons. com/testprep**.

> **Important:** Usage of the coupon code to access online content is intended for the original purchaser of the book and not for resellers or library patrons. Access will expire 18 months after the copyright date printed in this title.

WHAT TO STUDY: TACHS AND HSPT®

Parts III and IV of this book provide TACHS and HSPT content for you to review. Use the table below to determine which chapters to study for your test.

Chapter #	Title	TACHS	HSPT®
	Part III: Verbal Skills		
6	Synonyms	X	X
7	Antonyms		X
8	Analogies		X
9	Logic		X
10	Reading	X	X
11	Spelling	X	
12	Punctuation and Capitalization	X	X
13	Usage	X	X
14	Composition and Expression	X	X
	Part IV: Quantitative and Nonverbal Skills		
15	Mathematics	X	X
16	Series Reasoning		X
17	Comparisons and Ability Questions	X	X

SPECIAL STUDY FEATURES

You will find the following kinds of special study features scattered throughout the book:

Overview

Each chapter begins with a bulleted overview listing the topics to be covered in the chapter. This will allow you to quickly target the areas in which you are most interested.

Summing It Up

Each chapter ends with a point-by-point summary that captures the most important points contained in the chapter. This provides a convenient way to review key points.

 Tips point out valuable information you need to know when taking the TACHS and HSPT exams. Tips provide quick and simple hints for selecting the correct answers for the most common question types.

 Alerts identify potential pitfalls in the testing format or question types that can cause common mistakes in selecting answers.

Notes address information about the test structure itself.

 Cautions provide warnings, such as common grammatical errors or possible errors in computation or formulas that can result in choosing incorrect answers.

Word List and List of Synonyms and Antonyms

Questions that require a robust knowledge of vocabulary appear throughout both of these exams. The broader, more varied, and more accurate your vocabulary knowledge, the better your chances of answering questions quickly and correctly. To help you with this task, we've put together a list of about 500 commonly used words that may appear on your exam, including hundreds of related words—words that are variants of the primary words or words that share a common word root. We've also included a list of synonyms and antonyms for many of the terms on the word list as well as additional terms. You'll find the word list and the list of synonyms and antonyms at the back of the book. We hope they will enhance your vocabulary study for any of the Catholic high school entrance exams. You will also find a convenient tear-out sheet of math and geometry formulas to help you with memorization.

Looking for Additional Practice? Check out Peterson's Test Prep Subscriptions

Our subscription plans allow you to study as quickly as you can, or as slowly as you'd like. How does it work? Subscribers get unlimited usage of our entire test prep catalogue for over 150 exams, including important exams for students preparing for high school entrance exams like the TACHS, HSPT, SSAT, and ISEE. For more information, go to **www.petersons.com/testprep/high-school-entrance-exams**.

GIVE US YOUR FEEDBACK

Peterson's publishes a full line of books—test prep, career preparation, education exploration, and financial aid. Peterson's publications can be found at high school guidance offices, college libraries and career centers, and your local bookstore and library. Peterson's books are also available for purchase online at **petersons.com**.

We welcome any comments or suggestions you may have about this publication. Your feedback will help us make education dreams possible for you—and others like you.

YOU'RE WELL ON YOUR WAY TO SUCCESS

Remember that knowledge is power. By using this book you will be studying the most comprehensive guide available.

The *first step* to acing your high school entrance exam is to know the structure and format of the exam you're going to take inside and out, including all the basics you need to know.

We *know* you're eager to get to the test practice and review, but having a thorough understanding of the exam from top to bottom will give you a real advantage—and put you ahead of the test-taking competition. We'll go carefully through each exam—the TACHS and the HSPT®—and guide you through each step so you'll be confident and prepared for test day success. Let's get started!

TOP 10 WAYS TO RAISE YOUR SCORE

When it comes to taking your entrance exam, some test-taking skills will do you more good than others. There are concepts you can learn, techniques you can follow, and tricks you can use that will help you to do your very best. Here are our picks for the top 10 ways to raise your score:

1. **Regardless of which plan you will follow, get started by reading Part I to familiarize yourself with the test formats.**

2. **Make sure to complete the exercises in each chapter you read.**

3. **When you are one third of the way through your preparation, take a practice test.** Make sure you are applying new test-taking strategies.

4. **It's a good idea to have a dictionary nearby while taking the practice test or studying the review sections of this book.** If you come across a word you don't know, circle it and look it up later.

5. **Revisit problematic chapters and chapter summaries.**

6. **After you have completed all the study sections, take your second practice test.** You should find the second practice test much easier now, and, after your study and practice, you should be able to answer more questions than you could on the first practice test.

7. **If you have the time, you might find it instructive to take the practice tests for the other exams.** For example, if you're required to take the TACHS, you might also test yourself with the HSPT® exam.

8. **During the last phase of your study, review the practice tests.**

9. **Be sure to read the test-taking techniques in Chapter 3 for additional tips to help you on the day of the exam.**

10. **The night before your exam, RELAX.** You'll be prepared.

PART I
TACKLING THE EXAMS

All About the New York City Test for Admission into Catholic High Schools (TACHS)

OVERVIEW

- **Registering for the TACHS**
- **TACHS Format and Focus**
- **TACHS Test Day Checklist**
- **Summing It Up**

The Test for Admission into Catholic High Schools (TACHS) is the entrance test for eighth-grade students who want to attend a Catholic high school in the Diocese of Brooklyn/Queens or Archdiocese of New York City. The TACHS is a multiple-choice exam that lasts about 2 hours, including time to give directions. There are no breaks during the TACHS.

If you are currently in the eighth grade and plan to attend a Catholic high school in this area, you'll take the TACHS exam as part of your admissions application. If, however, you plan to enter a school in this area as a tenth, eleventh, or twelfth grader, you *don't need* to take the TACHS. Instead, you'll apply directly to the high school you wish to attend.

Along with your school records, your TACHS score is sent to the principals of up to three high schools that you're applying to, so they can make an admissions decision. Unlike the ACT and SAT, the official TACHS Handbook says **you may take the TACHS only once.** This is an important test, but don't worry—we'll help you fully prepare for it!

1

REGISTERING FOR THE TACHS

There are two ways to register for the TACHS:

1. **Online**—Visit **http://www.tachsinfo.com/howtoregister.aspx** to register online. This process is open to students, parents, guardians, and principals. This is the preferred method of registration, as there is no waiting involved. After you're registered, you can have your confirmation instantly emailed to you. Be sure to print your confirmation and bring it with you on test day.

2. **By phone**—Students, parents, and guardians can also register for the TACHS by calling 1-866-61TACHS and speaking with a representative who will guide you through the process. As of this writing, the hours for phone registration are Monday through Friday, from 8:00 a.m. to 7:00 p.m., and Saturday and Sunday from 10 a.m. to 2 p.m., Eastern Standard Time. Options for non-English-speaking callers are available. Once you're registered, you'll get a verbal confirmation. You can also ask to have your confirmation emailed. We recommend printing this confirmation email and bringing it with you on test day.

Upon registration, you'll receive an Admit Card confirming your test site. You *must* bring this Admit Card with you on the day of the test. When you receive your card, make sure you follow all directions for completion—this includes choosing the three high schools that will receive your score. The card also requires your parent's signature. Then check to confirm that all the information is accurate, including:

- Your name and address
- The date and time of your exam
- Your scheduled test site name and address (this may not match the high school that you wish to attend)

If there are any errors on your Admit Card, make sure you follow the directions for making corrections when it arrives.

TIP
THE OFFICIAL TACHS STUDENT HANDBOOK
Download or browse a copy of the TACHS Student Handbook for detailed information about exam contents and requirements, as well as information about scholarships and financial aid for Catholic high schools throughout New York City: **https://tachsinfo.com/handbook.aspx**

2020 TACHS Registration

Mark your calendars—the next registration period for the TACHS opens on **August 26, 2020.**

Complete registration information, including important dates, registration procedures, registration fees, and testing locations can be found online at **www.tachsinfo.com**.

TACHS Exam Fee

The current fee for taking the TACHS is $65. This is a *nonrefundable* fee, and includes a copy of the student handbook, test materials, and up to three score reports for the Catholic high schools of your choice. Please note that if you register by phone, a credit card payment is required.

Special Exam Accommodations

There is an option for extended testing time (time and a half) for students who have a documented need. Those who will need extra time are required to submit an eligibility form. The form is in the student handbook you'll receive after you register. Pay careful attention to the deadline and instructions for submitting the form.

If you think you may have an issue with accessibility—such as difficulty with stairs or doorways—please contact your diocesan office before exam day.

TACHS FORMAT AND FOCUS

The TACHS is a multiple-choice exam that tests your knowledge in the following key areas: **reading, written expression, mathematics,** and **general reasoning ability**. The questions you see will match the content a typical eighth-grade student should have mastered. It's not designed to trick you, give you impossible challenges, or test your patience. So, breathe easy!

Questions on the TACHS will have either four or five answer choices, with alternating letter options ('A, B, C, D, E' or 'J, K, L, M, N'). Your job is to pick the choice that best answers each question.

The following is a general overview of what you can expect on each subtest of the TACHS.

The TACHS Reading Subtest (35 minutes long)

The Reading subtest of the TACHS features several passages of varying length. Your task is to read and answer questions that test your factual, interpretive, and evaluative understanding of the text. Some passages will be fiction; these might include fables, narrative stories, and excerpts from previously published works. Others will be nonfiction; these may include topics like science and social studies.

It's important to note that the exam will test your ability to comprehend what you read, *not* your general understanding of the topics, such as social studies or science. For the most part, you'll be asked to infer or generalize about what you read. You may also be asked to identify the meaning of words or phrases in their literary context, to identify the main idea of a passage, and to determine what should come next in the story. Reading the text closely is your greatest ally here.

Let's look at a sample reading question:

NOTE

While the practice tests presented in the book and online reflect the *content* you will find on the TACHS, the question sequence, time allotment, and number of questions found within each subtest are subject to change.

1

Directions: This is a test of how well you understand what you read.

Read the following passage and then answer the questions. Four choices are given for the question. Choose the answer that you think is better than the others.

Paul Grisham, as a young boy, sold newspapers on the street corner to help his family. He went to work before sunrise, worked until it was time for school, and then returned home after school. Paul walked everywhere he went, regardless of the weather. The work ethic he developed as a youngster contributed to his eventual financial success as an adult.

Which of the following can be inferred about Paul's family when he was a child?

    A. Paul's family had very little money.

    B. Paul's family was very wealthy.

    C. Paul's family lived in the country.

    D. Paul's family was very large.

The correct answer is A. Paul worked before school and "walked everywhere he went." It can be inferred from the passage that he worked because he needed the money and walked because the family had no other means of transportation.

The TACHS Written Expression Subtest (30 minutes long)

The Written Expression subtest of the TACHS will test your skills in the proper use of Standard English. The questions cover sentence structure, organization, clarity, effectiveness or appropriateness of expressions, spelling, capitalization, punctuation, usage, and expression.

The first part of the test features pieces of writing followed by questions about how the writing should be changed. The second part features short pieces of writing with mistakes that you'll need to identify.

Let's look at a sample written expression question:

Directions: This is a test about writing in Standard English.

Four answers are given for this question. Choose the answer that you think is better than the others.

    J. Clarisse, though a fast runner, a match for her cousin Arnold she was not.

    K. Though she was fast; Clarisse was a runner but was no match for her cousin Arnold.

    L. Though Clarisse was a fast runner, she was no match for her cousin Arnold.

    M. As a runner, though fast, a match for her cousin Arnold Clarisse was not.

The correct answer is L. In this sentence, the clause "though Clarisse was a fast runner" is followed by a comma, which is the correct punctuation.

The TACHS Mathematics Subtest (40 minutes long)

The Mathematics subtest of the TACHS tests your ability to solve math problems. For each math question, you'll be given a set of choices and will need to choose the correct answer.

Topics covered on the Mathematics subtest include geometry, measurement, algebraic patterns and connections, number sense and operations, data analysis, probability, and statistics. Questions can involve the use of formulas, equations, word problems, symbols, operations, estimation, data interpretation, and working with charts and graphs.

Let's look at a sample mathematics question:

Directions: This is a test of your knowledge and understanding of math.

Four answers are given for this question. Choose the answer that you think is better than the others.

Gail has $\frac{2}{3}$ as many french fries as Mindy. Mindy has 12 french fries. How many french fries does Gail have?

   A. 8

   B. 9

   C. 10

   D. Not given

The correct answer is A. $\frac{2}{3} \times 12 = 8$

The TACHS Ability Subtest (32 minutes long)

The Ability subtest of the TACHS exam will test your abstract reasoning abilities—skills you have honed both in the classroom and in everyday life. Question types in this section include Paper Folding, Figure Classification, and Figure Matrices. You'll be presented with visual tasks that require you to generalize from one item or series of items to another. Don't worry if this sounds different or new to you; the exam is testing general reasoning skills here, not academic knowledge. Identifying patterns within a series and looking ahead to logical outcomes are the skills required in this section.

1

Let's look at a sample figure classification question:

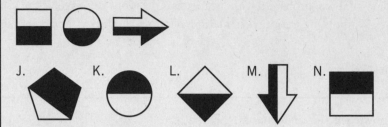

Directions: In the following question, the first three figures are alike in certain ways. Choose the figure that corresponds to the first three figures.

The correct answer is L. Each of the figures is divided in half with its bottom shaded.

TACHS TEST DAY CHECKLIST

You already know how important it is to study and prepare for the TACHS. But it's *equally* important to know what you must—and must not—bring to your test center on the day of your exam; this will help avoid any unpleasant delays or surprises.

What to bring on exam day:

- ✓ Your fully completed Admit Card
- ✓ A form of identification (e.g., a student ID or library card)
- ✓ A few sharpened No. 2 pencils with good erasers

What *not* to bring on exam day:

- ✗ Notes, notebooks, or scratch paper
- ✗ Food or beverages
- ✗ Battery-operated or electronic devices including calculators, watches, phones, tablets, and laptop computers

Summing It Up

- The Test for Admission into Catholic High Schools (TACHS) is the entrance examination for eighth-grade students who want to attend a Catholic high school in the Diocese of Brooklyn/Queens or the Archdiocese of New York City.

- Along with your school records, your TACHS score will be sent to the principals of up to three high schools you're applying to; this will allow them to make a proper decision.

- The TACHS is a multiple-choice exam that lasts about 2 hours and is designed to test your knowledge in the following key areas: reading, written expression, mathematics, and general reasoning ability.

- The difficulty level of TACHS questions will be on par with what a typical eighth-grade student should have mastered.

- You have two options for TACHS registration: Online (recommended) and by phone.

- Be sure to bring these on exam day:

  - Your fully completed Admit Card

  - A form of identification (e.g., a student ID or library card)

  - A few sharpened No. 2 pencils with good erasers

- Be sure **NOT** to bring these on exam day:

  - Notes, books, or scratch paper

  - Food or beverages

  - Battery-operated or electronic devices, including calculators, watches, phones, tablets, or laptops

Chapter 2

All About the High School Placement Test (HSPT®)

OVERVIEW

- **Registering for the HSPT®**
- **How the HSPT® Is Scored**
- **HSPT® Format and Focus**
- **Summing It Up**

Like TACHS, the Scholastic Testing Service High School Placement Test—HSPT for short—is part of the admissions process for many Catholic high schools. The HSPT is a multiple-choice, 298-question exam designed to test your **reading, mathematics**, **verbal**, **quantitative**, and **language skills**.

There's also an optional forty-question test in either science, mechanical aptitude, or religion. Because many schools do not use any of the optional tests, and because these test results are *not* included as part of your composite score, this book doesn't cover the optional tests in depth. To give you some idea of what you can expect on an optional test, you'll find an outline of the Science test at the end of this section. The outline shows you the typical structure and scope of the optional tests. If you need to take one of the optional tests, be sure to get study advice from the schools you want to attend.

The exam takes about 2 hours and 30 minutes; along with your school records, your HSPT score will be sent to the high schools you're applying to, so they can make an admissions decision. Keep reading, and we'll help you prepare for success on this important exam!

Closed vs. Open HSPT

There are two different kinds of HSPT exams: the Closed HSPT and the Open HSPT. The Closed HSPT is administered by the school but scored by the Scholastic Testing Service (STS), the official HSPT creators and administrators. Closed HSPT scores are compared to national standard distribution norms, so nationwide percentiles can be computed. The Open HSPT is administered and scored by the school, so STS does not deal directly with student results. The Open HSPT uses old versions of the Closed HSPT.

2

The Pre-HSPT is an edition of the Closed HSPT designed to help seventh-grade students prepare for the HSPT. Families with seventh-grade students interested in taking the Pre-HSPT should contact the student's current school to see if the test is offered.

REGISTERING FOR THE HSPT®

The HSPT is ordered and administered by individual schools or dioceses throughout the country. To schedule the HSPT, contact the school you want to attend and ask about its registration process.

Unlike other standardized admissions exams, the STS does not have set days for testing. Rather, individual schools and dioceses determine their own test days. For more information, contact the school where you'd like to take the HSPT.

The STS strongly recommends that each student take the HSPT only once. However, each school can allow a student to retest due to extenuating circumstances; this process is handled on a case-by-case basis.

Special Exam Accommodations

Each school administering the HSPT has its own policy regarding special exam accommodations. The STS suggests that if a student needs any accommodations, the parents or guardians should contact the schools directly for additional information.

Upon a school's request, the STS does provide large-print test booklets and answer sheets for visually impaired test takers. If your child requires large-print materials, please contact the school where you are taking the test, which will contact STS.

TIP

You *don't* lose points for incorrect answers on the HSPT—this means you should try to answer *every* question you encounter on test day, even if you need to guess! Visit **http://www.ststesting.com/hsp/index.html** for more information.

HOW THE HSPT® IS SCORED

High schools nationwide use score results on the HSPT to make admissions decisions, scholarship award selections, and curriculum placement determinations. That said, there are no set guidelines for how schools should use score results, empowering each school to set its own rules for evaluating your scores.

To determine your HSPT scores, the number of questions you answered correctly on each of the subtests are added up, which will give you a set of *raw scores*. Your raw scores are then converted into standardized scores and national percentile rankings for each subtest ranging from one to 99, clearly showing how you stack up against other test takers nationwide.

Your HSPT® Score Report

Each individual school, cooperative, or diocese decides on the type of score report it wishes to receive, its process for distributing scores, and what information will be shared and distributed to test takers.

If a test taker is taking the HSPT at a school that is part of a cooperative of several high schools, they may have the option of sending their scores to several schools by coding their answer sheets accordingly.

HSPT® FORMAT AND FOCUS

As mentioned previously, the HSPT is a multiple-choice exam with five distinct sections:

1. Verbal Skills
2. Quantitative Skills
3. Reading
4. Mathematics
5. Language Skills

You'll have approximately 2 hours and 30 minutes to answer the 298 questions you'll encounter on test day. Let's take a closer look at each of the sections on the exam.

Verbal Skills Section (16 minutes long)

The Verbal Skills Section of the HSPT is designed to measure your ability to perform reasoning tasks that involve the use of words. This is a core performance ability that spans a wide array of content areas, including language, reading, and various areas within social studies.

The following is a breakdown of the topics you will encounter in the HSPT Verbal Skills section:

- Analogy
- Logic
- Verbal Classifications
- Synonyms
- Antonyms

Let's look at a sample verbal skills question:

Directions: Mark one answer—the answer you think is best—for the problem.

Throw is to ball as shoot is to

    A. policeman.

    B. kill.

    C. arrow.

    D. hunting.

The correct answer is C. This analogy describes an action-to-object relationship. You *throw* a ball, and you *shoot* an arrow.

> **NOTE**
>
> While the practice tests presented in this book and online are much like the *content* you will find on the actual test, the sequence, time allotment, and number of questions found within each section will vary from one HSPT test session to the next.

Quantitative Skills Section (30 minutes long)

The quantitative component measures your ability to answer reasoning problems involving numbers and quantities. This is a core performance ability that spans a wide array of content areas, including mathematics and science.

The cognitive skills you've acquired and built up thus far, both in the classroom and in your everyday life, are tested during this section of the exam.

The following is a breakdown of the topics you will encounter in the HSPT Quantitative Skills section:

- Sequence
- Reasoning
- Geometric Comparison
- Non-Geometric Comparison

The following geometric comparison is an example of a quantitative skills question:

Directions: Mark one answer—the answer you think is best—for the problem.

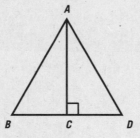

A. $\overline{AD}$ is greater than $\overline{CD}$.

B. $\overline{BA}$ and $\overline{AD}$ are each less than $\overline{BC}$.

C. $\overline{AB}$ is equal to $\overline{BC}$.

D. $\overline{AB}$ is equal to $\overline{AC}$ plus $\overline{BC}$.

The correct answer is A. The line drawn from point *A* to the base of triangle *ABD* divides the triangle into two right angles, one of which is ∠*ACD*. $\overline{AD}$ is the hypotenuse of this right triangle, whose length must be greater than the length of *CD*, the base of ∠*ACD*.

Reading Section (25 minutes long)

The Reading Section of the HSPT tests your overall reading comprehension, your recognition of key details and ideas, your ability to identify central thoughts and premises, how well you make logical inferences, and your understanding of vocabulary in context. This section tests the reading skills you've acquired in the classroom and in your everyday life.

2

Here is a breakdown of the topics you will encounter in the HSPT Reading Section:

Comprehension

- Vocabulary in Context
- Literal Comparison
- Inferential Comparison
- Main Idea
- Drawing Conclusions
- Reasoning
- Implied Characterization
- Critical Composition
- Author Purpose
- Compare/Contrast
- Predictions
- Fact vs. Fiction

Vocabulary

Let's look at a sample reading comprehension question:

Directions: Read the passage below and then answer the question. Four answers are given for the question. You are to choose the answer that you think is better than the others.

Sample Passage

Most of us know that physical exercise is important for a healthy lifestyle. We know that people who exercise live longer lives and resist many fatal diseases. We know, in short, that exercise is a good thing. What we might not realize, however, is exactly how *many* benefits physical activity provides. Research conducted by the Harvard University School of Public Health has shed light on this issue by describing the effects of exercise in detail.

   The Harvard® studies show that physical exercise helps prevent many diseases, including obesity, stroke, heart disease, and many types of cancers. Exercise increases our balance as well as the strength of our muscles and bones. Exercise helps us concentrate, enables us to burn more fat, keeps our joints healthy, and fortifies our immune systems. If all that weren't enough, exercise also has an important psychological benefit: it causes us to feel more positive and to maintain better moods.

2

Which of the following is true regarding the Harvard University School of Public Health?

    A. It conducted research studies showing that physical activity prevents many diseases.

    B. It ran many tests on exercise and published a book on the benefits of exercise.

    C. It developed technology to measure what happens to the joints of people who exercise.

    D. It ran scientific studies to examine how athletes can be harmed by too much exercise.

The correct answer is A. To answer a question like this one, it is helpful to re-read the part of the passage that contains the reference to the Harvard University School of Public Health. This reference occurs at the end of the first paragraph and the beginning of the second one. We learn that the Harvard University School of Public Health has conducted research about the benefits of exercise. According to paragraph two, the school's studies have shown that "physical exercise helps prevent many diseases," so choice A is correct. Choice B is incorrect because we're never told that the Harvard University School of Public Health published a book on the benefits of exercise, just that it conducted research studies.

Mathematics Section (45 minutes long)

The Mathematics Section of the HSPT is designed to measure your ability to perform arithmetic operations, apply key math concepts, and utilize sound mathematical reasoning to solve problems. The math skills you've acquired and built up thus far, both in the classroom and in your everyday life, will be tested during this section of the exam.

Here is a breakdown of the topics you will encounter in the HSPT Mathematics Section:

Numbers & Numeration

- Procedural Operations
- Roots/Exponents/Place Values
- Ratios/Proportions
- Properties/Factors/Multiples
- Word Problems

Measurements

- Weight/Length/Dry/Liquid
- Metric/Monetary Conversions

Geometry

- Points/Lines/Angles
- Planes/Cubic Figures
- Perimeter/Area/Volume
- Diameter/Radius/Circumference
- Congruency/Symmetry/Pythagorean Theorem

Algebra

- Equality/Inequality
- Functions/Coordinates

Statistics & Probability

- Mean/Median/Mode/Range
- Probability/Concepts
- Data Graphs/Tables

Let's look at a sample measurements question:

Directions: Mark one answer—the answer you think is best—for the problem.

On a map, 1 inch represents 500 miles. How many miles apart are two cities that are $1\frac{1}{2}$ inches apart on the map?

A. 750

B. 1,000

C. 1,250

D. 1,500

The correct answer is A. If 1 inch = 500 miles, then $\frac{1}{2}$ inch = 250 miles. Therefore, $1\frac{1}{2}$ inches = 500 + 250 = 750 miles.

Language Skills Section (25 minutes long)

The Language Skills Section of the HSPT is designed to measure your knowledge of proper English language capitalization, punctuation, grammar, spelling, usage, and composition. The language skills you've acquired and built up thus far, both in the classroom and in your everyday life, will be tested during this section of the exam.

The following is a breakdown of the topics you will encounter in the HSPT Language Skills section:

Punctuation

Capitalization

Incorrect Usage

- Noun/Pronoun
- Verb/Adverb/Adjective
- Other Parts of Speech

Correct Usage

Spelling

Composition

Let's look at a sample incorrect usage question:

2

> **Directions:** Find the sentence that has an error in usage. If you find no mistake, mark D as your answer.
>
> **A.** Many children adopt the beliefs of their parents.
>
> **B.** "Is he always so amusing?" she asked.
>
> **C.** All the officers declined except she.
>
> **D.** *(No mistakes)*
>
> **The correct answer is C.** This sentence has an error in usage. The word *she* should be *her* since it acts as the object of the preposition *except.*

The Optional HSPT® Tests

Some schools might require that you take one of the three optional tests described at the beginning of this section: Mechanical Aptitude, Science, or Catholic Religion. If you must take an optional test, the test is chosen by the school, and, like the basic HSPT exam, the test will involve multiple-choice questions and answers.

Your score on the optional test will not be included with your score on the basic HSPT exam. Rather, the school will receive a report on your overall performance on the optional exam and a topic-by-topic evaluation of your performance. The school will use this information to place you in appropriate classes. It might also use the information to determine the background of the student body in preparing the curriculum for the following year.

The optional science test consists of 40 questions covering a wide variety of topics. The questions are not neatly categorized. For example, a biology question might be followed by a physics question, then a laboratory methods question might be followed by a chemistry question. The following outline gives you an idea of how many topics are covered on the science test.

DISTRIBUTION OF TOPICS ON HSPT® OPTIONAL SCIENCE TEST

Biological Sciences

- Plants
- Animals
- Life Processes
- Health and Safety
- Ecology

Earth Sciences

- Astronomy
- Geology
- Weather
- Air
- Water

Physical Sciences

- Matter and Energy
- Machines and Work
- Magnetism and Electricity
- Sound
- Heat and Light
- Chemistry

Implications of Scientific Technology

- Societal Benefits
- Technical Applications

Principles of Scientific Research and Experimentation

- Laboratory Methods
- Research Practices

Summing It Up

- The High School Placement Test (HSPT) is an entrance examination for eighth-grade students who want to attend a Catholic high school.

- Along with your school records, your HSPT score will be sent to the principals of the high schools to which you're applying, so that they can make an admissions decision.

- The HSPT exam takes about 2 hours and 30 minutes to complete 298 questions designed to test your reading, mathematics, verbal, quantitative, and language skills. There's also an optional 40-question test in either science, mechanical aptitude, or religion.

- The HSPT is ordered and administered by individual schools or dioceses throughout the country. Contact the school at which you'd like to take the test and ask for information about the registration process and special exam accommodations, if needed.

- High schools nationwide use score results on the HSPT to make admissions decisions, scholarship award selections, and curriculum placement determinations.

- Each individual school, cooperative, or diocese decides on the type of score report it wishes to receive, its process for distributing scores, and what information will be distributed to test takers.

Test-Taking Techniques

OVERVIEW

- **What to Expect When You Take the Exam**
- **Study Tips**
- **Tips for Answering Questions**
- **Summing It Up**

No test-preparation book is complete without a rundown of tried and true study and test-taking tips. Some of the techniques and tips listed here are common sense, but it never hurts to review them. For example, you should always get your materials together the night before the exam. Get a good night's sleep and get up early enough so that you're not rushing. In the morning, eat a healthy, "brain food" breakfast. Here are some more tips:

- The only materials you should bring are a few sharpened #2 pencils with clean erasers, your school ID or library card (or whatever would be accepted as identification), and your admission ticket (if you were issued one).

- Do not bring a calculator unless you were expressly told to bring one. Calculators are not permitted on most high school entrance exams.

- It is important to wear a watch even though the room will most likely have a clock. The clock might not be conveniently located for time-tracking. If calculators are not allowed, be sure that your watch does not have a calculator function, because all calculator watches will be confiscated for the duration of the exam. If your watch has an alarm, be sure to turn it off. (Note: you are not permitted to wear a watch for the HSPT exam.)

- Enter the room early enough to choose a comfortable seat. After you're settled, relax. You'll concentrate more and perform better on the test if you're comfortable. Besides, you studied hard for the exam, so what do you have to worry about?

WHAT TO EXPECT WHEN YOU TAKE THE EXAM

The first thing you will do is fill out forms. The exam administrator will give you detailed instructions for this procedure. Listen, read, and follow the directions; filling out forms is not timed, so don't rush. The exam will not begin until everyone has finished.

Next, the administrator will give you general instructions for taking the exam. You will be told how to recognize the stop and start signals. You will also find out what to do if you have a problem, such as breaking a pencil or finding a page missing from your test booklet. If you have any questions, ask them now, before the test begins.

When the signal is given, open your test booklet and:

3

- **Read all directions carefully.** The directions will probably be very similar to those in this book, but don't take anything for granted. Test makers periodically change the exams.

- **Read every word of every question.** Be alert for little words that might have a big effect on your answer—for example, words such as *not, most, all, every,* and *except.*

- **Read all the choices before you select an answer.** It is statistically true that the most errors are made when the correct answer is the last in the list. Too many people mark the first answer that seems correct without reading through all the choices to find the best answer.

STUDY TIPS

Where you study is just as important as *how* you study. Here are a few ideas to maximize the effectiveness of your study time.

- **Make an office.** Have one place, such as a desk or a favorite chair, devoted to study. Make sure the place is quiet, well-lit, and distraction-free (i.e. no Facebook or Snapchat).

- **Create a plan.** Use a planner to schedule what you need to study, as well as for how long.

- **Take your time.** Space your study schedule so you are not cramming a subject. Give your brain enough time to absorb each topic so you can retain all the information.

- **Keep it straight.** Use folders, binders, and notebooks to keep study materials sorted by topic.

- **Keep it up.** Don't just organize your study material—be organized with classwork and homework, too.

- **Make study cards.** Get a stack of 3×5 or 4×6 cards and a Sharpie or two. Write a key word, term, or problem on one side, and the answer on the other.

- **Make cheat sheets.** Writing something down (**not typing!**) forms stronger connections in the brain. Make study cards by hand and write things down in a notebook.

TIPS FOR ANSWERING QUESTIONS

One of the best test tips we can offer is this: Try to answer every question on the exam, especially if you're running out of time. If you answer every question—even if you guess wildly—you are more likely to earn a high score. There is no penalty for wrong answers on the TACHS or HSPT, so even a wild guess gives you a 20-25 percent chance for credit! Here are some tips for making an educated guess.

- An educated guess is worth more than a random guess. To make an educated guess, look carefully at the question and eliminate any answers that you're sure are wrong. Chances are that you will spot some obviously wrong answers among the choices for vocabulary, reading, and language questions. You will probably find some of the choices for math questions to be so far off as to make you chuckle. When it comes right down to it, you have a better chance of guessing correctly when you have three options instead of four or five. Your odds improve to 50/50 if you can guess between two choices.

- Eliminate all answers you know for certain are incorrect and work backward by process of deduction. This should leave you with fewer options to choose from.

- Keep alert for the moment when time is about to run out on the exam. In those last few seconds, pick one response—preferably not the first, because the first answer is often wrong—and mark all remaining blanks on your answer sheet with that same answer. Based on the law of averages, you should pick up a free point or two.

Another way to ensure success is to make sure you don't lose any points through carelessness. Here's a list of eleven suggestions that apply to any paper-and-pencil entrance exam, including the practice exams you'll take later in Part V.

1. Mark your answers by completely blackening the answer space of choice. Be sure not to make any marks outside the lines.

2. Mark only **one** answer for each question, even if you think that more than one answer is correct. If you mark more than one answer, you will receive no credit for that question.

3. If you change your mind, erase the answer completely. Leave no doubt as to which answer you meant to select.

4. Answer every question in the right place on the answer sheet. Make sure that the number on your answer sheet matches the number of the question you are answering. You could lose valuable time if you have to go back and change your answers.

5. Don't spend too much time on any one question, even if it's difficult. Pick an answer and move on. You can always mark the question in your test booklet and go back if time permits.

6. You are not required to answer every question; however, if you skip one, **be sure to skip the corresponding answer space.** Otherwise, you'll throw off your entire answer sheet. For that reason, it's safer to guess than to skip. Just mark the guesses in your test booklet so that you can go back and deliberate if you have time.

7. If you're using scratch paper (permitted on the HSPT), be sure to mark the answer on the answer sheet. Only the answer sheet is scored; the test booklet and the scratch paper are not.

8. Stay alert. Getting a good night's sleep and eating breakfast on the morning of the test will help you give your best effort.

9. If you don't finish a section before the time is up, don't worry. Few people can answer every question. If you are accurate, you might still earn a high score—even without finishing every test section.

10. Don't let performance on one section affect performance on other parts of the test. For example, if you don't think you did well on mathematics, try to forget it and move on. Worrying about a previous section will only cause unnecessary stress and confusion. Remember, only the correct answers count.

11. Check and recheck. If you finish any part before time is up, go back and check to be sure each question is answered in the right space and that there's only one answer for each question. Then return to the difficult questions and rethink them.

TIP
The machine that scores your test can only "read" the bubbles. Be sure to fill in the entire bubble and erase all stray marks.

Chapter 3: Test-Taking Techniques

Summing It Up

- Get organized. Set up a specific space for studying where you won't be distracted. Make a study plan, and use written materials such as index cards or "cheat sheets" to help you memorize important material.

- Assemble everything you'll need the night before your exam, including a few #2 pencils and a watch (calculator watches are not permitted). Don't bring a calculator unless you have been instructed to do so.

- Get a good night's sleep and get up early enough so you can eat breakfast and arrive at the testing center with plenty of time to spare. Enter the room early enough to find a comfortable seat and relax before the test begins. Be sure you are not dehydrated, as that can negatively affect your test performance.

- **READ.** Read all directions carefully, read every word of every question, and review all answer options before making a selection.

- **PRACTICE.** Practice all the question-answering tips in this chapter when you study and when you take the practice exams. This way, using the tips will have become second nature by the time you take the real exam.

Take a moment to ask yourself some simple questions about your understanding of the chapter:

Review: What did I learn?

Evaluate: What do I need to learn more about?

Plan: What can I do next to keep improving?

Based on your answers to those questions, adjust your study plan to dedicate additional time to the areas of weakness that you've identified.

PART II
DIAGNOSTIC TESTS

ANSWER SHEET: TACHS DIAGNOSTIC TEST

Reading

1. Ⓐ Ⓑ Ⓒ Ⓓ	11. Ⓐ Ⓑ Ⓒ Ⓓ	21. Ⓐ Ⓑ Ⓒ Ⓓ	31. Ⓐ Ⓑ Ⓒ Ⓓ	41. Ⓐ Ⓑ Ⓒ Ⓓ
2. Ⓙ Ⓚ Ⓛ Ⓜ	12. Ⓙ Ⓚ Ⓛ Ⓜ	22. Ⓙ Ⓚ Ⓛ Ⓜ	32. Ⓙ Ⓚ Ⓛ Ⓜ	42. Ⓙ Ⓚ Ⓛ Ⓜ
3. Ⓐ Ⓑ Ⓒ Ⓓ	13. Ⓐ Ⓑ Ⓒ Ⓓ	23. Ⓐ Ⓑ Ⓒ Ⓓ	33. Ⓐ Ⓑ Ⓒ Ⓓ	43. Ⓐ Ⓑ Ⓒ Ⓓ
4. Ⓙ Ⓚ Ⓛ Ⓜ	14. Ⓙ Ⓚ Ⓛ Ⓜ	24. Ⓙ Ⓚ Ⓛ Ⓜ	34. Ⓙ Ⓚ Ⓛ Ⓜ	44. Ⓙ Ⓚ Ⓛ Ⓜ
5. Ⓐ Ⓑ Ⓒ Ⓓ	15. Ⓐ Ⓑ Ⓒ Ⓓ	25. Ⓐ Ⓑ Ⓒ Ⓓ	35. Ⓐ Ⓑ Ⓒ Ⓓ	45. Ⓐ Ⓑ Ⓒ Ⓓ
6. Ⓙ Ⓚ Ⓛ Ⓜ	16. Ⓙ Ⓚ Ⓛ Ⓜ	26. Ⓙ Ⓚ Ⓛ Ⓜ	36. Ⓙ Ⓚ Ⓛ Ⓜ	46. Ⓙ Ⓚ Ⓛ Ⓜ
7. Ⓐ Ⓑ Ⓒ Ⓓ	17. Ⓐ Ⓑ Ⓒ Ⓓ	27. Ⓐ Ⓑ Ⓒ Ⓓ	37. Ⓐ Ⓑ Ⓒ Ⓓ	47. Ⓐ Ⓑ Ⓒ Ⓓ
8. Ⓙ Ⓚ Ⓛ Ⓜ	18. Ⓙ Ⓚ Ⓛ Ⓜ	28. Ⓙ Ⓚ Ⓛ Ⓜ	38. Ⓙ Ⓚ Ⓛ Ⓜ	48. Ⓙ Ⓚ Ⓛ Ⓜ
9. Ⓐ Ⓑ Ⓒ Ⓓ	19. Ⓐ Ⓑ Ⓒ Ⓓ	29. Ⓐ Ⓑ Ⓒ Ⓓ	39. Ⓐ Ⓑ Ⓒ Ⓓ	49. Ⓐ Ⓑ Ⓒ Ⓓ
10. Ⓙ Ⓚ Ⓛ Ⓜ	20. Ⓙ Ⓚ Ⓛ Ⓜ	30. Ⓙ Ⓚ Ⓛ Ⓜ	40. Ⓙ Ⓚ Ⓛ Ⓜ	50. Ⓙ Ⓚ Ⓛ Ⓜ

Written Expression

1. Ⓐ Ⓑ Ⓒ Ⓓ Ⓔ	14. Ⓙ Ⓚ Ⓛ Ⓜ	27. Ⓐ Ⓑ Ⓒ Ⓓ	40. Ⓙ Ⓚ Ⓛ Ⓜ
2. Ⓙ Ⓚ Ⓛ Ⓜ Ⓝ	15. Ⓐ Ⓑ Ⓒ Ⓓ	28. Ⓙ Ⓚ Ⓛ Ⓜ	41. Ⓐ Ⓑ Ⓒ Ⓓ
3. Ⓐ Ⓑ Ⓒ Ⓓ Ⓔ	16. Ⓙ Ⓚ Ⓛ Ⓜ	29. Ⓐ Ⓑ Ⓒ Ⓓ	42. Ⓙ Ⓚ Ⓛ Ⓜ
4. Ⓙ Ⓚ Ⓛ Ⓜ Ⓝ	17. Ⓐ Ⓑ Ⓒ Ⓓ	30. Ⓙ Ⓚ Ⓛ Ⓜ	43. Ⓐ Ⓑ Ⓒ Ⓓ
5. Ⓐ Ⓑ Ⓒ Ⓓ Ⓔ	18. Ⓙ Ⓚ Ⓛ Ⓜ	31. Ⓐ Ⓑ Ⓒ Ⓓ	44. Ⓙ Ⓚ Ⓛ Ⓜ
6. Ⓙ Ⓚ Ⓛ Ⓜ Ⓝ	19. Ⓐ Ⓑ Ⓒ Ⓓ	32. Ⓙ Ⓚ Ⓛ Ⓜ	45. Ⓐ Ⓑ Ⓒ Ⓓ
7. Ⓐ Ⓑ Ⓒ Ⓓ Ⓔ	20. Ⓙ Ⓚ Ⓛ Ⓜ	33. Ⓐ Ⓑ Ⓒ Ⓓ	46. Ⓙ Ⓚ Ⓛ Ⓜ
8. Ⓙ Ⓚ Ⓛ Ⓜ Ⓝ	21. Ⓐ Ⓑ Ⓒ Ⓓ	34. Ⓙ Ⓚ Ⓛ Ⓜ	47. Ⓐ Ⓑ Ⓒ Ⓓ
9. Ⓐ Ⓑ Ⓒ Ⓓ Ⓔ	22. Ⓙ Ⓚ Ⓛ Ⓜ	35. Ⓐ Ⓑ Ⓒ Ⓓ	48. Ⓙ Ⓚ Ⓛ Ⓜ
10. Ⓙ Ⓚ Ⓛ Ⓜ Ⓝ	23. Ⓐ Ⓑ Ⓒ Ⓓ	36. Ⓙ Ⓚ Ⓛ Ⓜ	49. Ⓐ Ⓑ Ⓒ Ⓓ
11. Ⓐ Ⓑ Ⓒ Ⓓ	24. Ⓙ Ⓚ Ⓛ Ⓜ	37. Ⓐ Ⓑ Ⓒ Ⓓ	50. Ⓙ Ⓚ Ⓛ Ⓜ
12. Ⓙ Ⓚ Ⓛ Ⓜ	25. Ⓐ Ⓑ Ⓒ Ⓓ	38. Ⓙ Ⓚ Ⓛ Ⓜ	
13. Ⓐ Ⓑ Ⓒ Ⓓ	26. Ⓙ Ⓚ Ⓛ Ⓜ	39. Ⓐ Ⓑ Ⓒ Ⓓ	

Answer Sheet

4

TACHS Diagnostic Test

Math

1. Ⓐ Ⓑ Ⓒ Ⓓ   11. Ⓐ Ⓑ Ⓒ Ⓓ   21. Ⓐ Ⓑ Ⓒ Ⓓ   31. Ⓐ Ⓑ Ⓒ Ⓓ   41. Ⓐ Ⓑ Ⓒ Ⓓ
2. Ⓙ Ⓚ Ⓛ Ⓜ   12. Ⓙ Ⓚ Ⓛ Ⓜ   22. Ⓙ Ⓚ Ⓛ Ⓜ   32. Ⓙ Ⓚ Ⓛ Ⓜ   42. Ⓙ Ⓚ Ⓛ Ⓜ
3. Ⓐ Ⓑ Ⓒ Ⓓ   13. Ⓐ Ⓑ Ⓒ Ⓓ   23. Ⓐ Ⓑ Ⓒ Ⓓ   33. Ⓐ Ⓑ Ⓒ Ⓓ   43. Ⓐ Ⓑ Ⓒ Ⓓ
4. Ⓙ Ⓚ Ⓛ Ⓜ   14. Ⓙ Ⓚ Ⓛ Ⓜ   24. Ⓙ Ⓚ Ⓛ Ⓜ   34. Ⓙ Ⓚ Ⓛ Ⓜ   44. Ⓙ Ⓚ Ⓛ Ⓜ
5. Ⓐ Ⓑ Ⓒ Ⓓ   15. Ⓐ Ⓑ Ⓒ Ⓓ   25. Ⓐ Ⓑ Ⓒ Ⓓ   35. Ⓐ Ⓑ Ⓒ Ⓓ   45. Ⓐ Ⓑ Ⓒ Ⓓ
6. Ⓙ Ⓚ Ⓛ Ⓜ   16. Ⓙ Ⓚ Ⓛ Ⓜ   26. Ⓙ Ⓚ Ⓛ Ⓜ   36. Ⓙ Ⓚ Ⓛ Ⓜ   46. Ⓙ Ⓚ Ⓛ Ⓜ
7. Ⓐ Ⓑ Ⓒ Ⓓ   17. Ⓐ Ⓑ Ⓒ Ⓓ   27. Ⓐ Ⓑ Ⓒ Ⓓ   37. Ⓐ Ⓑ Ⓒ Ⓓ   47. Ⓐ Ⓑ Ⓒ Ⓓ
8. Ⓙ Ⓚ Ⓛ Ⓜ   18. Ⓙ Ⓚ Ⓛ Ⓜ   28. Ⓙ Ⓚ Ⓛ Ⓜ   38. Ⓙ Ⓚ Ⓛ Ⓜ   48. Ⓙ Ⓚ Ⓛ Ⓜ
9. Ⓐ Ⓑ Ⓒ Ⓓ   19. Ⓐ Ⓑ Ⓒ Ⓓ   29. Ⓐ Ⓑ Ⓒ Ⓓ   39. Ⓐ Ⓑ Ⓒ Ⓓ   49. Ⓐ Ⓑ Ⓒ Ⓓ
10. Ⓙ Ⓚ Ⓛ Ⓜ   20. Ⓙ Ⓚ Ⓛ Ⓜ   30. Ⓙ Ⓚ Ⓛ Ⓜ   40. Ⓙ Ⓚ Ⓛ Ⓜ   50. Ⓙ Ⓚ Ⓛ Ⓜ

Ability

Figure Classification

1. Ⓐ Ⓑ Ⓒ Ⓓ Ⓔ   6. Ⓙ Ⓚ Ⓛ Ⓜ Ⓝ   11. Ⓐ Ⓑ Ⓒ Ⓓ Ⓔ   16. Ⓙ Ⓚ Ⓛ Ⓜ Ⓝ
2. Ⓙ Ⓚ Ⓛ Ⓜ Ⓝ   7. Ⓐ Ⓑ Ⓒ Ⓓ Ⓔ   12. Ⓙ Ⓚ Ⓛ Ⓜ Ⓝ   17. Ⓐ Ⓑ Ⓒ Ⓓ Ⓔ
3. Ⓐ Ⓑ Ⓒ Ⓓ Ⓔ   8. Ⓙ Ⓚ Ⓛ Ⓜ Ⓝ   13. Ⓐ Ⓑ Ⓒ Ⓓ Ⓔ   18. Ⓙ Ⓚ Ⓛ Ⓜ Ⓝ
4. Ⓙ Ⓚ Ⓛ Ⓜ Ⓝ   9. Ⓐ Ⓑ Ⓒ Ⓓ Ⓔ   14. Ⓙ Ⓚ Ⓛ Ⓜ Ⓝ   19. Ⓐ Ⓑ Ⓒ Ⓓ Ⓔ
5. Ⓐ Ⓑ Ⓒ Ⓓ Ⓔ   10. Ⓙ Ⓚ Ⓛ Ⓜ Ⓝ   15. Ⓐ Ⓑ Ⓒ Ⓓ Ⓔ   20. Ⓙ Ⓚ Ⓛ Ⓜ Ⓝ

Figure Matrices

1. Ⓐ Ⓑ Ⓒ Ⓓ Ⓔ   6. Ⓙ Ⓚ Ⓛ Ⓜ Ⓝ   11. Ⓐ Ⓑ Ⓒ Ⓓ Ⓔ   16. Ⓙ Ⓚ Ⓛ Ⓜ Ⓝ
2. Ⓙ Ⓚ Ⓛ Ⓜ Ⓝ   7. Ⓐ Ⓑ Ⓒ Ⓓ Ⓔ   12. Ⓙ Ⓚ Ⓛ Ⓜ Ⓝ   17. Ⓐ Ⓑ Ⓒ Ⓓ Ⓔ
3. Ⓐ Ⓑ Ⓒ Ⓓ Ⓔ   8. Ⓙ Ⓚ Ⓛ Ⓜ Ⓝ   13. Ⓐ Ⓑ Ⓒ Ⓓ Ⓔ   18. Ⓙ Ⓚ Ⓛ Ⓜ Ⓝ
4. Ⓙ Ⓚ Ⓛ Ⓜ Ⓝ   9. Ⓐ Ⓑ Ⓒ Ⓓ Ⓔ   14. Ⓙ Ⓚ Ⓛ Ⓜ Ⓝ   19. Ⓐ Ⓑ Ⓒ Ⓓ Ⓔ
5. Ⓐ Ⓑ Ⓒ Ⓓ Ⓔ   10. Ⓙ Ⓚ Ⓛ Ⓜ Ⓝ   15. Ⓐ Ⓑ Ⓒ Ⓓ Ⓔ   20. Ⓙ Ⓚ Ⓛ Ⓜ Ⓝ

Paper Folding

1. Ⓐ Ⓑ Ⓒ Ⓓ Ⓔ   4. Ⓙ Ⓚ Ⓛ Ⓜ Ⓝ   7. Ⓐ Ⓑ Ⓒ Ⓓ Ⓔ   10. Ⓙ Ⓚ Ⓛ Ⓜ Ⓝ

2. Ⓙ Ⓚ Ⓛ Ⓜ Ⓝ   5. Ⓐ Ⓑ Ⓒ Ⓓ Ⓔ   8. Ⓙ Ⓚ Ⓛ Ⓜ Ⓝ

3. Ⓐ Ⓑ Ⓒ Ⓓ Ⓔ   6. Ⓙ Ⓚ Ⓛ Ⓜ Ⓝ   9. Ⓐ Ⓑ Ⓒ Ⓓ Ⓔ

Answer Sheet

4

TACHS Diagnostic Test

Chapter 4

TACHS
Diagnostic Test

READING

50 Questions (35 Minutes)

Turn to the Reading section of your answer sheet to answer the questions in this section.

Directions: This is a test of how well you understand what you read.

- Read the passage below and then answer the questions.

- Four answers are given for each question. You are to choose the answer that you think is better than the others.

Questions 1–4 are based on the following passage.

Passage 1

Everything was white, from the top of Mount Franklin to the coast—forests, prairie, lake, river, beach. The waters of the Mercy ran under a vault of ice, which cracked and broke with a loud noise at every change of tide. Thousands of birds—ducks and wood-peckers—flew over the
Line surface of the lake. The rocks between which the cascade plunged to the borders of the Plateau
5 were blocked up with ice. One would have said that the water leaped out of a huge gargoyle, cut by some fantastic artist of the Renaissance. To calculate the damage done to the forest by this hurricane would be impossible until the snow had entirely disappeared.

Spilett, Pencroff, and Herbert took this opportunity to look after their traps and had hard work finding them under their bed of snow. There was danger of their falling in themselves; a
10 humiliating thing to be caught in one's own trap! They were spared this annoyance, however, and found the traps had been untouched; not an animal had been caught, although there were a great many footprints in the neighborhood, among others, very clearly impressed marks of claws.

Herbert at once classified these carnivora among the cat tribe, a circumstance which justified the engineer's belief in the existence of dangerous beasts on Lincoln Island. Doubtless these
15 beasts dwelt in the dense forests of the Far West; but driven by hunger, they had ventured as far as Prospect Plateau. Perhaps they scented the inhabitants of Granite House.

—Excerpt from *Mysterious Island*, by Jules Verne

Chapter 4: TACHS Diagnostic Test

1. In this passage the word *fantastic* most likely means

   A. good.

   B. unrealistic.

   C. terrible.

   D. funny.

2. Where does the passage take place?

   J. Mount Franklin

   K. Lincoln Island

   L. The Far West

   M. Prospect Plateau

3. Which of these phrases best describes Spilett, Pencroff, and Herbert?

   A. Brave

   B. Cowardly

   C. Annoying

   D. Dangerous

4. From this passage you can infer that the characters

   J. will soon leave the island.

   K. are experts at trapping animals.

   L. do not like animals.

   M. are in peril.

Questions 5–10 are based on the following passage.

PASSAGE 2

April's Charms

When April scatters coins of primrose gold
Among the copper leaves in thickets old,
And singing skylarks from the meadows rise,
To twinkle like black stars in sunny skies;

Line

5   When I can hear the small woodpecker ring
Time on a tree for all the birds that sing;
And hear the pleasant cuckoo, loud and long—
The simple bird that thinks two notes a song;

When I can hear the woodland brook, that could
10   Not drown a babe, with all his threatening mood:
Upon whose banks the violets make their home,
And let a few small strawberry blossoms come;

When I go forth on such a pleasant day,
One breath outdoors takes all my care away;
15   It goes like heavy smoke, when flames take hold
Of wood that's green and fill a grate with gold.

—*William H. Davies*

5. The poet believes that

   A. April is the only decent month.

   B. the cuckoo makes the prettiest sound.

   C. this particular day in April is extremely nice.

   D. skylarks ruin the view of the sky.

6. The second stanza describes

   J. the sounds of woodpeckers and cuckoos.

   K. the sound and appearance of skylarks.

   L. the appearance of the brook.

   M. the appearance of birds in a tree.

7. The poet likely

   A. enjoys seeing violets.

   B. prefers woodpeckers to cuckoos.

   C. has never eaten a strawberry.

   D. thinks the day is too cold.

8. When he writes, "April scatters coins of primrose gold / Among the copper leaves in thickets old," the poet means

   J. someone named April has dropped her coins.

   K. he sees golden rays of sunlight through the trees.

   L. he lives in a fantasy world where leaves are made of copper.

   M. the environment appears to be messy.

9. In this passage, *thickets* most likely means

   A. days.

   B. woods.

   C. copper.

   D. songs.

10. The tone of the poem is

    J. simple.

    K. threatening.

    L. heavy.

    M. pleasant.

Questions 11–16 are based on the following passage.

PASSAGE 3

Soups are a traditional part of Pennsylvania Dutch cooking and the Dutch housewife can apparently make soup out of anything. If she has only milk and flour she can still make rivel soup. However, most of their soups are sturdier dishes, hearty enough to serve as the major portion *Line* of the evening meal. One of the favorite summer soups in the Pennsylvania Dutch country is
5 Chicken Corn Soup. Few Sunday School picnic suppers would be considered complete without gallons of this hearty soup.

Many of the Pennsylvania Dutch foods are a part of their folklore. No Shrove Tuesday would be complete without raised doughnuts called "fastnachts." One of the many folk tales traces this custom back to the burnt offerings made by their old country ancestors to the goddess of
10 spring. With the coming of Christianity, the custom became associated with the Easter season and "fastnachts" are eaten on Shrove Tuesday to insure living to next Shrove Tuesday. Young dandelion greens are eaten on Maundy Thursday in order to remain well throughout the year...

The apple is an important Pennsylvania Dutch food. Dried apples form the basis for many typical dishes. Each fall barrels of apples are converted into cider. Apple butter is one of the
15 Pennsylvania Dutch foods which has found national acceptance. The making of apple butter is an all-day affair and has the air of a holiday to it. Early in the morning the neighbors gather and begin to peel huge piles of apples that will be needed. Soon the great copper apple butter kettle is brought out and set up over a wood fire. Apple butter requires constant stirring to prevent burning. However, stirring can be light work for a boy and a girl when they're young and the day
20 is bright and the world is full of promise. By dusk the apple butter is made, neighborhood news is brought up to date and hunger has been driven that much further away for the coming winter.

—Excerpt from *Pennsylvania Dutch Cooking*, by Unknown

11. Which of these sayings is best illustrated by this passage?

    A. "Necessity is the mother of invention."

    B. "Out with the old, in with the new."

    C. "Old habits die hard."

    D. "Too many cooks spoil the broth."

12. The word *hearty* most likely means

    J. energetic.

    K. enthusiastic.

    L. cheerful.

    M. substantial.

13. What are the Pennsylvania Dutch people most likely to eat on Shrove Tuesday?

    A. Rivel soup

    B. Chicken corn soup

    C. Fastnachts

    D. Dandelion greens

14. What is the purpose of burnt offerings?

    J. To appease the goddess of spring

    K. To eat at a Sunday school picnic

    L. To contact ancient ancestors

    M. To bake doughnuts called fastnachts

15. This passage is intended to be

A. informative.

B. persuasive.

C. humorous.

D. personal.

16. The phrase "the air of a holiday to it" is another way of saying which of the following?

J. It involves the giving of gifts.

K. It only happens once a year.

L. It is a fun event that communities enjoy together.

M. It occurs on the same day as Christmas.

Questions 17–22 are based on the following passage.

PASSAGE 4

Animals below the level of zoophytes and sponges are called Protozoa. The word obviously means "First Animals," but all that we can say is that the very simplest of them may give us some hint of the simplicity of the original first animals. For it is quite certain that the vast majority

Line of the Protozoa today are far too complicated to be thought of as primitive. Though most of

5 them are microscopic, each is an animal complete in itself, with the same fundamental bodily attributes as are manifested in ourselves. They differ from animals of higher degree in not being built up of the unit areas or corpuscles called cells. They have no cells, no tissues, no organs, in the ordinary acceptation of these words, but many of them show a great complexity of internal structure, far exceeding that of the ordinary cells that build up the tissues of higher animals.

10 They are complete living creatures that have not gone in for body-making.

—Excerpt from *The Outline of Science, Vol. 1*, by J. Arthur Thomson

17. What alternate title best expresses the main idea of the passage?

A. "The Only Complete Living Creature"

B. "The Complex First Animal"

C. "The Primitive Protozoa"

D. "It Is Quite Certain"

18. In this passage the word *fundamental* most likely means

J. useless.

K. complete.

L. basic.

M. unusual.

19. All the following characteristics of protozoa are mentioned in this passage *except* their

A. complexity.

B. appearance.

C. size.

D. internal structures.

20. Animals more complex than protozoa are made up primarily of

J. organs.

K. flesh.

L. cells.

M. bones.

21. What does the author mean when he states, "Animals below the level of zoophytes and sponges are called Protozoa"?

    A. Zoophytes and sponges are smaller than Protozoa.

    B. Zoophytes and sponges are more intelligent than Protozoa.

    C. Zoophytes and sponges are more dangerous than Protozoa.

    D. Zoophytes and sponges are more complex than Protozoa.

22. In this passage the word *exceeding* most likely means

    J. greater than.

    K. moving over.

    L. as much as.

    M. trying harder.

Questions 23–28 are based on the following passage.

Passage 5

An hour went by, and a second hour. The pale light of the short sunless day was beginning to fade, when a faint far cry arose on the still air. It soared upward with a swift rush, till it reached its topmost note, where it persisted, palpitant and tense, and then slowly died away. It might
Line have been a lost soul wailing, had it not been invested with a certain sad fierceness and hungry
5 eagerness. The front man turned his head until his eyes met the eyes of the man behind. And then, across the narrow oblong box, each nodded to the other.

    A second cry arose, piercing the silence with needle-like shrillness. Both men located the sound. It was to the rear, somewhere in the snow expanse they had just traversed. A third and answering cry arose, also to the rear and to the left of the second cry.

10   "They're after us, Bill," said the man at the front.

    His voice sounded hoarse and unreal, and he had spoken with apparent effort.

    "Meat is scarce," answered his comrade. "I ain't seen a rabbit sign for days."

    Thereafter they spoke no more, though their ears were keen for the hunting-cries that continued to rise behind them.

                     —Excerpt from *White Fang,* by Jack London

23. In this scene, Bill appears to be

    A. hungry.

    B. bored.

    C. angry.

    D. frightened.

24. The phrase *hunting-cries* probably refers to

    J. the sounds Bill and his friend are making.

    K. the sounds the animals are making.

    L. the sounds the rabbits are making.

    M. the sound the wind is making.

25. The characters were probably

   A. on a fun camping trip.

   B. spending several days outdoors.

   C. hunting for rabbits.

   D. escaped prisoners.

26. The person observing all of this is

   J. Bill.

   K. Bill's friend.

   L. a rabbit hunter.

   M. an unknown narrator.

27. The passage takes place as

   A. evening approaches.

   B. the day begins.

   C. the winter approaches.

   D. the summer is ending.

28. Which statement best reflects the main idea of the passage?

   J. "Never fear what you cannot see in the dark."

   K. "There is nothing to fear but fear itself."

   L. "Be respectful of nature, because nature has no respect for you."

   M. "Always let nature take its course."

Questions 29–34 are based on the following passage.

PASSAGE 6

The color of animals is by no means a matter of chance; it depends on many considerations, but in the majority of cases tends to protect the animal from danger by rendering it less conspicuous. Perhaps it may be said that if coloring is mainly protective, there ought to be but few brightly
Line colored animals. There are, however, not a few cases in which vivid colors are themselves pro-
5 tective. The kingfisher itself, though so brightly colored, is by no means easy to see. The blue harmonizes with the water, and the bird as it darts along the stream looks almost like a flash of sunlight; besides which, protection is not the only consideration. Let us now consider the prevalent colors of animals and see how far they support the rule.

Desert animals are generally the color of the desert. Thus, for instance, the lion, the ante-
10 lope, and the wild ass are all sand-colored. "Indeed," says Canon Tristram, "in the desert, where neither trees, brushwood, nor even undulation of the surface afford the slightest protection to its foes, a modification of color which shall be assimilated to that of the surrounding country is absolutely necessary. Hence, without exception, the upper plumage of every bird, whether lark, chat, sylvain, or sand grouse, and also the fur of all the smaller mammals and the skin of
15 all the snakes and lizards, is of one uniform sand color."

—Excerpt from *The Colors of Animals,* by Sir John Lubbock

TACHS Diagnostic Test

4

4

29. Based on the passage, *plumage* most likely means which of the following?

   A. Camouflage

   B. Color

   C. Fur

   D. Feathers

30. How does a kingfisher protect itself?

   J. It has a sharp beak it uses to peck at other animals.

   K. It flies too quickly for any other animal to catch it.

   L. Its enormous size keeps other animals from trying to hunt it.

   M. Its coloring causes it to blend in with its surroundings.

31. In paragraph 1, *conspicuous* most likely means

   A. hidden.

   B. realistic.

   C. visible.

   D. friendly.

32. All the following animals are mentioned in this passage *except*:

   J. Sand grouses

   K. Cobras

   L. Antelopes

   M. Lizards

33. The lion is adapted to blend in with

   A. the desert.

   B. grass.

   C. forests.

   D. country sides.

34. Based on this passage, which animal is most likely adapted to survive in a grassy environment?

   J. Grasshoppers

   K. Elephants

   L. Raccoons

   M. Skunks

Questions 35–40 are based on the following passage.

Passage 7

American independence, the beginnings of which we have just been considering, was accomplished after a long struggle. Many brave men fought on the battle-field, and many who never shouldered a musket or drew a sword exerted a powerful influence for the good of the patriot
Line cause. One of these men was Benjamin Franklin.

5   He was born in Boston in 1706, the fifteenth child in a family of seventeen children. His father was a candle-maker and soap-boiler. Intending to make a clergyman of Benjamin, he sent him, at eight years of age, to a grammar-school, with the purpose of fitting him for college. The boy made rapid progress, but before the end of his first school-year his father took him out on account of the expense, and put him into a school where he would learn more practical subjects,
10 such as writing and arithmetic. The last study proved very difficult for him.

    Two years later, at the age of ten, he had to go into his father's shop. Here he spent his time in cutting wicks for the candles, filling the moulds with tallow, selling soap in the shop, and acting the part of errand-boy.

    Many times he had watched the vessels sailing in and out of Boston Harbor, and often in
15 imagination had gone with them on their journeys. Now he longed to become a sailor, and, quitting the drudgery of the candle-shop, to roam out over the sea in search of more interesting life. But his father wisely refused to let him go. His fondness for the sea, however, took him frequently to the water, and he learned to swim like a fish and to row and sail boats with great skill. In these sports, as in others, he became a leader among his playmates.

20   With all his dislike for the business of candle-making and soap-boiling, and with all his fondness for play, he was still faithful in doing everything that his father's business required. His industry, together with his liking for good books and his keen desire for knowledge, went far toward supplying the lack of school training. He spent most of his leisure time reading and devoted his savings to collecting a small library.

25   His father, noting his bookish habits, decided to apprentice Benjamin to his older brother, James, a printer in Boston. Benjamin was to serve until he was 21 and to receive no wages until the last year. In this position he was able to see more books and made good use of his opportunities. Often, he would read far into the night, a borrowed book that had to be returned in the morning. He also wrote some verses and peddled them about the streets, until his father
30 discouraged him by ridiculing his efforts.

—Excerpt from *American Leaders and Heroes: A Preliminary Text-book in United States History,* by Wilbur F. Gordy

35. The author refers to Benjamin Franklin as "a leader among his playmates" because

    A. he was captain of an athletic team.

    B. he was stronger than the other children.

    C. the other children probably admired him.

    D. the other children feared him.

36. As used in sentence 2 of paragraph 1, what does the word *shouldered* most likely mean?

    J. Built

    K. Sold

    L. Threw

    M. Carried

37. Benjamin Franklin probably disliked making candles because

    A. the work was too difficult.

    B. he was not smart enough to make candles.

    C. he wanted to become a writer.

    D. it was not challenging work.

38. In the second sentence of paragraph 5, *keen* most likely means

    J. eager.

    K. intense.

    L. biting.

    M. blunt.

39. Why did Benjamin Franklin's father send him to apprentice for his brother, James?

    A. He wanted Benjamin to make more money than he did as a candle maker.

    B. He knew that Benjamin always wanted to become a printer.

    C. He could tell that Benjamin was interested in printed materials.

    D. He though Benjamin might learn to read if he worked as a printer.

40. What would be an appropriate alternate title for this passage?

    J. "Benjamin Franklin: The Early Years"

    K. "The Life of a Founding Father"

    L. "Benjamin Franklin: The Complete Biography"

    M. "The Art of Making Candles"

Questions 41–46 are based on the following passage.

PASSAGE 8

Like Art, Tea has its periods and its schools. Its evolution may be roughly divided into three main stages: the Boiled Tea, the Whipped Tea, and the Steeped Tea. We moderns belong to the last school. These several methods of appreciating the beverage are indicative of the spirit of the age *Line* in which they prevailed. For life is an expression, our unconscious actions the constant betrayal 5 of our innermost thought. Confucius said that "man hideth not." Perhaps we reveal ourselves too much in small things because we have so little of the great to conceal. The tiny incidents of daily routine are as much a commentary of racial ideals as the highest flight of philosophy or poetry. Even as the difference in favorite vintage marks the separate idiosyncrasies of different periods and nationalities of Europe, so the Tea-ideals characterize the various moods of Asian culture. 10 The Cake-tea which was boiled, the Powdered-tea which was whipped, the Leaf-tea which was steeped, mark the distinct emotional impulses of the Tang, the Sung, and the Ming dynasties of China. If we were inclined to borrow the much-abused terminology of art-classification, we might designate them respectively, the Classic, the Romantic, and the Naturalistic schools of Tea.

    The tea-plant, a native of southern China, was known from very early times to Chinese 15 botany and medicine. It is alluded to in the classics under the various names of Tou, Tseh, Chung, Kha, and Ming, and was highly prized for possessing the virtues of relieving fatigue, delighting the soul, strengthening the will, and repairing the eyesight. It was not only administered as an internal dose, but often applied externally in paste form to alleviate rheumatic pains. The Taoists claimed it as an important ingredient of the elixir of immortality. The Buddhists used 20 it extensively to prevent drowsiness during their long hours of meditation.

—Excerpt adapted from *The Book of Tea,* by Kakuzo Okakura

41. Who used tea to stay awake?

    A. Taoists

    B. Confucians

    C. Mohists

    D. Buddhists

42. In the fourth sentence of paragraph 1, the word *indicative* most likely means

    J. opposite.

    K. unrelated.

    L. representative.

    M. following.

43. How was tea administered to relieve rheumatic pains?

    A. As a paste

    B. Brewed in water

    C. As a pill

    D. As dry leaves

44. Which kind of tea was whipped?

    J. Powdered tea

    K. Cake tea

    L. Leaf tea

    M. Ming tea

45. In sentence 13 of the passage, the word *designate* most likely means

    A. solve.

    B. name.

    C. detail.

    D. move.

46. Based on this passage, which of the following is true?

    J. Tea is the most important influence on Chinese philosophy.

    K. The only correct Chinese name for tea is Chung.

    L. Tea was believed to have many uses in Chinese culture.

    M. Tea does not really repair weak eyesight.

Questions 47–50 are based on the following passage.

Passage 9

The western margin of this continent is built of a succession of mountain chains folded in broad corrugations, like waves of stone upon whose seaward base beat the mild, small breakers of the Pacific.

Line
5   By far the grandest of all these ranges is the Sierra Nevada, a long and massive uplift lying between the arid deserts of the Great Basin and the Californian exuberance of grain-field and orchard; its eastern slope, a defiant wall of rock plunging abruptly down to the plain; the western, a long, grand sweep, well watered and overgrown with cool, stately forests; its crest a line of sharp, snowy peaks springing into the sky and catching the *alpenglow* long after the sun has set for all the rest of America.

10   The Sierras have a structure and a physical character which are individual and unique. To Professor Whitney and his corps of the Geological Survey of California is due the honor of first gaining a scientific knowledge of the form, plan, and physical conditions of the Sierras.

            —Excerpt from *Mountaineering in the Sierra Nevada*, by Clarence King

4

TACHS Diagnostic Test

47. Why does the author claim the Sierra Nevada is the grandest of the western mountain ranges?

    A. It is huge with several unique features.

    B. It is the biggest of the mountain ranges.

    C. It has several snowy peaks.

    D. It is part of a great desert.

48. What was Professor Whitney's relationship with the Sierra Nevada range?

    J. He was the first person to discover it.

    K. He was the first person to climb it.

    L. He was the first person to record its features.

    M. He was the first person to measure it.

49. What makes up the eastern side of the Sierra Nevada range?

    A. Forests

    B. Rock

    C. A grain field

    D. An orchard

50. In the first sentence of paragraph 2, the word *arid* most likely means

    J. rainy.

    K. small.

    L. pleasant.

    M. dry.

STOP.

If you finish before time is up, you may check your work on this section only.
Do not turn to any other section in the test.

WRITTEN EXPRESSION

50 Questions (30 Minutes)

Turn to the Written Expression section of your answer sheet to answer the questions in this section.

Directions: This is a test of how well you can find mistakes in writing. You will be given questions that deal with spelling, capitalization, punctuation, usage, and expression. Based on the instructions given for each section, you will either choose the answer you think is better than the others or determine how to correct a mistake in the way words or sentences are used. If no correction is needed, choose the last answer choice.

For questions 1-10, identify the misspelled word. If all the words are spelled correctly, choose the last option, (*No mistakes*).

---

1. A. cantaloupe
   B. porcupine
   C. acquire
   D. explaination
   E. (*No mistakes*)

2. J. definitly
   K. license
   L. noticeable
   M. publicly
   N. (*No mistakes*)

3. A. seperate
   B. until
   C. calendar
   D. leisure
   E. (*No mistakes*)

4. J. jewelry
   K. accommodate
   L. priviledge
   M. restaurant
   N. (*No mistakes*)

5. A. camouflage
   B. foreign
   C. defendant
   D. grammar
   E. (*No mistakes*)

6. J. apology
   K. precede
   L. disappoint
   M. existance
   N. (*No mistakes*)

7. A. development
   B. pronounciation
   C. recommend
   D. knowledge
   E. (*No mistakes*)

8. J. occasion
   K. pleasant
   L. necessery
   M. labeled
   N. (*No mistakes*)

9. A. obstacle
   B. pallor
   C. escalater
   D. width
   E. (*No mistakes*)

10. J. generation
    K. frivolous
    L. overbearing
    M. tawnt
    N. (*No mistakes*)

Directions: For questions 11-25, identify the line of text that contains an error in capitalization, punctuation, usage, or expression. If there are no errors, choose the last option, (*No mistakes*).

11. **A.** In the movie *King Kong,*
    B. a giant gorilla climbs up the
    C. side of the Empire State building.
    D. (*No mistakes*)

12. **J.** We just got a new kitten,
    K. and my little sister gave him an
    L. adorable name Pookie.
    M. (*No mistakes*)

13. **A.** I asked my cousin Tim if
    B. he has ever read the poem "The Raven"
    C. by Edgar Allan Poe.
    D. (*No mistakes*)

14. **J.** The first chapter of Herman Melville's
    K. novel *Moby Dick*
    L. is called *Loomings.*
    M. (*No mistakes*)

15. **A.** "Fur Elise" is one of the most famous
    B. compositions by Ludwig van Beethoven,
    C. but no one really knows who elise is.
    D. (*No mistakes*)

16. **J.** Did you know that Khandi
    K. has an article in the latest addition
    L. of the school newspaper?
    M. (*No mistakes*)

17. **A.** Pluto was once considered to be a
    B. planet, but it has recently been
    C. demoted to a Planetoid.
    D. (*No mistakes*)

18. **J.** Mrs Shahi is going to
    K. be my art teacher
    L. next semester.
    M. (*No mistakes*)

19. **A.** My sister works in a glass factory
    B. on highway 61 called
    C. Super Glass Works, LTD.
    D. (*No mistakes*)

20. **J.** I haven't seen Jimmy,
    K. Maria said, despite just
    L. taking math class with him.
    M. (*No mistakes*)

21. **A.** This is not the same car
    B. we drove here, so our car must be
    C. parked someplace else?
    D. (*No mistakes*)

22. **J.** Willow is running for class
    K. president; Buffy is the captain of
    L. the cheerleading squad.
    M. (*No mistakes*)

23. **A.** When you pack for the trip,
    B. be sure to include, a warm sweater,
    C. a heavy jacket, and ski pants.
    D. (*No mistakes*)

24. **J.** Shara and Lashawn are going
    K. to that new movie on Saturday,
    L. and I really want to see it with her.
    M. (*No mistakes*)

25. **A.** Last year I attended JFK Junior
    B. High School, but next year I will be
    C. going to St. Mary's High School.
    D. (*No mistakes*)

Directions: For questions 26–30, choose the best way of expressing the idea.

26. J. They were anxious, the explorers were, because dangerous terrain they knew they were entering.

    K. The explorers, because they knew that they were entering dangerous terrain, were anxious.

    L. The explorers were anxious because they knew that they were entering dangerous terrain.

    M. The explorers, knowing that they were entering dangerous terrain, were anxious.

27. A. At the tournament, John, because he lost his confidence, fared poorly despite months of practice.

    B. Despite months of practice, John lost his confidence and fared poorly at the tournament.

    C. John, at the tournament, despite months of practice, lost his confidence and fared poorly.

    D. Losing his confidence, at the tournament despite months of practice, John fared poorly.

28. J. Putting aside their differences on the project allowed Marc and Jason to collaborate on it.

    K. Marc and Jason, once they put aside their differences on the project, collaborated.

    L. Collaborating on the project, Marc and Jason were able to once they put aside their differences.

    M. Marc and Jason were able to collaborate on the project once they put aside their differences.

29. A. The Louisiana Purchase and the Gold Rush sparked westward expansion in the nineteenth century.

    B. Sparking westward expansion were the Louisiana Purchase and the Gold Rush in the nineteenth century.

    C. The Louisiana Purchase in the nineteenth century and the Gold Rush sparked westward expansion.

    D. In the nineteenth century, westward expansion of the Louisiana Purchase and the Gold Rush sparked.

30. J. From Monday to Friday long hours my mother works, but she always makes plenty of time to spend with me on the weekend.

    K. My mother works long hours from Monday to Friday, but she always makes plenty of time to spend with me on the weekend.

    L. My mother, but she always makes plenty of time to spend with me on the weekend, from Monday to Friday works long hours.

    M. My mother long hours from Monday to Friday works, but she always makes plenty of time to spend with me on the weekend.

4

TACHS Diagnostic Test

4

Directions: For questions 31–50, choose the best answer based on the following paragraphs.

---

(1) Most photographers snap photos because they <u>wanted to capture</u> beautiful or interesting images. (2) However, Dorothea Lange had a higher purpose behind her work. (3) She took pictures of impoverished people during the Great Depression to expose the personal cost of the vast economic crisis. (4) She took pictures of unemployed people and migrant workers often with captions featuring quotations from the people in her pictures. (5) She performed her work as an investigative project for the U.S. Farm Security Administration, and it served as a powerful, unforgettable portrait of a difficult time in U.S. history.

31. What is the best way to write the underlined portion of sentence 1?

  A. want to capture

  B. wants to capture

  C. wanted to captured

  D. *(No change)*

32. Choose the best last sentence to add to this paragraph.

  J. Dorothea Lange was born on May 26, 1895, in Hoboken, New Jersey.

  K. The U.S. Farm Security Administration employed Dorothea Lange, and her pictures chronicled a tough time for America.

  L. For that reason, Dorothea Lange will always be remembered as a great artist and human being.

  M. Another great photographer is Ansel Adams, who is beloved for his landscape pictures and environmental work.

(1) However, collage is an art form that anyone can perform. (2) It simply involves taking existing pictures and reconfiguring them into interesting new images. (3) Some artists create collages by clipping pictures out of magazines and pasting them onto <u>oak tag; but collages</u> can also be made digitally using a computer. (4) A collage may follow a particular theme, or it may be a random assortment of pictures that capture the artist's fancy. (5) There are no rules to making a collage, which is another reason why it is such a fabulous and accessible art form.

33. Choose the best first sentence to add to this paragraph.

    A. Making collages is something anyone can do.

    B. Some people shy away from the arts because they do not know how to draw or sculpt.

    C. Art forms include painting, sculpting, drawing, making collages, dancing, making music, writing, and anything else that is creative.

    D. A collage artist must study for years to become good at his or her craft.

34. What is the best way to write the underlined portion of sentence 3?

    J. oak tag, but collages

    K. oak tag collages

    L. oak tag: but collages

    M. (No change)

(1) A rhinoceros may look like a huge, horned pig, or even a distant relative of horned <u>dinosaurs such as the triceratops</u>. (2) However, this animal is actually related to the horse. (3) It is a member of the odd-toed ungulates, which includes several other <u>animals horses, asses, and zebras</u>. (4) All of these creatures are characterized by their odd number of toes and the fact that they digest plant cellulose in their intestines instead of their stomachs. (5) A rhinoceros may be related to the horse, but it still might not be a smart idea to try to ride one!

35. What is the best way to write the underlined portion of sentence 1?

    A. dinosaurs such as the Triceratops

    B. Dinosaurs such as the triceratops

    C. Dinosaurs such as the Triceratops

    D. (No change)

36. What is the best way to write the underlined portion of sentence 3?

    J. animals: horses, asses, and zebras

    K. animals; horses, asses and zebras

    L. animals, horses, asses, and zebras

    M. (No change)

(1) *Dracula* is one of the most popular novels ever written. (2) It <u>tells the tail</u> of a mysterious Transylvanian count who is actually an ancient blood-drinking creature known as the vampire. (3) Yet as successful as *Dracula* was, its writer never managed to write another book that was as well-loved. (4) In fact, few people even read books such as *The Jewel of Seven Stars* and *Miss Betty*. (5) His final novel, <u>The lair of the white worm</u>, is considered almost laughably poor and borderline nonsensical. (6) So although Stoker had a major hit with his chilling tale of creeping vampires, he will forever be remembered as a one-hit wonder.

TACHS Diagnostic Test

4

37. What is the best way to write the underlined portion of sentence 2?

   A. tells the tale

   B. tells the tails

   C. tell the tail

   D. *(No change)*

38. What is the best way to write the underlined portion of sentence 5?

   J. *The Lair Of The White Worm*

   K. *The lair of The white worm*

   L. *The Lair of the White Worm*

   M. *(No change)*

(1) Finding a fossil from a long-extinct dinosaur is always an amazing discovery for scientists. (2) Few places are <u>as rife in fossils</u> as the southeast side of the Uinta Mountains. (3) That is why it has earned the title of Dinosaur National Monument! (4) Exploration of the site began in 1909 when paleontologist Earl Douglass first discovered an abundance of plant and animal fossils there. (5) Yet discoveries continue into the present age. (6) In 2010, a team of paleontologists discovered a previously unknown <u>herbivore called: *Abydosaurus mcintoshi*</u>. (7) However, you do not need to be a professional scientist to explore Dinosaur National Monument—just ask the explorers of all ages who view the 1,500 bones pulled from the site displayed at the Dinosaur Quarry Exhibit Hall!

39. What is the best way to write the underlined portion of sentence 2?

   A. as rich of fossils

   B. as rich in fossils

   C. as rife of fossils

   D. *(No change)*

40. What is the best way to write the underlined portion of sentence 6?

   J. herbivore called; *Abydosaurus mcintoshi*

   K. herbivore called *Abydosaurus mcintoshi*

   L. herbivore called—*Abydosaurus mcintoshi*

   M. *(No change)*

(1) The Taj Mahal is one of the most spectacular buildings in the world. (2) Although its name translates to "Crown of the Palace," the Taj Mahal is not actually a palace; it is a mausoleum entombing Mumtaz Mahal. (3) She was the wife of emperor <u>Shah Jahan of the Mughal empire</u>. (4) He so adored his wife that when she died, he had a massive, architecturally spectacular construction made to serve as her final resting place. (5) Two thousand artisans were required to build it at a cost of $827 million in contemporary US currency.

41. Choose the best final sentence to add to this paragraph.

    A. The Taj Mahal remains one of the most recognizable buildings in the world and an essential destination for visitors to Pradesh, India.

    B. Shah Jahan, who reigned from 1628 to 1658, commissioned the building of the Taj Mahal in 1632.

    C. Mumtaz Mahal's birth name was Arjumand Banu Begum, and she was born in Agra, a city on the banks of the Yamuna River in Uttar Pradesh.

    D. The Taj Mahal is designated a UNESCO World Heritage Site, and so is Dinosaur Provincial Park in Alberta, Canada.

42. What is the best way to write the underlined portion of sentence 3?

    J. Shah Jahan of the mughal empire

    K. Shah Jahan of the Mughal Empire

    L. shah Jahan of the Mughal Empire

    M. *(No change)*

(1) Considered one of the Seven Natural Wonders of the World, Paracutin is a cinder volcano that varies between 9,101 and 10,397 feet above ground. (2) Although it has been dormant since 1952, Paracutin is still considered to be an active volcano. (3) However, these are not the reasons it is considered a natural wonder. (4) The amazing thing about Paracutin is that its birth was actually witnessed by people. (5) While most volcanoes originated during prehistoric times, Paracutin dates back less than 80 years ago. (6) In fact, it is the youngest volcano in the world, which makes it wholly unique.

43. What is the best way to write the underlined portion of sentence 1?

    A. the Seven Natural Wonders Of the World

    B. the Seven Natural Wonders Of The World

    C. the seven natural wonders of the world

    D. *(No change)*

44. What is the best way to write the underlined portion of sentence 4?

    J. Paracutin is that it's birth

    K. Paracutin is that it is birth

    L. Paracutin is that its' birth

    M. *(No change)*

(1) If you enters any souvenir shop in New York City, you are likely to find abundant merchandise depicting the Statue of Liberty. (2) The statue is regarded as one of the most recognizable symbols of the Big Apple. (3) However, most people do not realize that the Statue of Liberty is technically not located in New York City. (4) In fact, it is not even located in the state of New York. (5) The Statue of Liberty is actually positioned within New Jersey, even though the statue is officially within the territorial jurisdiction of New York. (6) The Statue of Liberty can even be reached from ferries out of Jersey City's Liberty State Park, named in honor of the major but rather misunderstood New Jersey landmark.

45. What is the best way to write the underlined portion of sentence 1?

A. If you enter any

B. If they enters any

C. If we enters any

D. *(No change)*

46. What is the best way to write the underlined portion of sentence 6?

J. major. But rather misunderstood. New Jersey

K. major—but rather misunderstood—New Jersey

L. major; but rather misunderstood; New Jersey

M. *(No change)*

(1) People often travel to Hawaii for its natural beauty. (2) However, there is a human-made attraction that is just as lush and green and gorgeous <u>as any palm tree framed shore</u>. (3) On Honolulu's Dole Plantation, you will find the Pineapple Garden Maze. (4) It is the largest hedge maze in the world, spanning almost three acres of land. (5) To walk through all its paths is to walk almost two and a half miles. (6) While it is a marvelous place to simply stroll at a leisurely pace, some visitors race through the Pineapple Garden Maze as quickly as possible because those with the fastest exit time are allowed to sign their names at the entrance of the maze. (7) <u>Its considered quite</u> an honor among maze enthusiasts.

47. What is the best way to write the underlined portion of sentence 2?

A. as any palm tree-framed-shore

B. as any palm-tree framed shore

C. as any palm tree-framed shore

D. *(No change)*

48. What is the best way to write the underlined portion of sentence 7?

J. It's considered quite

K. Its' considered quite

L. It is' considered quite

M. *(No change)*

(1) With the enacting of the Emergency Quota Act of 1921, the United States drastically restricted immigration, especially from non-Northern European countries. (2) Many saw the act as discriminatory and in need of revision. (3) This <u>revision finally is occurring in 1965</u> when New York Representative Emanuel Celler proposed the Immigration and Nationality Act. (4) The new act removed the racial and national specifics of the Emergency Quota Act, allowing more diverse immigration into the United States. (5) With support from Senators Phillip Hart and Ted Kennedy, the bill passed heralded the age of a more welcoming America.

49. What is the best way to write the underlined portion of sentence 3?

   A. revision finally will be occurring in 1965

   B. revision finally occurred in 1965

   C. revision finally occurs in 1965

   D. *(No change)*

50. What is the best way to write sentence 5?

   J. With support from Senators Phillip Hart and Ted Kennedy, the bill passed and heralded the age of a more welcoming America.

   K. With support from Senators Phillip Hart and Ted Kennedy, the bill passed, heralded the age of a more welcoming America.

   L. With support from Senators Phillip Hart and Ted Kennedy.

   M. *(No change)*

STOP.

If you finish before time is up, you may check your work on this section only.
Do not turn to any other section in the test.

4

TACHS Diagnostic Test

MATHEMATICS
50 Questions (40 Minutes)

Turn to the Mathematics section of your answer sheet to answer the questions in this section.

Directions: Four answers are given for each problem. Choose the best answer.

---

1. Which of these is equivalent to $(5 \times 10^4) + (3 \times 10^2) + (1 \times 10^1) + (4 \times 10^{-2})$?

   A. 531.4

   B. 5,031.004

   C. 5,031.04

   D. 50,310.04

2. What is the sum of four squared and three cubed?

   J. 16

   K. 17

   L. 27

   M. 43

3. The ratio of bathrooms to bedrooms in a mansion is 2:3. If there are 18 bedrooms, how many bathrooms are there?

   A. 9

   B. 12

   C. 15

   D. 21

4. Which of these is equal to $5\frac{11}{25}$?

   J. 0.522

   K. 2.2

   L. 5.22

   M. 5.44

5. Compute: $1.111 - 0.919$

   A. 0.108

   B. 0.192

   C. 0.202

   D. 0.292

6. Which of these numbers is composite?

   J. 17

   K. 23

   L. 51

   M. 71

7. Which of these statements is true?

   A. $1 - (-4) < 4 - (-2)$

   B. $(-2)(3) > (-1)(-6)$

   C. $6 \div \left(-\frac{1}{2}\right) > \left(\frac{1}{4}\right) \div \left(-\frac{1}{4}\right)$

   D. $-(5 - 3) = -5 - 3$

8. The ratio of camp counselors to campers is 1:25. If there are 9 counselors, how many campers are there?

   J. 34

   K. 125

   L. 225

   M. 450

9. Compute: $2\left(\frac{5}{2} - 2\right) \div \frac{1}{2}$

   A. $\frac{1}{2}$

   B. 1

   C. 2

   D. 6

10. Solve for x: $x + \dfrac{5}{4} = \dfrac{17}{8}$

   J. $\dfrac{27}{8}$

   K. 3

   L. $\dfrac{7}{8}$

   M. $\dfrac{17}{20}$

Use the following diagram for Questions 11 and 12:

A family has several tasks to complete in preparation for Halloween each year. The pie chart below shows the time devoted to each of these tasks.

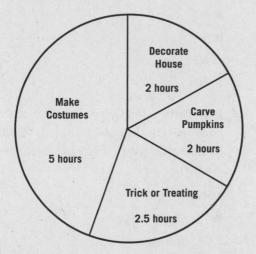

11. How much total time is spent preparing for Halloween each year?

   A. 5 hours

   B. 7.5 hours

   C. 11.5 hours

   D. 13.5 hours

12. What is the approximate percentage of the total time spent on trick-or-treating?

   J. 17%

   K. 35%

   L. 43%

   M. 22%

13. Which of these is NOT equal to $(3 + 4)^2$?

   A. $(3 + 4)(3 + 4)$

   B. $3^2 + 2 \cdot 3 \cdot 4 + 4^2$

   C. $(3 + 4)(4 + 3)$

   D. $3^2 + 4^2$

14. What is the perimeter of the rhombus *ABCD*?

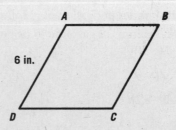

   J. 12 inches

   K. 24 inches

   L. 36 inches

   M. 18 inches

15. A batch of brownies takes $\dfrac{2}{3}$ hour to bake. If Cherie bakes 4 batches of brownies, one at a time, each day for 3 days, how many hours total is spent baking?

   A. 2 hours

   B. 4 hours

   C. 6 hours

   D. 8 hours

16. A credit card company charges a 4% balance transfer fee. If you want to transfer a balance of $2,100 to this credit card, what fee would you pay?

   J. $40

   K. $84

   L. $400

   M. $840

4

TACHS Diagnostic Test

17. 4 hours minus 1 hour, 59 minutes, 58 seconds equals

    A. 2 hours, 2 seconds.

    B. 3 hours, 1 minute, 2 seconds.

    C. 2 hours, 1 minute, 1 second.

    D. 3 hours, 2 seconds.

18. If it is p miles from home to school, how many round trips can be made if your car gets q miles per gallon of gasoline and there are 5 gallons of gasoline in its tank?

    J. $\dfrac{5q}{2p}$

    K. $5q + 2p$

    L. $\dfrac{q}{p}$

    M. $\dfrac{5}{2} + pq$

19. Compute: $\left(-\dfrac{1}{2}\right)\cdot(-6)\div\left(-\dfrac{3}{2}\right)$

    A. $-\dfrac{9}{2}$

    B. -2

    C. 2

    D. $\dfrac{9}{4}$

20. Find x:

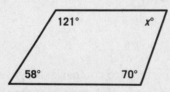

    J. 58°

    K. 70°

    L. 111°

    M. 121°

Use the following stacked bar chart for Questions 21–23:

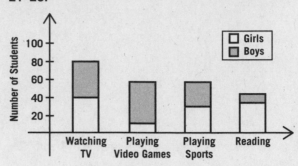

21. How many boys selected "Watching TV" as their favorite activity?

    A. 20

    B. 40

    C. 60

    D. 80

22. For which activity is there the largest difference between the number of girls selecting it as their favorite and the number of boys doing so?

    J. Watching TV

    K. Playing video games

    L. Playing sports

    M. Reading

23. What is the ratio of the number of boys to the number of girls selecting "Playing Sports" as their favorite activity?

    A. 3:6

    B. 2:1

    C. 3:2

    D. 1:1

Use the following chart for Questions 24 and 25:

Three traffic officers record the number of speeding tickets they issue to drivers each week for six weeks. The results are as follows:

Week	Officer Ken	Officer Michelle	Officer Pat
1	8	6	1
2	5	10	2
3	0	3	1
4	7	4	10
5	11	3	9
6	2	8	6

24. How many more tickets did Officer Michelle issue than Officer Ken during this six-week period?

J. 1
K. 4
L. 5
M. 7

25. During which week were the least number of tickets issued?

A. Week 3
B. Week 1
C. Week 5
D. Week 6

26. 500% of 0.01 is _____.

J. 0.05
K. 0.5
L. 5
M. 50

27. The temperature is 96° on the beach at 1 p.m. on Monday. If the temperature decreases by 25% by 5 a.m. Tuesday morning and then increases by 10% by noon that same day, what is the approximate temperature at noon on Tuesday?

A. 72°
B. 76°
C. 79°
D. 82°

28. If $x = -1$ and $y = 2$, what is the value of $(y - x)^3$?

J. 1
K. 9
L. 27
M. 81

29. Which of these equals $2^5 \cdot 3^2$?

A. $(2 \cdot 3)^{5+2}$
B. $(2 \cdot 3)^{5 \cdot 2}$
C. $(2 \cdot 5)(2 \cdot 3)$
D. $2^3 \cdot 6^2$

Use the following graph for Questions 30 and 31:

The number of weighted lunges that Nancy and Laura completed during a workout session each day of a certain week is shown below.

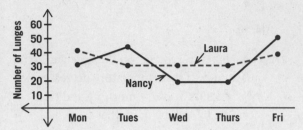

30. What is the difference between the number of lunges Nancy completed and the number Laura completed during this five-day period?

   J. 0

   K. 10

   L. 20

   M. 30

31. What fraction of the total number of lunges that Laura completed did she complete on Friday?

   A. $\frac{3}{17}$

   B. $\frac{4}{17}$

   C. $\frac{2}{11}$

   D. $\frac{4}{5}$

32. What is the area of the shaded region inside the square *ABCD*?

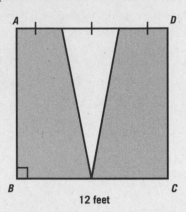

   J. 48 square feet

   K. 96 square feet

   L. 120 square feet

   M. 144 square feet

33. What is the complete set of factors common to 12, 18, and 48?

   A. {1, 3, 6, 12, 18}

   B. {1, 2, 3, 4, 6}

   C. {1, 2, 3, 6}

   D. {1, 2, 3, 12}

34. What is the area of the shaded region pictured below?

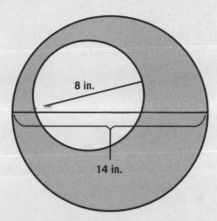

J. 6π square inches

K. 33π square inches

L. 49π square inches

M. 132π square inches

35. Which of the following does *not* result in an integer?

A. $9 \div \dfrac{1}{4}$

B. $2 - 16$

C. $\left(\dfrac{1}{2}\right)^2$

D. $\dfrac{5 + 11}{5 + 3}$

36. In what quadrant of the *xy*-plane does the point $(-5, 6)$ lie?

J. Quadrant I

K. Quadrant II

L. Quadrant III

M. Quadrant IV

37. Find the value of *x*:

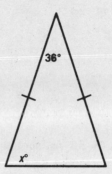

A. $54°$

B. $72°$

C. $90°$

D. $144°$

38. Stella leaves her home at 5 a.m. for a road trip to the beach. She arrives at the hotel at 1 p.m. If she drove 560 miles, what was her average speed?

J. 60 miles per hour

K. 65 miles per hour

L. 70 miles per hour

M. 80 miles per hour

39. Rick likes playing classic video games. He plays three rounds of a game and earns the following scores: 6,500; 13,000; and 16,500. What is his average score for these three games?

A. 9,000

B. 11,500

C. 12,000

D. 13,000

4

TACHS Diagnostic Test

40. If x is an odd integer, which of these is also an odd integer?

J. $x + 2$

K. $2x$

L. $x + 1$

M. $\dfrac{x}{2}$

For Questions 41–50, estimate the answer without writing any calculations down.

41. What is the closest estimate for $(8.04)^2$?

A. 62

B. 65

C. 68

D. 70

42. What is the closest estimate for $4(1.7 + 8.1) + 3(12.1 + 7.6)$?

J. 60

K. 80

L. 90

M. 100

43. What is the closest estimate to $8,112 - 4,978$?

A. 2,000

B. 3,000

C. 4,000

D. 5,000

44. What is the closest estimate to

$$4\frac{7}{8} + 7\frac{1}{16} + 9\frac{8}{9}?$$

J. 20

K. 22

L. 25

M. 30

45. A recipe calls for 9 ounces of canola oil. If the recipe were made 32 times, how many ounces of canola oil would be needed?

A. 40

B. 100

C. 288

D. 400

46. A survey of local teachers revealed that 5% were not in favor of the field trip to the city art museum. If 612 teachers responded to the survey, about how many were not in favor of the field trip?

J. 30

K. 45

L. 60

M. 75

47. What is the closest estimate to 286×193?

A. 30,000

B. 40,000

C. 60,000

D. 100,000

48. What is the closest estimate to 39.08 ÷ 2.13?

    J. 15

    K. 20

    L. 40

    M. 80

49. Tim bowled nine games and acquired a total of 1,819 points. What is the best estimate of the average number of points he scored per game?

    A. 190

    B. 192

    C. 195

    D. 200

50. It takes Cooper 8 minutes to complete an exercise circuit. If he completed 9 circuits, how long did it take him?

    J. 17 minutes

    K. 58 minutes

    L. 72 minutes

    M. 90 minutes

STOP.

If you finish before time is up, you may check your work on this section only.

Do not turn to any other section in the test.

4

TACHS Diagnostic Test

ABILITY
50 Questions (32 Minutes)
Figure Classification

Turn to the Ability section of your answer sheet to answer the questions in this section.

Directions: In questions 1–20, the first three figures are alike in certain ways. Choose the answer choice that best corresponds to the first three figures.

4

1.

A. B. C. D. E.

2.

J. K. L. M. N.

3.

A. B. C. D. E.

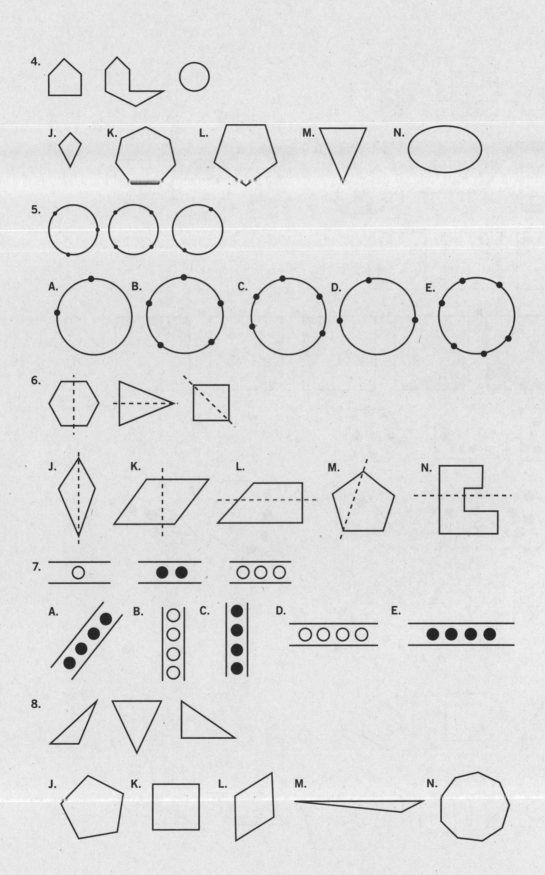

4.

J.   K.   L.   M.   N.

5.

A.   B.   C.   D.   E.

6.

J.   K.   L.   M.   N.

7.

A.   B.   C.   D.   E.

8.

J.   K.   L.   M.   N.

TACHS Diagnostic Test

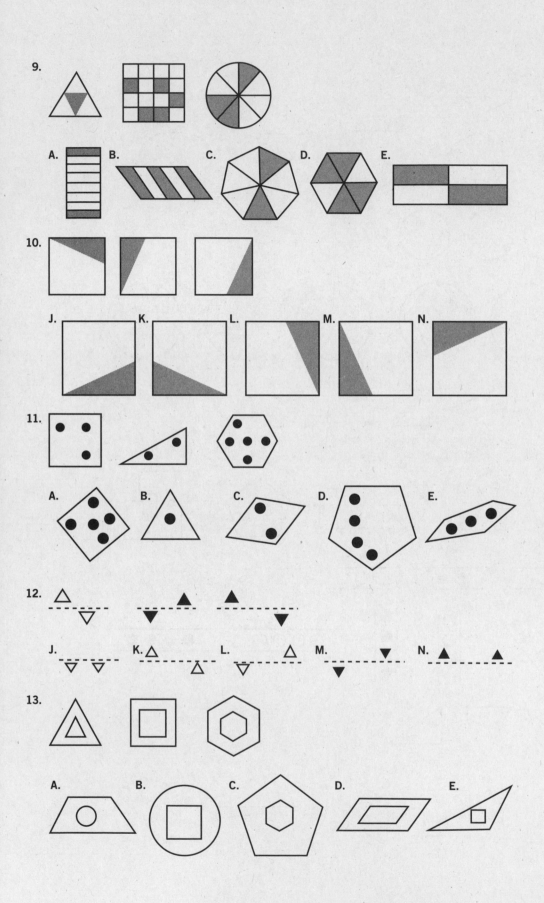

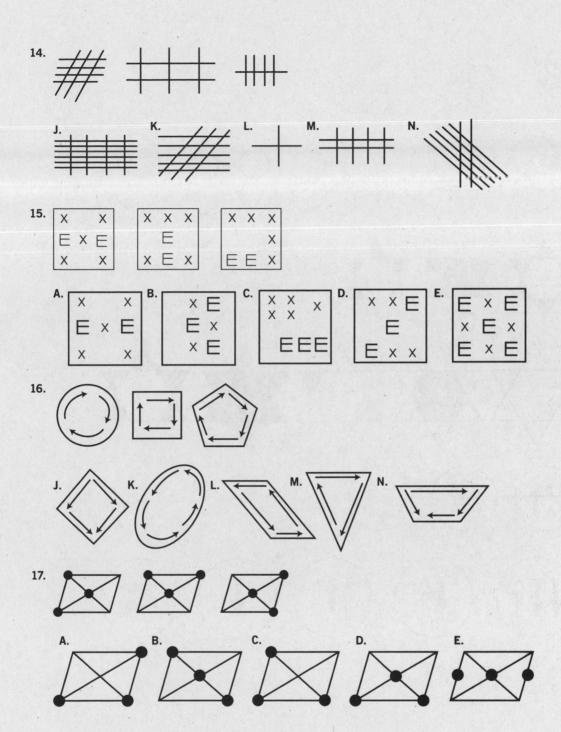

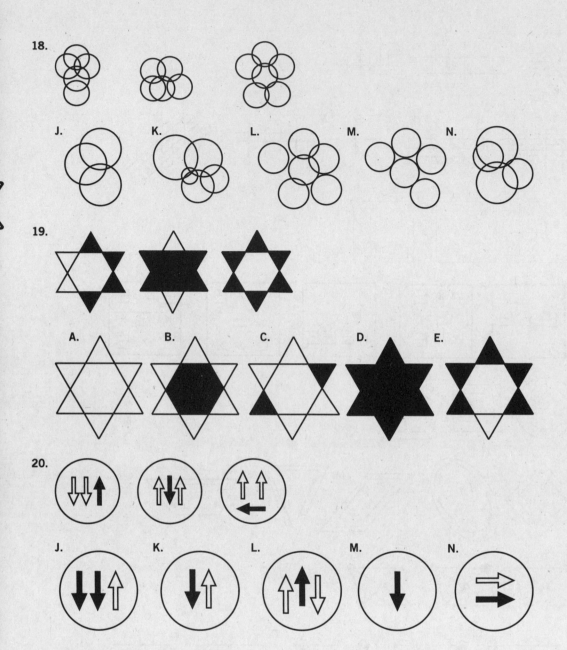

18.

J.   K.   L.   M.   N.

19.

A.   B.   C.   D.   E.

20.

J.   K.   L.   M.   N.

PART II: Diagnostic Tests

Figure Matrices

Directions: In questions 1–20, select the image that would continue the pattern or sequence.

1.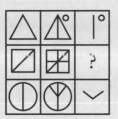

A. B. C. D. E.

2.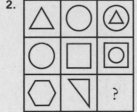

J.  K. L. M. N.

3.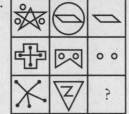

A. B. C. D. E.

TACHS Diagnostic Test

4

4.

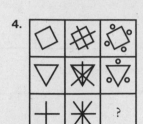

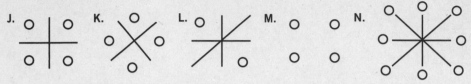

5.

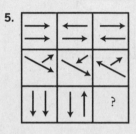

A.   B.   C.   D.   E.

6.

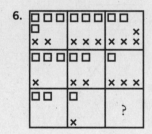

7.

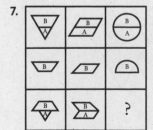

A.   B.   C.   D.   E.

8.

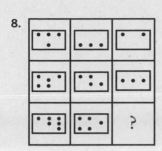

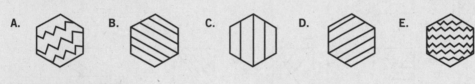

J.   K.   L.   M.   N.

9.

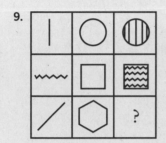

A.   B.   C.   D.   E.

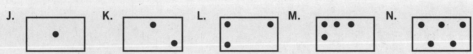

10.

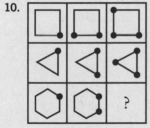

J.   K.   L.   M.   N.

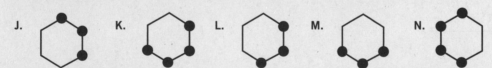

11.

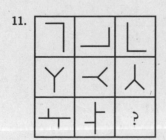

A.   B.   C.   D.   E.

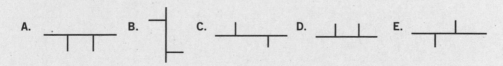

4

TACHS Diagnostic Test

12.

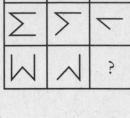

J. 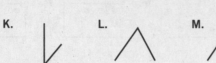 K. L. M. N.

13.

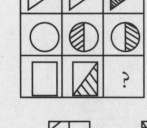

A. B. C. D. E.

14.

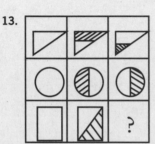

J. 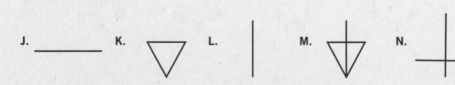 K. L. M. N.

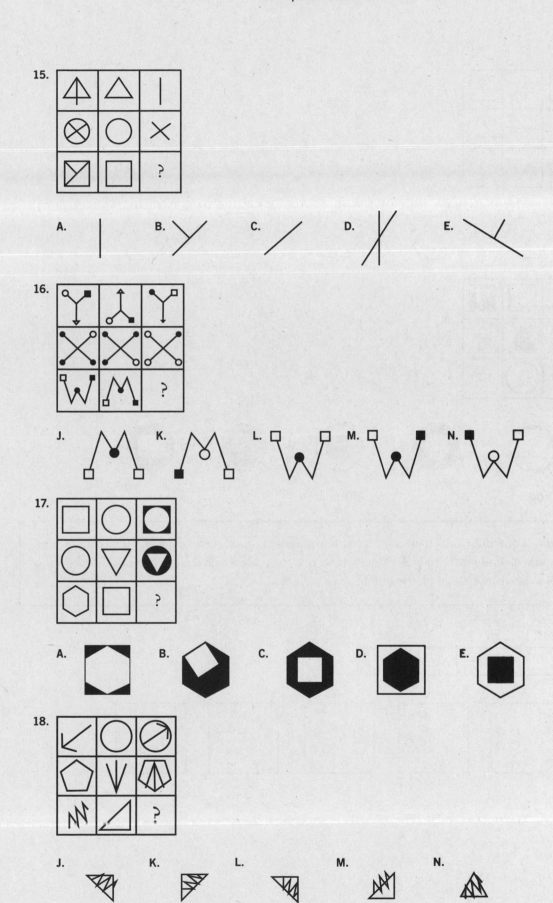

15.

A.   B.   C.   D.   E.

16.

J.   K.   L.   M.   N.

17.

A.   B.   C.   D.   E.

18.

J.   K.   L.   M.   N.

4

TACHS Diagnostic Test

19.

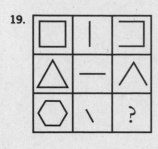

A. B. C. D. E.

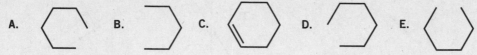

20.

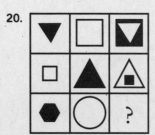

J. K. L. M. N.

Paper Folding

Directions: In questions 1–10, look at the top row to see how a square piece of paper is folded and where holes are punched into it. Then look at the bottom row to decide which answer choice shows how the paper will look when it is completely unfolded.

1.

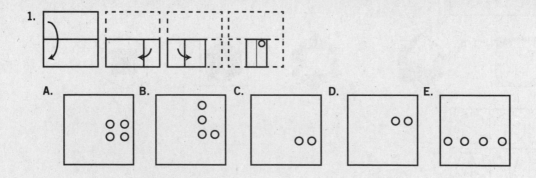

A. B. C. D. E.

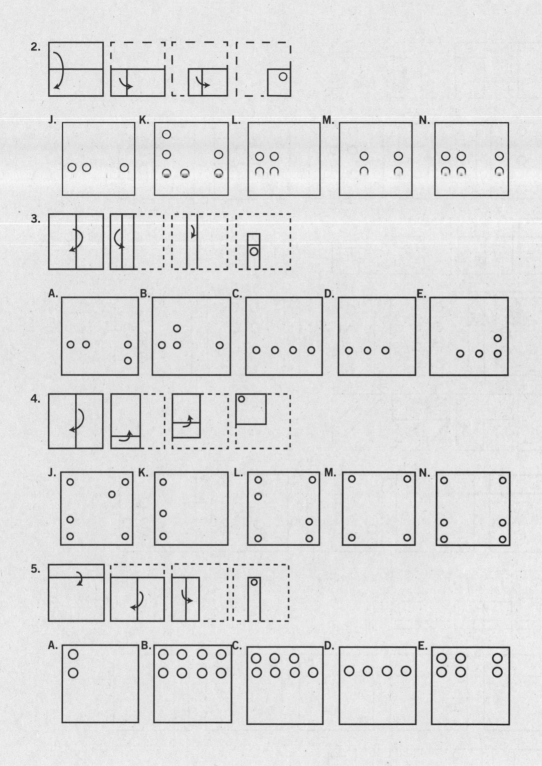

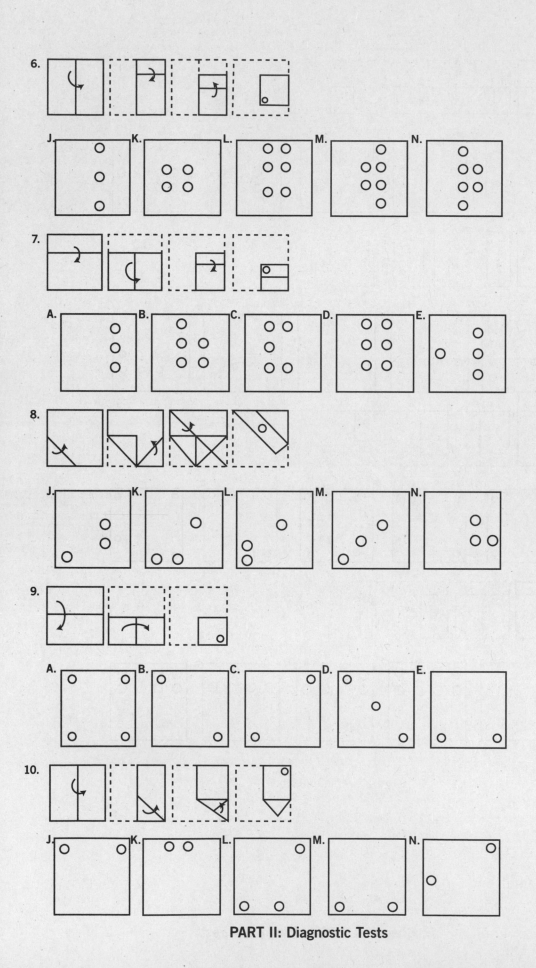

ANSWER KEYS AND EXPLANATIONS
Reading

1. B	11. A	21. D	31. C	41. D
2. K	12. M	22. J	32. K	42. L
3. A	13. C	23. D	33. A	43. A
4. M	14. J	24. K	34. J	44. J
5. C	15. A	25. B	35. C	45. B
6. J	16. L	26. L	36. M	46. L
7. A	17. B	27. A	37. D	47. A
8. K	18. L	28. L	38. K	48. L
9. B	19. B	29. D	39. C	49. B
10. M	20. L	30. M	40. J	50. M

1. **The correct answer is B.** The word *fantastic* is used to refer to an artist who sculpts unrealistic creatures such as gargoyles. While *fantastic* can sometimes be used to mean "extremely good," choice A is too mild a word to ever be a synonym of *fantastic*. Choice C is the opposite of *fantastic*, and *funny* (choice D) is not a synonym of *fantastic* either.

2. **The correct answer is K.** All the reader knows is that the passage takes place on Lincoln Island. While the narrator refers to Mount Franklin (choice J), the Far West (choice L), and Prospect Plateau (choice M), there is no evidence that the characters are actually in any of these locations in this particular passage.

3. **The correct answer is A.** According to the narrator, Spilett, Pencroff, and Herbert risked falling into the traps, but they decided to check them anyway, and since they faced such risks but still did what they had to do, they can be characterized as brave. Choice B can be eliminated since *cowardly* is the opposite of *brave*. The narrator refers to an annoyance that the three men might have faced, but he does not actually refer to the men as annoying, so choice C is incorrect. While the three men do something dangerous (choice D), they are not dangerous themselves.

4. **The correct answer is M.** Herbert believes that dangerous beasts with large claws are stalking the island, so it is likely that the characters are in peril. There is no evidence in the passage that supports choice J. Since the characters have not caught any animals in this passage, there is no reason to draw the conclusion in choice K. The characters are trying to trap animals because they are afraid that there are dangerous ones on the island, not because they do not like animals in general, so choice L is not the best answer.

5. **The correct answer is C.** The poem describes how a particular day in April makes the poet feel happy, so choice C is the best answer. Choices A and B reach extreme conclusions that the information in the poem does not support. While the poet refers to how skylarks change the view of the sky, he does not suggest that the skylarks ruin the view, so choice D lacks support.

6. **The correct answer is J.** In the second stanza, the poet describes the sounds of woodpeckers and cuckoos. Choice K refers only to the second couplet of the first stanza. Choice L describes the third stanza, not

the first one. In the second stanza, the poet describes sounds, not appearances, so choice M is incorrect.

7. **The correct answer is A.** As a whole, the poem describes all of the pleasant things the poet sees during his walk. Since he mentions violets among those things, it is reasonable to conclude that the poet enjoys seeing violets. The other answer choices all reach conclusions that information in the poem does not support.

8. **The correct answer is K.** Choice K is the likeliest interpretation of the figurative language in the poem's opening couplet. Choice J is too literal a translation of that opening couplet, and April is a month, not a person, in this poem. Choice L is also too literal. Choice M misinterprets the author's use of the word *scattered*; he thinks the environment looks nice, not messy.

9. **The correct answer is B.** In the first stanza, the poet is talking about leaves. That should provide a clue that he is talking about the woods. Evidence in the poem does not support the other answer choices.

10. **The correct answer is M.** The poet spends the poem discussing all of the nice things he sees and hears and the pleasant way they make him feel. While the poet uses the words *simple* (choice J), *threatening* (choice K), and *heavy* (choice L) in the poem, none of them conveys the niceness of the day in April he describes.

11. **The correct answer is A.** The first paragraph of the passage explains how a cook, who only has a few ingredients, can still create a soup out of it. Eating is a necessity, and the desire to eat causes these cooks to create—or invent—a meal out of them. Therefore, the saying "Necessity is the mother of invention" suits the passage well. The passage is about the importance of tradition and old ways, but choices B and C put a negative spin on

tradition and old ways, so they are not the best answers. While the passage is about cooking, there is nothing in the passage that supports the saying in choice D.

12. **The correct answer is M.** Each of the answer choices can be used as a synonym for *hearty*, but only *substantial* makes sense in this context since *hearty* is used to describe soup. One would not refer to a soup as energetic (choice J), enthusiastic (choice K), or cheerful (choice L).

13. **The correct answer is C.** According to the passage, "No Shrove Tuesday would be complete without raised doughnuts called 'fastnachts.'" The author does not provide a day on which rivel soup (choice A) is traditionally eaten. Chicken corn soup (choice B) is traditionally eaten in the summertime, and dandelion greens (choice D) are traditionally eaten on Maundy Thursday.

14. **The correct answer is J.** According to the passage, "No Shrove Tuesday would be complete without raised doughnuts called 'fastnachts.' One of the many folk tales traces this custom back to the burnt offerings made by their old country ancestors to the goddess of spring." Chicken corn soup, not burnt offerings, is eaten at Sunday school picnics, so choice K is incorrect. Ancient ancestors made burnt offerings to the goddess of spring; burnt offerings were not used to contact these ancestors, so choice L is incorrect as well. Burnt offerings are not ingredients in fastnachts (choice M) either.

15. **The correct answer is A.** The sole purpose of the passage is to inform the reader about traditional Pennsylvania Dutch cooking. It is not intended to persuade the reader to do anything, so choice B is incorrect. It is not particularly funny, so choice C is incorrect as well. It is not written from the first-person point of view, so it cannot be personal (choice D).

16. **The correct answer is L.** A holiday is a fun event a community can enjoy together, and this is how the author describes the making of apple butter in the third paragraph. Choice J describes certain holidays, but it does not describe the making of apple butter. The author never suggests that apple butter can be made on only one day of the year, so choice K is incorrect. The author does not suggest that it can only be made on Christmas, so choice M is also incorrect.

17. **The correct answer is B.** The passage is about how the protozoa (which means "first animal") may seem simple but is actually complex, and this title suits that theme well. This also eliminates choice C. While the passage identifies protozoa as "complete living creatures," it never suggests that there are no other such creatures, so choice A would make a misleading title. Choice D is a random phrase from the passage that fails to capture its main idea in any meaningful way.

18. **The correct answer is L.** As it is used in the passage, *fundamental* means "basic." Almost no body parts are useless, so choice J is incorrect. Since *fundamental* is used to compare the body parts of a protozoa to those of a person, choice K has to be incorrect since human bodies are not identical to those of protozoa. There is no reason to believe the body attributes in question are unusual, so choice M is not the best answer.

19. **The correct answer is B.** The author never describes how protozoa look. However, their complexity (choice A), microscopic size (choice C), and internal structures (choice D) are all mentioned in the passage.

20. **The correct answer is L.** According to the passage, protozoa "differ from animals of higher degree in not being built up of the unit areas or corpuscles called cells." The passage offers no evidence that animals more complex than protozoa are primarily made up of organs (choice J), flesh (choice K), or bones (choice M).

21. **The correct answer is D.** When the author states that "Animals below the level of zoophytes and sponges are called Protozoa," he means that zoophytes and sponges are more complex than protozoa. The opposite of choice A is true. The author is not referring to intelligence, and sponges do not have brains, so they cannot be more intelligent than protozoa, in any event; therefore, choice B is incorrect. The author is not referring to levels of danger either, so choice C is incorrect as well.

22. **The correct answer is J.** The phrase "great complexity" is a clue that the word *exceeding* means "greater than." The other answer choices do not make as much sense if used in place of *exceeding* in the passage.

23. **The correct answer is D.** Bill feels that animals are after him, and his voice is hoarse. These details are clues that he is frightened. The man with Bill suggests that the animals are hungry; he does not suggest that Bill is hungry, so choice A is not the best answer. Bill is too concerned to be bored, so choice B is not the best answer. He does not seem particularly angry, so choice C is not a strong answer either.

24. **The correct answer is K.** The phrase "hunting-cries" possibly refers to the sounds that animals are making. Bill and his friend hear the sounds; they are not making them, so choice J is incorrect. Bill's friend says there is no sign of rabbits, so choice L does not make sense. Wind is never mentioned in the passage, so choice M is not the likeliest answer.

25. **The correct answer is B.** Bill's friend says that he hadn't seen a rabbit in days, and the men seem to be in danger from animals with no way to escape them by going indoors. Therefore, choice B is the most logical conclusion. Choice A is too specific,

and the situation in this passage is not very fun. Choice C is also too specific; although rabbits are mentioned in the passage, there is no evidence that the men are actually hunting rabbits. There is no evidence to support choice D either.

26. **The correct answer is L.** This passage is written from the third-person point of view, which is an unknown narrator. Neither Bill (choice J) nor Bill's friend (choice K) is telling his own story in this passage. There is no rabbit hunter in this passage, so choice M is incorrect.

27. **The correct answer is A.** The passage states, "The pale light of the short sunless day was beginning to fade," which supports the idea that it takes place as evening is approaching. This eliminates choice B. There are no clues regarding which season it is, so choices C and D can be eliminated too.

28. **The correct answer is L.** The men in this passage are out in nature, and they are in danger of being harmed by wild animals, so this phrase captures the idea in the passage well. Choices J and K imply that the men have nothing to fear, when they are in very real danger. Choice M refers to nature, but it fails to reflect the main idea of the passage in any meaningful way.

29. **The correct answer is D.** The passage draws a parallel between the fur of mammals and the plumage of birds. Since fur covers mammals, plumage must cover birds, and feathers cover birds. Therefore, choice D is correct and choice C can be eliminated. While plumage can be used as camouflage (choice A) or have color (choice B), neither of these words defines it as *feathers* does.

30. **The correct answer is M.** Choice M is confirmed by the discussion of the kingfisher in the first paragraph of the passage. Choices J and L are never mentioned in the passage. While the author does suggest that the

kingfisher flies fast, he discusses a different way the bird protects itself.

31. **The correct answer is C.** The passage discusses how animals use their coloring to make them more difficult to see, so if its coloring makes an animal less conspicuous, then it makes that animal less visible. Choice A is the opposite of *conspicuous*. The passage simply provides no evidence to support choice B or choice D.

32. **The correct answer is K.** All of these animals are mentioned in the second paragraph except for cobras. While snakes are mentioned, the specific snake called the cobra is not.

33. **The correct answer is A.** The passage mentions lions among the animals that have adapted to blend into a desert environment. The other environments are not mentioned in the passage.

34. **The correct answer is J.** The passage is all about how the coloring of animals helps them to survive by camouflaging them in their given environments. Since grasshoppers are green like grass, choice J is the best answer. The other answer choices do not describe green animals.

35. **The correct answer is C.** Based on information in the passage, Benjamin Franklin had many skills and, for these, the other children probably admired him. While he may have been athletic, choice A reaches a specific conclusion the passage does not support. Choice B reaches an extreme conclusion, since Franklin's abilities are never compared to those of the other children. While some people fear their leaders, there is no reason to believe the other children feared Benjamin Franklin.

36. **The correct answer is M.** *Shouldered* means "carried." The other answer choices would not make much sense if used in place of *shouldered* in paragraph 1.

37. The correct answer is D. The passage shows that Franklin was a very bright boy with many skills, but the process of making candles seems like dull work that required running errands for other people. Therefore, it is reasonable to conclude that the work was not challenging enough for him. This eliminates choices A and B. While Franklin did become a writer as an adult, there are no clues that this would happen in the passage, so choice C lacks supporting evidence.

38. The correct answer is K. As it is used in the context of paragraph 5, *keen* means "intense." *Eager* (choice J) and *biting* (choice L) can be used as synonyms for *keen*, but they do not fit this particular context. *Blunt* (choice M) is the opposite of *keen*.

39. The correct answer is C. Benjamin Franklin's father knew his son was "bookish," which means Benjamin liked reading printed materials such as newspapers and books. According to the passage, the apprenticeship was mostly unpaid, so choice A is unlikely and never given as a reason in the passage. There is no evidence for choice B either. Benjamin already knew how to read, so choice D is incorrect.

40. The correct answer is J. The passage as a whole is about Benjamin Franklin's youth, so choice J is the best answer. Choices K and L imply that the passage is about Franklin's entire life, which it is not. Although Benjamin Franklin helped make candles when he was a boy, choice M implies that the passage is more about making candles than it is about Benjamin Franklin, which is inaccurate.

41. The correct answer is D. According to the final sentence of the passage, Buddhists used tea "extensively to prevent drowsiness during their long hours of meditation." Taoists used tea as an elixir of immortality, so choice A is incorrect. While Confucius is mentioned in the passage, Confucians are not, so choice

B is incorrect. Mohists are not mentioned either, which eliminates choice C.

42. The correct answer is L. The word *indicative* means "representative." *Opposite* (choice J) and *unrelated* (choice K) are almost antonyms of *indicative*. *Following* (choice M) suggests a sequence of events that the passage does not support.

43. The correct answer is A. According to the passage, tea was "often applied externally in paste form to alleviate rheumatic pains." While the passage does indicate that people drank tea by saying that it was taken as an "internal dose," the author never suggests that tea was brewed in water to relieve rheumatic pains, so choice B is incorrect. Administering tea in pill form (choice C) or as dry leaves (choice D) is never mentioned in the passage.

44. The correct answer is J. According to the passage, powdered tea was whipped. Cake tea (choice K) was boiled, and leaf tea (choice L) was steeped. *Ming* is the name of a dynasty, not a kind of tea, so choice M is incorrect.

45. The correct answer is B. After stating that teas can be designated, the author names a few different teas, which is a clue that *designate* means "to name." Choices A, C, and D would not make sense if used in place of *designate* in the sentence.

46. The correct answer is L. The passage details many uses of tea in Chinese culture. While the author references philosophy, the passage provides no strong evidence to support the extreme conclusion in choice J. The author provides a number of names for tea but does not suggest that any of the names are the "only correct" one for tea, so choice K is not the best answer. The passage states that tea was believed to be capable of repairing weak eyesight; it does not comment on whether or not this is true, so choice M lacks supporting evidence.

47. **The correct answer is A.** The author notes that the Sierra Nevada is grand because it is "long and massive," which means that it is huge, and then describes its many unique features. Choice B reaches a conclusion that the passage does not support. The author states only that the Sierra Nevada is huge; he does not say that it is the biggest. Choice C mentions only one of the details about the Sierra Nevada, and it is not a particularly unique one among mountain ranges. Choice D describes the features on one side of the Sierra Nevada; this is not a feature of the mountain range itself.

48. **The correct answer is L.** According to the passage, Professor Whitney was the first person to gain "a scientific knowledge of the form, plan, and physical conditions of the Sierras," which supports choice L. There is no support for choices J, K, or M.

49. **The correct answer is B.** According to the passage, the range's eastern slope is "a defiant wall of rock plunging abruptly down to the plain." Forests are found on the western range, so choice A is incorrect. Choices C and D describe the features on one side of the Sierra Nevada; these are not features of the mountain range itself.

50. **The correct answer is M.** The author describes a desert as "arid," and deserts are dry. Deserts are not rainy, so choice J can be eliminated. *Small* (choice K) and *pleasant* (choice L) are not words associated with deserts, so there are no context clues to suggest that either of these words is a synonym of *arid*.

Written Expression

1. D	11. C	21. C	31. A	41. A
2. J	12. L	22. M	32. L	42. K
3. A	13. D	23. B	33. B	43. D
4. L	14. L	24. L	34. J	44. M
5. E	15. C	25. D	35. D	45. A
6. M	16. K	26. L	36. J	46. K
7. B	17. C	27. B	37. A	47. C
8. L	18. J	28. M	38. L	48. J
9. C	19. B	29. A	39. B	49. B
10. M	20. J	30. K	40. K	50. J

1. **The correct answer is D.** The correct spelling is *explanation*.

2. **The correct answer is J.** The correct spelling is *definitely*.

3. **The correct answer is A.** The correct spelling is *separate*.

4. **The correct answer is L.** The correct spelling is *privilege*.

5. **The correct answer is E.** *No mistakes*

6. **The correct answer is M.** The correct spelling is *existence*.

7. **The correct answer is B.** The correct spelling is *pronunciation*.

8. **The correct answer is L.** The correct spelling is *necessary*.

9. **The correct answer is C.** The correct spelling is *escalator*.

10. **The correct answer is M.** The correct spelling is *taunt*.

11. **The correct answer is C.** *Building* is part of the name of the structure, so it should be capitalized.

12. **The correct answer is L.** The clarifying information—the kitten's name—needs to be introduced with a colon in this sentence.

13. **The correct answer is D.** *No mistakes*

14. **The correct answer is L.** While the title of a novel should be italicized, a chapter title should be placed within quotation marks.

15. **The correct answer is C.** *Elise* is someone's name, so it should be capitalized.

16. **The correct answer is K.** There is a spelling error in this sentence. *Addition* means "something added"; *edition* means "an issue of a periodical, such as a school newspaper."

17. **The correct answer is C.** *Planetoid* is not a proper noun, so it should not be capitalized.

18. **The correct answer is J.** An abbreviated title such as *Mrs.* needs to end with a period.

19. **The correct answer is B.** Since Highway 61 is the proper name of a specific road, it should be capitalized.

20. **The correct answer is J.** The line "I haven't seen Jimmy" is something Maria said, and quotes belong within quotation marks.

21. **The correct answer is C.** This sentence is a declarative statement, so it should end with a period, not a question mark.

22. **The correct answer is M.** *No mistakes*

23. **The correct answer is B.** There should not be a comma at the beginning of the list. Therefore, the comma after *include* is misplaced.

24. **The correct answer is L.** There is a pronoun/antecedent error in this sentence. *Shara* and *Lashawn* are two people, yet *her* is a singular pronoun. It should be replaced with *them*.

25. **The correct answer is D.** *No mistakes*

26. **The correct answer is L.** This sentence expresses the ideas clearly: "The explorers were anxious because they knew that they were entering dangerous terrain." Its independent and dependent clauses are separate, distinct, and straightforward.

27. **The correct answer is B.** This sentence expresses the ideas clearly: "Despite months of practice, John lost his confidence and fared poorly at the tournament." The subject immediately follows a brief introductory phrase, and it is not separated from the predicate by any clauses or phrases.

28. **The correct answer is M.** This sentence expresses the ideas directly and concisely: "Marc and Jason were able to collaborate on the project once they put aside their differences." The plural subject begins the sentence and is immediately followed by the verb, which helps to clearly convey the action taking place.

29. **The correct answer is A.** This sentence expresses the ideas directly and concisely: "The Louisiana Purchase and the Gold Rush sparked westward expansion in the nineteenth century." The compound subject begins the sentence and is immediately followed by the verb, which helps to clearly convey the action taking place.

30. **The correct answer is K.** This sentence expresses the ideas directly and concisely: "My mother works long hours from Monday to Friday, but she always makes plenty of time to spend with me on the weekend." The subject begins the sentence, and it is immediately followed by a verb, which helps to clearly convey the action taking place.

31. **The correct answer is A.** Use of the present-tense verb *snap* establishes this sentence in the present tense, but *wanted* is in the past tense. The best way to correct this problem is to write the verb in the present tense as *want*.

32. **The correct answer is L.** This sentence does the best job of wrapping up the passage by naming Lange again and summing up her significance. Choice J is information that

would make much more sense earlier in the passage since it describes the beginning of a life. Choice K basically just rewords sentence 5 and introduces no new information. Choice M changes the topic from Dorothea Lange to another photographer.

33. **The correct answer is B.** Sentence 1 begins with the word *However*, which indicates that it introduces an exception to the sentence that would precede it, and choice B is something to which sentence 1 would be an exception. Choice A just rewords sentence 1, so it is unnecessary. Choice C simply lists art forms without providing information that would be followed by *However*. Choice D states the opposite of sentence 1.

34. **The correct answer is J.** Sentence 3 is a compound sentence with two independent clauses, and clauses should be connected with a semicolon only if there is no conjunction. However, these clauses are connected with the conjunction *but*, so the correct punctuation is a comma, not a semicolon. Choice K would turn sentence 3 into a run-on. A colon is used to introduce a list or a clarifying word; it is not used to connect independent clauses. Therefore, choice L is incorrect.

35. **The correct answer is D.** *No change.* Neither *dinosaurs* nor *triceratops* is a proper name, so neither word should be capitalized. Sentence 1 is correct as written.

36. **The correct answer is J.** Sentence 3 ends with a list, and a colon is used to introduce a list. A semicolon (choice K) separates complete clauses in a compound sentence; a comma (choice L) is used to separate items in a list.

37. **The correct answer is A.** There is a word choice error in sentence 2. A tail is the body part on the back of an animal. However, this sentence is referring to a story, and *tale* means "story." Neither making the word *tail* plural

(choice B) nor changing the word *tells* to the plural form *tell* (choice C) corrects that error.

38. **The correct answer is L.** When capitalizing a title, all of the words are capitalized except for articles and prepositions in the center of the title. Only choice L is capitalized correctly. Choice J capitalizes the article and preposition in the center of the title. Choice K capitalizes the article in the center of the title and fails to capitalize the words *Lair, White,* and *Worm*.

39. **The correct answer is B.** There is a word choice error in the original sentence, because the correct phrase is "rife with," not "rife in." Therefore, the best way to correct this sentence is to replace *rife* with *rich*, which has a similar meaning but works with the preposition *in*.

40. **The correct answer is K.** A colon would be necessary to introduce the dinosaur's name only if the word *called* did not already serve that introductory function. The best fix is to delete the unnecessary punctuation altogether.

41. **The correct answer is A.** This sentence effectively confirms the idea that the Taj Mahal is a significant site. Choice B is a detail that should have appeared earlier in the passage, not at the passage's end. Choice C would also work better earlier in the passage, but since it focuses on details about Mumtaz Mahal when the passage is really about the Taj Mahal, it is somewhat unnecessary information. Choice D starts as a strong concluding sentence, but its second clause provides unnecessary information about another UNESCO World Heritage Site that has nothing to do with the passage's main idea.

42. **The correct answer is K.** The entire name of the empire, the *Mughal Empire*, is a proper noun, so both words should be capitalized. Choice J fails to capitalize either word. Choice L capitalizes both words but fails to capitalize *Shah*, which should be capitalized since it is a title.

43. **The correct answer is D.** *Seven Natural Wonders of the World* is the official title of a series of spectacular natural features of the earth, so it should be capitalized. However, prepositions, such as *of*, and articles, such as *the*, should not be capitalized in titles unless they are the first word of the title.

44. **The correct answer is M.** *No change. It's* is a contraction of *it is*; *its* is the possessive form of *it*, which is what is required in sentence 4.

45. **The correct answer is A.** As sentence 1 is originally written, there is a pronoun-verb error. Choice A corrects that error by changing the verb *enters* to *enter*. Choices B and C create different pronoun-verb errors.

46. **The correct answer is K.** The phrase "but rather misunderstood" is nonessential additional information, so it should be set off from the rest of the sentence. Choice K corrects the original sentence's lack of punctuation by offsetting the phrase with em dashes. Choice J converts the original sentence into three fragments. Choice L incorrectly uses semicolons to offset the nonessential information.

47. **The correct answer is C.** In sentence 2, *palm tree framed* is a compound adjective, so it needs a hyphen to connect *tree* and *framed*.

However, there should not be a hyphen between a compound adjective and the noun it modifies, so choice A is incorrect. Choice B places the hyphen incorrectly.

48. **The correct answer is J.** *Its* is the possessive form of *it*; *it's* is a contraction of *it is*, which is what is required in sentence 7. Writing out *it is* completely would solve the problem if an unnecessary apostrophe were not added to it, as in choice L.

49. **The correct answer is B.** Sentence 3 describes something that happened in the past, so the verb needs to be written in the past tense as *occurred*. Choice A rewrites it in the future tense, and choice C writes it in the present tense.

50. **The correct answer is J.** As originally written, the independent clause in sentence 5 has a compound predicate (*passed* and *heralded*) that is not joined correctly. Choice J corrects this error by adding the conjunction *and* between the two verbs. A comma would not be used to join a two-verb compound predicate, so choice K is incorrect. Choice L reduces the run-on to a fragment and deletes relevant information.

Answers 4

TACHS Diagnostic Test

Mathematics

1. D	11. C	21. B	31. B	41. B
2. M	12. M	22. K	32. L	42. M
3. B	13. D	23. D	33. C	43. B
4. M	14. K	24. J	34. K	44. K
5. B	15. D	25. A	35. C	45. C
6. L	16. K	26. J	36. K	46. J
7. A	17. A	27. C	37. B	47. C
8. L	18. J	28. L	38. L	48. K
9. C	19. B	29. D	39. C	49. D
10. L	20. L	30. K	40. J	50. L

1. **The correct answer is D.** The given expression equals $50{,}000 + 300 + 10 + 0.04 = 50{,}310.04$.

2. **The correct answer is M.**
$4^2 + 3^3 = 16 + 27 = 43$

3. **The correct answer is B.** Let x be the number of bathrooms. Set up and solve the proportion $\frac{2}{3} = \frac{x}{18}$. Cross-multiply to get $36 = 3x$. Finally, dividing by 3 yields $x = 12$.

4. **The correct answer is M.**
$5\frac{11}{25} = 5 + \frac{11}{25} = 5 + \frac{44}{100} = 5.44$

5. **The correct answer is B.**
$1.111 - 0.919 = 0.192$

6. **The correct answer is L.** Since $51 = 3(17)$, it is not prime. So, it must be composite, which means it has factors other than 1 and itself.

7. **The correct answer is A.** Observe that $1 - (-4) = 1 + 4 = 5$ and $4 - (-2) = 4 + 2 = 6$. Since $5 < 6$, the inequality in A is true.

8. **The correct answer is L.** Multiply 9 times 25 to conclude that 225 is the number of campers.

9. **The correct answer is C.** Use the order of operations:

$$2\left(\frac{5}{2} - 2\right) \div \frac{1}{2} = 2\left(\frac{1}{2}\right) \div \frac{1}{2} = 1 \div \frac{1}{2} = 1 \cdot 2 = 2$$

10. **The correct answer is L.** Subtract $\frac{5}{4}$ from both sides to get the following:

$$x + \frac{5}{4} = \frac{17}{8}$$
$$x = \frac{17}{8} - \frac{5}{4}$$
$$x = \frac{17}{8} - \frac{10}{8}$$
$$x = \frac{7}{8}$$

11. **The correct answer is C.** Add the number of hours in each wedge to get $5 + 2 + 2 + 2.5 = 11.5$ hours.

12. **The correct answer is M.** 2.5 hours are spent trick-or-treating, and there are 11.5 hours total. So, the percentage of the time spent trick-or-treating is $\frac{2.5}{11.5} \times 100\% \approx 22\%$.

13. **The correct answer is D.** Note that $(3 + 4)^2 = 7^2 = 49$, while $3^2 + 4^2 = 9 + 16 = 25$. Therefore they are not equal.

14. **The correct answer is K.** All four sides of a rhombus have the same length. So, the perimeter is $4(6) = 24$ inches.

15. **The correct answer is D.** Multiply $\frac{2}{3}$ times 4 times 3 to get 8 hours.

16. **The correct answer is K.** 4% of $2,100 is $0.04(\$2{,}100) = \$84$.

17. The correct answer is A.

3 $\overset{3}{\cancel{4}}$ hours	$\overset{59/60}{\cancel{0}}$ minutes	$\overset{60}{\cancel{0}}$ seconds
$-$ 1 hour	59 minutes	58 seconds
2 hours	0 minutes	2 seconds

18. The correct answer is J. One round trip is $2p$ miles. The car can travel $5q$ miles on 5 gallons of gasoline. So, the number of round trips that can be made is $\dfrac{5q}{2p}$.

19. The correct answer is B. Use the order of operations:

$$\left(-\frac{1}{2}\right) \cdot (-6) \div \left(-\frac{3}{2}\right) =$$

$$3 \div \left(-\frac{3}{2}\right) =$$

$$3 \cdot \left(-\frac{2}{3}\right) = -2$$

20. The correct answer is L. The sum of the four interior angles of a trapezoid is 360°. So, $x° + 121° + 58° + 70° = 360°$. This is equivalent to $249° + x° = 360°$. So, x = 111°.

21. The correct answer is B. The length of the shaded portion of the bar above "Watching TV" is $80 - 40 = 40$.

22. The correct answer is K. The number of boys selecting "Playing Video Games" as their favorite activity is 50, while the number of girls selecting this as their favorite activity is 10. The difference is 40, which is larger than the other three differences.

23. The correct answer is D. The number of boys and the number of girls selecting "Playing Sports" as their favorite activity is both 30. So the ratio is 1:1.

24. The correct answer is J. Officer Michelle issued 34 tickets and Officer Ken issued 33 tickets during this six-week period. So the difference in the number of tickets issued is $34 - 33 = 1$.

25. The correct answer is A. Add the cells in each row. The smallest sum occurs in Week 3.

26. The correct answer is J. Since 500% of 1 = 5, it follows that 500% of 0.01 is $5(0.01) = 0.05$.

27. The correct answer is C. The temperature at 5 a.m. Tuesday is $96° - 0.25(96°) = 96° - 24° = 72°$. So the temperature at noon that same day is $72° + 0.10(72°) = 72° + 7.2° \approx 79°$.

28. The correct answer is L. $(2 - (-1))^3 = 3^3 = 27$

29. The correct answer is D. Simplify as follows:

$$2^5 \cdot 3^2 = 2 \cdot 2 \cdot 2 \cdot 2 \cdot 2 \cdot 3 \cdot 3$$
$$= 2 \cdot 2 \cdot 2 \cdot (2 \cdot 3) \cdot (2 \cdot 3)$$
$$= 2 \cdot 2 \cdot 2 \cdot 6 \cdot 6$$
$$= 2^3 \cdot 6^2$$

30. The correct answer is K. Nancy completed $30 + 40 + 20 + 20 + 50 = 160$ lunges, and Laura completed $40 + 30 + 30 + 30 + 40 = 170$ lunges. So, the difference is $170 - 160 = 10$.

31. The correct answer is B. Laura completed 40 lunges on Friday and a total of 170 lunges for the week. So, the fraction completed on Friday is $\dfrac{40}{170} = \dfrac{4}{17}$.

32. The correct answer is L. The area of the entire square is $(12)(12) = 144$ square feet. The base of the unshaded triangle is 4 feet (since $\overline{AD}$ is divided into three congruent segments, and one of them is the base of the unshaded triangle). Since its height is 12 feet, the area of the unshaded triangle is $\dfrac{1}{2}(4)(12) = 24$ square feet. So the area of the shaded region is $144 - 24 = 120$ square feet.

33. The correct answer is C.

Factors of 12: 1, 2, 3, 4, 6, 12

Factors of 18: 1, 2, 3, 6, 9, 18

Factors of 48: 1, 2, 3, 4, 6, 8, 12, 16, 24, 48

The complete set of factors common to all three is {1, 2, 3, 6}.

Answers

4

TACHS Diagnostic Test

34. **The correct answer is K.** The radius of the large circle is 7 inches, so its area is $\pi \cdot 7^2$ = 49π square inches. The radius of the small inner circle is 4 inches, so its area is $\pi \cdot 4^2 =$ 16π. So, the area of the shaded region is 49π $- 16\pi = 33\pi$ square inches.

35. **The correct answer is C.** $\left(\dfrac{1}{2}\right)^2 = \dfrac{1}{2} \cdot \dfrac{1}{2} = \dfrac{1}{4}$, which is not an integer.

36. **The correct answer is K.** The point is plotted as follows:

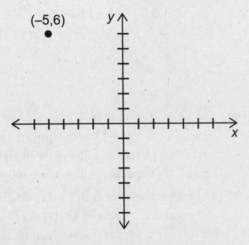

37. **The correct answer is B.** The triangle is isosceles, so the base angles are congruent; call both of their measures $x°$. Since the sum of the three interior angles of a triangle is 180°, we have $36° + x° + x° = 180°$. Solve for x as follows:

$$36° + x° + x° = 180°$$
$$36° + 2\left(x°\right) = 180°$$
$$2\left(x°\right) = 144°$$
$$x° = 72°$$

38. **The correct answer is L.** The number of hours she travels is 8. So, the average speed is $560 \div 8 = 70$ miles per hour.

39. **The correct answer is C.** Add the three scores and divide the sum by 3:

$$\frac{6,500 + 13,000 + 16,500}{3} = \frac{36,000}{3} = 12,000$$

40. **The correct answer is J.** If you start with an odd integer and add 1 to it, you get an even integer. If you add 1 to this, you get another odd integer. So, adding 2 to an odd integer gives an odd integer.

41. **The correct answer is B.** $8^2 = 64$, and since 8.04 is slightly larger than 8, it follows that 8.04^2 is closer to 65 than it is to 62.

42. **The correct answer is M.** The expression is approximately $4(10) + 3(20) = 100$.

43. **The correct answer is B.** The expression is approximately $8,000 - 5,000 = 3,000$.

44. **The correct answer is K.** The expression is approximately $5 + 7 + 10 = 22$.

45. **The correct answer is C.** The number of ounces of canola oil needed to make 32 batches would be 9×32, or 288.

46. **The correct answer is J.** Approximate 612 as 600. Since 10% of 600 is 60, it follows that 5% of 600 is half of this, or 30.

47. **The correct answer is C.** The expression is approximately $300(200) = 60,000$.

48. **The correct answer is K.** The expression is approximately $40 \div 2 = 20$.

49. **The correct answer is D.** Approximate 1,819 as 1,800 and divide by 9. Doing so, the expression is approximately $1,800 \div 9 = 200$. Since 1,819 is greater than 1,800, the average would be a little higher than that, but 200 is the closest option.

50. **The correct answer is L.** Multiply 8 times 9 to get 72 minutes.

Ability

Figure Classification

1. E	5. B	9. B	13. D	17. D
2. K	6. J	10. K	14. N	18. J
3. A	7. E	11. D	15. A	19. D
4. J	8. M	12. L	16. M	20. L

1. **The correct answer is E.** All figures are comprised of line segments and no curves.

2. **The correct answer is K.** All figures are closed regions comprised of five line segments.

3. **The correct answer is A.** The interiors of the figures are cut in half and the shading is done using line segments perpendicular to the line used to cut the figure in half.

4. **The correct answer is J.** All the given figures are small. Since choice J is small and the other four are large, it is the logical choice.

5. **The correct answer is B.** The points on the circles of the given figures are equally spaced around the entire circle.

6. **The correct answer is J.** The figures are symmetric about the dotted line shown.

7. **The correct answer is E.** The pattern exhibited in the figures is one unshaded circle between two parallel horizontal lines, then two shaded circles between two parallel horizontal lines, then three unshaded circles between two parallel horizontal lines. Following this pattern, the next logical choice should be four shaded circles between two parallel horizontal lines.

8. **The correct answer is M.** The given figures are all triangles.

9. **The correct answer is B.** An odd number of congruent portions of each of the given figures are shaded.

10. **The correct answer is K.** The given figures are all rotations about the center point of the square. The figure in choice K is obtained by rotating the second given figure 90 degrees counterclockwise.

11. **The correct answer is D.** All figures contain one shaded circle fewer than the number of sides of which the figure is comprised.

12. **The correct answer is L.** The pairs of triangles in each of the given figures are obtained by translating the leftmost triangle to the right and then reflecting it over the dotted line.

13. **The correct answer is D.** The inner and outer shapes in each figure are similar (that is, the inner one is a smaller version of the outer shape).

14. **The correct answer is N.** The figures are comprised of two sets of intersecting lines which, when added, equal an odd number of lines.

15. **The correct answer is A.** The ratio of X's to E's is 5:2.

16. **The correct answer is M.** The arrows inside each of the figures all point in a clockwise direction, and no two figures are similar.

17. **The correct answer is D.** The given figures all contain the same internal configuration, with circles included at vertices to form a triangle pattern that encompasses a quarter of the figure's area.

18. **The correct answer is J.** All pattern options feature interlocking circles of equal size. In choices K and N the circles are different sizes. In choice L two of the circles are not interlocked with the rest. In choice M all the circles are touching, but none of them interlock with one another.

19. **The correct answer is D.** This pattern features a hexagram with a decreasing number of unshaded parts. The first is missing

three parts, the second two parts, and the third one part. Choice D would continue this pattern because it's a hexagram that's missing zero parts. Choice A is missing all parts, choice B is missing six parts, choice C is missing 5 parts, and choice E is missing 2 parts.

20. **The correct answer is L.** Each circle includes two white arrows and one black arrow in its interior.

Figure Matrices

1. B	**5.** E	**9.** D	**13.** D	**17.** C
2. N	**6.** K	**10.** L	**14.** L	**18.** L
3. D	**7.** C	**11.** C	**15.** B	**19.** D
4. J	**8.** M	**12.** J	**16.** N	**20.** K

1. **The correct answer is B.** The pattern across the rows is to start with a figure (either empty or bisected), add something to it, and then put only what was added in the final column. Doing so here yields choice B.

2. **The correct answer is N.** The pattern across the rows is to insert a smaller version of the figure in the first square inside the figure in the second square to get the figure for the third square. Choice N is a better option than choices K or M, as it preserves the orientation of the original triangle.

3. **The correct answer is D.** The pattern across the rows has nothing to do with the first column! The third square is simply the interior figure from the second square.

4. **The correct answer is J.** The pattern across the rows is to start with the figure in the first square, insert intersecting lines to get the figure in the second square, and then replace those lines with circles that appear at the ends of each of the segments that appeared in the second square.

5. **The correct answer is E.** The pattern across the rows is to start with two arrows in the first square, change the direction of one of the arrows to get the second square, and then change the direction of both arrows from what they were in the second square to get the figure in the third square.

6. **The correct answer is K.** The pattern across the rows is to remove one square and add one X to go from the first to the second figure, and then do the same to go from the second to the third figure.

7. **The correct answer is C.** This time, the pattern occurs in the columns, not the rows. The pattern going down the columns is to start with a figure and remove the bottom portion labeled A to get the second square. Then to get the figure in the third square, add the removed figure A portion back to a horizontally flipped figure B of the image found in the second square.

8. **The correct answer is M.** The pattern across the rows is to remove one circle from the interior to go from the first to the second square. Then, do the same to go from the second to the third square.

9. **The correct answer is D.** The pattern across the rows is to use the type of segment (and the direction of the segment, i.e., horizontal, diagonal, zig zag, vertical, etc.) in the first square to shade the interior of the figure in the second square to get the figure in the third square.

10. **The correct answer is L.** The pattern across the rows is to affix the next consecutive vertex of the figure moving in a clockwise fashion to go from the first to the second square. Then, do the same thing to go from the second to the third square.

11. **The correct answer is C.** The figures in a row are all rotations by a multiple of 90 degrees of each other.

12. **The correct answer is J.** The pattern across the rows is to remove the leftmost or bottom segment of the figure to go from the first to the second square. Then, do the same thing to go from the second to the third square.

13. **The correct answer is D.** The pattern across the rows is to start with a figure in the first square, divide it in half, and then shade half of it using diagonal line segments to get the figure in the second square. Then, to get the third square, shade the opposite portion of the figure from the second square using line segments in a different direction from those used in the second square.

14. **The correct answer is L.** The pattern across the rows is to start with a figure in the first square, and add something to it to get the second square. The third square is simply what you added in the second square.

15. **The correct answer is B.** The pattern across the rows is to start with a figure containing some line segments. To get the second square, remove those interior line segments to get an empty figure. To get the third square, put only the interior line segments that appear in the first square.

16. **The correct answer is N.** The pattern across the rows can be determined from the first to the third squares in this case. Here, the figure in the third square is the same as the one in the first square with the exception that the small shapes affixed to the ends of the line segments have opposite shading. The exercise does make a change from column one to column two, but it is not relevant to the third column.

17. **The correct answer is C.** The pattern across the rows is to insert the figure from the second square inside the figure in the first square and shade the region around it to get the figure in the third square.

18. **The correct answer is L.** The pattern across the rows is to insert the figure from the first square into the figure in the second square, and then turn the combined image upside down to arrive at the figure in the third square. In choice J, the zigzag line is rotated, but not turned upside down. In choice K, the triangle is rotated 90 degrees, but not turned upside down like the hexagon from the original matrix. In choice M, neither the zigzag nor the triangle have been turned upside down correctly. And choice N is incorrect because it gives us an equilateral triangle instead of a right triangle.

19. **The correct answer is D.** The pattern across the rows here is to remove the segment from column two from the shape in column one. In addition, the segment that is removed must be in the same orientation as shown in the second square. Choice A is incorrect because it subtracts the line segment from the right side of the shape, not the left side. Choice B is incorrect because it removes two lines of the hexagon instead of one. Choice C is incorrect because it adds a line segment to the hexagon instead of subtracting, and choice E is incorrect because it removes a line from the top instead of the hexagon instead of the lower left side.

20. **The correct answer is K.** The pattern across the rows is simply to place the shape from column one inside the shape from column two, and then reverse the shading. Choice J is incorrect because the size of the hexagon increased instead of staying the same. Choice L is incorrect because the circle should be solid and the hexagon transparent, not the other way around. Choice M is also incorrect for this reason, plus the size of the hexagon has been altered. Finally, choice N is incorrect because the hexagon in the middle of the circle has been rotated 60 degrees.

Answers 4

TACHS Diagnostic Test

Paper Folding

1. A	**3.** C	**5.** B	**7.** D	**9.** A
2. N	**4.** N	**6.** K	**8.** M	**10.** J

1. **The correct answer is A.** The third fold in this exercise does not reach across far enough to be included in the hole punch, so the final hole pattern is only affected by the first two folds. As such, four sheets are being punched and the folds are perpendicular. So there are four holes in the shape of a square.

2. **The correct answer is N.** Six sheets are being punched. One sheet is missed since the second fold didn't overlap it. This explains the missing hole between the other three that have been punched.

3. **The correct answer is C.** Four sheets are being punched and the folds are all in the same direction. So, the holes line up along a single column.

4. **The correct answer is N.** Six sheets are being punched in the form of two parallel columns since the folds are made in perpendicular directions. One sheet is missed since the second fold didn't overlap it. This explains the missing hole between the other three that have been punched.

5. **The correct answer is B.** Eight sheets are being punched and so there are eight holes.

6. **The correct answer is K.** Only four sheets are being punched because there is no overlap between the second and third folds, so there are four holes.

7. **The correct answer is D.** Six sheets are being punched and the hole never reaches the leftmost edge of the square by the way the folds are being made. So, it cannot be choice C and hence, must be D.

8. **The correct answer is M.** Three sheets are being punched in parallel, diagonal folds, so the holes must align in a diagonal column format.

9. **The correct answer is A.** Four sheets are being punched, so there are four holes, one in each corner, that are reflections of each other over the fold.

10. **The correct answer is J.** The only fold affecting where the holes will appear is the first one since the paper never reaches the top half of the square after subsequent folds. So there are two holes in the upper corners of the square.

SCORE SHEET

Although your actual exam scores will not be reported as percentages, it might be helpful to convert your test scores to percentages so that you can see at a glance where your strengths and weaknesses lie. The numbers in parentheses represent the questions that test each skill.

Subject	# Correct ÷ # of questions	× 100 = _____ %
Reading		
Vocabulary/Word Relationships (1, 9, 12, 16, 18, 22, 24, 29, 31, 36, 38, 42, 45, 50)	_____ ÷ 14 = _____	× 100 = _____ %
Details/Main Idea/Structure (2, 6, 10, 14, 15, 17, 19, 20, 26, 27, 28, 30, 32, 33, 40, 41, 43, 44, 46, 48, 49)	_____ ÷ 21 = _____	× 100 = _____ %
Inference/Understanding (3, 4, 5, 7, 8, 11, 13, 21, 23, 25, 34, 35, 37, 39, 47)	_____ ÷ 15 = _____	× 100 = _____ %
TOTAL READING SKILLS	_____ ÷ 50 = _____	× 100 = _____ %
Written Expression		
Spelling and Capitalization (1, 2, 3, 4, 5, 6, 7, 8, 9, 10, 11, 15, 17, 19, 25, 35, 37, 38, 42, 43)	_____ ÷ 20 = _____	× 100 = _____ %
Punctuation (12, 13, 14, 18, 20, 21, 22, 23, 34, 36, 40, 44, 46, 47, 48	_____ ÷ 15 = _____	× 100 = _____ %
Grammar (16, 24, 31, 45, 49)	_____ ÷ 5 = _____	× 100 = _____ %
Usage and Composition (26, 27, 28, 29, 30, 32, 33, 39, 41, 50)	_____ ÷ 10 = _____	× 100 = _____ %
TOTAL WRITTEN EXPRESSION SKILLS	_____ ÷ 50 = _____	× 100 = _____ %
Mathematics		
Arithmetic (1, 2, 3, 4, 5, 6, 7, 8, 9, 13, 15, 16, 19, 26, 27, 29, 33, 35, 39, 41, 42, 43, 44, 46, 47, 48, 49, 50)	_____ ÷ 28 = _____	× 100 = _____ %
Algebra (10, 18, 28, 36, 40)	_____ ÷ 5 = _____	× 100 = _____ %
Data Analysis (11, 12, 21, 22, 23, 24, 25, 30, 31)	_____ ÷ 9 = _____	× 100 = _____ %
Geometry and Measurement (14, 17, 20, 32, 34, 37, 38, 45)	_____ ÷ 8 = _____	× 100 = _____ %
TOTAL MATHEMATICS SKILLS	_____ ÷ 50 = _____	× 100 = _____ %
Ability		
Figure Classification (1, 2, 3, 4, 5, 6, 7, 8, 9, 10, 11, 12, 13, 14, 15, 16, 17, 18, 19, 20)	_____ ÷ 20 = _____	× 100 = _____ %
Figure Matrices (1, 2, 3, 4, 5, 6, 7, 8, 9, 10, 11, 12, 13, 14, 15, 16, 17, 18, 19, 20)	_____ ÷ 20 = _____	× 100 = _____ %
Paper Folding (1, 2, 3, 4, 5, 6, 7, 8, 9, 10)	_____ ÷ 10 = _____	× 100 = _____ %
TOTAL ABILITY SKILLS	_____ ÷ 50 = _____	× 100 = _____ %

Study Reference Guide

Subject	Chapter	Page
Reading	Chapter 10: Reading	199
Written Expression	Chapter 11: Spelling	235
	Chapter 12: Punctuation and Capitalization	243
	Chapter 13: English Usage	257
	Chapter 14: Language Composition and Expression	275
Mathematics	Chapter 15: Mathematics	285
Ability	Chapter 17: Comparisons and Ability Questions	397

ANSWER SHEET: HSPT® DIAGNOSTIC TEST

Verbal Skills

1. Ⓐ Ⓑ Ⓒ Ⓓ 13. Ⓐ Ⓑ Ⓒ 25. Ⓐ Ⓑ Ⓒ Ⓓ 37. Ⓐ Ⓑ Ⓒ Ⓓ 49. Ⓐ Ⓑ Ⓒ Ⓓ

2. Ⓐ Ⓑ Ⓒ Ⓓ 14. Ⓐ Ⓑ Ⓒ 26. Ⓐ Ⓑ Ⓒ Ⓓ 38. Ⓐ Ⓑ Ⓒ Ⓓ 50. Ⓐ Ⓑ Ⓒ Ⓓ

3. Ⓐ Ⓑ Ⓒ Ⓓ 15. Ⓐ Ⓑ Ⓒ 27. Ⓐ Ⓑ Ⓒ Ⓓ 39. Ⓐ Ⓑ Ⓒ Ⓓ 51. Ⓐ Ⓑ Ⓒ Ⓓ

4. Ⓐ Ⓑ Ⓒ Ⓓ 16. Ⓐ Ⓑ Ⓒ 28. Ⓐ Ⓑ Ⓒ Ⓓ 40. Ⓐ Ⓑ Ⓒ Ⓓ 52. Ⓐ Ⓑ Ⓒ Ⓓ

5. Ⓐ Ⓑ Ⓒ Ⓓ 17. Ⓐ Ⓑ Ⓒ 29. Ⓐ Ⓑ Ⓒ Ⓓ 41. Ⓐ Ⓑ Ⓒ Ⓓ 53. Ⓐ Ⓑ Ⓒ Ⓓ

6. Ⓐ Ⓑ Ⓒ Ⓓ 18. Ⓐ Ⓑ Ⓒ 30. Ⓐ Ⓑ Ⓒ Ⓓ 42. Ⓐ Ⓑ Ⓒ Ⓓ 54. Ⓐ Ⓑ Ⓒ Ⓓ

7. Ⓐ Ⓑ Ⓒ Ⓓ 19. Ⓐ Ⓑ Ⓒ 31. Ⓐ Ⓑ Ⓒ Ⓓ 43. Ⓐ Ⓑ Ⓒ Ⓓ 55. Ⓐ Ⓑ Ⓒ Ⓓ

8. Ⓐ Ⓑ Ⓒ Ⓓ 20. Ⓐ Ⓑ Ⓒ 32. Ⓐ Ⓑ Ⓒ Ⓓ 44. Ⓐ Ⓑ Ⓒ Ⓓ 56. Ⓐ Ⓑ Ⓒ Ⓓ

9. Ⓐ Ⓑ Ⓒ Ⓓ 21. Ⓐ Ⓑ Ⓒ 33. Ⓐ Ⓑ Ⓒ Ⓓ 45. Ⓐ Ⓑ Ⓒ Ⓓ 57. Ⓐ Ⓑ Ⓒ Ⓓ

10. Ⓐ Ⓑ Ⓒ Ⓓ 22. Ⓐ Ⓑ Ⓒ 34. Ⓐ Ⓑ Ⓒ Ⓓ 46. Ⓐ Ⓑ Ⓒ Ⓓ 58. Ⓐ Ⓑ Ⓒ Ⓓ

11. Ⓐ Ⓑ Ⓒ 23. Ⓐ Ⓑ Ⓒ Ⓓ 35. Ⓐ Ⓑ Ⓒ Ⓓ 47. Ⓐ Ⓑ Ⓒ Ⓓ 59. Ⓐ Ⓑ Ⓒ Ⓓ

12. Ⓐ Ⓑ Ⓒ 24. Ⓐ Ⓑ Ⓒ Ⓓ 36. Ⓐ Ⓑ Ⓒ Ⓓ 48. Ⓐ Ⓑ Ⓒ Ⓓ 60. Ⓐ Ⓑ Ⓒ Ⓓ

Quantitative Skills

61. Ⓐ Ⓑ Ⓒ Ⓓ 73. Ⓐ Ⓑ Ⓒ Ⓓ 85. Ⓐ Ⓑ Ⓒ Ⓓ 97. Ⓐ Ⓑ Ⓒ Ⓓ 109. Ⓐ Ⓑ Ⓒ Ⓓ

62. Ⓐ Ⓑ Ⓒ Ⓓ 74. Ⓐ Ⓑ Ⓒ Ⓓ 86. Ⓐ Ⓑ Ⓒ Ⓓ 98. Ⓐ Ⓑ Ⓒ Ⓓ 110. Ⓐ Ⓑ Ⓒ Ⓓ

63. Ⓐ Ⓑ Ⓒ Ⓓ 75. Ⓐ Ⓑ Ⓒ Ⓓ 87. Ⓐ Ⓑ Ⓒ Ⓓ 99. Ⓐ Ⓑ Ⓒ Ⓓ 111. Ⓐ Ⓑ Ⓒ Ⓓ

64. Ⓐ Ⓑ Ⓒ Ⓓ 76. Ⓐ Ⓑ Ⓒ Ⓓ 88. Ⓐ Ⓑ Ⓒ Ⓓ 100. Ⓐ Ⓑ Ⓒ Ⓓ 112. Ⓐ Ⓑ Ⓒ Ⓓ

65. Ⓐ Ⓑ Ⓒ Ⓓ 77. Ⓐ Ⓑ Ⓒ Ⓓ 89. Ⓐ Ⓑ Ⓒ Ⓓ 101. Ⓐ Ⓑ Ⓒ Ⓓ

66. Ⓐ Ⓑ Ⓒ Ⓓ 78. Ⓐ Ⓑ Ⓒ Ⓓ 90. Ⓐ Ⓑ Ⓒ Ⓓ 102. Ⓐ Ⓑ Ⓒ Ⓓ

67. Ⓐ Ⓑ Ⓒ Ⓓ 79. Ⓐ Ⓑ Ⓒ Ⓓ 91. Ⓐ Ⓑ Ⓒ Ⓓ 103. Ⓐ Ⓑ Ⓒ Ⓓ

68. Ⓐ Ⓑ Ⓒ Ⓓ 80. Ⓐ Ⓑ Ⓒ Ⓓ 92. Ⓐ Ⓑ Ⓒ Ⓓ 104. Ⓐ Ⓑ Ⓒ Ⓓ

69. Ⓐ Ⓑ Ⓒ Ⓓ 81. Ⓐ Ⓑ Ⓒ Ⓓ 93. Ⓐ Ⓑ Ⓒ Ⓓ 105. Ⓐ Ⓑ Ⓒ Ⓓ

70. Ⓐ Ⓑ Ⓒ Ⓓ 82. Ⓐ Ⓑ Ⓒ Ⓓ 94. Ⓐ Ⓑ Ⓒ Ⓓ 106. Ⓐ Ⓑ Ⓒ Ⓓ

71. Ⓐ Ⓑ Ⓒ Ⓓ 83. Ⓐ Ⓑ Ⓒ Ⓓ 95. Ⓐ Ⓑ Ⓒ Ⓓ 107. Ⓐ Ⓑ Ⓒ Ⓓ

72. Ⓐ Ⓑ Ⓒ Ⓓ 84. Ⓐ Ⓑ Ⓒ Ⓓ 96. Ⓐ Ⓑ Ⓒ Ⓓ 108. Ⓐ Ⓑ Ⓒ Ⓓ

Answer Sheet

5

HSPT® Diagnostic Test

Answer Sheet 5

HSPT® Diagnostic Test

Reading

Comprehension

113. Ⓐ Ⓑ Ⓒ Ⓓ   121. Ⓐ Ⓑ Ⓒ Ⓓ   129. Ⓐ Ⓑ Ⓒ Ⓓ   137. Ⓐ Ⓑ Ⓒ Ⓓ   145. Ⓐ Ⓑ Ⓒ Ⓓ
114. Ⓐ Ⓑ Ⓒ Ⓓ   122. Ⓐ Ⓑ Ⓒ Ⓓ   130. Ⓐ Ⓑ Ⓒ Ⓓ   138. Ⓐ Ⓑ Ⓒ Ⓓ   146. Ⓐ Ⓑ Ⓒ Ⓓ
115. Ⓐ Ⓑ Ⓒ Ⓓ   123. Ⓐ Ⓑ Ⓒ Ⓓ   131. Ⓐ Ⓑ Ⓒ Ⓓ   139. Ⓐ Ⓑ Ⓒ Ⓓ   147. Ⓐ Ⓑ Ⓒ Ⓓ
116. Ⓐ Ⓑ Ⓒ Ⓓ   124. Ⓐ Ⓑ Ⓒ Ⓓ   132. Ⓐ Ⓑ Ⓒ Ⓓ   140. Ⓐ Ⓑ Ⓒ Ⓓ   148. Ⓐ Ⓑ Ⓒ Ⓓ
117. Ⓐ Ⓑ Ⓒ Ⓓ   125. Ⓐ Ⓑ Ⓒ Ⓓ   133. Ⓐ Ⓑ Ⓒ Ⓓ   141. Ⓐ Ⓑ Ⓒ Ⓓ   149. Ⓐ Ⓑ Ⓒ Ⓓ
118. Ⓐ Ⓑ Ⓒ Ⓓ   126. Ⓐ Ⓑ Ⓒ Ⓓ   134. Ⓐ Ⓑ Ⓒ Ⓓ   142. Ⓐ Ⓑ Ⓒ Ⓓ   150. Ⓐ Ⓑ Ⓒ Ⓓ
119. Ⓐ Ⓑ Ⓒ Ⓓ   127. Ⓐ Ⓑ Ⓒ Ⓓ   135. Ⓐ Ⓑ Ⓒ Ⓓ   143. Ⓐ Ⓑ Ⓒ Ⓓ   151. Ⓐ Ⓑ Ⓒ Ⓓ
120. Ⓐ Ⓑ Ⓒ Ⓓ   128. Ⓐ Ⓑ Ⓒ Ⓓ   136. Ⓐ Ⓑ Ⓒ Ⓓ   144. Ⓐ Ⓑ Ⓒ Ⓓ   152. Ⓐ Ⓑ Ⓒ Ⓓ

Vocabulary

153. Ⓐ Ⓑ Ⓒ Ⓓ   158. Ⓐ Ⓑ Ⓒ Ⓓ   163. Ⓐ Ⓑ Ⓒ Ⓓ   168. Ⓐ Ⓑ Ⓒ Ⓓ   173. Ⓐ Ⓑ Ⓒ Ⓓ
154. Ⓐ Ⓑ Ⓒ Ⓓ   159. Ⓐ Ⓑ Ⓒ Ⓓ   164. Ⓐ Ⓑ Ⓒ Ⓓ   169. Ⓐ Ⓑ Ⓒ Ⓓ   174. Ⓐ Ⓑ Ⓒ Ⓓ
155. Ⓐ Ⓑ Ⓒ Ⓓ   160. Ⓐ Ⓑ Ⓒ Ⓓ   165. Ⓐ Ⓑ Ⓒ Ⓓ   170. Ⓐ Ⓑ Ⓒ Ⓓ
156. Ⓐ Ⓑ Ⓒ Ⓓ   161. Ⓐ Ⓑ Ⓒ Ⓓ   166. Ⓐ Ⓑ Ⓒ Ⓓ   171. Ⓐ Ⓑ Ⓒ Ⓓ
157. Ⓐ Ⓑ Ⓒ Ⓓ   162. Ⓐ Ⓑ Ⓒ Ⓓ   167. Ⓐ Ⓑ Ⓒ Ⓓ   172. Ⓐ Ⓑ Ⓒ Ⓓ

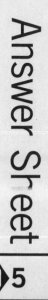

Mathematics

175. Ⓐ Ⓑ Ⓒ Ⓓ	188. Ⓐ Ⓑ Ⓒ Ⓓ	201. Ⓐ Ⓑ Ⓒ Ⓓ	214. Ⓐ Ⓑ Ⓒ Ⓓ	227. Ⓐ Ⓑ Ⓒ Ⓓ
176. Ⓐ Ⓑ Ⓒ Ⓓ	189. Ⓐ Ⓑ Ⓒ Ⓓ	202. Ⓐ Ⓑ Ⓒ Ⓓ	215. Ⓐ Ⓑ Ⓒ Ⓓ	228. Ⓐ Ⓑ Ⓒ Ⓓ
177. Ⓐ Ⓑ Ⓒ Ⓓ	190. Ⓐ Ⓑ Ⓒ Ⓓ	203. Ⓐ Ⓑ Ⓒ Ⓓ	216. Ⓐ Ⓑ Ⓒ Ⓓ	229. Ⓐ Ⓑ Ⓒ Ⓓ
178. Ⓐ Ⓑ Ⓒ Ⓓ	191. Ⓐ Ⓑ Ⓒ Ⓓ	204. Ⓐ Ⓑ Ⓒ Ⓓ	217. Ⓐ Ⓑ Ⓒ Ⓓ	230. Ⓐ Ⓑ Ⓒ Ⓓ
179. Ⓐ Ⓑ Ⓒ Ⓓ	192. Ⓐ Ⓑ Ⓒ Ⓓ	205. Ⓐ Ⓑ Ⓒ Ⓓ	218. Ⓐ Ⓑ Ⓒ Ⓓ	231. Ⓐ Ⓑ Ⓒ Ⓓ
180. Ⓐ Ⓑ Ⓒ Ⓓ	193. Ⓐ Ⓑ Ⓒ Ⓓ	206. Ⓐ Ⓑ Ⓒ Ⓓ	219. Ⓐ Ⓑ Ⓒ Ⓓ	232. Ⓐ Ⓑ Ⓒ Ⓓ
181. Ⓐ Ⓑ Ⓒ Ⓓ	194. Ⓐ Ⓑ Ⓒ Ⓓ	207. Ⓐ Ⓑ Ⓒ Ⓓ	220. Ⓐ Ⓑ Ⓒ Ⓓ	233. Ⓐ Ⓑ Ⓒ Ⓓ
182. Ⓐ Ⓑ Ⓒ Ⓓ	195. Ⓐ Ⓑ Ⓒ Ⓓ	208. Ⓐ Ⓑ Ⓒ Ⓓ	221. Ⓐ Ⓑ Ⓒ Ⓓ	234. Ⓐ Ⓑ Ⓒ Ⓓ
183. Ⓐ Ⓑ Ⓒ Ⓓ	196. Ⓐ Ⓑ Ⓒ Ⓓ	209. Ⓐ Ⓑ Ⓒ Ⓓ	222. Ⓐ Ⓑ Ⓒ Ⓓ	235. Ⓐ Ⓑ Ⓒ Ⓓ
184. Ⓐ Ⓑ Ⓒ Ⓓ	197. Ⓐ Ⓑ Ⓒ Ⓓ	210. Ⓐ Ⓑ Ⓒ Ⓓ	223. Ⓐ Ⓑ Ⓒ Ⓓ	236. Ⓐ Ⓑ Ⓒ Ⓓ
185. Ⓐ Ⓑ Ⓒ Ⓓ	198. Ⓐ Ⓑ Ⓒ Ⓓ	211. Ⓐ Ⓑ Ⓒ Ⓓ	224. Ⓐ Ⓑ Ⓒ Ⓓ	237. Ⓐ Ⓑ Ⓒ Ⓓ
186. Ⓐ Ⓑ Ⓒ Ⓓ	199. Ⓐ Ⓑ Ⓒ Ⓓ	212. Ⓐ Ⓑ Ⓒ Ⓓ	225. Ⓐ Ⓑ Ⓒ Ⓓ	238. Ⓐ Ⓑ Ⓒ Ⓓ
187. Ⓐ Ⓑ Ⓒ Ⓓ	200. Ⓐ Ⓑ Ⓒ Ⓓ	213. Ⓐ Ⓑ Ⓒ Ⓓ	226. Ⓐ Ⓑ Ⓒ Ⓓ	

Language

239. Ⓐ Ⓑ Ⓒ Ⓓ	251. Ⓐ Ⓑ Ⓒ Ⓓ	263. Ⓐ Ⓑ Ⓒ Ⓓ	275. Ⓐ Ⓑ Ⓒ Ⓓ	287. Ⓐ Ⓑ Ⓒ Ⓓ
240. Ⓐ Ⓑ Ⓒ Ⓓ	252. Ⓐ Ⓑ Ⓒ Ⓓ	264. Ⓐ Ⓑ Ⓒ Ⓓ	276. Ⓐ Ⓑ Ⓒ Ⓓ	288. Ⓐ Ⓑ Ⓒ Ⓓ
241. Ⓐ Ⓑ Ⓒ Ⓓ	253. Ⓐ Ⓑ Ⓒ Ⓓ	265. Ⓐ Ⓑ Ⓒ Ⓓ	277. Ⓐ Ⓑ Ⓒ Ⓓ	289. Ⓐ Ⓑ Ⓒ Ⓓ
242. Ⓐ Ⓑ Ⓒ Ⓓ	254. Ⓐ Ⓑ Ⓒ Ⓓ	266. Ⓐ Ⓑ Ⓒ Ⓓ	278. Ⓐ Ⓑ Ⓒ Ⓓ	290. Ⓐ Ⓑ Ⓒ Ⓓ
243. Ⓐ Ⓑ Ⓒ Ⓓ	255. Ⓐ Ⓑ Ⓒ Ⓓ	267. Ⓐ Ⓑ Ⓒ Ⓓ	279. Ⓐ Ⓑ Ⓒ Ⓓ	291. Ⓐ Ⓑ Ⓒ Ⓓ
244. Ⓐ Ⓑ Ⓒ Ⓓ	256. Ⓐ Ⓑ Ⓒ Ⓓ	268. Ⓐ Ⓑ Ⓒ Ⓓ	280. Ⓐ Ⓑ Ⓒ Ⓓ	292. Ⓐ Ⓑ Ⓒ Ⓓ
245. Ⓐ Ⓑ Ⓒ Ⓓ	257. Ⓐ Ⓑ Ⓒ Ⓓ	269. Ⓐ Ⓑ Ⓒ Ⓓ	281. Ⓐ Ⓑ Ⓒ Ⓓ	293. Ⓐ Ⓑ Ⓒ Ⓓ
246. Ⓐ Ⓑ Ⓒ Ⓓ	258. Ⓐ Ⓑ Ⓒ Ⓓ	270. Ⓐ Ⓑ Ⓒ Ⓓ	282. Ⓐ Ⓑ Ⓒ Ⓓ	294. Ⓐ Ⓑ Ⓒ Ⓓ
247. Ⓐ Ⓑ Ⓒ Ⓓ	259. Ⓐ Ⓑ Ⓒ Ⓓ	271. Ⓐ Ⓑ Ⓒ Ⓓ	283. Ⓐ Ⓑ Ⓒ Ⓓ	295. Ⓐ Ⓑ Ⓒ Ⓓ
248. Ⓐ Ⓑ Ⓒ Ⓓ	260. Ⓐ Ⓑ Ⓒ Ⓓ	272. Ⓐ Ⓑ Ⓒ Ⓓ	284. Ⓐ Ⓑ Ⓒ Ⓓ	296. Ⓐ Ⓑ Ⓒ Ⓓ
249. Ⓐ Ⓑ Ⓒ Ⓓ	261. Ⓐ Ⓑ Ⓒ Ⓓ	273. Ⓐ Ⓑ Ⓒ Ⓓ	285. Ⓐ Ⓑ Ⓒ Ⓓ	297. Ⓐ Ⓑ Ⓒ Ⓓ
250. Ⓐ Ⓑ Ⓒ Ⓓ	262. Ⓐ Ⓑ Ⓒ Ⓓ	274. Ⓐ Ⓑ Ⓒ Ⓓ	286. Ⓐ Ⓑ Ⓒ Ⓓ	298. Ⓐ Ⓑ Ⓒ Ⓓ

Answer Sheet

5

HSPT® Diagnostic Test

Chapter 5

HSPT®
Diagnostic Test

VERBAL SKILLS

60 Questions (16 minutes)

Turn to the Verbal Skills section of your answer sheet to answer the questions in this section.

Directions: This test measures your performance on reasoning tasks involving the use of words. This ability is related to performance in language, reading, and social studies-related tasks.

Mark one answer—that answer you think is best—for each problem.

1. Brown is to dirt as blue is to
   A. tree.
   B. sky.
   C. cloud.
   D. black.

2. Stove is to cook as bed is to
   A. run.
   B. sheet.
   C. sleep.
   D. laugh.

3. Glass is to window as wall is to
   A. house.
   B. beach.
   C. winter.
   D. car.

4. First is to last as beginning is to
   A. entrance.
   B. question.
   C. cup.
   D. end.

5. Dirty is to clean as interested is to
   A. bored.
   B. certain.
   C. silly.
   D. funny.

6. Hair is to head as leaves are to
   A. grow.
   B. green.
   C. tree.
   D. grass.

5

HSPT® Diagnostic Test

7. Finger is to hand as toe is to

   A. foot.
   B. nail.
   C. skin.
   D. knuckle.

8. Elevator is to lift as scale is to

   A. pound.
   B. machine.
   C. needle.
   D. weigh.

9. Bouquet is to vase as ice cube is to

   A. cold.
   B. bottle.
   C. tray.
   D. water.

10. Desk is to chair as jacket is to

    A. tie.
    B. pants.
    C. torso.
    D. elegant.

11. Bill is taller than Ingrid. Ingrid is taller than Charles. Charles is taller than Bill. If the first two statements are true, the third is

    A. true.
    B. false.
    C. uncertain.

12. The red car has a black roof. The blue car has a blue roof. All the cars are just one color. If the first two statements are true, the third is

    A. true.
    B. false.
    C. uncertain.

13. Alan has more books than Desmond. Liara has fewer books than Desmond. Alan has more books than Liara. If the first two statements are true, the third is

    A. true.
    B. false.
    C. uncertain.

14. Gerald has blond hair. Suzanne has blond hair. All the kids in Gerald's class have blond hair. If the first two statements are true, the third is

    A. true.
    B. false.
    C. uncertain.

15. All the vegetables in the soup are green. All the fruit in the salad is red. All the vegetables and fruit in the meal are green or red. If the first two statements are true, the third is

    A. true.
    B. false.
    C. uncertain.

16. Miles runs faster than Bea. Bea runs faster than Clarence. Miles runs faster than Clarence. If the first two statements are true, the third is

    A. true.
    B. false.
    C. uncertain.

17. A computer is more expensive than a chair. A chair is less expensive than an oven. A computer is more expensive than an oven. If the first two statements are true, the third is

    A. true.
    B. false.
    C. uncertain.

18. Grace ate more strawberries than Anna. Anna ate as many strawberries as Patrice. Grace ate more strawberries than Patrice. If the first two statements are true, the third is

A. true.

B. false.

C. uncertain.

19. Dogs live longer than mosquitoes. Elephants live longer than dogs. Elephants live longer than mosquitoes. If the first two statements are true, the third is

A. true.

B. false.

C. uncertain.

20. Shirley got a better grade on the math test than Yuri. Yuri got a better grade on the English test than Barry. Shirley got a better grade on the math test than Barry. If the first two statements are true, the third is

A. true.

B. false.

C. uncertain.

21. Pablo is hungrier than Jann. Jann is as hungry as Kira. Kira is as hungry as Pablo. If the first two statements are true, the third is

A. true.

B. false.

C. uncertain.

22. The brown horse is bigger than the white horse. The grey horse is bigger than the brown horse. The grey horse is smaller than the white horse. If the first two statements are true, the third is

A. true.

B. false.

C. uncertain.

23. Which word does *not* belong with the others?

A. Hammer

B. Screwdriver

C. Basket

D. Wrench

24. Which word does *not* belong with the others?

A. Watch

B. Sing

C. Talk

D. Whisper

25. Which word does *not* belong with the others?

A. Hopeful

B. Perspective

C. Positive

D. Optimistic

26. Which word does *not* belong with the others?

A. Cello

B. Violin

C. Guitar

D. Trumpet

27. Which word does *not* belong with the others?

A. Run

B. Leap

C. Sit

D. Stroll

28. Which word does *not* belong with the others?

A. Eraser

B. Marker

C. Pen

D. Paint brush

HSPT® Diagnostic Test

5

29. Which word does *not* belong with the others?

A. Earth
B. Moon
C. Venus
D. Jupiter

30. Which word does *not* belong with the others?

A. Oven
B. Blender
C. Refrigerator
D. Television

31. Which word does *not* belong with the others?

A. Milk
B. Ham
C. Butter
D. Ice cream

32. Which word does *not* belong with the others?

A. Snake
B. Squirrel
C. Mouse
D. Rat

33. Which word does *not* belong with the others?

A. Mustard
B. Pepper
C. Salsa
D. Ketchup

34. Which word does *not* belong with the others?

A. Florida
B. Michigan
C. New York
D. Los Angeles

35. Which word does *not* belong with the others?

A. Dress
B. Sock
C. Pocketbook
D. Necklace

36. Which word does *not* belong with the others?

A. Handlebars
B. Seat
C. Bicycle
D. Wheels

37. Which word does *not* belong with the others?

A. Dresser
B. Clothing
C. Suitcase
D. Wardrobe

38. Which word does *not* belong with the others?

A. Bulldozer
B. Dump truck
C. Backhoe
D. Bus

39. An *artificial* tree is

A. new.
B. beautiful.
C. natural.
D. fake.

40. An *audible* hum is

A. heard.
B. quiet.
C. melodic.
D. unpleasant.

41. An *elementary* understanding is

   A. educational.

   B. basic.

   C. complex.

   D. perfect.

42. An *absurd* excuse is

   A. convincing.

   B. silly.

   C. weak.

   D. tired.

43. A *pungent* odor is

   A. strong.

   B. lovely.

   C. different.

   D. constant.

44. A *gradual* change is

   A. necessary.

   B. permanent.

   C. sudden.

   D. slow.

45. A *hilarious* story is

   A. troubling.

   B. long.

   C. dull.

   D. funny.

46. An *ignorant* opinion is

   A. smart.

   B. created.

   C. uninformed.

   D. popular.

47. A *jubilant* reaction is

   A. sad.

   B. controlled.

   C. thrilled.

   D. cruel.

48. A *sinister* plot is

   A. careful.

   B. evil.

   C. original.

   D. stylish.

49. A *misplaced* item is

   A. broken.

   B. simple.

   C. close.

   D. lost.

50. A *lucid* idea is

   A. clear.

   B. foolish.

   C. stupid.

   D. flawed.

51. A *humongous* hill is

   A. cluttered.

   B. dusty.

   C. huge.

   D. average.

52. Lavish means the *opposite* of

   A. plain.

   B. elegant.

   C. profitable.

   D. attractive.

5

HSPT® Diagnostic Test

53. Partial means the *opposite* of

    A. open.

    B. orderly.

    C. whole.

    D. normal.

54. Deteriorate means the *opposite* of

    A. liken.

    B. expect.

    C. improve.

    D. oppose.

55. Flair means the *opposite* of

    A. secret.

    B. unjust.

    C. darkness.

    D. inability.

56. Squander means the *opposite* of

    A. undo.

    B. save.

    C. approve.

    D. proceed.

57. Accurate means the *opposite* of

    A. mistaken.

    B. expected.

    C. useful.

    D. absent.

58. Escalate means the *opposite* of

    A. punctual.

    B. arise.

    C. obey.

    D. decrease.

59. Renounce means the *opposite* of

    A. discard.

    B. obvious.

    C. accept.

    D. redo.

60. Tumult means the *opposite* of

    A. calm.

    B. wild.

    C. turn.

    D. trouble.

STOP.

If you finish before time is up, you may check your work on this section only.
Do not turn to any other section in the test.

5

HSPT® Diagnostic Test

QUANTITATIVE SKILLS

52 Questions (30 minutes)

Turn to the Quantitative Skills section of your answer sheet to answer the questions in this section.

> **Directions:** This test measures the ability to perform reasoning problems involving numbers and quantities. This ability is related to performance in mathematics, sciences, and other areas dealing with numbers.
>
> Mark one answer—that answer you think is best—for each problem.

61. Look at this series: _____, 6, 10, 14, 18, ... What number should come first?

A. 0

B. 2

C. 4

D. 10

62. What number is 8 less than 3 cubed?

A. 1

B. 17

C. 19

D. 27

63. Examine the isosceles right triangle ABC below and choose the best answer.

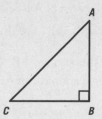

A. $\overline{AB}$ and $\overline{BC}$ have the same length, and $\overline{BC}$ is longer than $\overline{AC}$.

B. $\overline{AB}$, $\overline{BC}$, and $\overline{AC}$ all have the same length.

C. $\overline{AC}$ and $\overline{BC}$ have the same length, and $\overline{AB}$ is shorter than $\overline{AC}$.

D. $\overline{AB}$ and $\overline{BC}$ have the same length, and $\overline{AB}$ is shorter than $\overline{AC}$.

64. Look at this series: QXR SXT UXV ____ YXZ. What letter group should fill the blank in the middle of the series?

A. WXV

B. WXZ

C. WXX

D. WXY

65. Examine A, B, and C. Find the best answer.

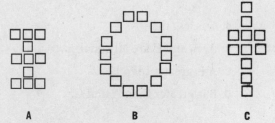

A. A and B each has more squares than C.

B. A and C have the same number of squares.

C. C has more squares than B.

D. B and C each has fewer squares than A.

66. What number is twice $\frac{2}{3}$ of 24?

A. 8

B. 16

C. 18

D. 32

67. Look at this series: 81, 27, 9, 3, ...
What number should come next?

    A. –3

    B. 0

    C. $\frac{1}{3}$

    D. 1

68. Look at this series: 202, 200, 196, 190, 182, ...
What number should come next?

    A. 170

    B. 172

    C. 176

    D. 180

69. Examine A, B, and C. Choose the best answer.

    A. 82

    B. 9 × 7

    C. 67

    A. C is less than A.

    B. A, B, and C are all equal.

    C. A is greater than B.

    D. B is greater than A and C.

70. Examine A, B, and C. Choose the best answer.

    A.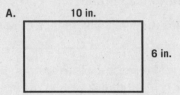

    B.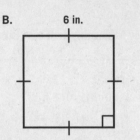

    C.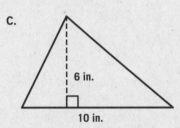

    A. The area of A and the area of C are equal, and the area of B is less than the area of C.

    B. The area of C is less than the area of B, and the area of B is less than the area of A.

    C. The area of C is less than the area of B, and the area of A is less than the area of B.

    D. A, B, and C all have the same area.

71. Look at this series: A, B, A, BB, A, BBB, ...
What term should come next?

    A. A

    B. AA

    C. BB

    D. BBBB

72. Look at this series: ARD, DAR, RDA, ARD, ... What term should come next?

A. ARD

B. DAR

C. RAD

D. RDA

73. What number is 40% of the sum of 2.1 and 1.9?

A. 1.6

B. 4.0

C. 4.4

D. 16

74. Examine A, B, and C. Choose the best answer.

    A. $(7 - 3)^2$

    B. $7^2 - 3^2$

    C. $(3 - 7)^2$

A. A = B and C < A

B. A = B = C

C. A = C and A < B

D. C < A < B

75. The product of 2 and what number, when subtracted from 1, leaves 5?

A. −3

B. −2

C. 6

D. 8

76. Look at this series: Z, YY, X, WW, V, ... What term should come next?

A. T

B. TT

C. U

D. UU

77. Look at this series: 3, 4, 9, 6, 27, _____, 81, 10. What term should fill in the blank?

A. 8

B. 18

C. 29

D. 36

78. Examine the square and find the best answer.

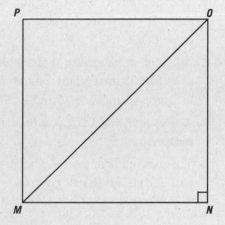

A. $\overline{MN}$ is equal to $\overline{MO}$.

B. $\overline{MO}$ minus $\overline{MN}$ is equal to $\overline{ON}$.

C. ∠OMP is greater than ∠ONM.

D. $\overline{MO}$ is greater than $\overline{MP}$.

5

HSPT® Diagnostic Test

79. Consider the diagram below and choose the best answer.

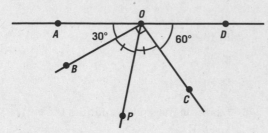

A. The sum of the measures of angles *AOB* and *DOC* is greater than the measure of angle *BOC*.

B. The sum of the measures of angles *DOC* and *COP* is greater than the sum of the measures of angles *AOB* and *POB*.

C. Angles *AOP* and *DOP* have the same measure.

D. The sum of the measures of angles *POC* and *COD* is less than 90 degrees.

80. Examine A, B, and C. Choose the best answer.

   A. 3^4

   B. 4^3

   C. 3×4

   A. A = C and B < A

   B. A = B = C

   C. C < B and B = A

   D. C < B and B < A

81. Look at this series: 28, 23, 18, 13, ... What number should come next?

   A. 1

   B. 3

   C. 6

   D. 8

82. Examine A, B, and C. Choose the best answer.

   A. 6×10^2

   B. $\dfrac{6}{10}$

   C. 0.60

   A. B is equal to C

   B. A is less than B

   C. C is greater than A and B

   D. B is greater than A

83. Look at this series:

   $$\frac{3}{4}, \frac{6}{16}, \frac{12}{64}, \underline{\hspace{1cm}}, \frac{48}{512}.$$

   What term should fill in the blank?

   A. $\dfrac{24}{256}$

   B. $\dfrac{48}{256}$

   C. $\dfrac{24}{128}$

   D. $\dfrac{48}{128}$

84. One-third of what number leaves two less than $\dfrac{2}{3}$ of that number?

   A. $\dfrac{1}{3}$

   B. $\dfrac{2}{3}$

   C. 2

   D. 6

85. Look at the series: D2, G10, J50, ... What term should come next?

   A. K500

   B. L60

   C. M100

   D. M250

86. Consider the following diagram in which the circle is centered at O and choose the best answer.

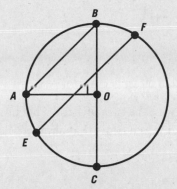

A. $\overline{BO}$ and $\overline{BA}$ have the same length.

B. $\overline{AO}$ is longer than $\overline{CO}$.

C. $\overline{BC}$ is longer than $\overline{EF}$.

D. The sum of the lengths of AB and AO is equal to the length of BC.

87. Look at the series: CY, DX, EW, ...

What term should come next?

A. FU

B. FV

C. GV

D. GY

88. One-fourth the sum of 1 and what number is one-half the sum of 2 and $\frac{1}{2}$?

A. $\frac{1}{5}$

B. $\frac{1}{4}$

C. 4

D. 5

89. Look at this series: 3, 4, 0, 8, −3, 16, ... What two numbers should come next?

A. 6, 20

B. −6, 32

C. 0, 32

D. 3, 28

90. Examine A, B, and C. Choose the best answer.

A. 200% of 0.1

B. 50% of 1

C. 25% of 10

A. $A > B$ and $B = C$

B. $A = B$ and $B < C$

C. $A < B$ and $B < C$

D. $A > B$ and $B > C$

91. Examine figures A, B, and C. Choose the best answer.

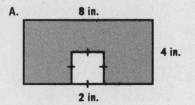

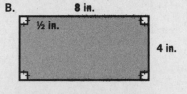

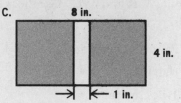

A. The area of A equals the area of C, and the area of B is greater than the area of A.

B. The area of A is less than the area of B, and the area of B is less than the area of C.

C. The area of B is less than the area of C, and the area of C is less than the area of A.

D. A, B, and C all have the same area.

92. Look at this series: 0.5J, 1.2M, 1.9P, 2.6S, ...
    What term should come next?

    A. 3.1T
    B. 3.3U
    C. 3.3V
    D. U3.3

93. Three-fourths of what number is $\frac{4}{3}$?

    A. $\frac{1}{4}$
    B. $\frac{9}{16}$
    C. $\frac{3}{4}$
    D. $\frac{16}{9}$

94. Look at this series: 7, 8, 10, 11, 13, 14, ...
    What number should come next?

    A. 14
    B. 16
    C. 17
    D. 19

95. Examine A, B, and C. Choose the best
    answer.

    A. Four times the square of 4
    B. Half the cube of 4
    C. Twice the cube of 3

    A. A = B and B < C
    B. A > C and C > B
    C. C > B and B > A
    D. A = B = C

96. Look at this series: 0.04, 0.20, 1, _____,
    _____, 125. What terms should fill in the two
    blanks?

    A. 2, 10
    B. 5, 25
    C. 5, 50
    D. 6, 30

97. Twice the sum of 4 and what number is the
    same as 4 times that number?

    A. 2
    B. 4
    C. 6
    D. 8

98. Examine A, B, and C. Choose the best
    answer.

    A. 6(4 + 2)
    B. $(4 + 2)^2$
    C. (6 × 4) + 2

    A. C is greater than B.
    B. C is less than A and B.
    C. A is less than B.
    D. A, B, and C are all equal.

99. Look at this series: 1, $\frac{3}{2}, \frac{5}{3}, \frac{7}{4}$, ...
    What two terms should come next?

    A. $\frac{9}{5}, \frac{11}{6}$
    B. $\frac{8}{5}, \frac{9}{6}$
    C. $\frac{8}{6}, \frac{9}{7}$
    D. $\frac{10}{5}, \frac{14}{6}$

5   HSPT® Diagnostic Test

100. Examine A, B, and C. Choose the best answer.

    A. 0.03×10^3

    B. 0.003×10^4

    C. 0.3×10^2

A. A = B = C

B. A < B < C

C. A = B and C > B

D. B > C and A > B

101. Look at this series: 2, 4, 7, 14, 17, 34, ... What number should come next?

    A. 35

    B. 36

    C. 37

    D. 39

102. One-half of what number equals the product of 4 and that number?

    A. 0

    B. $\dfrac{1}{8}$

    C. $\dfrac{2}{3}$

    D. $\dfrac{3}{2}$

103. Examine A, B, and C. Choose the best answer.

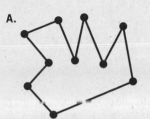
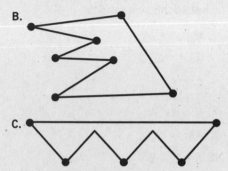

A. A, B, and C all have the same number of vertices.

B. C and B have the same number of edges.

C. A has two more edges than B.

D. The number of vertices A has is equal to the sum of the number of vertices B and C have.

104. Look at this series: 3D, E8, 3F, G8, _____, _____, ... What two terms should come next?

    A. 3H, I8

    B. H3, 8I

    C. H8, 3I

    D. 3I, J8

105. Look at this series: $\dfrac{2}{27}, \dfrac{3}{4}, \dfrac{2}{9}, \dfrac{4}{5}, \dfrac{2}{3}, \dfrac{5}{6}, \ldots$ What term should come next?

    A. $\dfrac{6}{7}$

    B. $\dfrac{7}{8}$

    C. 2

    D. 6

5

HSPT® Diagnostic Test

106. The sum of 6 and what number equals the square of the sum of 2 and 4?

    A. 6
    B. 14
    C. 30
    D. 32

107. Assume that $0 < z < 1$. Examine A, B, and C. Choose the best answer.

    A. $2z$
    B. z^2
    C. z^3

    A. $C < B < A$
    B. $A < B < C$
    C. $A < C < B$
    D. $B > A$ and $B > C$

108. Look at this series: 2, CC, 4, CCCC, 6, _____, ... What term should come next?

    A. CCCCCCCC
    B. CCCCCC
    C. 8
    D. 12

109. Three less than what number equals one-half the square of 4?

    A. 5
    B. 7
    C. 11
    D. 19

110. Examine A, B, and C. Choose the best answer.

    A. $2 \div \dfrac{1}{10} \div 5$
    B. $2 \div \left(\dfrac{1}{10} \div 5 \right)$
    C. $\left(2 \div \dfrac{1}{10} \right) \div 5$

    A. $A = B = C$
    B. $A < B$ and $B < C$
    C. $A < C$ and $C < B$
    D. $A = C$ and $A < B$

111. Look at this series: 1.2, 2.1, 1.8, 2.7, 2.4, ... What two terms should come next?

    A. 2.1, 3.0
    B. 2.7, 1.8
    C. 2.9, 2.6
    D. 3.3, 3.0

112. The sum of twice a number and three times that number is five less than the square of 10. What is the number?

    A. 3
    B. 19
    C. 95
    D. 105

STOP.

If you finish before time is up, you may check your work on this section only.
Do not turn to any other section in the test.

PART II: Diagnostic Tests

READING

62 Questions (25 minutes)

Comprehension

Turn to the Reading Comprehension section of your answer sheet to answer the questions in this section.

> **Directions:** Read each passage carefully. Then mark one answer—the answer you think is best—for each item.

Questions 113-122 refer to the following passage.

In order to better understand what it is that makes people purchase particular items or be drawn to certain products, the business world conducts psychological research about buyer behavior. Researchers want to learn as much as they can about the actions that people take when they are
Line in the purchasing process. Much of market research revolves around uncovering the factors that
5 influence how and why people make purchasing decisions.

One of the ways in which companies conduct market research is through the use of surveys. A survey is a questionnaire that asks respondents for information, including their demographic characteristics. A survey might ask if a person is male or female, for instance. It might also ask for the individual's approximate age, income level, marital information, the number of persons
10 living in the household, and the number of children living at home. All of this information gives the company administering the survey a general profile or picture of the background of the person responding.

Then, depending on the type of products or services that the company specializes in, a survey will typically ask respondents about their behavioral patterns in a certain area. For
15 example, a company that produces fabric softener might ask survey respondents if they own a washing machine or not, how often they do the laundry, how many loads per week they do, or perhaps whether or not they use fabric softener.

As another example, a fast-food company might be interested in the types of food that people most frequently buy when they go through a drive-through. Or, they might ask if respondents
20 prefer sandwiches with chicken or beef. They might inquire about what kinds of salad dressing a person eats most frequently.

All of this information is collected so that companies can track the behavior of buyers. Businesses want to know about respondents' demographic characteristics in order to build a profile of the kind of person who most frequently buys their products or shops at their stores.
25 If companies can track how their buyers make decisions, they can gain a much stronger understanding of the psychological motivations that drive people's purchases. They can also tailor their advertisements in order to attract the attention of their target customers by designing their ads to have the greatest appeal for potential buyers.

Market research involves more than administering questionnaires and surveys, however.
30 Companies and corporate researchers can also investigate what colors and designs people find most appealing in product packaging. They can further inquire about the types of advertising and marketing messages that buyers are most likely to remember and respond to as they make their purchasing decisions.

35 Companies can also hold focus groups in which they ask groups of people about their preferences, opinions, or responses concerning different types of products—from food to cleaning supplies to electronics. Businesses collect the responses of these focus groups and use the data to construct advertisements and marketing campaigns in ways that are designed to be appealing, based on the focus groups' results. Though not as effective as surveys, focus groups are still a popular way to conduct market research.

40 Sometimes market researchers even ask buyers to test new products. They might ask a subject to use a certain new shampoo. The results of consumer tests such as these can influence whether a new product ever actually makes it onto the shelves for people to buy or not.

113. What is the passage mainly about?

A. It focuses on how people make decisions concerning a company's products.

B. It mainly discusses how advertisers test new products.

C. It explains the various ways that companies conduct market research.

D. It discusses people's preferences concerning their shopping decisions.

114. According to the passage, what is one of the main ways that companies collect market research information?

A. Through the use of surveys

B. Through the use of secret shoppers

C. Through the use of role playing

D. Through the use of psychological evaluations

115. As used in the passage, the word *demographic* in paragraph 2 most nearly means

A. superior.

B. problematic.

C. likeable.

D. group.

116. Why does the author mention fabric softener in paragraph 3?

A. To describe how many consumers make decisions concerning purchases

B. To give an example of a product that might be the subject of market research

C. To discuss the product that is the most common subject of market research

D. To explain why buyers like the product based on historical market research

117. According to the passage, why do market research surveys collect demographic information?

A. To be able to track customers' purchases with the company over time

B. To keep careful records in a database so that the company can sell this information

C. To compile information about people most likely to purchase the company's products

D. To be able to tell why purchasers like certain colors better than other colors

118. According to the passage, companies hold focus groups to

A. develop ideas for new products.

B. collect data for constructing advertising campaigns.

C. influence the people in the groups to buy new products.

D. find out which products are the most marketable.

119. We can infer from the information provided in the passage that the author would most likely characterize market research as

    A. useful.

    B. invasive.

    C. untrustworthy.

    D. ingenious.

120. Which of the following pieces of information would make the discussion of product testing in the final paragraph clearer and more focused?

    A. How market researchers asked subjects to try the new shampoo

    B. The specific name of the new shampoo

    C. How many people the market researchers asked to try the new shampoo

    D. How market researchers follow up with a subject who uses the new shampoo

121. Based on the information provided in the passage, we can predict that readers who decide to become involved in market research will

    A. find the process of product testing exciting.

    B. make better informed decisions about the products they buy.

    C. help companies decide how to market their products.

    D. become mistrustful of the ways that products are marketed.

122. According to the passage, compared to surveys, focus groups are

    A. more popular forms of market research.

    B. completely useless forms of market research.

    C. superior forms of market research.

    D. less effective forms of market research.

5

Questions 123–132 refer to the following passage.

Whenever we hear the name of Napoleon mentioned, or see it printed in a book, it is usually in connection with a hard-fought victory on the battlefield. He certainly spent most of his life in the camp, and enjoyed the society of soldiers more than that of courtiers. The thunder of guns,
Line the charge of cavalry, and the flash of bayonets as they glittered in the sun, appealed to him with
5 much the same force as music to more ordinary folk. Indeed, he himself tells us that "the cries of the dying, the tears of the hopeless, surrounded my cradle from the moment of my birth."

We are apt to forget that this mighty conqueror, whom Carlyle calls "our last great man," had a childhood at all. He was born ... on the 15th August 1769 to be exact, in the little town of Ajaccio, the capital of picturesque Corsica. This miniature island rises a bold tree-covered rock
10 in the blue waters of the Mediterranean, fifty miles west of the coast of Italy. It had been sold to France by the Republic of Genoa the previous year, but the inhabitants had fought for their independence with praiseworthy determination. Then civil war broke out, and the struggle finally ended three months before the birth of the boy who was to become the ruler of the conquering nation. The Corsicans had their revenge in time, although in a way very different
15 from what they could have expected.

Letizia Bonaparte, Napoleon's mother, was as beautiful as she was energetic, and her famous son never allowed anyone to speak ill of her. "My excellent mother," said he, not long before his death, "is a woman of courage and of great talent ... she is capable of doing everything for me," and he added that the high position which he attained was due largely to the careful way
20 in which she brought him up.

Napoleon was Letizia's fourth child, two having died in infancy, while Joseph, the surviving son, was still unable to toddle when the latest addition to the family was in his cradle. His father was a happy-go-lucky kind of man of good ancestry, a lawyer by profession, who on the landing of the French had resigned the pen for the sword. He enlisted in the army raised by Pascal
25 Paoli to defend the island, for the Corsicans were then a very warlike people and much sought after as soldiers, and it is supposed by some that he acted as Paoli's secretary. It is certain that the patriot showed him marked favor, which was never repaid.

—Excerpt from *The Story of Napoleon*, by Harold F. B. Wheeler

123. The main contrast in the passage is between

A. Napoleon's adult life and the person he was in his personal life.

B. Napoleon's mother and Napoleon's father.

C. what Napoleon said about his mother and how he actually treated her.

D. the soldiers Napoleon commanded and the people in his family.

124. According to the passage, how many miles was Corsica from the west coast of Italy?

A. 10

B. 20

C. 40

D. 50

125. The passage states that Corsica was formerly the property of

   A. Ajaccio.

   B. the Republic of Genoa.

   C. France.

   D. Carlyle.

126. According to the passage, Napoleon's victories on the battlefield were generally

   A. easily won.

   B. difficult to achieve.

   C. few and far between.

   D. impossible to count.

127. In the last sentence of the final paragraph, "It is certain that the patriot showed him marked favor, which was never repaid," the word *patriot* refers to

   A. Napoleon's father.

   B. Napoleon Bonaparte.

   C. Letizia Bonaparte.

   D. Pascal Paoli.

128. As used in the passage, the word *apt* in paragraph 2 most nearly means:

   A. appropriate.

   B. clever.

   C. quick.

   D. right.

129. Based on the information provided in the passage, we can infer that the author would most likely compare Napoleon to

   A. his mother.

   B. his brother.

   C. other Corsicans.

   D. Carlyle.

130. Based on the information provided in the passage, what is the most likely explanation why Napoleon misrepresented his childhood?

   A. He wanted to present the idea that he was always a fierce warrior.

   B. He was embarrassed about his mother and father.

   C. He could not remember what his childhood was actually like.

   D. He was a weak soldier and wanted his enemies to think he was stronger than he was.

131. Based on the information provided in the passage, the "high position" mentioned in paragraph 3 most likely refers to a

   A. soldier.

   B. ruler.

   C. king.

   D. secretary.

132. The main idea of the passage is

   A. Napoleon was his parents' fourth child, and two of his siblings died in infancy.

   B. the years before Napoleon became a conqueror are not usually discussed.

   C. Napoleon spent most of his life on the battlefield where he won many battles.

   D. Napoleon was born on August 15, 1769, in the town of Ajaccio.

5

HSPT® Diagnostic Test

Questions 133–142 refer to the following passage.

Newspapers were once thought to have been first published in England in 1583 when Queen Elizabeth was monarch. What was believed to have been the first newspaper was called the *English Mercurie*, published in London by a man named Christopher Barker. However, this
Line paper was actually a hoax perpetrated 200 years later by Philip Yorke and Thomas Birch. They
5 submitted the newspaper they printed up to the British Museum in 1766, and it was soon accepted as historical fact. Ironically, the newspaper's purpose was to serve as a counterpoint to false reports!

The first real publications to have some sort of news-reporting purpose actually appeared in England in the 1600s. However, the main purpose of these papers was not to report current
10 events: they were actually owned by various political parties, and these papers were generally intent on stimulating loyalty to a particular political party or stirring outage against the opposing party.

While these papers varied quite a bit in the quality of their writing, there were some unusual consistencies when it came to their titles. References to Mercury and birds was an odd recurring
15 theme in these titles, which included the *Scots Dove*, the *Parliament Kite*, the *Screech Owle*, the *Parliamentary Screech Owle*, *Mercurius Acheronticus*, *Mercurius Democritus*, and *Mercurius Mastix*. The implication was that these papers reached the public with the latest news as quickly as a darting bird or an ancient Roman god best known for his incredible speed. Of course, in a modern age in which the latest news is released across the internet as soon as it occurs, these
20 publications of more than 400 years ago were not nearly as on top of their times.

133. Which of the following is the best title for this passage?

A. "Mercury and Birds"

B. "The Speed of the Internet"

C. "The First 'Newspapers' in England"

D. "The Story of the *English Mercurie*"

134. The main purposes of England's first newspapers include

A. relaying current events.

B. discussing birds.

C. reporting on sporting events.

D. conveying political agendas.

135. The *English Mercurie* was unusual because it

A. discredited false reports.

B. was the first newspaper in England.

C. was not a real newspaper.

D. was accepted by the British Museum.

136. When the article says it is ironic that the purpose of the *English Mercurie* was to expose false stories, it is referring to the fact that the *English Mercurie*

A. was not published regularly.

B. exposed many false stories.

C. was never printed at all.

D. was a hoax.

137. Newspapers published during the 1600s are described as

A. inconsistent in quality.

B. entirely fake.

C. quickly delivered.

D. brilliantly written.

138. Of the following common characteristics of early English newspapers, the one that is not mentioned is

    A. a title that references birds.

    B. a title that references Mercury.

    C. the presence of a political agenda.

    D. the refusal to publish political attacks.

139. Based on how it's used in paragraph 1 of the passage, the word *perpetrated* most nearly means

    A. committed.

    B. continued.

    C. covered.

    D. related.

140. Based on the information provided in the passage, we can conclude that

    A. the author does not consider any of the newspapers discussed in the passage to be proper newspapers.

    B. the author believes that modern newspapers should be more like the ones discussed in the passage.

    C. the author believes the internet is the only worthwhile place to obtain news today.

    D. the author does not think there was any difference among the newspapers published during the 1600s.

141. We can infer from the information provided in the passage that the *English Mercurie* is like

    A. a current events report on a television news channel.

    B. a rare and precious jewel displayed in a museum.

    C. a story that is too ridiculous to believe.

    D. a man in a costume trying to convince people he is a monster.

142. According to the passage, which of the following words would have been least likely to be included in the title of a newspaper in 1600s England?

    A. Eaglet

    B. Falcon

    C. Hen

    D. Sparrow

HSPT® Diagnostic Test

5

Questions 143–152 refer to the following passage.

Sound consists of three significant dimensions: speed, loudness, and frequency. Sound can travel through different media, such as air, for example. But it can also travel through water and even solids. After all, can you remember being inside a building but hearing a fire truck's
Line siren outside? That is an example of how sound can travel through a solid. The sound travels
5 through the solid matter of the building—its bricks or limestone, for instance.

It can take sound longer to travel through liquids, and especially through solids, than it might take the same sound to travel through gases or the air. This explains why it sometimes seems as if you can hear a siren sooner when you are standing outside than you can when you are inside a building. This can also be what causes sounds to seem odd or modified when heard
10 underwater.

Sound is made up of waves. This wave structure explains why the loudness of a sound can change as a person moves in relation to the sound. To go back to the siren example, as a fire truck drives closer to a building, the sound of its siren becomes louder. This increase in intensity has to do with the amplitude, or size, of the sound wave. As the fire truck moves away from
15 the building, the sound of the siren becomes softer, since the listener is now farther away from the sound source.

Finally, the frequency of a sound makes the sound seem higher or lower in pitch. Only sounds that fall into a certain range are discernible by human hearing. That range is 20 to 20,000 hertz (Hz). Instrumental orchestras must tune before performing to make sure that their
20 instruments are pitched at a specific frequency, so that the notes all match when the instruments play together. The tuning note that often sounds prior to an orchestra performance is an A. Usually, the frequency of this note is pitched right around 440 Hz. That is at the lower end of the frequency range that many human beings can hear.

143. What is the passage mainly about?

A. It focuses on how sound properties change because of position.

B. It discusses the properties associated with sound.

C. It explains ideas about why sounds become louder.

D. It talks generally about why pitches are used in certain ways for music.

144. As used in the passage, the word *media* in paragraph 1 most nearly means

A. substances.

B. artistic materials.

C. newspapers.

D. communication devices.

145. According to the passage, sound waves can take longer to travel through which of the following?

A. Air and gases

B. Liquids and solids

C. Air and liquids

D. Gases and solids

146. According to the passage, what causes an approaching fire truck's siren to first sound louder and then to become softer again?

    A. The pitch of the siren as the truck moves past

    B. The listener's location inside or outside a building

    C. The frequency of the siren as the truck moves past

    D. The proximity of the listener to the siren

147. Why does a siren seem to be heard sooner when a person is standing outside a building, according to the passage?

    A. The sound waves do not have to travel through the solid medium of a building.

    B. The sound waves do not have to travel through the liquid medium of a river.

    C. The person is physically more distant from the siren, so the siren is louder.

    D. The pitch of the siren sounds different to a listener outside the building.

148. Based on how it's used in the paragraph 2 of the passage, the word *modified* most nearly means

    A. changed.

    B. described.

    C. lost.

    D. clarified.

149. Based on how they're described in the passage, the way sound travels through a wall can best be compared to the way

    A. volume can be adjusted.

    B. clouds pass throughout the day.

    C. light travels through the atmosphere.

    D. liquid seeps through a cloth.

150. Based on the passage, we can say that a sound wave

    A. changes size as its source moves further away.

    B. cannot be heard through solid material.

    C. is difficult to create in the right pitch.

    D. is more pleasant when heard from far away.

151. What is the author's purpose for discussing the musical note A in paragraph 4?

    A. To make the passage more interesting by including a reference to music

    B. To use it as an example of a sound at the lower end of sounds people can hear

    C. To illustrate how flawed human hearing can be

    D. To prove that certain animals have much better hearing than most people do

152. Based on the information in the passage, we can infer that compared to light, sound is

    A. more difficult to block.

    B. more difficult to discern.

    C. more common in everyday life.

    D. more important to sense.

5

HSPT® Diagnostic Test

Vocabulary

Turn to the Vocabulary section of your answer sheet to answer the questions in this section.

Directions: Choose the word that means the same or nearly the same as the underlined word.

---

153. an <u>articulate</u> speaker

   A. expressive

   B. boastful

   C. daring

   D. unusual

154. <u>curtail</u> the program

   A. begin

   B. appreciate

   C. enrich

   D. shorten

155. <u>lucrative</u> profession

   A. demanding

   B. profitable

   C. common

   D. exciting

156. great <u>elation</u>

   A. achievement

   B. joy

   C. interest

   D. appeal

157. a strong <u>adversary</u>

   A. effort

   B. support

   C. opponent

   D. attraction

158. <u>adjourn</u> the meeting

   A. discontinue

   B. organize

   C. direct

   D. schedule

159. effective <u>technique</u>

   A. discipline

   B. equipment

   C. instructor

   D. method

160. <u>amend</u> the rules

   A. create

   B. sketch

   C. change

   D. follow

161. <u>delete</u> the text

   A. enter

   B. write

   C. erase

   D. consider

162. a <u>sentimental</u> mood

   A. emotional

   B. bland

   C. normal

   D. serious

163. a <u>cordial</u> encounter

   A. brief

   B. friendly

   C. tense

   D. sudden

164. a <u>sluggish</u> movement

   A. boring

   B. quick

   C. easy

   D. slow

165. an <u>erroneous</u> explanation

  A. wrong
  B. unusual
  C. original
  D. timely

166. to <u>withhold</u> information

  A. reveal
  B. deny
  C. believe
  D. possess

167. a <u>frivolous</u> purchase

  A. necessary
  B. expensive
  C. silly
  D. smart

168. an <u>oppressive</u> government

  A. balanced
  B. fake
  C. controlling
  D. kind

169. a <u>valiant</u> decision

  A. foolish
  B. cowardly
  C. frightening
  D. brave

170. to <u>eliminate</u> waste

  A. expand
  B. remove
  C. revise
  D. create

171. a <u>lamentable</u> ending

  A. positive
  B. common
  C. final
  D. sad

172. a <u>slovenly</u> roommate

  A. neat
  B. punctual
  C. sloppy
  D. sleepy

173. a <u>wayward</u> kid

  A. naughty
  B. cute
  C. champion
  D. fast

174. a <u>vibrant</u> design

  A. dark
  B. bright
  C. unattractive
  D. gorgeous

STOP.

If you finish before time is up, you may check your work on this section only.
Do not turn to any other section in the test.

MATHEMATICS

64 Questions (45 minutes)

Turn to the Mathematics Concepts section of your answer sheet to answer the questions in this section.

> **Directions:** Mark one answer—the answer you think is best—for each problem. You may use scratch paper when working on these problems.

175. Which number is fifty million thirty?

A. 50,030

B. 50,000,030

C. 50,030,000

D. 50,000,000,030

176. Complete the proportion: $\dfrac{5}{20} = \dfrac{\frac{1}{3}}{\square}$

A. $\dfrac{1}{4}$

B. $\dfrac{3}{4}$

C. $\dfrac{4}{3}$

D. 4

177. Find the area of the triangle ABC:

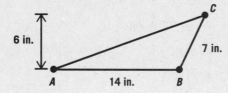

A. 28 square inches

B. 42 square inches

C. 56 square inches

D. 84 square inches

178. To which of these is 0.05% equal?

A. 0.0005

B. $\dfrac{1}{200}$

C. $\dfrac{1}{20}$

D. 5

179. Fill in the blank with the appropriate symbol: $\dfrac{5}{8}\ \square\ \dfrac{5}{9}$

A. <

B. >

C. =

D. ≡

180. Which of these triples could be the angles of an isosceles right triangle?

A. 50°, 50°, 80°

B. 90°, 32°, 58°

C. 60°, 60°, 60°

D. 45°, 45°, 90°

181. Suppose a bag contains 7 tiles marked: A, X, K, B, E, E, M. If you select one tile from the bag without looking, what is the probability that you do *not* choose a vowel?

A. $\dfrac{3}{7}$

B. $\dfrac{4}{7}$

C. 3

D. 4

182. How many milliliters are in 5 liters?

A. 5

B. 500

C. 1,000

D. 5,000

183. Write 784 in expanded form, using exponents.

    A. $(7 \times 10^2) + (8 \times 10) + 4$

    B. $(7 \times 10^3) + (8 \times 10^2) + (4 \times 10)$

    C. $(7 \times 10^0) + (8 \times 10) + (4 \times 10)$

    D. None of the above

184. If *PQRS* is a parallelogram, what is the sum of the two topmost angles?

    A. 90

    B. 180

    C. 270

    D. 360

185. In the following expression, what is "3" called?

    $$(3x + 1)(x + 2)$$

    A. Coefficient

    B. Variable

    C. Expression

    D. Factor

186. A factory makes 200 cameras per day. How many days will it take the factory to make about 997 cameras?

    A. 5

    B. 11

    C. 53

    D. Not given

187. The ratio of 1 hour to 120 seconds is

    A. 6 to 24

    B. 18 to 1

    C. 30 to 1

    D. 120 to 1

188. Which is the shortest length?

    A. 90 millimeters

    B. 10 centimeters

    C. 10 inches

    D. 1.5 feet

189. What digit is in the ten thousandths place of the decimal 95,287.01364?

    A. 3

    B. 5

    C. 6

    D. 9

190. What is the mode of the data set 0, 0, 0, 1, 2, 3, 4?

    A. 0

    B. 1

    C. $1\frac{3}{7}$

    D. 2

191. A dog's toy box contains four tennis balls, five stuffed animals, three chew bones, and one rope. What is the probability that a dog chooses a tennis ball from the toy box?

    A. $\frac{1}{13}$

    B. $\frac{4}{13}$

    C. $\frac{5}{13}$

    D. $\frac{9}{13}$

192. Which of the following is a pair of reciprocals?

    A. $(12, -12)$

    B. $(0, 0)$

    C. $\left(3\frac{3}{4}, \frac{4}{15}\right)$

    D. $(5^2, 2^5)$

5

HSPT® Diagnostic Test

5 HSPT® Diagnostic Test

193. If a number is divisible by 12, it must also be divisible by which of the following?

   A. 6
   B. 10
   C. 18
   D. 24

194. What is the least common multiple of 12 and 18?

   A. 2
   B. 6
   C. 36
   D. 204

195. Compute:

$$\begin{array}{r} 4 \text{ hours} \quad 12 \text{ minutes} \quad 10 \text{ seconds} \\ - \ 1 \text{ hour} \quad 58 \text{ minutes} \quad 20 \text{ seconds} \\ \hline \end{array}$$

   A. 2 hours 13 minutes 50 seconds
   B. 2 hours 47 minutes 30 seconds
   C. 3 hours 12 minutes 40 seconds
   D. 3 hours 46 minutes 10 seconds

196. What value of x makes this inequality true?

$$-3x > -1$$

   A. $\frac{1}{3}$
   B. 0
   C. 1
   D. 2

197. Fill in the box to make the statement true:

$$-1 - \boxed{} = 2$$

   A. −3
   B. −1
   C. 1
   D. 3

198. What is the circumference of this circle?

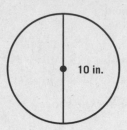

   A. 10π inches
   B. 20π inches
   C. 25π inches
   D. 100π inches

199. There are 60 minutes in one hour. To convert from hours to minutes, you would

   A. divide by 60.
   B. multiply by 60.
   C. subtract 60.
   D. add 60.

200. Which of these statements is false?

   A. $\frac{10 + 4}{2} = \frac{10}{2} + 4$
   B. $(4 + 6) - 2 = 4 + (6 - 2)$
   C. $\frac{3 \cdot 7}{4 \cdot 5} = \frac{3}{4} \cdot \frac{7}{5}$
   D. $5(8 - 2) = 5(8) - 5(2)$

201. There are 3 teaspoons in 1 tablespoon, and 8 tablespoons in 0.5 cup. How many teaspoons are in 1 cup?

   A. 16
   B. 24
   C. 48
   D. 64

202. Maria can paddle a kayak at a maximum speed of 8 miles per hour in still water. If she is paddling downstream with a current that has speed x miles per hour, what is her maximum speed?

   A. $8 + x$ miles per hour

   B. $8x$ miles per hour

   C. $8 - x$ miles per hour

   D. $x - 8$ miles per hour

203. How many sixths are in $6\frac{2}{3}$?

   A. $\frac{10}{9}$

   B. $\frac{26}{3}$

   C. 36

   D. 40

204. Which of these time durations does *not* equal the other three?

   A. 360 minutes

   B. 6 hours

   C. 2,160 seconds

   D. 0.25 day

205. Ken is deciding on materials to use for a fencing project. There are 6 different board patterns from which to choose, 3 different end posts, and 5 different types of wood. How many different combinations of board pattern, end post, and wood type are there from which to choose?

   A. 21

   B. 30

   C. 90

   D. 180

206. 100 inches = _____ yards

   A. $2\frac{7}{9}$

   B. $33\frac{1}{3}$

   C. 300

   D. 1,200

207. Which of these represents the ratio of 12 cats to 18 dogs?

   A. 2:3

   B. 3:2

   C. 4:9

   D. 18:12

208. Compute 0.04×0.04.

   A. 0.000016

   B. 0.0016

   C. 0.016

   D. 0.16

209. If $0 < x < 1$, then which of the following must be true?

   A. $x - \frac{1}{2} > 0$

   B. $2x > 1$

   C. $x^2 - 1 < 0$

   D. $1 - 2x < 0$

210. What is the median of this data set?
   5, 0, 0, 10, 20

   A. 0

   B. 5

   C. 7

   D. 20

211. A side of a rhombus has a length of 5 inches. What is its perimeter?

   A. 10 inches

   B. 15 inches

   C. 20 inches

   D. Cannot be determined

212. What is 200% of $\frac{3}{5}$?

   A. $\frac{5}{6}$

   B. $1\frac{1}{5}$

   C. 12

   D. 120

213. Simplify: $12 - 3 \times 3 - 1$

   A. 2

   B. 3

   C. 18

   D. 26

214.

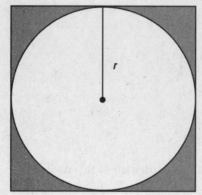

In the figure shown, the length of r is 3 centimeters. The area of the shaded portion of the square is approximately

   A. $5\frac{1}{4}$ sq. centimeters

   B. $7\frac{1}{6}$ sq. centimeters

   C. $7\frac{3}{4}$ sq. centimeters

   D. 10 sq. centimeters

215. Sandra buys two coffee mugs and four bags of coffee beans. If one coffee mug costs c dollars and one bag of coffee beans costs d dollars, what is the total cost of her purchase, in dollars?

   A. $c + d$

   B. $2cd$

   C. $2c + 4d$

   D. $8cd$

216. Consider the following line:

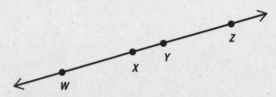

The length of XY is one-fourth the length of WZ; WX and YZ have the same length, and the length of WX is 3 meters. What is the length of WZ?

   A. 2 meters

   B. 4 meters

   C. 6 meters

   D. 8 meters

217. Simplify: $\frac{5}{8} \div 10 - 5 \times \frac{3}{8}$

   A. $-\frac{29}{16}$

   B. $-\frac{1}{4}$

   C. $\frac{3}{64}$

   D. $\frac{35}{8}$

218. If a is a nonzero number, which of these operations, when performed on a, will result in the number 0?

   A. Divide by 0.

   B. Multiply by the reciprocal of a.

   C. Multiply by $-a$.

   D. Subtract a.

219. What is the average of this list of numbers: 0.040, 0, 0.40, 4.00

   A. 0

   B. 0.22

   C. 1.11

   D. 1.48

220. If $a = -1$, $b = -\dfrac{1}{2}$, and $c = -2$, what is the value of $c(a - b)^2$?

   A. -1

   B. $-\dfrac{1}{2}$

   C. $\dfrac{1}{2}$

   D. 1

221. Solve for x: $3.7x - 1.2 = 58$

   A. 12

   B. 15.35

   C. 16

   D. 18.70

222. If Andrea spends $1\dfrac{3}{4}$ hours per day training for a marathon and she trains 5 days per week, how many hours does Andrea train for the marathon each week?

   A. $5\dfrac{1}{4}$

   B. $6\dfrac{1}{2}$

   C. $8\dfrac{3}{4}$

   D. 9

223. Alicia invests $2,000 and earns 8 percent interest on her investment in one year. What is the total amount of her investment after one year?

   A. $2,008

   B. $2,080

   C. $2,160

   D. $2,225

224. The time remaining for a video to come to its end is described by a time bar 4 inches long on the bottom of the monitor. If $\dfrac{1}{2}$ inch corresponds to 1 minute, 45 seconds, how long is the video?

   A. 10 minutes, 45 seconds

   B. 12 minutes, 30 seconds

   C. 14 minutes

   D. 16 minutes, 15 seconds

225. If it rains, there is a 30% chance that a school bus will run late. What is the probability that the school bus will not run late if it rains?

   A. 0.30

   B. 0.50

   C. 0.70

   D. 1.00

226. Felix earns $4,200 per month. He pays 22% in various taxes. Of the amount remaining, he invests 15% in different stocks. What amount of money remains, to the nearest dollar, after these amounts are subtracted?

   A. $2,646

   B. $2,785

   C. $3,276

   D. $3,425

5

HSPT® Diagnostic Test

227. Compute: $3\frac{3}{4} \div \frac{4}{3}$

A. $2\frac{13}{16}$

B. 3

C. $3\frac{8}{9}$

D. 5

228. For five weeks over the summer, Neera earned weekly paychecks at her part-time job. The amount of each paycheck was $101.65, $79.23, $84.67, $121.33, and $77.62. What was her average paycheck for those five checks?

A. $92.90

B. $94.16

C. $99.47

D. $101.30

229. Compute: $2 \div 0.004$

A. 0.008

B. 8

C. 500

D. 2,000

230. Which of these figures need not have a 90-degree angle?

A. Rectangle

B. Right triangle

C. Square

D. Parallelogram

231. Which of the following is not a factor of 36?

A. 4

B. 6

C. 9

D. 10

232. What is 40 reduced by 20%?

A. 8

B. 20

C. 32

D. 48

233. Find the area of the following figure.

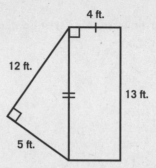

A. 48 square feet

B. 52 square feet

C. 78 square feet

D. 82 square feet

234. Solve for b: $(b-2)(b+5) = 0$

A. −2 and −5

B. −2 and 5

C. 2 and −5

D. 2 and 5

235. If $xy - 7 = 56$, and $x = 7$, $y =$

A. 3

B. 7

C. 9

D. 12

236. Consider the following region:

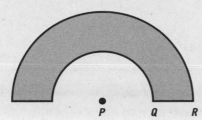

Assume the following:

$\overline{PQ}$ is the radius of the inner semicircle and has measure 3 meters.

$\overline{PR}$ is the radius of the outer semicircle and has measure 8 meters.

Find the perimeter of the shaded region.

A. $(11\pi + 5)$ meters

B. $(11\pi + 10)$ meters

C. 21π meters

D. $(22\pi + 10)$ meters

237. The cost of a new sink is reduced from $350 to $275. By approximately what percent has the price been reduced?

A. 21%

B. 27%

C. 35%

D. 75%

238. The square root of 141 is between

A. 11 and 12.

B. 20 and 22.

C. 41 and 100.

D. 70 and 71.

STOP.

If you finish before time is up, you may check your work on this section only.
Do not turn to any other section in the test.

LANGUAGE

60 Questions (25 minutes)

Turn to the Language section of your answer sheet to answer the questions in this section.

> **Directions:** In questions 239–277, look for errors in capitalization, punctuation, or usage. Mark the answer choice that contains the error. If you find no mistake, mark D on your answer sheet.

239. A. "I'm not sure who lives there," she said.
   B. Zach is a student here, isn't he?
   C. You cannot drive on this street. It is for pedestrian's only.
   D. *(No mistakes)*

240. A. He finished his homework on Friday so that he could relax all weekend.
   B. Who's in charge of graduation this year?
   C. Amy missed the bus she was late for school.
   D. *(No mistakes)*

241. A. Mr. Wolfe, who was my French teacher last year, is leading the trip to Paris.
   B. I don't like living in a small town. I prefer the city life.
   C. How many students in this class ride the bus to school?
   D. *(No mistakes)*

242. A. When we finished the hike, we were all very tired?
   B. "We parked the car behind the building," she said.
   C. If the weather is bad, we'll have to change our plans.
   D. *(No mistakes)*

243. A. Julia wrote their name in the book.
   B. The dog drank from its water bowl.
   C. That is not my book; it's hers.
   D. *(No mistakes)*

244. A. We shall now proceed into the next room.
   B. I cannot concieve of a better excuse.
   C. The teacher led the class into the auditorium.
   D. *(No mistakes)*

245. A. Will you stop shouting!
   B. Is that your cousin Gary?
   C. The night air is chilly, so be sure to wear a jacket.
   D. *(No mistakes)*

246. A. That is not mine; it is her's.
   B. Paul's brother is in my class this year, but Paul is in a different class.
   C. The dog's collar is brown; the cat's color is red.
   D. *(No mistakes)*

247. A. Jasmine likes apples; Davy prefers oranges.
   B. My dad is an artist; my mom is a lawyer.
   C. The bat actually flies; but the flying squirrel only glides.
   D. *(No mistakes)*

248. A. My little brother hates the taste of broccoli.
   B. This cantalope tastes really sweet.
   C. Spinach tastes better fresh than it does when it's boiled.
   D. *(No mistakes)*

249. **A.** How many of the *Star Wars* movies have you seen?

   B. The first book of the *Lord of the Rings* trilogy is *The Fellowship of the Ring*.

   C. My father read *Alice's Adventures in Wonderland* to me when I was a small child.

   D. *(No mistakes)*

250. **A.** The best way to avoid mistakes is to do your homework slowly and carefully.

   B. The boat rocked on the waves violently as the wind howled over the sea's surface.

   C. That prettily dress is the nicest one in my closet.

   D. *(No mistakes)*

251. **A.** The drummer beat out the rhythm of the song.

   B. Having a well-developed conscience helps you to make the right decisions.

   C. There is an embarrassing picture of me in that photo album!

   D. *(No mistakes)*

252. **A.** The film crew included a director, a camera operator, actors and actresses, and a sound person.

   B. The school orchestra has numerous musicians; cellists, violinists, brass players, woodwind players, and percussionists.

   C. The artist works with paints, pencils, clay, metal, and many other tools and materials.

   D. *(No mistakes)*

253. **A.** My parents are driving me to the play in they minivan.

   B. Greta asked her sister for help with her homework.

   C. My family is having Thanksgiving dinner at our house this year.

   D. *(No mistakes)*

254. **A.** My favorite ice cream flavor is pistachio.

   B. I keep my sissors in the same drawer as my pencils and erasers.

   C. That dog may look vicious, but it is as gentle as a lamb.

   D. *(No mistakes)*

255. **A.** "Listen," Francine began, "because I do not want to have to repeat myself."

   B. The song "You're So Sweet" was playing the night my grandparents fell in love.

   C. I started reading a story called "The Long, Long Night," but it was so long that I couldn't finish it before bedtime!

   D. *(No mistakes)*

256. **A.** The glass broke; I used a plastic cup instead.

   B. All of my clothing was dirty; I spent the day washing laundry.

   C. The song was not very good; I changed the radio to a different station.

   D. *(No mistakes)*

257. **A.** This is the chapter the teacher expects us to read tonight.

   B. I would of called you but my phone was not working.

   C. We talked of the good times we had when we were kids.

   D. *(No mistakes)*

258. **A.** The cats are prowling through the night.

   B. The stars are twinkling in the sky.

   C. The trees leaves are falling.

   D. *(No mistakes)*

259. A. At this school, we are committed to excellense.

    B. That advertisement is trying to convince you to buy something you don't need.

    C. Tyrese exceeds in every competition in which he competes.

    D. *(No mistakes)*

260. A. My guitar string broke, so I need to take a trip to the music store to buy a new one.

    B. The temperature is too hot, so I am thinking about swimming instead of sitting on the sand.

    C. Bernie is organizing his books alphabetically by author, on the shelf.

    D. *(No mistakes)*

261. A. There is a noticeable flaw in this structure.

    B. Do you have an arguement you'd like to present?

    C. When you most feel like giving up, that is when you must persevere.

    D. *(No mistakes)*

262. A. If you are going to Lisa's house, please gave her this note for me.

    B. I wish you could have met Helga, because she would like you.

    C. They are studying for a test they are taking next week.

    D. *(No mistakes)*

263. A. Regardless of your plans, you still have to clean up your room.

    B. We would have gone to your party, but we thought it was going to be next week!

    C. I insure that you will have a good time.

    D. *(No mistakes)*

264. A. My brother (he's our family's worst back-seat driver) is getting his first car.

    B. Those clouds (stratus and nimbostratus, I think) make the sky look ominous.

    C. That movie (which I was tricked into seeing) was much too scary for me.

    D. *(No mistakes)*

265. A. Do not run on the ice—it is very thin!

    B. Where is Janice going on vacation.

    C. This magazine is already two months old.

    D. *(No mistakes)*

266. A. We learned about president John F. Kennedy in history class.

    B. The senator participated in an important vote this morning.

    C. I am writing a letter to my congressperson.

    D. *(No mistakes)*

267. A. The only way to acheive anything is to try.

    B. I have a lot of respect for your mother.

    C. There is a small cemetery at the end of the street.

    D. *(No mistakes)*

268. A. My favorite novel is *Emma*.

    B. The movie *The Incredibles* is very funny!

    C. This song is called *Honey*.

    D. *(No mistakes)*

269. A. Either you like that color or you don't.

    B. The coach will choose either Tricia or me to be team captain.

    C. Neither Grace or Yuri was in class today.

    D. *(No mistakes)*

270. A. I spent the entire weekend worked.

 B. We went to the bowling alley, but it was closed.

 C. The day was incredibly cold, but the birds still sang.

 D. *(No mistakes)*

271. A. Will you stop talking so loudly?

 B. I cannot hear you!

 C. Is there no end to this day?

 D. *(No mistakes)*

272. A. Keith was born in Febuary.

 B. I think you misspelled that word.

 C. My sister is as mischievous as a pixie!

 D. *(No mistakes)*

273. A. She insisted on meeting you.

 B. This is the first time we talked since a long time.

 C. Iris has been building this birdhouse for two weeks.

 D. *(No mistakes)*

274. A. First we're going to the movies; then we're going out to dinner.

 B. Being selected to join the band will depend on how I perform at the audition.

 C. I had the opportunity to go to the park on Saturday or Sunday, and I chose the later.

 D. *(No mistakes)*

275. A. Today the weather is lovely, but tomorrow it is supposed to rain.

 B. There are shrubs on the front lawn, and there are tall trees in the backyard.

 C. Either I am going to study art or I am going to study music when I go to college.

 D. *(No mistakes)*

276. A. If you want to get into the building, you will need to bring your id.

 B. According to the American Medical Association, smoking is bad for you.

 C. We're going to have a big celebration, and all of my aunts and uncles are coming to it!

 D. *(No mistakes)*

277. A. I will check my calendar to see if I am free that day.

 B. I am defiantly interested in hearing about your day.

 C. I have no knowledge of what you are saying.

 D. *(No mistakes)*

278. Choose the sentence that demonstrates correct usage.

 A. The twins are asking her mother for permission to go to the party.

 B. Cora and Luis are taking they dog to the veterinarian.

 C. The group is naming itself The Community Cleaners.

 D. The toys need new batteries so it can work again.

279. Choose the best word to join the thoughts together.

 Alan and his family always visit the Statue of Liberty _____ they are in New York.

 A. unless

 B. until

 C. whenever

 D. after

HSPT® Diagnostic Test

5

280. Choose the sentence that demonstrates correct usage.

    A. I am renewed my library card today.

    B. I came to the dance a little late.

    C. The teacher will stayed after school to tutor students.

    D. The football team will traveled to another city for their next game.

281. Choose the word that best completes this sentence.

    Lisette was in a bad mood, so she answered Marvin's question more _____ than she would have if she were feeling better.

    A. abruptly

    B. slowly

    C. casually

    D. horribly

282. Choose the sentence that demonstrates correct usage.

    A. Curtis rides his motorcycle to their job every day.

    B. Beatrice is washing the shirt they wore last night at the Laundromat.

    C. Han thinks I forgot his birthday, but I'm actually planning a surprise party for him!

    D. Glenda wants to visit her cousin Ralph, but she cannot remember its address.

283. Which of the following sentences offers the *least* support for the topic "Why we must recycle"?

    A. Recycling prevents air pollution by reducing the amount of new plastics factories produce.

    B. Recycling reduces global warming by cutting down on the release of carbon dioxide that occurs when producing aluminum.

    C. Recycling prevents water pollution by eliminating some of the garbage in landfills that releases contaminated material into ground water.

    D. Recycling is something that anyone can do simply by separating recyclable plastics, metals, and papers from non-recyclable trash.

284. Choose the sentence that demonstrates correct usage.

    A. Because she gets good grades, Anna is going to a great college.

    B. He was feeling ill, he stayed home from school today.

    C. Bryant still occupies the house in which he was born or so do I.

    D. She is my friend, then I did not hesitate to help her.

285. Choose the word that best completes this sentence.

    The cat found a warm stream of sunlight and laid herself down _____ it.

    A. beneath

    B. within

    C. between

    D. of

286. Choose the sentence that demonstrates correct usage.

    A. The shirts pattern is a little too garish for me.

    B. The moon's glow is particularly lovely tonight.

    C. The birds feathers only appear blue; there is no actual blue pigment in them.

    D. The books cover is starting to come apart from the binding.

287. Which of these expresses the idea most clearly?

    A. This picture does not fit this frame, so I'll have to get a new one.

    B. This picture does not fit this frame, a new frame I'll have to get.

    C. This picture does not fit this frame, so I'll have to get a new frame.

    D. So I'll have to get a new frame, this picture does not fit this frame.

288. Choose the sentence that demonstrates correct usage.

    A. The bird flew in the birdhouse.

    B. The firefighter went into save the puppy.

    C. I finished my project in two hour's time.

    D. I don't care for this brand of juice.

289. Choose the pair of sentences that best develops this topic sentence.

    All high school students should perform mandatory community service.

    A. High school students are generally irresponsible because they have too much free time on their hands. They are in dire need of things to keep them busy.

    B. More and more people are living to advanced ages. High school students would perform an invaluable service by volunteering in senior citizen centers.

    C. High school curricula should develop civic responsibility as well as academic proficiency. Mandatory community service would help achieve these noble aims.

    D. Studies indicate that teenagers who participate in a diverse range of activities do well in college. High school curricula should therefore include more varied activities.

290. Choose the sentence that demonstrates correct usage.

    A. Victoria did hers homework on Sunday night.

    B. Tiana and Paolo are moving into her new house today.

    C. This is not my book; it is your's.

    D. We decided not to buy this house because it has a bad foundation.

291. Which of these expresses the idea most clearly?

A. The batteries in the remote control are dead I am going to have to replace them.

B. The batteries in the remote control are dead, so I am going to have to replace them.

C. So I am going to have to replace them, the batteries in the remote control are dead.

D. The batteries in the remote control are dead, so I am going to have to.

292. Choose the sentence that demonstrates correct usage.

A. To slowly work is to do a careful job.

B. The wind blew mighty during the storm.

C. The horse's mane flowed down its back beautifully.

D. The students grumbled when they learned loudly about the upcoming test.

293. Which sentence does *not* belong in the paragraph?

(1) Sometimes businesses in developing countries have not figured out the best ways to produce their goods. (2) FINE, an association of fair-trade networks, helps such companies run their businesses as responsibly as possible. (3) A business that receives fair trade approval meets certain standards regarding environmental concerns and fair treatment of their workers. (4) My local supermarket sells fair-trade coffee in aisle 7.

A. Sentence 1

B. Sentence 2

C. Sentence 3

D. Sentence 4

294. Choose the sentence that demonstrates correct usage.

A. I am going to the beach with Margaret and him.

B. If his wants his ball, he is going to have to look for it.

C. Garreth has the odd habit of talking about hisself in the third person.

D. What is her doing in the attic?

295. Which sentence does *not* belong in the paragraph?

(1) Doctors without Borders is a charitable organization that provides medical aid in troubled regions of the world. (2) "What would you like for your birthday this year?" Darren's mom asked. (3) "I have everything I could want," Darren replied. (4) "Maybe this year you could just make a donation to a worthy charity in my name."

A. Sentence 1

B. Sentence 2

C. Sentence 3

D. Sentence 4

296. Choose the sentence that demonstrates correct usage.

A. The spider spun its web intricate.

B. The sticker fell off the book because its glue was too drily.

C. The harp resounded lovely in the concert hall.

D. Writing a poem was a challenging task, but I performed it happily.

297. Which of the following sentences offers the *least* support to the topic "Why students should have after-school jobs"?

A. They can earn money for school supplies.

B. They can learn the value of having responsibilities.

C. They can get jobs close to their homes.

D. They can learn new skills on the job.

298. Choose the sentence that demonstrates correct usage.

A. If you have an moment, I'd like to talk to you.

B. Do you have a quarter I can borrow?

C. This glass has an crack in it.

D. Do you know a antonym of the word *loquacious*?

HSPT® Diagnostic Test

5

ANSWER KEYS AND EXPLANATIONS

Verbal Skills

1. B	13. A	25. B	37. B	49. D
2. C	14. C	26. D	38. D	50. A
3. A	15. C	27. C	39. D	51. C
4. D	16. A	28. A	40. A	52. A
5. A	17. C	29. B	41. B	53. C
6. C	18. A	30. D	42. B	54. C
7. A	19. A	31. B	43. A	55. D
8. D	20. C	32. A	44. D	56. B
9. C	21. B	33. B	45. D	57. A
10. B	22. B	34. D	46. C	58. D
11. B	23. C	35. C	47. C	59. C
12. B	24. A	36. C	48. B	60. A

1. **The correct answer is B.** This analogy is an object-characteristic relationship. Brown is the color of dirt; blue is the color of the sky.

2. **The correct answer is C.** This analogy is an object-purpose relationship. The purpose of a stove is to use it to cook; the purpose of a bed is to use it to sleep.

3. **The correct answer is A.** This analogy is a part-whole relationship. Glass is part of a window; a wall is part of a house.

4. **The correct answer is D.** This analogy is a sequence relationship. The first item in a series comes before the last item; the beginning of an event comes before the end.

5. **The correct answer is A.** This analogy is an antonym relationship. *Dirty* is the opposite of *clean*; *interested* is the opposite of *bored*.

6. **The correct answer is C.** This analogy is a part-whole relationship. Hair grows from the head; leaves grow from a tree.

7. **The correct answer is A.** This analogy is a part-whole relationship. A finger is a digit of the hand; a toe is a digit of the foot.

8. **The correct answer is D.** This analogy is an object-purpose relationship. Lifting is the purpose of an elevator; weighing is the purpose of a scale.

9. **The correct answer is C.** This analogy is an object-purpose relationship. A vase is used to contain a bouquet of flowers; an ice cube tray is used to contain ice cubes.

10. **The correct answer is B.** This analogy is an association relationship. A desk and a chair are included in a desk set; a jacket and pants are included in a suit set.

11. **The correct answer is B.** If Bill is taller than Ingrid, and she is taller than Charles, then Charles can't be taller than Bill. Therefore, the third statement is false.

12. **The correct answer is B.** Since we know that the red car is two colors because it has a black roof, all of the cars cannot be just one color. Therefore, the third statement is false.

13. **The correct answer is A.** Liara has the fewest books, so Alan must have more books than she does. Therefore, the third statement is true.

14. **The correct answer is C.** We do not know if Gerald and Suzanne are in the same class, or anything about the other children in Gerald's class, so there is no way to know if the final statement is true.

15. **The correct answer is C.** We do not know if the only vegetables and fruits served at the meal are in the soup and salad, so there is no way to know if the third statement is true.

16. **The correct answer is A.** Clarence is the slowest runner, so Miles must be faster than him. Therefore, the third statement is true.

17. **The correct answer is C.** We can only compare the chair to the computer and oven since we know only that it is the least expensive item. There are no clues regarding whether an oven or a computer is more expensive, so there is no way to know if the third statement is true.

18. **The correct answer is A.** Anna ate the fewest strawberries, and since Patrice ate as many strawberries as she did, Grace has to have eaten more strawberries than Patrice. Therefore, the third statement is true.

19. **The correct answer is A.** All of the animals in question live longer than mosquitoes. Therefore, the third statement is true.

20. **The correct answer is C.** There is no true statement about how well Shirley did on the math test, so there is no way to determine if the third statement is true.

21. **The correct answer is B.** Pablo is the hungriest, so he must be hungrier than Kira. Therefore, the third statement is false.

22. **The correct answer is B.** The grey horse must be the biggest since it is bigger than the brown horse, which is bigger than the white horse. Therefore, the third statement is false.

23. **The correct answer is C.** A hammer, a screwdriver, and a wrench are all tools. A basket is not a tool, so it does not belong with the other three words.

24. **The correct answer is A.** To sing, to talk, and to whisper all involve using your voice. To watch requires using your eyesight, not your voice, so *watch* does not belong with the other three words.

25. **The correct answer is B.** The word *perspective* refers to a particular viewpoint. The other three words all reflect positive attitudes or qualities.

26. **The correct answer is D.** A cello, a violin, and a guitar are all stringed instruments. A trumpet is a brass instrument.

27. **The correct answer is C.** To run, leap, or stroll all involve movement. To sit does not.

28. **The correct answer is A.** A marker, a pen, and a paint brush all make marks. An eraser removes marks.

29. **The correct answer is B.** Earth, Venus, and Jupiter are all planets. The moon is not.

30. **The correct answer is D.** An oven, a blender, and a refrigerator are all appliances for storing or preparing food; a television has nothing to do with food.

31. **The correct answer is B.** Milk, butter, and ice cream are all dairy products. Ham is meat.

32. **The correct answer is A.** A squirrel, mouse, and rat are rodents. A snake is a reptile.

33. **The correct answer is B.** Mustard, salsa, and ketchup are all sauces; pepper is a spice.

34. **The correct answer is D.** Florida, Michigan, and New York are all states. Los Angeles is a city.

35. **The correct answer is C.** A dress, a sock, and a necklace are all things to wear. A pocketbook is not worn.

36. **The correct answer is C.** Handlebars, a seat, and wheels are all part of a bicycle. The bicycle is the object, itself.

37. **The correct answer is B.** A dresser, a suitcase, and a wardrobe are containers. Clothing is what is stored in those containers.

38. **The correct answer is D.** A bulldozer, a dump truck, and a backhoe are all construction vehicles. A bus is a transportation vehicle.

39. **The correct answer is D.** An artificial tree is fake.

40. **The correct answer is A.** An audible hum is heard.

41. **The correct answer is B.** An elementary understanding is basic.

42. **The correct answer is B.** An absurd excuse is silly.

43. **The correct answer is A.** A pungent odor is strong.

44. **The correct answer is D.** A gradual change is slow.

45. **The correct answer is D.** A hilarious story is funny.

46. **The correct answer is C.** An ignorant opinion is uninformed.

47. **The correct answer is C.** A jubilant reaction is thrilled.

48. **The correct answer is B.** A sinister plot is evil.

49. **The correct answer is D.** A misplaced item is lost.

50. **The correct answer is A.** A lucid idea is clear.

51. **The correct answer is C.** A humongous hill is huge.

52. **The correct answer is A.** *Lavish* means "extravagant"; the opposite is *plain*.

53. **The correct answer is C.** *Partial* means "incomplete"; the opposite is *whole*.

54. **The correct answer is C.** *Deteriorate* means "to worsen"; the opposite is to *improve*.

55. **The correct answer is D.** *Flair* means "skill"; the opposite is *inability*.

56. **The correct answer is B.** *Squander* means "to waste"; the opposite is to *save*.

57. **The correct answer is A.** *Accurate* means "correct"; the opposite is *mistaken*.

58. **The correct answer is D.** *Escalate* means "to increase"; the opposite is to *decrease*.

59. **The correct answer is C.** *Renounce* means "reject"; the opposite is *accept*.

60. **The correct answer is A.** *Tumult* means "commotion"; the opposite is *calm*.

Quantitative Skills

61. B	72. B	83. A	93. D	103. B
62. C	73. A	84. D	94. B	104. A
63. D	74. C	85. D	95. B	105. C
64. C	75. B	86. C	96. B	106. C
65. B	76. D	87. B	97. B	107. A
66. D	77. A	88. C	98. B	108. B
67. D	78. D	89. B	99. A	109. C
68. B	79. B	90. C	100. A	110. D
69. C	80. D	91. A	101. C	111. D
70. B	81. D	92. C	102. A	112. B
71. A	82. A			

61. **The correct answer is B.** The pattern is to add 4 to a term to get the next one in the series. Since you add 4 to 2 to get 6, the first term must be 2.

62. **The correct answer is C.** $3^3 - 8 = 27 - 8 = 19$

63. **The correct answer is D.** Since the triangle is isosceles, $\overline{AB}$ and $\overline{BC}$ have the same length. Since the triangle is right, $\overline{AC}$ is the hypotenuse, and its length is greater than the length of each leg, specifically $\overline{AB}$.

64. **The correct answer is C.** This series consists of the letters of the alphabet in alphabetical order, beginning with the letter Q. The letter X appears in the middle of each set of three letters.

65. **The correct answer is B.** Count the number of squares in A, B, and C. The figures in A and C each have 11 squares, and the figure in B has 14 squares.

66. **The correct answer is D.** When solving a math problem expressed in words, look for key terms such as *twice* or *double* that indicate you will need to **multiply** a quantity by 2. Also be sure to recognize when when you see the word *of* in connection with a fraction, it also means to **multiply** a number by that fraction.

$$2 \times \left(\frac{2}{3} \times 24\right) = 2 \times (16) = 32$$

67. **The correct answer is D.** The pattern is to divide a term by 3 to get the next term. So, the next term is $3 \div 3 = 1$.

68. **The correct answer is B.** The pattern in the series is to subtract 2 from the first term to get the second term, subtract 4 from the second term to get the third term, subtract 6 from the third term to get the fourth term, etc. So, to get the sixth term, subtract 10 from the fifth term, 182, to get 172.

69. **The correct answer is C.** Calculate the value of A and B. The value of A is 8×8, or 64. The value of B is 9×7, or 63. The only true statement is that A is greater than B.

70. **The correct answer is B.** The area of A is $(6)(10) = 60$ square inches. The area of B is $(6)(6) = 36$ square inches. The area of C is $\frac{1}{2}(6)(10) = 30$ square inches. So, the area of C is less than the area of B, and the area of B is less than the area of A.

71. **The correct answer is A.** The 1st, 3rd, 5th, etc., terms are all just "A." Since the term sought is the 7th one, it must be A.

72. **The correct answer is D.** This series consists of the three letters A-R-D in constant rotation. In each succeeding group of letters, the last letter of the previous group moves

Answers 5 HSPT® Diagnostic Test

to the beginning of the group, and the other two letters move to the right, so the letter that was last in the previous group becomes the first letter of the next. After ARD, the D must move to the beginning, and the next group must begin with D followed by AR.

73. **The correct answer is A.** The sum of 2.1 and 1.9 is 4.0. Forty percent of 4.0 is 4.0(0.04) = 1.6.

74. **The correct answer is C.** Note that $(7-3)^2 = 4^2 = 16$, $7^2 - 3^2 = 49 - 9 = 40$, and $(3-7)^2 = 4^2 = 16$. So A = C and A < B.

75. **The correct answer is B.** Let x be the number. It satisfies the equation $1 - 2x = 5$. Solve for x:

$$1 - 2x = 5$$
$$-2x = 4$$
$$x = -2$$

76. **The correct answer is D.** The pattern is that each term involves the previous letter in the alphabet, and the 1st, 3rd, 5th, etc., terms use just one letter while the 2nd, 4th, 6th, etc., terms use two letters. Since the missing term is the 6th one, it must be UU.

77. **The correct answer is A.** The 3rd and 5th terms are obtained by multiplying the previous term by 3, while the 2nd, 4th, 6th, etc., terms are obtained by adding 2 to the previous term. Since the missing term is the 6th one, we add 2 to 6 to get 8.

78. **The correct answer is D.** The diagonal $\overline{MO}$ forms two right triangles. The hypotenuse of a right triangle is always its longest side, so $\overline{MO}$ must be greater than $\overline{MP}$.

79. **The correct answer is B.** Angles *POC* and *POB* both have measures of 45 degrees. So, the sum of the measures of angles *DOC* and *POC* is 105 degrees, while the sum of the measures of angles *AOB* and *POB* is 75 degrees.

80. **The correct answer is D.** Observe that $3^4 = 3 \times 3 \times 3 \times 3 = 81$, $4^3 = 4 \times 4 \times 4 = 64$, and $3 \times 4 = 12$. So, C < B < A.

81. **The correct answer is D.** The pattern in this series is formed by subtracting 5 from each number.

82. **The correct answer is A.** Calculate the value of A and B. The value of A is 6×10^2, or 6×100, which equals 600. The value of B is $6 \div 10$, or 0.60. Therefore, B is equal to C.

83. **The correct answer is A.** The pattern is to multiply the numerator of the previous term by 2 and the denominator by 4. Doing so here yields $\frac{12 \times 2}{64 \times 4} = \frac{24}{256}$.

84. **The correct answer is D.** Let x be the number. Then, x satisfies the equation $\frac{1}{3}x = \frac{2}{3}x - 2$. Solve for x:

$$\frac{1}{3}x = \frac{2}{3}x - 2$$
$$0 = \frac{1}{3}x - 2$$
$$2 = \frac{1}{3}x$$
$$x = 6$$

85. **The correct answer is D.** The pattern is to skip two letters from the previous term and to multiply the number portion of the previous term by 5. Doing so here yields M250.

86. **The correct answer is C.** The diameter is the longest chord of a circle. Since $\overline{BC}$ passes through the center, it is a diameter; since $\overline{EF}$ does not pass through the center, it is not a diameter. So, the length of *BC* is greater than the length of *EF*.

87. **The correct answer is B.** The pattern is that the first letter goes forward in the alphabet by one letter, and the second letter goes backward in the alphabet by one letter. Doing so here yields FV.

88. **The correct answer is C.** Let x be the number. Then, x satisfies the equation $\frac{1}{4}(1 + x) = \frac{1}{2}\left(2 + \frac{1}{2}\right)$. Solve for x:

$$\frac{1}{4}(1+x) = \frac{1}{2}\left(2+\frac{1}{2}\right)$$

$$\frac{1}{4}(1+x) = \frac{1}{2}\left(\frac{5}{2}\right)$$

$$\frac{1}{4}(1+x) = \frac{5}{4}$$

$$1+x = 5$$

$$x = 4$$

89. **The correct answer is B.** The 3rd, 5th, etc., terms are obtained by subtracting 3 from the previous term, while the 2nd, 4th, 6th, etc., terms are obtained by multiplying the previous term by 2. Since we are asked for the 7th and 8th terms, we subtract 3 from −3 to get −6 as the 7th term and multiply 16 by 2 to get 32 for the 8th term.

90. **The correct answer is C.** 200% = 2, so 200% of 0.1 is 2(0.1) = 0.2.

   50% = 0.5, so 50% of 1 is 0.5(1) = 0.5.

   25% = 0.25, so 25% of 10 is 0.25(10) = 2.5. Therefore, A < B < C.

91. **The correct answer is A.** The area of the shaded region in A = 32 − 2(2) = 28 square inches.

   The area of the shaded region in B = 32 − $4\left(\frac{1}{2}\right)^2$ = 32 − 1 = 31 square inches. The area of the shaded region in C = 32 − 4(1) = 28 square inches.

   So, the area of A equals the area of C, and the area of B is greater than the area of A.

92. **The correct answer is C.** The pattern is to add 0.7 for the number portion and to skip two letters for the letter portion. Doing so yields 3.3V.

93. **The correct answer is D.** Remember, when you see the word *of* in connection with a fraction, it means you need to multiply the number that follows by that fraction. Let x be the number. Then, x must satisfy the equation $\frac{3}{4}x = \frac{4}{3}$.

   Solve for x:

$$\frac{3}{4}x = \frac{4}{3}$$

$$x = \frac{4}{3}\cdot\frac{4}{3}$$

$$x = \frac{16}{9}$$

94. **The correct answer is B.** The pattern in this series is +1, +2, +1, +2, and so on. Adding 2 to 14 gives the sum 16.

95. **The correct answer is B.** Note:

   A: $4 \times 4^2 = 64$

   B: $\frac{1}{2}\left(4^3\right) = \frac{1}{2}(64) = 32$

   C: $2 \times 3^3 = 2 \times 27 = 54$

   So, A > C > B.

96. **The correct answer is B.** The pattern is to multiply by 5 to get the next term. Doing so here yields 1(5) = 5 for the 4th term and 5(5) = 25 for the 5th term.

97. **The correct answer is B.** Let x be the number. Then, x must satisfy the equation $2(x + 4) = 4x$. Solve for x:

$$2(x + 4) = 4x$$

$$2x + 8 = 4x$$

$$8 = 2x$$

$$x = 4$$

98. **The correct answer is B.** Calculate the value of A, B, and C. The value of A is $6 \times (4 + 2)$, or 6×6, which equals 36. The value of B is $(4 + 2) \times (4 + 2)$, or 6×6, which also equals 36. The value of C is $(6 \times 4) + 2$, or $24 + 2$, which equals 26. Therefore, C is less than A and B.

99. **The correct answer is A.** The pattern is to increase the numerator by 2 and the denominator by 1. Doing so here yields $\frac{9}{5}$ for the 5th term and $\frac{11}{6}$ for the 6th term.

100. **The correct answer is A.** For each of these expressions, the exponent on the 10 tells the number of places to the right to move the decimal point. In each case, moving the

decimal point the indicated number of places results in the number 30. So, A = B = C.

101. **The correct answer is C.** The pattern in this series is ×2, +3, ×2, +3, and so on.

102. **The correct answer is A.** Remember, when you see the word *of* in connection with a fraction, it means you need to multiply the number that follows by that fraction. Let x be the number. Then, x must satisfy the equation $\frac{1}{2}x = 4x$. The only value of x that can make this true is $x = 0$.

103. **The correct answer is B.** The figures in C and B both have seven edges (i.e., a segment between two consecutive vertices).

104. **The correct answer is A.** The pattern is to alternate between 3 in the first slot and 8 in the second slot of a term for the number portion, and to increase the letter portion by 1 each time. Doing so here yields the next two terms as being 3H and I8.

105. **The correct answer is C.** The 3rd and 5th terms are obtained by multiplying the previous term by 3, while the 2nd, 4th, 6th, etc., terms are obtained by adding 1 in the numerator and denominator of the previous term. Since we are asked for the 7th term, we multiply $\frac{2}{3}$ by 3 to get 2.

106. **The correct answer is C.** Let x be the number. Then, x must satisfy the equation $x + 6 = (2 + 4)^2$. Solve for x:

$$x + 6 = (2 + 4)^2$$
$$x + 6 = 6^2$$
$$x + 6 = 36$$
$$x = 30$$

107. **The correct answer is A.** Since $0 < z < 1$, it follows that multiplying both sides of $z < 1$ by z produces $z^2 < z$. Doing that again shows that $z^3 < z^2$. Since $z < 2z$, we see that $z^3 < z^2 < z < 2z$, so we know that C < B < A.

108. **The correct answer is B.** The 2nd, 4th, 6th, etc., terms are obtained by affixing two more

C's to the previous term in that list. Doing so here yields CCCCCC.

109. **The correct answer is C.** Let x be the number. Then, x must satisfy the equation $x - 3 = \frac{1}{2} \cdot 4^2$. Solve for x:

$$x - 3 = \frac{1}{2} \cdot 4^2$$
$$x - 3 = \frac{1}{2} \cdot 16$$
$$x - 3 = 8$$
$$x = 11$$

110. **The correct answer is D.** Using the order of operations, expressions A and C are equal:

$$2 \div \frac{1}{10} \div 5 = \left(2 \div \frac{1}{10}\right) \div 5$$
$$= 2 \times 10 \div 5$$
$$= 20 \div 5$$
$$= 4$$

Positioning the parentheses differently in B results in a different solution.

$$2 \div \left(\frac{1}{10} \div 5\right) = 2 \div \left(\frac{1}{10} \times \frac{1}{5}\right)$$
$$= 2 \div \left(\frac{1}{50}\right)$$
$$= 2 \times 50 = 100$$

So, A = C and A < B.

111. **The correct answer is D.** The pattern is to alternate between adding 0.9 and subtracting 0.3. Since we are asked for the 6th and 7th terms, we add 0.9 to 2.4 to get 3.3 for the 6th term. Then, subtract 0.3 from this to get 3.0 for the 7th term.

112. **The correct answer is B.** Let x be the number. Then, x satisfies the equation $2x + 3x = 10^2 - 5$. Solve for x:

$$2x + 3x = 10^2 - 5$$
$$5x = 100 - 5$$
$$5x = 95$$
$$x = 19$$

READING

Comprehension

113. C	121. C	129. C	137. A	145. B
114. A	122. D	130. A	138. D	146. D
115. D	123. A	131. B	139. A	147. A
116. B	124. D	132. B	140. A	148. A
117. C	125. B	133. C	141. D	149. D
118. B	126. B	134. D	142. C	150. A
119. A	127. D	135. C	143. B	151. B
120. D	128. C	136. D	144. A	152. A

113. **The correct answer is C.** The passage is mainly about the various ways that companies conduct market research. Choice A is incorrect because the passage explains how companies find out this information instead of how people make their decisions. The passage mainly describes various ways to conduct market research, so choices B and D can be eliminated.

114. **The correct answer is A.** In the beginning of the passage, the author explains that one of the main ways that companies conduct market research is through the distribution of surveys. The passage focuses on how market research is conducted, so choices C and D can be eliminated.

115. **The correct answer is D.** The second sentence in paragraph 2 uses *demographic* to refer to characteristics of a group. Gender and marital status are group characteristics mentioned in the sentence that follows, giving a clue as to the context. This eliminates *problematic* (choice B). Choices A and C also do not fit the context and can be eliminated.

116. **The correct answer is B.** The author mentions fabric softener in paragraph 3 to give an example of a product that might be the subject of market research. This example helps explain why a survey might contain certain types of questions.

117. **The correct answer is C.** The author states in paragraph 5 that companies ask for demographic information from survey respondents in order to understand what type of person is most likely to purchase their products. With this information, companies can build consumer profiles of potential customers.

118. **The correct answer is B.** According to information in paragraph 7, a main reason to hold focus groups is to collect data for constructing advertising campaigns. The passage never indicates that focus groups are held to develop ideas for new products (choice A), influence the people in the groups to buy new products (choice C), or find out which products are the most marketable (choice D).

119. **The correct answer is A.** This passage maintains a neutral tone, and since the author is never critical of market research and presents its purposes matter-of-factly, choice A is the best answer. The author never expresses opinions strong enough to justify the conclusions that she or he believes market research is invasive (choice B), untrustworthy (choice C), or ingenious (choice D).

120. **The correct answer is D.** As written, the final paragraph does not present a clear idea of what product testing entails since there is no indication of what happens after the subject tries the new shampoo; choice D would

clarify the product testing process. However, the way researchers went about approaching subjects (choice A), the name of the shampoo (choice B), and the number of people asked to try the new shampoo (choice C) would not clarify this example intended to explain the purpose of product testing.

121. **The correct answer is C.** The passage focuses on how companies use market research to figure out the most effective ways to market their products, so choice C is the most logical answer. While choices A, B, and D are possible, they imply that the passage focuses on how market research affects the subjects involved, when it really focuses on how market research affects companies' marketing decisions.

122. **The correct answer is D.** According to paragraph 7, surveys are more effective than focus groups. This eliminates choice C, which suggests that the opposite of this is true. The popularity of particular forms of marketing research is not discussed in the passage, so there is no support for choice A. While focus groups are not as effective as surveys, choice B reaches an extreme conclusion that the passage simply does not support.

123. **The correct answer is A.** The passage draws a distinction between Napoleon's imposing reputation as a blood-thirsty conqueror and the fact that in his personal life he had a simple childhood and loved his mother. There is no contrast between Napoleon's father and mother in the passage, so choice B cannot be correct. Choice C is incorrect because the passage draws no contrast between how Napoleon spoke of his mother and how he treated her. The passage is not about the contrasts between people who were involved with Napoleon; it is about contrasts within Napoleon's personal story, so choice D is incorrect.

124. **The correct answer is D.** This information is given in paragraph 2: "He was born ... on the 15th August 1769 to be exact, in the little town of Ajaccio, the capital of picturesque Corsica. This miniature island rises a bold tree-covered rock in the blue waters of the Mediterranean, fifty miles west of the coast of Italy."

125. **The correct answer is B.** This information can be found in paragraph 2, which states that Corsica "...had been sold to France by the Republic of Genoa." Since Corsica was sold to France, France cannot be Corsica's former owner, so choice C is incorrect. Ajaccio is a town on Corsica, it is not the island's former owner, so choice A is incorrect. According to the passage, Carlyle is the name of a person, not the previous owner of Corsica, so choice D is incorrect.

126. **The correct answer is B.** The opening paragraph describes Napoleon's victories on the battlefield as "hard-fought," which supports choice B; if they were not difficult to achieve, he would not have had to fight so hard. This contradicts the answer in choice A. The passage implies that Napoleon fought many battles, which contradicts choice C. Choice D is an extreme answer that the passage simply does not support.

127. **The correct answer is D.** In the final paragraph, the word *patriot* refers to Pascal Paoli. It does not refer to Napoleon's father (choice A), Napoleon himself (choice B), or Napoleon's mother (choice C).

128. **The correct answer is C.** While each answer choice can be used a synonym for *apt*, only *quick* (choice C) makes sense in this context.

129. **The correct answer is C.** The author characterizes both Napoleon and Corsicans in general as "warlike," so choice C is the best answer. However, there is no indication that Napoleon's mother (choice A) or his brother Joseph (choice B) were much like Napoleon.

There is no information at all about Carlyle aside from his opinion of Napoleon, so choice D does not make sense.

130. **The correct answer is A.** Napoleon had a reputation for being a fierce warrior, so it is likely that he misrepresented his childhood to support that reputation. The passage is clear about Napoleon's love for his mother, so choice B lacks strong support. There is no evidence that Napoleon simply could not remember his childhood, so choice C is not the best answer. The passage supports the idea that Napoleon was a fierce warrior, so choice D cannot be correct.

131. **The correct answer is B.** Earlier in the passage, Napoleon is identified as the future ruler of France, so the "high position" must refer to that. While he was a soldier, this is not as high a position as a ruler, so choice A is not the best answer. The passage only states that he was a ruler; it does not say that he was a king, so choice C is not the best answer either. Choice D seems to make the mistake that the person with the high position was Napoleon's father, not Napoleon, himself.

132. **The correct answer is B.** The passage is set up as an explanation of Napoleon's early years since they are not usually discussed. Choices A and D are just minor details in the passage. The detail in choice C is mentioned only to set up a discussion of Napoleon's life before he set foot on the battlefield.

133. **The correct answer is C.** The passage is focused mainly on the first purported papers in England, and since most of them did not function as modern newspapers do, the word *newspapers* is placed within quotes. While the titles of many of these papers referred to birds or Mercury, this is too minor a detail to serve as a fitting title, so choice A is not the best answer. The internet is mentioned only as a contrast to the newspapers of hundreds of years ago, so choice B would

not be a fitting title. Only the first paragraph discussed the *English Mercurie*, and the best title should capture the idea of the whole passage, so choice D is not the best title.

134. **The correct answer is D.** The passage states that early newspapers in England were mostly intent on conveying the agenda of political parties. Choices A and C are purposes of today's newspapers, but these purposes are not discussed in the passage. While many of the titles of England's first papers referred to birds, there is no suggestion that the papers actually discussed birds, so choice B is incorrect.

135. **The correct answer is C.** According to the passage, the *English Mercurie* was a hoax, which means it was not real. This fact contradicts the conclusion in choice B. While it was supposedly a discredited false report, this is not what set it apart from actual newspapers. While the British Museum did accept the *English Mercurie*, this is not the main factor that set it apart from other newspapers.

136. **The correct answer is D.** Irony is when an opposite occurs to humorous effect, and the fact that the *English Mercurie* was supposed to have exposed false stories when it, itself, was false, is ironic. While the fake newspaper was not published regularly, this is not necessarily ironic, so choice A is incorrect. It did not actually expose false stories either, so choice B is incorrect, too. However, the newspaper was printed, otherwise it could not be accepted by the British Museum, so choice C is incorrect.

137. **The correct answer is A.** According to paragraph 3, newspapers "varied quite a bit in the quality of their writing." This contradicts the conclusion in choice D. While the *English Mercurie* was entirely fake, these later newspapers were not, so choice B is incorrect. The passage indicates only that their titles were intended to emphasize the idea

that these newspapers were quickly delivered to the public; it does not actually say that they really were all that quick, so choice C is not the best answer.

138. **The correct answer is D.** The passage indicates that many of these early English papers did publish attacks against political opponents, so choice D is correct. This fact also contradicts choice C. The passage states that many of the first English newspapers had titles that referenced birds or Mercury, so choices A and B are incorrect.

139. **The correct answer is A.** A hoax is something that is committed, so choice A is the best answer. Choice B seems to have confused *perpetrated* with *perpetuated*. Choice C seems to have confused it with *permeated*. Choice D seems to have confused it with *pertained.*

140. **The correct answer is A.** The author seems to believe that a proper newspaper reports current events, and this is not the main purpose of any of the newspapers discussed in the passage. This contradicts choice B. The author states only that the internet delivers news quickly; there is no implication that it delivers more credible news than the newspapers in 1600s England did. The author indicates that there are differences in the writing quality among the newspapers discussed in the passage, so choice D is incorrect.

141. **The correct answer is D.** The *English Mercurie* was a hoax, and choice D refers to another kind of hoax. Choice A is the opposite of that. While the *English Mercurie* was accepted by a museum, choice B fails to take the phoniness of the *English Mercurie* into account. Many people believed that the *English Mercurie* was really England's first newspaper, so choice C does not really capture what it is like.

142. **The correct answer is C.** Many of the titles of early English newspapers referenced fast

birds of flight, and though a hen is a bird, it does not conjure images of speedy delivery. The birds referenced in the other answer choices do.

143. **The correct answer is B.** The passage is mainly about the various properties of sound. Choice A is incorrect because this represents just one component of the passage, as does choice D. The author discusses the speed, loudness, and frequency of sound, so choice C can be eliminated.

144. **The correct answer is A.** Air is a medium, or intervening substance, through which sound is transmitted; therefore, choice A is the correct answer. Choices B, C, and D do not fit the context of the passage.

145. **The correct answer is B.** The passage explains in paragraph 2 that sound waves can take longer to move through liquids and solids than through gases or air, so choices A, C, and D can be eliminated.

146. **The correct answer is D.** The author describes how a siren gradually gets louder as it moves toward a building and then becomes softer again as it passes the building. This is because of the listener's proximity in relation to the siren's distance on a moving fire truck.

147. **The correct answer is A.** The passage mentions in paragraph 2 that a siren sometimes seems to be heard sooner when the listener is outside because the sound does not have to travel through the solid medium of a building. It takes longer for sound waves to travel through solids than through the air.

148. **The correct answer is A.** *Modified* means "changed." The other answer choices would not make sense if used in place of *modified* in paragraph 2 of the passage.

149. **The correct answer is D.** A wall is a solid object and so is a cloth. The way volume can be adjusted does not compare to the passing of sound through a wall, so choice A is not the best answer. A day is not a solid object, so

choice B is incorrect. The atmosphere is not solid either, so choice C is incorrect as well.

150. **The correct answer is A.** The passage indicates that a sound wave is the size of a sound, and that as a source of noise moves further away, it becomes more difficult to hear. This supports the conclusion in choice A. This fact also eliminates choice B. Musicians like those described in the passage create sounds in specific pitches, so choice C does not make much sense. Choice D is a matter of opinion and dependent on the sound in question, so it is not the best answer.

151. **The correct answer is B.** The author discusses the musical note A in paragraph 4

only to use it as an example of a sound at the lower end of sounds people can hear. The author is less concerned with making the passage more interesting (choice A) or suggesting that human hearing is flawed (choice C). Since the passage never discusses the hearing of animals other than people, choice D is not the best answer.

152. **The correct answer is A.** Light cannot pass through walls, but sound can. There is no evidence to support the ideas that sound is more difficult to discern (choice B), common in everyday life (choice C), or important to sense (choice D) than light is.

Vocabulary

153. A	**158.** A	**163.** B	**167.** C	**171.** D
154. D	**159.** D	**164.** D	**168.** C	**172.** C
155. B	**160.** C	**165.** A	**169.** D	**173.** A
156. B	**161.** C	**166.** B	**170.** B	**174.** B
157. C	**162.** A			

153. **The correct answer is A.** *Expressive* is a synonym for *articulate*. Other synonyms include *eloquent*, *fluent*, and *well-spoken*.

154. **The correct answer is D.** *Shorten* is a synonym for *curtail*. Other synonyms include *limit*, *reduce*, and *curb*.

155. **The correct answer is B.** *Profitable* is the closest in meaning to the word *lucrative* among the four choices. Other synonyms include *productive*, *high-paying*, and *money-making*.

156. **The correct answer is B.** *Joy* is a synonym for the word *elation*. Other synonyms include *happiness*, *delight*, and *ecstasy*.

157. **The correct answer is C.** *Opponent* is a synonym for *adversary*. Other synonyms include *enemy*, *competitor*, and *rival*.

158. **The correct answer is A.** *Discontinue* is a synonym of *adjourn*. Other synonyms include *stop*, *finish*, and *suspend*.

159. **The correct answer is D.** *Method* is a synonym for the word *technique*. Other synonyms include *procedure* and *system*.

160. **The correct answer is C.** *Change* is a synonym for the word *amend*. Other synonyms include *alter* and *modify*.

161. **The correct answer is C.** *Erase* is a synonym for the word *delete*. Other synonyms include *remove* and *cancel*.

162. **The correct answer is A.** *Emotional* is a synonym for the word *sentimental*. Other synonyms include *maudlin* and *romantic*.

163. **The correct answer is B.** *Friendly* is a synonym for the word *cordial*. Other synonyms include *pleasant* and *warm*.

164. **The correct answer is D.** *Slow* is a synonym for the word *sluggish*. Other synonyms include *listless* and *slothful*.

165. **The correct answer is A.** *Wrong* is a synonym for the word *erroneous*. Other synonyms include *mistaken* and *invalid*.

166. **The correct answer is B.** *Deny* is a synonym for the word *withhold*. Other synonyms include *refuse* and *hold back*.

167. **The correct answer is C.** *Silly* is a synonym for the word *frivolous*. Other synonyms include *thoughtless* and *trivial*.

168. **The correct answer is C.** *Controlling* is a synonym for the word *oppressive*. Other synonyms include *cruel* and *harsh*.

169. **The correct answer is D.** *Brave* is a synonym for the word *valiant*. Other synonyms include *courageous* and *heroic*.

170. **The correct answer is B.** *Remove* is a synonym for the word *eliminate*. Other synonyms include *abolish* and *get rid of*.

171. **The correct answer is D.** *Sad* is a synonym for the word *lamentable*. Other synonyms include *terrible* and *appalling*.

172. **The correct answer is C.** *Sloppy* is a synonym for the word *slovenly*. Other synonyms include *messy* and *careless*.

173. **The correct answer is A.** *Naughty* is a synonym for the word *wayward*. Other synonyms include *unruly* and *disobedient*.

174. **The correct answer is B.** *Bright* is a synonym for the word *vibrant*. Other synonyms include *vivid* and *brilliant*.

Mathematics

175. B	188. A	201. C	214. C	227. A
176. C	189. C	202. A	215. C	228. A
177. B	190. A	203. D	216. D	229. C
178. A	191. B	204. C	217. A	230. D
179. B	192. C	205. C	218. D	231. D
180. D	193. A	206. A	219. C	232. C
181. B	194. C	207. A	220. B	233. D
182. D	195. A	208. B	221. C	234. C
183. A	196. B	209. C	222. C	235. C
184. B	197. A	210. B	223. C	236. B
185. A	198. A	211. C	224. C	237. A
186. A	199. B	212. B	225. C	238. A
187. C	200. A	213. A	226. B	

175. **The correct answer is B.** The ten million's place is the eighth digit from the right, and the tens place is the second digit from the right. So, the number is 50,000,030.

176. **The correct answer is C.** Solve for the box as follows:

First, put the fraction on the left side of the equation in lowest terms:

$$\frac{5}{20} = \frac{\frac{1}{3}}{\square}$$

$$\frac{1}{4} = \frac{\frac{1}{3}}{\square}$$

Then, get rid of the fraction on both sides of the equation by multiplying by the bottom terms of each: 4 on the left side and the ☐ on the right side:

$$\frac{4}{1} \times \frac{1}{4} \times \square = \frac{\frac{1}{3}}{\square} \times \square \times \frac{4}{1}$$

This simplifies to the following:

$$1 \times \square = \frac{1}{3} \times \frac{4}{1}$$

Simplify further to get the final answer:

$$\square = \frac{4}{3}$$

177. **The correct answer is B.** The height is 6 inches and the base is 14 inches. The area is $\frac{1}{2}(6)(14) = 42$ square inches.

178. **The correct answer is A.**

$$0.05\% = \frac{0.05}{100} = 0.0005$$

179. **The correct answer is B.** Since the fractions have the same numerator, the one with the smaller denominator has the larger overall value. So, $\frac{5}{8} > \frac{5}{9}$.

180. **The correct answer is D.** A right triangle has a 90-degree angle. The sum of the two remaining angles is 90, and they must have the same measure since the triangle is isosceles. So the other two angles each measure 45 degrees.

181. **The correct answer is B.** There are 4 tiles that are not vowels. Since each of the 7 tiles is equally likely to be chosen, the probability is $\frac{4}{7}$.

182. **The correct answer is D.** 1 liter = 1,000 milliliters. So, 5 liters = 5,000 milliliters.

183. **The correct answer is A.** The number 784 can be written as $(7 \times 10^2) + (8 \times 10) + 4$. The number 10^2 equals 100, so $7 \times 10^2 = 700$. The value of 8×10 is 80. Add the three numbers together to double check the result: $700 + 80 + 4 = 784$.

184. **The correct answer is B.** A property of parallelograms says that the sum of the measures of same-side interior angles is 180 degrees.

185. **The correct answer is A.** A number in front of a variable is called a coefficient.

186. **The correct answer is A.** The factory makes 200 cameras per day, so it would make 1,000 cameras in 5 days. It would take 5 days for the factory to make about 997 cameras.

187. **The correct answer is C.** The components of this problem must be stated in the same units. There are 60 minutes in an hour and 60 seconds in a minute. Therefore, 1 hour equals 60×60, or 3,600 seconds. The ratio of 3,600 to 120 is simplified to 30 to 1.

188. **The correct answer is A.** Note that 1.5 feet = 18 inches, and 90 millimeters = 9 centimeters. Since 10 centimeters is less than 10 inches, we have A < B < C < D.

189. **The correct answer is C.** The ten-thousandths place is four places after the decimal point. Here, that digit is 6.

190. **The correct answer is A.** The value that occurs most often in the data set is 0.

191. **The correct answer is B.** There are 13 toys total, 4 of which are tennis balls. So, the probability of the dog selecting one is $\frac{4}{13}$.

192. **The correct answer is C.** The reciprocal of a fraction is the fraction inverted. To find the answer, you would have to rewrite $3\frac{3}{1}$ as an improper fraction, $\frac{15}{4}$. The fraction $\frac{15}{4}$ is the reciprocal of $\frac{4}{15}$.

193. **The correct answer is A.** Since 12 is divisible by 6, the number must also be divisible by 6.

194. **The correct answer is C.** The smallest number into which both 12 and 18 divide evenly is 36; this is the least common multiple.

195. **The correct answer is A.** Borrow 1 minute to perform the subtraction in the second's column, and then borrow 1 hour to perform the subtraction in the minute's column:

$$\begin{array}{r} {}^{3}\cancel{4}\text{ hours} \quad {}^{71}\cancel{12}\text{ minutes} \quad {}^{70}\cancel{10}\text{ seconds} \\ -\quad 1\text{ hour} \qquad 58\text{ minutes} \qquad 20\text{ seconds} \\ \hline 2\text{ hours} \qquad 13\text{ minutes} \qquad 50\text{ seconds} \end{array}$$

196. **The correct answer is B.** Any number less than $\frac{1}{3}$ makes this inequality true.

197. **The correct answer is A.**

$-1 - (-3) = -1 + 3 = 2$

198. **The correct answer is A.** The diameter is 10 inches, so the circumference is 10π inches.

199. **The correct answer is B.** The conversion factor is $\dfrac{x \text{ hours}}{} \times \dfrac{60 \text{ minutes}}{1 \text{ hour}}$. So, you multiply by 60.

200. **The correct answer is A.** You must divide both numbers in the numerator by 2 when splitting into two fractions.

201. **The correct answer is C.** Since 8 tablespoons equals $\frac{1}{2}$ cup, it follows that 16 tablespoons equals 1 cup. So, there are 3(16) teaspoons = 48 teaspoons in 1 cup.

202. **The correct answer is A.** Since Maria is paddling downstream with the current, her speed is increased by the speed of the current by x miles per hour. So, her maximum speed would be $8 + x$ miles per hour.

203. **The correct answer is D.**

$$\frac{6\frac{2}{3}}{\frac{1}{6}} = \frac{20}{3} \div \frac{1}{6} = \frac{20}{3} \times 6 = 40$$

204. **The correct answer is C.** Note that 0.25 day $= 0.25 \times 24 = 6$ hours, and 6 hours $= 6 \times 60 = 360$ minutes, but 360 minutes $= 360 \times 60 = 21{,}600$ seconds.

205. **The correct answer is C.** The number of combinations is $3 \times 5 \times 6 = 90$.

206. **The correct answer is A.** Since 1 yard = 36 inches, we have

$$\frac{100 \text{ inches}}{} \times \frac{1 \text{ yard}}{36 \text{ inches}} = \frac{100}{36} \text{ yards}$$
$$= 2\frac{7}{9} \text{ yards}$$

207. **The correct answer is A.** The ratio is $\frac{12}{18} = \frac{2}{3}$, which can be written as 2:3.

208. **The correct answer is B.** $0.04(0.04) = 0.0016$

209. **The correct answer is C.** If you square a number that is between 0 and 1, the result is also between 0 and 1. Symbolically, this is written as $x^2 < 1$, which is equivalent to $x^2 - 1 < 0$.

210. **The correct answer is B.** Arrange the data in increasing order: 0, 0, 5, 10, 20. The median is the value in the middle, namely 5.

211. **The correct answer is C.** All four sides of a rhombus have the same length. The perimeter is $5(4) = 20$ inches.

212. **The correct answer is B.** Since 200% is equal to 2, 200% of $\frac{3}{5}$ is $2\left(\frac{3}{5}\right) = \frac{6}{5} = 1\frac{1}{5}$.

213. **The correct answer is A.** Use the order of operations: $12 - 3 \times 3 - 1 = 12 - 9 - 1 = 3 - 1 = 2$.

214. **The correct answer is C.** To find the area of the shaded portion, subtract the area of the circle from the area of the square. The area of the circle can be found using the formula $A = \pi r^2$. The area of the circle is therefore $\pi(3)^2$, or 3.14×9, which equals approximately 28.26 square centimeters.

The diameter of the circle is equal to the length of the side of the square. The radius of the circle measures 3 centimeters, so the diameter of the circle is twice that, or 6 centimeters. The area of the square can be found using the formula $A = s^2$. The area of the square is 6×6, or 36 square centimeters.

The area of the shaded portion equals $36 - 28.26$, or 7.74 square centimeters, which is closest to $7\frac{3}{4}$ square centimeters.

215. **The correct answer is C.** The cost of two coffee mugs is $2c$ dollars, and the cost of four bags of coffee beans is $4d$ dollars. The cost of her purchase is $2c + 4d$ dollars.

216. **The correct answer is D.** Label the given lengths as follows:

Note that $\frac{3}{4}$ of the length of WZ equals $3\text{ m} + 3\text{ m} = 6\text{ m}$.

So, the length of WZ equals $\frac{4}{3}(6) = 8$ meters.

217. **The correct answer is A.** Use the order of operations:

$$\frac{5}{8} \div 10 - 5 \times \frac{3}{8} = \frac{5}{8} \times \frac{1}{10} - 5 \times \frac{3}{8}$$
$$= \frac{1}{16} - \frac{15}{8}$$
$$= \frac{1 - 30}{16}$$
$$= -\frac{29}{16}$$

218. **The correct answer is D.** For any number a, $a - a = 0$.

219. **The correct answer is C.**

$$\frac{0.040 + 0 + 0.40 + 4.00}{4} = \frac{4.44}{4} = 1.11$$

220. **The correct answer is B.**

$$-2\left(-1 - \left(-\frac{1}{2}\right)\right)^2 = -2\left(-\frac{1}{2}\right)^2 = -2\left(\frac{1}{4}\right) = -\frac{1}{2}$$

221. **The correct answer is C.** Solve the equation by isolating the variable x on one side:

$$3.7x = 58 + 1.2$$
$$3.7x = 59.2$$
$$x = \frac{59.2}{3.7}$$
$$x = 16$$

222. **The correct answer is C.**

$$1\frac{3}{4} \times 5 = 8\frac{3}{4} \text{ hours each week}$$

223. **The correct answer is C.** The amount of interest earned in one year is $2,000 \times 0.08$, or $160. The total value of Alicia's investment after one year is $2,000 + $160, or $2,160.

224. **The correct answer is C.** Let x be the length of the entire video. Solve the following proportion:

$$\frac{\frac{1}{2}\text{ inch}}{105\text{ seconds}} = \frac{4\text{ inches}}{x\text{ seconds}}$$
$$\frac{1}{2}x = 4(105)$$
$$x = 2(4)(105)$$
$$x = 840$$

Since there are 60 seconds in 1 minute, 840 seconds $= \frac{840}{60} = 14$ minutes.

225. **The correct answer is C.** The probability of a complement of an event is one minus the probability of the event. So, $1 - 0.3 = 0.7$ is the probability that the school bus will not run late.

226. **The correct answer is B.** The amount Felix pays in taxes is $($4,200)(0.22) = 924. The amount remaining after this is deducted is $4,200 - $924 = $3,276$. Of this, he invests 15%, which is $($3,276)(0.15) = 491.40. So, the amount remaining is $3,276 - $491.40 = $2,784.60, which rounds to $2,785.

227. **The correct answer is A.**

$$3\frac{3}{4} \div \frac{4}{3} = \frac{15}{4} \div \frac{4}{3} = \frac{15}{4} \times \frac{3}{4} = \frac{45}{16} = 2\frac{13}{16}$$

228. **The correct answer is A.** To find the average, add the sum of the paychecks and divide by 5. The sum of the paychecks is $101.65 + $79.23 + $84.67 + $121.33 + $77.62, which equals $464.50. The average paycheck equals $464.50 ÷ 5, or $92.90.

229. **The correct answer is C.**

$$2 \div 0.004 = 2 \times \frac{1}{0.004}$$
$$= 2 \times \frac{1}{\frac{4}{1,000}}$$
$$= 2 \times \frac{1,000}{4}$$
$$= 500$$

230. **The correct answer is D.** A parallelogram need only have two pairs of parallel sides. The angles opposite congruent sides are congruent but need not have a measure of 90 degrees.

231. **The correct answer is D.** 36 cannot be divided evenly by 10.

232. **The correct answer is C.** 20% of 40 equals $40(0.2) = 8$. So 40 reduced by 20% is $40 - 8 = 32$.

233. **The correct answer is D.** The area of the triangle portion of the figure is $\frac{1}{2}(12)(5) = 30$ square feet. The area of the rectangle portion of the figure is $4(13) = 52$ square feet. So, the area of the figure is $30 + 52 = 82$ square feet.

234. **The correct answer is C.** Set each factor equal to zero and solve for b:

$b - 2 = 0$ has solution $b = 2$

$b + 5 = 0$ has solution $b = -5$

235. **The correct answer is C.** Substitute 7 into the equation for x. Then solve for y:

$$xy - 7 = 56$$
$$7y - 7 = 56$$
$$7y = 56 + 7$$
$$7y = 63$$
$$y = 9$$

236. **The correct answer is B.** The perimeter of the outer semicircle is $\frac{1}{2}(2\pi \cdot 8) = 8\pi$ meters, the perimeter of the inner semicircle is $\frac{1}{2}(2\pi \cdot 3) = 3\pi$ meters, and the two horizontal segments on the bottom of the figure each has a length of 5 meters. So, the perimeter of the entire figure is $(8\pi + 3\pi + 5 + 5) = (11\pi + 10)$ meters.

237. **The correct answer is A.** The percent reduction is $\frac{350 - 75}{350} = \frac{275}{350} \approx 0.21$, or about 21%.

238. **The correct answer is A.** Since $121 < 141 < 144$ and $\sqrt{121} = 11$ and $\sqrt{144} = 12$, it follows that $\sqrt{141}$ is between 11 and 12.

Language

239. C	251. D	263. C	275. D	287. C
240. C	252. B	264. D	276. A	288. D
241. D	253. A	265. B	277. B	289. C
242. A	254. B	266. A	278. C	290. D
243. A	255. D	267. A	279. C	291. B
244. B	256. D	268. C	280. B	292. C
245. A	257. B	269. C	281. A	293. D
246. A	258. C	270. A	282. C	294. A
247. C	259. A	271. D	283. D	295. A
248. B	260. C	272. A	284. A	296. D
249. D	261. B	273. B	285. B	297. C
250. C	262. A	274. C	286. B	298. B

239. **The correct answer is C.** There should not be an apostrophe before the *s* in *pedestrians* because it is a plural noun, not a singular possessive noun.

240. **The correct answer is C.** Choice C is a run-on sentence. It contains two independent clauses joined with no punctuation. One way to correct this sentence would be to add a comma followed by a coordinating conjunction: Amy missed the bus, and she was late for school.

241. **The correct answer is D.** *No mistakes.* The sentences are correctly punctuated.

242. **The correct answer is A.** The sentence should end with a period because it is a statement, not a question.

243. **The correct answer is A.** Julia is just one person, so this sentence should have the singular pronoun *her*, not the plural *their*.

244. **The correct answer is B.** The correct spelling is *conceive*.

245. **The correct answer is A.** This is a question, not a declarative sentence, so it needs to end with a question mark.

246. **The correct answer is A.** There is a possessive pronoun error in the first sentence. The

possessive form of *her* is *hers* without an apostrophe.

247. **The correct answer is C.** Either a semicolon or a conjunction such as *but* is used to join the clauses in a compound sentence. Both should not be used.

248. **The correct answer is B.** The correct spelling is *cantaloupe*.

249. **The correct answer is D.** *No mistakes.* All the sentences are capitalized correctly.

250. **The correct answer is C.** An adverb should modify a verb, yet in this sentence, the adverb *prettily* modifies the noun *dress*. The word should be written in its adjective form: *pretty*.

251. **The correct answer is D.** *No mistakes.* All the words in these sentences are spelled correctly.

252. **The correct answer is B.** The list in choice B is not introduced correctly; it should begin with an introductory word or a colon, not a semicolon.

253. **The correct answer is A.** The minivan belongs to the speaker's parents, so the sentence requires the possessive form of the pronoun *they*: *their*.

254. The correct answer is B. The correct spelling is *scissors*.

255. The correct answer is D. *No mistakes.* Each sentence uses quotations correctly.

256. The correct answer is D. *No mistakes.* Each sentence uses semicolons correctly.

257. The correct answer is B. There is a word choice error in this sentence. This sentence mistakenly uses the preposition *of* as a helping verb. It should have used *have* instead of *of*.

258. The correct answer is C. In this sentence, the leaves belong to the tree, so *trees* should be in its possessive form: *tree's*. Without the apostrophe, it is in its plural form.

259. The correct answer is A. There is a spelling error in this sentence. The correct spelling is *excellence*.

260. The correct answer is C. The comma in this sentence is unnecessary.

261. The correct answer is B. There is a spelling error in this sentence. The correct spelling is *argument*.

262. The correct answer is A. The introductory phrase of this complex sentence describes action that will take place in the future, but the verb *gave* is in the past tense in the second clause. The best fix would be to replace *gave* with *give*.

263. The correct answer is C. There is a word choice error in this sentence. *Insure* means to protect, but the writer clearly uses it to mean "guarantee." The author probably intended to use the word *ensure*.

264. The correct answer is D. *No mistakes.* There are no errors in parentheses use in these sentences.

265. The correct answer is B. This sentence is a question, so it should end with a question mark, not a period.

266. The correct answer is A. *President* is John F. Kennedy's title in this sentence, so it should be capitalized.

267. The correct answer is A. There is a spelling error in this sentence. The correct spelling is *achieve*.

268. The correct answer is C. Although the titles of novels and movies should be italicized, the titles of songs should be placed within quotations without italics. The song should be written as "Honey," not *Honey*.

269. The correct answer is C. This sentence uses an incorrect *neither/nor* construction. It should be written: "Neither Grace nor Yuri was in class today."

270. The correct answer is A. Although the sentence describes something that happened in the past (last weekend), it requires the present participle of *work* (*working*) to show that the speaker spent the entire weekend working.

271. The correct answer is D. *No mistakes.* Each sentence is punctuated correctly.

272. The correct answer is A. There is a spelling error in this sentence. The correct spelling is *February*.

273. The correct answer is B. There is a preposition error in this sentence. When describing a duration of time, the correct preposition to use is *for*, not *since*.

274. The correct answer is C. There is a word choice error in this sentence. *Later* means something that has happened beyond now; *latter* means the last thing mentioned, which is what this sentence requires.

275. The correct answer is D. *No mistakes.* Each sentence uses conjunctions correctly.

276. The correct answer is A. In this sentence, *id* is an acronym meaning identification, and acronyms need to be capitalized: ID.

277. The correct answer is B. There is a word choice error in this sentence. *Defiantly* means "rebelliously," which does not make much sense in this context. It's clear that the speaker intended to use *definitely*, which means "certainly."

278. **The correct answer is C.** This sentence demonstrates correct usage. The other answer choices contain incorrect pronoun choices.

279. **The correct answer is C.** The word *whenever* joins the thoughts together in a timeframe that is logical. Choices A, B, and C represent impossibilities.

280. **The correct answer is B.** Choice B is the only answer that does not have a verb-tense error. Choices A, C, and D describe actions that take place in the present or future, yet all choices use a past-tense verb.

281. **The correct answer is A.** When someone is in a bad mood, that person is likely to be impatient, and speaking abruptly or rudely is a sign of impatience. Choices B and C do not imply impatience at all. Choice D may suggest something bad, such as a bad mood, but it would be odd to describe the way someone answered a question as "horribly."

282. **The correct answer is C.** Choice C is the only sentence without a pronoun error. Choice A matches the antecedent subject *Curtis* with the plural pronoun *their*. Choice B matches the singular antecedent *Beatrice* with the plural pronoun *they*. Choice D matches the human antecedent *Ralph* with the non-human pronoun *its*.

283. **The correct answer is D.** While choices A, B, and C describe great benefits of recycling, choice D focuses only on how easy it is to recycle. It does not support the topic as strongly as the other answer choices do.

284. **The correct answer is A.** Choice A is the only sentence that uses a conjunction correctly. The other sentences all contain conjunction errors. Choice B lacks any conjunction, so it is a comma splice. Choice C uses *or* instead of *and*, which makes the

clauses seem like a choice even though they do not have that kind of relationship. Choice D uses the conjunction *then*, which makes it seem as though the clauses share a sequential relationship, when in reality they share a consequential relationship.

285. **The correct answer is B.** The preposition that makes the most sense is *within*. Lying beneath (choice A) a stream of sunlight would not be as warm as lying right within it. Since there is only one stream of sunlight, the cat cannot lie between it (choice C). "Lying of" (choice D) something does not make grammatical sense.

286. **The correct answer is B.** An apostrophe is needed to show possession, and choice B is the only one that uses an apostrophe correctly. Choices A, C, and D all need possessive nouns but feature plural nouns.

287. **The correct answer is C.** Only choice C is expressed clearly. It is unclear whether the speaker plans to get a new picture or a new frame in choice A. Choice B has awkward syntax and is a run-on. Switching the clauses renders the sentence confusing, so choice D is not the best answer.

288. **The correct answer is D.** Only choice D uses a preposition correctly. Choice A should use *into*, not *in*, since *in* is used to show a position, and *into* is used to show where something is going. Conversely, Choice B should use *in to*, as *to* is part of the infinitive "to save," not part of the preposition *into*. Choice C should use "hours' time," not "hour's time"; the apostrophe is needed *after* the *s* in the plural *hours*.

289. **The correct answer is C.** Both sentences tell us why community service is beneficial to high school students and support the argument that it should be mandatory. Choice A is a statement of opinion and a biased generalization. Choice B digresses into a narrow aspect of community service—the

elderly—and fails to express why community service should be mandatory. Choice D does not specifically address or develop the statement introduced in the topic sentence.

290. **The correct answer is D.** Only choice D uses its pronoun correctly. Choice A uses the possessive pronoun *hers,* even though the word is not used to show possession. Choice B uses the singular pronoun *her,* even though "Tiana and Paolo" is a plural antecedent. Choice C uses an apostrophe in a pronoun that should not have one: *yours.*

291. **The correct answer is B.** Only choice B is expressed correctly. Choice A uses neither a punctuation-conjunction combination nor proper standalone punctuation (either a semicolon or a dash), so it is a run-on. Choice C reverses the clauses, making it seem as though the batteries dying is a consequence of having to replace them. Choice D is a fragment since the sentence does not explain what the speaker must do.

292. **The correct answer is C.** Only choice C uses its adverb correctly. Choice A makes the mistake of a split infinitive since it places the adverb *slowly* between *to* and the verb it should modify. Choice B uses an adjective, *mighty,* to modify a verb, *blew;* but an adverb should modify a verb. Choice D misplaces the adverb *loudly,* making it seem as though it modifies *learned* instead of *grumbled.*

293. **The correct answer is D.** For the most part, this passage is informative and not personal, but sentence 4 shifts that purpose and tone with irrelevant information about the writer's local supermarket.

294. **The correct answer is A.** Only choice A uses its pronoun correctly. Choice B uses the possessive pronoun *his* when the non-possessive *he* should follow *If.* Choice C uses a non-existing pronoun (*hisself*); the correct reflexive pronoun is *himself.* Choice D uses the possessive pronoun *her* when the non-possessive *she* is required.

295. **The correct answer is A.** The paragraph is mostly a fictional dialogue between a boy and his mother. Sentence 1 supplies an informative detail that is only marginally related to the topic Darren and his mother discuss. It does not belong in this paragraph.

296. **The correct answer is D.** Only choice D uses an adverb correctly. Choice A uses the adjective *intricate* to modify the verb *spun* when the adverb *intricately* is required. Choice B uses the adverb *drily* to modify the noun *glue,* but an adjective should be used to modify a noun. *Resounded* is a verb, and an adverb—not an adjective such as *lovely*—should modify a verb; therefore, choice C is incorrect.

297. **The correct answer is C.** Each answer choice supports the topic well except for choice C, which explains an approach to finding an after-school job rather than the value of having an after-school job.

298. **The correct answer is B.** Choice B is the only sentence that uses the correct article. Choices A and C are incorrect because *an* should be used only to indicate a word that begins with a vowel. Choice D is incorrect because *a* should be used to indicate a word that begins with a consonant, not a vowel such as the *a* at the beginning of *antonym.*

SCORE SHEET

Although your actual exam scores will not be reported as percentages, it might be helpful to convert your test scores to percentages so that you can see at a glance where your strengths and weaknesses lie. The numbers in parentheses represent the questions that test each skill.

Subject	# Correct ÷ # of questions	× 100 = _____ %
Verbal Analogies (1, 2, 3, 4, 5, 6, 7, 8, 9, 10)	÷ 10 =	× 100 = _____ %
Synonyms (39, 40, 41, 42, 43, 44, 45, 46, 47, 48, 49, 50, 51)	_____ ÷ 13 = _____	× 100 = _____ %
Logic (11, 12, 13, 14, 15, 16, 17, 18, 19, 20, 21, 22)	_____ ÷ 12 = _____	× 100 = _____ %
Verbal Classification/Word Knowledge (23, 24, 25, 26, 27, 28, 29, 30, 31, 32, 33, 34, 35, 36, 37, 38)	_____ ÷ 16 = _____	× 100 = _____ %
Antonyms (52, 53, 54, 55, 56, 57, 58, 59, 60)	_____ ÷ 9 = _____	× 100 = _____ %
TOTAL VERBAL SKILLS	_____ ÷ 60 = _____	× 100 = _____ %
Number Series/Sequences (61, 64, 67, 68, 71, 72, 76, 77, 81, 83, 85, 87, 89, 92, 94, 96, 99, 101, 104, 105, 108, 111)	_____ ÷ 22 = _____	× 100 = _____ %
Geometric Comparisons (63, 65, 70, 78, 79, 86, 91, 103)	_____ ÷ 8 = _____	× 100 = _____ %
Nongeometric Comparisons (69, 74, 80, 82, 95, 98, 100, 107, 110)	_____ ÷ 10 = _____	× 100 = _____ %
Number Manipulation/Reasoning (62, 66, 73, 75, 84, 88, 90, 93, 97, 102, 106, 109, 112)	_____ ÷ 12 = _____	× 100 = _____ %
TOTAL QUANTITATIVE SKILLS	_____ ÷ 52 = _____	× 100 = _____ %
Reading—Comprehension (113–152)	_____ ÷ 40 = _____	× 100 = _____ %
Reading—Vocabulary (153–174)	_____ ÷ 22 = _____	× 100 = _____ %
TOTAL READING SKILLS	_____ ÷ 62 = _____	× 100 = _____ %
Mathematics—Concepts (175–198)	_____ ÷ 24 = _____	× 100 = _____ %
Mathematics—Problem-Solving (199–238)	_____ ÷ 40 = _____	× 100 = _____ %
TOTAL MATHEMATICS SKILLS	_____ ÷ 64 = _____	× 100 = _____ %
Capitalization, Punctuation, Spelling, and Grammar (239–277)	_____ ÷ 39 = _____	× 100 = _____ %
Usage and Composition (278–298)	_____ ÷ 21 = _____	× 100 = _____ %
TOTAL LANGUAGE SKILLS	_____ ÷ 60 = _____	× 100 = _____ %

Study Reference Guide

Subject	Chapter	Page
Verbal Skills	Chapter 6: Synonyms	161
	Chapter 7: Antonyms	173
	Chapter 8: Analogies	181
	Chapter 9: Verbal Logic	191
Quantitative Skills	Chapter 16: Series Reasoning	377
	Chapter 17: Comparisons and Ability Questions	397
Reading	Chapter 10: Reading	199
Mathematics	Chapter 15: Mathematics	285
Language	Chapter 11: Spelling	235
	Chapter 12: Punctuation and Capitalization	243
	Chapter 13: English Usage	257
	Chapter 14: Language Composition and Expression	275

PART III
VERBAL SKILLS

Chapter 6

Synonyms

OVERVIEW

- **Tips for Answering Synonym Questions**
- **Summing It Up**
- **Exercises: Synonyms**
- **Answer Keys and Explanations**

Synonym questions test your understanding of words. You are asked to choose another word that has the same, or nearly the same, meaning as the word given. On the HSPT, synonyms are tested in the Verbal Skills section and the Reading section under Vocabulary. On the TACHS, synonyms are tested in the Reading section under Vocabulary. Each exam may indicate the synonym in a different fashion. For example, some exams will identify the word they want you to match by italicizing or capitalizing the word, then ask you to choose a synonym from the answer choices. Other exams will use the word in a sentence, usually identifying the synonym in question by italicizing, underlining, or capitalizing the word, and then ask you to select a matching synonym from the answer choices. For example:

The surface of the *placid* lake was smooth as glass.

    A. cold

    B. muddy

    C. deep

    D. calm

The correct answer is D. In this example, the word *calm* is the correct choice. The nice thing about a sentence example is that it provides contextual clues that make it easier to figure out the synonym's meaning. When you read that the lake was "smooth as glass" you can infer that while the lake *might* have been muddy, deep, or cold, it *must* have been calm. That makes choice D the best answer.

TIPS FOR ANSWERING SYNONYM QUESTIONS

Here's a tip to use when choosing the answer for a synonym question: If the word is given in a sentence, try substituting the choices in the place of the indicated word. This process can help you find and check your answer.

Sometimes the italicized or underlined word has multiple meanings, which can make the contextual clues of the sentence even more important. Consider the following question:

The camel is sometimes called the ship of the *desert*.

   A. abandon

   B. ice cream

   C. sandy wasteland

   D. leave

The correct answer is C. Here, the context in the sentence is crucial to the word's definition. Without the sentence, you would not know whether the word *desert* is to be pronounced *de-sert'*, which means to leave or to abandon, or *des'-ert*, which means a sandy wasteland. If you are not sure of your spelling, the sentence can also spare you the confusion of *desert* versus *dessert*, the latter of which is the last course of a meal.

On the other hand, the phrase or sentence might be of little or no use in helping you choose the correct synonym. The sentence might help you to determine the part of speech for the word in question, but not its meaning, as in the following example:

The robbery suspect had a *sallow* complexion.

   A. ruddy

   B. pale

   C. pock-marked

   D. freckled

The correct answer is B. The sentence shows you the proper use of the word *sallow*. It is an adjective used to describe a complexion, but the sentence gives no clue that *sallow* means "pale." You either know the meaning of the word or you must guess. When the given word isn't part of a sentence, or if the sentence doesn't help define the word, your best option may be to guess. Don't guess blindly, however; first, you need to make sure there are no other clues that could lead you to the correct answer.

6

TIP

Make a habit of writing down unfamiliar words, reading them out loud, listening to their pronunciation, and using them in conversation. The more ways you use information (auditory, visually, etc.), the more places your brain will store it, making it easier to recall when needed.

Perhaps you have seen the word used, but aren't sure what it means. Look carefully. Do you know the meaning of any part of the word? If you can associate the word with something else you've read or you know, you might be able to find the answer. An example:

Remedial most nearly means

    A. reading.

    B. slow.

    C. corrective.

    D. special.

The correct answer is C. Your association is probably "remedial reading." That association can help you, but it can also lead you astray. *Remedial* does not mean "reading." *Remedial* is an adjective—*reading* is the noun it modifies. Slow readers might receive remedial reading instruction in special classes that are intended to improve poor reading skills. Do you see the word *remedy* in *remedial?* You know that a remedy is a cure or a correction for an ailment. If you combine all the information you now have, you can choose *corrective* as the word that most nearly means "remedial."

Sometimes you can find the correct answer to a synonym question by eliminating answers you know are wrong. If you can eliminate even one of the answers, you have a 33 percent chance (1 in 3) of choosing correctly, rather than a 25% chance (1 in 4). Eliminate two incorrect answers, and you have a 50% chance of choosing correctly. For example:

Infamous most nearly means

    A. well-known.

    B. poor.

    C. disgraceful.

    D. young.

The correct answer is C. The first word you see when you look at *infamous* is *famous.* *Famous,* of course, means well-known. Because *in-*, meaning "not," is a negative prefix, you should be looking for a negative word as your answer. By knowing that you're looking for a negative word, you can eliminate choice A, *well-known.* A person who is not well-known may or may not be poor. You should carefully consider the other choices before choosing *poor* (choice B). *Young* (choice D) probably can be eliminated for the same reasons. Though many young people are not famous, the terms aren't necessarily synonymous. Disgrace, however, is a negative kind of fame. A person who behaves disgracefully is known for bad behavior and is thus "infamous." Therefore, choice C becomes the best answer for this question.

6

TIP
Use the prefix, root, and suffix of unknown words to uncover their meanings. As part of your prep, spend some time studying common Latin and Greek prefixes (*anti-*, *bi-*, *ex-*), roots (*dem-*, *liber-*, *omni-*) and suffixes (*-able*, *-cracy*, *-logy*) to increase your chances of understanding unfamiliar vocabulary.

6

All the previous suggestions can help you use clues to determine the meaning of words and find their synonyms. But many synonym questions give no clues at all. The best way to minimize the number of synonym questions that you simply cannot answer is to learn as many vocabulary words as you can. One way to increase your vocabulary is to work with a dictionary when preparing for your exam. Another is to read everything you can during the time before your exam. When you run into a word that's unfamiliar, look it up. If you run across a word you don't know while doing the practice exams, circle the word and look it up later. Look up words you find in the reading passages, new words from among the answer choices, words you find in the explanations, and words you meet in the study chapters. Looking up words for yourself and relating them to your own life is the best way to learn them. After defining a new word, write a sentence that creates a strong image. Your long-term memory excels with visual information, so creating images (especially those that are weird and wild) will help you more easily store the word and its meaning for later use.

If you understand every word in this book, you are well on your way to a broad-based vocabulary and should be able to handle not only the synonym questions, but the other verbal questions as well.

Summing It Up

- When choosing an answer for a synonym question, if the given word is in a sentence you should try substituting the answer choices in the place of the indicated word.

- When the given word is in a sentence, there are several ways to select the best answer. Look for contextual clues to determine which meaning of the word is being used. Determine which part of speech the word is, and look for an answer choice of the same part of speech.

- When you don't know the meaning, try to take the word apart. Look for prefixes, suffixes, and the root word.

- Eliminate answers that you know are wrong and concentrate on the others.

6

Take a moment to ask yourself some simple questions about your understanding of the chapter:

Review: What did I learn?

Evaluate: What do I need to learn more about?

Plan: What can I do next to keep improving?

Based on your answers to those questions, adjust your study plan to dedicate additional time to the areas of weakness that you've identified.

EXERCISES: SYNONYMS

Exercise 1

> **Directions:** In the following questions, choose the word that means the same as or about the same as the underlined word.

1. a display of <u>affluence</u>
   - A. power
   - B. wealth
   - C. glibness
   - D. junction

2. the <u>gloss</u> of her lips
   - A. goblet
   - B. shadow
   - C. shine
   - D. blush

3. a <u>wary</u> neighbor
   - A. boastful
   - B. cautious
   - C. weak
   - D. flexible

4. a thrilling <u>encounter</u>
   - A. meeting
   - B. bar
   - C. ledge
   - D. spaceship

5. to <u>concede</u> one's guilt
   - A. hide
   - B. invent
   - C. admit
   - D. contradict

6. to <u>emerge</u> from hiding
   - A. bury
   - B. come out
   - C. join
   - D. show anger

7. to <u>teem</u> with humanity
   - A. abound
   - B. play
   - C. group
   - D. adolescent

8. to <u>permit</u> to attend
   - A. discourage
   - B. allow
   - C. drive
   - D. card

9. an <u>indifferent</u> politician
   - A. confused
   - B. involved
   - C. charismatic
   - D. neutral

10. a <u>recurrent</u> theme
    - A. refined
    - B. resultant
    - C. electrifying
    - D. returning

11. on the <u>verge</u> of disaster

 A. boat
 B. force
 C. brink
 D. violence

12. to <u>ponder</u> deeply

 A. peruse
 B. think
 C. delay
 D. reveal

13. <u>aspire</u> to succeed

 A. hope
 B. breathe
 C. exhaust
 D. plot

14. an <u>era</u> of apathy

 A. mistake
 B. war
 C. place
 D. age

15. <u>temerity</u> to speak out

 A. fear
 B. nerve
 C. flutter
 D. cowardice

16. a <u>feat</u> of great renown

 A. body part
 B. celebration
 C. big meal
 D. achievement

17. <u>zest</u> for adventure

 A. enthusiasm
 B. fluency
 C. garment
 D. haste

18. a <u>plaintive</u> sound

 A. musical
 B. famous
 C. mournful
 D. patient

19. to view with <u>consternation</u>

 A. dismay
 B. telescope
 C. relief
 D. pretense

20. <u>flagrant</u> disobedience

 A. disguised
 B. glaring
 C. repeated
 D. perfumed

6

Exercise 2

Directions: Choose the word or phrase that has the same or nearly the same meaning as the underlined word or group of words.

1. The veracity of her story is without doubt.

   A. persistence

   B. truthfulness

   C. poetry

   D. horror

2. The drawings were completely identical.

   A. twin

   B. unclear

   C. breathtaking

   D. alike

3. In our cellar, we accumulate old clothes.

   A. affirm

   B. donate

   C. refurbish

   D. collect

4. This legislation will transform the railroad system.

   A. improve

   B. electrify

   C. change

   D. sell

5. Candy will gratify the baby.

   A. satisfy

   B. fatten

   C. excite

   D. teach

6. The arena was girded with ribbons.

   A. protected

   B. established

   C. decorated

   D. encircled

7. How shall we quell the rebellion?

   A. begin

   B. cushion

   C. crush

   D. fire

8. His face looked pale and sickly.

   A. wan

   B. gabled

   C. paltry

   D. ponderous

9. The father was stern and impersonal with his children.

   A. gaudy

   B. gruff

   C. opinionated

   D. endeared

10. The meaning of the text was inscrutable to laymen.

    A. comprehensible

    B. loud

    C. mysterious

    D. enjoyable

11. Let us <u>hoist</u> the banner now.

    A. raise
    B. lower
    C. wave
    D. fold

12. The town took <u>drastic</u> measures to ensure its security.

    A. well-informed
    B. ill-advised
    C. haphazard
    D. extreme

13. The newscaster <u>alluded to</u> the weather forecast.

    A. changed
    B. complained about
    C. praised
    D. referred to

14. The strength of the cord <u>exceeds</u> government standards.

    A. surpasses
    B. equals
    C. challenges
    D. falls short of

15. The <u>austere</u> forest cabin appealed to the pioneers.

    A. simple
    B. sturdy
    C. extravagant
    D. hidden

16. I wish that you would stop <u>beating around the bush</u>.

    A. running in circles
    B. avoiding the subject
    C. cleaning up the dirt
    D. repeating the same thing over and over

17. I generally accept Jim's pronouncements with <u>a grain of salt</u>.

    A. some question
    B. criticism
    C. pleasure
    D. relief

18. That explanation is little more than <u>an old wives' tale</u>.

    A. a deliberate falsehood
    B. a half-truth
    C. feminist propaganda
    D. folklore

19. The medicine man shared his <u>tried and true</u> remedy with me.

    A. new and unusual
    B. tested and proven
    C. experimental
    D. unorthodox but effective

20. You should not <u>look a gift horse in the mouth</u>.

    A. question authority
    B. quibble over details
    C. expose yourself to danger
    D. be suspicious of good fortune

6

ANSWER KEYS AND EXPLANATIONS

Exercise 1

1. B	**5.** C	**9.** D	**13.** A	**17.** A
2. C	**6.** B	**10.** D	**14.** D	**18.** C
3. B	**7.** A	**11.** C	**15.** B	**19.** A
4. A	**8.** B	**12.** B	**16.** D	**20.** B

1. **The correct answer is B.** *Affluence* is a synonym for *wealth*. *Influence* is a synonym for *power* (choice A). *Glibness* (choice C) means being talkative in a smooth, somewhat insincere way, and *confluence* is a synonym for *junction* (choice D).

2. **The correct answer is C.** *Gloss* is brightness, polish, or shine.

3. **The correct answer is B.** To be wary means to be cautious or careful, particularly in dangerous situations.

4. **The correct answer is A.** An encounter is a face-to-face meeting.

5. **The correct answer is C.** To concede is to admit or to acknowledge.

6. **The correct answer is B.** To emerge is to come out. The word *emerge* is almost opposite to the word *merge*, which means "join."

7. **The correct answer is A.** To teem is to abound or to overflow. If you selected *group* (choice C), you might have been thinking about the homonym *team*. *Adolescent* (choice D) is incorrect because the word is *teem*, not *teen*.

8. **The correct answer is B.** The word *permit*, pronounced *per-mit'*, means allow. If the word were pronounced *per'-mit*, it would mean license (which is not offered as a choice), but in no event would it mean "discourage," "drive," or "card."

9. **The correct answer is D.** To be indifferent is to be neutral or disinterested in something.

10. **The correct answer is D.** That which is recurrent returns from time to time.

11. **The correct answer is C.** *Verge* means "brink or threshold."

12. **The correct answer is B.** To ponder is to think or to consider. *Peruse* (choice A) means to read.

13. **The correct answer is A.** To aspire is to hope or to desire. To breathe is to respire.

14. **The correct answer is D.** An era is an age or period. Read carefully to avoid careless mistakes such as reading *err* or *area* and incorrectly selecting *mistake* (choice A) or *place* (choice C).

15. **The correct answer is B.** Temerity is audacity or nerve. Timorousness is timidity, fear, or cowardice.

16. **The correct answer is D.** A feat is an achievement. Beware of homonyms (words that sound the same) when choosing synonyms (words that mean the same).

17. **The correct answer is A.** *Zest* means "relish," "gusto," or "enthusiasm."

18. **The correct answer is C.** *Plaintive* means "mournful" or "melancholy."

19. **The correct answer is A.** Consternation is amazement or dismay that throws one into confusion.

20. **The correct answer is B.** *Flagrant* means "glaring" or "conspicuously objectionable." The word meaning "perfumed" (choice D) is *fragrant*.

Exercise 2

1. B	**5.** A	**9.** B	**13.** D	**17.** A
2. D	**6.** D	**10.** C	**14.** A	**18.** D
3. D	**7.** C	**11.** A	**15.** A	**19.** B
4. C	**8.** A	**12.** D	**16.** B	**20.** D

1. **The correct answer is B.** Veracity is truth-fulness or accuracy. *Persistence* (choice A) would be a synonym for *tenacity*.

2. **The correct answer is D.** *Identical* means "same," "alike," or "exactly alike." Identical twins are genetically the same, but *twin* (choice A) is not a synonym for *identical*.

3. **The correct answer is D.** To accumulate is to collect or to amass.

4. **The correct answer is C.** To transform means to change. A transformer converts electrical currents, but the word *transform* has nothing to do with electricity (choice B). If the railroad system is transformed, it may be improved (choice A), but the change in itself is no guarantee.

5. **The correct answer is A.** To gratify is to indulge, to please, or to satisfy.

6. **The correct answer is D.** *Girded* means "encircled."

7. **The correct answer is C.** To quell is to put down, to suppress, or to crush.

8. **The correct answer is A.** *Wan* means "pale, sickly, or feeble."

9. **The correct answer is B.** *Gruff* means "rough or stern."

10. **The correct answer is C.** Something that is inscrutable is mysterious or not easy to interpret.

11. **The correct answer is A.** To hoist is to raise or to lift.

12. **The correct answer is D.** *Drastic* means "extreme or severe."

13. **The correct answer is D.** To allude is to make indirect reference or to refer.

14. **The correct answer is A.** To exceed is to surpass.

15. **The correct answer is A.** Something that is austere is simple and not fancy in appearance and character.

16. **The correct answer is B.** *Beating around the bush* means talking about irrelevant topics or raising side issues to avoid addressing important issues in a given scenario.

17. **The correct answer is A.** When one takes something with "a grain of salt," one does not accept it at face value but questions details, motives, or conclusions.

18. **The correct answer is D.** *An old wives' tale* is a story or explanation that has been handed "from woman to woman" as an oral tradition until it becomes folklore.

19. **The correct answer is B.** *Tried and true* means "tested and proven."

20. **The correct answer is D.** Quite literally, the expression means that because one does not know the mood of a horse one has been given, one should not risk sticking one's head in its mouth; furthermore, one should accept a gift as a gift without questioning its value (checking the quality of its teeth). In other words, be happy with what you get and don't be suspicious of good fortune.

6

Antonyms

OVERVIEW

- **Tips for Answering Antonym Questions**
- **Summing It Up**
- **Exercises: Antonyms**
- **Answer Keys and Explanations**

Antonym questions are like synonym questions in that they test your understanding of words. Antonym questions, however, are a bit trickier because they challenge you to demonstrate your mental flexibility as well as your verbal skills. On the HSPT, antonym questions appear on the Verbal Skills portion of the exam.

The task in an antonym question is to define the indicated word and pick its *opposite*. That sounds simple enough, right? Here's where it gets tricky: Where there's no true opposite, you must choose the word or phrase that is most *nearly* opposite. Where there appears to be more than one opposite, you must choose the *best opposite*. You must resist choosing an associated word or phrase that is different in meaning but is not a true opposite. After you define a word, you must then take care to choose its *antonym*, not its *synonym* (the word or phrase that is most similar in meaning).

Let's try an example.

Inaudible means the *opposite* of

  A. invisible.

  B. bright.

  C. loud.

  D. clear.

You might not know the meaning of the word *inaudible*, but you may recognize some of the word's parts. You might know that the prefix *in-* typically means "not." You also might recognize a part of *audio* in the word, and you know that the audio of your TV is the sound. You might also see *-able* in *-ible* and thereby reconstruct "not sound-able" or "not heard."

BEWARE! This is the point at which your reasoning can easily lead you astray. If you associate the word with your TV, you might think, "The opposite of 'not heard' is 'not seen' or *invisible*, choice A." That's wrong because those are not true opposites. You might also associate "not heard" with "not seen" and select choice B, *bright,* as the opposite of "not seen." Wrong again. Finally, you might think of *inaudible* as "hard to hear" and select choice D, *clear. Clear* would not be a bad answer, but choice C, *loud,* is better and is indeed the best answer. The best opposite of *inaudible* is *loud.* Now you know how tricky finding the right answer can be! That's why it's best to remember exactly what you're looking for as you reject or choose an answer.

TIPS FOR ANSWERING ANTONYM QUESTIONS

Thankfully, there is a sound approach to handling antonym questions if you're not sure of the correct answer. After carefully reading the word and its four answer choices, run through the following four possibilities.

Possibility #1

You know the meaning of the word, but none of the answer choices seems correct.

- Perhaps you misread the word. Are there other words that look like the word in the question? For example, did you mistake *revelation* for *revaluation* or *compliment* for *complement?*

- Perhaps you read the word correctly but accented the wrong syllable. Some words have alternative pronunciations with vastly different meanings. Remember *de-sert'* and *des'-ert?*

- Perhaps you are dealing with a single word that can be used as two different parts of speech and therefore has two entirely unrelated meanings. A *moor* (noun) is a boggy wasteland; to *moor* (verb) is to secure a ship or a boat in place; and the proper noun *Moor* refers to the Muslim conquerors of Spain.

- Perhaps the word can appear as different parts of speech with numerous meanings and shades of meaning within each of these. *Fancy* (noun) can mean inclination, love, notion, whim, taste, judgment, or imagination. *Fancy* (verb) can mean to like, to imagine, and to think. *Fancy* (adjective) can mean whimsical, ornamental, and extravagant. Your task is to choose *one* of the four choices that is opposite to *one* of the meanings of the word *fancy.*

Possibility #2

You do not know the meaning of the word, but it appears to contain prefix, suffix, or root clues. Examine those clues to deduce your answer. For example, the word *inaudible* uses the prefix *in-*, which means "not," so look for the best opposite of "not audible."

Possibility #3

You do not know the meaning of the word and can see no clues, but you have a feeling that the word has some specific positive or negative connotation. Play your hunch and choose a word with the opposite connotation.

Possibility #4

You are stumped. There is no penalty for guessing on the HSPT exam so, when all else fails, guess. If you can eliminate one or more of the choices, you improve your odds of guessing correctly. Eliminate choices wherever you can, choose from the remaining options, and move on. There's no need to waste time on a question for which you cannot figure out the answer.

Summing It Up

- Antonym questions are trickier than synonym questions because they ask you to define the indicated word and choose its opposite—or the word or phrase that is most nearly opposite.

- When you think you know the meaning of the given word but can't find the answer, go back and check the following: Did you misread the word? Did you accent the wrong syllable? Can the word be used as two different parts of speech? Does the word have multiple meanings?

- If you don't know the meaning of the word, look for prefixes, suffixes, and root words. Be sure you are clear on the context and look for the opposite meaning.

- Before guessing, try to eliminate as many answer choices as possible. Consider connotation and the part of speech.

Take a moment to ask yourself some simple questions about your understanding of the chapter:

Review: What did I learn?

Evaluate: What do I need to learn more about?

Plan: What can I do next to keep improving?

Based on your answers to those questions, adjust your study plan to dedicate additional time to the areas of weakness that you've identified.

EXERCISES: ANTONYMS

Exercise 1

Directions: Choose the best answer.

---

1. Accelerate means the *opposite* of
   A. stop.
   B. slow.
   C. quicken.
   D. hasten.

2. Docile means the *opposite* of
   A. active.
   B. health.
   C. probable.
   D. teachable.

3. Candor means the *opposite* of
   A. frankness.
   B. doubt.
   C. deception.
   D. enthusiasm.

4. Nomadic means the *opposite* of
   A. secret.
   B. anonymous.
   C. stationary.
   D. famous.

5. Heed means the *opposite* of
   A. agree.
   B. ignore.
   C. listen.
   D. analyze.

6. Defy means the *opposite* of
   A. desire.
   B. embrace.
   C. fight.
   D. abscond.

7. Gorge means the *opposite* of
   A. duck.
   B. diet.
   C. stuff.
   D. valley.

8. Curtail means the *opposite* of
   A. curry.
   B. open.
   C. shorten.
   D. extend.

9. Initiate means the *opposite* of
   A. instruct.
   B. begin.
   C. terminate.
   D. invade.

10. Craven means the *opposite* of
    A. brave.
    B. greedy.
    C. hungry.
    D. nervous.

11. Clamor means the *opposite* of

   A. ugliness.

   B. beauty.

   C. silence.

   D. dishonor.

12. Rouse means the *opposite* of

   A. lull.

   B. alarm.

   C. complain.

   D. weep.

13. Credible means the *opposite* of

   A. believable.

   B. unbelievable.

   C. honorable.

   D. dishonorable.

14. Thorough means the *opposite* of

   A. around.

   B. circumvented.

   C. incomplete.

   D. inside.

15. Wooden means the *opposite* of

   A. iron.

   B. slippery.

   C. rubbery.

   D. green.

7

Exercise 2

Directions: Choose the best answer.

1. Succumb means the *opposite* of

   A. arrive.

   B. yield.

   C. eat.

   D. conquer.

2. Divert means the *opposite* of

   A. instruct.

   B. include.

   C. bore.

   D. amuse.

3. Admonish means the *opposite* of

   A. review.

   B. scare.

   C. praise.

   D. tease.

4. Diminish means the *opposite* of

   A. lessen.

   B. begin.

   C. complete.

   D. expand.

5. Brazen means the *opposite* of

   A. frozen.

   B. meek.

   C. rustproof.

   D. leaky.

6. Intent means the *opposite* of

   A. alfresco.

   B. busy.

   C. uninterested.

   D. shy.

Chapter 7: Antonyms

7. Erode means the *opposite* of
   A. weaken.
   B. restore.
   C. combat.
   D. color.

8. Lavish means the *opposite* of
   A. filthy.
   B. elegant.
   C. squander.
   D. conserve.

9. Aloof means the *opposite* of
   A. sociable.
   B. humble.
   C. public.
   D. ignorant.

10. Elated means the *opposite* of
    A. on time.
    B. tardy.
    C. ideal.
    D. depressed.

11. Furnish means the *opposite* of
    A. dress.
    B. decorate.
    C. remove.
    D. polish.

12. Ostracize means the *opposite* of
    A. include.
    B. shun.
    C. hide.
    D. delight.

13. Exorbitant means the *opposite* of
    A. priceless.
    B. worthless.
    C. reasonable.
    D. straight.

14. Chastise means the *opposite* of
    A. dirty.
    B. cleanse.
    C. praise.
    D. straighten.

15. Profit means the *opposite* of
    A. gain.
    B. money.
    C. suffer.
    D. disgust.

ANSWER KEYS AND EXPLANATIONS
Exercise 1

1. B	**4.** C	**7.** B	**10.** A	**13.** B
2. A	**5.** B	**8.** D	**11.** C	**14.** C
3. C	**6.** B	**9.** C	**12.** A	**15.** C

1. **The correct answer is B.** To accelerate is to quicken or to hasten. Its best opposite is *slow*. *Accelerate* implies that the object was already in motion. *Stop* would be the opposite if the original word had meant "to put into motion" and not "to increase speed."

2. **The correct answer is A.** *Docile* means "calm and easily led." Of the choices offered, its best opposite is *active*.

3. **The correct answer is C.** Candor is frankness or honesty; its opposite is *deception*.

4. **The correct answer is C.** *Nomadic* means "wandering;" its opposite is *stationary*, which means staying in one place. The other words have nothing to do with movement or lack of movement.

5. **The correct answer is B.** To heed means "to pay close attention to something." To ignore something is the opposite. *Listen* is a close match for *heed*, but it is not the opposite.

6. **The correct answer is B.** To defy is to challenge, and its opposite is *embrace*. In this case, *embrace* means "to accept." When reviewing answer options, try to think of all possible meanings for each word choice.

7. **The correct answer is B.** To gorge oneself is to overeat; the opposite is to diet. You could be forgiven for interpreting *gorge* as a landscape feature similar to a canyon, and therefore selecting *valley* as its opposite. However, in a situation where context is lacking, it is usually wise to give preference to the verb or adjective, rather than the noun. Most verbs and adjectives have clear opposites, while nouns are less definite.

8. **The correct answer is D.** To curtail is to shorten; the opposite is to extend.

9. **The correct answer is C.** To initiate is to begin; its opposite is to end or to terminate.

10. **The correct answer is A.** *Craven* means "fearful" or "having a lack of courage." Being brave is the direct opposite of this.

11. **The correct answer is C.** *Clamor* is noise; its opposite is *silence*. You must read carefully. *Clamor* is not *glamour*.

12. **The correct answer is A.** To rouse is to awaken; to lull is to soothe and cause to sleep.

13. **The correct answer is B.** *Credible* means "believable;" its opposite is *unbelievable*. *Honorable* and *dishonorable* are choices designed to mislead you, under the assumption you will confuse *credible* with *creditable*. If you spot that connection, you can eliminate those choices, giving you a better chance of selecting the correct answer.

14. **The correct answer is C.** One meaning of *thorough* is to cover everything or all the important points; its opposite would be *incomplete*. *Circumvented* (choice B) also implies lack of thoroughness, but is not so clearly the opposite of *thorough*.

15. **The correct answer is C.** *Wooden* means "stiff and unbending;" its opposite, *rubbery*, means "flexible."

7

Chapter 7: Antonyms

Exercise 2

1. D	**4.** D	**7.** B	**10.** D	**13.** C
2. C	**5.** B	**8.** D	**11.** C	**14.** C
3. C	**6.** C	**9.** A	**12.** A	**15.** C

1. **The correct answer is D.** To succumb is to yield or to give in; the opposite is to conquer.

2. **The correct answer is C.** To divert is to amuse (think *diversion*); the opposite is to bore. To divert also means "to change the direction of," but no opposite to this meaning is offered.

3. **The correct answer is C.** To admonish means to criticize or reprimand; the opposite is to praise.

4. **The correct answer is D.** To diminish is to lessen. Therefore, the opposite is to expand. As with most antonym questions, one of the choices means the same (or nearly the same) as the word in question, in this case, *lessen* (choice A). This allows you to quickly eliminate at least one answer option.

5. **The correct answer is B.** *Brazen* means "bold or impudent;" its opposite is *meek*.

6. **The correct answer is C.** To be intent is to be engrossed or determined (think *intense*); the opposite is to be uninterested.

7. **The correct answer is B.** To erode means "to whither or wear away," often gradually, or over time. The opposite of this is to restore, meaning "to bring back to pristine condition."

8. **The correct answer is D.** To lavish is to spend profusely or to squander; the opposite is to conserve.

9. **The correct answer is A.** One who is aloof is distant or reserved; an opposite type of person is sociable. *Humble* (choice B) is tempting, but it is a better antonym for *arrogant*. The word *aloof* does not involve snobbery or arrogance, but rather a distant or nonsocial attitude, making *sociable* the best choice for an opposite.

10. **The correct answer is D.** *Elated* means "joyful" and "jubilant"; the opposite is *depressed*. Note that answer choices A and B are there to mislead you in case you mistakenly associate *elated* with lateness, rather than it's actual meaning.

11. **The correct answer is C.** To furnish is to provide; its opposite is to remove.

12. **The correct answer is A.** To ostracize is to shut out or to exclude; the opposite is to include.

13. **The correct answer is C.** *Exorbitant* means "excessive;" its opposite is *reasonable*.

14. **The correct answer is C.** To chastise is to scold; the opposite is to praise.

15. **The correct answer is C.** To profit is to benefit; the opposite is to suffer.

Chapter 8

Analogies

OVERVIEW

- **Tips for Answering Analogy Questions**
- **Summing It Up**
- **Exercises: Analogies**
- **Answer Keys and Explanations**

Verbal analogy questions on the HSPT will test your ability to see relationships between words and apply those relationships accordingly. It is a test of your ability to think things through clearly and logically.

Depending on the exam, verbal analogy questions might be presented in several different ways. On the HSPT exam, you are given a pair of words that are related in a certain way. Then you are given a third word and four answer choices to create a second word pair. The correct answer choice will have the same relationship to the third word as that shared by the example words. For example:

8

Man is to boy as woman is to

  A. child.

  B. sister.

  C. girl.

  D. offspring.

The correct answer is C. The completed analogy reads "man is to boy as woman is to girl." A woman is an adult girl, just as a man is an adult boy.

Regardless of the form an analogy takes, the task is always the same: define the relationships between words and then apply those relationships to a different set of words.

TIPS FOR ANSWERING ANALOGY QUESTIONS

The first step in tackling an analogy question is to define the first set of words and determine their relationship. Most often you will know the meanings of both words, but if you're not sure, make a guess and move on to the next step. Your next step will be to determine how those two words are related. Here's an example: Suppose you are confronted with an analogy question that begins *brim* is to *hat*. *Brim* and *hat* are immediately associated in your mind; a *brim* is a part of a *hat*, so the relationship between the two is that of a part to the whole.

ALERT!

Don't be fooled by similar words in the analogy questions. You're looking for similar relationships, not similar words.

Now look at the third word in the analogy question and the four answer choices available. Start by crossing off the answers you know are incorrect. By process of elimination, you will find a word that has the same relationship to the third word that the first set has. The analogy question would look like this:

Brim is to hat as hand is to

   A. glove.

   B. finger.

   C. foot.

   D. arm.

The correct answer is D. To figure out the answer, consider each answer choice in turn. *Hand* is certainly associated with *glove* (choice A), but in no way is a hand part of a glove. *Hand* and *finger* (choice B), are certainly associated and, indeed, a *finger* is part of a *hand*. But BEWARE! Look again at the relationship of the first two words: *Brim* is a part of *hat*, or in other words, *hat* is the whole of which *brim* is a part. The relationship in choice B is the reverse of the relationship of the first two words. *Hand* is the whole and *finger* is the part. Your answer must maintain the same relationship in the same sequence as the original pair.

The relationship of *hand* and *foot* (choice C) is only one of association, not of part to whole. This answer is no more likely to be correct than choice A. In fact, because you have found two answers that have equal chances of being incorrect, you now know that neither of them is the answer you are looking for. There must be a best answer.

A *hand* is part of an *arm* in the same way that a *brim* is part of a *hat*, or the *arm* is the whole of which a *hand* is a part in the same way that *hat* is the whole of which a *brim* is the part. When you've spotted this, you know that choice D is the *best* answer.

TIP

What if none of the answer pairs seems exactly right? Just remember: The directions tell you to choose the *best* answer. The correct answer won't necessarily be a perfect fit, but it will work better than the other choices.

So, the process consists of the following five steps:

1. Define the initial terms.
2. Describe the initial relationship.
3. Eliminate incorrect answers.
4. Refine the initial relationship, if necessary.
5. Choose the best of the remaining answer choices.

Usually your biggest problem in solving an analogy question will involve narrowing your choices down to the *best* answer. Sometimes, however, your difficulty will be in finding just one answer you think is correct. If this happens, you need to shift gears and redefine your initial relationship. Let's look at another analogy example.

Consider an analogy that begins "letter is to word." Initially, you will probably think, "A letter is part of a word; therefore, the relationship is that of part to whole." If the relationship of the third word to any of the choices is also part to whole, then all is well. However, suppose the question looks like this:

Letter is to word as song is to

    A. story.

    B. music.

    C. note.

    D. orchestra.

The correct answer is C. Three choices offer an association relationship; clearly, you should go along with a more refined definition of the relationship. No choice offers a whole of which a song might be a part (such as an opera). Therefore, you must return to the original pair of words and consider other relationships between letter and word. If letter refers to "written communication," rather than "letter of the alphabet," then a word is part of a letter and the relationship of the first to the second is the whole to a part. Then the answer becomes clear: A song is the whole of which *note* (choice C), is the part. The relationship of *song* and *note* is the same as that of *letter* and *word*.

Analogy questions are challenging, but they can be fun to solve. Here's a list of a few of the most common word relationships found in analogies.

- part to whole, e.g., *branch* to *tree*
- whole to part, e.g., *ocean* to *water*
- cause and effect, e.g., *germ* to *disease*
- effect and cause, e.g., *honors* to *study*
- association, e.g., *bat* to *ball*
- degree, e.g., *hut* to *mansion*
- sequence, e.g., *elementary* to *secondary*
- function, e.g., *teacher* to *student*
- characteristic, e.g., *wise* to *owl*
- antonym, e.g., *bad* to *good*
- synonym, e.g., *spring* to *jump*
- purpose, e.g., *mask* to *protection*

8

TIP

Know the six most common analogy connections:
1. Characteristic
2. Purpose
3. Antonym
4. Part to Whole
5. Whole to Part
6. Degree

Analogy questions also present many opportunities for error if every answer is not given careful consideration. Here are some of the most common pitfalls to avoid:

- Reversal of sequence of the relationship:

  - Part to whole is *not* the same as whole to part.
  - Cause to effect is *not* the same as effect to its cause.
  - Smaller to larger is *not* the same as larger to smaller.
  - Action to object is *not* the same as object to action.

- Confusion of relationship:

  - Part to part (*geometry* to *calculus*) with part to whole (*algebra* to *mathematics*)
  - Cause and effect (*fire* to *smoke*) with association (*man* to *woman*)
  - Degree (*drizzle* to *downpour*) with antonyms (*dry* to *wet*)
  - Association (*walk* to *limp*) with synonyms (*eat* to *consume*)

- Grammatical inconsistency: The grammatical relationship of the first two words must be retained throughout the verbal analogy. A wrong analogy would be *imprisoned* is to *convict* as *cage* is to *parrot*. While the meaningful relationship exists, the analogy is not parallel in construction. A correct analogy of this sort would have to read *prison* is to *convict* as *cage* is to *parrot,* or *imprisoned* is to *convict* as *caged* is to *parrot*. In analogy questions, you must create a pair that is grammatically consistent with the first pair, as well as being correct in definition and meaning.

- Concentration on the meanings of words instead of on their relationships: In this type of error, you see *gear* to *transmission,* and you think of *car* as the common relationship instead of spotting the part-to-part relationship; gears are part of the transmission. When looking for an analogy for the word *piston*, and the list of answers include *car* and *engine*, you might pick *car*, when the better answer is *engine*.

Remember: The key to answering verbal analogy questions lies in the relationship between the first two words!

If you struggle with finding the relationship between the words of the initial pair, you might find it useful to mentally reverse their order. If this works, remember to mentally reverse the order of the third and fourth terms as well, to maintain the relationship in your answer.

8

TIP

Turn the analogy pairs into sentences to help you see the connection. Then fit the answer pairs into the same sentence until you find the one that works best.

PART III: Verbal Skills

Summing It Up

- Analogies are tested on the HSPT exam.
- Follow these steps: define the initial terms, describe the initial relationship, eliminate incorrect answers, refine the initial relationship, and choose the best answer.
- Study and learn the twelve types of analogy questions: part to whole, whole to part, cause and effect, effect and cause, association, degree, sequence, function, characteristic, antonym, synonym, and purpose.

Take a moment to ask yourself some simple questions about your understanding of the chapter:

Review: What did I learn?

Evaluate: What do I need to learn more about?

Plan: What can I do next to keep improving?

Based on your answers to those questions, adjust your study plan to dedicate additional time to the areas of weakness that you've identified.

8

EXERCISES: ANALOGIES

Exercise 1

> **Directions:** In the following questions, the first two words are related to each other in a certain way. The third and fourth words must be related to each other in the same way. Choose a word from among the four choices that is related to the third word in the same way that the second word is related to the first.

1. Gasoline is to petroleum as sugar is to
   A. sweet.
   B. oil.
   C. plant.
   D. cane.

2. Fly is to spider as mouse is to
   A. cat.
   B. rat.
   C. rodent.
   D. trap.

3. Volcano is to crater as chimney is to
   A. smoke.
   B. fire.
   C. flue.
   D. stack.

4. Petal is to flower as fur is to
   A. coat.
   B. rabbit.
   C. warm.
   D. woman.

5. Retreat is to advance as timid is to
   A. bold.
   B. cowardly.
   C. fearful.
   D. shy.

6. Ledger is to accounts as journal is to
   A. pen.
   B. territory.
   C. book.
   D. observations.

7. Picture is to see as speech is to
   A. view.
   B. enunciate.
   C. hear.
   D. soliloquize.

8. Soprano is to high as bass is to
   A. guitar.
   B. bad.
   C. low.
   D. fish.

9. Addition is to addend as subtraction is to
   A. difference.
   B. sum.
   C. subtrahend.
   D. minus.

10. Obese is to eat as elected is to
    A. advertise.
    B. run.
    C. count.
    D. fraud.

8

11. Acute is to chronic as temporary is to

A. persistent.

B. sick.

C. pretty.

D. narrow.

12. Sleeves are to shirt as legs are to

A. shoes.

B. slacks.

C. hats.

D. closets.

13. Chariot is to charioteer as automobile is to

A. passenger.

B. engine.

C. motor.

D. driver.

14. Team is to league as player is to

A. piano.

B. team.

C. tournament.

D. football.

15. Honor is to citation as speeding is to

A. citation.

B. hurry.

C. race.

D. stop.

Exercise 2

Directions: In the following questions, the first two words are related to each other in a certain way. The third and fourth words must be related to each other in the same way. Choose from among the four choices the word that is related to the third word in the same way that the second word is related to the first.

1. Net is to fisherman as gun is to

A. bullet.

B. policeman.

C. deer.

D. hunter.

2. *Hamlet* is to Shakespeare as telephone is to

A. Bell.

B. telegraph.

C. iPhone.

D. Verizon.

3. Distracting is to noise as soothing is to

A. medicine.

B. music.

C. volume.

D. bleeding.

4. Year is to calendar as hour is to

A. decade.

B. minute.

C. clock.

D. month.

5. Father is to brother as mother is to

   A. daughter.

   B. sister.

   C. aunt.

   D. niece.

6. Words are to books as notes are to

   A. songs.

   B. letters.

   C. pianos.

   D. fragrances.

7. Pungent is to odor as shrill is to

   A. whisper.

   B. sound.

   C. piercing.

   D. shriek.

8. Present is to birthday as reward is to

   A. accomplishment.

   B. medal.

   C. punishment.

   D. money.

9. Mouse is to mammal as lizard is to

   A. fish.

   B. scale.

   C. camouflage.

   D. reptile.

10. Sky is to ground as ceiling is to

    A. floor.

    B. roof.

    C. top.

    D. plaster.

11. Food is to nutrition as light is to

    A. watt.

    B. bulb.

    C. electricity.

    D. vision.

12. Actor is to play as musician is to

    A. guitarist.

    B. performer.

    C. instrument.

    D. concert.

13. Square is to triangle as cube is to

    A. circle.

    B. line.

    C. ball.

    D. pyramid.

14. Abacus is to calculator as propeller is to

    A. jet.

    B. airplane.

    C. mathematics.

    D. flight.

15. Dizziness is to vertigo as fate is to

    A. adversity.

    B. order.

    C. destiny.

    D. pride.

ANSWER KEYS AND EXPLANATIONS
Exercise 1

1. D	4. B	7. C	10. B	13. D
2. A	5. A	8. C	11. A	14. B
3. C	6. D	9. C	12. B	15. A

1. **The correct answer is D.** The relationship is that of the product to its source. Gasoline comes from petroleum; sugar comes from cane. Although you could argue that sugar also comes from a plant (choice C), cane is a more direct and specific relationship, much like the relationship between gasoline and petroleum.

2. **The correct answer is A.** The relationship is that of the eaten to the eater. The fly is eaten by the spider; the mouse is eaten by the cat. Refine this analogy to eating in order to solve it. If you were to consider only catching, then you would not be able to distinguish between the cat and the trap.

3. **The correct answer is C.** The relationship is functional. The crater contains the vent(s) for a volcano; the flue is the vent for a chimney.

4. **The correct answer is B.** The relationship is that of part to whole. A petal is part of a flower; fur is part of a rabbit. Fur might be part of a coat, but it is not a necessary part, so *rabbit* makes a better analogy.

5. **The correct answer is A.** The relationship is that of antonyms. *Retreat* is the opposite of *advance*; *timid* is the opposite of *bold*.

6. **The correct answer is D.** This analogy involves a functional relationship. A ledger stores and maintains accounts for businesses. A journal stores and maintains observations for individuals.

7. **The correct answer is C.** This is another variety of object-to-action relationship. You see a picture; you hear a speech.

8. **The correct answer is C.** The relationship is that of synonyms or definition. A soprano voice is high; a bass voice is low. While *bass* has multiple meanings, you must define the word in context of the relationship among the first two words.

9. **The correct answer is C.** The relationship is that of the whole to a part. The addend is one term of an addition problem; the subtrahend is one term of a subtraction problem.

10. **The correct answer is B.** This is essentially a cause-and-effect relationship. You cannot become obese if you do not eat; you cannot be elected if you do not run.

11. **The correct answer is A.** The relationship is that of antonyms. *Acute* means sudden and short; *chronic* means always present. *Temporary* is the opposite of *persistent*.

12. **The correct answer is B.** This is a part-to-whole relationship—sleeves are a part of a shirt. *Legs*, therefore, must be a part of the correct answer. Review the answer choices: legs are a part of slacks, which completes the analogy.

13. **The correct answer is D.** The relationship is that of object and actor. The charioteer drives the chariot; the driver drives the automobile. You must consider the action in this analogy in order to differentiate between *driver* and *passenger*.

14. **The correct answer is B.** The relationship is that of the part to the whole. The team is part of the league; the player is part of the team.

8

15. **The correct answer is A.** This analogy is probably more difficult than any you will get. The trick lies in the fact that *citation* has two distinct meanings. The relationship is that of cause to effect. When you are being honored, you receive a citation, which is a formal document describing your achievements. When you are stopped for speeding, you receive a citation, which is an official summons to appear in court.

Exercise 2

1. D	4. C	7. B	10. A	13. D
2. A	5. B	8. A	11. D	14. A
3. B	6. A	9. D	12. D	15. C

1. **The correct answer is D.** This relationship does not fall into a category with a precise name. The fisherman uses a net for his sport; the hunter uses a gun for his sport. The policeman also uses a gun, but not for sport. You must refine the relationship to eliminate all but one choice.

2. **The correct answer is A.** This is a creation-creator relationship. Shakespeare is the creator (author) of *Hamlet*; the telephone is an invention of Alexander Graham Bell.

3. **The correct answer is B.** The relationship is that of effect to its cause. Noise is distracting; music is soothing.

4. **The correct answer is C.** This is a functional relationship. Years are measured on a calendar; hours are measured on a clock.

5. **The correct answer is B.** The relationship of *father* to his same-sex sibling, *brother*, is analogous to the relationship of *mother* to her same-sex sibling, *sister*.

6. **The correct answer is A.** The relationship is of parts to wholes. Words are parts of books; notes are parts of songs.

7. **The correct answer is B.** The relationship is that of an adjective to the noun it modifies. An odor may be described as pungent, though there are many other adjectives you could use. A sound may be described as shrill, though certainly not all sounds are shrill. *Shriek* is not the best answer because a shriek is always shrill sound.

8. **The correct answer is A.** This is a purpose relationship. The purpose of a present is to celebrate a birthday; the purpose of a reward is to celebrate an accomplishment.

9. **The correct answer is D.** The relationship is one of classification. A mouse is a mammal; a lizard is a reptile.

10. **The correct answer is A.** The relationship is one of antonyms. *Sky* is the opposite of *ground*; *ceiling* is the opposite of *floor*.

11. **The correct answer is D.** The relationship is that of cause and effect. Food promotes nutrition; light promotes vision.

12. **The correct answer is D.** This analogy highlights a part-to-whole relationship. An actor is a part of a play performance, and a musician is a part of a concert performance.

13. **The correct answer is D.** You might loosely state the relationship as four is to three. A square is a four-sided plane figure in relation to a triangle, which is a three-sided plane figure. A cube is a solid figure based on a square; a pyramid is a solid figure based on a triangle.

14. **The correct answer is A.** The relationship is sequential. An abacus is an earlier, more primitive calculator; a propeller is an earlier, less sophisticated means of propulsion than a jet.

15. **The correct answer is C.** The relationship is that of synonyms. Vertigo is dizziness; destiny is fate. One's fate may well be to suffer adversity, but fate is not necessarily negative.

Chapter 9

Logic and Verbal Classification

OVERVIEW

- HSPT® Exam Logic
- HSPT® Exam Verbal Classification
- Summing It Up
- Exercise 1: Logic
- Exercise 2: Verbal Skills
- Answer Keys and Explanations

The HSPT exam will put your logical thinking and verbal reasoning skills to the test by presenting logic and verbal classification questions. Both question types appear within the HSPT Verbal Skills section.

Logic questions require you to extract indisputable information from a series of short sentences. The verbal classification questions present four words and ask you to determine which of the words doesn't fit with the other three.

HSPT® EXAM LOGIC

Logic questions on the HSPT exam take a slightly different form than other questions on the exam. In these questions, you're given a series of sentences. You are then asked to determine if—based on the truth of the other sentences—the final sentence is **A.** true, **B.** false, or **C.** uncertain. If it is not possible to determine whether the final sentence is true or false, then the correct answer is choice C.

9

TIP

Visualization and diagramming are valuable tools for understanding relationships. Try drawing out and labeling the relationships described by the sentences. Or, if there's no room to draw, create a mental picture of the actions described by the sentences and then select the relevant answer.

Let's look at an example of an HSPT logic exam question:

The black horse jumped over more hurdles than the spotted horse. The white horse jumped over more hurdles than the spotted horse. The white horse jumped over more hurdles than the black horse. If the first two statements are true, the third statement is

   A. true.

   B. false.

   C. uncertain.

The correct answer is C. From the first two statements, we know that both the black horse and the white horse jumped over more hurdles than the spotted horse. This is all that we know. The first two statements do not give us any information about the comparative achievements of the black horse and the white horse. The third statement can be neither affirmed nor denied based on the first two statements.

HSPT® EXAM VERBAL CLASSIFICATION

Here's another type of verbal skills question you'll find on the HSPT. In Verbal Classification questions, you are presented with four words and asked to determine which of the words doesn't fit with the other three. Here's an example:

Which word does *not* belong with the others?

   A. crack

   B. cleave

   C. split

   D. pare

The correct answer is D. The first three words are synonyms. All refer to dividing something by opening it into two or more pieces. Choice D, on the other hand, refers to opening by peeling off the outer layer (to pare is to peel). The key to answering this kind of question lies in figuring the relationship among three of the words. There are many possible relationships. The words could be synonyms; they may express the same idea in varying degrees; they may be similar parts of speech; or they may serve similar functions in a sentence. It is up to you to recognize the relationship and select your answer accordingly.

Summing It Up

- The HSPT exam tests different types of logic in its Verbal Skills section using logic and verbal classification questions.

  - Logic questions give you a series of sentences, then ask you to determine if—based on the truth of the other sentences—the final sentence is **A.** true, **B.** false, or **C.** uncertain. If it is not possible to determine whether the final sentence is true or false, then the correct answer is choice **C.**

  - Verbal Classification questions present you with four words and asked to determine which of the words doesn't fit with the other three.

- For HSPT exam logic questions, you have only three answer choices.

Take a moment to ask yourself some simple questions about your understanding of the chapter:

Review: What did I learn?

Evaluate: What do I need to learn more about?

Plan: What can I do next to keep improving?

Based on your answers to those questions, adjust your study plan to dedicate additional time to the areas of weakness that you've identified.

Try your hand at using the reasoning processes we have just taught you as you tackle the exercises in this chapter. Answer keys and explanations follow the Verbal Classification exercise.

EXERCISE 1: LOGIC

Directions: Choose the best answer.

1. George is older than Bob. Fred is younger than George. Bob is older than Fred. If the first two statements are true, the third statement is

   A. true.

   B. false.

   C. uncertain.

2. Group A sings higher than Group C. Group B sings lower than Group C. Group A sings higher than Group B. If the first two statements are true, the third statement is

   A. true.

   B. false.

   C. uncertain.

3. Percolator coffee is weaker than electric-drip coffee. Extractor coffee is stronger than electric-drip coffee. Percolator coffee is stronger than extractor coffee. If the first two statements are true, the third statement is

   A. true.

   B. false.

   C. uncertain.

4. Red kites fly higher than yellow kites. Yellow balloons fly higher than red kites. Yellow kites fly higher than yellow balloons. If the first two statements are true, the third statement is

   A. true.

   B. false.

   C. uncertain.

5. The New York team lost fewer games than the Boston team. The Boston team won more games than the Baltimore team, but not as many games as the New York team. The Baltimore team lost the fewest games. If the first two statements are true, the third statement is

   A. true.

   B. false.

   C. uncertain.

6. The history book has more pages than the poetry book, but fewer pages than the math book. The math book has more pages than the science book but fewer pages than the English book. The poetry book has the fewest pages. If the first two statements are true, the third statement is

   A. true.

   B. false.

   C. uncertain.

7. Edward reads faster than Amanda. Lindsey reads slower than Edward, but not slower than Amanda. Lindsey and Amanda read at the same pace. If the first two statements are true, then the third statement is

   A. true.

   B. false.

   C. uncertain.

8. The widget factory sold more items than the gizmo factory sold. The gadget factory sold more items than the widget factory sold. The gizmo factory sold more items than the gadget factory sold. If the first two statements are true, then the third statement is

   A. true.

   B. false.

   C. uncertain.

9. Stefen has traveled to 16 countries. Meredith has traveled to fewer countries than Stefen, but more than Aiden. Aiden has been to the fewest number of countries. If the first two statements are true, then the third statement is

   A. true.

   B. false.

   C. uncertain.

10. US Route 1 is longer than US Route 5. US Route 66 is less than 80 miles longer than US Route 1. US Route 66 is longer than US Route 5. If the first two statements are true, then the third statement is

    A. true.

    B. false.

    C. uncertain.

EXERCISE 2: VERBAL CLASSIFICATION

> **Directions:** Choose the word that doesn't belong with the others.

1. Which word does *not* belong with the others?

   A. ceiling

   B. window

   C. floor

   D. wall

2. Which word does *not* belong with the others?

   A. orange

   B. apple

   C. tomato

   D. carrot

3. Which word does *not* belong with the others?

   A. emotion

   B. love

   C. anger

   D. disappointment

4. Which word does *not* belong with the others?

   A. destroy

   B. brick

   C. construct

   D. connect

5. Which word does *not* belong with the others?

   A. medicine

   B. healing

   C. therapy

   D. surgery

6. Which word does *not* belong with the others?

   A. orange

   B. brown

   C. red

   D. purple

7. Which word does *not* belong with the others?

   A. bottle

   B. canteen

   C. cup

   D. plate

8. Which word does *not* belong with the others?

   A. smart phone

   B. console

   C. laptop

   D. tablet

9. Which word does *not* belong with the others?

   A. noun

   B. gerund

   C. apostrophe

   D. verb

10. Which word does *not* belong with the others?

   A. glider

   B. skateboard

   C. bicycle

   D. scooter

9

ANSWER KEYS AND EXPLANATIONS

Exercise 1: Logic

1. C	3. B	5. C	7. C	9. A
2. A	4. B	6. C	8. B	10. A

1. **The correct answer is C.** We know only that George is the oldest. There is no way to tell whether Bob is older than Fred, or Fred is older than Bob.

2. **The correct answer is A.** Group A sings the highest of the three.

3. **The correct answer is B.** Extractor coffee is the strongest, electric drip comes next, and percolator is the weakest.

4. **The correct answer is B.** Balloons appear to fly higher than kites.

5. **The correct answer is C.** We know for certain that the Baltimore team *won* the fewest games, but without information about how many games were played, we have no knowledge of how many games the Baltimore team *lost*.

6. **The correct answer is C.** The English book has the most pages, followed by the math book. The history book has more pages than the poetry book. However, we do not have enough information to rank the science book; it might have more or fewer pages than the poetry book.

7. **The correct answer is C.** We know Edward reads faster than Amanda and Lindsey, but we do not know how fast Amanda and Lindsey read.

8. **The correct answer is B.** The gadget factory sold more than the widget factory sold, and the widget factory sold more than the gizmo factory sold.

9. **The correct answer is A.** Meredith traveled to more countries than Aiden did, but still not as many as Stefen did.

10. **The correct answer is A.** US Route 66 is longer than Route 1, which is longer than Route 5.

Exercise 2: Verbal Classification

1. B	3. A	5. B	7. D	9. C
2. D	4. B	6. C	8. B	10. A

1. **The correct answer is B.** The window is transparent or, at the very least, translucent, and it is probably movable as well. All the other choices are solid, opaque, and fixed.

2. **The correct answer is D.** The carrot is a root vegetable. All the other choices are seed-bearing fruits.

3. **The correct answer is A.** The other three choices (love, anger, and disappointment) are all actual emotions.

4. **The correct answer is B.** This is a verbal classification question, so you must determine which of the words doesn't fit with the other three. *Brick* is a noun; the other three choices are verbs.

5. **The correct answer is B.** Medicine, therapy, and surgery are all procedures leading to healing.

6. **The correct answer is C.** Red is a primary color; all the others (orange, brown, and purple) are red-based mixtures.

7. **The correct answer is D.** Bottle, canteen, and cup are all used to hold water, but a plate holds food.

9

8. **The correct answer is B.** Smart phones, laptops, and tablets all have their own screens. A console needs to be connected to a screen.

9. **The correct answer is C.** The apostrophe is a punctuation mark. The others are all parts of speech.

10. **The correct answer is A.** Gliders fly through the air while skateboards, bicycles, and scooters roll on wheels.

9

Chapter 10

Reading

OVERVIEW

- **How to Improve Your Reading Skills**
- **Tips for Answering Reading Comprehension Questions**
- **Summing It Up**
- **Exercises: Reading**
- **Answer Keys and Explanations**

Both the TACHS and HSPT exam include sections on reading comprehension. The format for reading questions on each exam differs from the other question types you've learned about so far. Here, you'll be presented with reading passages followed by a series of questions based on the text. The questions test not only how well you understand what you read on the surface, but how well you interpret the passage's meaning and the author's intent. These questions also test how well you draw conclusions based on what you've read.

Reading quickly is crucial to success on the reading comprehension sections of an exam, but so is comprehension. You won't be able to answer questions based on a passage if you don't allow yourself enough time to read it. Even if you can read the passage through once, you must have enough time left over to reread the selection for detailed questions.

10

HOW TO IMPROVE YOUR READING SKILLS

One of the best techniques for increasing your reading speed and comprehension is also one of the techniques that will help you improve your vocabulary—*reading*. The best way to increase your reading speed between now and the actual exam is to read as much as possible. Read everything in sight: newspapers, magazines, novels, billboards, nutrition labels, instruction manuals, etc. Newspaper reading is an especially good way to sharpen your skills. And don't just stop after the opening paragraph! Push yourself to read the whole story and give it your full attention as you read. Only by reading a complete work will you be able to properly analyze and understand it. If your mind wanders while you're reading, your comprehension is likely to wander, too.

To read with understanding, your eyes must occasionally stop on the page. Most people stop on each word because that is the way reading is taught in the early grades. But once you know how to read well, this method wastes a great deal of time. The key to increasing your reading speed is to take in more words each time your eyes stop. If there's a line with ten words and you're able to read it by stopping only twice instead of ten times, you'll be reading approximately five times faster than you do now. As with most things in life, the only effective way to improve is with practice.

TIP

Read actively! This means marking the text, summarizing paragraphs, and writing down questions as they come. Active reading helps you better comprehend and remember information in the text.

If you have a habit of softly speaking words as you read, *break that habit now*! This habit is called *subvocalizing*, and no matter how fast you can talk, you can read faster if you stop subvocalizing. Some people chew gum to stop subvocalizing. For others, just being aware of the habit is enough to help them correct it. Not only will it slow you down, but if you're reading aloud during your exam, the administrator may ask you to stop so you don't disturb others who are taking the test.

In building your reading speed, try moving your index finger or pencil tip underneath the line you are reading. Because your eyes tend to move as quickly as your pencil, you will not stop on every word. You will not regress (look back), and you probably will not subvocalize. However, what you might do is concentrate on your pencil and not on the reading passage. We recommend practicing this technique before trying it out on your test. Start with one finger or the point of your pencil at the second or third word in a line and stop before it hits the last word. Your peripheral vision (what you see at the edges) will pick up the first and last words in the lines, and you'll save time by not having to focus on them directly.

Pay closer attention to words. Earlier in this section, we advised you to use a dictionary while reading to alleviate confusion and strengthen vocabulary. That exercise helps with reading comprehension questions as well. Vocabulary and reading comprehension are closely related. You can't grow your vocabulary without reading. And you can't comprehend a text without a firm grasp of the words the author is using. When you look up words, study their roots, their prefixes, and their suffixes so you can apply all you know whenever you meet a word that's unfamiliar.

Don't forget to check out the Word List in the back of this book.

NOTE

The reading comprehension section of the HSPT and TACHS exams requires that you read quickly and fully comprehend the text. The best way to increase reading speed is to read as much as possible between now and the time of the exam.

TIPS FOR ANSWERING READING COMPREHENSION QUESTIONS

- Begin by reading the questions—not the answer choices, just the questions themselves. With an idea of what the questions will be asking, you'll be able to read with greater focus.

- Skim the passage to get a general idea of the subject matter and pick up any clues about text's meaning. Pay special attention to the first and last sentences of each paragraph, as they often state the main idea of the passage.

- Reread the passage while giving attention to smaller details like point-of-view. Be alert for hints as to what the author finds important. Phrases such as *Note that . . .*, *Of importance is . . .*, and *Do not overlook . . .* give clues to what the writer is stressing.

- If the author quotes material from another source, be sure that you understand the quote's purpose. Does the author agree or disagree with what he's quoting?

- If you find that questions commonly trick you, try predicting the answer before looking at the options. This will force you to recall what you read and reduce the likelihood of falling for a trick answer.

- Carefully read each question or incomplete statement and determine exactly what you need to look for. Watch for negatives or all-inclusive words such as *always, never, all, only, every, absolutely, completely, none, entirely,* and *no.*

- Read all four answer options. Avoid rushing to choose the first answer that appears correct. Eliminate the obviously incorrect choices first, then reread the remaining choices and refer to the passage, if necessary, to determine the *best* answer.

- Don't confuse a *true* answer with the *correct* answer—just because an answer is true doesn't mean it's the only true answer or that it's correct. Avoid involving personal or emotional judgments when finding your answers. Even if you disagree with the author, or spot a factual error in the passage, you must answer based on what's stated or implied in the text.

- There's always an excellent reason why the right answer is right: It will be directly supported by the passage. Meanwhile, wrong answers distort details from the passage or fail to align them with the goal of the question. Always ensure you have good reasons for selecting your answer and eliminating others.

- Don't spend too much time on one question. If looking back at the passage doesn't help you figure it out, eliminate the obviously-wrong answers and choose from those that remain. Then forget about it for the time being and move on.

TIP

Many people find it helpful to review the questions before reading the passage, as it gives them an idea of what to look for prior to reading the text.

Summing It Up

- The reading comprehension section is called Reading on the HSPT (under the Comprehension section) and on the TACHS. Each test presents reading passages followed by a series of questions.

- To do well on this section, you will need to be able to read quickly. If you do not read quickly, study the section "How to Improve Your Reading Skills" in this chapter.

- Study and remember all of the steps for answering reading comprehension questions: read over the question, skim the passage for the main idea, reread the passage with attention to specific details and point of view. Carefully read each question or incomplete statement, read all four answer choices, and don't spend too much time on any one question.

Take a moment to ask yourself some simple questions about your understanding of the chapter:

Review: What did I learn?

Evaluate: What do I need to learn more about?

Plan: What can I do next to keep improving?

Based on your answers to those questions, adjust your study plan to dedicate additional time to the areas of weakness that you've identified.

Now try the following exercises (you can find answers and explanations after Exercise 2).

EXERCISES: READING

Directions: The following questions are based on several reading passages. Each passage is followed by a series of questions. Read each passage carefully, then answer the questions. You may reread the passage as often as you wish. When you have finished answering the questions based on one passage, go right on to the next passage.

Exercise 1

Questions 1–4 refer to the following passage.

Henry Ford was a natural businessman, even as a youngster. Ford grew up in Michigan in the 1860s. When he was 11 years old, he was given a watch for his birthday. Young Ford was so enthralled by the watch that he managed to develop his own timepiece a year later. He set about attempting to sell the homemade watches at every opportunity for $1 each. That might not seem like much to us now, but remember that Ford only made about $1.10 per day when he took his first job at age 17.

According to the biography produced by the Edison and Ford Winter Estates, the most notable event that inspired Ford to begin working with automobiles happened when Ford was 13. Ford and his father were riding together in a wagon when they saw a steam engine moving down the road. The engine had been attached to wheels to propel itself. When Ford saw the engine, he became very excited and asked the engine's driver all about the machine. From this the idea of a self-propelled vehicle took root in Ford's mind.

Ford gained his first experience in the auto industry when he was 17, when he moved to Detroit and took his first job. Ford was fired after only a short time at that job. He angered the senior employees in the company because he was able to make repairs in about 30 minutes that took the other employees five hours!

1. Which of the following best describes Henry Ford?

   A. Even as a youngster, Ford was better at mechanics than at business.

   B. From the time of his first job, Ford was an efficient worker.

   C. Ford was fired from his first job for not working very hard.

   D. As a business owner, Ford had a way of making his workers dissatisfied.

2. Which of the following describes Ford's first experience as a business owner?

   A. He gained his first experience working in the auto industry when he was 17.

   B. As early as age 13, he was very interested in how steam engines operated.

   C. He started his first business selling watches when he was just 12 years old.

   D. He started an auto business that earned more than $1 million within four years.

3. Which statement best expresses the main idea of this selection?

   A. Henry Ford's innovation helped develop the American auto industry.

   B. Henry Ford started his career as a watchmaker.

   C. Henry Ford had a strong aptitude for business and industry from childhood.

   D. Ford started life as a low-wage laborer in an auto factory.

4. Which of the following best describes Ford's watch-making business?

   A. Ford sold his watches very cheaply.

   B. Ford was able to make several watches a day.

   C. Ford was able to earn enough money from his watches to leave home.

   D. Ford sold his watches for a relatively high price.

Questions 5–13 refer to the following passage.

The music of Mozart has had a significant impact on the world, and it still does to this day. Although Mozart died very young, at the age of 35, he wrote more compositions during his short lifetime than any other composer in history. He was so skilled as a musician that we find it difficult to comprehend the stories we hear of his talents today. His skill allowed him to leave a musical legacy that not only delighted audiences but had a great impact on the future of music as well.

Perhaps the most notable aspect of Mozart's career is how young he was when he started. From the time that Mozart was three years old, it was clear that he was extraordinarily gifted. He was considered a child <u>prodigy</u> because of his stunning musical talents. He began to play the piano at age three, and he composed his first music at the age of four. Mozart had an excellent ear for music, even at this very young age.

Mozart's efforts changed music in many ways. One of the most important changes that Mozart helped to contribute was expanding the different types of music that existed during his time. Before Mozart began composing, there was only one major form of music, known as the *sonata*. A sonata is a musical piece written for one or two solo instruments, consisting of three or four separate parts, called movements. At that time, composers wrote sonatas either for the violin or for the keyboard. The movements within these sonatas were also small, without much development.

Through his writing, Mozart greatly increased the types of music that were written and performed. He helped add forms such as symphonies, concertos, quartets, and trios. Mozart also wrote sonatas, but he added depth to the sonatas and gave them more structure. In part, he was able to do this because he had been exposed to many different types of music during his travels as a young boy. He combined the musical styles that he learned during his stays in Germany, France, Italy, and other regions in Austria.

PART III: Verbal Skills

5. Which statement best reflects the main idea of the passage?

   A. Mozart started his musical career when he was extremely young: he learned to play the piano when he was only three years old.

   B. Mozart was an extremely talented musician and composer whose contributions have had a significant impact on music.

   C. Mozart greatly increased the types of music that were written and performed, adding symphonies, concertos, quartets, and trios to the sonata form that already existed.

   D. Mozart wrote a great number of musical works during his lifetime, but his music was not appreciated until after his death.

6. The word *prodigy* in this context means a

   A. person with exceptional skills.

   B. person who is slower than most.

   C. person with a scientific mind.

   D. person who shows great kindness.

7. How did Mozart's sonatas differ from previous sonatas written before Mozart's time?

   A. Mozart's sonatas were more entertaining than the previous sonatas.

   B. Mozart's sonatas had more depth and more structure than the previous sonatas.

   C. Mozart's sonatas were composed more quickly than the previous sonatas.

   D. Mozart's sonatas were more difficult to play than the previous sonatas.

8. According to the passage, which statement is true of Mozart's compositions?

   A. No other composer in history has equaled his output.

   B. He wrote more symphonies than any other composer in history.

   C. His compositions all had at least three parts.

   D. All his compositions were sonatas.

9. According to the passage, what did Mozart accomplish before the age of 5?

   A. He learned to play the trumpet and piano.

   B. He composed a sonata for the violin and piano.

   C. He was introduced to the royal court in Vienna.

   D. He learned to play the piano and wrote his first composition.

10. According to the passage, many of Mozart's musical compositions had three or four separate parts, known as

    A. elements.

    B. solos.

    C. movements.

    D. aspects.

11. According to the passage, a sonata is a musical composition for

    A. an orchestra with a piano solo.

    B. a stringed instrument and a woodwind.

    C. trios and quartets.

    D. one or two instruments.

10

12. According to the passage, as a boy, Mozart traveled through which countries outside of his homeland?

    A. England, France, and Italy

    B. France, Italy, and Germany

    C. Germany, Austria, and Italy

    D. Austria, France, and Italy

13. According to the passage, Mozart's travels as a young boy

    A. brought him fame and wealthy patrons.

    B. exposed him to disease, causing his death at the age of 35.

    C. exposed him to many different types of music.

    D. helped him learn several languages.

Questions 14–20 refer to the following passage.

When I was growing up during the Depression, I lived on a farm in New Jersey with my grandmother and grandfather. Aunt Frieda was my youngest aunt; she lived in New York City with her husband, my Uncle Stuart, and she frequently wrote letters to my grandmother and grandfather. My grandparents didn't speak any English, so I always translated the correspondence for them from English into Italian.

One day, when I was about fifteen, I saw that the letters from my Aunt Frieda were coming written in Uncle Stuart's handwriting. I realized that Aunt Frieda wasn't really writing them, but I didn't say anything to my grandmother or grandfather because I didn't want to worry them. My grandmother was a real worrier, and I didn't want her to get upset, so I continued to read the letters to her as if they were coming from Aunt Frieda.

That went on for several weeks, until we had a visit from my Aunt Grace, who was Aunt Frieda's older sister. Aunt Grace told me that she had just visited Aunt Frieda. I asked my Aunt Grace what was wrong with Aunt Frieda, and Aunt Grace replied, "Your Aunt Frieda has had an eye operation. She's recuperating just fine, and she's planning a visit to see *Nana* very soon."

Shortly after that, I received a letter from Uncle Stuart informing me that he and Aunt Frieda were coming to visit. On the day they arrived, the moment I saw their car, I said to my grandmother, "*Nana*, I have something to tell you about Aunt Frieda. Now I don't want to worry you—Aunt Frieda is fine, but she's had an operation on her eye. She went to the hospital in Philadelphia to have the surgery done."

My grandmother was beginning to get visibly upset, and I did my best to calm her down. We were all standing on the front porch when Aunt Frieda and Uncle Stuart drove up. When Aunt Frieda exited the car, she was walking <u>gingerly</u>, like someone who couldn't see very well. I kept trying to keep my grandmother calm.

Nana behaved outwardly, but she cried silently to herself. When my Aunt Frieda got out of the car, all that my *Nana* said was, "Your own mother—you keep a secret from your own mother—your mother was supposed to be there by your side!" She kept repeating it over and over, but that was all she said.

I imagine that part of the reason why *Nana* would become so upset when she felt powerless was because she was accustomed to having everything go her way. Unlike my grandmother, my grandfather was a very quiet man who lived a routine, predictable life: he did his work, ate dinner, and went to bed. My grandmother, on the other hand, was absolutely in charge, and it was clear that she controlled the money, the decisions—she controlled everything. She was smart as a whip, too.

14. The word *gingerly* in this context means

    A. confidently.

    B. cautiously.

    C. recklessly.

    D. naturally.

15. How is the author's grandfather different from his grandmother?

    A. His grandfather doesn't have many dreams, while his grandmother dreams often.

    B. His grandfather becomes sick easily, while his grandmother is very healthy.

    C. His grandfather tends to be controlling, while his grandmother is usually relaxed.

    D. His grandfather tends to be very quiet, while his grandmother gets easily agitated.

16. How did the author know that Aunt Frieda had stopped writing letters to his grandmother?

    A. His Aunt Grace told him that Aunt Frieda had stopped writing.

    B. Aunt Frieda's letters were written in Italian and not in English.

    C. His grandmother stopped receiving any letters from Aunt Frieda.

    D. The letters began coming in Uncle Stuart's handwriting.

17. From the passage, we can infer that the author considered *Nana* to be

    A. cut off from her children because she couldn't speak English.

    B. withdrawn and fearful of the outside world.

    C. the authority figure in the household.

    D. submissive to her husband's decisions.

18. When *Nana* sees Aunt Frieda, her main feeling is

    A. confusion, because she did not know about the eye operation.

    B. relief, because the operation was a success.

    C. anger, because she had been tricked into thinking Frieda wrote the letters.

    D. powerlessness, because Frieda did not tell her about the operation.

19. In the passage, the author regards *Nana* as someone who is

    A. fragile but easily soothed.

    B. intelligent but easily worried.

    C. intelligent but lacking in formal education.

    D. educated but easily deceived.

20. When the author asks Aunt Grace why Aunt Frieda is not writing the letters, the tone of Aunt Grace's answer is intended to be

    A. reassuring.

    B. consoling.

    C. alarming.

    D. distressing.

10

Questions 21–25 refer to the following passage.

On entering the amphitheater, new objects of wonder presented themselves. On a level spot in the center was a company of odd-looking personages playing at nine-pins. They were dressed in a quaint, outlandish fashion, some wore short doublets, others jerkins, with long knives in their belts, and most of them had enormous breeches, of a type similar to that of the guide's. Their visages, too, were peculiar, one had a large beard, broad face, and small piggish eyes. The face of another seemed to consist entirely of nose and was surmounted by a white sugar-loaf hat set off with a little red cock's tail. They all had beards of various shapes and colors. There was one who seemed to be the commander. He was a stout old gentleman, with a weather-beaten countenance; he wore a lace doublet, broad belt and hangar, high crowned hat and feather, red stockings, and high-heeled shoes with roses in them. The whole group reminded Rip of the figures in an old <u>Flemish</u> painting, in the parlor of the village parson, which had been brought over from Holland at the time of the settlement.

What seemed particularly odd to Rip was that though these folks were evidently amusing themselves, yet they maintained the gravest faces, the most mysterious silence, and were the most melancholy party of pleasure he had ever witnessed. Nothing interrupted the stillness of the scene but the noise of the balls, which, whenever they were rolled, echoed along the mountains like rumbling peals of thunder.

—from *Rip Van Winkle*, by Washington Irving

21. Looking at this scene, the observer is apparently

  A. fascinated.

  B. frightened.

  C. repulsed.

  D. bored.

22. The word *Flemish* possibly refers to

  A. something from the area near Holland.

  B. the village parson.

  C. a certain painter.

  D. an old-fashioned parlor.

23. The characters were probably playing

  A. a game like bowling.

  B. soccer.

  C. a type of baseball.

  D. golf.

24. The person observing all of this is

  A. Flemish.

  B. a parson.

  C. melancholic.

  D. Rip.

25. The observer was surprised that the

  A. men's beards were of so many shapes and colors.

  B. men appeared to be so serious while they were playing a game.

  C. leader was so stout.

  D. rolling balls sounded like thunder.

10

Questions 26–31 refer to the following passage.

Author Ben Wiens defines energy simply as "the ability to create a force over a distance some time in the future." The term energy, Wiens notes, was developed only about 200 years ago, by a scientist named Thomas Young. In Young's time, energy was thought to be the ability to do physical work, like the work that an axe can do when it comes down on a log with force and <u>severs</u> the log in two. In Young's time, according to Wiens, work was defined as "a force acting over a distance." When a person uses his energy to run, for instance, he is showing an example of a force acting over a distance.

As scientists began to research energy more carefully, they realized that energy was more than just the ability to do physical work. They started to see energy as the *potential* to do work as well. One scientist named James Prescott Joule believed that the ability to do work was stored within the molecules of matter. Joule stated in 1830 that molecules contained very small forms of energy. These forms of energy could not be seen by the naked eye, according to Joule, but they did exist.

In 1905, Albert Einstein made an important contribution to our study of energy. During Einstein's time, scientists knew that matter was made up of smaller parts, such as molecules and atoms. Einstein believed, however, that molecules and atoms were not the smallest parts of matter. He stated that molecules and atoms were made up of energy. He saw them as large groups of energy particles. Some of these energy particles were even able to transfer energy between different types of matter.

Thanks to Einstein's work, energy became much better understood by modern scientists. Since the time of Thomas Young, work had been recognized as force acting over a distance. Einstein showed that energy is the *ability to create* force over any distance. In other words, according to Wiens, energy is "the ability to do work sometime in the future." It is the stored potential to be able to complete work.

10

26. Which statement best reflects the main idea of the passage?

    A. Scientists once believed that molecules and energy were the smallest parts of matter, but now they believe that molecules and atoms themselves are made up of even smaller energy particles.

    B. Scientists once defined energy as the ability to do physical work, but they now define it as the stored potential to complete work at some time in the future.

    C. Because of the work of Albert Einstein, modern scientists now have a better understanding of energy than did earlier scientists.

    D. Our understanding of energy developed from the work of three scientists: Thomas Young, James Prescott Joule, and Albert Einstein.

27. The word *severs* in the first paragraph means

    A. prepares.

    B. unites.

    C. splits.

    D. covers.

28. Which statement reflects the view of both James Prescott Joule and Albert Einstein?

    A. Molecules are the smallest parts of matter.

    B. Energy cannot be seen with the naked eye, so it does not exist.

    C. Energy is the ability to do physical work in the present moment.

    D. Molecules of matter are made up of energy.

29. According to the passage, Albert Einstein

   A. showed that energy is the ability to create force over any distance.

   B. showed that energy was made up of small particles called atoms.

   C. developed a way to view energy with the naked eye.

   D. developed the term "energy" about 200 years ago.

30. How did Albert Einstein's view of energy differ from that of Thomas Young?

   A. Einstein's view was more comprehensive than Young's, because Einstein saw energy as the potential to be able to do work.

   B. Einstein's view was more concrete than Young's, because Einstein saw energy as the ability to do physical work.

   C. Einstein's view was the opposite of Young's, because Einstein saw energy as the ability to do physical work.

   D. Einstein's view was more developed than Young's, because Einstein believed that molecules and atoms were the smallest parts of matter.

31. According to the passage, James Prescott Joule believed that the ability to do work

   A. could transfer between molecules.

   B. was constantly changing.

   C. was unable to be stored.

   D. was stored within matter.

10

PART III: Verbal Skills

Questions 32–36 refer to the following passage.

In 1911, an American named Hiram Bingham made a magnificent discovery in the Andes Mountains of Peru. Hidden deep in the Andean jungle and surrounded by mountain peaks lay the lost city of Machu Picchu, a sacred religious site built by the Inca Indians. Machu Picchu is located 43 miles northwest of a Peruvian city called Cusco. Cusco was conquered by the Spanish in 1532, but no mention was made of the remarkable city. Until Bingham's discovery in 1911, no one in the West knew that Machu Picchu even existed. Now, almost a century later, Machu Picchu is the best-known archeological site in South America.

Archeologists believe that when Machu Picchu was built around 1460, it was not built as a city. Instead, they believe, it was built as the royal estate of an Incan ruler named Pachacuti Inca Yupanqui. Machu Picchu doubled as the ruler's home and a religious retreat. It's located so high in the mountains—with an altitude of 8,000 feet—that it probably didn't have a military or host any major businesses.

Judging from the massive size of the "city," it must have housed many people during its day. Machu Picchu is made up of about 200 buildings. Most of these buildings were used as homes, but some were used as temples or for storage. Today, archeologists believe that about 1,200 people lived in the area of Machu Picchu and that most of these people were women, children, and priests.

32. How did Westerners learn of the existence of Machu Picchu?

   A. The site was discovered in 1911 by an American named Hiram Bingham.

   B. The site was discovered in 1420 by an Inca ruler named Pachacuti Inca Yupanqui.

   C. The site was discovered in 1532 by the Spanish, who conquered the Incas.

   D. The site was discovered in 1532 by an explorer named Cusco.

33. In this passage, Machu Picchu can best be described as

   A. a mythical city.

   B. the center of the Aztec Empire.

   C. the lost city of the Incan Empire.

   D. an example of Spanish colonization.

34. According to the passage, Machu Picchu is the

   A. largest archaeological site in South America.

   B. oldest archaeological site in South America.

   C. highest archaeological site in South America.

   D. most famous archaeological site in South America.

35. Archaeologists believe that the purpose of Machu Picchu was to serve as a

   A. home and religious retreat for the Incan ruler and his court.

   B. monastery exclusively for the use of Incan priests.

   C. fortress for Incan warriors.

   D. marketplace for traders from other parts of the Incan Empire.

10

36. Located near Machu Picchu, the city of Cusco was

    A. also lost, abandoned, and rediscovered like Machu Picchu.

    B. conquered by the Spanish.

    C. built around 1460.

    D. the burial site of Pachacuti Inca Yupanqui.

Questions 37–41 refer to the following passage.

Glutamate, or glutamic acid, is one of the amino acids present in our bodies. It serves as a neurotransmitter within the human body. As a neurotransmitter, glutamate works by sending signals to certain neurons, or nerve cells, located in the brain, spinal cord, and nervous system. Some researchers, such as Russell Blaylock and James South, have argued that glutamate is not safe to eat when added to food. When present in the blood in high levels, these researchers believe glutamate can destroy some types of brain cells.

How does this process of cell destruction occur? Neurotransmitters as a group fall into two types: those that *cause* nerve cells to act, and those that *stop* nerve cells from acting. Glutamate is one of the neurotransmitters that cause nerve cells to act. Although glutamate is commonly used, it is normally present in the brain in very small amounts. When gluten levels rise nerve cells in the brain to become too active, leading to destruction of the cells.

Since glutamate is found naturally in the body, the brain has ways of keeping glutamate levels in the brain from rising too high. One of these ways is a system called the *blood-brain barrier*. The blood-brain barrier was designed, writes Blaylock, to protect the brain against moderate increases of glutamate. It stops working as well when faced with large amounts of glutamate, such as those that enter the bloodstream when a person eats foods containing flavor enhancers.

Glutamate that is found naturally in foods does not pose as much of a risk of creating high levels of glutamate in the brain. This is because glutamate found naturally in foods occurs in its "bound" form, which means that it is bonded with other amino acids.

37. Which of the titles below best expresses the main idea of this selection?

    A. "The Effect of Glutamate on the Brain"

    B. "Glutamate as a Building Block of Cells"

    C. "Glutamate: The Most Common Neurotransmitter"

    D. "FDA Research on Glutamate"

38. How does excess glutamate in the brain destroy brain cells?

    A. It slows down the activity of nerve cells in the brain.

    B. It causes deterioration in the blood-brain barrier that protects the brain.

    C. It causes nerve cells in the brain to become overactive.

    D. It stops the hypothalamus from functioning.

39. Which type of glutamate does not pose much of a risk of creating high levels of glutamate in the brain?

   A. Glutamate in its free form

   B. Monosodium glutamate

   C. Hydrolyzed vegetable protein

   D. Glutamate that is bonded with other amino acids

40. As a neurotransmitter, glutamate

   A. stops nerve cells from acting.

   B. causes nerve cells to act.

   C. creates a barrier protecting the brain.

   D. slows down the brain's processing.

41. Glutamate in the brain

   A. helps strengthen the blood-brain barrier.

   B. blocks signals to nerve cells.

   C. is more potent in its bound form.

   D. is normally found in very small amounts.

10

Questions 42–45 refer to the following passage.

Janessa could not have had a tougher time falling asleep last night and woke up feeling exhausted. She has never been able to control the excitement she felt for an upcoming event, and she tossed and turned in bed until the sun rose that morning. Today was the day of her class trip to the Hopkins Planetarium. She did her best to shake off her tiredness and get ready for what she hoped would be a fun-filled day with her friends.

After getting dressed, Janessa raced down the stairs and nearly tripped over Marmalade, the families' orange tabby cat, which could almost always be found sleeping at the foot of the staircase.

"Slow down Janessa, or you might trip and fall!" Janessa's mom said. "Sit down, catch your breath, and have some breakfast."

"Sorry mom, I'm just excited." Janessa replied. "I've been looking forward to our trip to the planetarium for weeks!" Janessa took her usual seat at the kitchen table and rocked back and forth with excitement as her mom prepared a plate with scrambled eggs, toast, and bacon, which she placed in front of Janessa.

"I know you're excited," said Janessa's mom. "What part are you looking forward to the most?"

"I'm SO glad you asked me that!" Janessa beamed. "I hear they have the best presentation on black holes anywhere, and when they zoom in on the Milky Way solar system you can see HUNDREDS of stars and…" Janessa swung her hand wildly and knocked her plate onto the ground. It crashed, sending the uneaten food all over the floor.

Janessa's father came racing into the room. "What happened?" he asked.

"I think I got too excited…" Janessa replied. With that, her parents looked at each other and laughed.

"I tried to tell you, when people get too excited, they sometimes get careless" Janessa's mom said. Janessa's parents started cleaning up the mess.

"I know, I know… I just can't help it!" replied Janessa. "Dad, can you drive me to school? I can't wait to get there!"

Janessa's dad laughed and shook his head. "Some lessons are harder to learn than others," he said. "Ok, let's get in the car."

Janessa and her father got in the car and headed toward the school. The whole ride over, Janessa talked about the things she's been learning about in science class: the layers of the Earth, the planets, and photosynthesis. While her father paid careful attention to the road, Janessa spoke enthusiastically about her plans for her science project this year—a real working volcano—and got so excited that she gave herself the hiccups.

"Janessa, your mother and I tried to tell you—you have to try not to get too excited!"

"I know, I know…" Janessa said.

When Janessa arrived at school, she joined her classmates in the auditorium. Her teacher, Mrs. Ashton, had the students line up for the bus, but Janessa could hardly stand still. There was just one last thing before everyone could get on the bus and go to the planetarium. The teacher needed to collect the permission slips. Janessa fished around in her pockets and came up empty. At that moment, she learned the lesson that her parents were trying to teach her that morning.

42. According to the story, why was Janessa so tired that morning?

   A. She had a big test she was nervous about.

   B. She felt sick and couldn't fall asleep.

   C. She was too excited to sleep.

   D. Her cat kept waking her up during the night.

43. When Janessa's father says, "Some lessons are harder to learn than others," he means

   A. science is one of the most difficult subjects in school.

   B. you must study hard to do well on class exams.

   C. some students are smarter than others.

   D. sometimes it takes a person a long while to learn something.

44. Janessa was learning all the following things in science class *except*

   A. photosynthesis.

   B. magnetism.

   C. the layers of the Earth.

   D. the planets.

45. What lesson did Janessa finally learn at the end of the story?

   A. When someone gets too excited, they sometimes get careless and make mistakes.

   B. When someone stays up too late and wakes up tired, they are always more forgetful.

   C. When you don't eat a good breakfast in the morning, you're more likely to have accidents.

   D. It's difficult to forgive someone when they make mistakes, so try not to make mistakes very often.

10

Questions 46–50 refer to the following passage.

There used to be a saying in business that "if you make a better mousetrap, the world will beat a path to your door." This advice suggested to manufacturers that if they made a better product, and the product would be destined to sell. Unfortunately, this piece of advice <u>erroneously</u> ignored the role that prices play in affecting what consumers buy. It turns out that that role is very important.

In 1956, a better mousetrap *was* built by a company called the Pioneer Tool and Die Company. The mousetrap did not require the use of any bait (such as cheese), and it did not have any odor. It was a much higher quality product than the wooden mousetraps that households had been using. However, this mousetrap did not sell very well, and the company eventually stopped producing it. The key reason why consumers failed to buy the mousetrap was its price. The product sold for $29.95, compared to $0.07 for a plain wooden mousetrap.

The Pioneer Tool and Die Company set a high price for their better mousetraps because the mousetraps had more advanced features than regular mousetraps. The company learned from this experience, however, that people really did not care about the "better" qualities that were built into Pioneer mousetraps. At least, consumers did not value these qualities enough to pay a higher price for them. It turns out that consumers were really only willing to pay about 7 cents for an ordinary wooden mousetrap. These ordinary mousetraps sold the best.

When consumers refused to buy Pioneer mousetraps, Pioneer took their mousetraps off the market. It received a strong message from consumers that consumers did not want expensive mousetraps with lots of bells and whistles. Instead, consumers preferred a simple mousetrap at a very inexpensive cost.

10

46. The word *erroneously* in this context means

- **A.** bizarrely.
- **B.** mistakenly.
- **C.** wisely.
- **D.** quickly.

47. What happened to the expensive mousetraps produced by Pioneer Tool and Die Company?

- **A.** They were taken off the market.
- **B.** The company continues to produce them today.
- **C.** The company made them less expensive.
- **D.** The company made them easier to use.

48. Which is the most appropriate title for this passage?

- **A.** "A Cheaper Mousetrap"
- **B.** "A Successful Mousetrap"
- **C.** "An Electric Mousetrap"
- **D.** "A Better Mousetrap"

49. According to this passage, mousetraps preferred by consumers cost

- **A.** about $30.00.
- **B.** less than 10 cents each.
- **C.** 70 cents each.
- **D.** nothing, because they could be made at home.

50. The phrase "bells and whistles" in the last paragraph refers to the

A. sound the Pioneer Tool and Die mousetrap made when it snapped shut.

B. sleek and modern appearance of the Pioneer Tool and Die mousetrap.

C. fancy features on the Pioneer Tool and Die mousetrap.

D. fact that the Pioneer Tool and Die mousetrap did not use cheese for bait.

Exercise 2

Directions: Read each selection, then answer the questions that follow.

Questions 1–5 refer to the following passage.

Nowadays, the compound fluoride is found inside most American homes. It is the main ingredient in most toothpastes and has been used by dentists to help prevent tooth decay. The fluoride that is now used in dental care was developed as a result of the discovery of an element known as fluorine.

The discovery of fluorine began with the early work of Georg Bauer. Bauer was a German physician who studied the diseases of mine workers in the 1500s. In his work, Bauer described how a mineral known as "fluorspar" was used by miners in creating metal from ore. Fluorspar is a mineral found in nature in several different varieties. The purple version of fluorspar looks like amethyst, and the green version looks like emeralds.

In the 1600s and 1700s, scientists working with fluorspar saw that when the mineral was heated, it gave off a gas, which could create etchings in glass. However, it was not until 1771 that fluoric acid was discovered by a Swedish chemist named Carl Wilhelm Scheele. Once fluoric acid was discovered, the next step was to isolate the element fluorine. Many scientists unsuccessfully tried to isolate fluorine in dangerous experiments that cost some researchers their lives. The scientist who gets credit for isolating fluorine was a French chemist named Henri Moissan, who produced the element in 1886. Moissan's work was so significant that he won the Nobel Prize in chemistry in 1906.

Fluorine is a highly destructive, pale yellow gas. It participates in reactions with almost all substances, including gold and platinum. It explodes when it is mixed with hydrogen, and it causes glass, metals, ceramics, carbon, and water to burn with a bright flame. Even the salts of fluorine, known as fluorides, are very dangerous and should never be touched, inhaled, or swallowed.

10

1. What does the author mean when he states in paragraph 3 that certain experiments designed to isolate fluorine "cost some researchers their lives?"

   A. Some researchers spent their entire lives trying to isolate fluorine.

   B. Some researchers spent a great deal of money trying to isolate fluorine.

   C. Some researchers died in these experiments to try to isolate fluorine.

   D. Some researchers took on large amounts of debt to fund the experiments.

2. Which mineral was most important to the discovery of fluorine?

   A. Diamond

   B. Floures

   C. Emerald

   D. Fluorspar

3. Which of the following conclusions can be drawn about flourides?

   A. It is safer for researchers to touch flourides than to breathe in their fumes.

   B. Researchers should remember that flourides are more harmful than fluorine gas.

   C. Researchers should ensure that flouride fumes are released into the laboratory.

   D. Researchers should avoid contact with fluoride compounds.

4. Which of the following titles best expresses the main idea of this passage?

   A. "The Development of Toothpaste"

   B. "The Discovery of Fluorine"

   C. "The Dangers of Scientific Experiments"

   D. "The Isolation of Chemical Elements"

5. In the passage, fluorine is described as an element

   A. that is dangerous and should be banned before it takes more lives.

   B. for which no practical use has ever been discovered.

   C. that is dangerous but also has practical uses.

   D. that is extremely rare and valuable to most nations.

10

Questions 6–11 refer to the following passage.

The Berlin Wall was built in Berlin, Germany in 1961. It was built during the height of the Cold War, which was a period of tension between communist and democratic countries. At that time, the city of Berlin was divided into two parts. One part, the eastern part, had a communist government, and the other part (the western part) had a democratic government. Between 1949 and 1961, over 2 million people escaped from East Berlin to the western parts of Germany to be free from communism. The Berlin Wall was built to prevent East Germans from escaping.

The wall was an imposing landmark. It was built of concrete right in the middle of the city and topped with barbed wire. It was guarded by police with guns, and it separated East Berlin from West Berlin for twenty-eight years. During this time, it symbolized the strong division between communism and democracy.

Then, in 1989, all that changed. The wall was torn down due to riots by the people of East Berlin. The breach in the wall started during a visit by Mikhail Gorbachev, who was then head of the Soviet Union. Gorbachev was visiting East Germany to celebrate the country's 40th anniversary of communist government. When Gorbachev arrived, he was met with protesters. The East German people were unhappy with communism, and they chose this event to protest. On November 9, 1989, the protesters broke through the Berlin Wall. They demanded to be let into West Germany. The East German government crashed. The wall was quickly torn down, and millions of East Germans poured into West Germany.

For many years, the Berlin Wall had served not just as a symbol of the division between communism and democracy but also as a symbol of the Soviet Union's power. The Soviet Union had been the leader of the communist countries in Eastern Europe. When the Berlin Wall was destroyed, Soviet power soon declined also.

10

6. According to the author, what caused the fall of the Berlin Wall?

   A. Riots by the people of East Berlin

   B. Protests by the Soviet people

   C. The Cold War between the Soviet Union and the United States

   D. Striking workers in Poland

7. Which statement is true, according to the passage?

   A. The building of the Berlin Wall led to the Cold War.

   B. The Berlin Wall was necessary to protect West Germany from communism.

   C. The destruction of the Berlin Wall led to the decline of the Soviet Union.

   D. Soviet leader Mikhail Gorbachev caused the destruction of the Berlin Wall.

8. The Berlin Wall was built to

   A. prevent West Germans from entering East Germany.

   B. control trade between East and West Germany.

   C. prevent East Germans from escaping to West Germany.

   D. divide the city into four sections.

9. Soviet leader Mikhail Gorbachev visited East Berlin in November 1989 to

   A. put down protests of communism.

   B. celebrate the 40th anniversary of the Russian Revolution.

   C. conduct negotiations with West Germany.

   D. celebrate 40 years of communist rule in East Germany.

10. The wall was built of

A. stone topped with steel spikes.

B. concrete topped by barbed wire.

C. brick topped with iron spikes.

D. steel topped by barbed wire.

11. The wall was built in 1961 during a period of tension between democratic and communist nations commonly known as

A. the nuclear arms race.

B. détente.

C. the Red Scare.

D. the Cold War.

Questions 12–18 refer to the following passage.

Science is so much a part of our world today that we take it for granted as having always existed. As hard as it may be for us to believe, science in fact did not always exist. It was "invented" in the 1600s, and it went through many different developments before becoming the process that we utilize today.

The birth of modern science is usually traced back to the work of an English philosopher named Sir Francis Bacon. Before Bacon's time, scientific theories as we know them did not exist. Instead, ideas that were considered knowledge were based upon faith, and most came from the philosophies of the church. Bacon was very opposed to this approach to knowledge. He disliked the notion that knowledge could be based simply on beliefs or on the ideas of the church. He searched for a way of developing knowledge that he felt was more reliable.

Bacon was very interested in the facts that could be gained from simply observing what goes on around us in the physical world. He believed that observing the physical world would produce much more reliable knowledge than simply making up knowledge based on beliefs. In 1620, Bacon published a book containing his ideas on the importance of developing knowledge through observation of nature. This book, called *The New Organon*, created a foundation for what is now known as "empirical" science, or science that comes from observing that which can be perceived through our senses.

Bacon's approach came to be known by the name *inductivism*. Inductivism is the idea that theories about science can be developed from observing events. In the inductivist approach, the scientist views a series of repeating events and draws a general conclusion from these events. The scientist takes this conclusion to be true *because* it is based on experience. A scientist using the inductivist approach might conclude, for instance, that "all swans are white," based solely on the fact that all swans that he has previously observed are white.

12. Which of the following titles best expresses the main idea of this passage?

A. "Understanding the Scientific Method"

B. "Bacon and the Development of Science"

C. "Testing Hypotheses and Theories"

D. "The History of Sir Francis Bacon"

13. Why did Sir Francis Bacon search for a way to develop knowledge based on observing the physical world?

   A. He believed that knowledge based on observing similar, repeated events was unreliable.

   B. He believed that knowledge based on the principle of inductivism was unreliable.

   C. He believed that knowledge based on faith, or the ideas of the church, was unreliable.

   D. He believed that knowledge based on the principle of falsification was unreliable.

14. Bacon's approach to science was known as

   A. inductivism.

   B. positivism.

   C. radicalism.

   D. relativism.

15. Before Bacon, scientific knowledge was based on

   A. concepts from astronomy.

   B. rigorous testing.

   C. legal precepts.

   D. the ideas of the church.

16. Bacon's book, *The New Organon*, focused on

   A. refining knowledge that is based on personal beliefs.

   B. developing knowledge that can be perceived through the senses.

   C. revising the ideas of political leaders of Bacon's time.

   D. practicing strict scientific discipline in all research.

17. Which of the following would Bacon be most likely to accept as scientific knowledge?

   A. Ideas based on church doctrine

   B. Untested philosophical concepts

   C. Theories based on empirical facts

   D. A hypothesis based on opinion

18. Inductivist theories are developed from

   A. observing events.

   B. scientific mistakes.

   C. ongoing debates.

   D. experimental competitions.

10

Questions 19–23 refer to the following passage.

The animal kingdom is filled with interesting and wondrous creatures—both big and small—and among them is the awe-inspiring hippopotamus. The hippo, or *Hippopotamus amphibious*, is an herbivorous mammal that typically resides in sub-Saharan regions of Africa. The name "hippopotamus" has ancient Greek origins, meaning "river horse," despite bearing little resemblance to the other animals of the same name. Hippos have existed on Earth for several million years, with the earliest known fossilized examples dating back approximately 16 million years.

If you've ever seen a hippo, there's little chance that you'd forget it. They are among the largest and heaviest land mammals that currently exist on Earth, behind only elephants and rhinoceroses. The average weight of this undeniably prodigious animal, which stands at approximately 5 feet tall, is approximately 3,500 lbs. What do these large animals eat? Surprisingly, their diet largely consists of creeping grass, reeds, green shoots, and other vegetation.

Hippos have a smooth, cylindrical shape that's nearly hairless; high-set eyes, ears, and nostrils; large tusk-filled jaws; and distinctively squat, dainty legs (with webbed feet) for such a rotund animal. Their unique physical characteristics suit their semiaquatic lifestyle quite well—hippos spend a great deal of time staying cool in nearby rivers and lakes.

Some individuals mistakenly assume that these jolly-looking animals come with a sweet, harmless personality. They couldn't be more wrong! Despite appearances, hippos have garnered quite a reputation for unpredictable displays of vicious, aggressive behavior. They are capable of surprising bursts of speed (up to 19 mph) and are more than willing to use the immense power of their huge jaws to crush any foe who threatens their territory or safety. Few animals—living or extinct—can match the sheer bite force of the hippopotamus.

The relationship between humans and hippos could best be characterized as tenuous at best. Despite their penchant for fierceness, hippos are still threatened by poachers who are on the hunt for ivory. And humans aren't free from hippo harm; hippos have been known to randomly attack boats and hurt their unlucky passengers. It's safe to say that hippos and humans are best served when they maintain a safe and respectful distance from each other.

19. What title best expresses the main idea of the passage?

   A. "The Wide World of Large Animals"

   B. "A Closer Look at Sub-Saharan Africa"

   C. "Getting to Know the Hippopotamus"

   D. "The Strange Relationship between Humans and Hippos"

20. All the following characteristics of the hippopotamus are mentioned in the passage *except*

   A. a keen intelligence.

   B. aggressive behavior.

   C. surprising speed.

   D. strong jaws.

21. Based on paragraph 2 of the passage, what does *prodigious* most likely mean?

   A. Quite angry

   B. Very big

   C. Short tempered

   D. Fiercely loyal

22. What does the author mean when he states in paragraph 5 that the "relationship between humans and hippos could best be characterized as tenuous at best"?

    A. There is a history of mutual aggression between humans and hippos.

    B. Humans have long enjoyed learning more about how hippos live.

    C. Both humans and hippos enjoy staying cool while swimming in lakes.

    D. Humans rarely have opportunities to see hippos in their native habitat.

23. According to the information provided in the passage, which of the following meals would most likely appeal to a hippopotamus?

    A. Meat from a gazelle

    B. River trout

    C. A ripe pineapple

    D. Grazeable grass

Questions 24–28 refer to the following passage.

THE RHODORA

In May, when sea-winds pierced our solitudes,
I found the fresh Rhodora in the woods,
Spreading its leafless blooms in a damp nook,
To please the desert and the sluggish brook.
The purple petals, fallen in the pool,
Made the black water with their beauty gay;
Here might the red-bird come his plumes to cool,
And court the flower that cheapens his array.
Rhodora! if the sages ask thee why
This charm is wasted on the earth and sky,
Tell them, dear, that if eyes were made for seeing,
Then Beauty is its own excuse for being:
Why thou wert there, O rival of the rose!
I never thought to ask, I never knew:
But, in my simple ignorance suppose
The self-same Power that brought me there brought you.

—*Ralph Waldo Emerson*

24. The poet is impressed with the beauty of

    A. the sea.

    B. the woods.

    C. a bird.

    D. a flower.

25. When the poet says that the flower cheapens the array of the red-bird, he means that the

    A. bird gets nothing from the flower.

    B. flower gets nothing from the bird.

    C. color of the flower is brighter than that of the bird.

    D. bird ruins the flower.

10

26. In saying "This charm is wasted on the earth and sky," the poet means that

   A. the earth and sky do not appreciate beauty.

   B. no one sees a flower that blooms deep in the woods.

   C. wise men sometimes ask foolish questions.

   D. the bird does not even notice the beauty of the flower.

27. The poet believes that

   A. flower petals pollute the water.

   B. red birds are garish.

   C. beauty exists for its own sake.

   D. sea-wind is refreshing.

28. The poet probably

   A. is an insensitive person.

   B. dislikes solitude.

   C. is a religious person.

   D. is ignorant.

10

ANSWER KEYS AND EXPLANATIONS

Exercise 1

1. B	11. D	21. A	31. D	41. D
2. C	12. B	22. A	32. A	42. C
3. C	13. C	23. A	33. C	43. D
4. D	14. B	24. D	34. D	44. B
5. B	15. D	25. B	35. A	45. A
6. A	16. D	26. B	36. B	46. B
7. B	17. C	27. C	37. A	47. A
8. A	18. D	28. D	38. C	48. D
9. D	19. B	29. A	39. D	49. B
10. C	20. A	30. A	40. B	50. C

1. **The correct answer is B.** The passage tells us that Henry Ford was fired from his first job because he worked so quickly. This shows that Ford was a very efficient worker, as choice B states. The passage shows that Ford was very interested in mechanics as a youngster, but it never states that Ford was better at mechanics than at business, so choice A is incorrect.

2. **The correct answer is C.** We're told in paragraph 1 that Ford started his first business selling watches the year after he was 11, which means he started selling them when he was 12 years old. Choice A shows that Ford started working in the auto industry when he was 17, but this company wasn't a business that Ford owned.

3. **The correct answer is C.** The passage tells us that Henry Ford was a "natural business-man," meaning that an aptitude for and interest in business were part of his life from his earliest years. This idea is developed through various examples of Ford's ambitions and talents throughout his youth. Choice B is incorrect because although the passage describes the watch-making business Ford engaged in as a boy, it also covers his entry into the auto industry in his late teens.

4. **The correct answer is D.** The passage tells us that Ford sold each watch for $1.00 and points out that Ford only earned $1.10 a day at his first job in the auto industry. Therefore, he sold his watches for almost a full day's wage for a factory worker, making $1.00 a relatively high price for that time. Though the passage later tells us that Ford was an efficient worker, it does not state how long it took him to make a watch, so choice B is not the correct answer.

5. **The correct answer is B.** This main idea question requires you to locate the sentence that best describes the main point of the *entire* passage. This passage starts by describing Mozart's gifts as a musician and a composer, and then it explains his contribution to music. Choice B summarizes the main point clearly as it states: "Mozart was an extremely talented musician and composer whose contributions have a significant impact on music."

6. **The correct answer is A.** This question asks you to define the meaning of *prodigy*, a word that you may not be familiar with. When you are faced with unfamiliar words, you can use clues from the sentence to help you define them. If necessary, you can reread the part of

10

the passage that the sentence was taken from to gain more clues about the meaning of the vocabulary word.

The sentence that contains the word *prodigy* tells us that Mozart was highly musically talented. Paragraph 2 tells us how gifted he was as a child. The word *prodigy* must therefore mean "a child who is talented or gifted." Choice A comes closest to this meaning, so it is correct.

7. **The correct answer is B.** This is a "compare and contrast" question. It asks you to identify the difference between Mozart's sonatas and the sonatas that were written before his time.

   The answers to compare-and-contrast questions are often embedded directly in the text. If you look back to the part of the passage that describes sonatas (paragraphs 3 and 4), you will find a sentence that explains how Mozart wrote sonatas: "Mozart also wrote sonatas, but he added depth to the sonatas and gave them more structure." This sentence describes the main difference between Mozart's sonatas and the sonatas that existed previously, which is reflected in answer choice B.

8. **The correct answer is A.** The passage states in the first paragraph that Mozart wrote more compositions than any other composer in history. The passage does not state how many symphonies he wrote compared to other composers, nor does it state the number of movements he included in his compositions, so choices B and C are incorrect. The passage does make it clear that Mozart wrote a variety of compositions, so choice D is incorrect.

9. **The correct answer is D.** The passage states that Mozart learned to play the piano at the age of 3 and composed his first work at the age of 4. The passage does not state the nature of the composition, so choice B is

incorrect. Nor does the passage indicate the he learned to play the trumpet, which makes choice A incorrect as well.

10. **The correct answer is C.** The passage states that the separate parts of a musical composition are called movements. The words *elements* and *aspects* can be synonyms for parts, but the passage does not mention these words when describing musical compositions, so choices A and D are incorrect.

11. **The correct answer is D.** Paragraph 3 tells us that a sonata is a composition for one or two solo instruments. It does not state that the instruments must be a stringed instrument and a woodwind, so choice B is incorrect.

12. **The correct answer is B.** Although the passage does not specifically state that Mozart was born in Austria, the phrase "other regions in Austria," indicates that Mozart resided in a part of Austria, making choices C and D incorrect. The other countries mentioned in the passage are Germany, France, and Italy. England is not mentioned, so choice A is also incorrect.

13. **The correct answer is C.** The passage states that Mozart's travels exposed him to many types of music, which helped him compose sonatas with more depth and structure, as stated in choice C. The passage does not mention that he learned any foreign languages during those travels, so choice D is incorrect.

14. **The correct answer is B.** This "vocabulary" question asks you to identify the meaning of a word that you may not be familiar with. In such cases, the best way to define such a word is by using the context of the sentence to help you. Sometimes it can also be helpful to reread the paragraph that the sentence came from to get more clues about the meaning of the vocabulary word.

    In this case, we're told that Aunt Frieda has recently had surgery on her eye. She is coming to visit her mother after the surgery. When she exits the car, she walks like someone who can't see very well. Someone who can't see very well would probably walk in a *careful* manner, so we're looking for a word that has a meaning similar to *careful*. Answer choice B, *cautiously*, is close in meaning to *careful*, and it makes sense in the context of this sentence.

15. **The correct answer is D.** This "compare and contrast" question asks you to identify the difference between two of the characters in the story. In this case, the character of the grandfather is described in the last paragraph of the passage. The author states that his grandfather was "a very quiet man who lived a routine, predictable life." We know that the author's grandmother, on the other hand, became upset very easily whenever things didn't go her way. Choice D summarizes this difference between the characters nicely.

16. **The correct answer is D.** This question concerns one specific detail from the passage. The correct answers to detail questions are given directly within the passage. If you can't remember the answer, you can find it by rereading the necessary part of the passage. At the beginning of paragraph 2, the author tells us that "One day, when I was about fifteen, I saw that the letters from my Aunt Frieda were coming written in Uncle Stuart's handwriting. I realized that Aunt Frieda wasn't really writing them . . . " The author knew that Aunt Frieda wasn't writing the letters because he could tell that the handwriting belonged to his Uncle Stuart.

17. **The correct answer is C.** The passage states that *Nana* controlled the family finances and made most of the decisions, so choice C is the correct answer. Choice A is incorrect because, although she did not speak English, the author translated the letters from her children, so she was not cut off from them.

18. **The correct answer is D.** The author describes *Nana* as "crying inside" and feeling "powerless" when she sees Aunt Frieda and repeatedly saying that as a mother she should have been with her child at the hospital, making choice D the correct answer. Although it might make sense to suspect that she was also a little angry, she does not seem angry at the author about the deception regarding the letters, so choice C is incorrect.

19. **The correct answer is B.** When the letters started coming in Uncle Stuart's handwriting, the author did not inform Nana because she was easily worried, as is noted in paragraph 2: "My grandmother was a real worrier, and I didn't want her to get upset…" At the end of the passage, the author remarks that she was also "smart as a whip," making choice B the correct answer. The author does not reveal how much formal education she had, so choices C and D are incorrect.

20. **The correct answer is A.** Aunt Grace tells the author that Aunt Frieda is "recovering just fine," a reassuring statement that makes choice A the correct answer. Choice B is incorrect because "console" means to comfort another person at a time of grief, sorrow, or disappointment. Choice D is also incorrect because Aunt Grace's response is intended to be reassuring to the author, even though *Nana* later finds the news distressing.

21. **The correct answer is A.** If necessary, reread the selection. Clearly, the observer is fascinated by the scene before him. He gives no indication of being frightened or repulsed and is far too interested to be bored.

22. **The correct answer is A.** The Flemish painting was brought over from Holland.

23. **The correct answer is A.** At the beginning of the selection, the game is being played on a level spot with nine pins. At the end of the passage, balls are rolled, presumably at the pins. This is a variety of bowling.

10

24. The correct answer is D. Because paragraph 2 starts with, "What seemed particularly odd to Rip," we can assume that Rip is the observer. All the other choices *could* be true, but we have no confirming evidence in the selection, whereas the selection does tell us that the man's name is Rip.

25. The correct answer is B. In the first sentence of the last paragraph, Rip found it "particularly odd" that the men maintained such grave faces while evidently amusing themselves.

26. The correct answer is B. This question asks you to identify the main idea, or main point, of the entire passage. The correct answer will be broad enough to cover the entire passage, but narrow enough to describe its specific message. It must also describe this specific message accurately.

This passage basically provides us with a comparison of two views of energy: the original view, developed 200 years ago, and the current view now held by scientists. Paragraph 1 tells us that the original view, developed by Thomas Young, held that energy was "the ability to do physical work." The last paragraph tells us that the current view, developed by Albert Einstein, is that energy is "the stored potential to be able to complete work." This point is best summarized in choice B.

27. The correct answer is C. The word *severs* is found in the first paragraph of the passage. Here, we are presented with a definition of the term *energy*. We are told that the term *energy* was developed by a scientist named Thomas Young, who originally believed that energy was the ability to do physical work. Energy, Young thought, was like the work that an axe does when it comes down on a log and cuts the log into two pieces. The force of the axe acts on the log to break it in two.

You're looking for a word with a meaning similar to "cuts" or "breaks." *Splits* is the best option here because it reflects the action an axe takes when it divides a log in two.

28. The correct answer is D. To answer this question, you must identify a statement that reflects the views of *both* Joule and Einstein. The correct answer must express a belief shared by each scientist. If an answer choice contains the view of only one of the scientists, or neither of them, that choice will be incorrect.

Choice D reflects a belief that was held by both Joule and Einstein. Both scientists believed that molecules and atoms were made up of energy. Paragraph 2 tells us that Joule thought that "molecules contained very small forms of energy." Paragraph 3 tells us that Einstein thought that "molecules and atoms were made up of energy."

29. The correct answer is A. The last half of the passage is the place to look for the answer to this question. If we go back and reread paragraphs 3 and 4, we see that Einstein made two important discoveries that helped change our view of energy. First, as paragraph 3 tells us, he helped us understand that molecules and atoms were made up of large groups of energy particles. Second, as paragraph 4 states, Einstein broadened our definition of energy to "the ability to create force over any distance." This second discovery is mentioned in choice A.

Choice B is incorrect because it reflects the opposite of Einstein's view. Einstein did not show that energy was made up of atoms; on the contrary, he showed that molecules and atoms were made up of energy. Choice C is also incorrect, because the passage never states that Einstein invented a way to view energy with the naked eye. Finally, choice D is incorrect, because it is false, based on the passage. Einstein did not develop the term

10

energy. It is true that this term was developed about 200 years ago, as the passage tells us in paragraph 1, but it was developed by Thomas Young, not Einstein.

30. **The correct answer is A.** This question asks you to compare two views about energy that are given in the passage. The first view is that of Einstein, given toward the end of the passage. The second view is that of Thomas Young, given at the beginning of the passage. To answer the question, then, you must understand the difference between the two views.

The passage tells us in paragraph 1 that Young saw energy as the ability to do physical work. It then tells us in the last paragraph that Einstein saw energy as the stored potential to complete physical work. In other words, Young believed that energy was the ability to do work now, whereas Einstein saw it as the ability to do work at some time in the future. Einstein's view is stated accurately only in choice A.

31. **The correct answer is D.** Paragraph 2 describes Joule's beliefs about the ability to do work. It states that Joule believed "the ability to do work was stored within the molecules of matter," as stated in choice D.

32. **The correct answer is A.** To answer this question, you must identify the factor that enabled Western people to learn that Machu Picchu existed. Paragraph 1 tells us that Machu Picchu was discovered by an American named Hiram Bingham in 1911, and that "Until Bingham's discovery in 1911, no one in the West knew that Machu Picchu even existed." Westerners learned about the site because of Bingham's discovery, so choice A is the best answer.

33. **The correct answer is C.** The passage focuses on the rediscovery of Machu Picchu, after it was lost to history for many centuries. It was not mentioned in Spanish accounts of the Inca, so choice D is incorrect. The term

mythical refers to something that doesn't exist, making choice A incorrect. The Aztecs are not mentioned in the passage, so choice B is incorrect.

34. **The correct answer is D.** The passage states that Machu Picchu is the most well-known archaeological site in South America. The passage does not compare or contrast it with other archaeological sites, so we are not given enough information to determine if it is the largest, oldest, or highest in altitude.

35. **The correct answer is A.** The passage states that archaeologists believe the site was used as both a home and religious retreat, making choice A the correct answer. The high altitude made it unlikely that it could have any military or business value, so choices C and D are incorrect. The passage makes it clear that women and children also occupied Machu Picchu, so choice B is also incorrect.

36. **The correct answer is B.** The passage states that Cusco was conquered by the Spanish in 1532, though the Spanish apparently made no mention of Machu Picchu in their records. The passage does not state when Cusco was built or where Pachacuti Inca Yupanqui is buried, so choices C and D are incorrect.

37. **The correct answer is A.** The passage describes how glutamate works and how it can destroy certain types of brain cells. It addresses the impact of glutamate on the brain, so "The Effect of Glutamate on the Brain" is the best title. Choices B, C, and D aren't mentioned in the passage.

38. **The correct answer is C.** The correct answer can be found in the last sentence of paragraph 2: "When levels of glutamate become high, this prompts nerve cells in the brain to become too active, which leads to destruction of the cells." Excess glutamate destroys brain cells by causing nerve cells in the brain to become too active, so choice C is correct.

10

39. **The correct answer is D.** Paragraph 4 tells us that glutamate found naturally in foods poses a low risk of causing high levels of glutamate in the brain. It goes on to explain that natural glutamate is bonded with other amino acids, so choice D is correct.

40. **The correct answer is B.** Paragraph 2 states that there are two types of neurotransmitters: those that *cause* nerve cells to act and those neurotransmitters that *stop* nerve cells from acting. Glutamate is one of the neurotransmitters that cause nerve cells to act.

41. **The correct answer is D.** Paragraph 2 states that glutamate is normally present in the brain in very small amounts. Choice B is incorrect, because paragraph 1 states that glutamate *sends* signals to nerve cells rather than blocking them.

42. **The correct answer is C.** The passage states that Janessa had a tough time falling asleep last night and woke up tired because she has never been able to control the excitement she feels for an upcoming event, and this was the morning of her class trip, which she was very excited about. There is no mention of an upcoming test, so choice A is incorrect. The story did not mention that Janessa was sick or that her cat kept her up that night, so choices B and D are also incorrect.

43. **The correct answer is D.** When Janessa's father said, "Some lessons are harder to learn than others," he was talking about what Janessa's mother had said—that when people get too excited, they sometimes get careless. He meant that sometimes people make mistakes multiple times before learning their lesson, so choice D is the correct answer. There is no mention that he thinks science is the toughest subject in school, so choice A is incorrect. He also doesn't talk about studying hard to do well on exams, even if he thinks that's true, so choice B is incorrect. He also says nothing about some students being smarter than others, so choice C is also incorrect.

44. **The correct answer is B.** Use the information provided in the passage to answer this question. While riding in the car to school, Janessa talks to her father about the things she's learning in science class. The only topic she doesn't mention among the answer choices is magnetism (choice B).

45. **The correct answer is A.** At the end of the story, after checking her pockets for the trip permission slip and realizing she forgot it at home, Janessa finally realized the truth of what her parents were telling her that morning: if you get too excited, you may get careless and make mistakes, such as forgetting something. The lessons in the other answer choices may be important and worth learning, but they are not what Janessa finally realized when she discovered that she didn't have the trip permission slip.

46. **The correct answer is B.** To answer this question, it is helpful to first reread the paragraph that contains the sentence with the word *erroneously*. The sentence comes near the end of the first paragraph. Paragraph 1 tells us that some people used to believe that "if you build a better product, that product will definitely sell." It was discovered, however, that this idea was false.

Sentence 3 of the paragraph tells us that the piece of advice was wrong because it "ignored the role that prices play in affecting what consumers buy." We are therefore looking for a definition of *erroneously* that means something like "incorrectly." *Mistakenly* best fits the definition that we're looking for.

47. **The correct answer is A.** Companies used to believe that people would always buy better products if those products were available on the market. This belief, however, turned out not to be true, as the Pioneer company learned. The Pioneer Tool and Die Company built a very high-quality mousetrap, but people wouldn't buy it because it was too

expensive. The company therefore stopped producing or selling it.

48. **The correct answer is D.** The passage focuses on the fact that the Pioneer Tool and Die Company built a mousetrap that was better than others on the market, making choice D the correct answer. The mousetrap was not inexpensive, nor was it a successful product, so choices A and B are incorrect. The passage does not indicate if any of the features of the new mousetrap were powered by electricity, so choice C is also incorrect.

49. **The correct answer is B.** The passage states that the mousetraps most consumers preferred cost about seven cents each, making choice B the correct answer. Although it

is possible that mousetraps could be made at home, the passage does not address that issue, so choice D is incorrect.

50. **The correct answer is C.** The passage uses the phrase "bells and whistles" as a metaphor for the fancy features of the Pioneer Tool and Die mousetrap in contrast to the plain and simple one preferred by consumers, making choice C the correct answer. The passage does not state anything about the sounds the mousetrap made or its appearance, so choices A and B are incorrect. Choice D is also incorrect, because although this is one feature of the Pioneer mousetrap, the phrase "lots of bells and whistles" refers to multiple features of the device.

Exercise 2

1. C	7. C	13. C	19. C	24. D
2. D	8. C	14. A	20. A	25. C
3. D	9. D	15. D	21. B	26. B
4. B	10. B	16. B	22. A	27. C
5. C	11. D	17. C	23. D	28. C
6. A	12. B	18. A		

1. **The correct answer is C.** Paragraph 3 tells us that it was difficult to isolate fluorine because fluorine was very dangerous and destructive. The statement that it "cost some researchers their lives" tells us that certain researchers died during these destructive experiments.

2. **The correct answer is D.** This question is what is known as a "detail" question. It asks about a detail from the passage. The correct answer to detail questions will always be contained in the passage. In this case, paragraph 2 tells us that the discovery of fluorine began with a scientist named Georg Bauer, who first described a mineral known as "fluorspar." The third paragraph then tells us that scientists working with fluorspar saw that when the mineral was heated, it gave

off a gas. It took years to isolate the element fluorine, but the process started with the research on fluorspar by Bauer.

3. **The correct answer is D.** This last paragraph of the passage lets us know that fluorides are extremely dangerous and that they should never be touched, inhaled, or swallowed. The last paragraph is warning us that fluorides could harm the human body upon contact. Choice D reflects this conclusion, so it is correct.

4. **The correct answer is B.** The passage deals primarily with the discovery and isolation of fluorine, making choice B the correct answer. Choice D, which refers to chemical elements in general, is incorrect because fluorine is the only element that the passage discusses in detail. Toothpaste and the dangers

encountered by those experimenting with fluorine are details in the passage that contribute to the main idea, but choices A and C do not reflect the emphasis of the passage.

5. **The correct answer is C.** The passage describes a practical use for fluorine as fluoride in toothpaste in the first paragraph and warns of its dangers in pure form in the last paragraph, making choice C the correct answer. The passage does not discuss the rarity or monetary value of fluorine, so choice D is incorrect.

6. **The correct answer is A.** This "cause and effect" question asks you to identify the factor that *caused* the Berlin Wall to fall. To answer it, you should first reread the paragraph that describes the destruction of the wall. Paragraph 3 tells us (in sentence 2) that the wall was torn down due to riots by the people of East Berlin, so choice A is the correct answer.

7. **The correct answer is C.** The last paragraph states that the Berlin Wall was a symbol of the Soviet Union, and that the destruction of the wall soon led to a decline of Soviet power. Although Gorbachev was present when protestors first broke though the wall, the passage does not state that he was the cause of that protest, making choice D incorrect.

8. **The correct answer is C.** Paragraph 1 states that the wall was built to prevent East Germans from escaping to West Germany. The passage states that the city had already been divided before the wall was built, and it was divided into two parts, so choice D is incorrect.

9. **The correct answer is D.** Paragraph 2 states that Gorbachev's visit was prompted by the 40th anniversary of communist rule in East Germany. The Russian Revolution occurred much earlier in 1917 and is not mentioned in the passage, making choice B incorrect.

10. **The correct answer is B.** The second paragraph of the passage states that the wall was an "imposing landmark" built of concrete topped with barbed wire.

11. **The correct answer is D.** The term *Cold War* is mentioned in paragraph 1. This term refers to the period roughly between the end of World War II in 1945 and the fall of the Soviet Union in 1989, when the democratic countries led by the United States and the communist countries led by the Soviet Union engaged in a conflict without direct military confrontation.

12. **The correct answer is B.** The passage discusses Francis Bacon's contributions to the development of science. Choice B best reflects this content. Choice D is incorrect, because it is too narrow. Choice C is outside the scope of the passage.

13. **The correct answer is C.** To answer this "cause and effect" question, you must identify the *reason* why Francis Bacon chose to look for a new approach to knowledge. Why did he wish to develop an approach based on the observation of physical events? The answer to this question is revealed for us in paragraphs 2 and 3 of the passage. These paragraphs tell us that before Bacon's time, knowledge was based on the beliefs of the church. Bacon did not like the idea of basing knowledge only on faith or belief. The last sentence of paragraph 2 tells us that Bacon "searched for a way of developing knowledge that he felt was more reliable." This sentence suggests that Bacon felt that knowledge based on the beliefs of the church was *not* very reliable, so choice C is correct.

14. **The correct answer is A.** Paragraph 4 of the passage tells us that Bacon's approach came to be known by the name *inductivism*.

15. **The correct answer is D.** According to paragraph 2, scientific knowledge before Bacon's time was based on religious ideas and the

doctrine of the church. Ideas that were considered knowledge were based on faith, so choice D is correct.

16. **The correct answer is B.** The answer to this question is in paragraph 3. *The New Organon*, published in 1620, became the foundation for what we know today as the "empirical" sciences. It addressed how to develop knowledge gained from observing that which can be perceived through the senses, making B the correct answer. Choice D is incorrect, because the passage does not mention that the book emphasized practicing strict scientific discipline in all research.

17. **The correct answer is C.** To answer this inference question, you must draw on information given in the passage to make a logical deduction. Bacon did not support scientific ideas based on church doctrine, so choice A is incorrect. He advocated that science should be based on empirical research, or what could be observed through the senses, so choice C is the correct answer.

18. **The correct answer is A.** Sentence 2 of paragraph 4 tells us that inductivism is the idea that theories about science can be developed from observing events. Choices B, C, and D are incorrect, because these factors are not mentioned as important for inductivism.

19. **The correct answer is C.** The clear focus of the passage is the hippopotamus, including its behavioral and physical characteristics. Therefore, the best choice for a title would be "Getting to Know the Hippopotamus." Although Sub-Saharan Africa (choice B) and a few large animals (choice A) are mentioned in the passage, they are small supporting details. There is no mention of the relationship between humans and hippos as being strange, so choice D is incorrect.

20. **The correct answer is A.** The passage discusses a variety of the hippo's common characteristics, including its aggressive behavior

(choice B), surprising speed (choice C), and strong jaws (choice D). The only characteristic among the answer choices that isn't mentioned in the passage is a keen intelligence.

21. **The correct answer is B.** The sentence in which the word *prodigious* appears discusses the immense size and weight of the hippopotamus. Based on the context, it can be determined that *prodigious* means "very large."

22. **The correct answer is A.** The tenuous, or uncertain, relationship between humans and hippos, as described by the author, refers to the acts of aggression that have come from both sides. According to the passage, human poachers have hunted hippos for their ivory, and hippos have been known to attack boats filled with people. Therefore, choice A is the correct answer.

23. **The correct answer is D.** Information on the dietary habits of the hippopotamus is provided in paragraph 2. There we are told that the herbivorous mammal's diet "largely consists of creeping grass," which makes *grazeable grass* the correct answer. Hippos do not eat meat or fish, and there's no mention of pineapple or other fruits in the passage, so choices A, B, and C are incorrect.

24. **The correct answer is D.** The poem really is an ode to the flower.

25. **The correct answer is C.** The poet is saying that while the bird is splendid, the flower is even more beautiful.

26. **The correct answer is B.** The flower blooms deep in the woods where, except for the occasional wanderer like himself, no one sees it.

27. **The correct answer is C.** "Then beauty is its own excuse for being."

28. **The correct answer is C.** In saying "The self-same Power that brought me there brought you," the poet is expressing his faith in a Supreme Being that created man and nature.

10

Chapter 11

Spelling

OVERVIEW

- **Tips for Improving Your Spelling Skills**
- **Twenty-Four Spelling Rules**
- **Summing It Up**
- **Exercises: Spelling**
- **Answer Keys and Explanations**

The HSPT and TACHS exams both include several test questions that check spelling skills. In these questions, you are presented with a series of answer choices. Some of the choices contain sentences, but the last choice will always be "No Mistakes." You are asked to read the sentences and check for errors in capitalization, punctuation, usage, or spelling. If you believe the text contains no errors, choose "No Mistakes."

Spelling is a weakness for many students. The ability to spell well does not seem to be directly related to any measurable factor, including intelligence; many very intelligent people struggle with spelling. A few fortunate individuals are just natural spellers—they can hear a word and instinctively spell it correctly. Most people, however, must memorize rules and spellings, and rely on a dictionary.

Here are some tips to help improve your spelling, followed by a list of spelling rules. Use them to prepare for spelling questions on the HSPT and TACHS exams and to ensure a good score.

11

TIPS FOR IMPROVING YOUR SPELLING SKILLS

You can improve your spelling by keeping a list of words that you spell incorrectly or need to look up repeatedly. Add to this list whenever you find a word you can't spell. Set aside a few minutes to study spelling and write down each word correctly ten times. If you know how to type, type each word ten times, too. Let your hands get used to the feeling of spelling a difficult word correctly. Let your eye become accustomed to seeing a difficult word spelled correctly. Ask someone to read your list aloud to you on occasion and try writing them correctly. Frequent self-testing of problematic words should help you learn the correct spellings. On the day before the test, read back over your list carefully.

Another way to improve your spelling is to develop mnemonic devices. A mnemonic device is a private clue that you develop to help you remember something. For example, if you have trouble spelling the word *friend*, you might find it helpful to remember the sentence, "A friend is true to the *end*." This little sentence will help you remember to place the "i" before the "e." If you have trouble distinguishing between *here* and *hear*, try a sentence like, "To listen is to hear with an ear." If you confuse the spellings *principle* and *principal*, remember (whether you believe it or not), "The princi*pal* is your *pal*." And finally, this cute mnemonic device might help you spell "misspells" correctly: "*Miss Pell* never *misspells*." When you have trouble spelling a word, try inventing your own mnemonic device. Then you'll have a built-in "prompter" when you encounter spelling questions on the exam.

Much of spelling must simply be learned. Fortunately, there are some rules that apply to the spelling of root words and other rules that apply to the adding of suffixes. The following list presents some of the 24 most useful spelling rules and some of the most common exceptions to those rules. Try to learn them all! The explanations that go with the spelling exercises, as well as the exam questions that test spelling, refer to these rules by number when they apply.

TWENTY-FOUR SPELLING RULES

1. *i* before *e*
   Except after *c*
   Or when sounded like *ay*
   As in *neighbor* or *weigh*.
   Exceptions: Neither, leisure, foreigner, seized, weird, heights.

2. If a word ends in *y* preceded by a vowel, keep the *y* when adding a suffix.
   Examples: day, days; attorney, attorneys

3. If a word ends in *y* preceded by a consonant, change the *y* to *i* before adding a suffix.
   Examples: try, tries, tried; lady, ladies
   Exceptions: To avoid double *i*, retain the *y* before -*ing* and -*ish*.
   Examples: fly, flying; baby, babyish

4. A silent *e* at the end of a word is usually dropped before a suffix beginning with a vowel.
   Examples: dine + ing = dining
   locate + ion = location
   use + able = usable
   offense + ive = offensive
   Exceptions: Words ending in *ce* and *ge* retain *e* before -*able* and -*ous* in order to retain the soft Sounds of *c* and *g*.
   Examples: eace + able = peaceable
   courage + ous = courageous

5. A silent *e* is usually kept before a suffix beginning with a consonant.
   Examples: care + less = careless
   late + ly = lately
   one + ness = oneness
   game + ster = gamester

6. Some exceptions must simply be memorized. Some exceptions to the last two rules are *truly, duly, rideable, argument, wholly, ninth, mileage, dyeing, acreage, canoeing*.

7. A one-syllable word that ends with a single consonant preceded by a single vowel doubles the final consonant before a suffix beginning with a vowel or before the suffix -*y*.

TIP

If spelling is difficult for you, don't be discouraged. Many intelligent people have had problems spelling, even highly regarded authors such as Agatha Christie, Ernest Hemingway, and Jane Austen. You can improve your spelling by using a dictionary each time you encounter a word you don't know and by testing yourself on words you often spell incorrectly.

11

Examples: hit, hitting; drop, dropped; big, biggest; mud, muddy; **but:** *help, helping* because *help* ends in two consonants; *need, needing, needy* because the final consonant is preceded by two vowels.

8. A word of more than one syllable that accents the last syllable and ends in a single consonant preceded by a single vowel doubles the final consonant when adding a suffix beginning with a vowel.
   Examples: begin, beginner; admit, admitted; **but:** *enter, entered* because the accent is not on the last syllable.

9. A word ending in *er* or *ur* doubles the *r* in the past tense if the word is accented on the last syllable.
   Examples: occur, occurred; prefer, preferred; transfer, transferred

10. A word ending in *er* does not double the *r* in the past tense if the accent falls before the last syllable.
    Examples: answer, answered; offer, offered; differ, differed

11. When *-full* is added to the end of a noun, the final *l* is dropped.
    Examples: cheerful, cupful, hopeful

12. All words beginning with *over* are one word.
    Examples: overcast, overcharge, overhear

13. All words with the prefix *self-* are hyphenated.
    Examples: self-control, self-defense, self-evident

14. The letter *q* is always followed by *u*.
    Examples: quiz, bouquet, acquire

15. Numbers from twenty-one to ninety-nine are hyphenated.

16. *Per cent* is *never* hyphenated. It may be written as one word (*percent*) or as two words (*per cent*).

17. *Welcome* is one word with one *l*.

18. *All right*, meaning "everything's good," is two words. *Alright* is a different word that means "okay" or "fine."

19. *Already* means "prior to some specified time." *All ready* means "completely ready."
    Example: By the time I was *all ready* to go to the play, the tickets were *already* sold out.

20. *Altogether* means "entirely." *All together* means "in sum" or "collectively."
    Example: There are *altogether* too many people to seat in this room when we are *all together*.

21. *Their* is the possessive of *they*.
    They're is the contraction for *they are*.
    There means *at that place*.
    Example: *They're* going to put *their* books over *there*.

22. *Your* is the possessive of *you*.
    You're is the contraction for *you are*.
    Example: *You're* certainly planning to leave *your* muddy boots outside.

23. *Whose* is the possessive of *who*.
    Who's is the contraction for *who is*.
    Example: Do you know *who's* ringing the doorbell or *whose* car is in the street?

24. *Its* is the possessive of *it*. *It's* is the contraction for it is.
    Example: *It's* I who lost the letter and *its* envelope.

11

Summing It Up

- The HSPT and the TACHS exams have several questions specifically on spelling.

- You are given some choices containing sentences; the last choice says "No mistakes." You must find the spelling error and choose that sentence, or choose "No mistakes" if all sentences are correct.

- Keep a list of words that you spell incorrectly or that you have to look up. Periodically write the words or have someone test you on them.

- Read the "Twenty-Four Spelling Rules" section and write some examples for yourself.

Take a moment to ask yourself some simple questions about your understanding of the chapter:

Review: What did I learn?

Evaluate: What do I need to learn more about?

Plan: What can I do next to keep improving?

Based on your answers to those questions, adjust your study plan to dedicate additional time to the areas of weakness that you've identified.

Now try the following exercises (you can find answers and explanations after Exercise 2).

EXERCISES: SPELLING

> **Directions:** Look for errors in spelling. Choose the letter of the sentence that contains the error. No question contains more than one sentence with a spelling error. If you find no error, choose D as your answer.

Exercise 1

1. **A.** In the teacher's absence, the pupils had an eraser fight.
   B. The laws of apartheid prohibited marriage between people of different races.
   C. We may be haveing a fire drill this afternoon.
   D. *(No mistakes)*

2. **A.** The Indian girl carried her papoose strapped to a board on her back.
   B. Christopher Columbus is credited with the discovary of America.
   C. Innocent victims should not have to stand trial.
   D. *(No mistakes)*

3. **A.** Mel's position in the chess match was not advantagous, and he was nervous.
   B. The welcome committee set up the registration booth by the entrance to the banquet hall.
   C. The manager was eager to review her subordinate's recommendation for increasing company revenue.
   D. *(No mistakes)*

4. **A.** Meet me at the bus depot promptly at four.
   B. On Saturday, we will have dinner at a restaurant.
   C. The whipping post was in use as punishment in Delaware until recent times.
   D. *(No mistakes)*

5. **A.** The shepherd would be lonely without his dog.
   B. The experiment served to confirm the hypothesis.
   C. The divinity fudge was truly deliscious.
   D. *(No mistakes)*

6. **A.** The golfer took a break after the nineth hole.
   B. Let me acquaint you with the new rules.
   C. The slugger wields a heavy bat.
   D. *(No mistakes)*

7. **A.** Biology is always a laboratory science.
   B. The short story is really a memoir.
   C. My neice will enter college in the fall.
   D. *(No mistakes)*

8. **A.** The currency of Mexico is the peso.
   B. The detective had the perfect disguise.
   C. Is there anything one can buy for a nickel?
   D. *(No mistakes)*

9. **A.** Our senator is a staunch supporter of the president.
   B. I heard a rumer that our principal is about to retire.
   C. A surgeon must have steady hands.
   D. *(No mistakes)*

11

10. **A.** To grow crops in the desert, we must irrigate daily.

    B. Most convenience stores have very long hours.

    C. There was a lovly centerpiece on the table.

    D. *(No mistakes)*

Exercise 2

Directions: Look for errors in spelling. Choose the letter of the sentence that contains the error. No question contains more than one sentence with a spelling error. If you find no error, choose **D** as your answer.

1. **A.** Your not going to believe what happened in class today.

    B. The new mother worried incessantly about her baby.

    C. The new computer programming will take place tonight.

    D. *(No mistakes)*

2. **A.** Carter was always running around the house.

    B. Rachel preferred to ride her bike to school.

    C. The cashier wieghed the fruit on the scale.

    D. *(No mistakes)*

3. **A.** Our senator is a staunch supporter of the president.

    B. I heard a rumor that our principal is about to retire.

    C. A surgeon must have steady hands.

    D. *(No mistakes)*

4. **A.** I can never remember how to spell your name.

    B. Next Sunday, we'll be traveling to my grandmother's home in Arizona.

    C. The family was so thrilled that you found they're missing dog.

    D. *(No mistakes)*

5. **A.** We carefully stuffed the letters into the envelopes.

    B. Abby was very hopefull that she passed the exam.

    C. The fog made it impossible to see where we were going.

    D. *(No mistakes)*

6. **A.** The robbery occured when the Mitchell family was out of town.

    B. I need to explain this to you from the beginning.

    C. The kidnapping suspect was brought to the police station for questioning.

    D. *(No mistakes)*

7. **A.** We're honoring the veterans in our community today.

    B. I couldn't tell who's writing was on the board.

    C. When we are all together, there won't be an empty chair.

    D. *(No mistakes)*

11

8. **A.** It's a mystery how some ancient and forgotten civilizations vanished.

   B. Shana was eager to recieve her final exam grade in geometry class.

   C. Milo's loud breathing in the library made it difficult for everyone to concentrate.

   D. *(No mistakes)*

9. **A.** Jason answered every question correctly.

   B. My teacher is always so cheerful, even on gloomy days.

   C. Paula's mother is taking a self-defense class.

   D. *(No mistakes)*

10. **A.** I keep forgetting to tell you the story.

    B. The attorneys agreed to settle the case before going to trial.

    C. We all enjoyed the delicious desert Melissa baked for us.

    D. *(No mistakes)*

11

ANSWER KEYS AND EXPLANATIONS

Exercise 1

1. C	3. A	5. C	7. C	9. B
2. B	4. D	6. A	8. D	10. C

1. **The correct answer is C.** The correct spelling is *having*. Rule 4 states: A silent *e* at the end of a word is usually dropped before a suffix beginning with a vowel.

2. **The correct answer is B.** The correct spelling is *discovery*. (The base word is *discover*. There is no reason to change the *e* to *a*.)

3. **The correct answer is A.** The correct spelling is *advantageous*. Remember that words ending in *ce* and *ge* retain *e* before *-able* and *-ous* in order to retain the soft sounds of *c* and *g*.

4. **The correct answer is D.** *No mistakes*

5. **The correct answer is C.** The correct spelling is *delicious*. (There is no *s* in the middle of this word.)

6. **The correct answer is A.** The correct spelling is *ninth*. Rule 6 states that some exceptions to the rules must simply be memorized, and "ninth" is an exception to the rule that a silent *e* is usually kept before a suffix beginning with a consonant.

7. **The correct answer is C.** The correct spelling is *niece*. Remember Rule 1: "*i* before *e* except after *c*."

8. **The correct answer is D.** *No mistakes*

9. **The correct answer is B.** The correct spelling is *rumor*. (No rule; just learn the spelling.)

10. **The correct answer is C.** The correct spelling is *lovely*. Rule 5 states that a silent *e* is usually kept before a suffix beginning with a consonant: love + ly = lovely.

Exercise 2

1. A	3. D	5. B	7. B	9. D
2. C	4. C	6. A	8. B	10. C

1. **The correct answer is A.** The correct spelling is *You're*. Rule 22 states: *Your* is the possessive of *you*. *You're* is the contraction for *you are*.

2. **The correct answer is C.** The correct spelling is *weighed*. See Rule 1: "*i* before *e* except after *c* or when sounded like *ay* as in *neighbor* or *weigh*."

3. **The correct answer is D.** *No mistakes*

4. **The correct answer is C.** The word *they're* should be *their*, the possessive of *they*. Rule 21 states: *Their* is the possessive of *they*. *They're* is the contraction for *they are*.

5. **The correct answer is B.** The correct spelling is *hopeful*. See Rule 11: When *-full* is added to the end of a noun, the final *l* is dropped.

6. **The correct answer is A.** The correct spelling is *occurred*. Rule 9 states: A word ending in *er* or *ur* doubles the *r* in the past tense if the word is accented on the last syllable.

7. **The correct answer is B.** The correct spelling is *whose*. Rule 23 states: *Whose* is the possessive of *who*. *Who's* is the contraction for *who is*.

8. **The correct answer is B.** The correct spelling is *receive*. Remember Rule 1: "*i* before *e* except after *c*."

9. **The correct answer is D.** *No mistakes*

10. **The correct answer is C.** The correct spelling is *dessert*. A good way to remember this is the mnemonic device: "Dessert is double delicious."

Chapter 12

Punctuation and Capitalization

OVERVIEW

- **Punctuation Rules**
- **Capitalization Rules**
- **Summing It Up**
- **Exercises: Punctuation and Capitalization**
- **Answer Keys and Explanations**

Along with spelling, the HSPT and the TACHS exams will test your knowledge of punctuation and capitalization. To help you review, check out the following lists of punctuation and capitalization rules. Because rules can be boring and difficult to study, we've broken them into categories to help you study in "chunks." Most will be familiar to you, but if you find anything surprising, or if you have trouble understanding any of the rules, be sure to talk to your teacher.

> **TIP**
>
> Every sentence must have a subject (something to perform an action), a verb (an action), and express a complete thought. If a phrase can be cut out of a sentence without affecting its grammar, that means it's nonrestrictive or "extra" information.

PUNCTUATION RULES

The Period

- Use a period at the end of a sentence that makes a statement, gives a command, or makes a "polite request" in the form of a question that does not require an answer.
  Examples: I am brushing up on my verbal skills.
  Study the chapter on verbs for a quiz tomorrow.
  Would you please read this list of words so that I may practice my spelling lesson.

- Use a period after an abbreviation and after an initial in a person's name.
  Examples: Gen. Robert E. Lee led the Confederate forces.
  Minneapolis and St. Paul are known as the "twin cities."
  Exception: Do not use a period after postal service state name abbreviations.
  Example: St. Louis, MO

- Use a period as a decimal point in numbers.
  Example: A sales tax of 5.5% amounts to $7.47 on a $135.80 purchase.

12

The Question Mark

- Use a question mark at the end of a direct and genuine question.
  Example: Why do you want to borrow that book?

- Do not use a question mark after an indirect question; use a period.
  Example: He asked if they wanted to accompany him.

- A direct and genuine question must end with a question mark even if the question is only part of a sentence.
  Example: "Dad, are we there yet?" the child asked.

- Use a question mark (within parentheses) to indicate uncertainty as to the correctness of a piece of information.
  Example: John Carver (first governor of Plymouth colony?) was born in 1575 and died in 1621.

The Exclamation Mark

- Use an exclamation mark to express uncommonly strong feelings or to convey extreme urgency.
  Examples: Congratulations! You broke the record.
  Rush! Perishable contents.

The Comma

TIP

Commas are often used to separate introductory phrases, clauses, names, or appositives from the rest of a sentence.

- The salutation of a personal letter is followed by a comma.
  Example: Dear Mary,

- The complimentary close of a letter is ordinarily followed by a comma, though this use is optional.
  Example: Cordially yours,

- An appositive must be set off by commas.
  Example: Jim Rodgers, my next-door neighbor, is an excellent baby-sitter.

- A noun of address is set apart by commas.
  Example: When you finish your homework, Jeff, please take out the garbage.

- Use commas to set off parenthetical words.
  Example: I think, however, that a move might not be wise at this time.

- When two or more adjectives modify a noun equally, all but the last must be followed by commas. If you can add the word *and* between the adjectives without changing the meaning of the sentence, then use commas.
  Example: The refined, tall, stern-looking man stood at the top of the stairs.

- An introductory phrase of five or more words must be separated by a comma.
  Example: Because the prisoner had a history of attempted jailbreaks, he was put under heavy guard.

- After a short introductory phrase, the comma is optional. The comma should be used where needed for clarity.

  Examples: As a child she was a tomboy. (comma unnecessary)

  To Dan, Phil was friend as well as brother. (comma clarifies)

  In 1978, 300 people lost their lives in one air disaster. (comma clarifies)

- A comma is not generally used before a subordinate clause that ends a sentence, though in long, unwieldy sentences like this one, use of such a comma is recommended.

- A comma precedes the coordinating conjunction unless the two clauses are very short.

  Examples: Kevin wanted to borrow a book from the library, but the librarian would not allow him to take it until he had paid his fines.

  Roy washed the dishes and Helen dried.

- Words, phrases, or clauses in a series are separated by commas. The use of a comma before *and* is optional. If the series ends in *etc.*, use a comma before *etc.* Do not use a comma after *etc.* in a series, even if the sentence continues.

  Examples: Coats, umbrellas, and boots should be placed in the closet at the end of the hall.

  Pencils, scissors, paper clips, etc. belong in your top desk drawer.

- A comma separates a short direct quotation from the speaker.

  Examples: She said, "I must be home by six."

  "Tomorrow I begin my new job," he told us.

- Use a comma as a substitute for omitted words and phrases, such as *of* or *of the*.

  Example: President, XYZ Corporation

- Use a comma to separate a name from a title or personal-name suffix.

  Examples: Paul Feiner, Chairman

  Carl Andrew Pforzheimer, Jr.

- Use a comma when first and last names are reversed.

  Example: Bernbach, Linda

- Use a comma to separate parts of dates or addresses.

  Example: Please come to a party on Sunday, May 9, at the Pine Tavern on Drake Road, Cheswold, Delaware.

  Exception: Do not use a comma between the postal service state abbreviation and the zip code.

  Example: Scarsdale, NY 10583

- A comma ordinarily separates thousands, millions, and billions.

  Example: 75,281,646

- A nonrestrictive adjective phrase or clause must be set off by commas. A nonrestrictive phrase or clause is one that can be omitted without changing the essential meaning of the sentence.

  Example: Our new sailboat, which has bright orange sails, is entirely seaworthy.

TIP

Subordinating conjunctions like *when*, *while*, and *although*, etc. signal the start of subordinate clauses—statements that have a subject and a verb but don't express a complete thought. "When I went to the library," for example, can't stand on its own. Complete the thought: "When I went to the library, I took my Peterson's test prep guide."

12

TIP

FANBOYS (For, And, Nor, But, Or, Yet, So) represent English's coordinating conjunctions. We use them to connect items in a list, compound subjects and verbs, and complete sentences.

Chapter 12: Punctuation and Capitalization

- A restrictive phrase or clause is vital to the meaning of a sentence and cannot be omitted. Do not set it off with commas.
  Example: A sailboat without sails is useless.

- A comma must be used if the sentence might be subject to incorrect interpretations without it.
  Example: He saw the woman who had rejected him, and blushed.

- If a pause would make the sentence clearer and easier to read, insert a comma.
  Examples: Inside the people were dancing. (confusing)
  Inside, the people were dancing. (clearer)
  After all crime must be punished. (confusing)
  After all, crime must be punished. (clearer)

TIP

The pause rule is not infallible, but it is your best resort when all other rules governing comma usage fail you.

The Hyphen

- Use a hyphen to divide a word that falls between the end of one line and the start of another.

- Hyphenate numbers twenty-one through ninety-nine.

- Use a hyphen to join two words serving together as a single adjective before a noun.
  Examples: We left the highway and proceeded on a well-paved road.
  That baby-faced man is considerably older than he appears to be.

- Use a hyphen with the prefixes *ex-*, *self-*, *all-*, and the suffix *-elect*.
  Examples: ex-Senator, self-appointed, all-State, Governor-elect

- Use a hyphen to avoid ambiguity.
  Example: After the custodian recovered the use of his right arm, he re-covered the office chairs.

- Use a hyphen to avoid awkward letter combinations, such as two "*i*'s" or "*l*'s" in a row.
  Examples: semi-independent; shell-like

- Refer to a dictionary if you're uncertain whether to write something as two words, a hyphenated word, or one word.

The Dash

- You may use a dash (—) or parentheses ( ) for emphasis or to set off an explanatory group of words.
  Examples: The tools of his trade—probe, mirror, cotton swabs—were neatly arranged on the dentist's tray.
  The ingredients (lettuce, tomato, and cucumber) were left on the counter.

- If the set-off expression ends a sentence, you only need one dash.
  Example: I couldn't believe he didn't fall off his skateboard after that last trick—a triple spin!

- Use a dash to mark a sudden break in thought that leaves a sentence unfinished.
  Example: He opened the door a crack and saw—

The Colon

- Use a colon after the salutation in a business letter.
  Example: Dear Board Member:

- Use a colon to separate hours from minutes.
  Example: The eclipse occurred at 10:36 a.m.

- A colon may introduce a list of items, a long quotation, or a question.
  Example: My question is this: Are you willing to punch a time clock?

The Semicolon

- A semicolon may be used to join two short, related independent clauses.
  Example: Anne is working at the front desk on Monday; Ernie will take over on Tuesday.

- Two main clauses must be separated by a conjunction or a semicolon; if not, they should be written as two separate sentences. A semicolon never precedes a coordinating conjunction. The same two clauses may be correctly written as follows:
  Autumn had come, and the trees were almost bare.
  Autumn had come; the trees were almost bare.
  Autumn had come. The trees were almost bare.

- A semicolon may be used to separate two independent clauses that are joined by an adverb such as *however, therefore, otherwise,* or *nevertheless.* The adverb must be followed by a comma.
  Example: You may use a semicolon to separate this clause from the next; however, you would not be incorrect if you chose to write this as two separate sentences.

  If you are uncertain about how to use the semicolon to connect independent clauses, write two sentences instead.

- A semicolon should be used to separate a series of phrases or clauses when each phrase or clause contains a comma.
  Example: The old gentleman's heirs were Margaret Whitlock, his half-sister; James Bagley, the butler; William Frame, his late cousin; Robert Bone; and his favorite charity, the Salvation Army.

The Apostrophe

- In a contraction, insert an apostrophe to replace the omitted letter or letters.
  Examples: have + not = haven't
  we + are = we're
  let + us = let's
  of the clock = o'clock
  class of 1985 = class of '85

> **TIP**
> Except for salutations or writing the time, a colon should be used after an independent clause. If there's not a complete sentence before the colon, you don't need it.

12

- The apostrophe, when used to indicate possession, means *belonging to everything left of the apostrophe.*
  Examples: lady's = belonging to the lady
  ladies' = belonging to the ladies
  children's = belonging to the children

To test for correct placement of the apostrophe, remove the apostrophe and add *of the.*

Examples: waiter's = of the waiter (correct)
childrens' = of the childrens (therefore incorrect)
girls' = of the girls (correct if it is the meaning intended)

Quotation Marks

- All directly quoted material must be bracketed by quotation marks. Words not quoted must remain outside the marks.
  Example: "If it is hot on Sunday," she said, "we will go to the beach."

- An indirect quote must not be enclosed by quotation marks.
  Example: She said that we might go to the beach on Sunday.

- When a multiple-paragraph passage is quoted, each paragraph of the quotation must begin with quotation marks; however, ending quotation marks are used only at the end of the last quoted paragraph.

- A period always goes inside the quotation marks, whether the quotation marks are used to denote quoted material, to set off titles (like chapters in a book or titles of short stories), or to isolate words used in a special sense.
  Examples: Jane explained: "The house is just around the corner."
  The first chapter of *The Andromeda Strain* is entitled "The Country of Lost Borders."

- A comma always goes inside the quotation marks.
  Examples: "We really must go home," said the dinner guests.
  If your skills have become "rusty," you must study before you take the test.
  Three stories in Kurt Vonnegut's *Welcome to the Monkey House* are "Harrison Bergeron," "Next Door," and "EPICAC."

- A question mark goes inside the quotation marks if it is part of the quotation. If the whole sentence containing the quotation is a question, the question mark goes outside the quotation marks.
  Examples: He asked, "Was the airplane on time?"
  What did you really mean when you said, "I do"?

- An exclamation mark goes inside the quotation marks if the quoted words are an exclamation, but outside the marks if the entire sentence including the quotation is an exclamation.
  Examples: The sentry shouted, "Drop your weapon!"
  Save us from our "friends"!

- A colon and a semicolon always go *outside* the quotation marks.
  Example: He said, "War is destructive"; she added, "Peace is constructive."

- Words used in an unconventional or ironic manner may be placed inside quotation marks.
  Example: A surfer who "hangs ten" is performing a tricky maneuver on a surfboard, not staging a mass execution.

12

- A quote within a quote can be identified using single rather than double quotation marks.
  Example: George said, "The philosophy 'I think, therefore I am' may be attributed to Descartes."

Capitalization Rules

- Capitalize the first word of a complete sentence.
  Example: Your desktop should appear neat and orderly.

- Capitalize the first word of a quoted sentence.
  Example: The teacher said, "Please write your name at the top of the paper."

  Exception: Do *not* capitalize the first word within quotation marks if it doesn't begin a complete sentence.

  Examples: "I was late," she explained, "because of the snow."
  Some groups would like to restrict certain liberties in the interest of "patriotism."

- Capitalize the letter *I* when it stands alone.

- Capitalize the first word, the last word, and all other important words in the title of a book, play, article, etc.
  Examples: *"The Mystery of the Green Ghost"*
  A Night at the Opera

- Capitalize a title when it applies to a specific person, group, or document (i.e. a proper noun).
  Examples: The President will give a press conference this afternoon.
  Senators Goldwater and Tower were leading figures in the Conservative Party.
  Should our Constitution be strictly interpreted?

- Do *not* capitalize a title if it's not referencing something or someone specific.
  Examples: Some congressmen are liberal; others are conservative.
  It would be useful for our club to write a constitution.

- Capitalize days of the week, months of the year, and holidays, but do *not* capitalize the seasons.
  Example: Labor Day, the last holiday of the summer, falls on the first Monday in September.

- Capitalize all proper names, including but not limited to: names of people, buildings, events, places and words formed using those places, organizations, and references to a sole God.
  Examples: John F. Smith
  Empire State Building
  Memorial Day
  Panama and Panamanian
  The United Fund
  Allah

- Capitalize the points of the compass only when referring to a specific area or place.
  Example: Many retired persons spend their winters in the South.

- Do *not* capitalize the points of the compass when they refer to a direction.
  Example: Many birds fly south in the winter.

12

- The only school subjects that are regularly capitalized are languages and specific place names used as modifiers.

  Example: Next year I will study French, biology, English literature, mathematics, European history, and ancient philosophy.

- A noun not regularly capitalized should be capitalized when it is used as part of a proper name.

  Example: Yesterday I visited Uncle Charles, my favorite uncle.

- In a letter:
  - Capitalize all titles in the address and closing.

    Examples: Mr. John Jones, President Mary Smith, Chairman of the Board

  - Capitalize titles, proper names, and first and last words in the salutation.

    Examples: Dear Dr. Williams, My dear Sir:

  - Capitalize only the first word in a complimentary closing.

    Example: Very truly yours,

12

Summing It Up

- The HSPT and the TACHS exams test your writing skills regarding punctuation and capitalization.
- To prepare for this section, you must PRACTICE. Read the rules listed in this chapter and practice them.

Take a moment to ask yourself some simple questions about your understanding of the chapter:

Review: What did I learn?

Evaluate: What do I need to learn more about?

Plan: What can I do next to keep improving?

Based on your answers to those questions, adjust your study plan to dedicate additional time to the areas of weakness that you've identified.

EXERCISES: PUNCTUATION AND CAPITALIZATION

Exercise 1

> **Directions:** Among the following sentences, look for errors in capitalization or punctuation. If you find no mistake, mark D.

1. **A.** He was not informed, that he would have to work overtime.
   B. The wind blew several papers off his desk.
   C. I believe this is the man whom you interviewed last week.
   D. *(No mistakes)*

2. **A.** If an employee wishes to attend the conference, she should fill out the necessary forms.
   B. Mr. Wright's request cannot be granted under any conditions.
   C. Charles Dole, who is a member of the committee, was asked to confer with commissioner Wilson.
   D. *(No mistakes)*

3. **A.** He is the kind of person who is always willing to undertake difficult assignments.
   B. The teacher entered the room and said, "the work must be completed today."
   C. The special project was assigned to Mary Green and me.
   D. *(No mistakes)*

4. **A.** Mr. Barnes, the bus dispatcher, has many important duties.
   B. We checked the addresses once more and sent the letters to the mailroom.
   C. Do you agree that this year's class is the best yet?
   D. *(No mistakes)*

5. **A.** Gerry had never been the type to run away from a challenge however his sister was the exact opposite and did not have a taste for adventure.
   B. Rhett, an excellent fisherman, brought his new pole, a tackle box full of lures, and a cooler full of cold sodas on his trip to the ocean.
   C. Mrs. Cromwell asked the waitress for the following items: a sharp steak knife, a glass of cold water, and a bottle of ketchup.
   D. *(No mistakes)*

6. **A.** Although I am willing to work on most holidays, I refuse to work on Labor Day.
   B. Every Tuesday afternoon, Joan volunteers at Children's Hospital.
   C. If you wish to be considered for the scholarship, you must file your application promptly.
   D. *(No mistakes)*

7. **A.** The new student asked the gym teacher if he could join the baseball team?
   B. Girl Scout Troop 71 will march in the parade.
   C. Mrs. Garcia asked Louisa and Henry to help bake cookies for the party.
   D. *(No mistakes)*

8. **A.** I find his study of the birds of North America to be fascinating.

   B. The doctor suggested that my grandfather go South for the winter to avoid frequent colds.

   C. Under the new rules, when do we revert to Eastern Standard Time?

   D. *(No mistakes)*

9. **A.** If you would like to spend the night, you may sleep in Tom's room.

   B. The attack on Pearl Harbor, on December 7, 1941, came as a complete surprise.

   C. "May I use the computer this afternoon," the boy asked?

   D. *(No mistakes)*

10. **A.** "If it rains on Friday," the boy mused, "the game may be played on Saturday instead."

    B. The child's new bicycle lay on its side near the curb.

    C. Whenever I drive on a New York street, I watch for potholes.

    D. *(No mistakes)*

Exercise 2

Directions: Among the following sentences, look for errors in capitalization or punctuation. If you find no mistake, mark D.

1. **A.** I used to live in St. Paul, Minnesota, but I now reside in St. Augustine, Florida.

   B. "I love to play the piano from morning till night," said the musician.

   C. Lily answered the teacher's question correctly she was so proud.

   D. *(No mistakes)*

2. **A.** Every memorial day, my mother takes my picture next to the flag in front of our home.

   B. Please submit an essay, two letters of recommendation, and the completed application form.

   C. The reporter asked the senator about the election results.

   D. *(No mistakes)*

3. **A.** "I forgot my running shoes and can't go to the gym today," she explained.

   B. The conference will be held in November in Asheville, North Carolina.

   C. Marie shared her extra candy with Sofia, Eddie, and me.

   D. *(No mistakes)*

4. **A.** Saul and his best friend Madison went to see *The Guiding Hand*, the newest movie at the Pekoe County Theater.

   B. After Nomi's physical examination, Dr. Pembroke said to her, "You are in excellent health."

   C. Aleck read the first seven chapters of the horror novel he purchased, *no turning back*, and couldn't sleep all night.

   D. *(No mistakes)*

12

5. A. Some students requested extra test-prep help before the important exam.

   B. The art teacher asked, "has anyone seen the new exhibit at the museum?"

   C. Heather recommended that the organization draft a new constitution.

   D. *(No mistakes)*

6. A. On their class trip to independence hall in Philadelphia, the students interviewed the actor who portrayed John Adams.

   B. Our tour guide said that the school is accredited by the Southern Association of Colleges and Schools.

   C. Please read the directions carefully, and hand in your test before the bell rings at 3:05.

   D. *(No mistakes)*

7. A. Students may study Chinese, French, German, or Spanish in their first year at our school.

   B. Mrs. Young frowned as she asked, "Why are you late today?"

   C. The childrens' shoes were under the leaves in the backyard.

   D. *(No mistakes)*

8. A. Julia handed out the twenty two new books to the students in her class.

   B. Annual events include Parents' Weekend in the fall and Alumni Weekend in the spring.

   C. Their dog, Quincy, always barked whenever anyone rang the doorbell.

   D. *(No mistakes)*

9. A. Because Ben lives so far from school, he needs to set his alarm to ring at 5 a.m. each day.

   B. The event for new students will be held on Monday August 28 in the new gymnasium.

   C. "Do you think we'll get to the party on time?" she asked me for the third time.

   D. *(No mistakes)*

10. A. "When you finish your homework," my mom said, "please set the table for dinner."

    B. I was surprised to learn that Adam and Andrew are twins; they certainly don't look alike at all.

    C. I am always sad when the hummingbirds fly south for the winter.

    D. *(No mistakes)*

12

ANSWER KEYS AND EXPLANATIONS

Exercise 1

1. A	3. B	5. A	7. A	9. C
2. C	4. D	6. D	8. B	10. D

1. **The correct answer is A.** There is no reason for a comma between the verb and its object. The sentence should read: He was not informed that he would have to work overtime.

2. **The correct answer is C.** Commissioner Wilson is a specific commissioner, and so the *C* must be capitalized.

3. **The correct answer is B.** The direct quote must begin with a capital *T*.

4. **The correct answer is D.** *No mistakes*

5. **The correct answer is A.** As written, this is a run-on sentence. Remember the following rule: A semicolon may be used to separate two independent clauses that are joined by

an adverb such as *however, therefore, otherwise,* or *nevertheless.*

6. **The correct answer is D.** *No mistakes*

7. **The correct answer is A.** This is a declaratory statement, not a direct question; it must end with a period.

8. **The correct answer is B.** Do not capitalize directions, only place names.

9. **The correct answer is C.** The boy's question needs to end with a question mark: "May I use the computer this afternoon?" The entire sentence is a simple statement that should end with a period.

10. **The correct answer is D.** *No mistakes*

Exercise 2

1. C	3. D	5. B	7. C	9. B
2. A	4. C	6. A	8. A	10. D

1. **The correct answer is C.** This is a run-on sentence. It contains two independent clauses joined with no punctuation. One way to correct this is to add a comma followed by a coordinating conjunction: Lily answered the teacher's question correctly, and she was so proud. Another option would be to use a semicolon: Lily answered the teacher's question correctly; she was so proud.

2. **The correct answer is A.** Holidays, along with days of the week and months of the year, should be capitalized, so the M and D in *Memorial Day* should be capitalized.

3. **The correct answer is D.** *No mistakes*

4. **The correct answer is C.** Book titles, such as *No Turning Back*, should be capitalized.

5. **The correct answer is B.** The first word in a quoted sentence should be capitalized. The sentence should read: The art teacher asked, "Has anyone seen the new exhibit at the museum?"

6. **The correct answer is A.** Independence Hall should be capitalized since it is the name of a building.

7. **The correct answer is C.** The apostrophe belongs before the s here. As noted earlier, when used to indicate possession, an apostrophe means "belonging to everything to the left of the apostrophe." In this case, *the children's shoes* means "the shoes belonging to the children."

12

8. **The correct answer is A.** Hyphenate numbers from twenty-one to ninety-nine. The number should appear as twenty-two.

9. **The correct answer is B.** Commas are needed to separate parts of dates, so the sentence in choice B should read: The event for new students will be held on Monday, August 28, in the new gymnasium.

10. **The correct answer is D.** *No mistakes*

12

Chapter 13

English Usage

OVERVIEW

- **Principles of Grammar**
- **Troublesome Words**
- **Summing It Up**
- **Exercises: English Usage**
- **Answer Keys and Explanations**

The HSPT and TACHS exams will test your expertise in language usage. HSPT lumps this subject with spelling, punctuation and capitalization, and composition in the Language Skills section. TACHS tests this subject in the Language section.

Language usage includes a student's grasp of correct English and how it's used. Your expertise in this area is based on years of reading and hundreds of hours of classroom instruction on grammar. In answering language usage questions, you may have to consider problems of agreement, double negatives, and dangling modifiers. Word choice, punctuation, tense, and case may also affect your decision on which answer is best.

The "Principles of Grammar" that follow may prove useful as you prepare for English usage questions. Just remember, a simple, direct statement is more effective than a wordy one.

PRINCIPLES OF GRAMMAR

Subject-Verb Agreement

- A verb must agree with its subject in number.
  Single subjects require singular verbs.

  Example: *She walks* to school every day.

  Plural subjects need plural verbs.

  Example: *They walk* home together.

- The number of the subject is not affected by a prepositional phrase that follows it.
  Examples: The girl *together with* her friends *walks* to school every day.
  One of the apples *is* rotten.

- In sentences beginning with *there* or *here*, the verb must agree with the noun that follows it.
  Examples: There *are* six *boys* in the class.
  There *is* the *paper* you're looking for.
  Here *is* the *book* you wanted.
  Here *are* the *books* you asked about.

13

- *Each, every, everyone, everybody, someone, somebody, anyone, anybody, no one, nobody, either,* and *neither* are singular and require singular verbs and pronouns.
  Example: *Everyone* on the team *thinks he can* win the prize.

- Singular subjects joined by *and* take a plural verb.
  Example: *John and Ted are* good friends.

- Two singular subjects joined by *or* or *nor* take a singular verb.
  Example: *Meg or Mary is* always first to answer.

- A singular and a plural subject joined by *or* or *nor* take a singular or plural verb, depending on which subject is nearer the verb.
  Examples: Neither Kim nor her *sisters are* ready yet.
  Neither her sisters nor *Kim is* ready yet.

- *Don't* is a contraction for *do not*. It is correct for first- and second-person singular and plural (*I don't, you don't, we don't*) and for third-person plural (*they don't*). Use *doesn't* with third-person singular pronouns or nouns.
  Examples: *It doesn't* matter to me.
  Bill doesn't know that song.

Pronoun Agreement

- A pronoun agrees with the words to which it refers in person (first, second, or third), number (singular or plural), and gender (masculine, feminine, or neuter).
  Examples: When the *boys* left, *they* took *their* books with *them*.
  Each *girl* must have *her* ticket.

- A pronoun following a linking verb must be in the subject form (*I, you, he, she, it, we, they*).
  Example: The woman in the photo *was she*.

- If a pronoun is the object of a preposition or an action verb, the pronoun must be in the object form (*me, you, him, her, it, us, them*).
  Examples: Would you like to go to the movies *with* John and *me*?
  The teacher *selected* Joan and *me* to lead the class.

- When a pronoun is used as an appositive, it must be in the same form as the word to which it refers. An appositive is a noun or pronoun that follows another noun or pronoun to identify or explain it.
  Example: Ms. Ross, *my adviser*, suggested that I apply to this school.

- If the appositive refers to a subject, use the subject form.
  Example: The two pilots, *Captain Miller* and *he*, sat in the cockpit. (*Captain Miller* and *he* are appositives referring to the subject. Therefore, the subject form, *he*, is required.)

- If the appositive refers to an object, use the object form.
  Example: The class chose two representatives—*Jeff* and *him*—to attend the meeting. (*Jeff* and *him* are appositives referring to *representatives*, the object of the verb *chose*. Therefore, the object form, *him*, is required.)

- A noun ending in *-ing* (a gerund) takes a possessive pronoun.
  Example: My mother objected to *my getting* home so late.

- Use the pronouns *who* and *whom* the same way you would use *he/she* and *him/her*. Use *who* wherever you could substitute *he* or *she*, and *whom* where you could substitute *him* or *her*.
  Examples: The prize was won by a man *who* everyone agreed was deserving of it.
  (Think: Everyone agreed *he* was deserving of it.)
  The woman *whom* they elected to be chairperson accepted with pleasure.
  (Think: They elected *her* to be chairperson.)

- *This* and *that* are singular and refer to singular words: *this kind* of book, *that sort* of book. *These* and *those* are plural and refer to plural words: *these kinds* of books, *those sorts of books*.

> **TIP**
> One way to decide between *who* and *whom* in a sentence is to ask yourself
> 1. "*Who* is performing the action?" and
> 2. "To *Whom* is the action done?"

Adjective and Adverb Usage

- Use adverbs to modify action verbs.
  Example: The car drove *slowly* and *carefully* (not *slow* and *careful*) on the icy road.

- Use an adjective after a linking verb.
  Example: The flower smelled *sweet* (not *sweetly*).

- Use the comparative form of an adjective or adverb (the form that ends in *-er* or uses the word *more*) when comparing two things.
  Examples: Jim runs *faster* than Joe.
  Beth is *taller* than Amy.

- Use the superlative form of an adjective or adverb (the form that ends in *-est* or uses the word *most*) when comparing more than two things.
  Examples: Of all the boys on the team, Jim runs *fastest*.
  Beth is the *tallest* girl in the class.

- Avoid double negatives.
  Examples: The rain was so heavy we *could hardly* see.
  (*not*: The rain was so heavy we *couldn't hardly* see.)
  They *don't have any* homework tonight.
  (*not*: They *don't have no* homework tonight.)

TROUBLESOME WORDS

13

There are a few groups of words that span the realms of spelling, punctuation, and usage. You probably have many of these under control. Others might consistently give you trouble. Your choice of the best version of a sentence might hinge upon your understanding of the correct uses of the words in these troublesome groups.

- **their, they're, there**
  Their is the possessive of *they*.

  Example: The Martins claimed *their* dog from the pound when they learned he was missing.

  They're is the contraction for *they are*.

  Example: Tom and Marie said that *they're* going skiing in February.

There means at that place.

Example: You may park your car over *there*.

This last form is also used in sentences or clauses where the subject comes after the verb.

Examples: *There* is no one here by that name.

There are some plates in the sink.

- **your, you're**
  Your is the possessive of *you*.

  Example: Didn't we just drive past *your* house?

  You're is the contraction for *you are*.

  Example: When we finish caroling, *you're* all invited inside for hot chocolate.

- **whose, who's**
  Whose is the possessive of *who*.

  Example: The handwriting is very distinctive, but I cannot remember *whose* it is.

  Who's is the contraction for *who is*.

  Example: *Who's* calling at this hour of night?

- **its, it's**
  Its is the possessive of *it*.

  Example: The injured cat is licking *its* wounds.

  It's is the contraction for *it is*.

  Example: *It's* much too early to leave for the airport.

- **which, who, that**
  Which as a relative pronoun refers only to objects.

  Example: This is the vase *which* the cat knocked over.

  Who and *whom* refer only to people.

  Example: The boy *who* won the prize is over there.

  That may refer to either objects or people. *That* is used only in restrictive clauses.

  Examples: This is the vase *that* the cat knocked over.

  The boy *that* won the prize is over there.

- **learn, teach**
  To *learn* is to *acquire* knowledge. To *teach* is to *impart* knowledge.

  Example: My mother *taught* me all that I have *learned*.

- **between, among**
  Between commonly applies to only two people or things.

  Example: Let us keep this secret *between you and me*.

  Among always implies that there are more than two.

  Example: The knowledge is secure *among the members* of our club.

Exception: Between may be used with more than two objects to show the relationship of each object to each of the others, as in "The teacher explained the difference *between* adjective, adverb, and noun clauses."

- **beside, besides**

  Beside is a preposition meaning *by the side of.*

  Example: He sat *beside* his sick father.

  When used as an adverb, besides means *in addition to.*

  Example: *Besides* his father, his mother also was ill.

- **lay, lie**

  The verb to *lay*, except when referring to hens, may be used only if you could replace it with the verb to *put*. At all other times, use a form of the verb to *lie.*

  Examples: You may *lay* the books upon the table.

  Let sleeping dogs *lie.*

- **many/much, fewer/less, number/amount**

  The use of *many/much, fewer/less, number/amount* is governed by a simple rule of thumb. If the object can be counted, use *many, fewer,* or *number.* If the object is thought of as a single mass or unit, use *much, less,* or *amount.*

  Examples: *Many* raindrops make *much* water.

  If you have *fewer* dollars, you have *less* money.

  The *amount* of property you own depends upon the *number* of acres in your lot.

- **I, me**

  The choice of *I* or *me* when the first-person pronoun is used with one or more proper names may be tested by eliminating the proper names and reading the sentence with the pronoun alone.

  Examples: John, George, Marylou, and (me *or* I) went to the movies last night. (By eliminating the names, you can readily choose *I went to the movies.*)

  It would be very difficult for Mae and (I *or* me) to attend the wedding. (Without *Mae*, it is clear that *difficult for me* is correct.)

- **as, like**

  As is a conjunction introducing a subordinate clause, while *like*, in cases where the two words are confused, is a preposition. The object of a preposition is a noun or phrase.

  Examples: Speeding is a traffic violation, *as* you should know. (*You* is the subject of the clause; *should* is its verb.)

  He behaves *like* a fool.

  She prefers green vegetables *like* spinach.

- **already, all ready**

  Already means *prior to some specified time.*

  Example: It is *already* too late to submit your application.

  All ready means *completely ready.*

  Example: The cornfield is *all ready* for the seed to be sown.

13

- **altogether, all together**

  Altogether means *entirely.*

  Example: It is *altogether* too foggy to drive safely.

  All together means *in sum* or *collectively.*

  Example: The family will be *all together* at the Thanksgiving dinner table.

- **two, to, too**

  Two is the *numeral* 2.

  Example: There are *two* sides to every story.

  To means *in the direction of.*

  Example: We shall go *to* school.

  Too means *more than* or *also.*

  Examples: It's *too cold* to go swimming today.
  We shall go, *too.*

13

Summing It Up

- The HSPT tests English usage in the Language Skills section along with spelling, punctuation and capitalization, and composition. The TACHS includes it in the Language section.

- Study, learn, and practice the "Principles of Grammar" given in this chapter. They will help you not only on the test but also throughout school and life.

Take a moment to ask yourself some simple questions about your understanding of the chapter:

Review: What did I learn?

Evaluate: What do I need to learn more about?

Plan: What can I do next to keep improving?

Based on your answers to those questions, adjust your study plan to dedicate additional time to the areas of weakness that you've identified.

Now try the following exercises (you can find answers and explanations after Exercise 3).

13

EXERCISES: ENGLISH USAGE

Exercise 1

Directions: In the following questions, choose which of the four sentences is constructed best. The answer keys and explanations follow Exercise 3.

1. **A.** It is the opinion of the commissioners that programs that include the construction of cut-rate municipal garages in the central business district is inadvisable.

    B. Having reviewed the material submitted, the program for putting up cut-rate garages in the central business district seemed likely to cause traffic congestion.

    C. The commissioners believe that putting up cut-rate municipal garages in the central business district is inadvisable.

    D. Making an effort to facilitate the cleaning of streets in the central business district, the building of cut-rate municipal garages presents the problem that it would encourage more motorists to come into the central city.

2. **A.** Since the report lacked the needed information, it was of no use to him.

    B. This report was useless to him because there were no needed information in it.

    C. Since the report did not contain the needed information, it was not real useful to him.

    D. Being that the report lacked the needed information, he could not use it.

3. **A.** In reviewing the typists' work reports, the job analyst found records of unusual typing speeds.

    B. It says in the job analyst's report that some employees type with great speed.

    C. The job analyst found that, in reviewing the typists' work reports, that some unusual typing speeds had been made.

    D. In the reports of typists' speeds, the job analyst found some records that are kind of unusual.

4. **A.** They do not ordinarily present these kind of reports in detail like this.

    B. A report of this kind is not hardly ever given in such detail as this one.

    C. This report is more detailed than what such reports ordinarily are.

    D. A report of this kind is not ordinarily presented in as much detail as this one is.

5. **A.** Elephants suck water through their long, flexible trunks and squirt it into their mouths.

    B. Every morning, Angel talks to his parrot Rudy while getting dressed for school.

    C. The high school football teams practices diligently every morning during the playing season.

    D. Each year, everyone on the team go to the awards banquet.

6. **A.** If properly addressed, the letter will reach my mother and I.

B. The letter had been addressed to myself and my mother.

C. I believe the letter was addressed to either my mother or I.

D. My mother's name, as well as mine, was on the letter.

7. **A.** The paper we use for this purpose must be light, glossy, and stand hard usage as well.

B. Only a light and a glossy, but durable, paper must be used for this purpose.

C. For this purpose, we want a paper that is light, glossy, but that will stand hard wear.

D. For this purpose, paper that is light, glossy, and durable is essential.

8. **A.** This kind of worker achieves success through patience.

B. Success does not often come to men of this type except they who are patient.

C. Because they are patient, these sort of workers usually achieve success.

D. This worker has more patience than any man in his office.

9. **A.** You have got to get rid of some of these people if you expect to have the quality of the work improve.

B. The quality of the work would improve if they would leave fewer people do it.

C. I believe it would be desirable to have fewer people doing this work.

D. If you had planned on employing fewer people than this to do the work, this situation would not have arose.

10. **A.** It is quite possible that we shall reemploy anyone whose training fits them to do the work.

B. It is probable that we shall reemploy those who have been trained to do the work.

C. Such of our personnel that have been trained to do the work will be again employed.

D. We expect to reemploy the ones who have had training enough that they can do the work.

Exercise 2

Directions: Choose the word or group of words that should go into the blank to make a correct sentence.

1. All the boys and Joyce took _____ baseball gloves to the ball game.

   A. her

   B. their

   C. his

   D. our

2. Dana was the _____ person who dared go into the haunted house.

   A. most only

   B. onliest

   C. sole only

   D. only

13

3. Molly and Brandon always knew that _____ wanted to add a swimming pool to their family home.

   A. she

   B. he

   C. them

   D. they

4. If Duncan had joined the soccer team, he _____ been the star.

   A. should have

   B. could of

   C. would of

   D. might have

5. Even before the wind had stopped, the rain _____ down.

   A. was slowed

   B. has been slowing

   C. had been slowing

   D. had been slowed

6. Last week, I had lunch with the girl _____ won the English prize.

   A. who

   B. whom

   C. which

   D. what

7. In choosing between chocolate and vanilla ice cream, I like chocolate ice cream _____.

   A. most

   B. best

   C. better

   D. more better

8. The jury is depending _____ the witness' statements.

   A. about

   B. of

   C. upon

   D. from

9. I would bring Grandma to visit you, _____ I have no car.

   A. except

   B. while

   C. because

   D. moreover

10. The little girl next door _____ on her swings all day.

    A. swinged

    B. swang

    C. swung

    D. has swinged

11. Neither Kenneth nor Larry _____ book report.

    A. has completed their

    B. have completed their

    C. have completed his

    D. has completed his

12. We had just finished shoveling the driveway _____ the plow came through again.

    A. if

    B. until

    C. when

    D. than

13

13. You must wait for the election results until we _____ the ballots.

A. had counted

B. have counted

C. are counting

D. have had counted

Directions: Make a complete sentence by choosing the words that should go into the blank.

---

14. After completing the lifesaving course, _____.

A. and taking both the written and practical exams

B. gaining months of practical experience as an apprentice

C. you will be eligible to take the examination

D. at the YMCA under the auspices of the Red Cross

15. Ella, a professional carpenter, _____.

A. building is something that Ella really enjoys doing

B. built her first bookcase when she was 20 years old

C. her first serious building project will be a maple table and chair set

D. at work Ella is learning how to build a residential cabin

Directions: Select the sentence that means the same or most nearly the same as the underlined sentences.

---

16. <u>The hiker was lost. A St. Bernard rescued him. It happened in the Alps.</u>

A. The hiker was rescued by a St. Bernard lost in the Alps.

B. The lost Alpine hiker was rescued by a St. Bernard.

C. The hiker in the lost Alps was rescued by a St. Bernard.

D. In the Alps, the hiker was rescued by a lost St. Bernard.

17. <u>Taxes are deducted from all wages. Workers who must work at night are paid overtime. The rate of tax to be withheld is fixed by law.</u>

A. The law requires that people who are paid overtime must pay taxes.

B. According to the law, people who work at night must be paid overtime and deduct taxes.

C. The tax rate on overtime pay is deducted from wages by law and is paid at night.

D. By law, a fixed rate of taxes is deducted from all wages, including those paid overtime for night work.

13

Directions: Choose the word or group of words that makes the second sentence have the same meaning as the underlined sentence.

18. <u>The accident victim was not only frightened but also in pain.</u>

The accident victim was _____.

A. neither frightened nor in pain

B. both frightened and in pain

C. either frightened or in pain

D. only frightened, not in pain

19. <u>I may go to the movies tomorrow if I baby-sit today.</u>

_____ baby-sitting today, I may go to the movies tomorrow.

A. By

B. While

C. Until

D. Once

20. <u>The criminal received consecutive sentences for his three crimes.</u>

The criminal has to serve his sentences _____.

A. all at once

B. after a period of delay

C. one at a time

D. with no opportunity for parole

21. <u>We bought the house; moreover, we bought the adjacent lot.</u>

We bought _____.

A. the house because we bought the lot next door

B. the lot because we bought the house next door

C. the house but not the lot next door

D. the house and the lot next door

Exercise 3

Directions: For questions 1–8, look for errors in grammar, usage, or composition. If you find no mistakes, mark choice D.

1. A. He got off of the horse.
   B. Your umbrella is better than mine.
   C. How could I be other than glad?
   D. *(No mistakes)*

2. A. No one was there except Charles.
   B. Your sample is the most satisfactory of all that I have seen.
   C. I couldn't hardly do it.
   D. *(No mistakes)*

3. A. There should be no secrets between you and me.
   B. I knew him to be the ringleader.
   C. Everyone has studied his lesson.
   D. *(No mistakes)*

4. A. There are a piano and a phonograph in the room.
   B. This is the man whom you interviewed last week.
   C. He is reported to be killed.
   D. *(No mistakes)*

13

5. **A.** I have met but one person.

   B. She is the tallest of the two girls.

   C. The child is able to shape the clay easily.

   D. *(No mistakes)*

6. **A.** I wish I were going to Mexico with you.

   B. Please loan me five dollars until payday.

   C. The audience was enthusiastic.

   D. *(No mistakes)*

7. **A.** Because of the downpour, the carnival was postponed.

   B. He walks up and said "Hello."

   C. I already anticipate the good time I shall have at camp.

   D. *(No mistakes)*

8. **A.** The couple promised to renew they're wedding vows in Las Vegas every year.

   B. It's important to place all of your garbage in the proper recycling bins, in order to be environmentally responsible.

   C. Without a proper identification tag, it's difficult to determine whose piece of luggage this is.

   D. *(No mistakes)*

Directions: For questions 9–14, choose the answer that best describes the group of words.

---

9. The worst feature of my summer camp was the food the next worst was the latrine.

   A. Run-on sentence

   B. Complete sentence

   C. *Not* a complete sentence

10. The man with the wart on the end of his nose gave his seat to the old woman.

   A. Run-on sentence

   B. Complete sentence

   C. *Not* a complete sentence

11. Driving across the country in order to meet a deadline.

   A. Run-on sentence

   B. Complete sentence

   C. *Not* a complete sentence

12. Once upon a time in a corner of the kitchen lived a small black cricket and the cricket made a lot of noise which annoyed the woman who lived in the house and so the woman swept the cricket out the door.

   A. Run-on sentence

   B. Complete sentence

   C. *Not* a complete sentence

13. Bob and his brother Ted, who is a Civil War buff, went to Gettysburg during summer vacation and studied the battlefield together.

   A. Run-on sentence

   B. Complete sentence

   C. *Not* a complete sentence

14. The strong wind suddenly increased to gale force and the sailboat to capsize.

   A. Run-on sentence

   B. Complete sentence

   C. *Not* a complete sentence

13

Directions: For questions 15–20, choose the sentence that is correctly written.

15. **A.** She had done much the people began to realize.

 B. When the people began to realize how much she had done.

 C. Soon the people began to realize how much she had done.

 D. The people began to realize and how much she had done.

16. **A.** Mounting the curb, the empty car crossed the sidewalk and came to rest against a building.

 B. The empty car mounts the curb, crossed the sidewalk, and will come to rest against a building.

 C. Mounting the curb when the empty car crosses the sidewalk and comes to rest against a building.

 D. The curb was mounted by the empty car and crossed the sidewalk and came to rest against a building.

17. **A.** I had forgotten my gloves realizing and returning to the theater.

 B. Because I will realize that I forgot my gloves, I returned to the theater.

 C. My gloves forgotten, realized, and returned to the theater.

 D. Realizing I had forgotten my gloves, I returned to the theater.

18. **A.** She learned that further practice will have had a good effect on her swimming ability.

 B. She learned that further practice would have a good effect on her swimming ability.

 C. Having learned and practiced had a good effect on her swimming ability.

 D. Learning and practicing to have a good effect on her swimming ability.

19. **A.** Assisting him his friend who lives in the next house.

 B. Assisting him and living in the next house his friend.

 C. His friend who lives in the next house assisting.

 D. He was assisted by his friend who lives in the next house.

20. **A.** The driver does all that it will be possible to do.

 B. The driver, having done all that was possible.

 C. The driver did all that it was possible to do.

 D. Doing all that is possible to do and driving.

13

ANSWER KEYS AND EXPLANATIONS

Exercise 1

1. C	3. A	5. A	7. D	9. C
2. A	4. D	6. D	8. A	10. B

1. **The correct answer is C.** Choice A has an agreement error (should be *programs . . . are*). Choice B is incorrect because the program did not review the material. Choice D is totally garbled.

2. **The correct answer is A.** In choice B, the subject of the second clause is *information*, which is singular. In choice C, the adverb should be *really*. *Being that*, in choice D, is not an acceptable form.

3. **The correct answer is A.** The indefinite pronoun *it* in choice B refers to nothing at all, so it means nothing. In choice C, the *that* after *found* should be omitted. Choice D uses colloquial language, which is unacceptable in Standard Written English.

4. **The correct answer is D.** Choice A contains an error of agreement (*these kind*). Choice B contains a double negative, *not hardly*. *What* is an extra word in choice C.

5. **The correct answer is A.** Remember, plural subjects require plural verb forms to be in proper agreement. The plural subject *elephants* requires the use of plural verbs: *suck* and *squirt*. Choice B is incorrect because *Rudy* is an appositive and should be set off in commas. Choice C is incorrect because *teams* is plural and would require the plural verb, *practice*. In choice D, *everyone* is a singular pronoun and would require the singular verb, *goes*.

6. **The correct answer is D.** Choices A and C use the subject-form pronoun, *I*, where the object-form, *me*, is required. In choice B, the object of the preposition *to* should be *me*, not *myself*.

7. **The correct answer is D.** The sentences in choices A, B, and C are not parallel in construction. All the words that modify *paper* should be in the same form.

8. **The correct answer is A.** In choice B, *men* is the implied subject of the verb *are*. Inserting the subject into the phrase, you can see that it must read . . . *except to those (men) who are patient*. Choice C contains an error of number; to be correct, the phrase must read either *this sort of worker* or *these sorts of workers*. In choice D, the comparison is incomplete. It must read *than any other man*.

9. **The correct answer is C.** Choice A is wordy. In choice B, the correct verb should be *have* in place of *leave*. In choice D, *arose* is incorrect; the correct form is *arisen*.

10. **The correct answer is B.** In choice A, *them* should be *him* or *her* because it refers to *anyone*, which is singular. Choices C and D are wordy and awkward. In addition, choice C uses the word *that* to refer to people, when the correct choice is *who*, to read *personnel who have been trained*.

13

Exercise 2

1. B	**6.** A	**10.** C	**14.** C	**18.** B
2. D	**7.** C	**11.** D	**15.** B	**19.** A
3. D	**8.** C	**12.** C	**16.** B	**20.** C
4. D	**9.** A	**13.** B	**17.** D	**21.** D
5. C				

1. **The correct answer is B.** The subject is plural, and the object is plural; therefore, the possessive pronoun must be plural. The subject is in the third person, not the first, so *their*, not *our*, is the correct word.

2. **The correct answer is D.** *Only* is an exclusive term. It cannot be modified in any way.

3. **The correct answer is D.** This sentence requires a plural pronoun to replace the plural subject in this sentence, *Molly and Brandon*. The pronoun *they* is the correct choice.

4. **The correct answer is D.** *Of* is not an auxiliary verb, so choices B and C are automatically incorrect. Choice D is more in tune with the nature of the sentence than is choice A.

5. **The correct answer is C.** To show that one past activity (the *slowing*) occurred before another past activity (the *stopping*) requires the *had been* construction (past perfect). *Had been slowed* (choice D) implies that an external force was working on the rain. *Had been slowing* more accurately describes the end of a storm.

6. **The correct answer is A.** *Who* is the subject of the verb *won*. (Think: *She* won the prize.) *Which* may only be used to apply to things. *What* is not a pronoun.

7. **The correct answer is C.** The comparison between two objects requires *more* or *better*. *More better* (choice D) is redundant and incorrect. *Most* and *best* (choices A and B) refer to comparison among three or more objects.

8. **The correct answer is C.** The proper idiomatic use is *depend on* or *depend upon*.

9. **The correct answer is A.** In this sentence, *except* serves as a conjunction. *But* would fit into the blank in the same way. The other choices make no sense in the context of the sentence.

10. **The correct answer is C.** The past tense of *swing* is *swung*.

11. **The correct answer is D.** The construction *neither/nor* creates a singular subject (or object). Because the subject is singular, both the verb and the possessive pronoun must be singular as well.

12. **The correct answer is C.** The sentence describes two activities in terms of their relationship in time. Only choice C makes sense.

13. **The correct answer is B.** A present activity that is dependent on a future activity requires that the future activity be stated in the present perfect, *have counted*.

14. **The correct answer is C.** The sentence fragment is nothing more than an introductory prepositional phrase. The completion must supply both subject and verb, and only choice C does that.

15. **The correct answer is B.** The correct answer must be in the proper tense. Since Ella is a professional carpenter, her first building project must have already occurred. *Built* is the correct past tense for this verb, which is appropriate for this sentence.

16. **The correct answer is B.** The correct answer must give correct information as to who was lost, where he was lost, and how he was

rescued. Choices A and D are confusing and sound like the dog was lost in the Alps. Choice C describes the Alps as lost, rather than the hiker.

17. **The correct answer is D.** The tax rate and the fact of withholding are established by law. Overtime pay is not established by law, but it does constitute wages subject to withholding.

18. **The correct answer is B.** The term *not only . . . but also* is inclusive.

19. **The correct answer is A.** The sentence is conditional and in reverse sequence: "I may do something tomorrow *if* I do something today." Reverse the sentence: "By doing something today, I may do something else tomorrow."

20. **The correct answer is C.** *Consecutive* means "one after the other." The word that means "all at the same time" is *concurrent*.

21. **The correct answer is D.** The word *moreover* simply means "in addition to" or "also." It does not imply any causality.

Exercise 3

1. A	5. B	9. A	13. B	17. D
2. C	6. B	10. B	14. C	18. B
3. D	7. B	11. C	15. C	19. D
4. C	8. A	12. A	16. A	20. C

1. **The correct answer is A.** *Off of* is an unacceptable construction: He got off the horse.

2. **The correct answer is C.** *Hardly* is a negative word, so *couldn't hardly* is an unacceptable double negative. The correct version would be *I could hardly do it.*

3. **The correct answer is D.** *No mistakes*

4. **The correct answer is C.** The activity began in the past (he *was* killed) and is completed in the present (is reported *now*). Therefore, the present perfect tense should be used. The sentence should read: "He is reported to *have been killed.*"

5. **The correct answer is B.** The comparison is between two girls; therefore, *taller,* not *tallest,* is correct.

6. **The correct answer is B.** *Loan* is a noun. The sentence requires the verb *lend.*

7. **The correct answer is B.** The two verbs should be in the same tense. He *walked* up and *said* "Hello."

8. **The correct answer is A.** *There, their,* and *there* are typically confused words. In this sentence, the possessive *their* is required.

9. **The correct answer is A.** The two complete, independent clauses must either be separated into two sentences or be joined by a semicolon.

10. **The correct answer is B.** This sentence is complete.

11. **The correct answer is C.** This is not a complete sentence. It is a sentence fragment that needs a subject: *Juan was driving across the country in order to meet a deadline.* The sentence could also be corrected by joining with an independent clause: *Driving across the country in order to meet a deadline, Juan raced along in his red convertible.*

12. **The correct answer is A.** There are actually three independent clauses here. The best correction would be to eliminate the first *and,* and to begin a second sentence with "The cricket." The second *and* should be eliminated and be replaced by a comma.

13

13. **The correct answer is B.** This sentence is complete.

14. **The correct answer is C.** The sentence fragment, as organized, calls for a compound verb: *increased* to gale force and *caused* the sailboat to capsize.

15. **The correct answer is C.** Choice A is a run-on sentence. Choice B is a sentence fragment. In choice D, the *and* is superfluous.

16. **The correct answer is A.** Choice B mixes tenses illogically. Choice C is a sentence fragment. In choice D, the curb crosses the street and comes to rest against the building.

17. **The correct answer is D.** No other choice makes sense.

18. **The correct answer is B.** Choice A confuses tenses; choices C and D are sentence fragments.

19. **The correct answer is D.** No other choice is a complete sentence.

20. **The correct answer is C.** Choice A confuses tenses; choices B and D are sentence fragments.

13

Chapter 14

Language Composition and Expression

OVERVIEW

- **Tips for Answering Language Composition and Expression Questions**
- **Summing It Up**
- **Exercise: Language Composition and Expression**
- **Answer Key and Explanations**

Your studies of spelling, punctuation, capitalization, and grammar all contribute to your skills in language expression, another crucial part of any entrance exam. Language expression, also called language composition, is a skill you'll use in all kinds of course work and exams in high school and college.

Although the exams covered in this book do not include essay questions, the TACHS and HSPT exams have found ways to test your language expression skills. These exams have tucked questions into test sections of English usage and language expression that are designed to test your potential for composition. Among these are questions that ask you to move a sentence to another location in the paragraph or to remove a sentence that does not belong. Other composition questions require you to identify topic sentences or choose the best development of topic sentences that are given.

Language expression is an area in which test makers are experimenting. New methods of testing these skills are likely to crop up in the next editions of many high school exams administered over the next few years.

TIPS FOR ANSWERING LANGUAGE COMPOSITION AND EXPRESSION QUESTIONS

Composition questions make up only a small portion of the exam, but those few questions might be among the most difficult and time-consuming on the test. Though you probably won't become an expert essayist in just a few weeks, you can familiarize yourself with some of the basic guidelines of composition, and you can learn how to address these questions on your exam. Language expression questions typically test topic development and appropriateness. The following sections give you some common-sense tips and guidelines to use when you encounter questions dealing with these areas of language expression.

14

Tackling Topic Development Questions

What do we mean by "development"? The concept is relatively simple, though the task can be a bit more difficult. Topic development requires that you be able to clearly understand the main point or idea of a paragraph or essay, and then recognize additional information that logically expands upon or further clarifies that main point or idea. Topic development is much like finishing a story that someone else has started.

Topic development questions come in several forms. Here are four tips that will help you tackle these questions on the exams:

1. If the question gives you a topic sentence and asks you to develop that sentence, your task is to choose a second and third sentence that best develop the idea presented in the first sentence. You aren't just choosing some sentences that refer to the same subject presented in the topic sentence. You have to choose the sentences that best expand upon or clarify the topic.

2. The question might give you an essay title and then ask that you choose a topic sentence that would best express the idea of that essay. You have to choose a sentence that relates well to the subject presented by the title and that is broad enough to allow for further development of a paragraph.

3. If the question gives you a title and asks you simply to choose a sentence that belongs under that title, you must weed out the sentences that are related to but not entirely relevant to the topic.

4. The occasional answer choice "None of these" complicates your task and makes the question much more difficult. On the other questions, you know that one of the answers is the best solution to topic development, and you can use the process of elimination to improve your odds of landing on the correct response. When you're faced with a "None of these" response, you might not be able to use your skills to find the right answer. If you can't find the answer to one of these questions, just move on. Don't let it hold you up too long.

Tackling Appropriateness Questions

Questions that ask whether a particular sentence is appropriate to a specific paragraph are, in a way, asking you to perform the same skills you use in topic development, but in reverse! With these questions, rather than choosing the best way to add to the information about a topic, you're asked to choose which information does or does not belong, or to determine where the best placement of that information might be.

If you can write a well-organized composition, then you know how to allocate ideas into paragraphs. Unfortunately, these are not skills you can develop right this minute. Take time to go over your returned written class work and learn from your teachers' comments. If you do not understand some comments or the reasons for some low grades, ask your teachers for explanations and help.

TIP

Well-organized paragraphs present one primary topic and make use of transitional words and phrases (like *consequently, therefore, while,* etc.) to shift from one sentence to another. Avoid introducing new concepts apart from the paragraph's main topic to minimize confusion.

14

Summing It Up

- The HSPT and TACHS exams use multiple-choice questions that ask you to move a sentence to another location in the paragraph, remove a sentence that does not belong, identify topic sentences, or choose the best development of topic sentences.

- Topic development requires that you be able to clearly understand the main point or idea and then recognize additional information that logically expands upon or further clarifies that main point or idea.

- Appropriateness questions ask you to choose which information does or does not belong or to determine where the best placement of that information might be.

Take a moment to ask yourself some simple questions about your understanding of the chapter:

Review: What did I learn?

Evaluate: What do I need to learn more about?

Plan: What can I do next to keep improving?

Based on your answers to those questions, adjust your study plan to dedicate additional time to the areas of weakness that you've identified.

Now try the following exercises (you can find answers and explanations after the exercise).

EXERCISE: LANGUAGE COMPOSITION AND EXPRESSION

Directions: Choose the pair of sentences that best develops the topic sentence.

1. Salting highways in winter is undoubtedly helpful to the motorist, yet this practice may actually cause a great deal of harm.

   A. Salt works more quickly than chemical ice melters because it does not require heat to go into action. Salt mixed with sand offers especially good traction.

   B. While melting the ice and eliminating slippery conditions, the same salt eats into the road surface itself, creating dangerous potholes. Further, the salty runoff leaches into the soil and kills surrounding vegetation.

   C. A small amount of salt is a dietary necessity, especially in hot, dry climates. Large amounts of dietary salt, however, lead to water retention and high blood pressure.

   D. Salt is inexpensive because it occurs abundantly in nature. Highways in the Rocky Mountains should have good safety records because they are so close to Utah, a great source of salt.

2. Mesa Verde is a great flat-topped mountain that rises dramatically above the surrounding Colorado desert.

   A. In contrast to this desert, Mesa Verde is fertile and well-watered, a green oasis to which men have been drawn since ancient times. Within the sheer cliff walls of these canyons, nature has carved out vast caverns in soft sandstone rock.

   B. In 1275, a severe 24-year drought hit the Mesa Verde area. The Cliff Dwellers, hounded by their relentless enemies and forces they could not comprehend, abandoned their cities and fields and fled from Mesa Verde.

   C. At Mesa Verde, the Ancestral Puebloans found favorable growing conditions. Navajo legends call them the *Anasazi*, the Ancient Ones or Ancient Enemies.

   D. Villages, towns, and ultimately great cities appeared on the mesa tops. Tools and implements became more diverse and elaborate.

14

3. They set fires for many different reasons. Sometimes a shopkeeper sees no way out of losing his business and sets fire to it to collect the insurance. Another type of arsonist wants revenge and sets fire to the home or shop of someone he feels has treated him unfairly.

   A. They don't look like criminals, but they cost the nation millions of dollars in property loss and sometimes loss of life.

   B. Arsonists of this type have even been known to help fight the fire.

   C. Arsonists are persons who set fires deliberately.

   D. Some arsonists just like the excitement of seeing the fire burn and watching the firefighters at work.

4. But you ought not to despise it, for it can help you and your family obtain many of the good things of life. It can buy an adequate diet, one of the basics of good health. It can make it easier for your children to secure an education. When necessary, it can provide medicine and medical care.

   A. Money can offer a great opportunity for you to help others.

   B. Money can be the means for a comfortable house, for travel, for good books, and for hobbies and recreation.

   C. Many people consider that amassing great wealth is a goal in itself.

   D. Certainly money should not be your chief aim in life.

5. (1) In a democratic state, people are allowed to have certain freedoms. (2) They can speak their views freely, even if these views are against the government. (3) Andrew Jackson, who served from 1829–1837, was the first president elected by the Democratic Party. (4) They can express their views freely in the media, such as newspapers. (5) Citizens are free to gather together in groups to discuss political or religious issues. (6) They can form political parties, and they can elect the people they choose to govern them. (7) In a democratic state, no one can be arrested for expressing their views about politics. (8) The role of the government is to keep its citizens secure and to protect their freedoms.

   A. Sentence 2
   B. Sentence 3
   C. Sentence 4
   D. Sentence 5

6. (1) Hermit crabs are aquatic crustaceans that often dwell in saltwater reefs and near shorelines. (2) Hermit crabs typically protect their soft, curved abdomens from potential predators by wearing a shell, which is usually salvaged from sea snails or bivalves. (3) Other creatures that have shells include turtles and armadillos. (4) Did you know that hermit crabs have gills, which need to stay wet so they can breathe?

   A. Sentence 1
   B. Sentence 2
   C. Sentence 3
   D. Sentence 4

14

7. Where should the sentence, "Prior to the Civil War, the steamboat was the center of life in the thriving Mississippi towns," be placed in the paragraph below?

(1) With the war came the railroads. (2) River traffic dwindled, and the white-painted vessels rotted at the wharves. (3) During World War I, the government decided to relieve rail congestion by reviving the long-forgotten waterways. (4) Today, steamers, diesels, and barges ply the Mississippi.

A. Before sentence 1

B. Between sentences 2 and 3

C. Between sentences 3 and 4

D. The sentence does not fit in this paragraph.

8. Where should the sentence, "It can damage the heart and also the blood vessels," be placed in the paragraph below?

(1) Patients with the condition known as "Type 2" diabetes suffer from the same basic problem as patients with "Type 1" diabetes. (2) In short, their bodies are not able to use the sugar in their blood very effectively. (3) This blood sugar, known as glucose, becomes very high in patients with diabetes, and it can cause many problems. (4) People with Type 2 diabetes usually have high blood pressure as well, which puts even more of a strain on the heart and circulatory system.

A. Between sentences 1 and 2

B. Between sentences 2 and 3

C. Between sentences 3 and 4

D. After sentence 4

9. Which of the following sentences best fits under the topic, "The Symbolic Use of Bears"?

A. Dancing bears provide a comical form of entertainment at street fairs.

B. Small children love to hug teddy bears because they are soft and warm.

C. The bear has long been the symbol of Russia.

D. None of these

10. Which topic is best for a one-paragraph theme?

A. Development and Decline of the Whaling Industry

B. The Effects of Automation Upon the Farming Industry

C. The Advantage of Using a Heavier Baseball Bat

D. None of these

14

ANSWER KEY AND EXPLANATIONS

1. B	3. C	5. B	7. A	9. C
2. A	4. D	6. C	8. C	10. C

1. **The correct answer is B.** Choice B picks up where the topic sentence leaves off. It explains how the salt is helpful and then gives examples of the harm caused by salt. Choice A is also not a bad one. This choice amplifies the action of salt on ice and tells of its beneficial effects. Choices C and D do not develop the topic sentence at all. If you were not offered choice B, you could choose choice A over choices C and D and have an acceptable answer. However, because you must choose the *best* from among all of the options, choice B is the answer.

2. **The correct answer is A.** The topic sentence introduces both Mesa Verde and the Colorado desert, and choice A flows naturally by contrasting Mesa Verde to the desert and then further describing Mesa Verde. A clear second-best choice is C. However, a transitional sentence would be desirable to introduce the *Anasazi.* Choices B and D do nothing to develop the topic sentence.

3. **The correct answer is C.** Most often, a definition makes a good topic sentence. This definition sets a good reference point for the pronoun, *they,* which begins the next sentence. Choices A and B cannot be first sentences since they refer to antecedents that aren't there. Choice D might serve as a topic sentence, but not as the topic sentence for this particular paragraph. Choice D would lead to a very different paragraph development.

4. **The correct answer is D.** Choice D as topic sentence sets up a nice contrast with the *but* that follows it. Choices A and B set up meaningless contrasts. Choice C makes a weak topic sentence, and it takes a broad perspective by mentioning "Many people," while the paragraph uses a more personal approach by addressing "you and your family." In addition, Choice C leaves an unclear reference for the "it" that is not to be despised.

5. **The correct answer is B.** Although this paragraph discusses the types of freedoms associated with democracies, it does not address specific politicians, political events, or political parties. Sentence 3 provides information about a former president, noting that he was a prominent member of the Democratic Party, which is not the focus of this paragraph.

6. **The correct answer is C.** This is an informative passage about the hermit crab; sentence 3 provides only tangential information about other animals that have shells, and therefore it does not belong in the paragraph.

7. **The correct answer is A.** The organization of this paragraph is chronological. Because the third sentence discusses relief of rail congestion during World War I, it is clear that the war of the first sentence is the Civil War. Events prior to the Civil War should be mentioned before events that happened during the Civil War.

14

8. **The correct answer is C.** The topic sentence introduces the subject of Type 2 diabetes and indicates that more information about this condition will follow. Elevated blood sugar levels and the resulting problems are mentioned in the second and third sentences, so a description of these problems would logically follow. Therefore, the sentence should be placed between sentences 3 and 4.

9. **The correct answer is C.** Choices A and B tell of actual uses of bears. Only choice C describes a bear as a symbol.

10. **The correct answer is C.** This is a limited topic that could be dealt with in one paragraph. The topic also lends itself to being one paragraph in a longer, more comprehensive essay. Choices A and B are much more involved, and would require significant background information; neither topic could be covered adequately in a single paragraph.

14

PART IV
QUANTITATIVE AND NONVERBAL SKILLS

Mathematics

OVERVIEW

15

Whether you love it or hate it, math will always be a part of your life. You will find mathematics questions on all scholastic aptitude and achievement tests, including Catholic high school entrance exams. On the HSPT, math questions include the categories of Mathematics and Quantitative Skills. On the TACHS, the questions are called Math.

In the pages that follow, we have condensed eight years of mathematics classes into a comprehensive review that touches on most of the topics covered in the exams. This is only a review, not a course. If you find that you're having difficulties with any mathematics topic, talk with a teacher or refer to your mathematics textbooks. This chapter helps you most by showing you what you *don't* know, so you can focus some of your test-prep time on reinforcing your skills in problem areas. The explanations that accompany the mathematics exercises are complete. These explanations will be a big help to you, because they help you understand the processes involved in finding the right answers to mathematics questions. For extra practice with math questions, complete the math sections of all the practice exams that follow.

The following sections in this part outline some of the basic mathematics rules, procedures, and formulas that you've learned over the past eight years of school. You also have an opportunity to practice your skills with some exercises, and you can judge your progress by checking your work against the answer explanations that follow the exercises. Work through these sections and the exercises carefully, and be honest with yourself about your accuracy and speed as you solve these problems. Note which problems are difficult for you as well as those that are easy. After you've completed this section, you'll know exactly which areas you need to strengthen.

MATH SYMBOLS

Math is a language, with terms, meanings, structure, and symbols. To succeed at math, you need to understand the language. Often, the symbols used in equations can be the biggest challenge. So that is where we will start this chapter.

Some, if not all, of these symbols are already familiar to you. It never hurts to review the symbols that go beyond addition and subtraction. Probably the easiest way to review the symbols, without doing math problems, is to review a list of symbols and their meanings.

Symbol	Meaning	Function	Example
+	Plus sign	Addition	$5 + 3 = 8$
−	Minus sign	Subtraction	$5 - 3 = 2$
×	Times sign	Multiplication	$5 \times 3 = 15$
•	Multiplication dot	Multiplication	$5 \cdot 3 = 15$
÷	Division	Division	$10 \div 5 = 2$
/	Division slash	Division	$10/5 = 2$
.	Period	Decimal point	5.3, 7.25
%	Percent	$5\% = 5/100 = 0.05$	$0.5 = 50\%$ $1.25 = 125\%$
<	Strict inequality	Less than	$3 < 5$

Symbol	Meaning	Function	Example
≤	Inequality	Less than or equal to	$5 \leq 5, 4 \leq 5$
>	Strict inequality	Greater than	$5 > 3$
≥	Inequality	Greater than or equal to	$5 \geq 5, 5 \geq 4$
( )	Parentheses	Solve within first	$3 + (2 + 1) + 2 = 3 + 3 + 2 = 8$
[ ]	Brackets	Solve within first	$3 + [2 + 1] + 2 = 3 + 3 + 2 = 8$
x^y	Power	Exponent	$3^2 = 3 \times 3 = 9$ $3^3 = 3 \times 3 \times 3 = 27$
√	Square root	$\sqrt{a} \cdot \sqrt{a} = a$	$\sqrt{9} = 3, \sqrt{16} = 4$
π	Pi constant	Ratio between the radius and circumference of a circle	$c = 2 \cdot \pi \cdot r$
∠	Angle	Formed by two rays	$CDE = 45°$
⦟	Measured angle	Formed by two rays	$DEF = 60°$
∟	Right angle	Right angle = 90°	$a = 90°$
°	Degree	A circle = 360°, ½ = 180°	$a = 45°$
!	Factorial	$n! = 1 \times 2 \times 3 \times 4 \times ... \times n$	$4! = 1 \times 2 \times 3 \times 4 = 24$

There are many more math symbols out there, but you probably won't see them for a few years.

PROPERTIES

Properties in math are rules that have been proven over time. Many of them may seem like common sense, and for the most part they are. Here's a list of properties, with definitions and examples.

- **Commutative Property:** in addition and multiplication, order does not affect outcome.

  - $7 + 8 = 8 + 7$
  - $3 \times 5 = 5 \times 3$
  - $2(6) = 6(2)$

- **Distributive Property:** given an equation, $a(b + c)$, you can distribute the value a to the values inside the parentheses.

  - $7(2 + 8) = 7 \times 2 + 7 \times 8 = 14 + 56 = 70$

- **Associative Property:** in addition and multiplication, changing how numbers are grouped will not change the result.

  - $2(5 \times 4) = 5(2 \times 4) = 4(2 \times 5)$
  - $3 + (5 + 2) = 2 + (3 + 5) = 5 + (2 + 3)$

15

- **Identity Property:** any number added to zero will not change; any number multiplied by 1 will not change.
    - $15 + 0 = 15$
    - $15 \times 1 = 15$

- **Reflexive Property:** a number is always equal to itself.
    - $a = a$
    - $2 = 2$
    - $\pi = \pi$

- **Symmetric Property:** if $a = b$, then $b = a$.
    - If $x = 10$, then $10 = x$

- **Transitive Property:** if $a = b$ and $b = c$, then $a = c$.
    - If $a = b$ and $b = 3 + 4$, then $a = 3 + 4$

- **Substitution Property:** if $a = b$, then a can be substituted for b.
    - If $a = 7$ and $b = 7$, then $a + 3 = 10$ and $b + 3 = 10$

- **Additive Identity:** any variable added to zero will remain unchanged.
    - $x + 0 = x$

- **Multiplicative Property of Zero:** any number multiplied by zero equals zero.
    - $1 \times 0 = 0$
    - $4{,}962 \times 0 = 0$

- **Multiplicative Inverse:** any number multiplied by its reciprocal will equal 1.
    - $2 \times \dfrac{1}{2} = 1$
    - $12 \times \dfrac{1}{12} = 1$

Now try the following exercises.

Test Yourself 1

Identify which math properties are demonstrated in the following equations. The answer keys and explanations follow **Test Yourself 30**.

1. $2(x + y) = 2x + 2y$
2. $3x = 3x$
3. $43a \times 0 = 0$
4. $10 \times 6 = 6 \times 10$
5. $73 = 0 + 73$
6. $x = y$, $y = 2(10)$, so $x = 2(10)$
7. $17(4 \times 3) = 4(3 \times 17)$
8. $0 + b = b$
9. $403 \times 1 = 403$
10. $14 \times (1/14) = 1$
11. $7 = a$, $x = 7$, so $x - 1 = 6$ and $a - 1 = 6$
12. $a = 250$, so $250 = a$

15

THE NUMBER LINE

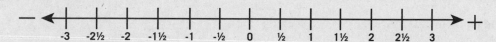

A *number line* is a convenient concept to keep as a mental picture. The number line above shows whole numbers and fractions greater than zero and less than zero. Numbers increase in size as you move to the right and decrease in size as you move to the left. The number line above has arrows at each end, meaning that the number line goes on infinitely in both positive and negative directions.

You can draw number lines to aid in basic mathematical calculations. You can use fractions, whole numbers, or decimals to name the intervals on the line. We suggest that you use number lines when dealing with signed (+, −) numbers and inequalities. To use a number line for signed numbers and inequalities, remember that values to the right of zero are positive, and values to the left of zero are negative. Given a problem such as 3 −2 = 1, we assume the 3 is positive (no sign means positive), and we treat the −2 as "negative 2" rather than "minus 2." Looking at the number line, when you move three whole numbers to the right and two whole numbers to the left, you have the answer, 1.

Here is a list of a few basic rules that you must master for speed and accuracy in mathematical computation. You will recognize many of these from the section on properties. These are the rules you should memorize well enough to have at your fingertips when needed:

Any number multiplied by 0 = 0.

$5 \times 0 = 0$

If 0 is divided by any number, the answer is 0.

$0 \div 2 = 0$

If 0 is added to any number, that number does not change.

$7 + 0 = 7$

If 0 is subtracted from any number, that number does not change.

$4 - 0 = 4$

If you multiply a number by 1, that number does not change.

$3 \times 1 = 3$

If you divide a number by 1, that number does not change.

$6 \div 1 = 6$

A number added to itself is doubled.

$4 + 4 = 8$

If you subtract a number from itself, the answer is 0.

$9 - 9 = 0$

If you divide a number by itself, the answer is 1.

$8 \div 8 = 1$

15

Once you have these rules memorized, you can write the answers to the questions in the following exercise as fast as you can read the questions.

Now try the following exercises.

Test Yourself 2

Write the answers to the following problems in the space provided. The answers and explanations follow **Test Yourself 30**.

1. $1 - 1 =$
2. $3 \div 1 =$
3. $6 \times 0 =$
4. $6 - 0 =$
5. $0 \div 8 =$
6. $9 \times 1 =$
7. $5 + 0 =$
8. $4 - 0 =$
9. $2 \div 1 =$
10. $7 - 7 =$

11. $8 \times 0 =$
12. $0 \div 4 =$
13. $1 + 0 =$
14. $3 - 0 =$
15. $5 \times 1 =$
16. $9 \div 1 =$
17. $6 + 6 =$
18. $4 - 4 =$
19. $5 \div 5 =$
20. $6 \times 1 =$

The more rules, procedures, and formulas you can memorize, the easier it will be to solve math problems on your exam and throughout life. Become thoroughly familiar with the rules in this section, and commit to memory as many as possible.

Moving the Decimal Point

When multiplying a number by 10, 100, 1,000, etc., move the decimal point to the right the number of spaces equal to the number of zeros in the multiplier. If the number being multiplied is a whole number, push the decimal point to the right by inserting the appropriate number of zeros.

$$0.36 \times 100 = 36$$
$$1.2 \times 10 = 12$$
$$5.0 \times 10 = 50$$
$$60.423 \times 100 = 6,042.3$$

When dividing a number by 10, 100, 1,000, etc., again count the zeros, but this time move the decimal point to the left.

$$123.0 \div 100 = 1.23$$
$$352.8 \div 10 = 35.28$$
$$16.0 \div 100 = 0.16$$
$$7.0 \div 1,000 = 0.007$$

15

Test Yourself 3

Write the answers to the following problems in the space provided. The answer keys and explanations follow **Test Yourself 30**.

1. $18 \times 10 =$
2. $5 \div 100 =$
3. $1.3 \times 1,000 =$
4. $3.62 \times 10 =$
5. $9.86 \div 10 =$

6. $0.12 \div 100 =$
7. $4.5 \times 10 =$
8. $83.28 \div 1,000 =$
9. $761 \times 100 =$
10. $68.86 \div 10 =$

ORDER OF OPERATIONS

TIP

Remember your order of operations with the acronym **PEMDAS**:

Parentheses
Exponents
Multiplication
Division
Addition
Subtraction

Some students use the mnemonic device "**P**lease **e**xcuse **m**y **d**ear **A**unt **S**ally."

One of the most important things to know when solving math problems is where to start. Fortunately, there are rules to explain what goes first. We call these rules the *order of operations*. At this stage of mathematics, there are only four rules to know. They are:

1. Operations within parenthesis
2. Operations with exponents and square roots
3. Multiplication and division
4. Addition and subtraction

In short, solve anything in parentheses first, going from hardest to easiest. As you go through calculations using the order of operations, note each step carefully to make sure you don't skip a step or forget anything along the way.

Let's look at a few examples.

- $(7 \times 2) + (8 - 2) = (14) + (6) = 20$ (Solve within the parenthesis before adding)
- $4^3 + (5 + 1) =$ (Parenthesis first)

  $4^3 + 6 = 64 + 6$ (Exponent, then addition)

- $6 - 8 \div 2 + 3 = 6 - 4 + 3$ (Multiplication and division first)

  $6 - 4 + 3 = 5$ (Then solve from left to right)

- $\sqrt{81} \times 5^2 - 45 \div 9 + 14 =$ (No parenthesis, so start with exponents and square roots)

  $9 \times 25 - 45 \div 9 + 14 =$ (Now solve multiplication and division)

  $225 - 5 + 14 = 234$ (Now solve addition and subtraction)

We just demonstrated the four orders of operations discussed here. As you go through these chapters on mathematics, you will come across other rules concerning order of operations. Add them to this section as you go, so you have a running list of rules for reference.

15

Order of Operations (other rules)

15

GREATEST COMMON FACTOR

The term Greatest Common Factor (or GCF) refers to the largest number that can be factored into two numbers cleanly—that is, without a remainder. For example, the greatest common factor of 10 and 15 is 5, for 10 and 20 the GCF is 10. How did we get those answers? Let's pick apart a pair of numbers.

Example: Find the GCF for (12, 8)

Solution: Factors for 12: 1, 2, 3, 4, 6, 12

Factors for 8: 1, 2, 4, 8

The common factors—the factors common to both sets of number—for 12 and 8 are 1, 2, and 4. The greatest (largest) of the group is 4, so that is your answer.

Example: Find the GCF for (28, 56)

Solution: Factors for 28: 1, 2, 4, 7, 14, 28

Factors for 56: 1, 2, 4, 7, 14, 28, 56

The greatest common factor the two numbers share is 28, which is your answer.

There may be number pairs, like (7, 13), that don't have anything other than 1 in common. When this happens, the numbers are relatively prime. Remember that a prime number is a number that is only divisible by itself and 1.

What about problems that have more than two numbers to factor? That just means you add another group of factors to choose from.

Example: Find the GCF for (28, 56, 84)

Solution: Factors for 28: 1, 2, 4, 7, 14, 28

Factors for 56: 1, 2, 4, 7, 14, 28, 56

Factors for 84: 1, 2, 3, 4, 6, 7, 12, 14, 21, 28, 42, 84

The numbers share 1, 2, 4, 7, 14, and 28 as common factors. The greatest common factor the three numbers share is 28, which is your answer.

Test Yourself 4

Find the Greatest Common Factor for each group of numbers. The answer keys and explanations follow **Test Yourself 30.**

1. (20, 75)
2. (14, 35)
3. (5, 13)
4. (30, 150)
5. (12, 78)

6. (13, 117)
7. (15, 25)
8. (6, 21)
9. (4, 12)
10. (24, 64)

> **CAUTION**
>
> Don't be confused by the term, "Greatest Common Divisor," as a divisor and a factor have the same meaning. They are both numbers that can divide into something.

15

RECIPROCALS

Reciprocals are as easy as flipping something over. Defined, a reciprocal is $\frac{1}{x}$ where x is the number in question. For example, the reciprocal of $5 = \frac{1}{5}$, or 0.2 as a decimal. Let's try a couple more.

Example: $\quad 17 = \frac{1}{17}$

$\qquad\quad 100 = \frac{1}{100}$

$\qquad\quad 42 = \frac{1}{42}$

It's seems pretty simple, and it is simple as long as you're dealing with whole numbers rather than fractions. One thing to think about with a whole number is that 17 is the same as $\frac{17}{1}$. That's a handy thing to remember, not only with reciprocals but any time you have a mix of whole numbers and fractions.

Speaking of fractions, finding the reciprocal of a fraction is done the same way. The reciprocal of $\frac{4}{5}$ is as easy as flipping the fraction over to get $\frac{5}{4}$. Let's look at a few more examples.

Examples: $\quad \frac{1}{8} = \frac{8}{1} = 8$

$\qquad\qquad \frac{2}{10} = \frac{10}{2} = 5$

$\qquad\qquad \frac{1}{0.25} = \frac{0.25}{1} = 0.25$

So, the rule of thumb with reciprocals is to divide by one or flip the numerator and denominator.

Test Yourself 5

Write the reciprocals to the following numbers in the space provided. The answer keys and explanations follow **Test Yourself 30.**

1. $72 =$

2. $\frac{1}{2} =$

3. $0.65 =$

4. $\frac{3}{36} =$

5. $-6 =$

15

DECIMALS

Decimals are a way of writing fractions using tenths, hundredths, thousandths, and so forth. If you can count money, make change, or understand a batting average, decimals should present no problem.

The most important step when writing decimals is placing the decimal point. The whole system is based on its location. Remember the decimal places? The chart below shows places for the number **1,236, 540.132456**.

When adding or subtracting decimals, you need to keep the decimal points in line. After you have lined up the decimal points, proceed with the problem the same way as with whole numbers, simply maintaining the location of the decimal point.

Example: Add 36.08 + 745 + 4.362 + 58.6 + 0.006.

Solution:
```
  36.08
745.
   4.362
  58.6
+  0.006
844.048
```

If you find it easier, you may fill in the spaces with zeroes. The answer will be unchanged.

```
 036.080
 745.000
 004.362
 058.600
+000.006
 844.048
```

Example: Subtract 7.928 from 82.1.

Solution:
```
  82.1      or      82.100
-  7.928          -  7.928
  74.172            74.172
```

15

Test Yourself 6

Write the answers to the following problems in the space provided. The answer keys and explanations follow **Test Yourself 30.**

1. $1.52 + 0.389 + 42.9 =$

2. $0.6831 + 0.01 + 4.26 + 98 =$

3. $84 - 1.9 =$

4. $3.25 + 5.66 + 9.1 =$

5. $17 - 12.81 =$

6. $46.33 - 12.1 =$

7. $51 + 7.86 + 42.003 =$

8. $35.4 - 18.21 =$

9. $0.85 - 0.16 =$

10. $7.6 + 0.32 + 830 =$

When multiplying decimals, ignore the decimal points until you reach the product. Then the placement of the decimal point is dependent on the sum of the places to the right of the decimal point in both the multiplier and number being multiplied.

$$\begin{array}{r} 1.482 \quad \text{(3 places to the right of decimal point)} \\ \times\ 0.16 \quad \text{(2 places to the right of decimal point)} \\ \hline 8892 \\ 14820 \\ \hline 0.23712 \quad \text{(5 places to the right of decimal point)} \end{array}$$

You cannot divide by a decimal. If the divisor is a decimal, you must move the decimal point to the right until the divisor becomes a whole number, an integer. Count the number of spaces you moved the decimal point in the divisor to the right, and move the decimal point in the dividend (the number being divided) the same number of spaces to the right. The decimal point in the answer should be directly above the decimal point in the dividend.

$$0.06\overline{)4.212} \quad 70.2$$

Decimal point moves two spaces to the right.

Test Yourself 7

Write the answers to the following problems in the space provided. The answer keys and explanations follow **Test Yourself 30.**

1. $3.62 \times 5.6 =$

2. $92 \times 0.11 =$

3. $18 \div 0.3 =$

4. $1.5 \times 0.9 =$

5. $7.55 \div 5 =$

6. $6.42 \div 2.14 =$

7. $12.01 \times 3 =$

8. $24.82 \div 7.3 =$

9. $0.486 \div 0.2 =$

10. $0.21 \times 12 =$

15

FRACTIONS

Fractions indicate parts of things. A fraction consists of a numerator and a denominator.

$$\frac{3}{4} \leftarrow \substack{\text{numerator} \\ \leftarrow \text{denominator}} \rightarrow \frac{7}{8}$$

The denominator tells you how many equal parts the object or number is divided into, and the numerator tells how many of those parts we are concerned with.

Example: Divide a baseball game, a football game, and a hockey game into convenient numbers of parts. Write a fraction to answer each equation.

   1. If a pitcher played two innings, how much of the whole baseball game did he play?

   2. If a quarterback played three quarters of a football game, how much of the whole game did he play?

   3. If a goalie played two periods of a hockey game, how much of the whole game did he play?

Solution 1:   A baseball game has nine parts (each an inning). The pitcher pitched two innings. Therefore, he played $\frac{2}{9}$ of the game. The denominator represents the nine parts the game is divided into; the numerator, the two parts we are concerned with.

Solution 2:   Similarly, there are four quarters in a football game, and a quarterback playing three of those quarters plays in $\frac{3}{4}$ of the game.

Solution 3:   There are three periods in hockey, and the goalie played in two of them. Therefore, he played in $\frac{2}{3}$ of the game.

Equivalent Fractions

Fractions having different denominators and numerators might represent the same amount. These are equivalent fractions. Even though the fractions don't look the same, their values can be the same.

For example, divide the following circle into two equal parts. Write a fraction to indicate how much of the circle is shaded.

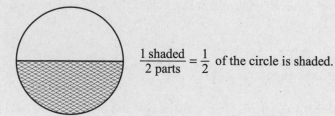

$\dfrac{1 \text{ shaded}}{2 \text{ parts}} = \dfrac{1}{2}$ of the circle is shaded.

15

The circle below is divided into four equal parts. Write a fraction to indicate how much of the circle is shaded.

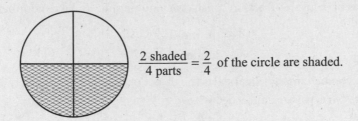

$\dfrac{2 \text{ shaded}}{4 \text{ parts}} = \dfrac{2}{4}$ of the circle are shaded.

This circle is divided into eight equal parts. Write a fraction to indicate how much of the circle is shaded.

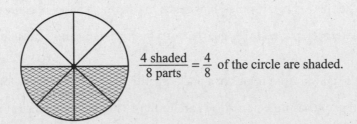

$\dfrac{4 \text{ shaded}}{8 \text{ parts}} = \dfrac{4}{8}$ of the circle are shaded.

In each circle, the same amount was shaded. This shows that there is more than one way to indicate one half of something.

The fractions $\dfrac{1}{2}$, $\dfrac{2}{4}$, and $\dfrac{4}{8}$ that you wrote are *equivalent fractions* because they all represent the same amount. Notice that the denominator is twice as large as the numerator in every case. Any fraction you write that has a denominator that is exactly twice as large as the numerator will be equivalent to $\dfrac{1}{2}$.

Example: Write other fractions equivalent to $\dfrac{1}{2}$.

Solution: Any fraction that has a denominator that is twice as large as the numerator: $\dfrac{3}{6}$, $\dfrac{5}{10}$, $\dfrac{6}{12}$, $\dfrac{32}{64}$, etc.

Example: Write other fractions equivalent to $\dfrac{1}{4}$.

Solution: Any fraction that has a denominator that is four times as large as the numerator: $\dfrac{2}{8}$, $\dfrac{4}{16}$, $\dfrac{5}{20}$, $\dfrac{15}{60}$, etc.

Example: Write other fractions equivalent to $\dfrac{2}{3}$.

Solution: Any fraction that has a denominator that is one and one-half times as large as the numerator: $\dfrac{4}{6}$, $\dfrac{10}{15}$, $\dfrac{14}{21}$, $\dfrac{16}{24}$, etc.

When you cannot divide the numerator and denominator of a fraction evenly by the same whole number (other than 1), the fraction is in its simplest form. In the examples above, $\dfrac{1}{2}$, $\dfrac{1}{4}$, and $\dfrac{2}{3}$ are in simplest form.

To write equivalent fractions where the numerator is not 1 requires one more step.

Example: What is the equivalent fraction for $\frac{4}{5}$ using 10 as a denominator?

Solution: Each $\frac{1}{5}$ is equivalent to $\frac{2}{10}$; therefore, $\frac{4}{5}$ is equivalent to $\frac{8}{10}$.

The quickest way to find an equivalent fraction is to divide the denominator of the fraction you want by the denominator you know. Take the result and multiply it by the numerator of the fraction you know. This becomes the numerator of the equivalent fraction.

Example: Rename $\frac{3}{8}$ as an equivalent fraction having 16 as a denominator.

Solution: $\frac{3}{8} = \frac{6}{16}$ $(16 \div 8 = 2; 2 \times 3 = 6)$

Example: Rename $\frac{3}{4}$ as equivalent fractions having 8, 12, 24, and 32 as denominators.

Solution: $\frac{3}{4} = \frac{6}{8}$ $(8 \div 4 = 2; 2 \times 3 = 6)$

$\frac{3}{4} = \frac{9}{12}$ $(12 \div 4 = 3; 3 \times 3 = 9)$

$\frac{3}{4} = \frac{18}{24}$ $(24 \div 4 = 6; 6 \times 3 = 18)$

$\frac{3}{4} = \frac{24}{32}$ $(32 \div 4 = 8; 8 \times 3 = 24)$

A fraction that has a numerator greater than the denominator is an *improper fraction*. A number expressed as an integer together with a proper fraction is a *mixed number*.

Examples of improper fractions include $\frac{3}{2}$, $\frac{12}{7}$, and $\frac{9}{5}$. Note that each is in simplest form because the numerator and denominator cannot be divided evenly by a number other than 1.

Examples of mixed numbers include $1\frac{1}{2}$, $1\frac{5}{7}$, and $1\frac{4}{5}$. We call these mixed numbers because they have a whole number part and a fractional part. These mixed numbers are equivalent to the improper fractions given previously. To rename a mixed number as an improper fraction is easy.

Example: Rename $2\frac{1}{4}$ as an improper fraction.

Solution: The whole number 2 contains 8 fourths. Add to it the $\frac{1}{4}$ to write the equivalent fraction $\frac{9}{4}$.

Another way of figuring this is to multiply the denominator of the fraction by the whole number and add the numerator.

Example: Rename $2\frac{1}{4}$ as an improper fraction.

Solution: $4 \times 2 = 8 + 1 = 9$; combined with the denominator, the result is $\frac{9}{4}$.

15

Chapter 15: Mathematics

To rename an improper fraction as a mixed number, just proceed backward.

Example: Rename $\frac{9}{4}$ as a mixed number.

Solution: Divide the numerator by the denominator and use the remainder (R) as the fraction numerator:

$$9 \div 4 = 2 \text{ R1 or } 9 \div 4 = 2\frac{1}{4}.$$

Adding and Subtracting Fractions

To add fractions with the same denominators, add the numerators and keep the common denominator.

Example: Add $\frac{1}{4} + \frac{3}{4} + \frac{3}{4}$.

Solution: When the denominators are the same, add the numerators to arrive at the answer, $\frac{7}{4}$ or simplify as $1\frac{3}{4}$.

To find the difference between two fractions with the same denominators, subtract the numerators, leaving the denominators alone.

Example: Find the difference between $\frac{7}{8}$ and $\frac{3}{8}$.

Solution: $\frac{7}{8} - \frac{3}{8} = \frac{4}{8}$ simplified to $\frac{4}{8} = \frac{1}{2}$.

To add or subtract fractions with different denominators, you must first find a *common denominator*. A common denominator is a number that can be divided by the denominators of all the fractions in the problem without a remainder. The process is the same as finding the greatest common factor. As you go through the upcoming exercises, look for the similarities to the GCF process. If you don't understand the steps coming up, go back and review the GCF section.

Example: Find a common denominator for $\frac{1}{4}$ and $\frac{1}{3}$.

Solution: Multiply the denominators to get $4 \times 3 = 12$. 12 can be divided by both 4 and 3:

$$\frac{1}{4} \text{ is equivalent to } \frac{3}{12}$$
$$\frac{1}{3} \text{ is equivalent to } \frac{4}{12}$$

We can now add the fractions because we have written equivalent fractions with a common denominator.

$$\frac{3}{12} + \frac{4}{12} = \frac{7}{12}$$

Therefore:

$$\frac{1}{4} + \frac{1}{3} = \frac{7}{12}$$

Seven-twelfths is in its simplest form because 7 and 12 do not have a whole number (other than 1) by which they are both divisible.

Example: Add $\frac{3}{8}$, $\frac{5}{6}$, $\frac{1}{4}$, and $\frac{2}{3}$.

Solution: Find a number into which all denominators will divide evenly. For 8, 6, 4, and 3, the best choice is 24. Now convert each fraction to an equivalent fraction having a denominator of 24:

$$\frac{3}{8} = \frac{9}{24} \quad (24 \div 8 = 3; \; 3 \times 3 = 9)$$

$$\frac{5}{6} = \frac{20}{24} \quad (24 \div 6 = 4; \; 4 \times 5 = 20)$$

$$\frac{1}{4} = \frac{6}{24} \quad (24 \div 4 = 6; \; 6 \times 1 = 6)$$

$$\frac{2}{3} = \frac{16}{24} \quad (24 \div 3 = 8; \; 8 \times 2 = 16)$$

Now add the fractions:

$$\frac{9}{24} + \frac{20}{24} + \frac{6}{24} + \frac{16}{24} = \frac{51}{24}$$

The answer, $\frac{51}{24}$, is an improper fraction; that is, the numerator is greater than the denominator. To rename the answer to a mixed number, divide the numerator by the denominator and express the remainder as a fraction.

$$\frac{51}{24} = 51 \div 24 = 2\frac{3}{24} = 2\frac{1}{8}$$

Test Yourself 8

Express your answers as simple mixed numbers in the space provided. The answer keys and explanations follow **Test Yourself 30**.

1. $\frac{2}{4} + \frac{3}{5} + \frac{1}{2} =$

2. $\frac{6}{8} - \frac{2}{4} =$

3. $\frac{1}{3} + \frac{1}{2} =$

4. $\frac{4}{5} - \frac{3}{5} =$

5. $\frac{7}{8} + \frac{3}{4} + \frac{1}{3} =$

6. $\frac{1}{2} + \frac{1}{4} + \frac{2}{3} =$

7. $\frac{5}{6} - \frac{1}{2} =$

8. $\frac{5}{8} - \frac{1}{3} =$

9. $\frac{5}{12} + \frac{3}{4} =$

10. $\frac{8}{9} - \frac{2}{3} =$

15

Multiplying and Dividing Fractions

When multiplying fractions, multiply numerators by numerators and denominators by denominators.

$$\frac{3}{5} \times \frac{4}{7} \times \frac{1}{5} = \frac{3 \times 4 \times 1}{5 \times 7 \times 5} = \frac{12}{175}$$

Try to work with numbers that are as small as possible. You can make numbers smaller by dividing out common factors. Do this by dividing the numerator of any one fraction and the denominator of any one fraction by the same number.

$$\frac{\overset{1}{\cancel{3}}}{\underset{2}{\cancel{4}}} \times \frac{\overset{1}{\cancel{2}}}{\underset{3}{\cancel{9}}} = \frac{1 \times 1}{2 \times 3} = \frac{1}{6}$$

In this case, we divided the numerator of the first fraction and the denominator of the second fraction by 3, while the denominator of the first fraction and the numerator of the second fraction were divided by 2.

To divide by a fraction, multiply by the reciprocal of the divisor.

$$\frac{3}{16} \div \frac{1}{8} = \frac{3}{\underset{2}{\cancel{16}}} \times \frac{\overset{1}{\cancel{8}}}{1} = \frac{3}{2} = 1\frac{1}{2}$$

TIP

You may have heard the phrase "copy dot flip flop." It's a nifty reminder that when you divide fractions you'll *copy* the first fraction, add a multiplication *dot*, then *flip flop* the second fraction so you can then multiply the fractions as you would normally.

Test Yourself 9

Divide out common factors wherever possible and express your answers in simplest form. The answer keys and explanations follow **Test Yourself 30**.

1. $\frac{4}{5} \times \frac{3}{6} =$

2. $\frac{2}{4} \times \frac{8}{12} \times \frac{7}{1} =$

3. $\frac{3}{4} \div \frac{3}{8} =$

4. $\frac{5}{2} \div \frac{3}{6} =$

5. $\frac{8}{9} \times \frac{3}{4} \times \frac{1}{2} =$

6. $\frac{7}{8} \div \frac{2}{3} =$

7. $\frac{4}{16} \times \frac{8}{12} \times \frac{10}{13} =$

8. $\frac{1}{6} \times \frac{7}{6} \times \frac{12}{3} =$

9. $\frac{3}{7} \div \frac{9}{4} =$

10. $\frac{2}{3} \div \frac{2}{3} =$

The fraction bar in a fraction means "divided by." To rename a fraction as a decimal, follow through on the division.

$$\frac{4}{5} = 4 \div 5 = 0.8$$

To rename a decimal as a percent, multiply by 100, move the decimal point two places to the right, and attach a percent sign.

$$0.8 = 80\%$$

Test Yourself 10

Rename each fraction, first as a decimal to three places, and then as a percent. The answer keys and explanations follow **Test Yourself 30**.

1. $\dfrac{2}{4} =$

2. $\dfrac{7}{8} =$

3. $\dfrac{5}{6} =$

4. $\dfrac{6}{8} =$

5. $\dfrac{3}{4} =$

6. $\dfrac{2}{3} =$

7. $\dfrac{3}{5} =$

8. $\dfrac{4}{10} =$

9. $\dfrac{1}{4} =$

10. $\dfrac{2}{5} =$

PERCENTAGES

One percent is one hundredth of something. The last syllable of the word *percent*, *-cent*, is the name we give to one hundredth of a dollar. Think of the word *century*, which is 100 years. Both share the root *cent*.

One percent of $1.00, then, is one cent. Using decimal notation, we can write one cent as $0.01, five cents as $0.05, twenty-five cents as $0.25, and so forth.

Twenty-five cents is equal to twenty-five hundredths of a dollar. Rather than say that something is so many hundredths of something else, we use the word percent. Twenty-five cents, then, is twenty-five percent of a dollar. We use the symbol % to stand for percent.

There is a relationship between decimals, fractions, and percentages. The following notes will help you to convert numbers from one of these forms to another:

1. To change a percentage to a decimal, remove the percent sign (%) and divide the number by 100.

   Example: $25\% = \dfrac{25}{100} = 0.25$

2. To change a decimal to a percentage, multiply by 100 and add the % sign.

   Example: $0.25 = 0.25\% \times 100 = 25\%$

3. To change a percentage to a fraction, remove the % sign and use that number as your numerator, with 100 as your denominator.

   Example: $25\% = \dfrac{25}{100} = \dfrac{1}{4}$

4. To change a fraction to a percentage, multiply by 100 and add the percent sign (%).

   Example: $\dfrac{1}{4} \times 100 = 25\%$

Percentage is not limited to comparing other numbers to 100. You can divide any number into hundredths and talk about percentage.

> **TIP**
>
> You can find a percentage with the following equation:
>
> $$\text{percentage} = \left(\frac{\text{part}}{\text{whole}}\right) \bullet 100.$$
>
> That equation can be flipped around algebraically to find that
>
> $$\text{part} = \text{whole} \bullet \left(\frac{\text{percentage}}{100}\right)$$
>
> or
>
> $$\text{whole} = \text{part} \div \left(\frac{\text{percentage}}{100}\right).$$

15

Example: Find 1% of 200.

Solution: 1% of 200 is 1/100, or 0.01, of 200.

Using decimal notation, we can calculate one percent of 200 by:

$200 \times 0.01 = 2$

Similarly, we can find a percentage of any number we choose by multiplying it by the correct decimal notation. For example:

Five percent of 50: $0.05 \times 50 = 2.5$
Three percent of 150: $0.03 \times 150 = 4.5$
Ten percent of 60: $0.10 \times 60 = 6$

Not all percentage measurements are between one percent and 100 percent. We may wish to consider less than one percent of something, especially if it is very large.

For example, if you were handed a book 1,000 pages long, and you were told to read one percent of it in five minutes, how much would you have to read?

$1000 \times 0.01 = 10$ pages

Quite an assignment! You might bargain to read one half of one percent, or one-tenth of one percent in the five minutes allotted to you.

Using decimal notation, we write one-tenth of one percent as 0.001, the decimal number for one thousandth. If you remember that a percent is one hundredth of something, you can see that one tenth of that percent is equivalent to one thousandth of the whole.

In percent notation, one tenth of one percent is 0.1%. On high school entrance exams, students often mistakenly think that 0.1% is equal to 0.1. As you know, 0.1% is equal to 0.001.

Sometimes we are concerned with more than 100% of something. You may ask, since 100% constitutes all of something, how can we speak of *more* than all of it?

Where things are growing, or increasing in size or amount, we may want to compare their new size to the size they once were. For example, suppose we measured the heights of three plants to be 6 inches, 9 inches, and 12 inches one week, and discover a week later that the first plant is still 6 inches tall, but the second and third ones are now 18 inches tall.

The 6-inch plant grew *zero percent* because it didn't grow at all. The second plant *added 100%* to its size. It doubled in height. The third plant *added 50%* to its height.

We can also say:

The first plant is 100% of its original height.
The second plant grew to 200% of its original height.
The third plant grew to 150% of its original height.

Here are some common percentage and fractional equivalents you should remember:

- Ten percent (10%) is one tenth $\left(\dfrac{1}{10}\right)$, or 0.10.

- Twelve and one-half percent (12.5%) is one eighth $\left(\dfrac{1}{8}\right)$, or 0.125.

> **TIP**
>
> When multiplying by percentages, students frequently mix up 0.1 and 0.1%. If you are trying to find 0.1% of something, you must multiply by 0.001, not 0.1, to get the correct answer.

15

- Twenty percent (20%) is one fifth $\left(\dfrac{1}{5}\right)$, or 0.20.

- Twenty-five percent (25%) is one quarter $\left(\dfrac{1}{4}\right)$, or 0.25.

- Thirty-three and one-third percent $\left(33\dfrac{1}{3}\%\right)$ is one third $\left(\dfrac{1}{3}\right)$, or $0.33\overline{3}$.

- Fifty percent (50%) is one half $\left(\dfrac{1}{2}\right)$, or 0.50.

- Sixty-six and two-thirds percent $\left(66\dfrac{2}{3}\%\right)$ is two thirds $\left(\dfrac{2}{3}\right)$, or $0.66\overline{6}$.

- Seventy-five percent (75%) is three quarters $\left(\dfrac{3}{4}\right)$, or 0.75.

Caution: When solving problems involving percentages, be careful of common errors:

- **Read the notation carefully.** 0.50% is *not* fifty percent, but one half of one percent.

- **Read the problem carefully** to look for increases or decreases in percentage.

- **Use common sense.** If you wish to find less than 100% of a number, your result will be smaller than the number you started with. For example, 98% of 50 is less than 50. Using common sense works in the other direction as well. For example, 70 is 40% of what number? The number you are looking for must be larger than 70, since 70 is only $\dfrac{40}{100}$ of it. Moreover, you can estimate that the number you are looking for will be a little more than twice as large as 70, since 70 is not quite half (50%) of that number.

To find a percent of a number, change the percent to a decimal and multiply the number by it.

Example: What is 5% of 80?

Solution: 5% of 80 = 80 × 0.05 = 4

To find out what a number is when given a percent of it, change the percent to a decimal and divide the given number by it.

Example: 5 is 10% of what number?

Solution: 5 ÷ 0.10 = 50

To find what percent one number is of another number, create a fraction by placing the part over the whole. Simplify the fraction if possible, then rename it as a decimal (remember the fraction bar means *divided by*, so divide the numerator by the denominator), and rename the answer as a percent by multiplying by 100, moving the decimal point two places to the right.

Example: 4 is what percent of 80?

Solution: $\dfrac{4}{80} = \dfrac{1}{20} = 0.05 = 5\%$

15

Test Yourself 11

Solve the following percentage problems in the space provided. The answer keys and explanations follow **Test Yourself 30**.

1. 10% of 32 =
2. 8 is 25% of what number?
3. 12 is what percent of 24?
4. 20% of 360 =
5. 5 is what percent of 60?

6. 12 is 8% of what number?
7. 6% of 36 =
8. 25 is 5% of what number?
9. 70 is what percent of 140?
10. What percent of 100 is 19?

PERCENT OF CHANGE

Ten percent off a $60 video game sounds pretty good, right? Well, sure. But do you have enough in your wallet to get the game? To know that, you must know how to calculate percent of change. For this, you need a good understanding of decimals, percentages, and fractions.

Let's figure out how much that video game will cost. First, we need the percent change formula.

$$\frac{\% \; change}{100} = \frac{difference}{original \; \#}$$

To get the new price, we need two pieces of information. We know the original price was $60, and the discount is ten percent. With that, we can fill the spaces in the formula.

$$\frac{10}{100} = \frac{x}{60}$$

From here, we cross-multiply.

$$\frac{10 \times 60 = 600}{100 \times x = 100x}, \text{ or } 600 = 100x, \text{ which reduces to } 6 = x.$$

Subtract this from the original price to find how much the game is now.

$60 - $6 = $54

What if you know the old price and the new, but you need to find the percent change between the two? Let's use that video game again. We know the original price was $60.00 and the new price is $54.00, so let's plug those figures into our percent change formula.

$$\frac{x}{100} = \frac{6}{60}$$

As before, we cross-multiply to obtain $600 = 60x$, which reduces to $10 = x$. The percent change in price is 10%.

15

Test Yourself 12

Using the percent change formula, find each requested value. The answer keys and explanations follow **Test Yourself 30**.

1. 25% of 90 =

2. 33% of 250 =

3. 10% of 500 =

4. 15% of 30 =

5. 45% of 400.5 =

Convert the following fractions to percentages and solve.

6. $\frac{1}{3}$ of 18 =

7. $\frac{4}{5}$ of 200 =

8. $\frac{1}{12}$ of 700 =

9. $\frac{1}{4}$ of 30 =

10. $\frac{1}{2}$ of 17.3 =

RATIOS

Ratios show the relationship between two or more items. For example, you have an 8 oz. glass of water and you add one ounce of lemon juice. That is a ratio, and we can express it as 8 oz. of water to 1 oz. lemon juice.

You can also write this as 8:1 or $\frac{8}{1}$. Let's look at a couple of examples.

Example: Write a ratio showing the number of tires (excluding the spare) on a car.

Solution: There are four tires on a car, so the ratio is 4:1.

Example: There are 25 students for every teacher. Show the ratio of students per teacher.

Solution: 25:1

Ratios like these can make scaling up easier, because whatever you do to one side, you do to the other. This is called *proportioning*.

Example: There are 25 students for every teacher (*t*). Show the ratio of students per teacher if you have 3 teachers.

Solution: Set up your proportion.

$$\frac{25}{1} = \frac{75}{t}$$

Multiply the two fractions to eliminate the denominator.

$$25 \times t = 75 \times 1$$

$$25t = 75$$

Divide both sides by 25 to solve for *t*

$$\frac{25t}{25} = \frac{75}{25}$$

$$t = 3$$

15

Chapter 15: Mathematics

Alternatively, you can also write the proportion like this:

$$3(25:1) = 3(25):3(1) = 75:3$$

An important thing to note is that order matters. Take the tires:car ratio of 4:1. If we slipped up and wrote that ratio as 1:4, then you start wondering how one tire fits on four cars. That would be a pretty bizarre-looking car.

Test Yourself 13

Write each problem as a ratio. The answer keys and explanations follow **Test Yourself 30.**

1. 4 miles to 1 bridge
2. 32 oz. of water per bottle
3. 3 reserved parking spots for every 17 parking spaces

4. 400 fish for every 2 pet stores
5. 9 tabs for each web browser, 3 browsers open

Ratios with More Than Two Items

When you bake biscuits, you have three core ingredients: three cups of flour, $1\frac{1}{3}$ cup of milk, and two eggs. If we express this as a ratio, it looks like this:

$$1:3:1\frac{1}{3}:2$$

What if you want to bake two batches of biscuits? The same rules apply as they did above. Take the above ratio and change the number of batches to 2. When you change the one element, in this case by multiplying the number of batches by 2, you must do the same to each element in the ratio.

$$2:6:2\frac{2}{3}:4$$

And now you know what goes into the batter for *two* batches of homemade biscuits.

Test Yourself 14

Write each problem as a ratio. The answer keys and explanations follow **Test Yourself 30.**

1. 7 lemons to 1 gallon of water to 3 cups sugar
2. 45 people to 4 clerks at 2 stores
3. 21 textbooks to 25 students for 1 teacher

4. 16 employees per field office in 1 district
5. 16 employees per field office in 1 district, in three districts

MEASUREMENT CONVERSIONS

Would you rather call something 5,280 feet or one mile? They both mean the same thing. But think about it for a second; one mile is something you understand. Dad drives nine miles, that makes sense to us. Dad driving 47,520 feet is quite a bit more difficult to comprehend. Being able to convert units of measurement is a necessary skill, both in the classroom and in life. Did you ever try baking a cake that calls for 144 teaspoons of flour? Or running 1.61 kilometers in gym class? Probably not, unless you already know 144 teaspoons is equal to three cups, or 1 mile is equal to 1.61 kilometers. Being able to convert one measurement into another can be a very valuable skill, indeed.

15

Here is a glossary of measurement terms and abbreviations. Below that is a list of common measurement conversions.

Metric System

- Millimeter = mm
- Centimeter = cm
- Meter = m
- Kilometer = km
- Milligram = mg
- Gram = g
- Kilogram = kg
- Milliliter = ml
- Milliliter = ml
- Liter = l
- Celsius = °C
- Fahrenheit = °F

Standard (US) System

- Inches = in. or "
- Feet = ft. or '
- Yard = yd.
- Miles = mi.

- Ounce = oz.
- Fluid Ounce = fl. oz.
- Pound = lb. or #
- Cup = c.
- Pint = pt.
- Quart = qt.
- Gallon = gal.

Common Conversions

- 1 km = 1,000 m = 100,000 cm = 1,000,000 mm
- 1 kg = 1,000 g = 1,000,000 mg
- 1 ft. = 12 in.
- 1 yd. = 3 ft. = 36 in.
- 1 mi. = 5,280 ft.
- 1 lb. = 16 oz
- 1 ton = 2,000 lbs.
- 1 gal. = 4 qts. = 16 c.

> **TIP**
>
> You're not expected to memorize all these conversions. But you should know the basics: quarts to gallons, meter to kilometer, ounces to pounds. Remember, the metric system is based on factors of ten; ten millimeters in a centimeter, 1,000 meters in a kilometer, etc.

Throughout most of the world, people use the metric system for measurements, while in the United States people use the standard measurement system. This can cause confusion when going from one system to another. When converting from one system to another, you need to know equivalent values. Here is a list of **common equivalencies**.

- 1 mi. = 1.96 km = 5,280 ft.
- 1 km = 0.62 mi. = 3,280.8 ft.
- 1 ft. = 30.48 cm = 304.8 mm
- 1 in. = 2.54 cm = 25.4 mm
- 1 m = 3.28 ft. = 39.37 in.
- 1 kg = 2.2 lbs. = 35.27 oz.

- 1 lb. = 0.453 kg = 453 g
- 1 gal. = 3.785 l
- 1 l = 0.264 gal. = 1.056 qt. = 4.2 c.
- 1°C = 33.8°F
- 1°F = −17.2°C
- 1°K = −272°C = −457.8°F

15

How to Convert

Knowing how many feet are in a kilometer is fine, but how do you put that bit of knowledge into use? Most of these are, "multiply this by that to get the other thing," the only real exceptions to that being going from Fahrenheit to Celsius and vice-versa. Before we go over the conversions for temperature, let's look at common conversions for length, weight, and volume.

Metric Unit Conversions		
Length and Distance		
when you know:	*multiply by:*	*to find:*
inches	2.5400	centimeters
feet	0.3048	meters
yards	0.9144	meters
miles	1.6093	kilometers
millimeters	0.0394	inches
centimeters	0.3937	inches
meters	3.2808	feet
meters	1.0936	yards
kilometers	0.6214	miles
Weight and Mass		
when you know:	*multiply by:*	*to find:*
ounces	28.3495	grams
pounds	0.4536	kilograms
short tons	0.9072	metric tons
kilograms	2.2046	pounds
metric tons	1.1023	short tons
Volume and Capacity (Liquid)		
when you know:	*multiply by:*	*to find:*
pints (U.S.)	0.4732	liters
quarts (U.S.)	0.9463	liters
gallons (U.S)	3.7853	liters
liters	2.1134	pints (U.S.)
liters	1.0567	quarts (U.S.)
liters	0.2642	gallons (U.S.)

15

For temperatures, let's use three specific values for our conversions: freezing, boiling, and body temperature. Those values are:

- Freezing: 32°F, 0°C
- Boiling: 212°F, 100°C
- Body temperature: 98.6°F, 37°C

Let's convert freezing from Fahrenheit to Celsius. The formula for converting Fahrenheit to Celsius is:

$$F - 32 \times 5 \div 9 = C$$

So, $32 - 32 \times 5 \div 9 = 0$, remembering the Multiplicative Property of Zero which states any number multiplied or divided by zero is equal to zero.

Going from Celsius to Fahrenheit requires doing the exact opposite. The formula for converting Celsius to Fahrenheit is:

$$C \times 9 \div 5 + 32 = F$$

If boiling water is 100°C, then $100 \times 9 \div 5 + 32 = 212$°F.

Test Yourself 15

Solve each conversion problem. The answer keys and explanations follow **Test Yourself 30**.

1. How many feet in a mile?
2. How many kilometers is 3,500 m?
3. How many qts. are in a 2-liter soda bottle?
4. How many inches is 17.78 cm?
5. How warm in Celsius is a 104°F bath?
6. How many feet are in 2 meters?
7. How many liters in one gallon?
8. A 180°C oven is what temperature in Fahrenheit?

ALGEBRA

If you are finishing the eighth grade this year, you might not yet have had a formal algebra class. Still, you have probably used algebraic terms and expressions, and you have probably solved simple equations. This section will review the skills you have acquired so far and will show you the kinds of questions you can expect to find on a high school entrance examination.

Signed Numbers

The number line exists to both sides of zero. Each positive number on the right of zero has a negative counterpart to the left of zero. The number line below shows the location of some pairs of numbers (+4, −4; +2, −2; +1, −1).

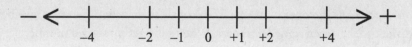

Because each number of a pair is located the same distance from zero (though in different directions), each has the same **absolute value**. Absolute value is symbolized by placing two vertical bars—one on either side of the number.

$$|+4| = |-4| = 4$$

The absolute value of +4 equals the absolute value of −4. Both are equivalent to 4. If you think of absolute value as the distance from zero, regardless of direction, you will understand it easily. The absolute value of any number, positive or negative, is expressed as a positive number.

Addition of Signed Numbers

> **TIP**
> To add signed numbers with the same sign, add the magnitudes of the numbers and keep the same sign. To add signed numbers with different signs, subtract the magnitudes of the numbers and use the sign of the number with the greater magnitude.

When we add two oppositely signed numbers having the same absolute value, the sum is zero.

$$(+10) + (-10) = 0$$
$$(-1.5) + (+1.5) = 0$$
$$(-0.010) + (+0.010) = 0$$
$$\left(+\frac{3}{4}\right) + \left(-\frac{3}{4}\right) = 0$$

If one of the two oppositely signed numbers is greater in absolute value, the sum is equal to the amount of that excess and carries the same sign as the number having the greater absolute value.

$$(+2) + (-1) = +1$$
$$(+8) + (-9) = -1$$
$$(-2.5) + (+2.0) = -0.5$$
$$\left(-\frac{3}{4}\right) + \left(+\frac{1}{2}\right) = -\frac{1}{4}$$

Test Yourself 16

Solve the following signed number addition problems. The answer keys and explanations follow **Test Yourself 30**.

1. $(+5) + (+8) =$
2. $(+6) + (-3) =$
3. $(+4) + (-12) =$
4. $(-7) + (+2) =$
5. $(-21) + (-17) =$
6. $(-9) + (-36) =$

7. $(+31) + (-14) =$
8. $(-16.3) + (-12.5) =$
9. $\left(-8\frac{1}{2}\right) + \left(+4\frac{1}{4}\right) =$
10. $(+66) + (-66) =$

Subtraction of Signed Numbers

Subtraction is the operation that finds the difference between two numbers, including the difference between signed numbers. When subtracting signed numbers, it is helpful to refer to a number line.

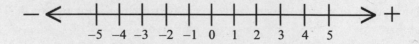

15

For example, if we wish to subtract +2 from +5, we can use the number line to see that the difference is +3. We give the sign to the difference that represents the direction we are moving along the number line from the number being subtracted to the number from which you are subtracting. In this case, because we are subtracting +2 from +5, we count three units in a positive direction from +2 to +5 on the number line.

When subtracting signed numbers:

- The distance between the two numbers gives you the absolute value of the difference.
- The direction you move from the number being subtracted to get to the number from which you are subtracting gives you the sign of the difference.

TIP
Change the sign of the number being subtracted and follow the rules for addition.

Example: Subtract −3 from +5.

Solution: Distance on the number line between −3 and +5 is 8 units.

Direction is from negative to positive—a positive direction.

Answer is +8.

Example: Subtract −6 from −8.

Solution: Distance on number line between −6 and −8 is 2 units.

Direction is from −6 to −8—a negative direction.

Answer is −2.

Example: Subtract +1.30 from −2.70.

Solution: Distance between +1.30 and −2.70 on the number line is 4.0.

Direction is from +1.30 to −2.70 —a negative direction.

Answer is −4.0.

A quick way to subtract signed numbers accurately involves placing the numbers in columns, reversing the sign of the number being subtracted and then adding the two.

Example: Subtract +26 from +15.

Solution: $+15 = +15$

$- +26 = -26$

$= -11$

Example: Subtract −35 from +10.

Solution: $+10 = +10$

$- -35 = +35$

$= +45$

Notice that in each of the examples, we found the correct answer by reversing the sign of the number being subtracted and then adding.

Test Yourself 17

Solve the following signed number subtraction problems. The answer keys and explanations follow **Test Yourself 30**.

1. $(-6) - (-12) =$
2. $(+17) - (-8) =$
3. $(+45) - (+62) =$
4. $(-34) - (+21) =$
5. $(+4) - (-58) =$

6. $(+75) - (+27) =$
7. $(-12.6) - (-5.3) =$
8. $\left(-15\frac{1}{4}\right) - \left(+26\frac{1}{4}\right) =$
9. $(-35) - (+35) =$
10. $(+56.1) - (+56.7) =$

Multiplication of Signed Numbers

Signed numbers are multiplied as any other numbers would be, with the following exceptions:

The product of two negative numbers is positive.

$$(-3) \times (-6) = +18$$

The product of two positive numbers is positive.

$$(+3.05) \times (+6) = +18.30$$

The product of a negative and positive number is negative.

$$\left(+4\frac{1}{2}\right) \times (-3) = -13\frac{1}{2}$$

$$(+1) \times (-1) \times (+1) = -1$$

Test Yourself 18

Solve the following signed number multiplication problems. The answer keys and explanations follow **Test Yourself 30**.

1. $(+5) \times (+8) =$
2. $(+12) \times (-3) =$
3. $(-6) \times (-21) =$
4. $(-4) \times (-10) =$
5. $(+3.3) \times (-5.8) =$

6. $(-7.5) \times (+4.2) =$
7. $\left(-6\frac{1}{2}\right) \times \left(-7\frac{1}{4}\right) =$
8. $(+9) \times (-1) =$
9. $(0) \times (-5.7) =$
10. $(-12) \times (-12) =$

15

Division of Signed Numbers

As with multiplication, the division of signed numbers requires you to observe three simple rules:

When dividing a positive number by a negative number, the result is negative.

$$(+6) \div (-3) = -2$$

When dividing a negative number by a positive number, the result is negative.

$$(-6) \div (+3) = -2$$

When dividing a negative number by a negative number or a positive number by a positive number, the result is positive.

$$(-6) \div (-3) = +2$$
$$(+6) \div (+3) = +2$$

Test Yourself 19

Solve the following signed number division problems. The answer keys and explanations follow **Test Yourself 30**.

1. $(+3) \div (-1) =$
2. $(+36) \div (+12) =$
3. $(-45) \div (-9) =$
4. $(-75) \div (+3) =$
5. $(+5.6) \div (-0.7) =$
6. $(-3.5) \div (-5) =$

7. $\left(+6\frac{1}{2}\right) \div \left(+3\frac{1}{4}\right) =$
8. $(-8.2) \div (-1) =$
9. $\left(+12\frac{1}{2}\right) \div \left(-12\frac{1}{2}\right) =$
10. $(0) \div (-19.6) =$

EQUATIONS

An equation is an equality. The values on either side of the equal sign in an equation must be equal. In order to learn the value of an unknown in an equation, do the same thing to both sides of the equation to leave the unknown on one side of the equal sign and its value on the other side.

Example: $x - 2 = 8$

Solution: Add 2 to both sides of the equation:

$$x - 2 + 2 = 8 + 2$$
$$x = 10$$

Example: $5x = 25$

Solution: Divide both sides of the equation by 5:

$$\left(\frac{{}^1\cancel{5}x}{\cancel{5}_1}\right) = \left(\frac{25}{5}\right)$$
$$x = 5$$

Example: $y + 9 = 15$

Solution: Subtract 9 from both sides of the equation:

$$y + 9 - 9 = 15 - 9$$
$$y = 6$$

Example: $a \div 4 = 48$

Solution: Multiply both sides of the equation by 4:

$$\cancel{4}\left(\frac{a}{\cancel{4}_1}\right) = 48 \times 4$$
$$a = 192$$

Sometimes more than one step is required to solve an equation.

Example: $6a \div 4 = 48$

Solution: First, multiply both sides of the equation by 4:

$$\frac{6a}{4} \times \frac{4}{1} = 48 \times 4$$
$$6a = 192$$

Then divide both sides of the equation by 6:

$$\frac{{}^1\cancel{6}a}{\cancel{6}_1} = \frac{192}{6}$$
$$a = 32$$

Test Yourself 20

Solve the following equations for x. The answer keys and explanations follow **Test Yourself 30**.

1. $x + 13 = 25$

2. $4x = 84$

3. $x - 5 = 28$

4. $x \div 9 = 4$

5. $3x + 2 = 14$

6. $\dfrac{x}{4} - 2 - 4 = 0$

7. $10x - 27 = 73$

8. $2x \div 4 = 13$

9. $8x + 9 = 81$

10. $2x \div 11 = 6$

15

STANDARD FORM AND SCIENTIFIC NOTATION

Standard form is something you've been using since you learned how to write numbers. Write the number one hundred. That is standard form—the usual way you'd write a number. In addition to being the way you've written numbers all your life, standard form is also an agreed-upon method of writing an equation. The standard form for equations has a couple of rules you need to know.

1. Always set an equation = 0.

   Example: $x = 7$ should have everything on the left of the equal sign, and 0 on the right:

   $x - 7 = 0$ is standard form.

2. Work from the highest exponent.

   Example: $7x^3 + 3x^6 - 5 + 4x^2$ should start with the highest exponent:

   $3x^6 + 7x^3 + 4x^2 - 5$

3. A linear equation is always $Ax + By = C$, where $C=0$.

Test Yourself 21

Put the following equations into standard form. The answer keys and explanations follow **Test Yourself 30**.

1. $x + 7 = 49$
2. $x = 4y$
3. $ab = 14c$
4. $4x^3 + 17x^5 - 2 - 4x^9$
5. $3x + 4y + 5 = 17$

Scientific notation uses exponents to write either very large or very small numbers. Let's use a very large number to explain this: 35 trillion. Written out in standard form, that is 35,000,000,000,000. Rather than writing out all those zeroes, we can use scientific notation: 3.5×10^{13}. To convert a number from standard form to scientific notation, imagine there's a decimal point at the end of that number. You must move that decimal point to the left until you have a number between one and ten. For 35 trillion, you move the decimal point 13 places to the left, giving you 3.5. To show that we moved the decimal point to the left, we multiply 3.5 by 10^{13}. Here are some more examples.

Example: Write 4 million in scientific notation.

Solution: 4,000,000.

   Move the decimal point to the left six spaces to get to a number between 1 and 10.

   4.000000

   Multiply 4 by 10 to the power of the number of zeroes you skipped over as you moved the decimal point to the left.

   4×10^6

Example: Write 735 trillion in scientific notation.

Solution: 735,000,000,000,000.

   Move the decimal to the left to get a number between 1 and 10.

   7.35000000000000

Multiply 7.35 by 10 to the number of units you skipped over as you moved the decimal point to the left. You can see here, when you move the decimal to the left, you skip over both zeroes and numerals, often referred to as *units* or *digits*.

$$7.35 \times 10^{14}$$

Example: Write 32,570,000,000 in scientific notation.

Solution: Move the decimal point to the left until you have a number between 1 and 10.

3.25700000000

Multiply by 10 to the power of the number of units you skipped over as you moved the decimal point to the left.

$$3.257 \times 10^{11}$$

You can also use scientific notation to write out very small numbers like 0.00000000000092. The two key differences between solving this versus the very large numbers are that (1) you are moving the decimal point to the right, and (2) your exponent is negative.

$$9.2 \times 10^{-13}$$

When the number is negative, be sure to make the scientific notation negative.

Example: −42,000,000

Solution: -4.2×10^7

Example: −0.00000000065

Solution: -6.5×10^{-10}

TIP

Moving the decimal point to the left gives a positive exponent. Moving the decimal to the right gives a negative exponent. Whether the number itself is positive or negative, the exponent's sign does not change.

Test Yourself 22

Write the following number in scientific notation. The answer keys and explanations follow **Test Yourself 30**.

1. 20,000,000,000
2. 5,150,000,000,000,000,000
3. 3,420

4. −0.00000008
5. −0.0000000000005

FACTORIALS

Factorials are a type of notation used when you need to multiply an integer by all the integers that come before it on a number line. For example, look at this:

$$5! = 5 \times 4 \times 3 \times 2 \times 1 = 320$$

In this example, we break down "five factorial." Let's solve the example:

$$5 \times 4 = 20$$
$$20 \times 3 = 60$$
$$60 \times 2 = 120$$
$$120 \times 1 = 120$$

Let's try a few questions.

Example: $3! =$

Solution: Write out the factorial and solve:

$3 \times 2 \times 1 = 6$

Example: $4! =$

Solution: Write out the factorial and solve:

$4 \times 3 \times 2 \times 1 =$
$12 \times 2 = 24$

Example: $8! =$

Solution: Write out the factorial and solve:

$8 \times 7 \times 6 \times 5 \times 4 \times 3 \times 2 \times 1 =$

We can multiply pairs of numbers:

$$56 \times 30 \times 12 \times 2 =$$
$$1,680 \times 24 = 40,320$$

Example: $10! =$

Solution: Write out the factorial and solve (again, multiply paired numbers):

$10 \times 9 \times 8 \times 7 \times 6 \times 5 \times 4 \times 3 \times 2 \times 1 =$
$90 \times 56 \times 30 \times 12 \times 2 = 3,628,800$

When adding factorials, it's not enough to add the numbers. Rather, you need to solve the factorials, then add those numbers together to make a new factorial.

Example: $2! + 3! =$ Solve each factorial

$(2 \times 1) + (3 \times 2 \times 1) =$
$2 + 6 = 8$

15

You will notice the answer is not written as a factorial. Remember, solving a factorial does not itself create a new factorial. Let's look at another example.

Example: $7! + 4! =$

$$(7 \times 6 \times 5 \times 4 \times 3 \times 2 \times 1) + (4 \times 3 \times 2 \times 1) =$$
$$5,040 + 24 = 5,064$$

So, what will happen if you just add the two factorials together? Let's look at the previous example.

Example: $7! + 4! = 11!$

$$11! = 11 \times 10 \times 9 \times 8 \times 7 \times 6 \times 5 \times 4 \times 3 \times 2 \times 1 = 39,916,800$$

> **TIP**
>
> Whenever you see a factorial in a problem, solve it first.

That's a big difference, so remember to solve the factorials before adding. Fortunately, the same rule applies for subtraction, multiplication, and division. So, you can put this step at the top of the Order of Operations discussed earlier in the chapter. Here are some sample problems.

Example: $4! - 3! =$

$$(4 \times 3 \times 2 \times 1) - (3 \times 2 \times 1) =$$
$$24 - 6 = 18$$

Example: $6! \times 2! =$

$$(6 \times 5 \times 4 \times 3 \times 2 \times 1) \times (2 \times 1) =$$
$$720 \times 2 = 1,440$$

Example: $\dfrac{6!}{4!} =$

$$\frac{6 \times 5 \times 4 \times 3 \times 2 \times 1}{4 \times 3 \times 2 \times 1} =$$

Fortunately, we have common factors in the numerator and denominator.

$$\frac{6 \times 5 \times \cancel{4 \times 3 \times 2 \times 1}}{\cancel{4 \times 3 \times 2 \times 1}} =$$

$$6 \times 5 = 30$$

15

Test Yourself 23

Write the answers to the following problems in the space provided. The answer keys and explanations follow **Test Yourself 30**.

1. $7! =$

2. $10! =$

3. $13! =$

4. $3! + 7! =$

5. $2! + 9! =$

6. $8! + 6! =$

7. $9! - 5! =$

8. $6! - 3! =$

9. $7! - 8! =$

10. $2! \times 3! =$

11. $3! \times 7! =$

12. $10! \times 4! =$

13. $5! \div 2! =$

14. $7! \div 4! =$

15. $9! \div 3! =$

GEOMETRY

Area of Plane Figures

Area is the space enclosed by a plane (flat) figure. A *rectangle* is a plane figure with four right angles. Opposite sides of a rectangle are of equal length and are parallel to each other. To find the area of a rectangle, multiply the length of the base of the rectangle by the length of its height. Always use square units to express area.

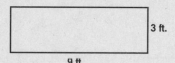

$A = bh$

$A = 9 \text{ ft.} \times 3 \text{ ft.}$

$A = 27 \text{ sq. ft.}$

A *square* is a rectangle in which all four sides are the same length. You find the area of a square by squaring the length of one side, which is the same as multiplying the square's length by its width.

$A = s^2$

$A = 4 \text{ in.} \times 4 \text{ in.}$

$A = 16 \text{ sq. in.}$

A *triangle* is a three-sided plane figure. You find the area of a triangle by multiplying the base by the altitude (height) and dividing by two.

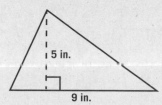

$A = \frac{1}{2}bh$

$A = \frac{1}{2}(9 \text{ in.})(5 \text{ in.}) = \frac{45}{2}$

$A = 22\frac{1}{2} \text{ sq. in.}$

15

A *circle* is a perfectly round plane figure. The distance from the center of a circle to its rim is its *radius*. The distance from one edge to the other through the center is its *diameter*. The diameter is twice the length of the radius.

Pi (π) is a mathematical value equal to approximately 3.14, or $\frac{22}{7}$; it is the ratio of the circle's circumference to its diameter. Pi (π) is frequently used in calculations involving circles. You find the area of a circle by squaring the radius and multiplying it by π. You may leave the area in terms of pi unless you are told what value to assign π.

4 cm.

$$A = \pi r^2$$
$$A = \pi (4\ \text{cm})^2$$
$$A = 16\pi\ \text{sq. cm}$$

Test Yourself 24

Find the area of each figure. Assume that any angle which appears to be a right angle *is* a right angle. The answer keys and explanations follow **Test Yourself 30**.

1.

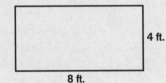

4 ft.

8 ft.

2.

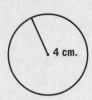

8 in.

7 in.

3.

1 mi.

4.

3 yd.

5 yd.

5.

2 cm.

6.

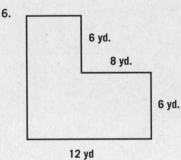

6 yd.

8 yd.

6 yd.

12 yd

7.   3 yd.

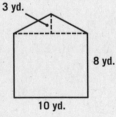

8 yd.

10 yd.

15

8.

9.

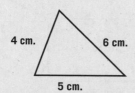

10.

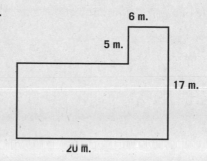

Perimeter of Plane Figures

The *perimeter* of a plane figure is the distance around the outside. To find the perimeter of a *polygon* (a plane figure bounded by line segments), just add the lengths of the sides.

3 in.

5 in.

$P = 3$ in. $+ 5$ in. $+ 3$ in. $+ 5$ in. $= 16$ in.

4 cm.   6 cm.

5 cm.

$P = 4$ cm. $+ 6$ cm. $+ 5$ cm. $= 15$ cm.

The perimeter of a circle is called the *circumference*. The formula for the circumference of a circle is πd or $2\pi r$, which are both, of course, the same thing.

$C = 2 \times 3 \times \pi = 6\pi$

Volume of Solid Figures

The volume of a solid figure is the measure of the space within. To find the volume of a solid figure, multiply the area of the base by the height or depth.

The volume of a rectangular solid is length × width × height. Volume is always expressed in cubic units.

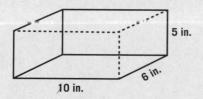

5 in.

10 in.   6 in.

$V = lwh$

$V = (10$ in.$)$ $(6$ in.$)$ $(5$ in.$)$

$V = 300$ cu. in.

15

The volume of a cube is the cube of one side.

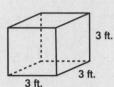

$V = s^3$

$V = (3 \text{ ft.})^3$

$V = 27 \text{ cu. ft.}$

The volume of a cylinder is the area of the circular base ($\pi r2$) times the height.

$V = \pi r^2 h$

$V = \pi (4 \text{ in.})^2 (5 \text{ in.})$

$V = \pi(16)(5) = 80\pi \text{ cu. in.}$

Test Yourself 25

Find the perimeter or volume of each figure as instructed. The answer keys and explanations follow **Test Yourself 30**.

1. Find the perimeter.

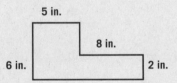

2. Find the volume.

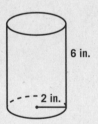

3. Find the circumference.

4. Find the volume.

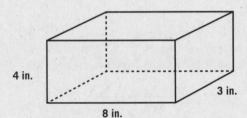

5. Find the volume.

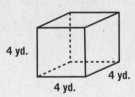

6. Find the perimeter.

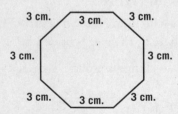

7. Find the perimeter.

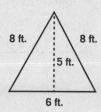

8. Find the perimeter.

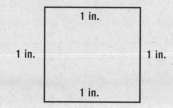

ANGLES

The sum of the angles of a straight line is 180°.

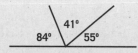

The sum of the angles of a triangle is 180°.

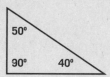

The sum of the angles of a rectangle is 360°.

The sum of the angles of a circle is 360°.

The sum of the angles of a polygon of *n* sides is $(n-2)180°$.

$$(8-2)(180°) = 6 \times 180° = 1{,}080°$$

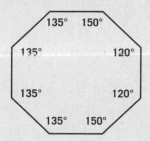

TIP

You can add angles just as you would add regular numbers. $60°+30° = 90°$

15

A *ray* is a line with an endpoint that extends to infinity. The endpoint is the origin of the line. Think of a ray of sunshine, in which the ray's endpoint (origin) is the sun, and the ray continues through space into infinity.

Bisecting rays are rays that divide larger angles into smaller ones. Since the rays are "bisecting," they divide the angle into two equal angles.

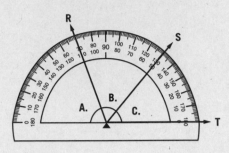

Here, we can see ray S bisecting the angle created by rays R and T. One thing to note, though, is that any bisecting ray should create two equal angles. Looking at the figure above, where should ray S read on the protractor for it to be a proper bisection? Ray R and ray T form a 100° angle, and since ray S bisects that angle, both of the new angles are 50° angles.

Test Yourself 26

Identify the size of the unlabeled angle in each figure. The answer keys and explanations follow **Test Yourself 30**.

1.

2.

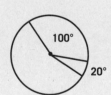

3.

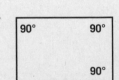

4.

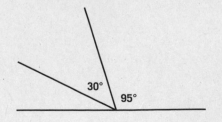

5.

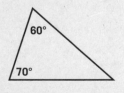

6.

7.

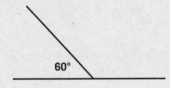

8.

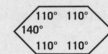

COORDINATE GEOMETRY

Coordinate geometry is used to locate and graph points and lines on a plane. The coordinate system is made up of two perpendicular number lines that intersect at 0. Any point on the plane has two numbers, or coordinates, that indicate its location relative to the number lines.

The *x*-coordinate is found by drawing a vertical line from the point to the horizontal number line (the *x*-axis). The number found on the *x*-axis is the *abscissa*.

The *y*-coordinate is found by drawing a horizontal line from the point to the vertical number line (the *y*-axis). The number found on the *y*-axis is the *ordinate*.

The two coordinates are always written in the order (*x*, *y*).

On the following graph, the *x*-coordinate of point A is 3. The *y*-coordinate of point A is 2. The coordinates of point A are given by the ordered pair (3, 2). Point B has coordinates (−1, 4). Point C has coordinates (−4, −3). Point D has coordinates (2, −3).

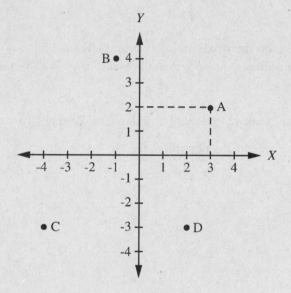

To graph a point whose coordinates are given, first locate the *x*-coordinate on the *x*-axis, then from that position move vertically the number of spaces indicated by the *y*-coordinate.

To graph (4, −2), locate 4 on the *x*-axis, then move −2 spaces vertically (2 spaces down, since the number is negative) to find the given point.

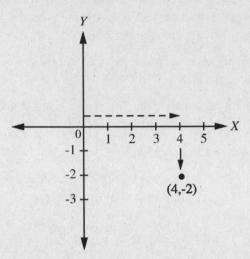

The point at which the *x*-axis and the *y*-axis meet has coordinates (0, 0) and is called the *origin*. Any point on the *y*-axis has 0 as its *x*-coordinate. Any point on the *x*-axis has 0 as its *y*-coordinate.

Test Yourself 27

Solve each graph. The answer keys and explanations follow **Test Yourself 30.**

1. In the graph below, the coordinates of point A are

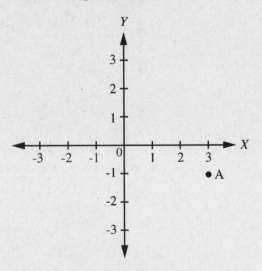

2. The coordinates of point P on the graph are

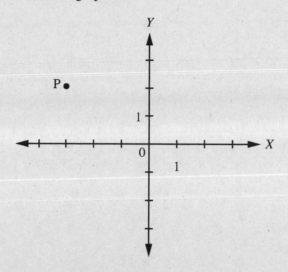

3. Which point is named by the ordered pair (5, 1)?

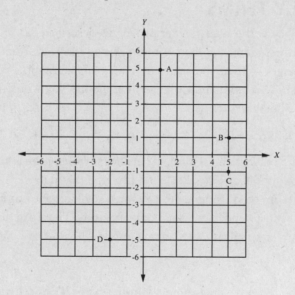

4. Which point might possibly have the coordinates (2,−3)?

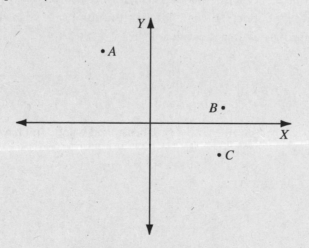

Chapter 15: Mathematics

5. The point with the coordinate (3, 0) is

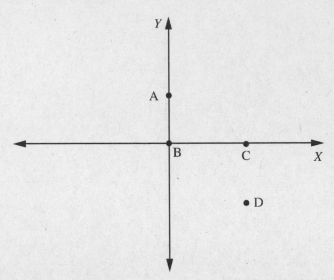

CENTRAL TENDENCY TERMS

Statistics is all about data. The central tendency terms help us describe a set of data. Have you ever had a teacher ask the class how many students did their homework every day last month? That is a statistic: out of the 26 students in the class, eight of them did their homework all last month. When you have a set of data points, like how often each student did homework over that month, you would have a data set of 26 numbers—one for each student—that is written as:

$$\{1, 2, 3, 4, 5, 6, 7, 8, 9, 10, 11, 12, 13, 14, 15, 16, 17, 18, 19, 20, 21, 22, 23, 24, 25, 26\}$$

Notice that the data points are between those squiggly brackets (which is an actual name for those, though they are generally referred to simply as *brackets*). Now, imagine that data set was made up of 26 random numbers. That could easily become confusing, especially when you have one hundred pieces of data, or 1,000, or 50,000. This is where the central tendency terms come in handy. There are three central tendency terms you'll be dealing with on your exam: mean, median, and mode.

Mean

The first term, mean, may be the one you are most familiar with; it's another word for average. Average means typical or middle, which is exactly what the mean is. It is also very easy to find. We find the mean by adding the numbers in the set of data, then dividing by the number of terms in that set. In the example above, we would find the mean by adding the data together $(1 + 2 + 3 + 4 + \dots)$ and divide that sum by the number of data points in the set.

$$\frac{351}{26} = 13.5$$

Your average then, is 13.5. You can do this with any data set, and you do not have to put all the data points in order. Just add, then divide.

15

Median

Median is another method to help make sense of a data set. Unlike the mean, the median is looking for the middle number in your data set, and not the average, although the two may be very close or even equal. To find the median, you must put all the data points in order.

$$\{7, 8, 9, 10, 11\}$$

The median is the number that is in the middle of the data set, which is 9 in this case. If you have an odd number of digits or data points, put them in order and find the one right in the middle. Easy.

Now, let's use the data set from earlier:

$$\{1, 2, 3, 4, 5, 6, 7, 8, 9, 10, 11, 12, 13, 14, 15, 16, 17, 18, 19, 20, 21, 22, 23, 24, 25, 26\}$$

You already know the median is the digit that appears right in the middle of the data set. In this case though, we have and even number of data points, and that means the median is two digits. If you have two numbers as the median, take those two and find the mean of the two. That is, when you have two numbers as the median, then the mean is exactly in the middle. For this data set, the median is $\{13, 14\}$.

$$13 + 14 = 27 \qquad 27 \div 2 = 13.5$$

The mean of those two numbers is 13.5, which happens to also be the median for the larger data set.

Mode

Mode is a bit different from the previous two. While the mean seeks the average of a data set, and the median seeks the middle digit in a data set when it's written in order, the mode wants to find the piece of data that shows up most often in a data set.

Let's take a set of data set of how many times per week a group of 26 students each brush his or her teeth. That would be written out as $\{5, 7, 8, 1, 4, 2, 5, 3, 9, 6, 5, 6, 5, 5, 4, 1, 7, 8, 2, 9, 2, 8, 5, 7, 4, 0\}$. That's a mess, so just like we did for finding the median, let's put this in order:

$$\{0, 1, 1, 2, 2, 2, 3, 4, 4, 4, 5, 5, 5, 5, 5, 5, 6, 6, 7, 7, 7, 8, 8, 8, 9, 9\}$$

Now, count how many times each number comes up.

$0 = 1$	$5 = 6$
$1 = 2$	$6 = 2$
$2 = 3$	$7 = 3$
$3 = 1$	$8 = 3$
$4 = 3$	$9 = 2$

Looking at this information, we see that the number 5 comes up in the data set six times, more often than any other number. That means the mode of that data set is 5. When would this be helpful information? If you want to show a trend (like brushing your teeth), knowing which value appears most frequently tells you which is the most popular. In this case, brushing five times a week is the most popular option.

And the kid that doesn't brush at all, ew.

Let's find the mode for another set of data: This time, how many pages each student reads at home every night. Your data set is $\{3, 3, 4, 4, 4, 5, 5, 7, 7, 7, 8, 8, 9, 11, 11, 12, 12, 12, 12, 12, 12, 17, 23\}$. Counting the frequency for each number in the set, 12 is the number that occurs most often, meaning more students read 12 pages each night than any other amount.

Another practical application would be if you have several cases of playing cards in four different colors: red, green, blue, and black. If you decide to sell the decks, and you keep track of what color decks sell the most, that's the mode. Looking at the mode would tell you if the green decks are most often purchased, while the blue ones hardly sell. If this becomes your business, knowing which decks sell the most can help you know which decks to stock more often, and which ones to stock less often.

Test Yourself 28

Find the mean, median, and mode for the number set provided. The answer keys and explanations follow **Test Yourself 30.**

{37, 46, 49, 11, 40, 32, 3, 39, 6, 47, 40, 4, 35}

1. Mean =
2. Median =
3. Mode =

{31, 1, 20, 43, 21, 39, 31, 25, 31, 9, 28, 36, 28, 18, 12, 21, 29, 41, 28, 27, 31}

4. Mean =
5. Median =
6. Mode =

{12, 22, 7, 35, 3, 30, 12, 7, 13, 24, 12, 1, 11, 3, 17, 15}

7. Mean =
8. Median =
9. Mode =

> **TIP**
>
> If you struggle with word problems, try the CUBES strategy. **C**ircle important numbers, **u**nderline the question, **b**ox key words, **e**liminate extra information and **e**valuate what steps you should take, then **s**olve.

WORD PROBLEMS

Two common kinds of word problems that you might encounter on high school entrance examinations are *rate, time, and distance problems* and *work problems*.

Rate, Time, and Distance Problems

The basic formula used in solving problems for distance is $D = RT$ (Distance = Rate × Time).

Use this formula when you know rate (speed) and time.

To find rate, use $R = \dfrac{D}{T}$ (Rate = Distance ÷ Time).

To find time, use $T = \dfrac{D}{R}$ (Time = Distance ÷ Rate).

Study the following problems:

Example: Two hikers start walking from the city line at different times. The second hiker, whose speed is 4 miles per hour, starts 2 hours after the first hiker, whose speed is 3 miles per hour. Determine the amount of time and distance that will be consumed before the second hiker catches up with the first.

Solution 1: Since the first hiker has a 2-hour head start and is walking at the rate of 3 miles per hour, he is 6 miles from the city line when the second hiker starts.

Rate × Time = Distance

Subtracting 3 miles per hour from 4 miles per hour gives us 1 mile per hour, or the difference in the rates of speed of the two hikers. In other words, the second hiker gains 1 mile on the first hiker in every hour.

Because there is a 6-mile difference to cut down and it is cut down 1 mile every hour, the second hiker will need 6 hours to overtake his companion. In this time, he will have traveled $4 \times 6 = 24$ miles. The first hiker will have been walking 8 hours, since he had a 2-hour head start, $8 \times 3 = 24$ miles.

Solution 2: One excellent way to solve distance (or mixture) problems is to organize all of the data in a chart. For distance problems, make columns for rate, time, and distance and make separate lines for each moving object. In the problem about the two hikers, the chart technique works like this:

STEP 1: Draw the chart.

	Rate	× Time	= Distance
Hiker 1			
Hiker 2			

STEP 2: Since the problem states that Hiker 1 is traveling at 3 miles per hour and Hiker 2 is traveling at 4 miles per hour, enter these two figures in the Rate column.

	Rate	× Time	= Distance
Hiker 1	3 mph		
Hiker 2	4 mph		

STEP 3: The problem does not tell us how long each hiker traveled, but it does say that Hiker 1 started 2 hours before Hiker 2. Therefore, if we use the unknown x to represent the number of hours Hiker 2 traveled, we can set Hiker 1's time as $x + 2$. Enter these two figures in the Time column.

	Rate	× Time	= Distance
Hiker 1	3 mph	$x + 2$	
Hiker 2	4 mph	x	

STEP 4: Using the formula $D = R \times T$, we can easily find each hiker's distance by multiplying the figures for rate and time already in the chart.

For Hiker 1: $3(x + 2) = 3x + 6$

For Hiker 2: $4(x) = 4x$

15

	Rate	×	Time	=	Distance
Hiker 1	3 mph		$x + 2$		$3x + 6$
Hiker 2	4 mph		x		$4x$

STEP 5: When the two hikers meet, each will have covered the same distance. Using this information, we can set up an equation:

Distance covered by Hiker 1		Distance covered by Hiker 2
$3x + 6$	$=$	$4x$

Solving this equation for x, we find that $x = 6$. This means that Hiker 1 has walked for $6 + 2 = 8$ hours when Hiker 2 catches up to him.

STEP 6: Because Hiker 1 started 2 hours earlier than Hiker 2, Hiker 2 will have walked for 6 hours to catch up to Hiker 1.

STEP 7: Using this information, we can determine that Hiker 1 walked 8 hours at 3 miles per hour to cover 24 miles. Hiker 2 walked for 6 hours at 4 miles per hour to cover the same 24 miles.

Let's try another example:

Example: The same two hikers start walking toward each other along a road connecting two cities that are 60 miles apart. Their speeds are the same as in the preceding example, 3 and 4 miles per hour, respectively. How much time will elapse before they meet?

Solution 1: In each hour of travel toward each other, the hikers will cut down a distance equal to the sum of their speeds, $3 + 4 = 7$ miles per hour. To meet, they must cut down 60 miles, and at 7 miles per hour this would be:

$$\frac{D}{R} = T \quad \text{or} \quad \frac{60}{7} = 8\frac{4}{7} \text{ hours}$$

Solution 2: In this problem, we know that the distance traveled by Hiker 1 plus the distance traveled by Hiker 2 equals 60 miles and that the two hikers will have been traveling for the same length of time when they meet. Therefore, we set up an equation to represent this information and solve for x to find the time that will have elapsed before the two hikers meet:

$$3x + 4x = 60$$
$$7x = 60$$
$$x = 8\frac{4}{7}$$

The problem might also have asked: "How much distance must the slower hiker cover before the two hikers meet?" In such a case, we should have gone through the same steps plus one additional step:

The time consumed before meeting was $8\frac{4}{7}$ hours. To find the distance covered by the slower hiker, we merely multiply his rate by the time elapsed:

$$R \times T = D \qquad 3 \times 8\frac{4}{7} = 25\frac{5}{7}$$

Test Yourself 29

Solve the following word problems. The answer keys and explanations follow **Test Yourself 30**.

1. A sailor on leave drove to Yosemite Park from his home at 60 miles per hour. On his trip home, his rate was 10 miles per hour less, and the trip took 1 hour longer. How far is his home from the park?

2. Two cars leave a restaurant at the same time and travel along a straight highway in opposite directions. At the end of 3 hours, they are 300 miles apart. Find the rate of the slower car if one car travels at a rate 20 miles per hour faster than the other.

3. At 10:30 a.m., a passenger train and a freight train left from stations that were 405 miles apart and traveled toward each other. The rate of the passenger train was 45 miles per hour faster than that of the freight train. If they passed each other at 1:30 p.m., how fast was the passenger train traveling?

4. Susie left her home at 11 a.m. traveling along Route 1 at 30 miles per hour. At 1 p.m., her brother Richard left home and started after her on the same road at 45 miles per hour. At what time did Richard catch up to Susie?

5. How far can a man drive into the country if he drives out at 40 miles per hour, returns over the same road at 30 miles per hour, and spends 8 hours away from home, including a 1-hour stop for lunch?

6. At 10 a.m., two cars started traveling toward each other from towns 287 miles apart. They passed each other at 1:30 p.m. If the rate of the faster car exceeded the rate of the slower car by 6 miles per hour, find the rate in miles per hour of the faster car.

7. A driver covered 350 miles in 8 hours. Before noon he averaged 50 miles per hour, but after noon he averaged only 40 miles per hour. At what time did he leave?

8. At 3 p.m., a plane left New York City for Los Angeles traveling at 600 miles per hour. At 3:30 p.m., another plane left the same airport on the same route traveling at 650 miles per hour. At what time did the second plane overtake the first?

9. A scout troop left their campsite at 10 a.m. and walked on the park trail at 4 miles per hour. They returned on the same path at 2 miles per hour. If the troop arrived back at their campsite at 4 p.m., how many miles on the path did they walk?

10. Two cars leave the gas station at the same time and proceed in the same direction along the same route. One car gets an average 36 miles per hour and the other 31 miles per hour. In how many hours will the faster car be 30 miles ahead of the slower car?

Work Problems

Work problems generally involve two or more workers doing a job at different rates. The aim of a work problem is to predict how long it will take to complete a job if the number of workers increases or decreases. Work problems may also involve determining how fast pipes can fill or empty tanks. In solving pipe and tank problems, you must think of the pipes as workers.

In most work problems, a job is broken into several parts, each representing a fractional portion of the entire job. For each part represented, the numerator should represent the time actually spent working, while the denominator should represent the total time the worker needs to do the job alone. The sum of all the individual fractions must be 1 if the job is completed. The easiest way to understand this procedure is to carefully study the examples that follow. By following the step-by-step solutions, you will learn how to make your own fractions to solve the practice problems that follow and the problems you may find on your exam.

Example: If A does a job in 6 days, and B does the same job in 3 days, how long will it take the two of them, working together, to do the job?

Solution:

STEP 1: Write the fractions as follows.

$$\frac{\text{Time actually spent}}{\text{Time needed to do entire job alone}} \quad \overset{A}{\frac{x}{6 \text{ days}}} + \overset{B}{\frac{x}{3 \text{ days}}} = 1$$

The variable x represents the amount of time each worker will work when both work together. The number 1 represents the completed job.

STEP 2: Multiply all the terms by the same number (in this case, 6) in order to clear the fractions and work with whole numbers.

$$x + 2x = 6$$

STEP 3: Solve for x.

$$3x = 6$$

$$x = 2 \text{ days}$$

Working together, A and B will get the job done in 2 days.

Example: A and B, working together, do a job in $4\frac{1}{2}$ days. If B works alone, B can do the job in 10 days. How long would it take A to do the job working alone?

Solution:

STEP 1: Write the fractions as follows.

$$\frac{\text{Time actually spent}}{\text{Time needed to do entire job alone}} \quad \overset{A}{\frac{4.5 \text{ days}}{x \text{ days}}} + \overset{B}{\frac{4.5 \text{ days}}{10 \text{ days}}} = 1$$

STEP 2: Multiply all the terms by 10x to clear the fractions.

$$45 + 4.5x = 10x$$

STEP 3: Solve for x

$$45 = 5.5x$$

$$x = 8\frac{2}{11} \text{ or } 8.18 \text{ days}$$

It would take A nearly $8\frac{2}{11}$ days to do the job alone.

Example: If A can do a job in 6 days that B can do in $5\frac{1}{2}$ days, and C can do in $2\frac{1}{5}$ days, how long would the job take if A, B, and C were working together?

Solution:

STEP 1: This example is very similar to the first one. The number of workers is greater, but the procedure is the same. First write the fractions as follows.

$$\frac{\text{Time actually spent}}{\text{Time needed to do entire job alone}} \qquad \overset{\text{A}}{\frac{x}{6 \text{ days}}} + \overset{\text{B}}{\frac{x}{5.5 \text{ days}}} + \overset{\text{C}}{\frac{x}{2.2 \text{ days}}} = 1$$

Convert all the decimals to fractions; multiply the fractions so that you are working with whole numbers in the numerator and denominator.

$$\frac{x}{6} + \frac{2x}{11} + \frac{5x}{11} = 1$$

Remember that 1 represents the completed job regardless of the number of days involved.

STEP 2: Multiply all terms by 66 to clear the fractions.

$$11x + 12x + 30x = 66$$

STEP 3: Solve for x.

$$53x = 66$$

$$x = 1.245 \text{ days}$$

A, B, and C all working together at their usual rates would get the job done in about $1\frac{1}{4}$ days.

Example: One pipe can fill a pool in 20 minutes, a second pipe can fill the pool in 30 minutes, and a third pipe can fill it in 10 minutes. How long would it take the three pipes together to fill the pool?

Solution:

STEP 1: Treat the pipes as workers and write the fractions as follows:

$$\frac{\text{Time actually spent}}{\text{Time needed to do entire job alone}} \qquad \overset{\text{A}}{\frac{x}{20 \text{ mins.}}} + \overset{\text{B}}{\frac{x}{30 \text{ mins.}}} + \overset{\text{C}}{\frac{x}{10 \text{ mins.}}} = 1$$

STEP 2: Multiply all terms by 60 to clear the fractions.

$$3x + 2x + 6x = 60$$

STEP 3: Solve for x.

$$11x = 60$$

$$x = 5\frac{5}{11} \text{ min}$$

If the water flows from all three pipes at once, it will take $5\frac{5}{11}$ minutes to fill the pool.

15

Chapter 15: Mathematics

Test Yourself 30

Solve each of the following work problems. Answer keys and explanations follow **Test Yourself 30.**

1. John can complete a paper route in 20 minutes. Steve can complete the same route in 30 minutes. How long will it take them to complete the route if they work together?

2. Mr. Powell can mow his lawn twice as fast as his son Rick can. Together they do the job in 20 minutes. How many minutes would it take Mr. Powell to do the job alone?

3. Mr. White can paint his barn in 5 days. What part of the barn is still unpainted after he has worked for x days?

4. Mary can clean the house in 6 hours. Her younger sister Ruth can do the same job in 9 hours. In how many hours can they do the job if they work together?

5. A swimming pool can be filled by an inlet pipe in 3 hours. It can be drained by a drainpipe in 6 hours. By mistake, both pipes are opened at the same time. If the pool is empty, in how many hours will it be filled?

6. Mr. Jones can plow his field with his tractor in 4 hours. If he uses his manual plow, it takes 3 times as long to plow the same field. One day, after working with the tractor for 2 hours, he ran out of gas and had to finish with the manual plow. How long did it take to complete this job after the tractor ran out of gas?

7. Michael and Barry can complete a job in 2 hours when working together. If Michael requires 6 hours to do the job alone, how many hours does Barry need to do the job alone?

8. A girl can sweep the garage in 20 minutes, while her brother needs 30 minutes to do the same job. How many minutes will it take them to sweep the garage if they work together?

9. One printing press can print the school newspaper in 12 hours, while another press can print it in 18 hours. How long will the job take if both presses work simultaneously?

10. If John can do $\frac{1}{4}$ of a job in $\frac{3}{4}$ of a day, how many days will it take him to do the entire job?

15

TEST YOURSELF ANSWER KEYS AND EXPLANATIONS

Test Yourself 1

1. Distributive Property	4. Commutative Property	7. Associative Property	10. Multiplicative Inverse
2. Reflexive Property	5. Identity Property	8. Additive Identity	11. Substitution Property
3. Multiplicative Property of Zero	6. Transitive Property	9. Identity Property	12. Symmetric Property

Test Yourself 2

1. 0	5. 0	9. 2	13. 1	17. 12
2. 3	6. 9	10. 0	14. 3	18. 0
3. 0	7. 5	11. 0	15. 5	19. 1
4. 6	8. 4	12. 0	16. 9	20. 6

Test Yourself 3

1. 180	3. 1,300	5. 0.986	7. 45	9. 76,100
2. 0.05	4. 36.2	6. .0012	8. 0.08328	10. 6.886

Test Yourself 4

1. 5	3. 1	5. 6	7. 5	9. 4
2. 7	4. 30	6. 13	8. 3	10. 8

Test Yourself 5

1. $\frac{1}{72}$	2. 2	3. $\frac{1}{0.65}$	4. 12	5. $\frac{1}{-6}$

Test Yourself 6

1. 44.809	3. 82.1	5. 4.19	7. 100.863	9. 0.69
2. 102.9531	4. 18.01	6. 34.23	8. 17.19	10. 837.92

Test Yourself 7

1. 20.272	3. 60	5. 1.51	7. 36.03	9. 2.43
2. 10.12	4. 1.35	6. 3	8. 3.4	10. 2.52

15

Test Yourself 8

1. $\frac{32}{20} = 1\frac{12}{20} = 1\frac{3}{5}$

2. $\frac{2}{8} = \frac{1}{4}$

3. $\frac{5}{6}$

4. $\frac{1}{5}$

5. $\frac{47}{24} = 1\frac{23}{24}$

6. $\frac{17}{12} = 1\frac{5}{12}$

7. $\frac{2}{6} = \frac{1}{3}$

8. $\frac{7}{24}$

9. $\frac{14}{12} = 1\frac{2}{12} = 1\frac{1}{6}$

10. $\frac{2}{9}$

Test Yourself 9

1. $\frac{2}{5}$

2. $2\frac{1}{3}$

3. 2

4. $\frac{15}{3} = 5$

5. $\frac{1}{3}$

6. $\frac{21}{16} = 1\frac{5}{16}$

7. $\frac{5}{39}$

8. $\frac{7}{9}$

9. $\frac{4}{21}$

10. 1

Test Yourself 10

1. $0.5 = 50\%$

2. $0.875 = 87\frac{1}{2}\%$

3. $0.833 = 83\frac{1}{3}\%$

4. $0.75 = 75\%$

5. $0.75 = 75\%$

6. $0.666 = 66\frac{2}{3}\%$

7. $0.60 = 60\%$

8. $0.40 = 40\%$

9. $0.25 = 25\%$

10. $0.40 = 40\%$

Test Yourself 11

1. $32 \times 0.10 = 3.2$

2. $8 \div 0.25 = 32$

3. $\frac{12}{24} = \frac{1}{2} = 0.5 = 50\%$

4. $360 \times 0.20 = 72$

5. $\frac{5}{60} = \frac{1}{12} = 0.083\overline{3} = 8\frac{1}{3}\%$

6. $12 \div 0.08 = 150$

7. $36 \times 0.06 = 2.16$

8. $25 \div 0.05 = 500$

9. $\frac{70}{140} = \frac{1}{2} = 0.5 = 50\%$

10. $\frac{19}{100} = 0.19 = 19\%$

Test Yourself 12

1. 22.5

2. 82.5

3. 50

4. 4.5

5. 180.225

6. 6

7. 160

8. $58.33\overline{3}$

9. 7.5

10. 8.65

Test Yourself 13

1. 4:1

2. 32:1

3. 3:17

4. 400:2

5. 3(9:1) or 27:3

Test Yourself 14

1. 7:1:3	**2.** 45:4:2	**3.** 21:25:1	**4.** 16:1:1	**5.** 3(16:1:1) or 48:3:3

Test Yourself 15

1. 5,280 ft.	**3.** 2.11 qts.	**5.** 40°C	**7.** 3.785 l
2. 3.5 km	**4.** 7 in	**6.** 6.56 ft.	**8.** 356°F

Test Yourself 16

1. +13	**3.** −8	**5.** −38	**7.** +17	**9.** $-4\frac{1}{4}$
2. +3	**4.** −5	**6.** −45	**8.** −28.8	**10.** 0

Test Yourself 17

1. +6	**3.** −17	**5.** +62	**7.** −7.3	**9.** −70
2. +25	**4.** −55	**6.** +48	**8.** $-41\frac{1}{2}$	**10.** −0.6

Test Yourself 18

1. +40	**3.** +126	**5.** −19.14	**7.** $+47\frac{1}{8}$	**9.** 0
2. −36	**4.** +40	**6.** −31.5	**8.** −9	**10.** +144

Test Yourself 19

1. −3	**3.** +5	**5.** −8	**7.** +2	**9.** −1
2. +3	**4.** −25	**6.** +0.7	**8.** 8.2	**10.** 0

Test Yourself 20

1. $x = 12$	**3.** $x = 33$	**5.** $x = 4$	**7.** $x = 10$	**9.** $x = 9$
2. $x = 21$	**4.** $x = 36$	**6.** $x = 24$	**8.** $x = 26$	**10.** $x = 33$

Test Yourself 21

1. $x - 42 = 0$	**2.** $x - 4y = 0$	**3.** $ab - 14c = 0$	**4.** $-4x^9 + 17x^5 + 4x^3 - 2$	**5.** $3x + 4y - 12 = 0$

Test Yourself 22

1. 2×10^{10}	**2.** 5.15×10^{18}	**3.** 3.42×10^3	**4.** -8×10^{-8}	**5.** -5×10^{13}

15

Test Yourself 23

1. 5,040	**4.** 5,046	**7.** 362,760	**10.** 12	**13.** 60
2. 3,628,800	**5.** 362,882	**8.** 714	**11.** 30,240	**14.** 210
3. 6,227,020,800	**6.** 41,040	**9.** −35,280	**12.** 87,091,200	**15.** 60,480

Test Yourself 24

1. $A = bh$
   $A = 8 \times 4 = 32$ sq. ft.

2. $A = \frac{1}{2}bh$
   $A = \frac{1}{2}(7 \times 8)$
   $A = \frac{1}{2}(56) = 28$ sq. in.

3. $A = s^2$
   $A = 1^2 = 1$ sq. mi.

4. $A = \frac{1}{2}bh$
   $A = \frac{1}{2}(5 \times 3)$
   $A = \frac{1}{2}(15) = 7\frac{1}{2}$ sq. yds.

5. $A = \pi r^2$
   $A = \pi 2^2$
   $A = 4\pi$ sq. cm.

6. $A = bh$
   $A = 12 \times 6 + (12 - 8) \times 6$
   $A = 12 \times 6 + 4 \times 6$
   $A = 72 + 24 = 96$ sq. yds.

7. $A = bh$
   $A = 10 \times 8 = 80$ sq. yds.
   $A = \frac{1}{2}bh$
   $A = \frac{1}{2}(10 \times 3) = \frac{1}{2}(30)$
   $A = 15$ sq. yds.
   $80 + 15 = 95$ sq. yds.

8. $A = \pi r^2$
   $A = \pi 6^2$
   $A = 36\pi$ sq. ft.

9. $A = \frac{1}{2}bh$
   $A = \frac{1}{2}(26 \times 2) = \frac{1}{2}(52)$
   $A = 26$ sq. ft.

10. $A = bh$
    $A = 6 \times 5 + 20 \times (17 - 5)$
    $A = 6 \times 5 + 20 \times 12$
    $A = 30 + 240 = 270$ sq. m.

Test Yourself 25

1. $P = 6 + 5 + (6 - 2) + 8 + 2 + (8 + 5)$
   $P = 38$ inches

2. $V = \pi r^2 h$
   $V = \pi \times 2^2 \times 6$
   $V = \pi \times 4 \times 6$
   $V = 24\pi$ cubic inches

3. $C = 2\pi r$
   $C = 2 \times \pi \times 7$
   $C = 14\pi$ centimeters

4. $V = lwh$
   $V = 8 \times 3 \times 4$
   $V = 96$ cubic inches

5. $V = s^3$
   $V = 4^3 = 4 \times 4 \times 4$
   $V = 64$ cubic yards

6. $P = 3 + 3 + 3 + 3 + 3 + 3 + 3 + 3$
   $P = 24$ centimeters

7. $P = 8 + 8 + 6 = 22$ feet

8. $P = 1 + 1 + 1 + 1 = 4$ inches

Test Yourself 26

1. 80°	**3.** 90°	**5.** 140°	**7.** 180°
2. 240°	**4.** 55°	**6.** 120°	**8.** 50°

15

Test Yourself 27

1. **The correct answer is (3,–1).** A vertical line through A meets the *x*-axis at 3; therefore, the *x*-coordinate is 3. A horizontal line through A meets the *y*-axis at –1; therefore, the *y*-coordinate is –1. The coordinates of point A are (3,–1).

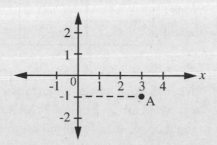

2. **The correct answer is (–3, 2).** Point P has coordinates $x = -3$ and $y = 2$.

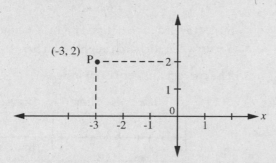

3. **The correct answer is point B.** Because both coordinates are positive numbers, the point must be located in the upper-right quadrant of the graph. Location along the *x*-axis is always stated first, so the correct answer is point B.

4. **The correct answer is point C.** Start by moving in a positive direction along the *x* axis. Then you must move along the *y*-axis in a negative direction. The actual number of spaces you move is irrelevant, since point C is the only possible answer.

5. **The correct answer is point C.** Again, make your moves in order. First move in the positive direction along the *x*-axis. Because the second coordinate is 0, make no move on the *y*-axis. Point C is your answer.

Test Yourself 28

1. 29.92	3. 40	5. 28	7. 14	9. 12
2. 37	4. 26.19	6. 31	8. 12	

15

Test Yourself 29

To solve any type of motion problem, it is helpful to organize the information in a chart with columns for Rate, Time, and Distance. A separate line should be used for each moving object. Be very careful of units used. If the rate is given in *miles per hour*, the time must be in hours and the distance will be in *miles*.

1. The correct answer is 300 miles.

	Rate ×	Time =	Distance
Going	60 mph	x	$60x$
Return	50 mph	$x + 1$	$50x + 50$

Let x = time of trip at 60 mph

The distances are, of course, equal.

$$60x = 50x + 50$$
$$10x = 50$$
$$x = 5$$

$R \times T = D$; 60 mph × 5 hours = 300 miles

2. The correct answer is 40 miles per hour.

	Rate ×	Time =	Distance
Slow Car	x	3	$3x$
Fast Car	$x + 20$	3	$3x + 60$

Let x = rate of slower car

$$\xleftarrow{\hspace{1cm}} \frac{3x+60+3x}{300 \text{ miles}} \xrightarrow{\hspace{1cm}}$$

$$3x + 3x + 60 = 300$$
$$6x = 240 \text{ mph}$$
$$x = 40 \text{ mph}$$

3. The correct answer is 90 miles per hour.

	Rate ×	Time =	Distance
Passenger	$x + 45$	3	$3x + 135$
Freight	x	3	$3x$

Let x = rate of freight train

$$3x + 135 + 3x = 405$$
$$6x = 270$$
$$x = 45$$
$$x + 45 = 45 + 45 = 90 \text{ mph}$$

4. The correct answer is 5 p.m.

	Rate ×	Time =	Distance
Susie	30	x	$30x$
Richard	45	$x - 2$	$45x - 90$

Let x = the time Susie traveled

Richard left 2 hours later than Susie, so he traveled for $x - 2$ hours. Since Richard caught up to Susie, the distances are equal.

$$30x = 45x - 90$$
$$90 = 15x$$
$$x = 6 \text{ hours}$$

Susie traveled for 6 hours. 11 a.m. + 6 hours = 5 p.m. when Richard caught up to her.

5. The correct answer is 120 miles.

	Rate ×	Time =	Distance
Going	40	x	$40x$
Return	30	$7 - x$	$210 - 30x$

Let x = time for trip out

Total driving time = 8 − 1 = 7 hours

Therefore, time for return trip = $7 - x$ hours

$$40x = 210 - 30x$$
$$70x = 210$$
$$x = 3 \text{ hours}$$

$R \times T = D$; 40 mph × 3 hours = 120 miles

15

6. **The correct answer is 44 miles per hour.**

	Rate	×	Time	=	Distance
Slow Car	x		3.5		$3.5x$
Fast Car	$x + 6$		3.5		$3.5(x + 6)$

Let x = rate of slow car

The cars traveled from 10 a.m. to 1:30 p.m., which is 3.5 hours.

$$3.5x + 3.5(x + 6) = 287$$
$$3.5x + 3.5x + 21 = 287$$
$$7x + 21 = 287$$
$$7x = 266$$
$$x = 38 \text{ mph}$$
$$x + 6 = 44 \text{ mph}$$

7. **The correct answer is 9 a.m.**

	Rate	×	Time	=	Distance
Before Noon	50		x		$50x$
After Noon	40		$8 - x$		$40(8 - x)$

Let x = hours traveled before noon

Note that the 8 hours must be divided into two parts.

$$50x + 40(8 - x) = 350$$
$$50x + 320 - 40x = 350$$
$$10x = 30$$
$$x = 3 \text{ hours}$$

If he traveled 3 hours before noon, he left at 9 a.m.

8. **The correct answer is 9:30 p.m.**

	Rate	×	Time	=	Distance
3 p.m. Plane	600		x		$600x$
3:30 p.m. Plane	650		$x - \frac{1}{2}$		$650(x - \frac{1}{2})$

Let x = travel time of the 3 p.m. plane.

The second plane traveled $\frac{1}{2}$ hour later.

$$600x = 650\left(x - \frac{1}{2}\right)$$
$$600x = 650x - 325$$
$$325 = 50x$$
$$x = 6\frac{1}{2} \text{ hrs}$$

The plane that left at 3 p.m. traveled for $6\frac{1}{2}$ hours. The time then was 9:30 p.m.

9. **The correct answer is 8 miles.**

	Rate	×	Time	=	Distance
Going	4		x		$4x$
Return	2		$6 - x$		$2(6 - x)$

Let x = time for a walk on the path

The scout troop was gone for 6 hours. Therefore, time of trip back = $6 - x$.

$$4x = 2(6 - x)$$
$$4x = 12 - 2x$$
$$6x = 12$$
$$x = 2 \text{ hours}$$

$R \times T = D$; 2 hours at 4 mph = 8 miles

10. **The correct answer is 6 hours.**

	Rate	×	Time	=	Distance
Faster Car	36		x		$36x$
Slower Car	31		x		$31x$

Let x = travel time

$$36x - 31x = 30$$
$$5x = 30$$
$$x = 6 \text{ hours}$$

15

Test Yourself 30

1. **The correct answer is 12 minutes.**

	John	Steve

   $$\frac{\text{Time actually spent}}{\text{Time needed to do entire job alone}} \quad \frac{x}{20} \quad + \quad \frac{x}{30} = 1$$

   Multiply all terms by 60 to clear the fractions.

   $$3x + 2x = 60$$
   $$5x = 60$$
   $$x = 12$$

2. **The correct answer is 30 minutes.**

   It takes Mr. Powell x minutes to mow the lawn. Rick alone will take twice as long, or $2x$ minutes.

	Mr. Powell	Rick

   $$\frac{\text{Time actually spent}}{\text{Time needed to do entire job alone}} \quad \frac{20}{x} \quad + \quad \frac{20}{2x} = 1$$

   Multiply all terms by $2x$ to clear the fractions.

   $$40 + 20 = 2x$$
   $$60 = 2x$$
   $$x = 30 \text{ minutes}$$

3. **The correct answer is $\frac{5-x}{5}$.**

   In x days, he has painted $\frac{x}{5}$ of the barn. To find what part is still unpainted, subtract the part completed from $\frac{5}{5}$.

   $$\frac{5}{5} - \frac{x}{5} = \frac{5-x}{5}$$

4. **The correct answer is $3\frac{3}{5} hrs$.**

	Mary	Ruth

   $$\frac{\text{Time actually spent}}{\text{Time needed to do entire job alone}} \quad \frac{x}{6} \quad + \quad \frac{x}{9} = 1$$

   Multiply all terms by 18 to clear the fractions.

   $$3x + 2x = 18$$
   $$5x = 18$$
   $$x = 3\frac{3}{5}$$

15

5. **The correct answer is 6 hours.**

	Inlet	Drain
$\dfrac{\text{Time actually spent}}{\text{Time needed to do entire job alone}}$	$\dfrac{x}{3}$ $-$	$\dfrac{x}{6} = 1$

Multiply all terms by 6 to clear the fractions.

$$2x - x = 6$$
$$x = 6$$

Note that the two fractions are subtracted because the drainpipe does not help the inlet pipe but rather works against it.

6. **The correct answer is 6 hours.**

	Tractor	Plow
$\dfrac{\text{Time actually spent}}{\text{Time needed to do entire job alone}}$	$\dfrac{2}{4}$ $+$	$\dfrac{x}{12} = 1$

You do not need to calculate the answer. Because half the job $\left(\dfrac{2}{4}\right)$ was completed by the tractor, the other half $\left(\dfrac{6}{12}\right)$ was done by the plow, and x, therefore, must equal 6.

7. **The correct answer is 3 hours.**

	Michael	Barry
$\dfrac{\text{Time actually spent}}{\text{Time needed to do entire job alone}}$	$\dfrac{2}{6}$ $+$	$\dfrac{2}{x} = 1$

Multiple all the terms by $6x$ to clear the fractions.

$$2x + 12 = 6x$$
$$12 = 4x$$
$$3 = x$$

8. **The correct answer is 12 minutes.**

	Girl	Brother
$\dfrac{\text{Time actually spent}}{\text{Time needed to do entire job alone}}$	$\dfrac{x}{20}$ $+$	$\dfrac{x}{30} = 1$

Multiply all the terms by 60 to clear the fractions.

$$3x + 2x = 60$$
$$5x = 60$$
$$x = 12$$

15

Chapter 15: Mathematics

9. **The correct answer is 7 hours, 12 minutes.**

	Fast Press		Slower Press	
$\dfrac{\text{Time actually spent}}{\text{Time needed to do entire job alone}}$	$\dfrac{x}{12}$	$+$	$\dfrac{x}{18}$	$= 1$

Multiply all the terms by 36 to clear the fractions.

$$3x + 2x = 36$$

$$5x = 36$$

$$x = 7.2 \text{ hours} = 7 \text{ hours } 12 \text{ minutes}$$

(To restate 7.2 hours as hours and minutes: 0.2 hours $= \dfrac{2}{10}$ or $\dfrac{1}{5} \times 60$ minutes $= 12$ minutes)

10. **The correct answer is 3 days.**

If John completes $\dfrac{1}{4}$ of the job in $\dfrac{3}{4}$ day, it will take him 4 times as long to do the entire job.

$$\frac{4}{1} \times \frac{3}{4} = 3$$

15

Summing It Up

- If you are having special difficulties with any mathematics topic, talk with a teacher or refer to any of your math textbooks.

- Use the exercises in this chapter to determine what you DON'T know well, and concentrate your study on those areas.

- When adding or subtracting decimals, it is important to keep the decimal points in line.

- The fastest way to find an equivalent fraction is to divide the denominator of the fraction you know by the denominator you want. Take the result and multiply it by the numerator.

- To change a percentage to a decimal, remove the percent sign (%) and divide by 100. To change a decimal to a percent multiply by 100 and add the % sign. To change a percentage to a fraction, divide by 100 and remove the % sign. To change a fraction to a percentage, multiply by 100 and add the %.

- When solving a percentage problem, be sure to read the notation carefully, read the problem carefully, and use common sense.

- Remember the number line when subtracting signed numbers.

- Memorizing some simple rules will help you to move through the test more quickly and with less anxiety. Some examples of those rules include: The product of two negative numbers is positive; the product of two positive numbers is positive; and the product of a negative number and a positive number is negative.

- Memorize the basic formulas of geometry. These may not be given to you on the test. For example, to find the area of a rectangle, you must multiply the length times the width, $A = lw$. The formulas are listed on the next page.

Take a moment to ask yourself some simple questions about your understanding of the chapter:

Review: What did I learn?

Evaluate: What do I need to learn more about?

Plan: What can I do next to keep improving?

Based on your answers to those questions, adjust your study plan to dedicate additional time to the areas of weakness that you've identified.

15

FORMULA SHEET

Perimeter

Add the lengths of the sides.

Square

$P = 4s$

Rectangle

$P = 2l + 2w$

Triangle

$P = s_1 + s_2 + s_3$

Circle (circumference)

$C = \pi d$ or $2 \pi r$

Area

Always express volume in square units. Multiply the length by the width.

Square

$A = s^2$

Rectangle

$A = bh$

Triangle

To find the area, multiply the length by the width, and divide by 2.

$A = \frac{1}{2}bh$

Circle

$A = \pi r^2$

Volume

Always express volume in cubic units.

Cube

$V = s^3$

Rectangle

$V = lwh$

Cylinder

$V = \pi r^2 h$

Angles

Straight line = 180°

Triangle = 180°

Rectangle = 360°

Square = 360°

Circle = 360°

Polygon = $(n-2)180°$ where n = # of sides

Pythagorean Theorem

$a^2 + b^2 = c^2$

Percent Change

$$\frac{\% \; change}{100} = \frac{difference}{original \; \#}$$

Percent to Decimal

$25\% = \frac{25}{100} = 0.25$

Reverse for Decimal to Percent

Percent to Fraction

$25\% = \frac{25}{100} = \frac{1}{4}$

Reverse for Fraction to Percent

Distance/Rate/Time

To find distance, use $D = RT$ (Distance = Rate × Time)

To find rate, use $R = \frac{D}{T}$ (Rate = Distance ÷ Time)

To find time, use $T = \frac{D}{R}$ (Time = Distance ÷ Rate)

A tear-out version of this formula guide is available in the appendix of this study guide on page 829.

15

EXERCISES: MATHEMATICS

Exercise 1

> **Directions:** In the following questions, work out each problem and mark the letter that corresponds to the correct answer. Answers follow Exercise 4.

1. 896
    $\times 708$

    A. 643,386
    B. 634,386
    C. 634,368
    D. 643,368

2. $9\overline{)4,266}$

    A. 447
    B. 474
    C. 475
    D. 477

3. $125.25
    0.50
    70.86
    $+\ 6.07$

    A. $200.68
    B. $201.68
    C. $202.68
    D. $202.69

4. $1,250.37
    $-\ \ \ 48.98$

    A. $1,200.39
    B. $1,201.38
    C. $1,201.39
    D. $1,201.49

5. $29\overline{)476.92}$

    A. 16.4445
    B. 16.4455
    C. 17.4445
    D. 17.4455

6. 28
    19
    17
    $+24$

    A. 87
    B. 88
    C. 89
    D. 90

7. $3.7\overline{)2,339.86}$

    A. 63.24
    B. 62.34
    C. 632.4
    D. 642.3

8. $45,286$

    $\times\ \ 4\frac{1}{5}$

    A. $190,021\frac{1}{5}$
    B. $190,201\frac{1}{5}$
    C. $190,202\frac{2}{5}$
    D. $190,234$

9. $8\frac{1}{6}$

  $-5\frac{2}{3}$

  A. $2\frac{1}{3}$

  B. $2\frac{1}{2}$

  C. $3\frac{1}{6}$

  D. $3\frac{2}{3}$

10. $\frac{1}{9} \times \frac{2}{3} \times \frac{7}{8} =$

  A. $\frac{6}{108}$

  B. $\frac{7}{108}$

  C. $\frac{12}{52}$

  D. $\frac{14}{27}$

11. $4\frac{1}{3}\overline{\smash{)}\frac{1}{4}}$

  A. $\frac{3}{52}$

  B. $\frac{5}{52}$

  C. $\frac{12}{52}$

  D. $17\frac{1}{3}$

12. 78,523

  21,457

  3,256

  $+\ \ 1,478$

  A. 104,714

  B. 104,814

  C. 105,714

  D. 105,814

13. 12,689

  $\times\ \ \ \ \ 37$

  A. 468,493

  B. 469,493

  C. 568,493

  D. 569.493

14. Find $6\frac{2}{3}\%$ of $13.50.

  A. $0.88

  B. $0.89

  C. $0.90

  D. $0.91

15. Rename $\frac{11}{16}$ as a decimal.

  A. 0.6578

  B. 0.6785

  C. 0.6875

  D. 0.8675

Chapter 15: Mathematics

353

Exercise 2

Directions: Work each problem on scratch paper or in the margins, then look at the answer choices. If your answer is among those choices, circle the letter before your answer. Answers follow Exercise 4.

1. 5,239
   × 706

   A. 68,107
   B. 398,164
   C. 3,698,734
   D. 3,708,734

2. 48,207
   ×   926

   A. 44,639,682
   B. 45,539,682
   C. 45,638,682
   D. 46,739,682

3. $4,628 \div 7 =$

   A. 660 R6
   B. 661
   C. 661 R1
   D. 662 R1

4. $419\overline{)5,063}$

   A. 11 R408
   B. 12 R9
   C. 12 R35
   D. 14 R81

5. $\$59.60 \div \$0.40 =$

   A. 0.149
   B. 1.49
   C. 14.9
   D. 149

6. $3.41 + 5.6 + 0.873 =$

   A. 4.843
   B. 9.883
   C. 15.264
   D. 17.743

7. 58,769
   −4,028

   A. 44,741
   B. 53,741
   C. 54,641
   D. 54,741

8. $0.3 \times 0.08 =$

   A. 0.0024
   B. 0.024
   C. 0.240
   D. 2.40

9. $0.33\overline{)9.9}$

   A. 0.3
   B. 3
   C. 30
   D. 33

10. 16% of 570 =

    A. 85.3
    B. 89.41
    C. 91.20
    D. 92

15

11. 135 is what percent of 900?

   A. 12%

   B. 15%

   C. 17.5%

   D. 19%

Directions: Express all fractions in lowest terms.

---

12. $\frac{3}{4} + \frac{3}{8} =$

   A. $\frac{7}{8}$

   B. $\frac{8}{9}$

   C. $1\frac{1}{8}$

   D. $1\frac{3}{8}$

13. $\begin{array}{r} 3\frac{1}{4} \\ 4\frac{1}{8} \\ +\ 4\frac{1}{2} \\ \hline \end{array}$

   A. $11\frac{5}{8}$

   B. $11\frac{3}{4}$

   C. $11\frac{7}{8}$

   D. 12

14. $\begin{array}{r} 10\frac{2}{3} \\ -\ 9\frac{1}{2} \\ \hline \end{array}$

   A. $\frac{13}{32}$

   B. $1\frac{1}{6}$

   C. $1\frac{1}{3}$

   D. $1\frac{1}{2}$

15. $\begin{array}{r} 14\frac{7}{24} \\ -\ 5\frac{2}{3} \\ \hline \end{array}$

   A. $8\frac{5}{8}$

   B. $8\frac{11}{12}$

   C. $9\frac{1}{3}$

   D. $9\frac{15}{24}$

16. $\frac{8}{15} \times \frac{3}{4} =$

   A. $\frac{1}{5}$

   B. $\frac{3}{10}$

   C. $\frac{2}{5}$

   D. $\frac{3}{5}$

15

17. $5\frac{1}{4} \times 2\frac{2}{7} =$

   A. $10\frac{3}{28}$

   B. $11\frac{3}{28}$

   C. $11\frac{4}{7}$

   D. 12

18. $\frac{3}{4}\overline{\smash{)}\frac{9}{16}}$

   A. $\frac{27}{64}$

   B. $\frac{7}{16}$

   C. $\frac{5}{8}$

   D. $\frac{3}{4}$

19. $(-12) + (+4) =$

   A. -16

   B. -8

   C. $+8$

   D. $+16$

20. $(-22) - (-18) =$

   A. -30

   B. -4

   C. $+6$

   D. $+13$

21. $(+7) \times (-7) =$

   A. -49

   B. -14

   C. 0

   D. $+1$

22. $(+56) \div (-7) =$

   A. -8

   B. -6

   C. $+6$

   D. $+8$

15

Exercise 3

Directions: Choose the correct answer to each problem and circle its letter. Answers follow Exercise 4.

1. Six girls sold the following numbers of boxes of cookies: 42, 35, 28, 30, 24, 27. What was the mean number of boxes sold?

    A. 26

    B. 29

    C. 30

    D. 31

2. The cost of sending a telegram is 52 cents for the first ten words and $2\frac{1}{2}$ cents for each additional word. The cost of sending a 14-word telegram is

    A. 62 cents.

    B. 63 cents.

    C. 69 cents.

    D. 87 cents.

3. A stock clerk has on hand the following items:

    500 pads worth 4 cents each
    130 pencils worth 3 cents each
    50 dozen rubber bands worth 2 cents per dozen

    If, from this stock, he issues 125 pads, 45 pencils, and 48 rubber bands, what would be the value of the remaining stock?

    A. $6.43

    B. $8.95

    C. $17.63

    D. $18.47

4. As an employee at a clothing store, you receive a 10% discount on all purchases. When the store has a sale, employees also receive the 20% discount offered to all customers. What would you have to pay for a $60 jacket bought on a sale day?

    A. $6

    B. $10.80

    C. $36

    D. $43.20

5. How many square yards of linoleum are needed to cover a floor having an area of 270 square feet?

    A. 24

    B. 28

    C. 30

    D. 33

6. If a pie is divided into 40 parts, what percent is one part of the whole pie?

    A. 0.4

    B. 2.5

    C. 4.0

    D. 25

7. A recipe for 6 quarts of punch calls for $\frac{3}{4}$ cups of sugar. How much sugar is needed for 9 quarts of punch?

    A. $\frac{5}{8}$ of a cup

    B. $\frac{7}{8}$ of a cup

    C. $1\frac{1}{8}$ cups

    D. $2\frac{1}{4}$ cups

15

8. How many yards of ribbon will it take to make 45 badges if each badge uses 4 inches of ribbon?

   A. 5

   B. 9

   C. 11

   D. 15

9. Oil once sold at $42\frac{1}{2}$ cents a quart. What was the cost of 4 gallons of oil?

   A. $6.50

   B. $6.60

   C. $6.70

   D. $6.80

10. A clerk can add 40 columns of figures an hour by using an adding machine. He can add 20 columns of figures an hour without using an adding machine. What is the total number of hours it will take the clerk to add 200 columns of figures if $\frac{3}{5}$ of the work is done by machine and the rest without the machine?

    A. 6 hours

    B. 7 hours

    C. 8 hours

    D. 9 hours

11. Two rectangular boards, each measuring 5 feet by 3 feet, are placed together to make one large board. How much shorter will the perimeter be if the two long sides are placed together than if the two short sides are placed together?

    A. 2 feet

    B. 4 feet

    C. 6 feet

    D. 8 feet

12. 1% of 8 =

    A. 8

    B. 0.8

    C. 0.08

    D. 0.008

13. When 81.3 is divided by 10, the quotient is

    A. 0.0813

    B. 0.813

    C. 8.13

    D. 813

14. +1 −1 +1 −1 +1 . . . and so on, where the last number is +1 has a sum of

    A. 0

    B. −1

    C. +1

    D. 2

15. If a plane travels 1,000 miles in 5 hours 30 minutes, what is its average speed in miles per hour?

    A. $181\frac{9}{11}$

    B. 200

    C. 215

    D. $191\frac{1}{5}$

16. A jacket that normally sells for $35 can be purchased on sale for 2,975 pennies. What is the rate of discount represented by the sale price?

    A. 5%

    B. 10%

    C. 15%

    D. 20%

15

17. Perform the indicated operations and express your answer in inches: 12 feet minus 7 inches, plus 2 feet 1 inch, minus 7 feet, minus 1 yard, plus 2 yards 1 foot 3 inches.

   A. 127 inches
   B. 128 inches
   C. 129 inches
   D. 131 inches

18. What is the value of x when $5x = 5 \times 4 \times 2 \times 0$?

   A. 6
   B. 8
   C. 0
   D. 1

19. A square has an area of 49 square inches. The number of inches in its perimeter is

   A. 7
   B. 28
   C. 14
   D. 98

20. $(3 + 4)^3 =$

   A. 21
   B. 91
   C. 343
   D. 490

21. A roll of carpeting will cover 224 square feet of floor space. How many rolls are needed to carpet a room 36' × 8' and another 24' × 9'?

   A. 2.25
   B. 4.50
   C. 2.50
   D. 4.25

22. A library contains 60 books on arts and crafts. If this is 0.05% of the total number of books on the shelves, how many books does the library own?

   A. 120,000
   B. 12,000
   C. 1,200,000
   D. 1,200

23. A court clerk estimates that the untried cases on the docket will occupy the court for 150 trial days. If new cases are accumulating at the rate of 1.6 trial days per day (Saturday and Sunday excluded) and the court sits 5 days a week, how many days' business will remain to be heard at the end of 60 trial days?

   A. 168 trial days
   B. 178 trial days
   C. 185 trial days
   D. 186 trial days

24. A house plan uses the scale $\frac{1}{4}$ inch = 1 foot, and in the drawing the living room is 7 inches long. If the scale changes to 1 inch = 1 foot, what will the length of the living room be in the new drawing?

   A. 18 inches
   B. 28 inches
   C. 30 inches
   D. 36 inches

25. A store sold suits for $65 each. The suits cost the store $50 each. The percentage of increase of selling price over cost is

   A. 40%
   B. $33\frac{1}{2}\%$
   C. $33\frac{1}{3}\%$
   D. 30%

15

26. A man borrowed $5,000 and agreed to pay $11\frac{1}{2}\%$ annual interest. If he repaid the loan in 6 months, how much interest would he pay?

   A. $2,875

   B. $5,750

   C. $287.50

   D. $575

27. After deducting a discount of 30%, the price of a coat was $35. What was the regular price of the coat?

   A. $116.67

   B. $24.50

   C. $50

   D. $42

28. Two cars start from the same point at the same time. One drives north at 20 miles an hour, and the other drives south on the same straight road at 36 miles an hour. How many miles apart are they after 30 minutes?

   A. Fewer than 10

   B. Between 10 and 20

   C. Between 20 and 30

   D. Between 30 and 40

29. During his summer vacation, a boy earned $14.50 per day and saved 60% of his earnings. If he worked 45 days, how much did he save?

   A. $391.50

   B. $287.93

   C. $402.75

   D. $543.50

30. The number of cubic feet of soil needed for a flower box 3 feet long, 8 inches wide, and 1 foot deep is

   A. 24

   B. 12

   C. $4\frac{2}{3}$

   D. 2

31. The scale of a certain map is 4 inches = 32 miles. The number of inches that would represent 80 miles is

   A. 8

   B. 12

   C. 10

   D. 16

32. The daily almanac report for one day during the summer stated that the sun rose at 6:14 a.m. and set at 6:06 p.m. Find the number of hours and minutes in the time between the rising and setting of the sun on that day.

   A. 11 hours, 52 minutes

   B. 12 hours, 8 minutes

   C. 11 hours, 2 minutes

   D. 12 hours, 48 minutes

33. One piece of wire is 25 feet 8 inches long and another is 18 feet 10 inches long. What is the difference in length?

   A. 6 feet, 10 inches

   B. 6 feet, 11 inches

   C. 7 feet, 2 inches

   D. 7 feet, 4 inches

15

34. If a vehicle is to complete a 20-mile trip at an average rate of 30 miles per hour, it must complete the trip in

    A. 20 minutes.
    B. 30 minutes.
    C. 40 minutes.
    D. 50 minutes.

35. A snapshot measures $2\frac{1}{2}$ inches by $1\frac{7}{8}$ inches. It is to be enlarged so that the longer dimension will be 4 inches. The length of the enlarged shorter dimension will be

    A. $2\frac{1}{2}$ inches.
    B. 3 inches.
    C. $3\frac{3}{8}$ inches.
    D. $2\frac{5}{8}$ inches.

36. An adult ski lift ticket costs twice as much as a child's. If a family of three children and two adults can ski for $49, what is the cost of an adult ticket?

    A. $7
    B. $10
    C. $12
    D. $14

37. A recipe calls for $1\frac{1}{2}$ cups of sugar. It is necessary to make eight times the recipe for a church supper. If 2 cups of sugar equal 1 pound, how many pounds of sugar will be needed to make the recipe?

    A. 4
    B. 6
    C. 8
    D. 10

38. In the fraction $\frac{1}{\Delta - 2}$, Δ can be replaced by all of the following except

    A. 0
    B. +3
    C. +2
    D. −2

39. If one pipe can fill a tank in $1\frac{1}{2}$ hours and another can fill the same tank in 45 minutes, how long will it take for the two pipes to fill the tank together?

    A. 1 hour
    B. $\frac{1}{2}$ hour
    C. $1\frac{1}{2}$ hours
    D. $\frac{1}{3}$ hour

40. Two cars are 550 miles apart and traveling toward each other on the same road. If one travels at 50 miles per hour, the other at 60 miles per hour, and they both leave at 1:00 p.m., what time will they meet?

    A. 4:00 p.m.
    B. 4:30 p.m.
    C. 5:45 p.m.
    D. 6:00 p.m.

15

Exercise 4

Directions: Choose the correct answer to each problem and circle its letter. Answers follow this exercise.

1. Any number that is divisible by both 5 and 6 is also divisible by
   A. 11
   B. 9
   C. 7
   D. 3

2. 3,482,613 rounded to the nearest million is
   A. 2,000,000
   B. 3,500,000
   C. 3,000,000
   D. 4,000,000

3. The number that is *not* a factor of 120 is
   A. 5
   B. 6
   C. 7
   D. 8

4. What is the place value of 3 in 4.9236?
   A. Hundredths
   B. Thousandths
   C. Ten thousandths
   D. Hundred thousandths

5. Which symbol belongs in the circle?
   0.0983 ○ 0.124
   A. <
   B. >
   C. =
   D. ≅

6. The greatest common factor of 24 and 12 is
   A. 2
   B. 4
   C. 6
   D. 12

7. 1,000% is equal to
   A. 0.0001
   B. 0.1
   C. 10
   D. 100

8. In the simplest form, $\frac{12}{16}$ is
   A. $\frac{3}{4}$
   B. $\frac{2}{3}$
   C. $\frac{2}{6}$
   D. $\frac{4}{8}$

9. $\frac{9}{25}$ is equal to
   A. 0.036
   B. 0.04
   C. 0.36
   D. 0.45

10. What number belongs in the box?
    $-5 + \square = 0$
    A. −5
    B. 0
    C. −1
    D. +5

11. $\sqrt{81}$ is equal to

   A. 8

   B. 9

   C. 18

   D. 40.5

12. Solve for $x: \frac{x}{2} + 3 = 15$

   A. 18

   B. 20

   C. 22

   D. 24

13. If $y + 2 > 10$, then y must be

   A. smaller than 10.

   B. smaller than 8.

   C. greater than 8.

   D. equal to 0.

14. If $a + b = 200°$, and $c + d + e + f = 140°$, what is the number of degrees in angle g?

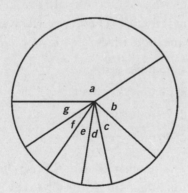

   A. 10°

   B. 20°

   C. 30°

   D. 45°

15. The area of the shaded portion of the rectangle below is

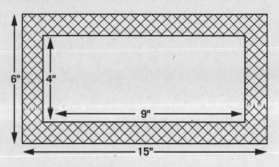

   A. 54 square inches.

   B. 90 square inches.

   C. 45 square inches.

   D. 36 square inches.

16. Which point shown below corresponds to (8, 3)?

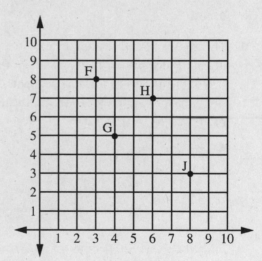

   A. Point F

   B. Point G

   C. Point H

   D. Point J

Chapter 15: Mathematics

Questions 17–23 are based on the following passage.

Mr. Shea, a shop teacher at the junior high school, owns a ski lodge in Vermont. The lodge is open to guests on weekends and during school vacations. Mr. Shea's regular rates, which include breakfast and dinner, are $25 per night for dormitory-style accommodations. He gives a 30 percent discount to all members of organized student groups from his community.

17. Sixteen members of Boy Scout Troop 60 and two of their leaders went on a ski weekend and stayed at Mr. Shea's lodge. The two-night cost of room and board for each boy was

   A. $25
   B. $35
   C. $50
   D. $60

18. The leaders shared a room instead of sleeping in the dormitory. The total bill for the two of them was $84 for the two nights. The surcharge per person for the semiprivate room was

   A. 7%
   B. 20%
   C. 32%
   D. 42%

19. Lift tickets cost $20 per day for adults and $14 per day for juniors (persons under 13 years of age). Five of the boys were 12 years old, while the others were older. What was the total cost of lift tickets for a day of skiing?

   A. $220
   B. $290
   C. $330
   D. $390

20. Among the boys, $\frac{1}{4}$ considered themselves to be expert skiers. Of those who were less experienced, $\frac{3}{4}$ took ski lessons. Of those who took ski lessons, $\frac{1}{3}$ rented ski equipment. How many boys rented ski equipment?

   A. 9
   B. 6
   C. 4
   D. 3

21. The mountain on which the troop skied had 27 trails served by a T-bar lift, two J-bar lifts, and three chair lifts. The proportion of trails to lifts was

   A. 5:1
   B. 7:2
   C. 9:3
   D. 9:2

22. One boy skied the length of a 4.6-mile trail in just under 14 minutes. His average speed was approximately

   A. 15 miles per hour.
   B. 20 miles per hour.
   C. 25 miles per hour.
   D. 30 miles per hour.

23. The bus chartered for the trip cost $250. The rooms and lift tickets totaled $1,304. The troop contributed $400 from its treasury to help defray expenses of the trip. If the rest was divided equally among the 16 boys and 2 leaders, how much did each individual pay?

   A. $64.11
   B. $71.13
   C. $75.28
   D. $83.07

15

Questions 24–28 refer to the following passage.

Applesville High School, an accredited 4-year institution (grades 9 to 12), is located on a picturesque 128-acre campus. At Applesville, the student-teacher ratio is 7:1, average class size is 15, and current annual tuition is $19,750. The historic library is located at the center of campus and has a collection of 30,000 volumes.

24. If $\frac{7}{8}$ of the campus is devoted to woods and gardens and the rest is developed for academic use, how many acres are used for academics?

   A. 16
   B. 32
   C. 48
   D. 96

25. This year, annual tuition is 7% higher than it was last year. Which expression represents last year's tuition?

   A. ($19,750)(1.07)
   B. $19,750 − (0.07)($19,750)
   C. ($19,750)(0.93)
   D. $\dfrac{\$19,750}{\$\;1.07}$

26. Of the 60 classes offered, 20 have an average class size of 21 students. What is the average size of the remaining classes?

   A. 9
   B. 12
   C. 15
   D. 21

27. Next year, Applesville will loan its rare book collection (2% of its volumes) to the local university. How many volumes will Applesville's library have on campus next year?

   A. 29,000
   B. 29,400
   C. 29,600
   D. 29,800

28. Excluding maintenance and administrative personnel, if there are 304 persons (teachers and students) at school, how many teachers work at Applesville High School?

   A. 7
   B. 14
   C. 38
   D. 152

Questions 29–32 refer to the following passage.

On an icy day, the Bergs' car skidded into a telephone pole and suffered two smashed doors and a broken drive shaft. After four weeks in a body shop, the car was fully repaired. The Bergs' insurance company paid the body shop's bill, less the $200 deductible, which the Bergs paid.

29. For what portion of the year were the Bergs unable to use their car?

   A. $\dfrac{1}{4}$
   B. $\dfrac{1}{10}$
   C. $\dfrac{1}{12}$
   D. $\dfrac{1}{13}$

15

30. In the year before the accident, the Bergs' insurance premium was $1,100. The year following the accident, their premium rose to $1,500. The new premium was about what percent of the old premium?

    A. $26\frac{2}{3}\%$

    B. $36\frac{1}{3}\%$

    C. $136\frac{1}{3}\%$

    D. 140%

31. To match the blue paint of the car, the man in the body shop had to add $1\frac{1}{2}$ ounces of black paint for each pint of blue paint. He used three gallons of blue paint on the car. What was the total amount of paint he used?

    A. $2\frac{1}{4}$ pints

    B. $21\frac{3}{4}$ pints

    C. 24 pints

    D. $26\frac{1}{4}$ pints

32. Three men of about equal efficiency were assigned to work on the Bergs' car. One man worked on the car full-time. He was always assisted by one of the other men. If the full-time man needed to complete the job alone, how many weeks would the car have been in the shop?

    A. 2 weeks

    B. 4 weeks

    C. 6 weeks

    D. 8 weeks

ANSWER KEYS AND EXPLANATIONS

Exercise 1

1. C	**4.** C	**7.** C	**10.** B	**13.** B
2. B	**5.** B	**8.** B	**11.** A	**14.** C
3. C	**6.** B	**9.** B	**12.** A	**15.** C

1. The correct answer is C.

$$\begin{array}{r} 896 \\ \times\ 708 \\ \hline 7,168 \\ 62,720 \\ \hline 634,368 \end{array}$$

2. The correct answer is B.

$$\begin{array}{r} 474 \\ 9\overline{)4,266} \\ \underline{36} \\ 66 \\ \underline{63} \\ 36 \\ \underline{36} \\ 0 \end{array}$$

3. The correct answer is C. $202.68

4. The correct answer is C. $1,201.39

5. The correct answer is B.

$$\begin{array}{r} 16.44551 \approx 16.4455 \\ 29\overline{)476.9200} \\ \underline{29} \\ 186 \\ \underline{174} \\ 129 \\ \underline{116} \\ 132 \\ \underline{116} \\ 160 \\ \underline{145} \\ 150 \\ \underline{145} \\ 50 \end{array}$$

6. The correct answer is D. 00

7. The correct answer is C.

$$\begin{array}{r} 63\ 2.39 \approx 632.4 \\ 3.7\overline{)2339.8\ 60} \\ \underline{222} \\ 119 \\ \underline{111} \\ 88 \\ 74 \\ \hline 146 \\ 111 \\ \hline 350 \\ 333 \\ \hline 17 \end{array}$$

8. The correct answer is B.

$$\frac{1}{5} = 0.20$$

$$\begin{array}{r} 45,286 \\ \times\ \ \ 4.20 \\ \hline 905,720 \\ 181,144 \\ \hline 190,201.20 = 190,201\frac{1}{5} \end{array}$$

9. The correct answer is B.

$$8\frac{1}{6} = 7\frac{7}{6}$$
$$-5\frac{2}{3} = 5\frac{4}{6}$$
$$\overline{\phantom{-5\frac{2}{3}=}\ 2\frac{3}{6} = 2\frac{1}{2}}$$

10. The correct answer is B.

$$\frac{1}{9} \times \frac{\overset{1}{\cancel{2}}}{3} \times \frac{7}{\underset{4}{\cancel{8}}} = \frac{7}{108}$$

15

11. The correct answer is A.

$$\frac{1}{4} \div 4\frac{1}{3} = \frac{1}{4} \div \frac{13}{3} = \frac{1}{4} \times \frac{3}{13} = \frac{3}{52}$$

12. The correct answer is A. 104,714. If you got this wrong, check how you added up each column again.

13. The correct answer is B.

$$
\begin{array}{r}
12,689 \\
\times 37 \\
\hline
88,823 \\
38,067 \\
\hline
469,493
\end{array}
$$

14. The correct answer is C.

$$\$13.50 \times 6\frac{2}{3}\% = \$13.50 \times 0.06\frac{2}{3}$$

$$= \frac{\$13.50}{1} \times \frac{0.20}{3}$$

$$= \frac{\$2.70}{3} = \$0.90$$

15. The correct answer is C.

$$
\frac{11}{16} = 16 \overline{)11.0000}^{\,0.6875}
$$
$$
\begin{array}{r}
9\,6 \\
\hline
1\,40 \\
1\,28 \\
\hline
120 \\
112 \\
\hline
80 \\
80
\end{array}
$$

Exercise 2

1. C	6. B	11. B	15. A	19. B
2. A	7. D	12. C	16. C	20. B
3. C	8. B	13. C	17. D	21. A
4. C	9. C	14. B	18. D	22. A
5. D	10. C			

1. The correct answer is C.

$$
\begin{array}{r}
5,239 \\
\times 706 \\
\hline
31,434 \\
3,667,300 \\
\hline
3,698,734
\end{array}
$$

2. The correct answer is A.

$$
\begin{array}{r}
48,207 \\
\times 926 \\
\hline
289,242 \\
964,140 \\
43,386,300 \\
\hline
44,639,682
\end{array}
$$

3. The correct answer is C.

$$
7 \overline{)4,628}^{\,661 \text{ R }1}
$$
$$
\begin{array}{r}
42 \\
\hline
42 \\
42 \\
\hline
08 \\
7 \\
\hline
1
\end{array}
$$

4. The correct answer is C.

$$
419 \overline{)5,063}^{\,12 \text{ R }35}
$$
$$
\begin{array}{r}
419 \\
\hline
873 \\
838 \\
\hline
35
\end{array}
$$

5. **The correct answer is D.**

$$\$0.40 \overline{)\,\$59.60\,}\quad\begin{array}{r}1\;49\\40\\\hline 19\;6\\16\;0\\\hline 3\;60\\3\;60\end{array}$$

6. **The correct answer is B.**

$$\begin{array}{r}3.410\\5.600\\+\,0.873\\\hline 9.883\end{array}$$

7. **The correct answer is D.** 54,741

8. **The correct answer is B.** 0.024

Add up the places to the right of the decimal point.

9. **The correct answer is C.**

$$.33 \overline{)\,9.90\,}\quad\begin{array}{r}30.\end{array}$$

10. **The correct answer is C.**

$$\begin{array}{r}570\\\times\,0.16\\\hline 34\,20\\570\\\hline 91.20\end{array}$$

11. **The correct answer is B.**

$135 \div 900 = 0.15 = 15\%$

12. **The correct answer is C.**

$$\begin{array}{r}\dfrac{3}{4}=\dfrac{6}{8}\\[6pt]+\,\dfrac{3}{8}=\dfrac{3}{8}\\[6pt]\hline \dfrac{9}{8}=1\dfrac{1}{8}\end{array}$$

13. **The correct answer is C.**

$$3\frac{1}{4}=3\frac{2}{8}$$
$$4\frac{1}{8}=4\frac{1}{8}$$
$$+\,4\frac{1}{2}=4\frac{4}{8}$$
$$\overline{11\frac{7}{8}}$$

14. **The correct answer is B.**

$$10\frac{2}{3}=10\frac{4}{6}$$
$$-\,9\frac{1}{2}=9\frac{3}{6}$$
$$\overline{1\frac{1}{6}}$$

15. **The correct answer is A.**

$$14\frac{7}{24}=14\frac{7}{24}=13\frac{31}{24}$$
$$-\,5\frac{2}{3}=\;5\frac{16}{24}=\;5\frac{16}{24}$$
$$\overline{8\frac{15}{24}=8\frac{5}{8}}$$

16. **The correct answer is C.**

$$\frac{^2\cancel{8}}{\cancel{15}_5}\times\frac{^1\cancel{3}}{\cancel{4}_1}=\frac{2}{5}$$

17. **The correct answer is D.**

$$5\frac{1}{4}\times 2\frac{2}{7}=\frac{^3\cancel{21}}{\cancel{4}_1}\times\frac{^4\cancel{16}}{\cancel{7}_1}=\frac{12}{1}=12$$

18. **The correct answer is D.**

$$\frac{9}{16}\div\frac{3}{4}=\frac{^3\cancel{9}}{\cancel{16}_4}\times\frac{^1\cancel{4}}{\cancel{3}_1}=\frac{3}{4}$$

19. **The correct answer is B.** When adding two numbers of unlike sign, subtract and assign the sign of the larger number.

15

20. **The correct answer is B.** Minus negative becomes plus positive. The problem then reads:

$$(-22) + (+18) = -4.$$

21. **The correct answer is A.** When multiplying two numbers of unlike signs, the product is always negative.

$$(7) \times (-7) = -49$$

22. **The correct answer is A.** When you divide two numbers of unlike sign, the quotient is always negative.

$$(+56) \div (-7) = -8$$

Exercise 3

1. D	9. D	17. C	25. D	33. A
2. A	10. B	18. C	26. C	34. C
3. D	11. B	19. B	27. C	35. B
4. D	12. C	20. C	28. C	36. A
5. C	13. C	21. A	29. A	37. B
6. B	14. C	22. A	30. D	38. C
7. C	15. A	23. D	31. C	39. B
8. A	16. C	24. B	32. A	40. D

1. **The correct answer is D.** To find the mean, add all the numbers and divide the sum by the number of terms.

   $42 + 35 + 28 + 30 + 24 + 27 = 186$

   $186 \div 6 = 31$

2. **The correct answer is A.**

   14 words = 10 words + 4 words

   10 words cost 52 cents

   4 words @ 2.5 cents = $4 \times 2.5 = 10$ cents

   52 cents + 10 cents = 62 cents

3. **The correct answer is D.**

   $500 - 125 = 375$ pads @ $0.04 = \$15.00$

   $130 - 45 = 85$ pencils @ $0.03 = \$2.55$

   50 dozen − 4 dozen = 46 dozen rubber bands @ $0.02 = \$0.92$

   $\$15 + \$2.55 + \$0.92 = \$18.47$

4. **The correct answer is D.**

   $\$60 \times 0.10 = \$6$ (employee discount)

   $\$60 - \$6 = \$54$

   $\$54 \times 0.20 = \$10.80$ (sale discount)

   $\$54 - \$10.80 = \$43.20$

5. **The correct answer is C.**

   9 square feet = 1 square yard

   270 square feet $\div 9 = 30$ square yards

6. **The correct answer is B.**

   The whole pie is 100%.

   Each part is $\dfrac{1}{40}$.

   $100 \div 40 = 2.5\%$

15

7. **The correct answer is C.** First, find out how much sugar one quart of punch needs.

$$\frac{3}{4} \text{ cups} \div 6 = \frac{3}{4} \div \frac{6}{1} = \frac{\cancel{3}^1}{4} \times \frac{1}{\cancel{6}_2} = \frac{1}{8}$$

For 9 quarts of punch:

$$9 \times \frac{1}{8} = \frac{9}{8} = 1\frac{1}{8}$$

8. **The correct answer is A.** 45 badges × 4 inches each = 180 inches needed. There are 36 inches in one yard. 180 inches ÷ 36 = 5 yards of ribbon needed.

9. **The correct answer is D.**

1 gallon = 4 quarts

4 gallons = 16 quarts

$16 \text{ quarts} \times 42\frac{1}{2} \text{ cents} = 16 \times \$0.425 = \$6.80$

10. **The correct answer is B.**

$\frac{3}{5}$ of 200 = 120 columns by machine @ 40 columns per hour = 3 hours

200 − 120 = 80 columns without machine @ 20 columns per hour = 4 hours

3 hours + 4 hours = 7 hours to complete the job

11. **The correct answer is B.** The perimeter of a rectangle = $2l + 2w$. If the two long sides are together, the perimeter will be 5 + 3 + 3 + 5 + 3 + 3 = 22.

If the two short sides are together, the perimeter will be 3 + 5 + 5 + 3 + 5 + 5 = 26.

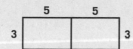

26 − 22 = 4 feet shorter

12. **The correct answer is C.** To remove a % sign, divide the number by 100.

Thus, $1\% = \frac{1}{100} = 0.01$. 1% of 8 is the same as 1% times $8 = 0.01 \times 8 = 0.08$.

13. **The correct answer is C.**

$$
\begin{array}{r}
8.13 \\
10{\overline{)81.30}} \\
\underline{80} \\
13 \\
\underline{10} \\
30 \\
\underline{30} \\
0
\end{array}
$$

14. **The correct answer is C.**

Each −1 cancels out the +1 before it.

Because the final term is +1, which is not canceled out by a −1, the sum is + 1.

15. **The correct answer is A.**

5 hours, 30 minutes = $5\frac{1}{2}$ hours

$1,000 \text{ miles} \div 5\frac{1}{2} \text{ hours} = 1,000 \div \frac{11}{2} =$

$1,000 \times \frac{2}{11} = 181\frac{9}{11}$ miles per hour

16. **The correct answer is C.**

2,975 pennies = $29.75

$35.00 − $29.75 = $5.25 amount of discount

Rate of discount $= \frac{5.25}{35} \times 100$

$= 0.15 \times 100$

$= 15\%$

15

17. **The correct answer is C.** First convert all the yards and feet into inches so that all addition and subtraction can be done using the same units.

$$12 \text{ feet} = 144 \text{ inches}$$
$$-7 \text{ inches} = -7 \text{ inches}$$
$$+2 \text{ feet}, 1 \text{ inch} = +25 \text{ inches}$$
$$-7 \text{ feet} = -84 \text{ inches}$$
$$-1 \text{ yard} = -36 \text{ inches}$$
$$+2 \text{ yards}, 1 \text{ foot}, 3 \text{ inches} = \underline{+87 \text{ inches}}$$
$$= 129 \text{ inches}$$

18. **The correct answer is C.** Any number multiplied by 0 equals 0. Since one multiplier on one side of the equals sign is 0, the product on that side of the sign must be 0.

$$5x = 5 \times 4 \times 2 \times 0$$
$$5x = 40 \times 0$$
$$5x = 0$$
$$x = 0$$

19. **The correct answer is B.**

Area of a square $= s^2$
$49 = 7^2$
One side $= 7$ inches
$P = 4s$
$P = 4 \times 7" = 28$ inches

20. **The correct answer is C.** First perform the operation within the parentheses. To cube a number, multiply it by itself three times.

$$(3 + 4)^3 = (7)^3 = 7 \times 7 \times 7 = 343$$

21. **The correct answer is A.**

First room:
   $36 \text{ ft.} \times 8 \text{ ft.} = 288 \text{ sq. ft.}$
Second room:
   $24 \text{ ft.} \times 9 \text{ ft.} = \dfrac{216 \text{ sq. ft.}}{504 \text{ sq. ft.}}$
$504 \div 224 = 2.25$ rolls needed

22. **The correct answer is A.**

0.05% of the total $(x) = 60$
$$0.0005x = 60$$
$$x = 60 \div 0.0005 = 120,000$$

23. **The correct answer is D.** If the court does a day's work every day, it will dispense with 60 days' worth of new cases. The excess work is $0.6 \times 60 = 36$ days of work. Add the 36 newly accumulated days of excess work to the backlog of 150 days of work to learn that the court will be 186 trial days behind.

24. **The correct answer is B.** $\frac{1}{4}$ inch $= 1$ foot, so 1 inch $= 4$ foot and the living room is $7 \times 4 = 28$ feet long. When the scale changes to 1 inch $= 1$ foot, the 28-foot living room will be 28 inches on the new drawing.

25. **The correct answer is D.** To find percent of change, subtract the original figure from the new figure to determine amount of change; then divide the amount of change by the original figure to determine percent of change.

$$\$65 - \$50 = \$15 \div 50 = 0.3 = 30\%$$

26. **The correct answer is C.** $11\frac{1}{2}\%$ of $5,000 is $575. Because he repaid the loan in one-half of a year, his interest payment is $575 \div 2 =$ $287.50.

27. **The correct answer is C.** If 30% has been deducted, $35 is 70% of the original price. To find out what a number is when a percent of it is given, rename the percent as a decimal and divide the given number by it.

$$\$35 \div 0.70 = \$50$$

28. **The correct answer is C.** One car went 20 mph for $\frac{1}{2}$ hour = 10 miles. The other went 36 mph for $\frac{1}{2}$ hour = 18 miles. Because they went in opposite directions, add the two distances to find the total number of miles apart: $10 + 18 = 28$.

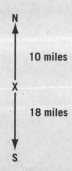

29. **The correct answer is A.** The boy worked 45 days × $14.50 per day, so he earned $652.50. He saved 60% of $652.50 = $391.50.

30. **The correct answer is D.** Rename 8 in. as $\frac{2}{3}$ ft. so that all measurements are in the same unit. Then multiply $l \times w \times h$.

$$3 \text{ ft.} \times \frac{2}{3} \text{ ft.} \times 1 \text{ ft.} = 2 \text{ cubic ft.}$$

31. **The correct answer is C.** 4 inches = 32 miles; therefore, 1 inch = $32 \div 4 = 8$ miles. 80 miles would be represented by 10 inches

32. **The correct answer is A.** You do not need to do complicated calculations to answer this question: $14 - 6 = 8$. The sun was above the horizon for 8 minutes less than 12 hours, which is 11 hours, 52 minutes ($60 - 8 = 52$).

33. **The correct answer is A.**

25 feet, 8 inches = 24 feet, 20 inches

18 feet, 10 inches = <u>18 feet, 10 inches</u>

6 feet, 10 inches

34. **The correct answer is C.** No calculations are needed here. Note that a 20-mile trip at 60 mph (which is 1 mile per minute) would take 20 minutes. Because the vehicle is traveling half as fast (30 miles per hour), the 20-mile trip should take twice as long, or 40 minutes.

35. **The correct answer is B.** This is a proportion problem. Set up the proportion as follows:

$$\frac{2\frac{1}{2}}{4} = \frac{1\frac{7}{8}}{?}$$

Substitute x for ?:

$$\frac{2\frac{1}{2}}{4} = \frac{1\frac{7}{8}}{x}$$

Cross-multiply:

$$2\frac{1}{2}x = 4 \times 1\frac{7}{8}$$

$$\frac{5}{2}x = \frac{60}{8}$$

Divide both sides by the coefficient of x and calculate:

$$x = \frac{60}{8} \div \frac{5}{2}$$

$$x = \frac{60}{8} \times \frac{2}{5}$$

$$x = 3$$

36. **The correct answer is A.** A child's ticket costs x dollars. Each adult ticket costs twice as much, or $2x$ dollars. $2(2x) = 2$ adult tickets; $3x = 3$ children tickets. Write a simple equation and solve for x.

$$2(2x) + 3x = \$49$$

$$4x + 3x = \$49$$

$$7x = \$49$$

$$x = \$7$$

$7 is the cost of a child's ticket; $14 is the cost of an adult's ticket.

37. **The correct answer is B.**

$1\frac{1}{2}$ cups sugar × 8 = 12 cups sugar

12 cups ÷ 2 cups per pound = 6 pound of sugar

38. **The correct answer is C.** By substituting +2 for the triangle, the denominator of the fraction becomes zero. A denominator of zero is undefined in mathematics.

15

39. The correct answer is B. The first pipe can fill the tank in $1\frac{1}{2}$ hours, or $\frac{3}{2}$ hours; that is, it can do $\frac{2}{3}$ of the job in 1 hour. The second pipe can fill the $\frac{x}{2}+3=15$ inutes, or $\frac{3}{4}$ of an hour, or it ca $\frac{x}{2}=15-3$ job in 1 hour. Together the pi $\frac{x}{2}=12$ ete $\frac{4}{3}+\frac{2}{3}=\frac{6}{3}$ of the job in 1 h $x=12\times 2$ r twice the job in 1 hour. Thererore, together the two pipes $x=24$ could fill the tank in $\frac{1}{2}$ hour.

$$y+2>10$$
$$y>10-2$$
$$y>8$$

40. The correct answer is D. The cars are traveling toward each other, so the distance between them is being reduced at $60 + 50$ or 110 miles per hour. At a rate of 110 miles per hour, 550 miles will be covered in 5 hours. If both cars left at 1:00 p.m., they should meet at 6:00 p.m.

Exercise 4

1. D	8. A	15. A	21. D	27. B
2. C	9. C	16. D	22. B	28. C
3. C	10. D	17. B	23. A	29. D
4. B	11. B	18. B	24. A	30. C
5. A	12. D	19. C	25. D	31. D
6. D	13. C	20. D	26. B	32. D
7. C	14. B			

1. **The correct answer is D.** Few numbers are divisible by both 5 and 6. Only multiples of 5×6 are divisible by both. Multiples of 5×6 are multiples of 30, which are all divisible by 3.

2. **The correct answer is C.** The seventh digit to the left of the decimal point is in the millions place. Because 482 is less than 500, round down.

3. **The correct answer is C.** 120 is not divisible by 7.

4. **The correct answer is B.** The place values are: four ones, nine tenths, two hundredths, three thousandths, six ten thousandths.

5. **The correct answer is A.** Look immediately to the right of the decimal point; 0 is less than 1.

6. **The correct answer is D.** The greatest number by which both 12 and 24 can be divided is 12.

7. **The correct answer is C.** To rename a percent as a decimal, move the decimal point two places to the left.

$$1000\% = 10.00$$

8. **The correct answer is A.** To simplify $\frac{12}{16}$ to simplest form, divide both numerator and denominator by 4.

9. **The correct answer is C.** The fraction bar in a fraction means "divided by."

$$9 \div 25 = 0.36$$

10. **The correct answer is D.** The positive and negative cancel each other out. Addition may be done in any order. To check this problem, reverse the order of the addends.

$$5 - 5 = 0$$

11. **The correct answer is B.** The square root of 81 is 9.

12. **The correct answer is D.**

13. **The correct answer is C.**

14. **The correct answer is B.** The sum of the angles of a circle equals 360°. Angles *a* through *f* total 340°. Angle *g* must be 20°.

15. **The correct answer is A.** The area of the entire rectangle is 6 inches × 15 inches = 90 square inches. The area of the unshaded portion is 4 inches × 9 inches = 36 square inches.

    90 square inches − 36 square inches = 54 square inches in the shaded portion.

16. **The correct answer is D.** In reading a graph, always read along the horizontal axis first.

17. **The correct answer is B.** The charge for one night is $25; for two nights, $50. The Boy Scouts receive a 30% discount, so they pay 70%. 70% of $50 = $35.

18. **The correct answer is B.** As part of the group, the leaders received the same 30% discount as the boys. If they had slept in the dormitory, they would have paid $35 each for the two nights. Their total bill (2 men, 2 nights) would have been $70. However, they paid extra for a semiprivate room. To find the percent of increase, subtract the original number from the new number and divide the difference by the original number.

    $84 − $70 = $14 ÷ $70 = 20%

19. **The correct answer is C.** Of the 18 people, there are 13 adults and 5 juniors. The adult tickets cost $20 × 13 = $260. The junior tickets cost $14 × 5 = $70. The total cost of lift tickets for one day is $260 + $70 = $330.

20. **The correct answer is D.** $\frac{1}{4}$ of 16 = 4 expert skiers. That leaves 16 − 4 = 12 less

experienced skiers. $\frac{3}{4}$ of 12 = 9 who took ski lessons. $\frac{1}{3}$ of 9 = 3 who rented equipment.

21. **The correct answer is D.** There were 27 trails and 6 lifts, which simplifies to 9:2.

22. **The correct answer is B.** The formula for determining rate is $\frac{D}{T}$. The distance skied is 4.6 miles. The time, just under 14 minutes, is approximately 0.25 hour.

    4.6 ÷ 0.25 = 18.4 miles per hour

    Because he skied the distance in slightly less than 0.25 hour, his average speed was very close to 20 miles per hour.

23. **The correct answer is A.** First add up the expenses:

    Rooms and lift tickets = $1,304
    Bus = +$250
    $1,554

    Subtract the troop contribution
    − $400
    $1,154

    Now divide by the 18 people:

    $1,154 ÷ 18 = $64.11 each

24. **The correct answer is A.** If $\frac{7}{8}$ of the campus is devoted to woods and gardens, then $\frac{1}{8}$ is used for academics.

15

25. **The correct answer is D.** Let x = tuition last year. This year's tuition is 7% greater:

$$1.07x = \$19{,}750$$

$$x = \frac{\$19{,}750}{1.07}$$

26. **The correct answer is B.** Average class size = (sum of the class sizes) ÷ (total number of classes). If 20 classes have an average size of 21 students, that's 20×21 students. Let x = average class size of the other 40 classes. Then:

$$\frac{(20)(21) + 40x}{60} = 15$$

Multiplying both sides by 60:

$$420 + 40x = 900$$
$$40x = 480$$
$$x = 12$$

Or, since we know that $\frac{1}{3}$ of the classes have an average size of 21, which is 6 above the given average size of 15, then the remaining $\frac{2}{3}$ of the classes (twice as many as $\frac{1}{3}$) must have an average size of 3 below 15: $15 - 3 = 12$.

27. **The correct answer is B.** The library has 30,000 volumes. Ten percent of 30,000 = 3,000. So, 2% = $\frac{3{,}000}{5} = 600$. The number of volumes left on campus next year will be $30{,}000 - 600 = 29{,}400$.

28. **The correct answer is C.** Based on the information given, the student-teacher ratio is 7:1. This means that for every 7 students, there is 1 teacher. So, we can let $7x$ = number of students and $1x$ = number of teachers.

Then:

$$7x + 1x = 304$$
$$8x = 304$$
$$x = 38$$

29. **The correct answer is D.** 4 weeks is

$$\frac{4}{52} = \frac{1}{13}.$$

30. **The correct answer is C.** Again find what percent one number is of another by creating a fraction. This time, the part that you want to know about happens to be larger than the whole.

$$\$1{,}500 \div 1{,}100 = 1.3636 \approx 136\frac{1}{3}\%$$

31. **The correct answer is D.** 3 gallons = 24 pints. $1\frac{1}{2}$ ounces of black paint $\times 24 = 36$ ounces of black paint. 36 ounces = $2\frac{1}{4}$ pints. 24 pints of blue + $2\frac{1}{4}$ pints of black = $26\frac{1}{4}$ pints of paint.

32. **The correct answer is D.** You do not have to calculate this problem. If you read carefully, you will see that 2 men worked full-time and the work took 4 weeks. If only one man (half the number) had worked, the job would have taken twice the time, or 8 weeks.

15

Chapter 16

Series Reasoning

OVERVIEW

- **Number Series**
- **Letter Series**
- **Mixed Series**
- **Tips for Answering Series Questions**
- **Summing It Up**
- **Exercises: Series Reasoning**
- **Answer Keys and Explanations**

Series reasoning questions crop up on the HSPT exam. These questions are in the Sequence section. Series reasoning questions—symbol series, number series, letter series, or mixed—test your ability to reason without words. These questions can be challenging, fun, or sometimes very frustrating.

Series questions are a lot like analogy questions—you remember, the questions that ask you to find the relationships between words. In series questions, you must determine the relationship between a series of symbols, numbers, or letters, and then choose the next item for the series.

This chapter gives you some in-depth instruction in working with series questions by showing you how to complete number and letter series. These are the most common kinds of series questions you'll encounter on the HSPT exam. The information and practice you get in this chapter will help you develop your own methods and strategies for solving these types of questions. What's more, you can use those same strategies to solve mixed series and even symbol series questions.

All series reasoning questions require the same concentration, the same logical thinking, and the same flexibility of approach. With any series reasoning question, you run the risk of working out a sequence only to find that the answer you would choose to complete the sequence is not among the choices. Don't be discouraged! Go back and determine what other relationship is reasonable.

NUMBER SERIES

Number series questions measure your ability to think numerically and recognize the relationship among numbers in a series. Even though this type of task might be new and unfamiliar to you, the actual mathematics of number series questions is not complicated. The problems involve nothing more than simple arithmetic and a few other mathematical concepts. What the questions do require of you is concentration; you must be able to see how the numbers in a series are related so that you can supply the next number in that series. You must be flexible enough in your thinking so that if the first pattern you consider for a series turns out to be invalid, you can try a different pattern.

16

There is a system with which to approach number series questions. First, look hard at the series. The pattern might be obvious to you right away. A series such as 1, 2, 3, 1, 2, 3, 1 . . . should not require any deep thought. Clearly, the sequence 1, 2, 3 is repeating. The next number in the series must be 2. You might also instantly recognize the pattern of a simple series into which one number periodically intrudes. An example of such a series is 1, 2, 15, 3, 4, 15, 5 . . . . The number 15 appears after each set of two numbers in a simple +1 series. The next number in this series is 6, followed by 15. Can you see why?

Test Yourself 1

Here are five series questions that you should be able to answer by inspection. Choose the number that should come next in the series. The answer keys and explanations appear after **Test Yourself 7**.

1. 12, 10, 13, 10, 14 . . .

   A. 9
   B. 10
   C. 14
   D. 15

2. 6, 21, 36, 6, 21 . . .

   A. 6
   B. 21
   C. 36
   D. 51

3. 9, 1, 9, 3, 9 . . .

   A. 4
   B. 5
   C. 6
   D. 8

4. 5, 8, 5, 8, 5 . . .

   A. 5
   B. 6
   C. 8
   D. 9

5. 10, 9, 8, 7, 6 . . .

   A. 4
   B. 5
   C. 6
   D. 7

Sometimes you might find that your ear is more adept than your eye. You might be able to "hear" a pattern or "feel" a rhythm more easily than you can "see" it. If you cannot immediately spot a pattern, try saying the series softly to yourself. First read the series through. If that does not help, try accenting the printed numbers and speaking the missing intervening numbers even more softly. Try grouping the numbers within the series into twos or threes. After grouping, try accenting the last number, or the first. If you read aloud 2, 4, 6, 8, 10, you will hear that the next number is 12. Likewise, if you see the series 31, 32, 33, 32, 33, 34, 33, and you group that series this way: 31, 32, 33/ 32, 33, 34/ 33 . . ., you will feel the rhythm. The series consists of three-number mini-series. Each mini-series begins with a number one higher than the first number of the previous mini-series. The next number of the above series is 34, then 35, and then the next step will be 34, 35, 36.

16

Test Yourself 2

You might be able to answer the next five series questions by inspection. If you cannot, try sounding them out. The answer keys and explanations appear after **Test Yourself 7**.

1. 1, 2, 5, 6, 9, 10, 13 . . .

   A. 14
   B. 15
   C. 16
   D. 17

2. 2, 3, 4, 3, 4, 5, 4 . . .

   A. 3
   B. 4
   C. 5
   D. 6

3. 10, 10, 12, 14, 14, 16 . . .

   A. 16
   B. 18
   C. 20
   D. 22

4. 1, 2, 3, 2, 2, 3, 3, 2, 3 . . .

   A. 1
   B. 2
   C. 3
   D. 4

5. 22, 20, 18, 20, 18, 16, 18 . . .

   A. 14
   B. 16
   C. 18
   D. 20

If you cannot hear the pattern of a series, the next step is to mark the degree and direction of change between the numbers. Most series progress by either + (plus) or − (minus) or a combination of both directions, so first try marking your changes in terms of + and −. If you cannot make sense of a series in terms of + and −, try × (times) and ÷ (divided by). You may mark the changes between numbers right on your exam paper, but be sure to mark the letter of the answer on your answer sheet when you figure it out. Even though they collect both your answer sheet and exam booklet, they only score your answer sheet.

Test Yourself 3

Try this next set of practice questions. If you cannot "see" or "hear" the pattern, mark the differences between the numbers to establish the pattern. Then continue the pattern to determine the next number of the series. The answer keys and explanations appear after **Test Yourself 7**.

1. 9, 10, 12, 15, 19, 24 . . .

   A. 25
   B. 29
   C. 30
   D. 31

2. 35, 34, 31, 30, 27, 26 . . .

   A. 22
   B. 23
   C. 24
   D. 25

16

3. 16, 21, 19, 24, 22, 27 . . .

   A. 20

   B. 25

   C. 29

   D. 32

4. 48, 44, 40, 36, 32, 28 . . .

   A. 27

   B. 26

   C. 25

   D. 24

5. 20, 30, 39, 47, 54, 60 . . .

   A. 65

   B. 66

   C. 68

   D. 70

Arithmetical series such as those above might be interrupted by a number that appears periodically or by repetition of numbers according to a pattern. For example: 3, 6, 25, 9, 12, 25, 15, 18, 25 . . . and 50, 50, 35, 40, 40, 35, 30, 30, 35 .... In these cases, you must search a bit harder to spot both the arithmetic pattern and the pattern of repetition. When choosing your answer, you must be alert to the interruption point in the pattern.

Test Yourself 4

Choose the number that should come next in the series. Do not repeat a number that has already been repeated, but do not forget to repeat before continuing the arithmetical pattern if repetition is called for at this point in the series. The answer keys and explanations appear after **Test Yourself 7**.

1. 10, 13, 13, 16, 16, 19 . . .

   A. 16

   B. 19

   C. 21

   D. 22

2. 2, 4, 25, 8, 16, 25, 32 . . .

   A. 25

   B. 32

   C. 48

   D. 64

3. 80, 80, 75, 75, 70, 70 . . .

   A. 60

   B. 65

   C. 70

   D. 75

4. 35, 35, 32, 30, 30, 27 . . .

   A. 25

   B. 26

   C. 27

   D. 28

5. 76, 70, 12, 65, 61, 12 . . .

   A. 12

   B. 54

   C. 55

   D. 58

16

LETTER SERIES

In letter series, each question consists of letters arranged according to a definite pattern. You must discover what that pattern is and then use that knowledge to determine which one of the four options completes the series. Letter series questions might be simple alphabetical progressions or intricate combinations that alternate between forward and backward steps.

Because each question is based on the twenty-six letters of the alphabet, it is a good idea write the alphabet in your booklet as you work. In addition, it is well worth your time to assign a number to each letter, jotting down the numbers from one to twenty-six directly under the letters. The seconds spent doing this might save you precious minutes as you work through the letter series.

There is more than one method of attack for letter series questions. You may solve these problems by inspection whenever possible. If that fails, try numerical analysis.

Inspection

The first line of attack should always be inspection; this is the quickest and easiest approach. Look at the letters. Are they progressing in normal or reverse alphabetical order? Are the letters consecutive, or do they skip one or more letters between terms? Are certain letters repeated?

Test Yourself 5

Here are some simple series that you should be able to solve by inspection only. The answer keys and explanations appear after **Test Yourself 7**.

1. d b f b h b j b l b

   A. b
   B. m
   C. n
   D. o

2. a b c c d e f f g h i

   A. f
   B. j
   C. k
   D. i

3. gij jlm mop

   A. prq
   B. prs
   C. rst
   D. qur

Numerical Analysis

If inspection does not make the answer apparent, try a numerical analysis of the series. Assign each letter in the series a numerical value according to its position in the alphabet. Write the direction and degree of difference between letters. Once you have done this, you will find yourself with a pattern of pluses and minuses like those you utilized for the numbers series questions.

16

Test Yourself 6

Choose the letter or group of letters that will continue the pattern or sequence. The answer keys and explanations appear after **Test Yourself 7**.

1. c d b e f d g h f i j

   A. h

   B. k

   C. f

   D. l

2. a b d g k p

   A. q

   B. u

   C. w

   D. v

3. mpt jmq gjn dgk

   A. cfj

   B. bei

   C. kos

   D. adh

MIXED SERIES

With mixed series, you must once again ask yourself, "What's happening? How are the numbers progressing? Up, or down? What about the letters? Are changes occurring in the relationships of numbers to letters? According to what pattern?"

Test Yourself 7

Choose the answer that will continue the pattern or sequence or that should fill in the blank in the series. The answer keys and explanations appear after this section.

1. RA_1T_2 RA_3T_4 RA_1T_2 RA_4T_5 _____

   A. RA_5T_6

   B. RA_5T_4

   C. RA_1T_2

   D. R_1AT_2

2. $L^2M_2N^2$ $O_3P^3Q_3$ $R^2S_2T^2$ _____ $X^2Y_2Z^2$

   A. $U_4V^4W_4$

   B. $T_3U^3V_3$

   C. $U^3V_3W^3$

   D. $V^4W_3X^4$

16

TEST YOURSELF ANSWER KEYS AND EXPLANATIONS

Test Yourself 1

1. B	2. C	3. B	4. C	5. B

1. **The correct answer is B.** The series is a +1 series with the number 10 inserted after each step of the series.

2. **The correct answer is C.** The sequence 6, 21, 36 repeats itself without changing.

3. **The correct answer is B.** This is a +2 series, with the number 9 appearing before each member of the series.

4. **The correct answer is C.** In this series, the sequence 5, 8 repeats.

5. **The correct answer is B.** This is a descending series; each number is one less than the one before it. You can call this a −1 series.

Test Yourself 2

1. A	2. C	3. B	4. D	5. B

1. **The correct answer is A.** If you pair the numbers, you can whisper the bracketed "missing numbers" to determine the pattern; 1, 2, [3, 4,] 5, 6, [7, 8,] 9, 10, [11, 12,] 13

   The next number to read aloud is 14, followed by a whispered 15, 16, and then aloud again for 17.

2. **The correct answer is C.** If you group the numbers into threes and read them aloud, accenting either the first or last number of each group, you should feel that each group of three begins and ends with a number one higher than the previous group.

   Read 2, 3, 4/ 3, 4, 5/ 4, 5, 6;
   or 2, 3, 4/ 3, 4, 5/ 4, 5, 6.

3. **The correct answer is B.** Once more, group the numbers into threes. This time, be certain to accent the third number in each group in order to sense the rhythm, and thereby the pattern, of the series:

   10, 10, 12/ 14, 14, 16/ 18 ....

4. **The correct answer is D.** In this series, the rhythm emerges when you accent the first number in each group:

   1, 2, 3/ 2, 2, 3/ 3, 2, 3/ 4, 2, 3, ...

5. **The correct answer is B.** Consider the first three terms 22, 20, 18. To obtain the next three terms, subtract 2 from each of these. Then, to get the next three terms after these, subtract 2 from each of *those* terms, and so on.

16

Test Yourself 3

1. C	2. B	3. B	4. D	5. A

1. **The correct answer is C.** The pattern here is that a number is added to each number in the series to get the next number. The "added" number starts with 1, and increases by 1 for each successive addition; 9 *(+1)*, 10 *(+2)*, 12 *(+3)*, 15 *(+4)*, 19 *(+5)*, 24 *(+6)*, 30 ....

2. **The correct answer is B.** The pattern for this series is to first subtract 1, then subtract 3, and then repeat this alternating pattern; 35 *(−1)*, 34 *(−3)*, 31*(−1)*, 30*(−3)*, 27*(−1)*, 26 *(−3)*, 23 ....

3. **The correct answer is B.** The pattern in this series is simply to add 5, then subtract 2; 16 *(+5)*, 21*(−2)*, 19 *(+5)*, 24 *(−2)*, 22 *(+5)*, 27 *(−2)*, 25 . . .

4. **The correct answer is D.** This series simply subtracts 4 to get each new member.

5. **The correct answer is A.** This series begins by adding 10, after which each successive addition is 1 less than the previous addition; 20 *(+10)*, 30 *(+9)*, 39 *(+8)*, 47 *(+7)*, 54 *(+6)*, 60 *(+5)*, 65 ....

Test Yourself 4

1. B	2. D	3. B	4. A	5. D

1. **The correct answer is B.** The series pattern here is to add 3, repeat that number, then add 3 again, repeat *that* number, and continue; 10 *(+3)*, 13 *(repeat)*, 13 *(+3)*, 16 *(repeat)*, 16 *(+3)*, 19 *(repeat)*, 19 ....

2. **The correct answer is D.** This series pattern includes an extraneous number that is repeated periodically. Specifically, 25 repeats itself every third number. The complete pattern is to multiply each number by 2, but insert 25 as every third entry; 2 *(×2)*, 4 *(×2)*, *25*, 8 *(×2)*, 16 *(×2)*, *25*, 32 *(×2)*, 64 ....

3. **The correct answer is B.** This pattern repeats each number once, and then subtracts 5; 80 *(repeat)*, 80 *(−5)*, 75 *(repeat)*, 75 *(−5)*, 70 *(repeat)*, 70 *(−5)*, 65 ....

4. **The correct answer is A.** This series contains three repeated steps: The pattern is to repeat the first number, subtract 3, then subtract 2. The pattern starts again by repeating the last number; 35 *(repeat)*, 35 *(−3)*, 32 *(−2)*, 30 *(repeat)*, 30 *(−3)*, 27 *(−2)*, 25 ....

5. **The correct answer is D.** This series starts by subtracting 6 from the initial number, and each successive subtraction is one less than the prior number. In addition, the number 12 is repeated every third number in the series; 76 *(−6)*, 70 *(−5)*, *12*, 65 *(−4)*, 61 *(−3)*, *12*, 58 ....

16

Test Yourself 5

1. C	2. D	3. B

1. **The correct answer is C.** The even terms of the sequence are always "b." The other terms start with "d" and skip a letter each time. So, the odd terms are d, f, h, j, l, n, p, r, ...

2. **The correct answer is D.** This is also a consecutive alphabetical progression, but here the third letter of each set repeats. Thus, we have abcc deff ghii. Because only one *i* is given in the original series, the next letter must be the second *i* needed to complete the third set.

3. **The correct answer is B.** This is a bit more difficult, but with the grouping already done for you, you should be able to solve it by inspection. The pattern is as follows: From the first letter, skip one, then let the next letter in sequence follow immediately. Start each new three-letter sequence with the last letter of the previous sequence. The missing sequence begins with the *p* of the previous sequence, skips one letter to *r*, then continues immediately with *s*.

Test Yourself 6

1. A	2. D	3. D

A	B	C	D	E	F	G	H	I	J	K	L	M	N	O	P	Q	R	S	T	U	V	W	X	Y	Z
1	2	3	4	5	6	7	8	9	10	11	12	13	14	15	16	17	18	19	20	21	22	23	24	25	26

1. **The correct answer is A.**

c	d	b	e	f	d	g	h	f	i	j	h
3	4	2	5	6	4	7	8	6	9	10	8

   +1 −2 +3 +1 −2 +3 +1 −2 +3 +1 −2

   Now it is obvious that the series progresses by the formula +1 −2 +3. According to this pattern, the next letter must be 10 −2, or 8, which corresponds to the letter *h*.

2. **The correct answer is D.**

a	b	d	g	k	p	v
1	2	4	7	11	16	22

   +1 +2 +3 +4 +5 +6

   The progression is obvious once placed into a format showing the numerical translation of the alphabet. The numeric difference between each member of the series starts with 1 and increases by 1 with each letter.

3. **The correct answer is D.**

m	p	t	j	m	q	g	j	n	d	g	k	a	d	h
13	16	20	10	13	17	7	10	14	4	7	11	1	4	8

   +3 +4 −10 +3 +4 −10 +3 +4 −10 +3 +4 −10 +3 +4

   This series has three steps; the pattern is +3, +4, −10. This series could be seen as groups of three in this instance; watch for questions in which the letters are pre grouped for you.

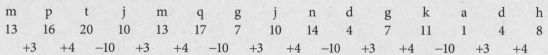

16

Test Yourself 7

1. C	2. A

1. **The correct answer is C.** A good solid look at the groupings within the series shows that the unit RA_1T_2 intervenes between the other units of the series. This unit is next in the series that is given to us, so there is no need to figure out the pattern of the other units; choice C is the correct answer.

2. **The correct answer is A.** The first thing that becomes clear in this mixed series is that the letters form a simple alphabetical progression. You can immediately narrow your choices to A and C. On the basis of the information given, there is no way to know whether the numbers in the missing unit should be 3s or 4s, but we do have information about their position with relation to the letters. The pattern of the groups in which the numbers are 2s is superscript, subscript, superscript. We are given only one group in which the numbers are not 2s, and the pattern in this case is subscript, superscript, subscript—the opposite of the groups with 2s. Because there is evidence of possible alternation of patterns—and we have already eliminated choices A and C—the proper choice is A, in which the pattern of the numbers is subscript, superscript, subscript.

16

TIPS FOR ANSWERING SERIES QUESTIONS

- Tackle the questions that seem easiest for you first. Questions generally tend to be arranged in order of difficulty, with the easiest questions first, but problems that might seem easy to some people might be more difficult to others, and vice versa. Answer quickly the questions that require little of your time, and leave yourself extra time for the more difficult questions.

- When you skip a question, put a mark before the question number in the test booklet and leave its answer space blank When you return to a question that you have skipped, be sure to mark its answer in the correct space. The time you spend checking to make sure that question and answer number are alike is time well spent.

- Follow the procedures outlined in this chapter. First, look for an obvious pattern. Second, sound out the series; if necessary, group the numbers or letters and sound out again. Third, write the direction and amount of change between the numbers or letters.

- If you do any figuring in the test booklet, be sure to mark the letter of the correct answer on your answer sheet. All answers must be marked on the answer sheet.

- If none of the answers given fits the rule you have figured out, try again. Try to figure out a rule that makes one of the four answers a correct one.

- Do not spend too much time on any one question. If a question seems impossible, skip it and come back to it later. A fresh look will sometimes help you find the answer. If you still cannot figure out the answer, guess. Remember that there is no penalty for a wrong answer on the HSPT exam.

- Keep track of time. Because there is no penalty for a wrong answer on the HSPT exam, you will want to answer every question. Leave yourself time to go back to the questions you skipped so that you can give them a second look. On the HSPT exam, if you are not finished as the time limit approaches, mark random answers for the remaining questions.

16

Summing It Up

- Series questions are in the Sequence category of the HSPT exam under Quantitative Skills.

- In series questions, you must determine the relationship among a series of symbols, numbers, or letters. Then, choose the next item for the series.

- First read the series through. If that does not help, try accenting the printed numbers and speaking the missing intervening numbers even more softly. Try grouping the numbers within the series into twos or threes. After grouping, try accenting the last number, or the first.

- It is a good idea to keep a copy of the alphabet in front of you as you work. In addition, it is helpful to assign a number to each letter, jotting down the numbers from 1 to 26 directly under the letters to which they correspond.

- Study and practice the series reasoning question tactics in this chapter. Remember: Answer the easy ones first; if you skip a question, make a mark on your answer sheet so you don't mark your answer sheet incorrectly. Follow the system described in this chapter—look, sound, and group series items. Don't spend too much time on any one question, and keep track of time. If you start to run out, remember that there is no penalty for guessing on the HSPT, and completing all the answers on the sheet—even randomly—may gain you points!

Take a moment to ask yourself some simple questions about your understanding of the chapter:

Review: What did I learn?

Evaluate: What do I need to learn more about?

Plan: What can I do next to keep improving?

Based on your answers to those questions, adjust your study plan to dedicate additional time to the areas of weakness that you've identified.

EXERCISES: SERIES REASONING

Exercise 1

> **Directions:** Choose the number that should come next or that should fill the blank in the series. The answer keys and explanations appear after Exercise 3.

1. 75, 75, 72, 72, 69, 69, . . .
   - A. 63
   - B. 66
   - C. 68
   - D. 69

2. 12, 16, 21, 27, 31, . . .
   - A. 33
   - B. 35
   - C. 36
   - D. 37

3. 22, 24, 12, 26, 28, 12, . . .
   - A. 12
   - B. 30
   - C. 34
   - D. 36

4. 13, 22, 32, 43, _____, 68
   - A. 53
   - B. 54
   - C. 55
   - D. 56

5. 4, 2, 1, $\frac{1}{2}$, $\frac{1}{4}$, . . .
   - A. 0
   - B. $\frac{1}{8}$
   - C. $\frac{3}{8}$
   - D. $\frac{1}{16}$

6. 100, 81, _____, 49, 36
   - A. 60
   - B. 64
   - C. 65
   - D. 75

7. 32, 25, 86, 32, 25, . . .
   - A. 5
   - B. 32
   - C. 68
   - D. 86

8. 51, 51, 30, 47, 47, 30, 43, . . .
   - A. 30
   - B. 41
   - C. 43
   - D. 45

9. 3 3 9 | 15 15 21 | 27 27 _____
   - A. 1
   - B. 27
   - C. 30
   - D. 33

10. 95 90 86 | 83 78 74 | 51 _____ 42
    - A. 45
    - B. 46
    - C. 47
    - D. 50

16

11. 1 5 1 | 2 6 2 | 3 ____ 3

    A. 0

    B. 3

    C. 4

    D. 7

12. 50 52 48 | 35 37 33 | ____ 14 10

    A. 9

    B. 11

    C. 12

    D. 15

13. 39 40 80 | 10 11 22 | 17 18 ____

    A. 9

    B. 33

    C. 36

    D. 38

14. 36 12 4 | 63 21 7 | ____ 36 12

    A. 72

    B. 85

    C. 97

    D. 108

Exercise 2

Directions: Choose the letter or group of letters that should come next or that should fill the blank in the series.

1. n n o p p q r r s t

    A. t

    B. u

    C. v

    D. r

2. a j e b u q i y e p a

    A. k

    B. d

    C. f

    D. w

3. d e f d g h i g j k l j m n o

    A. j

    B. m

    C. n

    D. o

4. a c d a a c d b a c d c a c

    A. a

    B. b

    C. c

    D. d

5. a d h l b e i m c f j

    A. l

    B. m

    C. n

    D. o

6. z a z c z f z j z

    A. g

    B. o

    C. z

    D. s

16

7. hat | mat | rat | bat | _____

   A. jat

   B. qat

   C. pat

   D. uat

8. mnp | hik | bce | _____ | kln

   A. uvx

   B. gij

   C. rqp

   D. xyz

9. ZWT WTQ TQN _____ NKH

   A. PNL

   B. NLJ

   C. MJG

   D. QNK

10. ABC IRS GNO DHI

   A. BDG

   B. FKL

   C. EJK

   D. NYZ

Exercise 3

Directions: Choose the answer that will continue the pattern or sequence or that should fill the blank in the series.

1. $STPR_1$ STP_1R_2 $STPR_3$ _____ $STPR_5$

   A. $STPR_4$

   B. STP_4R_5

   C. $ST_1P_2R_3$

   D. STP_2R_3

2. $F^1G_2H^3I_4G_6H^7I_8J^9H_4I^5J_6K^7I^3J_4K^5L_6$ _____

   A. $J^7K_8L^9M_{10}$

   B. $M^5N_6O^7P_8$

   C. $J^8K_9L^{10}M_{11}$

   D. $K^1L_3M^5N_9$

3. $D_4F_6H_8E_5G_7I_9$ _____ $K_{11}M_{13}O_{15}P_{16}R_{18}T_{20}$

   A. $J_{10}K_{11}L_{12}$

   B. $J_{10}L_{12}N_{14}$

   C. $J_{10}L_{11}N_{12}$

   D. $J_{10}K_{12}L_{14}$

4. $R^2D^2R^2D_2R_2D_2R_2D^2D^2R^2$ _____

   A. D_2R_2

   B. R^2D_2

   C. D^2R_2

   D. D. D_2R^2

16

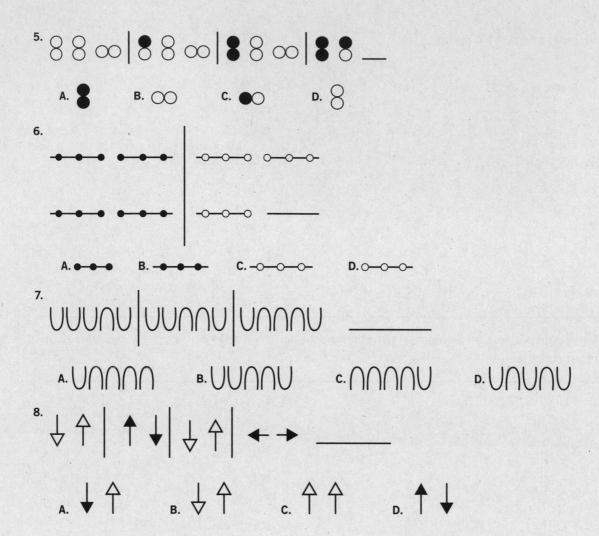

ANSWER KEYS AND EXPLANATIONS

Exercise 1

1. B	**4.** C	**7.** D	**10.** B	**13.** C
2. C	**5.** B	**8.** C	**11.** D	**14.** D
3. B	**6.** B	**9.** D	**12.** C	

1. **The correct answer is D.** The pattern is: repeat the number, −3; repeat the number, −3; repeat the number, −3. The next number must be 69 − 3 = 66.

2. **The correct answer is C.** The pattern repeats in groups of three; +4, +5, +6; +4, +5, +6. The next number must be 31 + 5, which is 36.

3. **The correct answer is B.** The basic pattern is a simple +2. The number 12 is inserted after each two terms of the series.

4. **The correct answer is C.** The numbers are large, but the progression is simple. If you mark the differences between numbers, you will recognize: +9, +10, +11, supply the +12 term, then continue with +13 to get the final number shown in the series to prove your answer.

5. **The correct answer is B.** This is a simple ÷2 series.

6. **The correct answer is B.** This series consists of the squares of the whole numbers in descending order.

7. **The correct answer is D.** This series follows no mathematical rule. You must solve it by inspection. The sequence 32, 25, 86 simply repeats.

8. **The correct answer is C.** The basic pattern is: repeat the number, −4; repeat the number, −4. The number 30 appears each time after the repeat and before the −4.

9. **The correct answer is D.** The entire series pattern is repeat, +6, +6; repeat, +6, +6. To answer the question, it is enough to recognize that the pattern within each segment of the series is: repeat, +6, +6.

10. **The correct answer is B.** Within each segment of the series, the pattern is −5, −4, −3. In the final segment, 51 − 5 = 46 − 4 = 42. The next number would be 39 (42 − 3).

11. **The correct answer is D.** You might see the pattern within each segment as +4, −4, or you might recognize by inspection or vocalization that each segment is simply a step up from the previous one.

12. **The correct answer is C.** Within each segment, the pattern is +2, −4. Because there is no overall pattern for the series, you must establish the pattern in the first two segments, then apply it in reverse to determine the first term in the last segment. Since the second term is two higher than the first, you can subtract 2 from the second term to determine the first; 14 − 2 = 12.

13. **The correct answer is C.** The pattern is +1, ×2.

14. **The correct answer is D.** In the first two segments, you can establish that the pattern is ÷3. When you reach the third segment, multiply the second term by 3 to achieve the number that when divided by 3 equals 36.

16

Exercise 2

1. A	**3.** B	**5.** C	**7.** C	**9.** D
2. A	**4.** D	**6.** B	**8.** A	**10.** C

1. **The correct answer is A.** This pattern alternates double and single letters in alphabetical order: nn o pp q rr s t. The next letter must be the second *t* needed to maintain the pattern.

2. **The correct answer is A.** In this series, each set of two letters is a vowel followed by a consonant that contains the sound of the vowel with which it is paired: aj eb uq iy ep a. The only consonant offered that contains the sound of *a* is *k*.

3. **The correct answer is B.** This series is an alphabetical progression of four-letter sequences where each fourth letter repeats the first letter of each sequence: defd ghig jklj mno. The missing letter is therefore the *m* needed to complete the fourth set.

4. **The correct answer is D.** This pattern consists of the letters *acd* followed by consecutive letters of the alphabet, starting with *a*. Thus: acda acdb acdc acd. The next letter must be *d*.

5. **The correct answer is C.** The best way to visualize this pattern is to assign the letters of the alphabet numbers from 1 to 26. This series then becomes:

a	d	h	l	b	e	i	m	c	f	j	n
1	4	8	12	2	5	9	13	3	6	10	14
	+3	+4	+4	−10	+3	+4	+4	−10	+3	+4	+4

The last number must be 10 + 4, which is 14, corresponding to the letter *n*. If you look at the numbers corresponding to each letter in each group of 4, you may notice that each item is one number higher than the group before.

6. **The correct answer is B.** Starting at the beginning of the alphabet, the space between even letters increases by one with each new letter:

a		c		f		j		o
	+2		+3		+4		+5	

The letter *z* is a constant between each term. The next step in this series must be five letters after *j*, which is *o*.

7. **The correct answer is C.** In this series, each set of three letters makes a word composed of a consonant plus *at*: hat, mat, rat, bat. The next segment, therefore, must consist of a consonant plus *at* that may be combined to form an English word. Choice C is the only answer option that forms a word. Another option would have been *cat*, but it is not among the answer choices.

8. **The correct answer is A.** The easiest way to solve this series is to verify the numerical relationship within segments. In each instance, the sequence is +1, +2. The only option that satisfies this sequence is u + 1 = v + 2 = x, or *uvx*.

9. **The correct answer is D.** Look at the alphabet written out before you. From *Z*, skip over two letters back to *W*, and from *W* skip back two more to *T*. In the next group, the procedure is exactly the same, and in each of the following groups as well. In addition, note that each succeeding group begins with the middle letter of the group before it. Thus, the missing group begins with the *Q* in the middle of the preceding group, continues with the skip of two back to *N*, and concludes with the further skip back to *K*.

16

10. **The correct answer is C.** It is very important to have written the entire alphabet and to have assigned each letter its numerical equivalent in order to choose the answer to this question.

ABC	IRS	GNO	DHI	EJK
1 2 3	9 18 19	7 14 15	4 8 9	5 10 11
×2 +1	×2 +1	×2 +1	×2 +1	×2 +1

Obviously, you must figure out the relationship on groups other than the first one, then confirm that the relationship of the first three letters is not simple alphabetical succession. It is also clear that no group of three bears any external relationship to any other group of three letters. Only the relationship within a group of three will determine the correct answer. Only choice C satisfies the ×2, +1 formula.

Exercise 3

1. D	3. B	5. B	7. C	8. B
2. A	4. C	6. D		

1. **The correct answer is D.** In all groupings, the letters are the same. You might assume that the answer choice will contain those same letters. When there is only one subscript number, it is at the end. When there are two, they follow the last and the next-to-last letter. Your best guess, if you can find reasonable choices to fit, is that the number pattern appears to alternate: one number, two numbers, one number, two numbers. Choices B and D might fit into this pattern. Then look for the rationale for the numbers themselves. The numbers of the second group add to make the number of the third. Because the numbers of choice D (2 and 3) add to make the number in the final group (5), this is the most logical choice.

2. **The correct answer is A.** By inspection, you can find the pattern of the letters. Each succeeding group of four picks up with the second letter of the preceding group and proceeds in alphabetical order. This means the next group must start with *J*, which narrows your answer choices to A or C. Now look at the numbers. Within each set of four, the numbers go in order, but there seems to be no rule by which numbers are assigned to succeeding groups. So you must look for a pattern of some sort. Note that even numbers always appear as subscripts and odd numbers are always superscripts. Now you know why choice A is the correct answer.

3. **The correct answer is B.** Some series questions are easier than others. The numbers that follow the letters are the numbers assigned to the letters according to their position in the alphabet. Immediately, you may narrow the correct answer possibility to choices A and B, since the numbers in choices C and D do not match their positions in the alphabet. Now look at the pattern of the letters. In each group, there is a skip-one pattern. Because choice A gives letters in sequence, the correct answer must be choice B.

4. **The correct answer is C.** In the first four groupings, the 2s position themselves in all possible combinations around the *R* and the *D*. The fifth group reverses the positions of *R* and *D* and appears to begin anew the circuit of 2s around the letters. The final group, then, should continue the rotation of the 2s, following in the same manner as when the letters were in their original position. Thus, the second *D R* should have the 2s placed in the same manner as the second *R D*—the first 2 at the top and the second 2 at the bottom.

16

5. **The correct answer is B.** As the pattern progresses, in each succeeding frame an additional circle is darkened. Thus, in the first, none; in the second, one; in the third, two; and in the fourth, three. Because three circles have already been darkened in the fourth frame, the frame must be completed with undarkened circles, horizontal as in all frames.

6. **The correct answer is D.** Because frames one and three are identical, you must assume that the pattern is of alternating identities, and that frames two and four must also be identical.

7. **The correct answer is C.** In the first three frames, the farthest-right figure is always a U shape. In the first frame, the next-to-last figure is upended; in the second frame, an additional figure is upended, reading from right to left; in the third frame, three figures are upended. Logically, as the series progresses, the fourth frame should include the four left-hand figures upended, with only the farthest right maintaining its position as a U.

8. **The correct answer is B.** The darkened figures seem to be following no particular pattern within themselves, but they do seem to be alternating frames with the undarkened figures. The positions of the undarkened arrows in the first and third frames are identical. There is no reason to expect their positions to change the next time they appear in the series. With the alternating dark, light pattern, the undarkened arrows are due to appear in the next frame, and only choice B maintains their same position as in the two previous appearances.

16

Comparisons and Ability Questions

OVERVIEW

- **Geometric Comparisons**
- **Nongeometric Comparisons**
- **Ability Questions**
- **Summing It Up**
- **Exercises: Comparisons**
- **Answer Key and Explanations**

The comparison questions in the Quantitative Skills section of the HSPT exam require a little bit of mathematical skill, a lot of patience, and logical thinking. You can't rush through any of these questions! To get the maximum number of right answers, you must study and count when you're answering geometric comparison questions.

For nongeometric comparison questions, you begin by performing all the operations. Then you work through the answer choices one by one, eliminating each statement that proves to be false, based on the facts of the problem. When you find what you think is the correct choice, you still need to continue trying all the other answers, as a check on your own reasoning. To give you a feel for these questions, let's work through a few together.

GEOMETRIC COMPARISONS

Geometric comparison questions ask you to compare values among multiple objects. It may be a comparison of the areas of three shapes, the shaded areas of three shapes, number of sides, and patterns, among others. Much like the series exercises in Chapter 16, geometric comparisons require your complete focus to spot the pattern(s) among the figures in the question. Some will be easier than others, but don't develop the idea that they are all going to be the same. That said, let's look at a couple of problems and identify techniques to help you solve them.

TIP
Carefully examine each shape to identify what element(s) change between each item and the next: measurement of a side, number of sides, how much of a shape is colored, and whether there is a pattern in the shapes.

17

TIP

Don't be afraid to draw on or label the diagrams to distinguish between the parts. Extend lines across the shapes and number parts to help yourself see how the shape is really divided.

1. Examine A, B, and C and find the best answer.

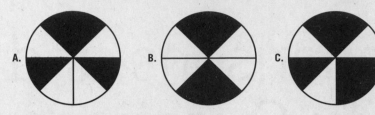

A. A is more shaded than B.

B. B is more shaded than A and less shaded than C.

C. A and B are equally shaded and less shaded than C.

D. A, B, and C are equally shaded.

The correct answer is C. This question asks how much of each circle is shaded. Begin by studying the three circles. Note that all three circles are divided into eight segments. If you count the number of shaded segments in each circle and write that number next to the circle, you will notice one specific detail: if you have counted accurately, you have written: A 4, B 4, C 5. Regardless of the pattern of shaded wedges, two of them have the same number of spaces shaded, while the third has one more wedge filled in. Now, read the statements one by one, paying attention to the words used, and mark true or false next to the letter of each statement. The statement in choice A is false because both A and B have four shaded segments. The statement in choice B must be false because it is not entirely true. B is indeed less shaded than C, but it is not more shaded than A. To be true, a statement must be 100 percent true. The statement in choice C is true. A and B are equally shaded (four each) and both are less shaded than C with its five shaded segments. Check out choice D just to be certain you have not made an error. No problem there, as the statement in choice D is clearly false.

2. The pie is divided into sixteen equal portions. Study the pie and find the best answer.

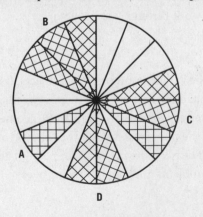

A. A plus D equals B plus C.

B. D minus A equals B minus C.

C. C minus D equals A.

D. B equals A plus C.

ALERT!

Make sure you look at each figure carefully. Without careful examination, an optical illusion could give you the wrong first impression.

17

The correct answer is C. Begin by counting the pie wedges in each portion; write the number of wedges next to the letter—A (1), B (3), C (3), D (2). Now perform the very simple arithmetic for each statement.

A. $1 + 2 = 3 + 3$; $3 = 6$—false

B. $2 - 1 = 3 - 3$; $1 = 0$—false

C. $3 - 2 = 1$—true

D. $3 = 1 + 3$; $3 = 4$—false

NONGEOMETRIC COMPARISONS

Nongeometric comparison questions test your ability to spot patterns with numbers or equations. Some might give you equations to solve, while others might give you a set of values. The object is to compare the values and equations against the response options. Like geometric comparisons, it is easier to actually see how it works than to try to explain all of the possible variations. So, let's look at a couple of nongeometric comparison questions.

1. Examine A, B, and C and find the best answer.

    A. $(5 \times 4) - 10$

    B. $(3 \times 6) + 4$

    C. $(8 \times 3) - 6$

A. $B = C > A$

B. $B > C > A$

C. $A > C$

D. $C > A > B$

Obviously, you must begin by performing the indicated operations.

    A. $(5 \times 4) - 10 = 20 - 10 = 10$

    B. $(3 \times 6) + 4 = 18 + 4 = 22$

    C. $(8 \times 3) - 6 = 24 - 6 = 18$

Now you can substitute these numbers for the letters in the four statements and choose the correct one.

A. 22 is equal to 18 and greater than 10—this is false, 22 is greater than 18.

B. 18 is greater than 10 but less than 22—this is true, 10 is less than 18, which is less than 22.

C. 10 is greater than 18—this is false, 10 is not greater than 18.

D. 10 is less than 18 but more than 22—this is false, 10 is not greater than 22.

The correct answer is B. We know this because each portion of the statement in choice B is true; 18 is greater than 10, and 18 is less than 22. Let's look at another problem.

17

Chapter 17: Comparisons and Ability Questions

2. Examine A, B, and C and find the best answer.

    A. 4^3

    B. 3^4

    C. $(3 \times 4)(4)$

A. $A > B > C$

B. $A = B > C$

C. $B > A > C$

D. $A = C < B$

First, perform the operations.

    A. $4^3 = 4 \times 4 \times 4 = 64$

    B. $3^4 = 3 \times 3 \times 3 \times 3 = 81$

    C. $(3 \times 4)(4) = 12 \times 4 = 48$

Substitute the numbers in the statements.

    A. 64 is greater than 81, which is greater than 48—false, 64 is less than 81.

    B. 64 equals 81, which is greater than 48—false, 64 is not equal to 81.

    C. 48 is smaller than 81, which is greater than 64—true, 81 is greater than both 64 and 48.

    D. 64 is equal to 48, which is smaller than 81—false, 64 is not equal to 48.

The correct answer is C. As soon as you hit a falsehood in an answer, no matter what comes before or after, that answer cannot be true.

You will have a chance to practice more geometric and nongeometric comparison questions in the exercise at the end of this chapter.

ABILITY QUESTIONS

If you are taking the TACHS, you will encounter questions in the Ability section. Questions in this section will assess the reasoning abilities you've developed through experiences both in and out of school, and will test your ability to reason using spatial and figure-based content. Unlike math or language arts questions, ability questions will highlight how well you use your reasoning skills to solve problems that you may or may not have learned in the classroom.

Ability questions come in three different formats: paper folding, figure classification, and figure matrices. Let's explore each of these question types.

Paper Folding

Paper folding questions test how well you can visualize what happens when holes are punched in a folded piece of paper. For these problems, you see a flat square piece of paper that folds one, two, or three times. You will observe each fold, presented in a sequence of folds and ending with one or more hole punches.

To successfully solve these problems, always assume that the paper fold is toward the front (toward you). The broken lines you will see indicate the original position of the paper prior to that fold, and the solid lines indicate the final position of the folded paper.

17

One or more holes appear in the paper after the last fold. You must mentally unfold the paper and determine the position of the holes that would then appear on the original square piece of paper. You then choose the pattern of circles indicating the position of these holes on the original square piece of paper.

In the answer choices, punched holes are based on an imaginary grid of 4 rows and 4 columns of circles, as shown:

These 16 positions represent the only possible final holes; no partial holes will appear in the final answer.

There are only four main type of folds:

1. A horizontal fold that occurs one-eighth, one-fourth, one-third, or one-half from the top or bottom edge of the square paper.

2. A vertical fold that occurs one-eighth, one-fourth, one-third, or one-half from the right or left edge of the square paper.

3. A fold along one of the two main diagonals of the square piece of paper.

4. A fold along a diagonal connecting the midpoints of adjacent sides.

The location in which the holes will appear is determined by the fold. If the paper folds vertically, then the holes will line up horizontally, and vice versa. After the first fold, the paper may fold one or two more times. The four types of folds are used in a wide variety of combinations, producing many different patterns of holes in the end product.

Paper folding questions can be quite difficult to follow, especially when there are multiple folds. However, there are some key details to watch out for that will help you eliminate answer choices.

1. **Keep track of the layers of paper that result from each fold**. Different parts of the folded paper following a fold can have a different number of layers—it depends on where the fold creates an overlap.

2. **Look at the symmetry of the first fold**. The final unfolding step is the opposite of that initial fold. So, any position with a hole on one side of the line of symmetry will result in a hole appearing in the corresponding position on the other side of the line of symmetry. You should immediately discard any answer choice that does not have that line of symmetry. You can see this in the following diagram:

3. **Remember that the number of holes in the result is directly related to the number of overlapping layers and the location of folds**. The number of layers of paper that overlap in the position where the hole was punched will affect the number of holes punched. A hole punched along a fold will result in two holes; if a hole is punched on an unfolded section, then it will result in one hole, not two.

17

Let's see these strategies in action by walking through two paper folding problems.

1. Determine the final hole pattern resulting from this sequence of folds and a hole punch.

The first fold divides the paper square in half from right to left, thereby producing two layers throughout the entire folded construct. Then, the paper folds in half from right to left, producing *four* layers throughout. Finally, the paper folds in half from top to bottom. All told, the entire folded construct is comprised of *eight* layers.

Now, the hole appears near the fold, going through all eight layers. Therefore, when you mentally unfold the paper you see eight holes. But where are they located?

If we mentally unfold the paper one step at a time, we first see that reversing the final fold reveals holes in these two positions:

Then, reversing the middle fold yields holes in four positions, as shown here:

Finally, reversing the very first fold shows holes in eight positions, as shown:

This last image is the final answer.

17

Let's try the next problem:

2. Determine the final hole pattern resulting from this sequence of folds and hole punches.

For the first step, the fold line is the diagonal line connecting the bottom-left and upper-right corners of the square piece of paper. The triangle formed below that line folds toward the bottom right corner. Visually, you can see that it divides the paper in two; however, you also know enough about geometry to realize that this is what happens when you fold a piece of paper in half—you get two equal halves.

In the second step (second square in the image) the triangle created in step one is folded in half again, this time moving the bottom-left corner to the upper-right corner. Keep track of how many layers are now present in the triangle (there are four).

In the third step we see that two holes have been punched through the folded paper—one through the center of the right edge, and another just below that. Now you need to mentally unfold the paper to see where the holes appear across the entire sheet of paper. You must unfold the paper in the reverse order of your initial folds. Undoing the second fold will cause the holes to reflect to the center and right of the bottom edge. Undoing the large diagonal fold will then reflect all four holes to the upper-left part of the page, as shown here.

Yes, paper folding questions require a lot of concentration and mental gymnastics. But with practice, you will learn to do the folds in your head just as easily as if you had the paper in your hands. So, grab a stack of construction paper and a hole punch and start practicing.

Figure Classification

In figure classification questions, three figures appear together that share some type of similarity. You must review the answer choices to find a figure that shares that similarity.

The following are some common ways in which the figures might be similar:

- The number of line segments or points that make up the figures may be similar. The figures could all have the same number, or have an even or an odd number of points or segments, etc. They may even increase or decrease in a pattern from one figure to the next.

- The alignment of the line segments that make up the figures may be the same. They may be parallel or perpendicular.

- The objects may be symmetrical, like a reflection across certain lines or rotations.

- The nature of the shapes must be considered, including dotted vs. solid borders or the type of shape (e.g., triangle, square, pentagon, and so on).

- The alignment and/or nature of shapes inside other shapes must be examined.

- The shaded portion of figures appearing across a row or down a column can be a factor, including the direction or slant of any shading lines.

If you have shapes within shapes, be sure to closely examine any relationships there. For example, let's look at the TACHS-style figure classification problem and walk through how to approach it.

1. Determine which answer exhibits the same characteristic as the three shapes shown here.

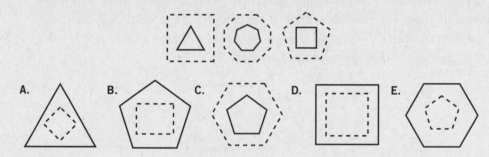

All three figures possess the following characteristics:

- The outer figure is comprised of dashed line segments;
- The inner figure is comprised of solid line segments; and
- The number of sides of the figure inside is *one less* than the number of segments of which the outer figure is comprised.

The correct answer is C. Choices A and D violate all three conditions, while choices B and E violate the first two conditions. Only choice C possesses all three characteristics exhibited in the original figures.

Let's look at another problem.

2. Determine which of the answer choices exhibits the same characteristic as the three shown:

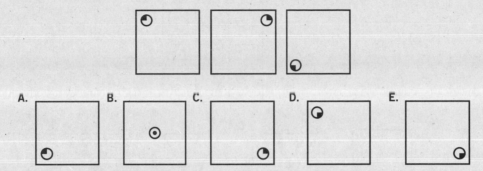

All three figures possess these characteristics:

- There is a circle in different corners of the square;
- Each circle has one quarter shaded; and
- The shaded portion corresponds to the location of that circle in the square—for example, the circle in the upper-right corner has the upper-right quarter shaded.

The correct answer is E. Choices A and D violate the first condition because those corners of the square already have a circle in them in one of the three given figures. In choice B, the circle is not in a corner. Choice C violates the third condition.

Figure Matrices

Figure matrices questions present you with a 3-by-3 matrix of figures. Most often, the figure in the bottom-right square will be missing. You need to determine which of the answer choices is the figure that completes the matrix. The figures are related by row or by column, or sometimes both.

The matrix uses the same pattern to produce the two complete rows or columns. The goal is to determine this pattern and apply it to identify the missing figure.

Just as with figure classification problems, the patterns can emerge in a variety of ways. For instance, there could be a change between adjacent entries in number, size, or position. Or, the pattern could add or remove a figure from another column to produce the third.

Once you work through several problems, you will get the feel for the types of patterns commonly assessed on the exam. Let's look at a few examples.

17

1. Determine which of the answer choices fits into the missing square so that either all three rows or all three columns exhibit the same pattern:

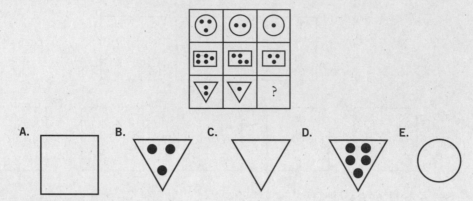

The correct answer is C. You can see the pattern repeating across the rows in this matrix. For both rows 1 and 2, the figure remains the same, but the number of dots contained within it decreases by one as you move from left to right in that row. As such, the answer choice that should fill in the missing cell is a triangle containing no dots. Choices A and E contain the correct number of points (none) but are not the same shape as the one used in the third row. Choices B and D contain the wrong number of points.

Let's look at another problem:

2. Determine which of the answer choices you should insert into the missing square so that either all three rows or all three columns exhibit the same pattern.

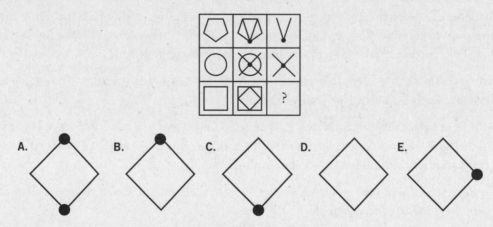

The correct answer is D. The pattern appears across rows in this matrix. In rows 1 and 2, you start with an empty figure and add something to it to get the second cell. To get the third cell, you mentally erase the original figure, leaving only the portion added in the second cell. As such, the answer choice that should fill in the missing cell is the diamond inserted inside the original square in the third row. And, there are no shaded vertices on this diamond. All the other answer choices have vertices darkened, but those are not part of the added element in the second cell of row 3.

You will have more opportunities to familiarize yourself with ability questions in the practice tests for the TACHS in Chapter 18. Be sure to read the explanations carefully—they can help you to understand the logic behind these question types and prepare you mentally for test day.

Summing It Up

- Comparison questions are in the Quantitative Skills section of the HSPT exam. You will get questions on geometric and nongeometric comparisons.

- Geometric comparisons require careful observation and counting to solve correctly.

- To solve nongeometric comparison questions, follow these three steps:

  1. Perform all the operations in the question.

  2. Work through all the answer choices one by one, and eliminate each statement that is false.

  3. When you think you have found the correct answer, continue until you have tried each answer choice.

- The TACHS Ability section includes three question types:

  1. **Paper folding**, which tests how well you can visualize what happens when you punch a hole in a folded piece of paper

  2. **Figure classification**, in which you must choose a figure that shares a similarity with three images presented in the question

  3. **Figure matrices**, which present a 3×3 matrix that you must complete by choosing the correct figure based on the pattern established in the matrix

Take a moment to ask yourself some simple questions about your understanding of the chapter:

Review: What did I learn?

Evaluate: What do I need to learn more about?

Plan: What can I do next to keep improving?

Based on your answers to those questions, adjust your study plan to dedicate additional time to the areas of weakness that you've identified.

17

EXERCISES: COMPARISONS

Directions: Examine A, B, and C and find the best answer. The answer key and explanations follow this exercise.

1.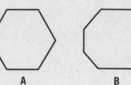

   A   B   C

   A. B and C have the same number of dots.

   B. A has fewer dots than B but more dots than C.

   C. C has more dots than A.

   D. B has more dots than A and C, which have the same number of dots.

2. The distance from X to Y is one inch.

   X ——————— Y X ～～～～ Y X ⌇⌇⌇⌇ Y
       A   B   C

   A. Lines A, B, and C are of equal length.

   B. Line A is longer than lines B and C, which are of equal length.

   C. Line B is shorter than line A but longer than line C.

   D. Line A is shorter than line C.

3.

   A   B   C

   A. C has more rings than A.

   B. A has the same number of rings as B.

   C. B and C have the same number of rings, which are more rings than A.

   D. B has fewer rings than either A or C.

4.

   A   B   C

   A. C has more corners than A.

   B. B has the same number of corners as C and more corners than A.

   C. A has fewer corners than B.

   D. A, B, and C all have the same number of corners.

5.

   A   B   C

   A. C is more shaded than B, which is more shaded than A.

   B. C is more shaded than A, which is not less shaded than B.

   C. B and C are equally shaded.

   D. A and B are equally shaded.

17

6. Examine the rectangle and find the best answer.

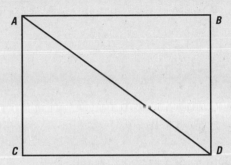

A. *AB* is equal to *CD*, which is longer than *AD*.

B. *BD* is shorter than *AC*.

C. *CD* is longer than *AD*.

D. *AC* is equal to *BD*.

7. Examine the graph and find the best answer.

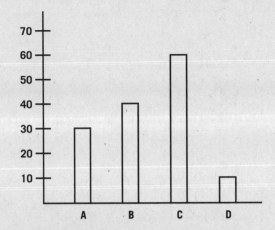

A. C plus D minus A equals B.

B. B plus D equals C.

C. A plus B equals C.

D. C minus D equals A plus B.

Directions: Examine A, B, and C and find the best answer.

---

8. **A.** 30% of 30

    B. 25% of 40

    C. 20% of 50

A. A = B = C

B. A = C > B

C. A = B < C

D. B = C > A

9. **A.** $(4 + 8) \times 10$

    B. $(8 + 10) \times 4$

    C. $(4 + 10) \times 8$

A. A > B < C

B. A = C > B

C. C > A, which is less than B

D. A = B = C

10. **A.** $(12 - 4) - 6$

    B. $(12 - 6) - 4$

    C. $12 - (6 - 4)$

A. C > A > B

B. C = A > B

C. A = B = C

D. A = B < C

11. **A.** $\frac{2}{3}$ of 27

    B. $\frac{2}{5}$ of 10

    C. $\frac{3}{7}$ of 28

A. B > A > X

B. B > C < A

C. B < C > A

D. A > C > B

17

12.　**A.** $\dfrac{2}{5}\%$

　　B. $\dfrac{2}{5}$

　　C. 0.04

A. $B > A > C$
B. $A < C < B$
C. $A = C < B$
D. $A = B = C$

13.　**A.** $(8 \div 2) \times 12$
　　B. $(15 \div 3) \times 10$
　　C. $(22 \div 1) \times 4$

A. $A > B < C$
B. $C > A > B$
C. $A = B < C$
D. $C > A < B$

14.　**A.** 160%
　　B. $\sqrt{256}$
　　C. 4^2

A. $A = B = C$
B. $B = C < A$
C. $C > B > A$
D. $A < C = B$

15. Both x and y are positive integers

　　A. $7(x + 2y)$
　　B. $7x + 2y$
　　C. $7(x + 2y) + 2x$

A. $C > B < A$
B. $B < C < A$
C. $A = B < C$
D. $C > A < B$

17

ANSWER KEY AND EXPLANATIONS

1. C	**4.** C	**7.** A	**10.** D	**13.** D
2. D	**5.** A	**8.** D	**11.** D	**14.** D
3. B	**6.** D	**9.** A	**12.** B	**15.** A

1. **The correct answer is C.** A has 10 dots, B has 12 dots, and C has 11 dots. 11 is greater than 10, so C has more dots than A. Test the other statements, and you will find them all false.

2. **The correct answer is D.** A straight line is the shortest distance between two points, so line A is the shortest line. Only choice D reflects this fact.

3. **The correct answer is B.** Each of the three figures has five rings, so any statement that speaks of more or fewer rings must be incorrect. Choice B does not mention figure C, but the statement regarding the other points is true, and therefore choice B is true.

4. **The correct answer is C.** Figures A and C are hexagons with 6 sides and 6 corners. Figure B is an octagon with 8 sides and 8 corners. The statement in choice C that figure A has fewer corners than figure B is correct.

5. **The correct answer is A.** C is exactly half shaded, B is somewhat less than half shaded, and A is very sparsely shaded. That is exactly the statement made in choice A.

6. **The correct answer is D.** In a rectangle, parallel sides are equal in length. Therefore, *AB* is equal to *CD*, and *AC* is equal to *BD*, so choice C is incorrect. *AD* is a hypotenuse. The hypotenuse is always the longest leg of a right triangle, which means *AD* cannot be shorter than any other line segment. This means choices A and C are incorrect.

7. **The correct answer is A.** Do the arithmetic to prove choice A; $60 + 10 - 30 = 40$. In other words, 40 equals 40, which is true. The other choices are all false.

8. **The correct answer is D.** Start by doing the arithmetic. For A, 30% of $30 = 9$; for B, 25% of $40 = 10$; and for C, 20% of $50 = 10$. Therefore, B and C are equal, and both are greater than A.

9. **The correct answer is A.** Do the arithmetic. For A, $12 \times 10 = 120$; for B, $18 \times 4 = 72$; and for C, $14 \times 8 = 112$. 120 is greater than 72, which is smaller than 112.

10. **The correct answer is D.** Do the arithmetic. For A, $8 - 6 = 2$; for B, $6 - 4 = 2$; and for C, $12 - 2 = 10$. A and B are equal but are far less than the 10 of C.

11. **The correct answer is D.** Do the math. For A, $\frac{2}{3}$ of $27 = 18$; for B, $\frac{2}{5}$ of $10 = 4$; and for C, $\frac{3}{7}$ of $28 = 12$. 18 is greater than 12, which is greater than 4. So, choice D is correct, as it states that A is greater than C, which is greater than B.

12. **The correct answer is B.** Convert all quantities to decimals. For A, $\frac{2}{5}\% = 0.4\% = 0.004$. For B, $\frac{2}{5} = 0.4$, and we are already given the decimal value of C. Checking against each of the answer options, choice B is correct in stating A < C < B.

13. **The correct answer is D.** Do the arithmetic. For A, $4 \times 12 = 48$; for B, $5 \times 10 = 50$; and for C, $22 \times 4 = 88$. Choice D correctly states that C > A < B, or 88 is greater than 48, which is less than 50.

14. **The correct answer is D.** Convert all quantities to decimals. For A, 160% = 1.6. Both B and C equal 16. Therefore, choice D is correct in stating A < C = B.

17

15. **The correct answer is A.** You could substitute numerical values for x and y and arrive at the correct answer, but it is unnecessary to work with numbers. Simply perform the algebraic multiplications to make your comparisons. For A, $7(x + 2y) = 7x + 14y$; for B, $7x + 2y = 7x + 2y$; and for C, $7(x + 2y) + 2x = 7x + 14y + 2x = 9x + 14y$. The resulting expressions make is easy to see that $9x + 14y$ is greater than $7x + 2y$, which is smaller than $7x + 14y$. That is what choice A states: C is greater than B, which is smaller than A.

17

PART V
SIX PRACTICE TESTS

ANSWER SHEET: TACHS PRACTICE TEST 1

Reading

1. Ⓐ Ⓑ Ⓒ Ⓓ   11. Ⓐ Ⓑ Ⓒ Ⓓ   21. Ⓐ Ⓑ Ⓒ Ⓓ   31. Ⓐ Ⓑ Ⓒ Ⓓ   41. Ⓐ Ⓑ Ⓒ Ⓓ
2. Ⓙ Ⓚ Ⓛ Ⓜ   12. Ⓙ Ⓚ Ⓛ Ⓜ   22. Ⓙ Ⓚ Ⓛ Ⓜ   32. Ⓙ Ⓚ Ⓛ Ⓜ   42. Ⓙ Ⓚ Ⓛ Ⓜ
3. Ⓐ Ⓑ Ⓒ Ⓓ   13. Ⓐ Ⓑ Ⓒ Ⓓ   23. Ⓐ Ⓑ Ⓒ Ⓓ   33. Ⓐ Ⓑ Ⓒ Ⓓ   43. Ⓐ Ⓑ Ⓒ Ⓓ
4. Ⓙ Ⓚ Ⓛ Ⓜ   14. Ⓙ Ⓚ Ⓛ Ⓜ   24. Ⓙ Ⓚ Ⓛ Ⓜ   34. Ⓙ Ⓚ Ⓛ Ⓜ   44. Ⓙ Ⓚ Ⓛ Ⓜ
5. Ⓐ Ⓑ Ⓒ Ⓓ   15. Ⓐ Ⓑ Ⓒ Ⓓ   25. Ⓐ Ⓑ Ⓒ Ⓓ   35. Ⓐ Ⓑ Ⓒ Ⓓ   45. Ⓐ Ⓑ Ⓒ Ⓓ
6. Ⓙ Ⓚ Ⓛ Ⓜ   16. Ⓙ Ⓚ Ⓛ Ⓜ   26. Ⓙ Ⓚ Ⓛ Ⓜ   36. Ⓙ Ⓚ Ⓛ Ⓜ   46. Ⓙ Ⓚ Ⓛ Ⓜ
7. Ⓐ Ⓑ Ⓒ Ⓓ   17. Ⓐ Ⓑ Ⓒ Ⓓ   27. Ⓐ Ⓑ Ⓒ Ⓓ   37. Ⓐ Ⓑ Ⓒ Ⓓ   47. Ⓐ Ⓑ Ⓒ Ⓓ
8. Ⓙ Ⓚ Ⓛ Ⓜ   18. Ⓙ Ⓚ Ⓛ Ⓜ   28. Ⓙ Ⓚ Ⓛ Ⓜ   38. Ⓙ Ⓚ Ⓛ Ⓜ   48. Ⓙ Ⓚ Ⓛ Ⓜ
9. Ⓐ Ⓑ Ⓒ Ⓓ   19. Ⓐ Ⓑ Ⓒ Ⓓ   29. Ⓐ Ⓑ Ⓒ Ⓓ   39. Ⓐ Ⓑ Ⓒ Ⓓ   49. Ⓐ Ⓑ Ⓒ Ⓓ
10. Ⓙ Ⓚ Ⓛ Ⓜ   20. Ⓙ Ⓚ Ⓛ Ⓜ   30. Ⓙ Ⓚ Ⓛ Ⓜ   40. Ⓙ Ⓚ Ⓛ Ⓜ   50. Ⓙ Ⓚ Ⓛ Ⓜ

Written Expression

1. Ⓐ Ⓑ Ⓒ Ⓓ Ⓔ   14. Ⓙ Ⓚ Ⓛ Ⓜ   27. Ⓐ Ⓑ Ⓒ Ⓓ   40. Ⓙ Ⓚ Ⓛ Ⓜ
2. Ⓙ Ⓚ Ⓛ Ⓜ Ⓝ   15. Ⓐ Ⓑ Ⓒ Ⓓ   28. Ⓙ Ⓚ Ⓛ Ⓜ   41. Ⓐ Ⓑ Ⓒ Ⓓ
3. Ⓐ Ⓑ Ⓒ Ⓓ Ⓔ   16. Ⓙ Ⓚ Ⓛ Ⓜ   29. Ⓐ Ⓑ Ⓒ Ⓓ   42. Ⓙ Ⓚ Ⓛ Ⓜ
4. Ⓙ Ⓚ Ⓛ Ⓜ Ⓝ   17. Ⓐ Ⓑ Ⓒ Ⓓ   30. Ⓙ Ⓚ Ⓛ Ⓜ   43. Ⓐ Ⓑ Ⓒ Ⓓ
5. Ⓐ Ⓑ Ⓒ Ⓓ Ⓔ   18. Ⓙ Ⓚ Ⓛ Ⓜ   31. Ⓐ Ⓑ Ⓒ Ⓓ   44. Ⓙ Ⓚ Ⓛ Ⓜ
6. Ⓙ Ⓚ Ⓛ Ⓜ Ⓝ   19. Ⓐ Ⓑ Ⓒ Ⓓ   32. Ⓙ Ⓚ Ⓛ Ⓜ   45. Ⓐ Ⓑ Ⓒ Ⓓ
7. Ⓐ Ⓑ Ⓒ Ⓓ Ⓔ   20. Ⓙ Ⓚ Ⓛ Ⓜ   33. Ⓐ Ⓑ Ⓒ Ⓓ   46. Ⓙ Ⓚ Ⓛ Ⓜ
8. Ⓙ Ⓚ Ⓛ Ⓜ Ⓝ   21. Ⓐ Ⓑ Ⓒ Ⓓ   34. Ⓙ Ⓚ Ⓛ Ⓜ   47. Ⓐ Ⓑ Ⓒ Ⓓ
9. Ⓐ Ⓑ Ⓒ Ⓓ Ⓔ   22. Ⓙ Ⓚ Ⓛ Ⓜ   35. Ⓐ Ⓑ Ⓒ Ⓓ   48. Ⓙ Ⓚ Ⓛ Ⓜ
10. Ⓙ Ⓚ Ⓛ Ⓜ Ⓝ   23. Ⓐ Ⓑ Ⓒ Ⓓ   36. Ⓙ Ⓚ Ⓛ Ⓜ   49. Ⓐ Ⓑ Ⓒ Ⓓ
11. Ⓐ Ⓑ Ⓒ Ⓓ   24. Ⓙ Ⓚ Ⓛ Ⓜ   37. Ⓐ Ⓑ Ⓒ Ⓓ   50. Ⓙ Ⓚ Ⓛ Ⓜ
12. Ⓙ Ⓚ Ⓛ Ⓜ   25. Ⓐ Ⓑ Ⓒ Ⓓ   38. Ⓙ Ⓚ Ⓛ Ⓜ
13. Ⓐ Ⓑ Ⓒ Ⓓ   26. Ⓙ Ⓚ Ⓛ Ⓜ   39. Ⓐ Ⓑ Ⓒ Ⓓ

Answer Sheet

Practice Test 1: TACHS

Math

1. Ⓐ Ⓑ Ⓒ Ⓓ   11. Ⓐ Ⓑ Ⓒ Ⓓ   21. Ⓐ Ⓑ Ⓒ Ⓓ   31. Ⓐ Ⓑ Ⓒ Ⓓ   41. Ⓐ Ⓑ Ⓒ Ⓓ
2. Ⓙ Ⓚ Ⓛ Ⓜ   12. Ⓙ Ⓚ Ⓛ Ⓜ   22. Ⓙ Ⓚ Ⓛ Ⓜ   32. Ⓙ Ⓚ Ⓛ Ⓜ   42. Ⓙ Ⓚ Ⓛ Ⓜ
3. Ⓐ Ⓑ Ⓒ Ⓓ   13. Ⓐ Ⓑ Ⓒ Ⓓ   23. Ⓐ Ⓑ Ⓒ Ⓓ   33. Ⓐ Ⓑ Ⓒ Ⓓ   43. Ⓐ Ⓑ Ⓒ Ⓓ
4. Ⓙ Ⓚ Ⓛ Ⓜ   14. Ⓙ Ⓚ Ⓛ Ⓜ   24. Ⓙ Ⓚ Ⓛ Ⓜ   34. Ⓙ Ⓚ Ⓛ Ⓜ   44. Ⓙ Ⓚ Ⓛ Ⓜ
5. Ⓐ Ⓑ Ⓒ Ⓓ   15. Ⓐ Ⓑ Ⓒ Ⓓ   25. Ⓐ Ⓑ Ⓒ Ⓓ   35. Ⓐ Ⓑ Ⓒ Ⓓ   45. Ⓐ Ⓑ Ⓒ Ⓓ
6. Ⓙ Ⓚ Ⓛ Ⓜ   16. Ⓙ Ⓚ Ⓛ Ⓜ   26. Ⓙ Ⓚ Ⓛ Ⓜ   36. Ⓙ Ⓚ Ⓛ Ⓜ   46. Ⓙ Ⓚ Ⓛ Ⓜ
7. Ⓐ Ⓑ Ⓒ Ⓓ   17. Ⓐ Ⓑ Ⓒ Ⓓ   27. Ⓐ Ⓑ Ⓒ Ⓓ   37. Ⓐ Ⓑ Ⓒ Ⓓ   47. Ⓐ Ⓑ Ⓒ Ⓓ
8. Ⓙ Ⓚ Ⓛ Ⓜ   18. Ⓙ Ⓚ Ⓛ Ⓜ   28. Ⓙ Ⓚ Ⓛ Ⓜ   38. Ⓙ Ⓚ Ⓛ Ⓜ   48. Ⓙ Ⓚ Ⓛ Ⓜ
9. Ⓐ Ⓑ Ⓒ Ⓓ   19. Ⓐ Ⓑ Ⓒ Ⓓ   29. Ⓐ Ⓑ Ⓒ Ⓓ   39. Ⓐ Ⓑ Ⓒ Ⓓ   49. Ⓐ Ⓑ Ⓒ Ⓓ
10. Ⓙ Ⓚ Ⓛ Ⓜ   20. Ⓙ Ⓚ Ⓛ Ⓜ   30. Ⓙ Ⓚ Ⓛ Ⓜ   40. Ⓙ Ⓚ Ⓛ Ⓜ   50. Ⓙ Ⓚ Ⓛ Ⓜ

Ability

Figure Classification

1. Ⓐ Ⓑ Ⓒ Ⓓ Ⓔ   6. Ⓙ Ⓚ Ⓛ Ⓜ Ⓝ   11. Ⓐ Ⓑ Ⓒ Ⓓ Ⓔ   16. Ⓙ Ⓚ Ⓛ Ⓜ Ⓝ
2. Ⓙ Ⓚ Ⓛ Ⓜ Ⓝ   7. Ⓐ Ⓑ Ⓒ Ⓓ Ⓔ   12. Ⓙ Ⓚ Ⓛ Ⓜ Ⓝ   17. Ⓐ Ⓑ Ⓒ Ⓓ Ⓔ
3. Ⓐ Ⓑ Ⓒ Ⓓ Ⓔ   8. Ⓙ Ⓚ Ⓛ Ⓜ Ⓝ   13. Ⓐ Ⓑ Ⓒ Ⓓ Ⓔ   18. Ⓙ Ⓚ Ⓛ Ⓜ Ⓝ
4. Ⓙ Ⓚ Ⓛ Ⓜ Ⓝ   9. Ⓐ Ⓑ Ⓒ Ⓓ Ⓔ   14. Ⓙ Ⓚ Ⓛ Ⓜ Ⓝ   19. Ⓐ Ⓑ Ⓒ Ⓓ Ⓔ
5. Ⓐ Ⓑ Ⓒ Ⓓ Ⓔ   10. Ⓙ Ⓚ Ⓛ Ⓜ Ⓝ   15. Ⓐ Ⓑ Ⓒ Ⓓ Ⓔ   20. Ⓙ Ⓚ Ⓛ Ⓜ Ⓝ

Figure Matrices

1. Ⓐ Ⓑ Ⓒ Ⓓ Ⓔ   6. Ⓙ Ⓚ Ⓛ Ⓜ Ⓝ   11. Ⓐ Ⓑ Ⓒ Ⓓ Ⓔ   16. Ⓙ Ⓚ Ⓛ Ⓜ Ⓝ
2. Ⓙ Ⓚ Ⓛ Ⓜ Ⓝ   7. Ⓐ Ⓑ Ⓒ Ⓓ Ⓔ   12. Ⓙ Ⓚ Ⓛ Ⓜ Ⓝ   17. Ⓐ Ⓑ Ⓒ Ⓓ Ⓔ
3. Ⓐ Ⓑ Ⓒ Ⓓ Ⓔ   8. Ⓙ Ⓚ Ⓛ Ⓜ Ⓝ   13. Ⓐ Ⓑ Ⓒ Ⓓ Ⓔ   18. Ⓙ Ⓚ Ⓛ Ⓜ Ⓝ
4. Ⓙ Ⓚ Ⓛ Ⓜ Ⓝ   9. Ⓐ Ⓑ Ⓒ Ⓓ Ⓔ   14. Ⓙ Ⓚ Ⓛ Ⓜ Ⓝ   19. Ⓐ Ⓑ Ⓒ Ⓓ Ⓔ
5. Ⓐ Ⓑ Ⓒ Ⓓ Ⓔ   10. Ⓙ Ⓚ Ⓛ Ⓜ Ⓝ   15. Ⓐ Ⓑ Ⓒ Ⓓ Ⓔ   20. Ⓙ Ⓚ Ⓛ Ⓜ Ⓝ

Paper Folding

1. Ⓐ Ⓑ Ⓒ Ⓓ Ⓔ   4. Ⓙ Ⓚ Ⓛ Ⓜ Ⓝ   7. Ⓐ Ⓑ Ⓒ Ⓓ Ⓔ   10. Ⓙ Ⓚ Ⓛ Ⓜ Ⓝ

2. Ⓙ Ⓚ Ⓛ Ⓜ Ⓝ   5. Ⓐ Ⓑ Ⓒ Ⓓ Ⓔ   8. Ⓙ Ⓚ Ⓛ Ⓜ Ⓝ

3. Ⓐ Ⓑ Ⓒ Ⓓ Ⓔ   6. Ⓙ Ⓚ Ⓛ Ⓜ Ⓝ   9. Ⓐ Ⓑ Ⓒ Ⓓ Ⓔ

Practice Test 1: TACHS

READING

50 Questions (35 minutes)

Turn to the Reading section of your answer sheet to answer the questions in this section.

Directions: This is a test of how well you understand what you read.

- Read the passages below and answer the questions.

- Four answers are given for each question. You must choose the answer that you think is better than the others.

Questions 1–4 are based on the following passage.

PASSAGE 1

Mrs. Rachel Lynde lived just where the Avonlea main road dipped down into a little hollow, fringed with alders and ladies' eardrops and traversed by a brook that had its source away back in the woods of the old Cuthbert place; it was reputed to be an intricate, headlong brook in its
Line earlier course through those woods, with dark secrets of pool and cascade; but by the time it
5 reached Lynde's Hollow it was a quiet, well-conducted little stream, for not even a brook could run past Mrs. Rachel Lynde's door without due regard for decency and decorum; it probably was conscious that Mrs. Rachel was sitting at her window, keeping a sharp eye on everything that passed, from brooks and children up, and that if she noticed anything odd or out of place she would never rest until she had ferreted out the whys and wherefores thereof.

10   There are plenty of people in Avonlea and out of it, who can attend closely to their neighbor's business by dint of neglecting their own; but Mrs. Rachel Lynde was one of those capable creatures who can manage their own concerns and those of other folks into the bargain.

—from *Anne of Green Gables* by Lucy Maud Montgomery

---

1. From the passage, the word *ferreted* most likely means

   A. avoided.

   B. stopped.

   C. completed.

   D. uncovered.

2. Where does the brook start?

   J. Avonlea

   K. The Cuthbert Place

   L. Lynde's Hollow

   M. The source is unknown

3. Which of these words best describes Mrs. Rachel Lynde?

   A. Mean

   B. Curious

   C. Sneaky

   D. Helpful

4. From the passage, you can infer that

   J. Avonlea is a large city.

   K. people in Avonlea live in fear of Mrs. Lynde.

   L. Avonlea is a place where people have many secrets.

   M. Avonlea is located near the woods.

Practice Test 1: TACHS

Questions 5–10 are based on the following passage.

PASSAGE 2

The Moon

The moon was but a chin of gold
A night or two ago,
And now she turns her perfect face
Upon the world below.

Line

5 Her forehead is of amplest blond;
Her cheek like beryl stone;
Her eye unto the summer dew
The likest I have known.

Her lips of amber never part;
10 But what must be the smile
Upon her friend she could bestow
Were such her silver will!

And what a privilege to be
But the remotest star!
15 For certainly her way might pass
Beside your twinkling door.

Her bonnet is the firmament,
The universe her shoe,
The stars the trinkets at her belt,
20 Her dimities of blue.

—Emily Dickinson

5. The poet believes that

  A. the moon is really a person.

  B. the moon is made of stone.

  C. the moon is beautiful.

  D. the moon only comes out in summer.

6. The first stanza describes

  J. how the moon changes.

  K. the change of the seasons.

  L. the location of the moon in the sky.

  M. the poet's own face.

7. The poet likely

  A. dislikes the outdoors.

  B. only goes out at night.

  C. studies astronomy.

  D. is interested in fashion.

8. In saying "The universe her shoe,/The stars the trinkets at her belt," the poet means that

J. the moon is old-fashioned.

K. the moon is cold and unfeeling.

L. the moon is the most important part of the sky.

M. the moon's beauty is fading.

9. Based on the passage, *firmament* most likely means

A. Earth.

B. top.

C. head.

D. sky.

10. The tone of this poem is

J. whimsical.

K. comic.

L. realistic.

M. sad.

Questions 11–16 are based on the following passage.

PASSAGE 3

Take a book, leave a book. That's the idea behind "little free libraries," which are small bird-house-like structures that contain bookshelves. These miniscule libraries are meant to be free community resources, letting neighbors share books they don't need anymore, or pick up a
Line new book to read.

5   These small libraries don't require a library card, or a special password for access. Usually, they are simple wooden cabinets (with a door to protect the books from the elements) that can be opened by anyone who comes along. Borrowing books is done on the honor system, in the hopes that the community will help maintain the library by adding to it and returning books when they're done. Many public areas like parks and beaches are starting to see these little
10 libraries pop up.

11. Which of these sayings is best illustrated by this passage?

A. Birds of a feather flock together.

B. You have to give a little to get a little.

C. Opportunity knocks.

D. Necessity is the mother of invention.

12. As used in sentence 3, *miniscule* most likely means

J. free.

K. underground.

L. tiny.

M. secret.

13. Based on the passage, who are likely to use the little free libraries?

A. People who read books online

B. People who want to read a variety of books

C. People who hate reading

D. People who already have library cards

14. What is the purpose of the door of the library?

J. To keep out rain

K. To keep out thieves

L. To keep out children

M. To keep books from falling

15. The passage is intended to be

A. humorous.

B. persuasive.

C. informative.

D. personal.

16. The phrase "honor system" is another way of saying which of the following?

J. All users are responsible for their own use of the library.

K. People who don't return books will be caught.

L. There is a security camera built into the library.

M. Only nice people can use the library.

Questions 17–22 are based on the following passage.

PASSAGE 4

The seasonal comings and goings of birds have excited the attention and wonder of all sorts of people in all ages and places. The oracles of Greece and the augurs of Rome wove them into ancient mythology. They are spoken of in the Books of Job and Jeremiah.

Line
5   Nevertheless, it has been difficult for many to believe that small birds, especially, are capable of migratory journeys. Aristotle was convinced that the birds that wintered in Greece were not new arrivals, but merely Greece's summer birds in winter dress. According to a belief persisting in some parts of the world to this day, swallows and swifts do not migrate, but spend the winter in hibernation. (Swifts and swallows do migrate, just as most other Northern Hemisphere birds do.) Another old and charming, but untrue, legend enlists the aid of the stork in getting small birds
10   to and from winter quarters: Small birds are said to hitch rides on the European stork's back.

It is clear why Northern Hemisphere birds fly south in the fall; they go to assure themselves of food and a more favorable climate for the winter months. It is also clear where most of the migrants come from and where they go. Years of bird-banding have disclosed the routes of the main migratory species.

15   But there are other aspects of migration that remain, for all our powers of scientific investigation, as puzzling and mysterious to modern man as to the ancients. Why do migrant birds come north each spring? Why don't they simply stay in the warm tropics the whole twelve months of the year? What determines the moment of departure for north or south? Above all, how do birds—especially species like the remarkable golden plover, which flies huge distances
20   directly across trackless ocean wastes—find their way?

17. Which of the following is the best title for this selection?

A. "The Solution of an Ancient Problem"

B. "Mysterious Migrations"

C. "The Secret of the Plover"

D. "Aristotle's Theory"

18. Bird-banding has revealed

J. the kinds of food birds eat.

K. why the birds prefer the tropics in the summer.

L. why birds leave at a certain time.

M. the routes taken by different types of birds.

19. Swallows and swifts

    A. remain in Greece all year.

    B. change their plumage in winter.

    C. hibernate during the winter.

    D. fly south for the winter.

20. The article proves that

    J. nature still has secrets that man has not discovered.

    K. the solutions of Aristotle are accepted by modern science.

    L. we live in an age that has lost all interest in bird lore.

    M. man has no means of solving the problems of bird migration.

21. How was it believed small birds were able to migrate long distances?

    A. African swallows bring hollow coconuts for small birds to ride in.

    B. Small birds rode in the mouths of European storks.

    C. Small birds were in a constant state of migration due to their short flight ranges.

    D. European storks allowed small birds to ride on their backs.

22. The main reason birds migrate is

    J. for vacation.

    K. to assure a good food supply and favorable climate.

    L. to satisfy their need to expand their habitat.

    M. so they can find potential mates.

Questions 23–28 are based on the following passage.

Passage 5

If you are asked the color of the sky on a fair day in summer, your answer will most probably be "blue." This answer is only partially correct. Blue sky near the horizon is not the same kind of blue as it is straight overhead. Look at the sky some fine day and you will find that the blue
Line sky near the horizon is slightly greenish. As your eye moves upward toward the zenith, you will
5 find that the blue changes into pure blue, and finally shades into a violet-blue overhead.

    Have you heard the story of a farmer who objected to the color of the distant hills in the artist's picture? He said to the artist, "Why do you make those hills blue? They are green, I've been over there and I know!" The artist asked him to do a little experiment. "Bend over and look at the hills between your legs." As the farmer did this, the artist asked, "Now what color are the
10 hills?" The farmer looked again, then he stood up and looked. "By gosh, they turned blue!" he said. It is quite possible that you have looked at many colors that you did not really recognize. Sky is not just blue; it is many kinds of blue. Grass is not plain green; it may be one of several varieties of green. A red-brick wall frequently is not pure red. It may vary from yellow-orange to violet-red in color, but to the unseeing eye it is just red brick.

23. Which title best expresses the ideas of this passage?

A. "The Summer Sky"

B. "Artists vs. Farmers"

C. "Recognizing Colors"

D. "Blue Hills"

24. At the zenith, the sky is usually

J. violet-blue.

K. violet-red.

L. greenish-blue.

M. yellow-orange.

25. The author suggests that

A. farmers are color-blind.

B. perceived color varies.

C. brick walls should be painted pure red.

D. some artists use poor color combinations.

26. The word *zenith* in paragraph 1 probably refers to

J. a color.

K. a point directly overhead.

L. a point on the horizon.

M. the hills.

27. The artist's experiment with the farmer shows that

A. farmers cannot tell the difference between colors.

B. artists use hypnosis to change other people's perception.

C. glancing at something and really seeing it can change how we perceive our environment.

D. artists like to make fun of people.

28. What should people do to understand the different shades of color?

J. Become artists

K. Look at more works of art

L. Stop trusting their own eyes

M. Open themselves to new perspectives

Questions 29–34 are based on the following passage.

PASSAGE 6

In a stressed-out world, yoga has become one of the most popular wellness practices around. It involves using a combination of body stretches, deep breathing techniques, and meditation to help practitioners achieve a state of inner well-being. People who practice yoga often report
Line feeling less stressed, having lower blood pressure, and feeling more in tune with their bodies.
5   Yoga has its roots in ancient India, where it originated around the 5th century BCE as a type of philosophical meditation practice. The name comes from the Sanskrit word *yuj*, which means "to join" or "to unite." Historically, yoga has been used as a way to achieve an equilibrium between body and mind.

It wasn't until the late 1900s that yoga began to take hold in the West, when Indian *gurus*,
10   or *yogis*, began to introduce the practice as a form of meditation. One of the most notable figures in this introduction was Swami Vivekananda, who brought Hindu culture to Chicago in 1893. In the 1980s, the practice of yoga truly caught on as a form of physical exercise, instead of philosophical meditation, and became popular as a type of body-mind workout.

29. Based on the passage, a yogi is likely which of the following?

   A. A novice yoga practitioner

   B. A yoga expert

   C. An Indian ruler

   D. A Sanskrit speaker

30. How did yoga become popular in the modern era?

   J. It was framed as exercise.

   K. It was a major philosophical trend in the West.

   L. Gurus were considered celebrities in the West.

   M. People became more interested in ancient Indian philosophy.

31. In paragraph 2, *equilibrium* most likely means

   A. yoga.

   B. breathing.

   C. balance.

   D. history.

32. All the following benefits of yoga are mentioned in the passage *except*

   J. stress relief.

   K. physical fitness.

   L. low blood pressure.

   M. increased intelligence.

33. As a practice, yoga originated in

   A. the United States.

   B. India.

   C. Europe.

   D. China.

34. Around when did yoga likely originate?

   J. 500 BCE

   K. 1893 CE

   L. 1900 CE

   M. 1980 CE

Questions 35–40 are based on the following passage.

Passage 7

Benjamin Franklin, one of the most prominent "founding fathers" in American history, is often credited with proposing that the new United States adopt the turkey as its national symbol. Instead of the turkey, the founders selected the majestic bald eagle, and Ben Franklin's sponsorship
Line of the humble turkey has become a bit of humorous lore over the centuries.

5   The only problem with this story? It's not actually true. Although he is credited with championing the turkey while the national symbol was being selected, Franklin did not suggest at the time that it should take its place on the new country's national seal. Rather, he thought that the eagle design on the national seal *looked* like a turkey, and he discussed this and wrote a more mild endorsement of the turkey in a later letter to his daughter:

10   "For the Truth the Turkey is in Comparison a much more respectable Bird, and withal a true original Native of America."

Yet over the years, the myth has persisted, and the image of Ben Franklin standing among the signers of the Constitution, passionately debating the nobility of the Great American turkey, has captured the American imagination in a way that few stories do.

35. Based on the information in the passage, the author refers to the turkey as "humble" because

    A. there are fewer turkeys than bald eagles in the United States.

    B. turkeys' personalities are different from bald eagles.

    C. turkeys are seen as less noble than bald eagles.

    D. turkeys were less expensive than bald eagles.

36. As used in the first sentence of paragraph 1, what does the word *prominent* most likely mean?

    J. Foolish

    K. Oldest

    L. Underrated

    M. Famous

37. The story about Ben Franklin and the turkey has likely survived because

    A. people find it humorous.

    B. the United States later voted to adopt the turkey as its symbol.

    C. the bald eagle turned out to be an unpopular choice.

    D. people agree with Ben Franklin.

38. In the third sentence of paragraph 2, *championing* most likely means

    J. winning.

    K. representing.

    L. racing.

    M. bringing.

39. Why did people think Ben Franklin supported the turkey as the national symbol?

    A. He gave a passionate speech about it in Congress.

    B. His letter about turkeys was taken out of context.

    C. His daughter told everyone he supported the turkey over the eagle.

    D. His fellow founding fathers spread it as a rumor.

40. An appropriate title for this passage would be

    J. "How the Bald Eagle Became the National Bird."

    K. "Ben Franklin: A Biography."

    L. "Letters from Ben Franklin."

    M. "The Myth of the Great American Turkey."

Practice Test 1: TACHS

Questions 41–46 are based on the following passage.

PASSAGE 8

You might not think of Hollywood stars as having much in common with inventors, but one American celebrity was both. Actress Hedy Lamarr, who appeared in more than 30 films between 1930 and 1950, was also a well-known "tinkerer" whose inventions have helped make
Line modern innovations possible.

5 Lamarr was born in Austria, but moved to the United States in the late 1930s to pursue a movie career. She appeared in famous films like *Samson and Delilah*, and went on to star in films alongside some of the biggest movie actors of the time, like Clark Gable and Bob Hope. Throughout her burgeoning Hollywood career, she kept up her lifelong hobby of taking things apart and tinkering with them, and devising new ways to approach engineering. The million-
10 aire Howard Hughes became one of the earliest supporters of her inventing career, when she developed ways to streamline his fleet of airplanes.

Her biggest invention came during World War II, when Lamarr worked on a coded form of radio communication which was used to guide Allied torpedoes to their targets. After the war, her contribution was largely forgotten—until her patented work ended up forming the
15 basis for Bluetooth®, GPS, Wi-Fi®, and other wireless forms of communication in the late 20th century and early 21st century. Although Lamarr, who passed away in 2000, is still best known for her glamorous on-screen career, she was truly a mother of modern technology. Lamarr was posthumously elected into the National Inventors Hall of Fame in 2014.

41. Who helped Hedy Lamarr's inventing career?

A. Clark Gable

B. Bob Hope

C. No one

D. Howard Hughes

42. In the third sentence of paragraph 2, the word *burgeoning* most likely means

J. growing.

K. stalled.

L. unsatisfying.

M. miraculous.

43. How did Lamarr's World War II-era technology lead to modern inventions?

A. She worked with engineers to develop new communication technology.

B. Her airplane designs are used now by the airline industry.

C. Her patents were used by modern inventors to develop communication technology.

D. She quit Hollywood and devoted the rest of her life to being an inventor.

44. What was the original purpose of the coding that eventually helped create Bluetooth® and Wi-Fi®?

J. Building a better airplane

K. Guiding military torpedoes

L. Improving film equipment

M. Developing GPS

45. In the last sentence of the passage, the word *posthumously* most likely means

A. collectively.

B. before long.

C. gratefully.

D. after death.

46. Based on the passage, which of the following was true?

J. All Hollywood celebrities have secret other careers.

K. Hedy Lamarr had a more complex career than most people realize.

L. Hedy Lamarr was a much better actress than inventor.

M. Most modern inventions were first developed during World War II.

Questions 47–50 are based on the following passage.

PASSAGE 9

The most famous baseball card doesn't have Babe Ruth on it, or Jackie Robinson, or any of the other players you might think of when you think about baseball greats. Instead, the most valuable baseball card in the world has the picture and name of someone you may never have
Line heard of: Honus Wagner.
5   Honus Wagner was a shortstop who played for the Pittsburgh Pirates for twenty-one seasons, from 1897 to 1917. But although his career was long, that's not why his baseball card has become so notorious. At the turn of the century, most baseball cards were produced by tobacco companies as promotions for cigarettes, featuring Major League Baseball players. Honus Wagner objected to having his picture used to sell tobacco, and he refused to allow the American
10   Tobacco Company to continue producing his card (known as the "T206 Honus Wagner"). By then, experts estimate, no more than 200 Honus Wagner cards had been distributed.

Since then, the price tag for this for this rare card has grown exponentially: in 2016, one of the few remaining Wagner cards sold at auction for $3.12 million—making it the most expensive baseball card in the world.

47. Why are Honus Wagner cards so valuable?

A. Wagner became the baseball player with the longest career.

B. They are the most common baseball card.

C. Wagner went on to become the greatest baseball player in history.

D. Only a very small number were ever produced.

48. What was the original purpose of baseball cards?

J. To promote baseball players

K. To promote a holiday

L. To promote Major League Baseball

M. To promote tobacco products

49. Today, there are how many T206 Honus Wagner cards in existence?

   A. More than 200

   B. None

   C. Fewer than 200

   D. Exactly 200

50. In the first sentence of paragraph 3, the word *exponentially* most likely means that the card's value increased

   J. quickly.

   K. slowly.

   L. not at all.

   M. more than anyone had expected.

STOP.

If you finish before time is up, you may check your work on this section only.
Do not turn to any other section in the test.

WRITTEN EXPRESSION

50 Questions (30 minutes)

Turn to the Written Expression section of your answer sheet to answer the questions in this section.

Directions: This is a test of how well you can find mistakes in writing.

- For the questions with mistakes in spelling, capitalization, and punctuation, choose the answer with the same letter as the **line** containing the mistake.

- For the questions with mistakes in usage and expression, choose the answer with the same letter as the **line** containing the mistake, or choose the word, phrase, or sentence that is better than the others.

- When there is no mistake or no change needed, choose the last answer choice.

---

1. **A.** involvment
   B. bologna
   C. organic
   D. matador
   E. (*No mistakes*)

2. **J.** redemption
   K. commitee
   L. claustrophobic
   M. malleable
   N. (*No mistakes*)

3. **A.** pseudonym
   B. placate
   C. anonymous
   D. suspishus
   E. (*No mistakes*)

4. **J.** retreave
   K. famished
   L. belligerent
   M. mnemonic
   N. (*No mistakes*)

5. **A.** compensate
   B. expression
   C. judgment
   D. fragile
   E. (*No mistakes*)

6. **J.** precious
   K. leverage
   L. credence
   M. beleivable
   N. (*No mistakes*)

7. **A.** flail
   B. appreshiate
   C. cognition
   D. statistics
   E. (*No mistakes*)

8. **J.** reccomendation
   K. cemetery
   L. finesse
   M. repetition
   N. (*No mistakes*)

9. **A.** ailment
B. onerous
C. pretense
D. manadgement
E. (*No mistakes*)

10. **J.** competetive
K. symbol
L. cringe
M. careening
N. (*No mistakes*)

11. **A.** Lake Huron,
B. one the of the great lakes of north America,
C. runs from Michigan in the United States to Ontario, a province in Canada.
D. (*No mistakes*)

12. **J.** Every morning without fail, Jackie purchases a copy of her favorite newspaper,
K. *The Beaverton Telegraph*, from Henri,
L. the local Merchant at the corner drugstore by the train station.
M. (*No mistakes*)

13. **A.** Isabelle watched her Dad's favorite movie,
B. *The Last City in the World*,
C. on her laptop as she lay on her living room couch.
D. (*No mistakes*)

14. **J.** Duncan and his friend Owen went to the local pet store,
K. Oakville Furry Friends,
L. and purchased a Rare spotted rabbit with the money he saved from his after-school job.
M. (*No mistakes*)

15. **A.** Reina's Dentist, Dr. Larissa Guerrero,
B. told Reina that she is going to need to have
C. her wisdom teeth removed next week.
D. (*No mistakes*)

16. **J.** Lara has not yet received her ticket for the concert
K. at the convention center next weekend,
L. but she is really looked forward to going next Tuesday.
M. (*No mistakes*)

17. **A.** Edsen hid his new headphones,
B. which he will buy from the music store at the mall,
C. from his younger sister Stephanie.
D. (*No mistakes*)

18. **J.** After he watching the new episode
K. of *Creature Hunters* on television,
L. Jacob felt that the ending was too predictable.
M. (*No mistakes*)

19. **A.** What are the most valuable life lessons
B. that you have learned during
C. your years in junior high school!
D. (*No mistakes*)

20. **J.** Boris asked his best friend Cynthia,
K. (Can I borrow four quarters?),
L. while they waited at the laundromat on Clarke Avenue.
M. (*No mistakes*)

21. **A.** The Empire State Building,
B. located in the heart of New York City,
C. is one of the most famous skyscrapers in the world?
D. (*No mistakes*)

Practice Test 1: TACHS

22.
J. After Jarrett's senior year of high school,

K. he plans to attend Georgetown university,

L. and major in computer science.

M. (*No mistakes*)

23.
A. Fiona's European vacation last summer

B. included stops at the canals of Venice, the Eiffel Tower in Paris,

C. and Buckingham Palace in London.

D. (*No mistakes*)

24.
J. Sabrina was terrified, of roller, coasters

K. and refused to even walk by one or look up

L. whenever she was at a carnival or amusement park.

M. (*No mistakes*)

25.
A. Louis memorized the quickest way

B. to get to their piano teacher's house:

C. take a right on Meadow Road and a left on Crasset Avenue.

D. (*No mistakes*)

Directions: For questions 26–30, choose the best way of expressing the idea.

26.
J. Drowned out by the fire trucks and their noise outside, no one can hear the value of hard work, dedication, and passion, the parts that discussed pursuing a goal, when Sheila's award acceptance speech reached the most important parts.

K. The most important parts of Sheila's award acceptance speech, the parts that discussed the value of hard work, dedication, and passion when pursuing a goal, were drowned out by the noise from the fire trucks outside.

L. The most important parts of the fire trucks outside was the noise delivered from the trucks that discussed Sheila's award acceptance speech, which contained parts about the value of pursuing a goal—including hard work, dedication, and passion.

M. When pursuing a goal, like Sheila did during the noise from the fire trucks outside, she showed hard work, dedication, and passion, which drowned out her important parts for the award acceptance speech and her values discussed.

27.
A. Party punch was Finn's nice enough bringing to the graduation celebration, and everyone loved his secret ingredient—pineapple juice, crowd-favorite limes, fruit punch, cherries.

B. Everybody loves graduation party secret ingredients, and Finn was nice enough to bring some of his to the party punch that was a crowd favorite, which contained limes, fruit punch, and pineapple juice.

C. Finn was nice enough to bring some of his crowd-favorite party punch, which was loved by everyone at the graduation celebration; it contained limes, fruit punch, cherries, and his secret ingredient—pineapple juice.

D. Was Finn, a crowd favorite at graduation celebrations, nice enough to bring his limes, fruit punch, cherries, and his secret ingredient—pineapple juice—to the contained party punch?

28. **J.** Completing the required certification exams will help you earn a degree in teaching and finish college, so you can plan after high school to get interested in pursuing a career as a teacher.

K. Teachers are interested in pursuing a career, so plan finishing required certification exams and earn a degree after high school in college teaching, if you are as well.

L. College teachers who finished high school complete the required certification exams, earn a pursuit in teaching careers, and finish college degrees in teaching.

M. If you're interested in pursuing a career as a teacher, your plan after high school should be to finish college, earn a degree in teaching, and complete the required certification exams.

29. **A.** Karina, who was running for student body president of Lakeville High School, promised her fellow students that if she were elected, there would be free snacks available every day in the cafeteria.

B. Who was Karina running for? Student body president, where free snacks would be available every day at Lakeville high school if elected, which she promised her fellow students every day in the cafeteria.

C. Every student body president in the cafeteria offered free available snacks every day, and Karina promised to run for her fellow students and for Lakeville High School.

D. The president of the cafeteria promised that free Lakeville High School snacks would be available every day for student body presidents and their fellow students, if Karina ran.

30. **J.** The winning gasoline-powered engine used old cooking oil and an ingenious new method for usable and environmentally friendly fuel, to win and develop the science competition.

K. The engine of the gasoline-powered science competition was the winner who developed and ingenious and environmentally friendly new method for converting usable old cooking oil.

L. The winner of the science competition developed an ingenious new method for converting old cooking oil into usable and environmentally friendly fuel for gasoline-powered engines.

M. The science competition winner was an ingenious new method for converting gasoline-powered engines into old and usable cooking oil that is environmentally friendly.

Directions: For questions 31–50, choose the best answer based on the following paragraphs.

(1) Do you know what's commonly accepted as the very first printed book? (2) The Gutenberg Bible <u>will be considered</u> to be the first major printed book in the world. (3) It was created in Europe in the mid-15th century using movable metal type. (4) Today, it is among the most valuable books in existence. (5) Fewer than 50 copies of the Gutenberg Bible are known to exist in the entire world.

31. What is the best way to write the underlined portion of sentence 2?

A. were considered

B. is considered

C. it's considered

D. (*No change*)

32. Choose the best last sentence to add to this paragraph.

J. The Gutenberg Bible sure is one rare book!

K. What other books are as old as the Gutenberg Bible?

L. Do you have books that are important to you?

M. The Gutenberg Bible sure is a large book!

(1) Spelunking, also known as "caving," is an intense and exciting physical activity that's popular around the world. (2) Spelunking involves the exploration of caves and cave systems, which presents a variety of challenges, not the least of which is the absence of natural light and the risk of unknown conditions. (3) Safety is an obvious issue for spelunkers, as <u>falling rock's</u>, extreme temperature shifts, unexpected falls, and even extreme exhaustion are concerns, not to mention getting lost. (4) Typical gear used during spelunking includes a headlamp, hardhat, water bottle, boots, and rock climbing equipment. (5) However, if you're experienced and follow safety protocols, cave exploration can be a wonderful pastime that tests your mental and physical abilities.

33. Choose the best first sentence to add to this paragraph.

A. Diamonds are often found in caves throughout the world.

B. Is there any place darker than inside a cave at night?

C. There was a large volcano eruption in 2015.

D. Have you ever heard of spelunking?

34. What is the best way to write the underlined portion of sentence 3?

J. falling rocks

K. falling's rock's

L. falling rocks'

M. (*No change*)

Practice Test 1: TACHS

(1) What do you know about the humble <u>ladybug</u>! (2) Well, you may be unaware of the wide variety of colors and patterns that ladybugs, or lady beetles, can be found sporting. (3) There are actually over 6,000 species of ladybug that have been found in nature, with the most common being either red, orange, or yellow in color. (4) The number and color of spots found on the wing covers of ladybugs can also vary wildly. (5) Ladybugs are widely considered to be useful creatures, as they typically eat a variety of crop-ravaging insects, such as <u>Aphids</u>.

35. What is the best way to write the underlined portion of sentence 1?

  A. ladybug.
  B. ladybug?
  C. ladybug;
  D. (*No change*)

36. What is the best way to write the underlined portion of sentence 5?

  J. aphid
  K. Aphid's
  L. aphids
  M. (*No change*)

(1) Is there an author <u>whose very Name</u> stirs up eerie chills and dark, moody Victorian settings like Edgar Allan Poe does? (2) Poe was a 19th century American author whose work is often categorized in the Gothic artistic genre. (3) Many of <u>their works</u> focus on death and the afterlife, and the sad darkness that often dwells deep in the human heart. (4) Among his most famous works is "The Raven," a poem in which a raven pays a nighttime visit to a lovelorn man who is slowly spiraling into madness as he laments the loss of his great love. (5) Did you know that Poe is widely considered to be the "father" of detective fiction, which would later give rise to such literary luminaries as Sir Arthur Conan Doyle and his most famous character, Sherlock Holmes?

37. What is the best way to write the underlined portion of sentence 1?

  A. whose very name
  B. who's very Name
  C. who is very name
  D. (*No change*)

38. What is the best way to write the underlined portion of sentence 3?

  J. their work
  K. his works
  L. its works
  M. (*No change*)

(1) Have you ever flown high in the sky without being on an airplane? (2) It may sound scary, but many hot air balloon <u>detractors</u> do just that whenever they feel an urge to soar high above the ground. (3) Hot air balloons are relatively simple in construction, and include a fabric "balloon," full of heated air, an onboard heat source (typically an open flame), and a basket. (4) Heating the volume of <u>air inside; the balloon</u> reduces the density of the air, as compared with the colder ambient air, thus making it more buoyant. (5) The record for the highest hot air balloon flight is currently a staggering 68,986 feet, and took place in India.

39. What is the best way to write the underlined portion of sentence 2?

   A. inventors

   B. collaborators

   C. enthusiasts

   D. (*No change*)

40. What is the best way to write the underlined portion of sentence 4?

   J. air inside the balloon

   K. air inside, the balloon

   L. air inside. The balloon

   M. (*No change*)

(1) Few man-made structures are as iconic and instantly recognizable as the Golden Gate Bridge, in San Francisco. (2) The colossal structure, which officially opened in 1937, connects Marin County to Northern San Francisco. (3) The Golden Gate Bridge is a <u>suspension bridge</u>, which means that the load-bearing portion of its construction is hung below vertically suspended suspension cables. (4) The Golden Gate Bridge is approximately 4,200 feet in length, and had been the longest suspension bridge span in the world until 1964. (5) Currently, the longest suspension bridge in the world is the Akashi Kaikyo Bridge in Japan.

41. Choose the best final sentence to add to this paragraph.

   A. San Francisco also has some of the most scenic parks in the country.

   B. The Akashi Kaikyo Bridge is 6,532 feet long.

   C. San Francisco is one of the most expensive cities to live in America.

   D. New York City is also home to several famous bridges.

42. What is the best way to write the underlined portion of sentence 3?

   J. Suspension Bridge

   K. Suspension bridge

   L. suspension Bridge

   M. (*No change*)

(1) It's hard to argue with the notion that giant sequoias are among the most ancient and majestic living organisms on Earth. (2) These gigantic trees have been known to live for thousands of years; the oldest known example of a giant sequoia is over 3,500 years old. (3) They are also widely considered to be not only the largest trees but also the largest living organisms (by volume) in the <u>entire World</u>. (4) Giant sequoias have been known to reach heights of over 300 feet in height and over 25 feet in diameter. (5) Although <u>it is only</u> found in small patches in California, because of its unmatched proportions the giant sequoia has made a lasting impression on the entire world.

43. What is the best way to write the underlined portion of sentence 3?

   A. Entire World

   B. Entire world

   C. entire world

   D. (*No change*)

44. What is the best way to write the underlined portion of sentence 5?

   J. he was

   K. they are

   L. we were

   M. (*No change*)

(1) Did you know that the first state in America to ratify the Constitution of the <u>United-States</u> is also one of the smallest? (2) Delaware, which has earned the nickname "The First State," is ranked 49th out of 50 states in terms of overall land area. (3) Only Rhode Island, also among the first Thirteen Colonies that would eventually form the United States of America, is smaller. (4) Interestingly, while a colony Rhode Island was the first to officially renounce <u>it's</u> allegiance to the British Crown. (5) This goes to show that you don't have to be a particularly large state to be an influential one!

45. What is the best way to write the underlined portion of sentence 1?

A. United States

B. united-states

C. United, States

D. (*No change*)

46. What is the best way to write the underlined portion of sentence 4?

J. It's

K. it is

L. its

M. (*No change*)

(1) The United States is chock full of <u>unique roadside attractions curious tourist sites and curious exhibits</u>. (2) The state of North Carolina is no exception, and if you find yourself travelling through the western part of the state with some time to spare, you may want to check out the American Museum of the House Cat. (3) This quirky little museum is entirely dedicated to the furry feline pet, and <u>youll find</u> over 10,000 cat-related objects to discover and enjoy during your visit here. (4) There is a wide array of objects on display, from statues and figurines to paintings, dolls, glassware, toys, and much more. (5) The objects range in age and obscurity—some are modern and easy-to-find objects, and some are quite rare and old, dating back to 600 BC!

47. What is the best way to write the underlined portion of sentence 1?

A. unique roadside attractions—curious tourist sites—and curious exhibits

B. unique roadside attractions, curious tourist sites, and curious exhibits

C. unique roadside attractions. Curious tourist sites. And curious exhibits

D. (*No change*)

48. What is the best way to write the underlined portion of sentence 3?

J. you'll find

K. you well find

L. youll' find

M. (*No change*)

(1) Few events in American history have so radically altered the concept and scope of the United States as the Louisiana Purchase did. (2) This agreement with France in 1803 <u>allow</u> the United States to officially acquire land that spans fifteen current states, including parts of Oklahoma, Iowa, Kansas, Arkansas, and Missouri, to name but a few. (3) In return for the land acquired under the Louisiana Purchase, France received fifty million francs and had a sizable portion of its debt to the United States cancelled. (4) Negotiation of the Louisiana Purchase Treaty between France and the United States was difficult at <u>times. With criticism</u> arising on both sides during the process. (5) However, it's hard to imagine what life in present-day United States would be like without the land that was acquired during this seminal negotiation.

49. What is the best way to write the underlined portion of sentence 2?

   A. allowing
   B. allowance
   C. allowed
   D. (*No change*)

50. What is the best way to write the underlined portion of sentence 4?

   J. times; with criticism
   K. times with; criticism
   L. times, with criticism
   M. (*No change*)

STOP.

If you finish before time is up, you may check your work on this section only.
Do not turn to any other section in the test.

Practice Test 1: TACHS

MATHEMATICS

50 Questions (40 minutes)

Turn to the Mathematics section of your answer sheet to answer the questions in this section.

Directions: Four answers are given for each problem. Choose the best answer.

---

1. Which of the following is *not* a factor of 20?

   A. 3

   B. 4

   C. 5

   D. 10

2. The fraction $\frac{2}{3}$ is approximately which of the following?

   J. 0.23

   K. 0.67

   L. $\frac{3}{2}$

   M. 23.67

3. Which of the following is *not* a prime number?

   A. 3

   B. 9

   C. 13

   D. 19

4. Which of the following is a multiple of 3?

   J. 29

   K. 39

   L. 49

   M. 89

5. What is the product of 43 and 100?

   A. 0.43

   B. 57

   C. 143

   D. 4,300

6. What is the difference between $\frac{7}{8}$ and $\frac{1}{2}$?

   J. $\frac{3}{8}$

   K. $\frac{6}{8}$

   L. $\frac{3}{4}$

   M. $\frac{6}{2}$

7. What is the sum of $(6 - 1) + (1 \times 5) + (10 \div 2) + (2.5 + 2.5)$?

   A. 15

   B. 20

   C. 25

   D. 125

8. Which of the following is *not* a multiple of 6?

   J. 72

   K. 112

   L. 182

   M. 246

9. Which of the following is the equivalent of $3 - (-6)$?

   A. −9

   B. −3

   C. 3

   D. 9

10. What is the least common multiple of 6, 12, and 72?

    J. 6

    K. 12

    L. 36

    M. 72

11. Jeff has 6 notebooks in his locker. Maggie has in her locker twice as many notebooks as Jeff. Darnell has in his locker twice as many notebooks as Maggie and Jeff combined. How many notebooks does Darnell have stuffed into his locker?

    A. 12

    B. 18

    C. 24

    D. 36

12. Baxter needed to replenish his supply of bottled water. The water dispenser in his kitchen holds 14 gallons of water. Baxter buys his water one half-gallon at a time at his local grocery store. How many half-gallon water purchases will Baxter need to make to fill his water dispenser?

    J. 7

    K. 14

    L. 21

    M. 28

13. McKenzie currently has $50 set aside to purchase a TV that costs $300. She earns $25 per week babysitting. How many weeks will it take her to earn enough money to buy the TV?

    A. 7

    B. 8

    C. 10

    D. 12

14. Sam's scooter gets 50 miles per gallon, and the scooter's gas tank holds 3 gallons of gasoline. If the gas tank in Sam's scooter is $\frac{2}{3}$ full, how many miles can Sam expect to travel before the tank is empty?

    J. 75

    K. 100

    L. 150

    M. 175

15. The rim on a basketball goal is 10 feet from the floor. If a player made 6 baskets, what is the sum of the distances that the ball would travel between the rim and the floor below?

    A. 60 feet

    B. 70 feet

    C. 160 feet

    D. Not given

16. Two hundred million, one hundred seventy-three thousand, sixty-three =

    J. 2,173,063

    K. 20,173,063

    L. 200,173,063

    M. 200,173,630

17. Seventeen million, sixty thousand, thirty-four =

    A. 17,634

    B. 1,760,034

    C. 17,060,034

    D. 17,600,034

18. 0.5% is equal to

    J. 0.005

    K. 0.05

    L. 0.5

    M. $\frac{1}{2}$

19. A group of 6 people raised $690 for charity. One person raised 35% of the total. What was the amount raised by the other 5 people?

A. $241.50

B. $445.50

C. $448.50

D. $449.50

20. If a pie is divided into 20 parts, what percent is one part of the whole pie?

J. 0.5%

K. 2.0%

L. 5%

M. 20%

21. Two angles of a triangle are 45° and 75°. What is the measure of the third angle?

A. 35°

B. 45°

C. 60°

D. 180°

22.

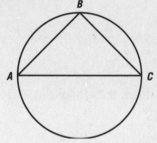

Isosceles $\triangle ABC$ is inscribed in a circle that has a diameter of 10 centimeters. The area of the triangle is

J. 12.5 sq. cm.

K. 25 sq. cm.

L. 50 sq. cm.

M. 78.5 sq. cm.

23. The volume of a small warehouse measuring 75 feet long, 50 feet wide, and 30 feet high is

A. 112,500 feet.

B. 112,500 square feet.

C. 112,500 cubic feet.

D. 1,112,500 cubic feet.

24. A department store marks up its clothing 80% over cost. If it sells blue jeans for $14, how much did the store pay for them?

J. $1.12

K. $7.78

L. $11.20

M. $17.50

25. The monthly finance charge on a charge account is $1\frac{1}{2}$% on the unpaid amount up to $500 and 1% on the unpaid amount over $500. What is the finance charge on an unpaid amount of $750?

A. $1.00

B. $10.00

C. $22.50

D. $100.00

26. What is the sum of $(8 \times 10^2) + (6 \times 10) + 2$ and $(5 \times 10^3) + (2 \times 10^2) + (8 \times 10) + 9$?

J. 6,041

K. 6,151

L. 50,041

M. 51,151

27. The set of common factors for 30 and 24 is

A. {1,2,3,6}.

B. {1,2,3,4,6}.

C. {1,2,4,6}.

D. {1,2,4,6,12}.

28. If the scale on a blueprint is $\frac{1}{4}$ inch = 1 foot, give the blueprint dimensions of a room that is actually 29 feet long and 23 feet wide.

J. $7\frac{1}{2}" \times 5\frac{1}{4}"$

K. $6\frac{3}{4}" \times 6"$

L. $7\frac{1}{4}" \times 5\frac{1}{2}"$

M. $7\frac{1}{4}" \times 5\frac{3}{4}"$

29. A scalene triangle has

A. no equal sides.

B. two equal sides.

C. two equal sides and one right angle.

D. three equal sides.

30. On a recent trip, the Smiths drove at an average speed of 55 miles per hour. If the trip took $5\frac{1}{2}$ hours, how many miles did they drive?

J. 302.5

K. 312.5

L. 320.5

M. 320.75

31. Audrey and Ginnie volunteer each month to drive meals to elderly people. The first month they volunteered, they delivered a total of 60 meals. The next month they delivered $33\frac{1}{3}$ percent more than they did the first month. The third month they delivered twice as many meals as the first two months combined. How many meals did the two girls deliver in the third month?

A. 80

B. 90

C. 160

D. 280

32. If Taylor earns $7.50 per hour, how many 40-hour weeks will he need to work to earn enough to buy a new computer system that costs $1,350?

J. 3

K. 4

L. $4\frac{1}{2}$

M. $12\frac{1}{2}$

33. Wallie wants to wallpaper her bedroom. Each roll of wallpaper covers 75 square feet of wall space. Her room has four walls that are 10 feet high and 15 feet wide. How many rolls of wallpaper will Wallie need to cover all four walls?

A. 2

B. 8

C. 16

D. 20

34. An amateur bowler practices daily and bowls four games per day. Today, his scores were 189, 243, 202, and 198. What was his average score?

J. 200

K. 208

L. 212

M. 220

35. Gee-Whiz electronics company exports 400,000 electronic devices each year. Gee-Whiz wants to merge with Go Electro, a new electronics company that exports 1,900 electronic devices each month. After the merger, how many electronic devices will the new company export per year?

A. 35,233

B. 401,900

C. 422,800

D. 6,333,333

Practice Test 1: TACHS

36. If 8 lb., 12 oz. of fruit were to be divided among eight people, how much would each receive?

   J. 10.5 oz.

   K. 13.5 oz.

   L. 1 lb., 1.5 oz.

   M. 2.0 lb.

37. In how much less time does a runner who finishes a marathon in 2 hours 12 minutes 38 seconds complete the race than a runner who finishes in 3 hours 2 minutes 24 seconds?

   A. 48 min. 56 sec.

   B. 49 min. 46 sec.

   C. 1 hr. 26 min. 12 sec.

   D. 1 hr. 51 min. 22 sec.

38. The drawing of a wheel in a book is done at $\frac{1}{16}$ scale. If the drawing is 1.8 inches in diameter, what is the wheel's diameter?

   J. 0.1125 inch

   K. 24 inches

   L. 28.8 inches

   M. 32 inches

39. If a man runs M miles in T hours, his speed is

   A. M/T

   B. $M + T$

   C. $M - T$

   D. MT

40. How many square yards are there in x rooms in a house, each having y square feet?

   J. $\dfrac{xy}{144}$

   K. $\dfrac{xy}{9}$

   L. $9xy$

   M. $144xy$

Directions: Use the charts provided to answer each question.

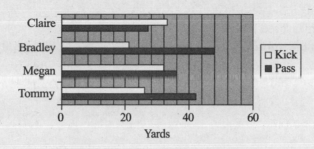

41. The city recently held a football skills competition at Barton Park. Based on the information in the chart above, which competitor passed the football the shortest distance?

    A. Claire

    B. Bradley

    C. Megan

    D. Tommy

42. Based on the information in the chart above, which competitor passed 4 more yards than he/she kicked the football?

    J. Claire

    K. Bradley

    L. Megan

    M. Tommy

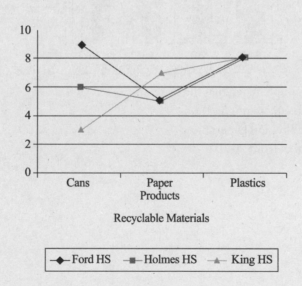

43. The City School District sponsored a week-long recycling campaign in which the three city high schools collected items to be recycled. The chart indicates the results of the campaign as measured in hundreds of pounds. Based on the information in the chart above, which of the high schools collected the most cans and paper products combined?

A. Ford HS

B. Holmes HS

C. King HS

D. Holmes HS and King HS

44. Based on the information in the chart above, what was the total weight of all plastics collected in the campaign?

J. 800 pounds

K. 1,600 pounds

L. 2,400 pounds

M. 6,900 pounds

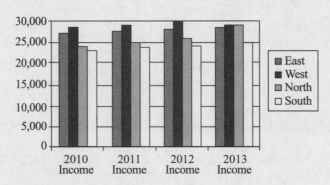

45. According to the bar graph above that illustrates per capita income by region in thousands of dollars, which region experienced the most income growth from 2010 to 2013?

A. East

B. West

C. North

D. South

Directions: For the following questions, estimate the answer in your head. No scratch work is allowed. Do *not* try to compute exact answers.

46. The closest estimate of 6,544 − 3,466 is .

    J. 1,000

    K. 2,000

    L. 3,000

    M. 4,000

47. The closest estimate of 82,122 ÷ 4,055 is _____.

    A. 20

    B. 200

    C. 2,000

    D. 20,000

48. The average class size at Kennedy High School is 31 students. There are 30 classes in session at any one time. About how many Kennedy High students are in class at any given time?

    J. 800

    K. 900

    L. 1,000

    M. Not given

49. The closest estimate of 3,988 + 2,177 is _____.

    A. 5,000

    B. 5,500

    C. 6,000

    D. 6,500

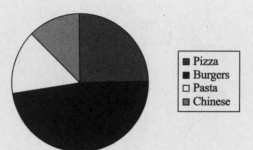

Favorite Foods of New York High School Seniors

50. According to the chart above, about what percent of New York high school seniors prefer burgers?

    J. 15%

    K. 25%

    L. 33%

    M. 50%

STOP.

If you finish before time is up, you may check your work on this section only.
Do not turn to any other section in the test.

Practice Test 1: TACHS

ABILITY

50 Questions (32 minutes)

Figure Classification

Turn to the Ability section of your answer sheet to answer the questions in this section.

Directions: In questions 1–20, the first three figures are alike in certain ways. Choose the answer choice that corresponds to the first three figures.

1.

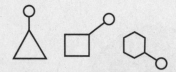

A.   B.   C.   D.   E.

2.

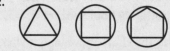

J.   K.   L.   M.   N.

3.

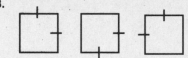

A.   B.   C.   D.   E.

4.

J.   K.   L.   M.   N.

5. =

A.   B.   C.   D.   E.

6.

J.   K.   L.   M.   N.

7.

A.  B.  C.  D.  E.

8.

J.   K.   L.   M.   N.

9.

A.   B.   C.   D.   E.

Practice Test 1: TACHS

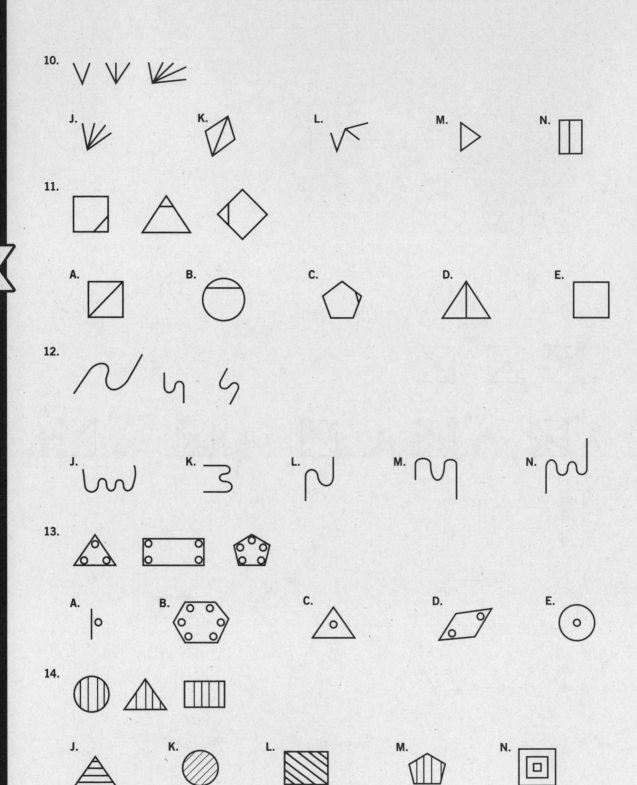

www.petersons.com

15.

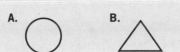

A.   B.   C.   D.   E.

16.

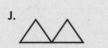

J.   K.   L.   M.   N.

17.

A.   B.   C.   D.   E.

18.

J.   K.   L.   M.   N.

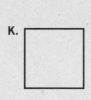

19.

A.   B.   C.   D.   E.

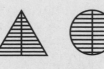

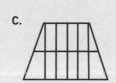

20.

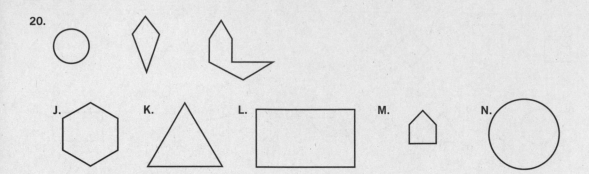

J.   K.   L.   M.   N.

Figure Matrices

Directions: In questions 1–20, find the figure that completes the matrix.

1.

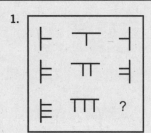

A.   B.   C.   D.   E.

2.

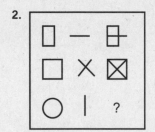

J.   K.   L.   M.   N.

3.

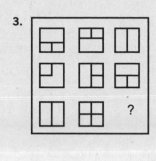

A.   B.   C.   D.   E.

4.

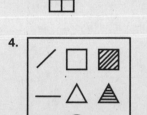

J.   K.   L.   M.   N.

5.

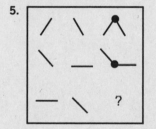

A.   B.   C.   D.   E.

6.

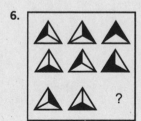

Practice Test 1: TACHS

Practice Test 1: TACHS

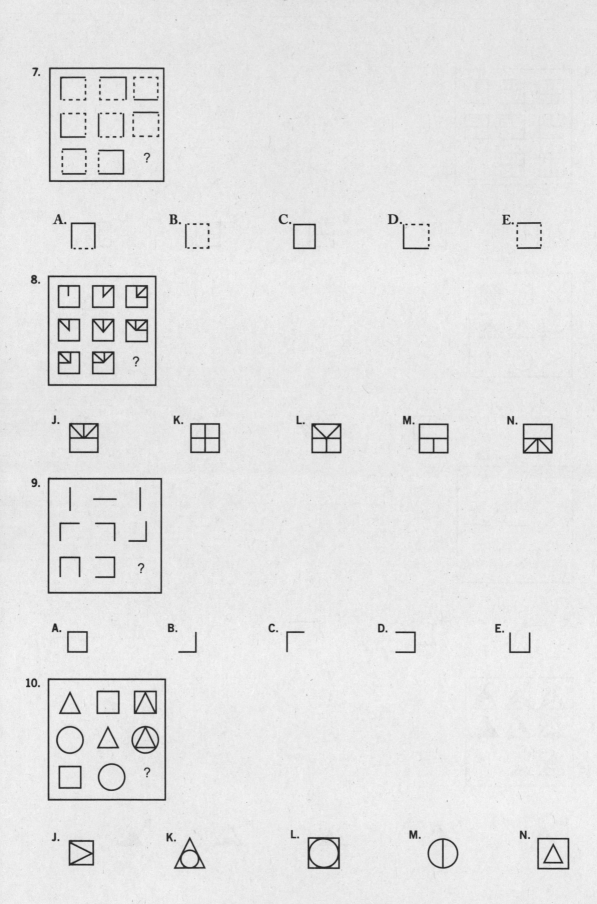

7.

A. B. C. D. E.

8.

J. K. L. M. N.

9.

A. B. C. D. E.

10.

J. K. L. M. N.

11.

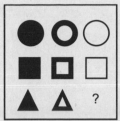

A. ⬠ B. △ C. ◬ D. ◎ E. ☐

12.

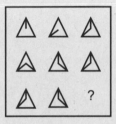

J. K. L. M. N.

13.

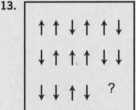

A. ↓ ↑ B. ↑ ↑ C. ↓ ↓ D. ↑ ↓ E. → ←

14.

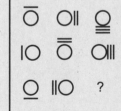

J. K. L. M. N.

15.

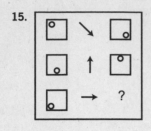

A.   B.   C.   D.   E.

16.

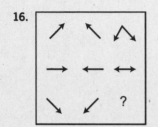

J.   K.   L.   M.   N.

17.

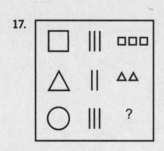

A.   B.   C.   D.   E.

18.

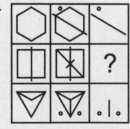

Practice Test 1: TACHS

19.

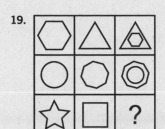

A.   B.  C.   D.   E.

20.

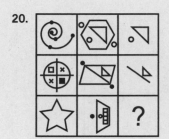

J.   K.   L.   M.   N.

Paper Folding

Directions: In questions 1–10, look at the top row to see how a square piece of paper is folded and where holes are punched into it. Then look at the bottom row to decide which answer choice shows how the paper will look when it is completely unfolded.

1.

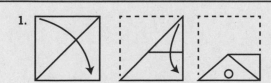

A. 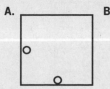 B.   C.   D.   E.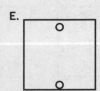

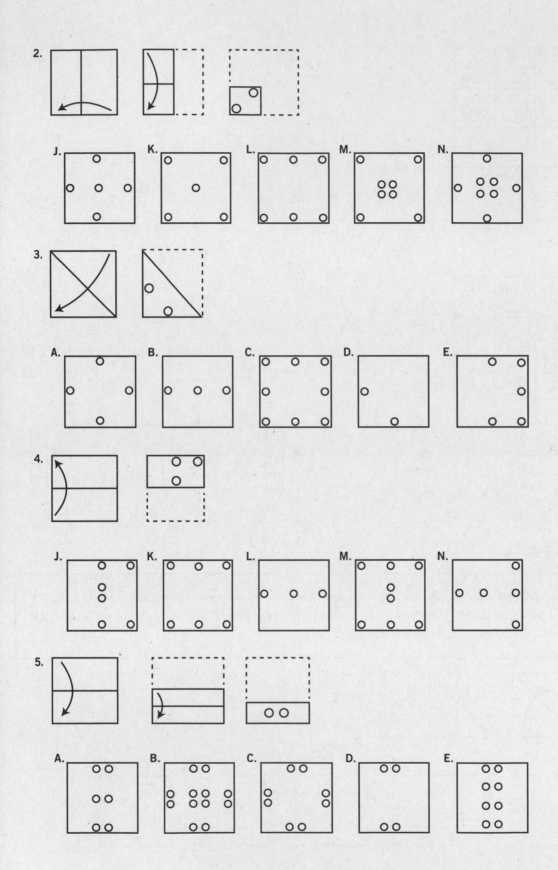

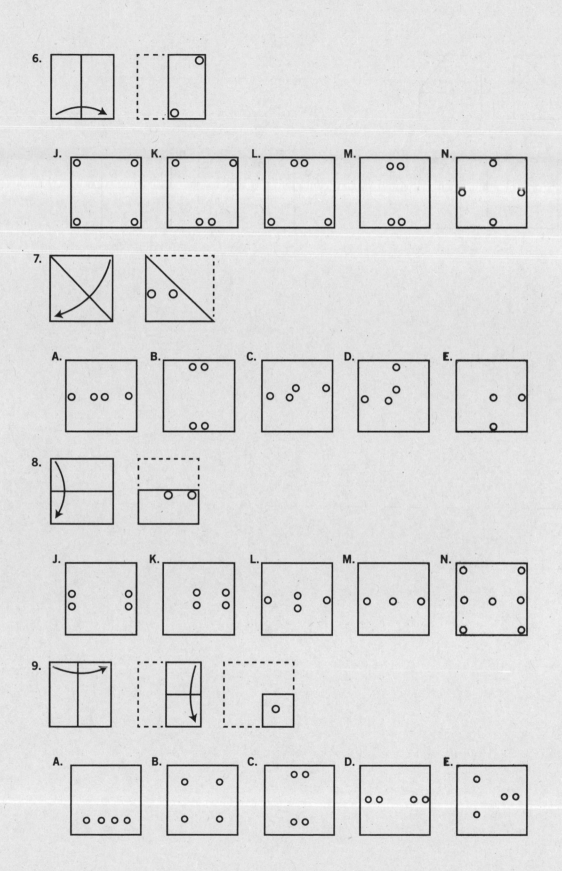

Practice Test 1: TACHS

10.

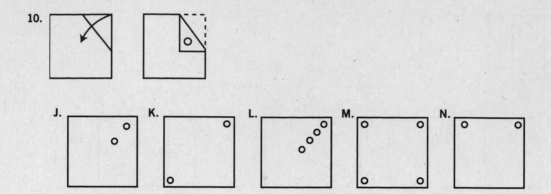

ANSWER KEYS AND EXPLANATIONS

Reading

1. D	11. B	21. D	31. C	41. D
2. K	12. L	22. K	32. M	42. J
3. B	13. B	23. C	33. B	43. C
4. M	14. J	24. J	34. J	44. K
5. C	15. C	25. B	35. C	45. D
6. J	16. J	26. K	36. M	46. K
7. C	17. B	27. C	37. A	47. D
8. L	18. M	28. M	38. K	48. M
9. D	19. D	29. B	39. B	49. C
10. J	20. J	30. J	40. M	50. J

1. **The correct answer is D.** The passage tells you that Mrs. Lynde is interested in knowing all that happens near her house, and the phrase "whys and wherefores" can clue you in that *ferreted* means "uncovered." Choice A doesn't fit because Mrs. Lynde is characterized as someone who wants to be in the know. Choice B is incorrect because there is no information that suggests she's against what is happening, just that she wants to know what is happening. Choice C is incorrect because, although Mrs. Lynde is described as observant, and therefore we can assume she obtains information, there is no indication that she seeks to "complete" anything.

2. **The correct answer is K.** Choice K is correct because the passage tells you that it "had its source away back in the woods of the old Cuthbert place." Choice J is incorrect because although the passage mentions that the town is Avonlea, there is not enough information to tell you that the brook starts in the town. Choice L is incorrect because the brook runs past Lynde's Hollow, but does not start there. Choice M is also incorrect because the passage explicitly says where the brook starts.

3. **The correct answer is B.** It's clear from the passage that the author is painting Mrs. Lynde as someone who wants to know exactly what is going on in her neighborhood, saying that nothing gets past her without investigation. The clearest support for choice B is this sentence: "Mrs. Rachel Lynde was one of those capable creatures who can manage their own concerns and those of other folks into the bargain." Choice A is incorrect because there is nothing that suggests Mrs. Lynde is spiteful about her neighbors. Choice D is similarly incorrect because the passage does not specifically say that Mrs. Lynde intends to help her neighbors; there is merely the statement that she can "manage" the concerns of others. Choice C is incorrect because there is not enough information to suggest that she is sneaky about seeking information; rather, the passage says that Mrs. Lynde is open about her interest in neighborhood happenings.

4. **The correct answer is M.** The only information that the reader is given about Avonlea in the passage is that people live there, and that the main road is located near the woods, so choice M is the choice best supported by the passage. Choice J is incorrect because there is no information about Avonlea's population

or how urban it is. Choice K is incorrect because there is no information about how people feel about Mrs. Lynde. Choice L is incorrect because, although we're told that Mrs. Lynde is interested in knowing all the details of what's going on with her neighbors, we're not told anything about what other people may be doing or hiding.

5. **The correct answer is C.** The poet is using figurative language to describe the moon. It is not likely that she actually believes the moon is made of stone or is actually a person, so this eliminates choices A and B. Although the poet describes the moon in terms of "summer dew," there is nothing to suggest that the poet really believes that the moon is only present during the summer.

6. **The correct answer is J.** By mentioning that the moon is different now than it was two days ago and suggesting that the moon now appears bigger ("now she turns her perfect face upon the world below"), the poet is describing the moon's phases over time, so choice J is correct. Choice K is incorrect because, although summer is mentioned later in the poem, it is in relation to the moon, not any other seasons. Choice L is incorrect because there is no information to suggest where the moon is located in the sky. Choice M is incorrect because the poet is using figurative language about the moon, not a literal description of her own face.

7. **The correct answer is C.** By giving such a detailed description of the moon, you can infer that the poet has spent a lot of time observing the sky and the moon. This eliminates choice A, given that the poet is describing outdoor elements. Choice B can be tempting because observing the moon requires nighttime observation, but there is nothing to suggest that the poet goes out only at night. The poem does describe the moon in terms of fashion, but there is no

indication that this is what interests the poet, so choice D is incorrect as well.

8. **The correct answer is L.** By suggesting that the rest of the sky is full of accessories to the moon, the poet is making the moon the most important part of the sky. The word *bonnet* may make you think that the poet is calling the moon old-fashioned, but she seems to be mentioning different kinds of clothing without making any kind of judgment, so choice J is incorrect. Stanzas 2 and 3 suggest that the moon is cold, but this is not indicated in the quoted stanza, so choice K is incorrect. These lines also do not say anything about whether the poet thinks the moon's beauty is fading, so choice M is incorrect as well.

9. **The correct answer is D.** In this stanza, the poet is describing things that can be found in the sky ("universe," "stars"). That should clue you in that *firmament* is also something that can be found in the sky, eliminating choice A.

10. **The correct answer is J.** The poet is trying to create a fanciful image of the moon as a beautiful woman. Choice J is the word that most closely recognizes this. The poet is not making fun of the moon or using jokes, so choice K doesn't really fit. The poet is not describing the moon literally, so choice L is incorrect. The poet does not seem to have any negative feelings like sadness or anger, so choice M does not fit the tone.

11. **The correct answer is B.** The first sentence of the passage—"take a book, leave a book"—essentially summarizes the concept in choice B. Choice A might be tempting because the author compares the little library to a birdhouse, but this is just a physical comparison. Choices C and D are incorrect because the passage does not suggest that little free libraries are a particularly innovative or essential invention.

12. **The correct answer is L.** The previous sentence calls the libraries "small" and "little," so it is likely that *miniscule* is a synonym for these words. The sentence already mentions that the library is "free," so it is unlikely that *miniscule* would mean "free" as well, so choice J is incorrect. Although the passage doesn't specifically say that the libraries aren't underground, it does say that these are often found in parks and beaches, which are open spaces, so choice K is incorrect. The passage also says that these are public resources, so choice M, *secret*, doesn't work either.

13. **The correct answer is B.** People who read online are unlikely to need or want physical books, so choice A is incorrect. The passage describes how people can get rid of their own books and read the ones that others donate, so choice B is the best answer. Choice C is unlikely, because people who hate reading are unlikely to seek out new books. The passage specifically says that you don't need a library card to belong to this type of library, so choice D is incorrect.

14. **The correct answer is J.** Paragraph 2 says that the door protects the books from "the elements," which includes rain. The paragraph also mentions that taking books is done on the honor system, which means that there is nothing keeping thieves from taking books and not bringing them back, so choice K is incorrect. There is also nothing in the passage that suggests children are not welcome to use the library, so choice L is also incorrect.

15. **The correct answer is C.** The tone is neutral, so there's no humor or personal narrative in the passage, which eliminates choices A and D. The author does not take a specific stance on free little libraries, so it is not meant to be persuasive (choice B). The author presents information about the libraries and their purpose, so the best answer is choice C.

16. **The correct answer is J.** "Honor system" means that there will be no security system watching to make sure that people don't steal the books, so choice J is the best answer. The idea is that people will leave books as well as take them and return the books they borrow, but if they do not, there is nothing in place like a security camera (choice L) to make sure that everyone is using the library correctly. Although one may assume that an honor system only works if people are "nice," this is not a condition that can be enforced, so choice M is incorrect.

17. **The correct answer is B.** The topic of the passage is bird migration and the mystery it has presented throughout the ages. Choice A is incorrect because the final paragraph states that there are still mysteries around bird migration. Choice C is incorrect because the focus of the passage is bird migration, not just the plover. Choice D is incorrect because Aristotle's theory was immediately disproven.

18. **The correct answer is M.** The last sentence of paragraph 3 makes this statement. Bird bands do not record types of food eaten or when birds begin their migration. Choice K is just ridiculous as there is no way to understand a bird's preferences.

19. **The correct answer is D.** This is stated within the parentheses in paragraph 2.

20. **The correct answer is J.** The final paragraph emphasizes this point. Choice K is untrue, while choice M refers to bird migration as a problem—which it is not. While choice L may seem true, it is not emphasized anywhere in the passage.

21. **The correct answer is D.** Despite evidence, some people still believe that small birds piggy-back on European storks. Choice B falsely suggests small birds climbed into a stork's mouth, while choice C suggests that small birds are in a constant state of

migration. Choice A is a silly answer as African swallows are non-migratory.

22. **The correct answer is K.** Birds migrate to warmer climates and to find reliable food sources. Birds do not migrate, nor are they expansionists, so choices J and L are incorrect. While birds may mate during migration, this is not the reason for migration, so choice M is incorrect.

23. **The correct answer is C.** The topic of the passage is how people recognize, or perceive, colors. The passage might highlight summer, but the same effects are visible at any time of the year, so choice A is incorrect. Choice B is incorrect, as farmers and artists are not in opposition over this subject. Choice D is incorrect because the topic is not the color, but how people perceive color.

24. **The correct answer is J.** Sentence 5 clearly states this.

25. **The correct answer is B.** You should be able to discern this from the passage, but if not you should be able to eliminate the other choices as ridiculous.

26. **The correct answer is K.** The phrase, "moves up toward the zenith" should lead you to the correct answer.

27. **The correct answer is C.** Choices A, B, and D are all ridiculous answers that you can eliminate quickly.

28. **The correct answer is M.** The experiment with the farmer demonstrates how shifting your perspective can change how you see something.

29. **The correct answer is B.** The passage tells you that yoga originated in India, and that it was brought to the West. It is not logical that a novice would be spreading yoga, so choice A is incorrect. Although the yogis are described as Indian, there is nothing to suggest that they are rulers, so choice C is incorrect. Although the original word *yoga* comes from Sanskrit, there is not enough

information to suggest that yogis were Sanskrit speakers, so choice D is incorrect.

30. **The correct answer is J.** In paragraph 3, the passage states that in the 1980s, yoga became popular as a type of exercise.

31. **The correct answer is C.** *Equilibrium* is a synonym for *balance*, so choice C is the correct answer.

32. **The correct answer is M.** Choices J, K, and L are all listed as physical benefits of yoga, but increased intelligence (choice M) is not one of the health benefits included in the passage.

33. **The correct answer is B.** We read in paragraph 2 of the passage that yoga originated in India. As for other locations, we learn that yoga came to Chicago in 1893, so choices A, C, and D are incorrect.

34. **The correct answer is J.** According to the passage, yoga first emerged in India in the 5th century BCE. Choices K, L, and M are all dates mentioned in the passage, but they refer to events occurring after yoga had spread beyond India.

35. **The correct answer is C.** The word *humble* is used here to draw a difference between the eagle (which was ultimately chosen) and the underdog recommendation, the turkey. There is not enough information in the passage to draw conclusions about the turkey and eagle populations (choice A), turkey and eagle personalities (choice B), or the price of each kind of bird (choice D).

36. **The correct answer is M.** *Prominent* means "noticeable" or "famous." Although the paragraph has a light-hearted tone, it does not attempt to make Benjamin Franklin appear foolish (choice J), nor does it mention his age (choice K). The passage seems to assume the reader knows something of Franklin's importance in history, but his status is not discussed—whether underrated (choice L) or not.

37. **The correct answer is A.** The author presents the turkey as a humorous symbol, playing up the differences between it and the bald eagle, suggesting that the humor in the story is what has helped it survive this long. There is no evidence in the passage to support choices B, C, or D.

38. **The correct answer is K.** The passage is clear that Franklin was not successful in supporting the turkey, so choice J is not correct. To champion means means to represent or sponsor something, so choice K is correct. *Racing* and *bringing* are not synonyms of *championing*, so choices L and M are not correct.

39. **The correct answer is B.** Ben Franklin compared the turkey to the bald eagle much later, although it has since been revised to suggest he always wanted the turkey as the national symbol. There is no evidence that he supported the turkey at the time of the debate, so choice A is incorrect. Although the letter discussing the turkey was sent to Ben Franklin's daughter, there is no suggestion that she had anything to do with the story being repeated, so choice C is incorrect. There is also no evidence that it was a rumor started by Ben Franklin's peers, so choice D is incorrect.

40. **The correct answer is M.** Of the choices, this one represents all of the passage. Choice J excludes the turkey altogether. Choice K is too broad, and choice L suggests that the entire passage is about Franklin's letters, when that is a small part of the passage.

41. **The correct answer is D.** Clark Gable and Bob Hope were fellow actors, but did not affect Lamarr's inventing career, so choices A and B are incorrect. The passage states that Howard Hughes *did* support her inventing career, making choice C incorrect.

42. **The correct answer is J.** The word *burgeoning* means "expanding" or "growing," so

choice J is correct. The passage describes how successful Lamarr's Hollywood career was, so from the context given, choices K and L are unlikely. Choice M is also incorrect, because there is nothing that suggests Lamarr's career was miraculous.

43. **The correct answer is C.** Paragraph 3 states that her patents and her work, not necessarily Lamarr herself, helped scientists develop those new technologies. There is no indication that she worked directly on these newer inventions, so choice A is incorrect. Although airplanes are given as an example of the kinds of inventions Lamarr worked on, there is no information in the passage that suggests the airplane designs are still in use, so choice B is incorrect. The passage says that her inventing career was "largely forgotten" in favor of her acting career, so choice D is incorrect.

44. **The correct answer is K.** Lamarr's invention was originally used for military purposes during World War II, as stated in paragraph 2.

45. **The correct answer is D.** *Posthumously* means "after death," so choice D is correct. You can use the dates as context: the passage says Lamarr died in 2000, but was elected into the National Inventors Hall of Fame in 2014, 14 years later.

46. **The correct answer is K.** The passage focuses only on Hedy Lamarr's particular career, so we have no way to know if J is true, making that choice incorrect. Choice K fits the entire passage the best, so it is the correct answer. The passage doesn't compare the success of her two careers, so choice L is incorrect. It also doesn't contain enough information about other inventions to conclude that M is true, so choice M is incorrect as well.

47. **The correct answer is D.** There were fewer cards available, which makes them more valuable. The passage states that choices A

and B are not true. The passage also suggests that Wagner is not one of the biggest names in baseball, so choice C is incorrect as well.

48. **The correct answer is M.** Paragraph 2 states that the baseball cards were produced by tobacco companies as a promotion for cigarettes. None of the other choices are backed up by the passage.

49. **The correct answer is C.** The passage says that "no more than 200" cards had been produced and distributed, and that there are "few remaining" now, so this eliminates choices A, B, and D.

50. **The correct answer is J.** *Exponentially* means "expanding at a steady and rapid rate."

Written Expression

1. A	11. B	21. C	31. B	41. B
2. K	12. L	22. K	32. J	42. M
3. D	13. A	23. D	33. D	43. C
4. J	14. L	24. J	34. J	44. K
5. E	15. A	25. B	35. B	45. A
6. M	16. L	26. K	36. L	46. L
7. B	17. B	27. C	37. A	47. B
8. J	18. J	28. M	38. K	48. J
9. D	19. C	29. A	39. C	49. C
10. J	20. K	30. L	40. J	50. L

1. **The correct answer is A.** The correct spelling is *involvement*.

2. **The correct answer is K.** The correct spelling is *committee*.

3. **The correct answer is D.** The correct spelling is *suspicious*.

4. **The correct answer is J.** The correct spelling is *retrieve*.

5. **The correct answer is E.** (*No mistakes*)

6. **The correct answer is M.** The correct spelling is *believable*.

7. **The correct answer is B.** The correct spelling is *appreciate*.

8. **The correct answer is J.** The correct spelling is *recommendation*.

9. **The correct answer is D.** The correct spelling is *management*.

10. **The correct answer is J.** The correct spelling is *competitive*.

11. **The correct answer is B.** In this sentence, "North America" is a proper noun and should be capitalized.

12. **The correct answer is L.** As written, *merchant* is a common noun that should be set in lowercase.

13. **The correct answer is A.** Although the name of Isabelle's father is a proper noun that should be capitalized, the word *dad* is a common noun that should be lowercased.

14. **The correct answer is L.** The word *rare* is a common noun, and there is no need to capitalize it.

15. **The correct answer is A.** Although the name of Reina's dentist (Dr. Larissa Guerrero) is a proper noun that must be capitalized, the word *dentist* is a common noun that should be written in lowercase.

16. **The correct answer is L.** As written, the action of Lara "looking forward" to the

concert is still occurring, so it should not be written in the past tense.

17. **The correct answer is B.** Since Edsen already has the new headphones, the act of purchasing them from the music store at the mall has already occurred and should be in the past tense: Edsen hid his new headphones, which he *had bought* from the music store at the mall, from his younger sister Stephanie.

18. **The correct answer is J.** Jacob has already "watched" the new episode of *Creature Hunters*, or else he would have been unable to comment on the ending. Therefore, the past tense is required here.

19. **The correct answer is C.** As written, the sentence is a question (the word *What* at the beginning is a good clue) and should be punctuated with a question mark.

20. **The correct answer is K.** Quotes, including dialog spoken by people in a sentence, should always be set in quotation marks: Boris asked his best friend Cynthia, "Can I borrow four quarters?" while they waited at the laundromat on Clarke Avenue.

21. **The correct answer is C.** The sentence, as written, is a statement of fact and not a question being posed, so it should end with a period, not a question mark.

22. **The correct answer is K.** The name of a university, like "Georgetown University," is a proper noun that should be capitalized.

23. **The correct answer is D.** (*No mistakes*)

24. **The correct answer is J.** The sentence contains incorrectly placed commas that introduce awkward pauses. It should be written as follows: Sabrina was terrified of roller coasters and refused to even walk by one or look up whenever she was at a carnival or amusement park.

25. **The correct answer is B.** As written, there is an error in agreement between a pronoun and the antecedent it is replacing. The pronoun *their* is a plural pronoun, but it's

replacing the singular noun *Louis*. The correct pronoun to use here is *his*.

26. **The correct answer is K.** This answer choice most clearly and effectively conveys the ideas in this sentence. The other answer choices introduce awkwardness or confusion into the ideas and are not appropriate options.

27. **The correct answer is C.** While the other answer choices are scattered and disorganized, choice C does the best job of clearly conveying the thoughts contained within this sentence.

28. **The correct answer is M.** This choice best shows the logical and chronological progression of ideas for those interested in pursuing a career as a teacher.

29. **The correct answer is A.** Choice A clearly expresses the information as intended in this sentence. The other choices are confusing and awkwardly written.

30. **The correct answer is L.** This choice makes it clear what's being discussed in the sentence, while the other choices mix thoughts in a confusing manner.

31. **The correct answer is B.** *The Gutenberg Bible* is a singular noun, and since the consideration here is current, the correct verb form here is *is*: "is considered." Choice A incorrectly utilizes a future tense. Choice C incorrectly uses the contraction *it's* (it is).

32. **The correct answer is J.** This paragraph discusses characteristics of the Gutenberg Bible, and ends with the fact that fewer than 50 copies are known to exist. Choice J reinforces the notion that the Gutenberg Bible is rare and is the best choice. Choices K and L are questions that start to shift focus away from the Gutenberg Bible. Choice M mentions the size of the Gutenberg Bible, which isn't discussed in this paragraph.

33. **The correct answer is D.** The focus of this paragraph is spelunking, and choice D most effectively introduces this core topic with a

question to draw in the reader. Choices A and B focus on superfluous details regarding darkness or caves and are not appropriate introductions. Choice C focuses on volcanoes, which are not discussed in this paragraph.

34. **The correct answer is J.** The sentence as written contains a possessive form of *rock*, which is inappropriate here. Choice J removes the apostrophe and creates the plural *rocks*, which is the correct answer for this context. Choices K and L also utilize incorrect possessive noun forms for this sentence.

35. **The correct answer is B.** This sentence is a question (the word *What* is a good clue) and should end in a question mark, which Choice B includes. The other choices utilize incorrect punctuation for this sentence.

36. **The correct answer is L.** *Aphids* is a common noun and should only be capitalized when at the beginning of a sentence. Choice L corrects this, and also utilizes the correct plural form of the word, since all aphids are being discussed here. Choice J uses the incorrect singular form. Choice K uses the incorrect possessive and capitalized form.

37. **The correct answer is A.** Choice A uses the correct form of the adjective *whose*, and correctly lowercases the common noun *name*. Choice B incorrectly utilizes the contraction *who's* ("who is"), and incorrectly capitalizes *Name*. Choice C incorrectly uses "who is" in this sentence.

38. **The correct answer is K.** As written, the underlined portion of the sentence utilizes the incorrect pronoun form. The antecedent, Edgar Allan Poe, is a singular masculine noun and requires the singular pronoun *his*, which Choice K uses. Choice J uses the incorrect plural pronoun (*their*) and noun form (*work*). Choice L uses the adjective *its*, which is incorrect given the context of the sentence.

39. **The correct answer is C.** As written, the word choice doesn't make logical sense. "Detractors" avoid utilizing something, so they wouldn't use hot air balloons when they feel the urge to soar above the ground. Choice C correctly fixes the problem, as "enthusiasts" would be the ones to happily use hot air balloons. Choices A and B also don't make sense given the context of the sentence.

40. **The correct answer is J.** As written, the underlined portion of the sentence contains superfluous punctuation, as semicolons should only be used to join independent clauses, which we do not have here. There is no internal punctuation required at this point in the sentence, so choice J is correct. The other answer choices introduce incorrect punctuation.

41. **The correct answer is B.** This paragraph currently ends by discussing the world's longest suspension bridge—but then doesn't tell us exactly how long that bridge is. Choice B provides the missing information. The other answer choices focus on minor details and do not conclude the paragraph effectively.

42. **The correct answer is M.** *No change.* The sentence is correct as written; "suspension bridge" is a common noun and should be capitalized only when used at the beginning of a sentence. The other answer choices add incorrect capitalization to the sentence.

43. **The correct answer is C.** The words *entire* and *world* are common nouns and should not be capitalized in this sentence; choice C corrects this mistake. The other answer choices contain incorrect capitalization.

44. **The correct answer is K.** In this sentence, giant sequoias in general are being discussed, so a plural pronoun and verb form are required. Choice K uses the correct plural form, "they are." Choices J, L, and M utilize incorrect pronoun and/or verb forms given the context of this sentence.

45. The correct answer is A. *United States*, a proper noun, should not be hyphenated. Choice A removes the hyphenation and is the correct answer. Choice B incorrectly lower-cases this proper noun and does not remove the erroneous hyphen. Choice C incorrectly adds a comma to this proper noun.

46. The correct answer is L. The sentence as written incorrectly includes the contraction *it's* ("it is"). The possessive adjective *its* is required here, so choice L is correct.

47. The correct answer is B. Items in a list, which is what we have at the underlined portion of this sentence, need to be separated by commas, so choice B is correct. Choice A incorrectly separates the list items with dashes. Choice C incorrectly separates the list items with periods.

48. The correct answer is J. Contractions such as *you'll* require the proper placement of an apostrophe, such as that shown in choice J. The other choices either don't create the contraction *you'll* properly or else incorrectly expand the contraction, which abbreviates "you will."

49. The correct answer is C. The past tense of the verb *to allow* is required here, as this action occurred in the past (in 1803, to be precise). Therefore, choice C is correct. Choice A uses an incorrect form of this verb, while choice B is a noun, not a verb, and is inappropriate here.

50. The correct answer is L. As written, the period creates a sentence fragment and is incorrect. Choice L fixes this problem and is the correct answer. Choices J and K are incorrect, as semicolons should be used only to separate independent clauses, which we don't have here.

Mathematics

1. A	11. D	21. C	31. D	41. A
2. K	12. M	22. K	32. L	42. L
3. B	13. C	23. C	33. B	43. A
4. K	14. K	24. K	34. K	44. L
5. D	15. A	25. B	35. C	45. C
6. J	16. L	26. K	36. L	46. L
7. B	17. C	27. A	37. B	47. A
8. K	18. J	28. M	38. L	48. K
9. D	19. C	29. A	39. A	49. C
10. M	20. L	30. J	40. K	50. M

1. The correct answer is A. 20 cannot be divided evenly by 3.

2. The correct answer is K. $\frac{2}{3}$ is the same as 0.67, rounded to the nearest hundredth.

3. The correct answer is B. 9 is divisible by three numbers: 1, 3, and 9. Since 9 is evenly divisible by a number other than 1 or itself, it is not a prime number.

4. The correct answer is K. 3 multiplied by 13 is 39. None of the other choices is evenly divisible by 3.

5. The correct answer is D. The term *product* means to multiply; $13 \times 100 = 4,300$.

6. The correct answer is J. $\frac{7}{8} - \frac{1}{2}$ is the same as $\frac{7}{8} - \frac{4}{8}$, which equals $\frac{3}{8}$.

7. **The correct answer is B.** Follow the order of operations; $(6 − 1 = 5) + (1 × 5 = 5) + (10 ÷ 2 = 5) + (2.5 + 2.5 = 5) = 5 + 5 + 5 + 5 = 20$.

8. **The correct answer is K.** Dividing 112 by 6 gives 18 remainder 4. Therefore, 112 is not a multiple of 6. The other choices all have a remainder of 0 when divided by 6.

9. **The correct answer is D.** Subtracting a negative is the same as adding a positive. $3 − (−6) = 3 + 6 = 9$

10. **The correct answer is M.** 72 is the lowest number of which 6, 12, and 72 are all factors.

11. **The correct answer is D.** Jeff has 6 notebooks. Maggie has $2 × 6$ notebooks. Jeff and Maggie combined have 18 notebooks. Darnell has $2 × 18$, or 36, notebooks.

12. **The correct answer is M.** Baxter needs two half-gallons for each gallon, or $2 × 14 = 28$.

13. **The correct answer is C.** Since she already has $50, she must earn $250 to be able to purchase the $300 TV. Divide $250 by $25 (the amount earned per week) to see that it will take her 10 weeks to earn this money.

14. **The correct answer is K.** A full tank would go 150 miles, since $3 × 50$ equals 150 miles. Sam's tank is only two-thirds full, so he can only drive two-thirds of that distance, or 100 miles:

$$\frac{2}{3} × 150 = 100$$

15. **The correct answer is A.** There would be 6 trips from rim to floor, so $6 × 10$ feet $= 60$ feet.

16. **The correct answer is L.** Remember, the hundreds place will not be mentioned if its value is zero.

17. **The correct answer is C.** Notice that the 6 is in the ten thousands place.

18. **The correct answer is J.** $1\% = 0.01$; one-half of 1 percent is written as 0.005.

19. **The correct answer is C.** One person raised 35% of $690, or $241.50 ($690 × 0.35 = 241.50). Subtract that amount from the total to get the amount raised by the others, which is $448.50 ($690 − $241.50 = 448.50).

20. **The correct answer is L.** The whole pie is 100%. Since each part is $\frac{1}{20}$ of the entire pie, divide 100% by 20 to get 5% ($100 ÷ 20 = 5\%$).

21. **The correct answer is C.** The sum of the angles of a triangle is always 180°. As such, the missing value x can be obtained by subtracting the total of the known values (45° and 75° = 120°) from 180°. The correct answer, therefore, is choice C, since 180° − 120° = 60°.

22. **The correct answer is K.** Note that the base of the triangle is the same as the diameter of the circle. Because $\triangle ABC$ is isosceles, its altitude is the same length as the radius of the circle. Use the formula for the area of a triangle, and substitute the correct values:

$$A = \frac{1}{2}bh$$
$$= \frac{1}{2} × 10 × 5$$
$$= 25 \text{ sq. cm.}$$

Choice K is the area of the circle.

23. **The correct answer is C.** These measurements describe a large rectangular room 30 feet high. Use the formula $V = l × w × h$ to find the volume:

$$V = 75 \text{ feet} × 50 \text{ feet} × 30 \text{ feet}$$
$$V = 112{,}500 \text{ cubic feet}$$

Choices A and B use the wrong units. Volume is always measured in *cubic* units.

24. **The correct answer is K.** A store markup of 100% would exactly double the price. An 80% markup almost doubles the price. The $14 jeans are priced at almost double their cost to the store, which means their original

cost would have been near $7. By estimation, the best answer is choice K. To figure precisely, remember that an 80% markup is the equivalent of multiplying the cost by 180%, or 1.80.

$$\text{cost} \times 1.80 = 14.00$$
$$\text{cost} = 14.00 \div 1.80$$
$$\text{cost} = \$7.78$$

25. **The correct answer is B.** The finance charge will be the sum of $1\frac{1}{2}$% of $500, plus 1% of $250. You can write this as follows: $(0.015 \times 500) + (0.01 \times 250) = 7.50 + 2.50 = \$10.00$

You can estimate the answer if you remember that *percent* means "hundredths of." One hundredth of $500 is $5.00; one hundredth of $250 is $2.50. The only answer near this sum is choice B, $10.00. Choices A and D would have resulted if you had misplaced a decimal point. Choice D is the result of multiplying $750 by $1\frac{1}{2}$% twice.

26. **The correct answer is K.** Calculate the first expression as $(8 \times 10^2) + (6 \times 10) + 2 = 862$, and then calculate the second expression to get $(5 \times 10^3) + (2 \times 10^2) + (8 \times 10) + 9 = 5{,}289$. Add the two results together to arrive at 6,151 (choice K).

27. **The correct answer is A.** The set of factors for 24 is:

$\{1,2,3,4,6,8,12,24\}$

The set of factors for 30 is:

$\{1,2,3,5,6,10,15,30\}$

Only four numbers appear in both sets. As such, the set of common factors is $\{1,2,3,6\}$, choice A.

28. **The correct answer is M.** For the length, 29 feet would be represented by 29 units of $\frac{1}{4}$ inch, resulting in $\frac{29}{4}$, or $7\frac{1}{4}$, inches. For the width, 23 feet would be represented

by 23 units of $\frac{1}{4}$ inch, resulting in $\frac{23}{4}$, or $5\frac{3}{4}$, inches.

29. **The correct answer is A.** A scalene triangle has no equal sides.

30. **The correct answer is J.**

$$\begin{aligned} \text{Distance} &= \text{Rate} \times \text{Time} \\ &= 55 \text{ mph} \times 5\frac{1}{2} \text{ hours} \\ &= 55 \text{ mph} \times 5.5 \text{ hours} \\ &= 302.5 \text{ miles} \end{aligned}$$

31. **The correct answer is D.** 60 meals in the first month plus $33\frac{1}{3}$ percent more meals in the second month $(60 + 20 = 80)$ equals 140 meals. In third month, they delivered 2×140, or 280 meals.

32. **The correct answer is L.** $7.50 \times 40 = \$300$. $\$1{,}350 \div \$300 = 4.5$, or $4\frac{1}{2}$ weeks.

33. **The correct answer is B.** There are $4 \times (10 \times 15 = 150)$ square feet of wall space, or 600 square feet. Divide by the capacity of each roll of wallpaper (75 square feet) to arrive at $600 \div 75 = 8$ rolls.

34. **The correct answer is K.** The average is $\frac{189 + 243 + 202 + 198}{4} = 208.$

35. **The correct answer is C.** Go Electro produces 1,900 devices per month; multiply this by 12 to find the annual number of devices they will add to the output, which is 22,800 devices per year. Add that amount to the current output (400,000) to calculate the new annual output, which is 422,800 devices.

36. **The correct answer is L.** You do not have to calculate this answer. If eight people share equally of 8 pounds and some ounces of fruit, each person would receive 1 pound and a few ounces. Only choice L is possible.

37. **The correct answer is B.** This is a subtraction problem. You must find the difference

between the lengths of time required to finish the race. As with other problems involving units of measurement, you must work carefully.

$$3 \text{ hr. } 2 \text{ min. } 24 \text{ sec.}$$
$$- 2 \text{ hr. } 12 \text{ min. } 38 \text{ sec.}$$

Because 38 seconds is larger than 24 seconds, and 12 minutes is larger than 2 minutes, borrow from the minutes' column and the hours' column and rewrite the problem as follows:

$$2 \text{ hr. } 61 \text{ min. } 84 \text{ sec.}$$
$$- 2 \text{ hr. } 12 \text{ min. } 38 \text{ sec.}$$
$$0 \text{ hr. } 49 \text{ min. } 46 \text{ sec.}$$

38. **The correct answer is L.** If the drawing is at a $\frac{1}{16}$ scale, it means that the drawing is $\frac{1}{16}$ the size of the actual wheel. Therefore, multiply the size of the drawing by 16 to arrive at choice L, or $1.8 \times 16 = 28.8$ inches.

39. **The correct answer is A.** This problem asks you to find speed or rate. Speed or rate is found by dividing the distance traveled (M) by the time required (T). The choice in which distance is divided by time is A.

40. **The correct answer is K.** There are 9 square feet in 1 square yard. So, y square feet equals $\frac{y}{9}$ square yards. Since there are x rooms with the same area, multiply this by x to get $x\left(\frac{y}{9}\right) = \frac{xy}{9}$ square yards.

41. **The correct answer is A.** The grey horizontal bars indicate how far each competitor passed the football, and each vertical line represents 4 feet. Claire passed for only 27 yards.

42. **The correct answer is L.** Megan passed for 36 yards and kicked 32 yards.

43. **The correct answer is A.** Ford HS collected 900 pounds of cans and 500 pounds of paper products, for a combined total of 1,400 pounds of can/paper recyclables. Holmes HS and King HS had can/paper totals of 1,100 pounds and 1,000 pounds, respectively.

44. **The correct answer is L.** Each of the three schools collected 800 pounds of plastics, totaling $800 \times 3 = 2,400$ pounds.

45. **The correct answer is C.** The income in the North grew from about $24,000 to nearly $29,000, the most of any region.

46. **The correct answer is L.** $6,544 - 3,466$ is approximately $6,500 - 3,500$, or 3,000.

47. **The correct answer is A.** $82,122 \div 4,055$ is approximately $80,000 \div 4,000$, or 20.

48. **The correct answer is K.** 31×30 is approximately 30×30, or 900.

49. **The correct answer is C.** $3,988 + 2,177$ is approximately $4,000 + 2,000$, or 6,000.

50. **The correct answer is M.** About half, or 50 percent, chose burgers.

Ability

Figure Classification

1. A	5. A	9. C	13. B	17. B
2. J	6. L	10. J	14. M	18. L
3. E	7. E	11. C	15. E	19. C
4. M	8. K	12. L	16. L	20. N

1. **The correct answer is A.** Each figure has a small circle connected by a segment to a vertex (a corner) of the shape. For all the other choices, the segment bisects one side of the figure, rather than connecting at a vertex.

2. **The correct answer is J.** Each figure has a regular polygon inscribed in a circle. When used in a mathematical context, *inscribed* means that one figure is placed within another in such a manner that it touches at as many points as possible. Note that in the example figures, the inner figures touch the circle at each corner. Choice K is a polygon inside a circle, but it is not inscribed like the examples.

3. **The correct answer is E.** Each square has segments splitting two adjacent sides.

4. **The correct answer is M.** Each shape is $\frac{1}{4}$ shaded.

5. **The correct answer is A.** Each figure consists of two parallel lines.

6. **The correct answer is L.** Each circle has two radii drawn that form a 90-degree angle.

7. **The correct answer is E.** In each of the figures, there are three circles on intersection points that form a triangle. It does not matter that some of the triangles contain two segments of the figure, while others contain only one.

8. **The correct answer is K.** Each figure is a rectangle. The only other rectangle among the answer choices is choice K.

9. **The correct answer is C.** Each figure consists of four small circles connected by means of three segments.

10. **The correct answer is J.** Each figure consists of segments all meeting at a single point.

11. **The correct answer is C.** Each figure consists of a polygon with a segment drawn to form a triangle at one of its angles.

12. **The correct answer is L.** Each figure is a curve that changes direction exactly twice.

13. **The correct answer is B.** Each figure is a polygon with a circle at each of its vertices.

14. **The correct answer is M.** Each of these figures is shaded with vertical stripes.

15. **The correct answer is E.** Each of these figures is a rectangle. A rectangle has four sides, so you can eliminate choices A, B, and D immediately. In addition, each of the angles in a rectangle must be a 90 degree angle, so choice C is incorrect. Choice E is a rectangle.

16. **The correct answer is L.** Each figure is split in half by and internal line to form two identical parts.

17. **The correct answer is B.** Each figure is a polygon.

18. **The correct answer is L.** Each of the examples is a closed figure with six sides, as is choice L.

19. **The correct answer is C.** Each of the example figures is bisected by a single line in one direction, and filled with multiple segments perpendicular to that line, as is choice C

20. **The correct answer is N.** The example figures include a circle and two irregular shapes. The answer choices do not include any irregular shapes, but they do include one circle, choice N.

Figure Matrices

1. B	5. A	9. E	13. A	17. E
2. M	6. L	10. L	14. K	18. K
3. C	7. B	11. B	15. A	19. C
4. J	8. J	12. M	16. J	20. J

1. **The correct answer is B.** Moving through the matrix from left to right rotates the shape clockwise by 90 degrees. Moving from top to bottom adds another segment to the image.

2. **The correct answer is M.** The third image in each row is just a combination of the first two images in that row. Notice that none of the images are rotated from one cell to the next, which makes choice M a better option that choice L.

3. **The correct answer is C.** The internal segments in the last square in each row are those that appear in one of the previous two images, but not both.

4. **The correct answer is J.** The third image in each row is obtained as follows: take the shape from the second position in the row, then shade it using segments parallel to the segment in the first position in the row.

5. **The correct answer is A.** The third image in each row is just the first two images in the row joined with a circle.

6. **The correct answer is L.** The shading in the third column consists of the sections that are shaded in either the first or second columns.

7. **The correct answer is B.** The solid segments in the third column are those that are not solid in either the first or second columns.

8. **The correct answer is J.** Moving left to right adds a segment that continues the current pattern in a clockwise manner. Similarly, moving top to bottom adds a segment that continues the pattern in a counterclockwise manner. Using either approach, the bottom-right image is the one shown in choice J.

9. **The correct answer is E.** Moving left to right across a row, the image rotates 90 degrees clockwise at each step. Moving top to bottom, a new segment is added at each step.

10. **The correct answer is L.** The image in the last position of each row is simply the previous two images in the row placed over each other.

11. **The correct answer is B.** Shapes are the same within a single row, and shading style is the same throughout a single column.

12. **The correct answer is M.** The internal segments in each triangle in the third column are visible based on the following rule: a segment is visible if it is visible in either the first or second triangles in the row, but not both.

13. **The correct answer is A.** Within each row, a move from the first to second image consists of reversing the first arrow and leaving the second arrow alone. Moving from the second to third column reverses both arrows.

14. **The correct answer is K.** A move from left to right consists of adding an extra segment and rotating the segments clockwise. A move from top to bottom is a rotation of 90 degrees counterclockwise.

15. **The correct answer is A.** The image in the first column is transformed by moving the circle in the direction indicted by the arrow in the second column; that arrow indicates both a vertical and horizontal movement. In the third row, the arrow does not indicate any vertical movement, only horizontal, so the circle needs to remain at the bottom of the figure.

16. **The correct answer is J.** The first two arrows in each row are reversed and joined to form the last image in the row.

17. **The correct answer is E.** The third figure in each row is multiple smaller versions of the first figure, and the number of smaller figures is determined by the number of segments in the second cell. The figures in the last column are placed side by side, which makes choice E a better option than choice B.

18. **The correct answer is K.** The figures in the middle of each row include all elements of the figures on both sides. Any elements not in the first column appear in the third.

19. **The correct answer is C.** The third figure in each row consists of the first figure placed inside the second figure.

20. **The correct answer is J.** The second figure in each row includes a polygon with various small shapes, circles, or line segments inside. The third figure in the row consists of the contents of that polygon. The first figure in each row (i.e., the entire first column) has no relation to the rest of the figures.

Paper Folding

1. A	3. A	5. E	7. D	9. B
2. M	4. J	6. K	8. K	10. J

1. **The correct answer is A.** The second fold has no effect on the result, since it does not overlap the only hole. The result needs to have two holes, at the centers of the bottom and left edges.

2. **The correct answer is M.** Unfolding the paper will result in each of the two holes being reflected first vertically and then horizontally. The hole near the center becomes four arranged around the center of the page, and the hole in the corner reflects to each of the other corners as well.

3. **The correct answer is A.** The hole on the bottom edge will be reflected to the center of the right edge, and the hole on the left edge will be reflected to the center of the top edge.

4. **The correct answer is J.** Each of the three holes on the folded page will reflect vertically across the center of the page.

5. **The correct answer is E.** When the last fold is undone, the two holes will reflect upward to become four, all still on the bottom half of the full page. Undoing the original fold will cause each of these four to reflect vertically upward again, creating two columns of four

holes immediately on either side of the page center.

6. **The correct answer is K.** Each of the two holes on the folded page will reflect horizontally across the vertical fold.

7. **The correct answer is D.** The horizontal row of two holes centered vertically in the page will reflect across the fold to become a vertical row of two holes centered horizontally in the page.

8. **The correct answer is K.** The two holes reflect over the fold onto the upper half of the page. Since they are near the fold, they will be near the fold on the other side as well.

9. **The correct answer is B.** The single hole in the center of the quarter-page will first reflect upward to be in the center of the upper-right quadrant. These two holes will then reflect across the vertical fold and end up in the centers of the lower-left and upper-left quadrants, respectively.

10. **The correct answer is J.** The small folded flap will, when unfolded, reflect the hole over the diagonal line and nearer to the corner.

SCORE SHEET

Although your actual exam scores will not be reported as percentages, it might be helpful to convert your test scores to percentages so that you can see at a glance where your strengths and weaknesses lie. The numbers in parentheses represent the questions that test each skill.

Subject	# Correct ÷ # of questions	× 100 = _____ %
Reading		
Vocabulary/Word Relationships: (1, 9, 12, 16, 18, 22, 24, 29, 31, 35, 36, 38, 42, 45, 50)	_____ ÷ 15 = _____	× 100 = _____ %
Details/Main Idea/Structure (2, 6, 10, 14, 15,17, 19, 20, 26, 27, 28, 30, 32, 33, 34, 39, 40, 41, 43, 44, 48, 49)	_____ ÷ 22 = _____	× 100 = _____ %
Inference/Understanding (3, 4, 5, 7, 8, 11, 13, 21, 23, 25, 37, 46, 47)	_____ ÷ 13 = _____	× 100 = _____ %
TOTAL READING SKILLS	_____ ÷ 50 = _____	× 100 = _____ %
Written Expression		
Spelling and Capitalization (1, 2, 3, 4, 5, 6, 7, 8, 9, 10, 11, 12, 13, 14, 15, 36, 37, 42, 43)	_____ ÷ 19 = _____	× 100 = _____ %
Punctuation (19, 20, 21, 22, 23, 24, 25, 34, 35, 40, 45, 46, 48, 50)	_____ ÷ 14 = _____	× 100 = _____ %
Grammar (16, 17, 18, 31, 38, 44)	_____ ÷ 6 = _____	× 100 = _____ %
Usage and Composition (26, 27, 28, 29, 30, 32, 33, 39, 41, 47, 49)	_____ ÷ 11 = _____	× 100 = _____ %
TOTAL WRITTEN EXPRESSION SKILLS	_____ ÷ 50 = _____	× 100 = _____ %
Mathematics		
Arithmetic (1, 2, 3, 4, 5, 6, 7, 8, 9, 10, 11, 12, 13, 14, 15, 16, 17, 18, 19, 25, 26, 27, 30, 33, 35, 36, 37, 46, 47, 48, 49)	_____ ÷ 31 = _____	× 100 = _____ %
Algebra (24, 31, 32, 39, 40)	_____ ÷ 5 = _____	× 100 = _____ %
Data Analysis (34, 41, 42, 43, 44, 45, 50)	_____ ÷ 7 = _____	× 100 = _____ %
Geometry and Measurement (20, 21, 22, 23, 28, 29, 38)	_____ ÷ 7 = _____	× 100 = _____ %
TOTAL MATHEMATICS SKILLS	_____ ÷ 50 = _____	× 100 = _____ %
Ability		
Figure Classification (1, 2, 3, 4, 5, 6, 7, 8, 9, 10, 11, 12, 13, 14, 15, 16, 17, 18, 19, 20)	_____ ÷ 20 = _____	× 100 = _____ %
Figure Matrices (1, 2, 3, 4, 5, 6, 7, 8, 9, 10, 11, 12, 13, 14, 15, 16, 17, 18, 19, 20)	_____ ÷ 20 = _____	× 100 = _____ %
Paper Folding (1, 2, 3, 4, 5, 6, 7, 8, 9, 10)	_____ ÷ 10 = _____	× 100 = _____ %
TOTAL ABILITY SKILLS	_____ ÷ 50 = _____	× 100 = _____ %

ANSWER SHEET: TACHS PRACTICE TEST 2

Reading

1. Ⓐ Ⓑ Ⓒ Ⓓ   11. Ⓐ Ⓑ Ⓒ Ⓓ   21. Ⓐ Ⓑ Ⓒ Ⓓ   31. Ⓐ Ⓑ Ⓒ Ⓓ   41. Ⓐ Ⓑ Ⓒ Ⓓ

2. Ⓙ Ⓚ Ⓛ Ⓜ   12. Ⓙ Ⓚ Ⓛ Ⓜ   22. Ⓙ Ⓚ Ⓛ Ⓜ   32. Ⓙ Ⓚ Ⓛ Ⓜ   42. Ⓙ Ⓚ Ⓛ Ⓜ

3. Ⓐ Ⓑ Ⓒ Ⓓ   13. Ⓐ Ⓑ Ⓒ Ⓓ   23. Ⓐ Ⓑ Ⓒ Ⓓ   33. Ⓐ Ⓑ Ⓒ Ⓓ   43. Ⓐ Ⓑ Ⓒ Ⓓ

4. Ⓙ Ⓚ Ⓛ Ⓜ   14. Ⓙ Ⓚ Ⓛ Ⓜ   24. Ⓙ Ⓚ Ⓛ Ⓜ   34. Ⓙ Ⓚ Ⓛ Ⓜ   44. Ⓙ Ⓚ Ⓛ Ⓜ

5. Ⓐ Ⓑ Ⓒ Ⓓ   15. Ⓐ Ⓑ Ⓒ Ⓓ   25. Ⓐ Ⓑ Ⓒ Ⓓ   35. Ⓐ Ⓑ Ⓒ Ⓓ   45. Ⓐ Ⓑ Ⓒ Ⓓ

6. Ⓙ Ⓚ Ⓛ Ⓜ   16. Ⓙ Ⓚ Ⓛ Ⓜ   26. Ⓙ Ⓚ Ⓛ Ⓜ   36. Ⓙ Ⓚ Ⓛ Ⓜ   46. Ⓙ Ⓚ Ⓛ Ⓜ

7. Ⓐ Ⓑ Ⓒ Ⓓ   17. Ⓐ Ⓑ Ⓒ Ⓓ   27. Ⓐ Ⓑ Ⓒ Ⓓ   37. Ⓐ Ⓑ Ⓒ Ⓓ   47. Ⓐ Ⓑ Ⓒ Ⓓ

8. Ⓙ Ⓚ Ⓛ Ⓜ   18. Ⓙ Ⓚ Ⓛ Ⓜ   28. Ⓙ Ⓚ Ⓛ Ⓜ   38. Ⓙ Ⓚ Ⓛ Ⓜ   48. Ⓙ Ⓚ Ⓛ Ⓜ

9. Ⓐ Ⓑ Ⓒ Ⓓ   19. Ⓐ Ⓑ Ⓒ Ⓓ   29. Ⓐ Ⓑ Ⓒ Ⓓ   39. Ⓐ Ⓑ Ⓒ Ⓓ   49. Ⓐ Ⓑ Ⓒ Ⓓ

10. Ⓙ Ⓚ Ⓛ Ⓜ   20. Ⓙ Ⓚ Ⓛ Ⓜ   30. Ⓙ Ⓚ Ⓛ Ⓜ   40. Ⓙ Ⓚ Ⓛ Ⓜ   50. Ⓙ Ⓚ Ⓛ Ⓜ

Written Expression

1. Ⓐ Ⓑ Ⓒ Ⓓ Ⓔ   14. Ⓙ Ⓚ Ⓛ Ⓜ   27. Ⓐ Ⓑ Ⓒ Ⓓ   40. Ⓙ Ⓚ Ⓛ Ⓜ

2. Ⓙ Ⓚ Ⓛ Ⓜ Ⓝ   15. Ⓐ Ⓑ Ⓒ Ⓓ   28. Ⓙ Ⓚ Ⓛ Ⓜ   41. Ⓐ Ⓑ Ⓒ Ⓓ

3. Ⓐ Ⓑ Ⓒ Ⓓ Ⓔ   16. Ⓙ Ⓚ Ⓛ Ⓜ   29. Ⓐ Ⓑ Ⓒ Ⓓ   42. Ⓙ Ⓚ Ⓛ Ⓜ

4. Ⓙ Ⓚ Ⓛ Ⓜ Ⓝ   17. Ⓐ Ⓑ Ⓒ Ⓓ   30. Ⓙ Ⓚ Ⓛ Ⓜ   43. Ⓐ Ⓑ Ⓒ Ⓓ

5. Ⓐ Ⓑ Ⓒ Ⓓ Ⓔ   18. Ⓙ Ⓚ Ⓛ Ⓜ   31. Ⓐ Ⓑ Ⓒ Ⓓ   44. Ⓙ Ⓚ Ⓛ Ⓜ

6. Ⓙ Ⓚ Ⓛ Ⓜ Ⓝ   19. Ⓐ Ⓑ Ⓒ Ⓓ   32. Ⓙ Ⓚ Ⓛ Ⓜ   45. Ⓐ Ⓑ Ⓒ Ⓓ

7. Ⓐ Ⓑ Ⓒ Ⓓ Ⓔ   20. Ⓙ Ⓚ Ⓛ Ⓜ   33. Ⓐ Ⓑ Ⓒ Ⓓ   46. Ⓙ Ⓚ Ⓛ Ⓜ

8. Ⓙ Ⓚ Ⓛ Ⓜ Ⓝ   21. Ⓐ Ⓑ Ⓒ Ⓓ   34. Ⓙ Ⓚ Ⓛ Ⓜ   47. Ⓐ Ⓑ Ⓒ Ⓓ

9. Ⓐ Ⓑ Ⓒ Ⓓ Ⓔ   22. Ⓙ Ⓚ Ⓛ Ⓜ   35. Ⓐ Ⓑ Ⓒ Ⓓ   48. Ⓙ Ⓚ Ⓛ Ⓜ

10. Ⓙ Ⓚ Ⓛ Ⓜ Ⓝ   23. Ⓐ Ⓑ Ⓒ Ⓓ   36. Ⓙ Ⓚ Ⓛ Ⓜ   49. Ⓐ Ⓑ Ⓒ Ⓓ

11. Ⓐ Ⓑ Ⓒ Ⓓ   24. Ⓙ Ⓚ Ⓛ Ⓜ   37. Ⓐ Ⓑ Ⓒ Ⓓ   50. Ⓙ Ⓚ Ⓛ Ⓜ

12. Ⓙ Ⓚ Ⓛ Ⓜ   25. Ⓐ Ⓑ Ⓒ Ⓓ   38. Ⓙ Ⓚ Ⓛ Ⓜ

13. Ⓐ Ⓑ Ⓒ Ⓓ   26. Ⓙ Ⓚ Ⓛ Ⓜ   39. Ⓐ Ⓑ Ⓒ Ⓓ

Answer Sheet

Practice Test 2: TACHS

Math

1. Ⓐ Ⓑ Ⓒ Ⓓ
2. Ⓙ Ⓚ Ⓛ Ⓜ
3. Ⓐ Ⓑ Ⓒ Ⓓ
4. Ⓙ Ⓚ Ⓛ Ⓜ
5. Ⓐ Ⓑ Ⓒ Ⓓ
6. Ⓙ Ⓚ Ⓛ Ⓜ
7. Ⓐ Ⓑ Ⓒ Ⓓ
8. Ⓙ Ⓚ Ⓛ Ⓜ
9. Ⓐ Ⓑ Ⓒ Ⓓ
10. Ⓙ Ⓚ Ⓛ Ⓜ

11. Ⓐ Ⓑ Ⓒ Ⓓ
12. Ⓙ Ⓚ Ⓛ Ⓜ
13. Ⓐ Ⓑ Ⓒ Ⓓ
14. Ⓙ Ⓚ Ⓛ Ⓜ
15. Ⓐ Ⓑ Ⓒ Ⓓ
16. Ⓙ Ⓚ Ⓛ Ⓜ
17. Ⓐ Ⓑ Ⓒ Ⓓ
18. Ⓙ Ⓚ Ⓛ Ⓜ
19. Ⓐ Ⓑ Ⓒ Ⓓ
20. Ⓙ Ⓚ Ⓛ Ⓜ

21. Ⓐ Ⓑ Ⓒ Ⓓ
22. Ⓙ Ⓚ Ⓛ Ⓜ
23. Ⓐ Ⓑ Ⓒ Ⓓ
24. Ⓙ Ⓚ Ⓛ Ⓜ
25. Ⓐ Ⓑ Ⓒ Ⓓ
26. Ⓙ Ⓚ Ⓛ Ⓜ
27. Ⓐ Ⓑ Ⓒ Ⓓ
28. Ⓙ Ⓚ Ⓛ Ⓜ
29. Ⓐ Ⓑ Ⓒ Ⓓ
30. Ⓙ Ⓚ Ⓛ Ⓜ

31. Ⓐ Ⓑ Ⓒ Ⓓ
32. Ⓙ Ⓚ Ⓛ Ⓜ
33. Ⓐ Ⓑ Ⓒ Ⓓ
34. Ⓙ Ⓚ Ⓛ Ⓜ
35. Ⓐ Ⓑ Ⓒ Ⓓ
36. Ⓙ Ⓚ Ⓛ Ⓜ
37. Ⓐ Ⓑ Ⓒ Ⓓ
38. Ⓙ Ⓚ Ⓛ Ⓜ
39. Ⓐ Ⓑ Ⓒ Ⓓ
40. Ⓙ Ⓚ Ⓛ Ⓜ

41. Ⓐ Ⓑ Ⓒ Ⓓ
42. Ⓙ Ⓚ Ⓛ Ⓜ
43. Ⓐ Ⓑ Ⓒ Ⓓ
44. Ⓙ Ⓚ Ⓛ Ⓜ
45. Ⓐ Ⓑ Ⓒ Ⓓ
46. Ⓙ Ⓚ Ⓛ Ⓜ
47. Ⓐ Ⓑ Ⓒ Ⓓ
48. Ⓙ Ⓚ Ⓛ Ⓜ
49. Ⓐ Ⓑ Ⓒ Ⓓ
50. Ⓙ Ⓚ Ⓛ Ⓜ

Ability

Figure Classification

1. Ⓐ Ⓑ Ⓒ Ⓓ Ⓔ
2. Ⓙ Ⓚ Ⓛ Ⓜ Ⓝ
3. Ⓐ Ⓑ Ⓒ Ⓓ Ⓔ
4. Ⓙ Ⓚ Ⓛ Ⓜ Ⓝ
5. Ⓐ Ⓑ Ⓒ Ⓓ Ⓔ

6. Ⓙ Ⓚ Ⓛ Ⓜ Ⓝ
7. Ⓐ Ⓑ Ⓒ Ⓓ Ⓔ
8. Ⓙ Ⓚ Ⓛ Ⓜ Ⓝ
9. Ⓐ Ⓑ Ⓒ Ⓓ Ⓔ
10. Ⓙ Ⓚ Ⓛ Ⓜ Ⓝ

11. Ⓐ Ⓑ Ⓒ Ⓓ Ⓔ
12. Ⓙ Ⓚ Ⓛ Ⓜ Ⓝ
13. Ⓐ Ⓑ Ⓒ Ⓓ Ⓔ
14. Ⓙ Ⓚ Ⓛ Ⓜ Ⓝ
15. Ⓐ Ⓑ Ⓒ Ⓓ Ⓔ

16. Ⓙ Ⓚ Ⓛ Ⓜ Ⓝ
17. Ⓐ Ⓑ Ⓒ Ⓓ Ⓔ
18. Ⓙ Ⓚ Ⓛ Ⓜ Ⓝ
19. Ⓐ Ⓑ Ⓒ Ⓓ Ⓔ
20. Ⓙ Ⓚ Ⓛ Ⓜ Ⓝ

Figure Matrices

1. Ⓐ Ⓑ Ⓒ Ⓓ Ⓔ
2. Ⓙ Ⓚ Ⓛ Ⓜ Ⓝ
3. Ⓐ Ⓑ Ⓒ Ⓓ Ⓔ
4. Ⓙ Ⓚ Ⓛ Ⓜ Ⓝ
5. Ⓐ Ⓑ Ⓒ Ⓓ Ⓔ

6. Ⓙ Ⓚ Ⓛ Ⓜ Ⓝ
7. Ⓐ Ⓑ Ⓒ Ⓓ Ⓔ
8. Ⓙ Ⓚ Ⓛ Ⓜ Ⓝ
9. Ⓐ Ⓑ Ⓒ Ⓓ Ⓔ
10. Ⓙ Ⓚ Ⓛ Ⓜ Ⓝ

11. Ⓐ Ⓑ Ⓒ Ⓓ Ⓔ
12. Ⓙ Ⓚ Ⓛ Ⓜ Ⓝ
13. Ⓐ Ⓑ Ⓒ Ⓓ Ⓔ
14. Ⓙ Ⓚ Ⓛ Ⓜ Ⓝ
15. Ⓐ Ⓑ Ⓒ Ⓓ Ⓔ

16. Ⓙ Ⓚ Ⓛ Ⓜ Ⓝ
17. Ⓐ Ⓑ Ⓒ Ⓓ Ⓔ
18. Ⓙ Ⓚ Ⓛ Ⓜ Ⓝ
19. Ⓐ Ⓑ Ⓒ Ⓓ Ⓔ
20. Ⓙ Ⓚ Ⓛ Ⓜ Ⓝ

Paper Folding

1. Ⓐ Ⓑ Ⓒ Ⓓ Ⓔ   4. Ⓙ Ⓚ Ⓛ Ⓜ Ⓝ   7. Ⓐ Ⓑ Ⓒ Ⓓ Ⓔ   10. Ⓙ Ⓚ Ⓛ Ⓜ Ⓝ

2. Ⓙ Ⓚ Ⓛ Ⓜ Ⓝ   5. Ⓐ Ⓑ Ⓒ Ⓓ Ⓔ   8. Ⓙ Ⓚ Ⓛ Ⓜ Ⓝ

3. Ⓐ Ⓑ Ⓒ Ⓓ Ⓔ   6. Ⓙ Ⓚ Ⓛ Ⓜ Ⓝ   9. Ⓐ Ⓑ Ⓒ Ⓓ Ⓔ

Answer Sheet

Practice Test 2: TACHS

Practice Test 2: TACHS

READING
50 Questions (35 minutes)

Turn to the Reading section of your answer sheet to answer the questions in this section.

Directions: This is a test of how well you understand what you read.

- Read the passages below and then answer the questions.

- Four answers are given for each question. You must choose the answer you think is better than the others.

Questions 1–6 are based on the following passage.

PASSAGE 1

My people are the people of Elu, the capital village of Ohafia in southeast Nigeria. Ours is a warrior tradition. We keep the tradition today primarily in name, but the warrior image is an important part of our identity, passed down through the generations.

Line
5   We learn the tradition of the warrior through the process of many rituals, each taught to us by our elders, who ensure that our identity is maintained. I remember the first step of my manhood, when I reached the age of eight and was finally ready for the *nnu nnu mbu*, a ritual that proves that you are ready to enter the world of men. It is a sweltering morning, and my family has been preparing for the ceremony since dawn. My father is absorbed in the task of dressing me in a fine costume befitting the occasion, and he looks down upon me with pride
10 as he completes his final touches and prepares me for show.

My father is beaming, and I feel his pride lift me as I move into the street to start the process of visiting others in the village who will honor me for my efforts. My chest swells and I hear my heart pounding in my ears, the blood rushing, as one by one I visit the huts of my kinfolk, receiving gifts of money and yams from each as they greet me. Some of the family members
15 from my mother's line are introduced to me during this ceremony for the first time. I feel the strength that comes with knowing that I am emerging into manhood.

1. How does the author's father feel about his son?

   A. He is confused by his son's behavior.

   B. He pays little attention to his son.

   C. He is proud of his son's accomplishments.

   D. He feels shamed by the actions of his son.

2. What happens when the author meets his mother's family?

   J. His family members urge him to continue his target practice.

   K. Some of his family members pretend that they do not know him.

   L. He receives gifts of money and yams from the family members.

   M. His family members come together to meet him in the village square.

3. From the passage, we can infer that

   A. The author's father was never proud of him before.

   B. The author and his father have a new way to bond.

   C. The author is closer to his father's family than his mother's family.

   D. The author is not interested in taking the warrior identity.

4. The village that the author lives in is

   J. Ohafia.

   K. Nigeria.

   L. Elu.

   M. unknown.

5. Based on the passage, we can conclude that

   A. the author still has further rituals to complete.

   B. the author is fully considered a man in his village.

   C. the author will move in with his mother's relatives.

   D. the author will soon be leaving his village.

6. Which of the following would be the best title for this passage?

   J. "Life in My Village"

   K. "My Journey into Manhood"

   L. "The Warrior Culture"

   M. "Money, Yams, and Manhood"

Questions 7–10 are based on the following passage.

Passage 2

Barrett had always dreamed of opening a photography studio. As soon as he finished photography school, he rented a small space in a strip mall just off the highway. For the first few years, he barely made ends meet. He took just enough photos to pay for rent and materials.

Line

5 Barrett knew his business was not going to be successful if he continued to do business the way he had since he opened his studio. He researched several business strategies before he made his decision. Barrett advertised a month-long special in the newspaper. He decided to reduce his standard pricing by one third for the entire month. He knew this was a calculated risk, but it was one he felt he had to take.

7. The phrase "made ends meet" is another way of saying which of the following?

   A. Opened the doors

   B. Took nice pictures

   C. Took care of customers

   D. Balanced the budget

8. If Barrett was struggling financially, why did he reduce his prices?

   J. He hoped to increase the number of customers.

   K. He was giving up.

   L. He was paying too many taxes.

   M. His research was faulty.

9. From the passage, we can infer that Barrett is

   A. lazy.

   B. unsuccessful.

   C. ambitious.

   D. not a good photographer.

10. Why is reducing his prices a risk?

   J. He might take just as many photos but make less money.

   K. He doesn't understand how business works.

   L. His rent and materials costs will go up.

   M. His research recommended against reducing prices.

Questions 11–16 are based on the following passage.

PASSAGE 3

History is full of "accidental inventions"—ingenious advances that were initially unintended but eventually served to benefit mankind in a variety of unique ways. Let's take a closer look at a few of these items, as well as their curious origins.

Line

5 Many of us take for granted having a microwave to cook and reheat food quickly. However, individuals were without this useful appliance until 1945, when an engineer named Percy Spencer accidentally cooked a chocolate bar in his pocket while tinkering with a magnetron for a radar-building project. This unexpected event led Spencer down an experimental path that ultimately resulted in the creation of the microwave oven.

Penicillin is an antibiotic used to treat a wide array of infections, and is widely considered
10 one of the most essential medications in the world today. But did you know that its discovery was due to a careless mistake by a scientist? In 1928, Alexander Fleming, a Scottish scientist, noticed a unique mold strain on a Petri dish that was mistakenly left open on a lab table; a mold strain that inhibited the growth of bacteria surrounding it. Rigorous scientific testing of the strange new mold followed, leading to one of the most significant scientific and medical
15 advances in history.

It's clear that scientific curiosity, when in the capable hands of an innovative thinker, can lead an individual down a path to greatness. But sometimes that path contains an unexpected detour, possibly due to a completely unforeseen mistake or accident, and the result changes history forever.

11. Based on the information in the passage, what do the microwave oven and penicillin have in common?

   A. Both the microwave and penicillin are essential inventions.

   B. Both required the work of professional inventors to create them.

   C. Both inventions are the direct result of an accident or mistake.

   D. Both would have eventually been invented, even if the accidents mentioned in the passage didn't occur.

12. As used in the passage, "an unexpected detour," most likely refers to

   J. a change in a driving route that leads to a new road.

   K. an unintended event leading to an innovation.

   L. an unlikely inventor who becomes famous.

   M. a world-changing invention that changes science.

13. As used in the passage, the word *inhibited* most likely means

   A. accelerated.

   B. shy.

   C. introverted.

   D. prevented.

14. All the following are accidental inventions *except*

   J. penicillin.

   K. the microwave.

   L. the Petri dish.

   M. All are accidental inventions.

15. Which of the following would be the best title for this passage?

   A. "Innovative Thinkers in Modern Science"

   B. "Happy Accidents"

   C. "Careless Mistakes"

   D. "Scientific Innovations of the 20th Century"

16. Which of the following is a lesson that we can learn from the passage?

   J. Be very careful when doing scientific research.

   K. Hide your mistakes.

   L. Don't be afraid to make mistakes.

   M. Every accident can change modern medicine.

Questions 17–22 are based on the following passage.

PASSAGE 4

With the increased use of e-mail and instant messaging, experts have struggled to make any substantial conclusions regarding the effects electronic communication has on computer users' social skills. Some experts in fields such as communications argue that e-mail and instant

Line messaging have increased the social skills of computer users because people now communicate

5 with each other more frequently than ever before. Others, however, maintain that computer users can hide behind their anonymity, thus allowing them to take on false personality traits and characteristics. Such experts further contend that the more communication takes place via e-mail and instant messaging, the less effective communication becomes in face-to-face settings. Experts on both sides of the debate do, however, agree that the frequency of communications

10 has increased since the advent of electronic correspondence, and that this alone should have some positive effect on the communication skills of computer users. After all, the adage says that practice makes perfect.

17. Which of the following would be the best title for the passage above?

   A. "The Problems with E-mail and Instant Messaging"

   B. "The Electronic Communications Revolution"

   C. "The Possible Effects of Electronic Communication on Communication Skills of Computer Users"

   D. "The Debate Over Instant Communications and Its Effects on E-mail"

18. The phrase "practice makes perfect" in the last sentence refers to which of the following?

   J. The increased frequency of electronic communication

   K. Public speaking engagements

   L. Practice with computer software

   M. Research conducted by experts in the field

19. How does anonymity decrease social skills?

   A. It prevents people from communicating at all.

   B. It lets people hide without working on their real-life communication skills.

   C. It means that people will grow mistrustful of everyone else.

   D. It decreases the frequency of communication.

20. Which of the following most affects electronic communication skills?

   J. Frequency of use

   K. E-mail

   L. Instant messaging

   M. Face-to-face conversation

21. Which of the following is seen as a drawback of electronic communication?

    A. Anonymity
    B. Bad grammar
    C. Bullying
    D. Forgetting how to talk face-to-face

22. As used in the passage, the word *adage* most likely means

    J. expert.
    K. dance.
    L. saying.
    M. book.

Questions 23–28 are based on the following passage.

PASSAGE 5

The reality TV craze that began bombarding viewers in the United States two decades ago apparently is here to stay, at least for several more years. Strangely, though, some people who watch reality TV still have not caught on to the fact that there is little to no reality in reality television
Line shows. Producers and directors often direct reality show stars to say particular things or act in
5 a particular manner. Filming stops frequently to re-shoot certain scenes or pieces of dialogue between cast members. People selected to be part of the reality show casts must sign contracts that require them to follow scores of rules. Furthermore, cast members cannot reveal any secrets of the show. The public, though, is still largely unaware of the many staged, contrived shows that are advertised as reality.

23. Which of the following is the main idea of the passage above?

    A. Reality shows are the most popular shows on TV.
    B. Reality shows lure watchers through fancy advertising slogans and cute stars.
    C. Reality TV consists of very little reality.
    D. Reality show cast members usually become big stars and famous celebrities.

24. The author of the passage above is most likely which of the following?

    J. A reality show winner
    K. A reality show producer
    L. A critic of reality TV
    M. An executive from a TV network

25. The author would most likely say that reality shows are

    A. authentic.
    B. deceptive.
    C. fleeting.
    D. fantastic.

26. All the following are evidence that reality shows are not real, *except*

    J. producers convince the stars to act a certain way.
    K. scenes are re-shot as necessary.
    L. stars are expected to keep details secret.
    M. shows are tightly scripted, not improvised.

27. Based on the passage, what do reality TV shows and regular TV shows most likely have in common?

    A. Cast members are sworn to secrecy.

    B. Both types of shows are staged.

    C. People expect both to be fake.

    D. Both types of shows are advertised as reality.

28. As used in the passage, the word *bombarding* most likely means

    J. shielding.

    K. flooding.

    L. attacking

    M. endangering.

Questions 29–36 are based on the following passage.

PASSAGE 6

While the Europeans were still creeping cautiously along their coasts, Polynesians were making trips between Hawaii and New Zealand, a distance of 3,800 miles, in frail canoes. These fearless sailors of the Pacific explored every island in their vast domain without even the simplest of navigational tools.

Line

5   In the daytime, the Polynesians guided their craft by the position of the sun, the trend of the waves and wind, and the flight of seabirds. At night, they used stars during long trips between island groups. Youths studying navigation learned to view the heavens as a cylinder on which the highways of navigation were marked. An invisible line bisected the sky from the North Star to the Southern Cross.

10   In addition to single canoes, the Polynesians often used twin canoes for transpacific voyages. The two boats were fastened together by canopied platforms that shielded passengers from sun and rain. Such crafts were remarkably seaworthy and could accommodate 60 to 80 people, in addition to water, food, and domestic animals. Some of these vessels had as many as three masts.

These Pacific *mariners* used paddles to propel and steer their canoes. The steering paddle

15   was so important that it was always given a personal name. Polynesian legends not only recite the names of the canoe and the hero who discovered a new island but also the name of the steering paddle he used.

29. Which title is best for this selection?

    A. "European Sailors"

    B. "The History of the Pacific Ocean"

    C. "The Study of Navigation"

    D. "Early Polynesian Navigation"

30. The Polynesians made trips to

    J. New Zealand.

    K. the Atlantic.

    L. the Southern Cross.

    M. Europe.

31. The word *mariner* means

    A. propeller.

    B. seaman.

    C. paddle.

    D. navigation.

32. This passage suggests that the Polynesians

    J. trained seabirds to guide their canoes.

    K. had seen a line in the sky that was invisible to others.

    L. used a primitive telescope to view the heavens.

    M. were astronomers as well as explorers.

33. The steering paddle was

    A. sometimes named after a Polynesian village.

    B. made from wood found floating in the ocean.

    C. always given a personal name.

    D. often replaced between journeys.

34. Of what use were dual canoes?

    J. They were primarily fishing vessels.

    K. They could carry passengers, food, and cargo.

    L. The chief and his family used them as leisure boats.

    M. They served as troop transport boats during times of war.

35. Based on the passage, we can infer that

    A. the Polynesians were skilled navigators.

    B. Polynesian canoes would often get lost on the Pacific Ocean.

    C. navigators could see invisible objects.

    D. they were afraid of traveling far from home.

36. What information do Polynesian legends state when referring to explorers?

    J. Route information, name of the Polynesian village, number of days

    K. Captain's log entries, weather, cargo brought home

    L. Name of the canoe, hero who discovered a new island, name of the steering paddle he used

    M. Type of wood used for the paddle, name of the paddle, name of the canoe

Questions 37–42 are based on the following passage.

PASSAGE 7

Was Phileas Fogg rich? Undoubtedly. But those who knew him best could not imagine how he had made his fortune, and Mr. Fogg was the last person to whom to apply for the information. He was not lavish, nor, on the contrary, avaricious; for, whenever he knew that money was needed

Line for a noble, useful, or benevolent purpose, he supplied it quietly and sometimes anonymously.

5 He was, in short, the least communicative of men. He talked very little, and seemed all the more mysterious for his taciturn manner. His daily habits were quite open to observation; but whatever he did was so exactly the same thing that he had always done before, that the wits of the curious were fairly puzzled.

Had he travelled? It was likely, for no one seemed to know the world more familiarly; there

10 was no spot so secluded that he did not appear to have an intimate acquaintance with it. He often corrected, with a few clear words, the thousand conjectures advanced by members of the club as to lost and unheard-of travellers, pointing out the true probabilities, and seeming as if gifted with a sort of second sight, so often did events justify his predictions. He must have travelled everywhere, at least in the spirit.

15 It was at least certain that Phileas Fogg had not absented himself from London for many years.

—Around the World in Eighty Days, by Jules Verne

37. As used in the passage, the word *avaricious* most likely means

A. generous.

B. wealthy.

C. stingy.

D. mean.

38. Phileas Fogg can best be described as

J. reserved.

K. unhappy.

L. sociable.

M. brave.

39. Based on the passage, which statement is true?

A. Phileas Fogg is secretive.

B. Phileas Fogg is knowledgeable about the world.

C. Phileas Fogg is a world traveler.

D. Phileas Fogg is unable to afford travel.

40. As used in the passage, the phrase *second sight* most likely means

J. psychic ability.

K. good eyesight.

L. intelligence.

M. experience.

41. The overall tone of the passage is

A. lighthearted.

B. somber.

C. critical.

D. harsh.

42. Based on the passage, we can infer that the author will be telling a story about

J. Phileas Fogg's wealth.

K. Phileas Fogg's friends.

L. Phileas Fogg's travels.

M. Phileas Fogg's reputation.

Questions 43–46 are based on the following passage.

PASSAGE 8

Up until the 1970s, the Brontosaurus was one of the most popular dinosaurs around, right alongside the Tyrannosaurus Rex. It was easily identified by its four legs, large cylindrical body, long neck, swooping tail, and small head. It even made it into pop culture, appearing in cartoons like *The Flintstones*. The Brontosaurus was one of the most prominent "thunder lizards." So what changed?

Line 5

It turns out the Brontosaurus may never have existed at all. Paleontologist O.C. Marsh was attempting to reconstruct an Apatosaurus skeleton in 1877, when he mistakenly attached the skull of a Camarasaurus to the Apatosaurus's body and believed he'd discovered a new dinosaur altogether—which he christened the Brontosaurus. Over the years, the Brontosaurus grew in popularity, but some paleontologists remained unconvinced. Eventually, the skull mistake was identified and corrected as a result of the work of paleontologists at the Carnegie Museum—and suddenly, the mighty Brontosaurus was no more.

10

43. Which of the following is the main idea of the passage?

A. Mistakes can create decades of "conventional wisdom" that eventually turn out to be untrue.

B. We don't know as much about dinosaurs as we think we do.

C. All dinosaur-related discoveries are suspect.

D. The Brontosaurus was very popular.

44. Who was most responsible for the myth of the Brontosaurus?

J. *The Flintstones*

K. Carnegie Museum

L. O.C. Marsh

M. none of these

45. A good title for this passage might be

A. "Finding the Apatosaurus."

B. "What Happened to the Brontosaurus?"

C. "Paleontology Today."

D. "Return of the Brontosaurus."

46. According to the passage, what kind of skull was attached to the wrong body?

J. Brontosaurus

K. Tyrannosaurus Rex

L. Camarasaurus

M. Apatosaurus

Questions 47–50 are based on the following passage.

PASSAGE 9

Tom presented himself before Aunt Polly, who was sitting by an open window in a pleasant rear-ward apartment, which was bedroom, breakfast-room, dining-room, and library, combined. The balmy summer air, the restful quiet, the odor of the flowers, and the drowsing murmur of the

Line bees had had their effect, and she was nodding over her knitting   for she had no company but

5   the cat, and it was asleep in her lap. Her spectacles were propped up on her gray head for safety. She had thought that of course Tom had deserted long ago, and she wondered at seeing him place himself in her power again in this intrepid way. He said: "Mayn't I go and play now, aunt?"

"What, a'ready? How much have you done?"

"It's all done, aunt."

10   "Tom, don't lie to me—I can't bear it."

"I ain't, aunt; it is all done."

Aunt Polly placed small trust in such evidence. She went out to see for herself; and she would have been content to find twenty percent of Tom's statement true. When she found the entire fence whitewashed, and not only whitewashed but elaborately coated and recoated, and even a

15   streak added to the ground, her astonishment was almost unspeakable.

—from *The Adventures of Tom Sawyer*, by Mark Twain

47. As used in the passage, the word *balmy* most likely means

A. chilly.

B. chaotic.

C. hostile.

D. pleasant.

48. What has Aunt Polly asked Tom to do?

J. Clean the house

K. Go outside

L. Help with knitting

M. Paint the fence

49. From the passage it is clear that

A. Aunt Polly trusts Tom.

B. Aunt Polly does not believe Tom.

C. Tom always does what he's asked.

D. Tom enjoys painting.

50. In the phrase "such evidence," the author is conveying what tone?

J. Sarcastic

K. Optimistic

L. Angry

M. Excited

STOP.

If you finish before time is up, you may check your work on this section only.

Do not turn to any other section in the test.

WRITTEN EXPRESSION

50 Questions (30 minutes)

Turn to the Written Expression section of your answer sheet to answer the questions in this section.

Directions: This is a test of how well you can find mistakes in writing.

- For the questions with mistakes in spelling, capitalization, and punctuation, choose the answer with the same letter as the line containing the mistake.

- For the questions with mistakes in usage and expression, choose the answer with the same letter as the line containing the mistake, or choose the word, phrase, or sentence that is better than the others.

- When there is no mistake or no change needed, select the last answer choice.

---

1. **A.** dictionery
   B. tragic
   C. vintage
   D. surprise
   E. *(No mistakes)*

2. **J.** vacation
   K. discovery
   L. collide
   M. patience
   N. *(No mistakes)*

3. **A.** fortress
   B. obtane
   C. complete
   D. interview
   E. *(No mistakes)*

4. **J.** invention
   K. coffee
   L. perswade
   M. employer
   N. *(No mistakes)*

5. **A.** disscuss
   B. manager
   C. exam
   D. advisory
   E. *(No mistakes)*

6. **J.** fortune
   K. traffic
   L. intrude
   M. messinger
   N. *(No mistakes)*

7. **A.** referee
   B. amature
   C. against
   D. believe
   E. *(No mistakes)*

8. **J.** cancellashun
   K. invest
   L. remark
   M. mall
   N. *(No mistakes)*

9. A. wander

B. mygrate

C. functional

D. disappear

E. *(No mistakes)*

10. J. mountain

K. progress

L. batter

M. profit

N. *(No mistakes)*

11. A. Jamey is going to College

B. at Outback University, which

C. is located in Australia.

D. *(No mistakes)*

12. J. The Mississippi river travels southward

K. toward the Gulf of Mexico

L. and passes many states along the way.

M. *(No mistakes)*

13. A. Jovan couldn't wait to have lunch

B. at the new Chinese Restaurant

C. on the corner of Ridge Street and Dey Road.

D. *(No mistakes)*

14. J. We're planning a nice dinner at the steak restaurant

K. to celebrate valentine's day; we're planning to watch

L. the movie *Shrek* after dinner.

M. *(No mistakes)*

15. A. You just can't beat a cold drink

B. or a few scoops of Ben and Jerry's

C. on a scorching-hot Summer day.

D. *(No mistakes)*

16. J. Mrs. Samson said that Archie,

K. her sister's third cousin, used to

L. live across the street from Taylor Swift.

M. *(No mistakes)*

17. A. The astronauts aboard the Apollo rocket

B. said that the moon looked much different in Space

C. than it did from on the ground.

D. *(No mistakes)*

18. J. He's so smart because he reads *Time* magazine

K. and the Newspaper in the morning

L. before he even gets to school.

M. *(No mistakes)*

19. A. She accompanied her mother

B. on a visit to father O'Reilly to

C. thank him for visiting her brother in the hospital.

D. *(No mistakes)*

20. J. The Dirt Road that wound through the woods

K. was just a few miles from Interstate 95,

L. which led to many major eastern cities.

M. *(No mistakes)*

Practice Test 2: TACHS

Directions: For questions 21 and 22, choose the best way of expressing the idea.

21. A. Eldridge liked to tinker in his workshop and often came up with new product ideas.

B. Eldridge, who liked to tinker in his workshop; he often came up with new product ideas.

C. In his workshop, Eldridge liked to tinker, where he often came up with new product ideas.

D. Often coming up with new product ideas, Eldridge liked to tinker in his workshop where he was.

22. J. The Garmin's house, their summer house in Maine, was built all month with a new bedroom by the carpenter.

K. In Maine, a summer house of the Garmin's, the carpenter spent all month building it—a new bedroom.

L. The carpenter spent all month building a new bedroom for the Garmins' summer house in Maine.

M. A summer house, which is the Garmin's, had a new bedroom built onto it by the carpenter, who spent all month building it.

Directions: For questions 23–50, choose the best answer based on the following paragraphs.

(1) Among the many scenic and storied lighthouses that still exist across the United States, there's one that stands above the rest—literally. (2) Cape Hatteras Lighthouse is America's tallest lighthouse, a 210-foot striped beacon to sailors and their sea vessels <u>since they were</u> first constructed in 1870. (3) It's located in a town called Buxton, on Hatteras Island—one of several islands that make up the Outer Banks along the coast of North Carolina. (4) <u>Obviously</u>, the current Cape Hatteras lighthouse is not the original; the original lighthouse was destroyed in 1862, during the Civil War. (5) Although the Cape Hatteras Lighthouse is the tallest in America, it currently ranks only 29th tallest in the world—it's dwarfed by the mammoth 436-foot Jeddah Lighthouse in Saudi Arabia.

23. What is the best way to write the underlined part of sentence 2?

A. when she was

B. when he were

C. since it was

D. *(No change)*

24. What is the best way to write the underlined part of sentence 4?

J. Therefore,

K. Interestingly,

L. In contrast,

M. *(No change)*

(1) Like many Impressionist painters working in France during the mid-to-late 19th century, Edgar Degas attempted to capture a fleeting moment in time on canvas. (2) Defined as an artistic movement in which painters tried to recreate the changing light and colors of a particular place and time, Impressionism featured heavy dabs of color painted with <u>bold, swift</u> strokes and subject matter rooted in nature. (3) Instead of painting the garden parties and floral landscapes embraced by his contemporaries, Degas preferred to paint a wide spectrum of human subjects. (4) Although best known for his depiction of <u>dancers especially</u> behind-the-scenes glimpses of ballerinas rehearsing or warming up backstage, he also painted everyday scenes of working-class Parisian life at racetracks and cafes.

25. What is the best way to write the underlined part of sentence 2?

A. bold swift

B. bold; swift

C. bold, Swift

D. *(No change)*

26. What is the best way to write the underlined part of sentence 4?

J. dancers. Especially

K. dancers, especially

L. dancers: especially

M. *(No change)*

(1) When we think of the fastest members of the animal kingdom, mammals often come to mind. (2) <u>Indeed,</u> cheetahs can sprint at over 70 mph, and greyhounds have been clocked at 46 mph. (3) A more unlikely candidate, however, claims the title of the fastest creature on the <u>Planet</u>—the peregrine falcon. (4) After soaring high above its prey, the peregrine falcon plunges into a hunting dive with ever-increasing velocity and speeds topping 200 mph. (5) Known as the *stoop*, this dizzying maneuver not only makes the peregrine falcon a highly effective predator, but also allows this bird of prey to attain record speeds during its free-falling descent.

27. What is the best way to write the underlined part of sentence 2?

A. Nonetheless,

B. Conversely,

C. Subsequently,

D. *(No change)*

28. What is the best way to write the underlined part of sentence 3?

J. Galaxy

K. planet

L. Hemisphere

M. *(No change)*

(1) Described as the most famous diamond in the world, the Hope Diamond is housed in the <u>Smithsonian Natural History museum</u> in Washington, DC (2) The Hope Diamond was formed about 1.1 billion years ago and was first discovered in India during the seventeenth century. (3) Pear-shaped and uncommonly large, the diamond is the size of a walnut with a brilliant, deep-blue color attributed to traces of boron found within its crystal structure. (4) Since its founding, the diamond has frequently changed hands as it traveled from India to France and Britain before reaching its final destination in the United States. (5) Legends of a supposed curse on those who have worn or owned the Hope Diamond <u>abound</u>, but these stories of troubles and misfortune have never been proven.

29. What is the best way to write the underlined part of sentence 1?

A. Smithsonian Natural History Museum

B. Smithsonian natural history museum

C. smithsonian natural history museum

D. (*No change*)

30. What is the best way to write the underlined part of sentence 5?

J. abounds

K. abounded

L. a bound

M. (*No change*)

(1) There are few more economically challenging events in American history than the Great Depression. (2) The Great Depression, which followed the stock market crash of 1929 and lasted until 1941, adversely affected the entire global economy. (3) Million's of people lost their jobs and livelihoods as a result of the Great Depression, and thousands of banks and tens of thousands of business failed during this time period. (4) It is estimated that the national Unemployment Rate in the United States rose to 25% or more, depending on analytical metrics used. (5) No demographic group was spared from this crisis—rich and poor, urban and rural dwellers, and young and old were all hit hard by this tragic event.

31. What is the best way to write the underlined portion of sentence 3?

A. Millions

B. millions

C. Millions'

D. (*No change*)

32. What is the best way to write the underlined portion of sentence 4?

J. Unemployment rate

K. unemployment rate

L. unemployment Rate

M. (*No change*)

(1) Few treats are as beloved among individuals both young and old as s'mores. (2) This popular and delicious snack, often made around campfires, typically consists of marshmallow and chocolate sandwiched between two graham crackers. (3) To make a classic s'more, the marshmallow; is heated over a fire and smashed against the chocolate covered graham cracker, and the chocolate melts from the heat of the marshmallow. (4) Once the other graham cracker is placed over the marshmallow and chocolate this gooey treat is ready to enjoy. (5) There's even a nationally recognized "National S'Mores Day."

33. What is the best way to write the underlined portion of sentence 3?

A. marshmallow. Is heated

B. marshmallow is heated

C. marshmallow is, heated

D. (*No change*)

34. Choose the best final sentence to add to this paragraph.

J. My favorite snack is popcorn covered in lots of melted butter.

K. Some people prefer eating trail mix when camping.

L. The commemorative day occurs on August 10th of each year.

M. Do you enjoy campfires?

(1) A visit to <u>new york city</u> would not be complete without a visit to Central Park. (2) This sprawling oasis in the heart of the Big Apple consists of approximately 843 acres of <u>lawns, lakes, trees, and walkways.</u> (3) The initial designs for the current incarnation of Central Park was conceptualized by famed landscape architect Frederick Law Olmstead. (4) Did you know that Central Park is the most visited park in the United States? (5) The park receives approximately 40 million visitors each year, and individuals from all over the world flock to the park to check out its beauty.

35. What is the best way to write the underlined portion of sentence 1?

   A. New York city

   B. New York City

   C. New york city

   D. (*No change*)

36. What is the best way to write the underlined portion of sentence 2?

   J. lawns lakes. Trees and walkways

   K. lawns lakes trees and walkways

   L. lawns; lakes trees; and walkways

   M. (*No change*)

(1) Plenty of time and attention is given to the largest and most impressive bodies of water on Earth, including the major oceans and Great Lakes. (2) However, have you ever heard of Roe River? (3) Roe River, which runs between the Missouri River and Giant Springs in Great Falls, Montana, is recognized by the <u>(Guinness Book of World Records)</u> as the world's shortest river. (4) Roe River is a humble 201 feet at its longest constant point, and ranges approximately 6-8 feet in depth. (5) In contrast, the <u>shortest</u> river in the world is the Amazon River, which runs for a staggering 4,345 miles.

37. What is the best way to write the underlined portion of sentence 3?

   A. *Guinness Book of World Records*

   B. "Guinness Book of World Records"

   C. Guinness Book of World Records

   D. (*No change*)

38. What is the best way to write the underlined portion of sentence 5?

   J. coldest

   K. ugliest

   L. longest

   M. (*No change*)

(1) Root beer, a popular and tasty North American beverage, has an interesting history. (2) This soft drink, which <u>will be traditionally made</u> using the root of the sassafras tree for years, was actually used for medicinal purposes by indigenous Native American people. (3) Following the Food and Drug Administration (FDA) ban of sassafras in commercial food and beverage products in 1960, many root beers started to be made using artificial flavoring. (4) Today, there is a wide variety of commercially available variants of root beer, and it is now produced in every state in <u>America?</u> (5) Although its origins can be traced to North America, where root beer's popularity is greatest, root beer is currently produced and sold in countries throughout Europe and Asia.

39. What is the best way to write the underlined portion of sentence 2?

A. have being traditionally making

B. is being traditionally make

C. has traditionally been made

D. (*No change*)

40. What is the best way to write the underlined portion of sentence 4?

J. America.

K. America;

L. America

M. (*No change*)

(1) It's a sad truth of history that collectively we often learn from mistakes. (2) The issues of worker safety <u>besides</u> employer accountability came under focus following the experience of the "Radium Girls." (3) The Radium Girls were a group of female <u>factory worker</u> who were tasked with painting watch dials in the early 20th century. (4) Although they were originally told that the paint was completely harmless, it actually contained deadly amounts of radium. (5) The incident helped to advance the labor rights movement, and in the wake of the unfortunate event industrial safety standards across the nation were improved.

41. What is the best way to write the underlined portion of sentence 2?

A. and

B. or

C. within

D. (*No change*)

42. What is the best way to write the underlined portion of sentence 3?

J. factory work

K. factory workers

L. factory working

M. (*No change*)

(1) One of the <u>worlds</u> most popular and widely played board games is also one of the oldest in existence. (2) Backgammon is a game played by two opponents in which pieces are moved based on dice rolls and the winner is the player who is able to remove all of his or her pieces from the board first, (3) The precise origin of the game is difficult to ascertain, but research suggests that versions of the game have existed for at least 5,000 years, stemming back to ancient Persia. (4) Today, scientists <u>is investigating</u> the implementation of computer software and artificial intelligence to challenge the best human players at the game.

43. What is the best way to write the underlined portion of sentence 1?

A. worlds'

B. World's

C. world's

D. (*No change*)

44. What is the best way to write the underlined portion of sentence 4?

J. are investigating

K. they're investigating

L. won't investigate

M. (*No change*)

(1) Harvard University, in Cambridge Massachusetts, <u>was established</u> in 1636, and originally primarily served to train clergymen. (2) The university is named after John Harvard, an English minister and one of the original benefactors of the university. (3) Each year, tens of thousands of elite students study and train across the university's eleven separate academic units. (4) Among Harvard's illustrious graduates are eight US presidents, more than 100 Nobel laureates, and several billionaires.

45. Choose the best first sentence to add to this paragraph.

A. Where do you plan to go to college after you graduate from high school?

B. Did you know that one of the most prestigious universities in the United States is also the oldest?

C. What are some good reasons for deciding to earn a college degree?

D. Do you live close to Cambridge Massachusetts, in the northeastern region of the United States?

46. What is the best way to write the underlined portion of sentence 1?

J. will be established

K. will establish

L. will be establishing

M. (*No change*)

(1) People all around the world enjoy eating garlic. (2) It's a popular addition to <u>sauces, soups; and stews,</u> and its flavor and aroma is unmistakable for any other food. (3) However, did you know that eating garlic also has a variety of health <u>benefits!</u> (4) It has been argued that regularly consuming garlic as part of a healthy diet can combat illnesses like colds and the flu, and can even reduce the risk of heart disease. (5) Garlic also contains a wealth of vitamins and nutrients including vitamin C, vitamin B6, selenium, and fiber.

47. What is the best way to write the underlined portion of sentence 2?

A. sauces; soups and stews

B. sauces. Soups and stews

C. sauces, soups, and stews

D. (*No change*)

48. What is the best way to write the underlined portion of sentence 3?

J. benefits;

K. benefits.

L. benefits?

M. (*No change*)

(1) One of the most famous obelisks in the world is the <u>Washington monument,</u> located at the National Mall in Washington, DC. (2) An obelisk is a towering, four-sided narrow monument that tapers as it rises and is topped with a pyramid-like structure. (3) The Washington Monument stands approximately 554 feet tall and is comprised of marble, bluestone gneiss, and granite. (4) It's currently the <u>world's; tallest,</u> obelisk and stone structure, and was built to commemorate George Washington, the first President of the United States. (5) However, it's not the world's oldest obelisk, as examples from Ancient Egypt are still standing tall.

49. What is the best way to write the underlined portion of sentence 1?

A. Washington Monument

B. washington monument

C. "Washington Monument"

D. (*No change*)

50. What is the best way to write the underlined portion of sentence 4?

J. world's, tallest

K. world's tallest

L. world's tallest;

M. (*No change*)

STOP.

If you finish before time is up, you may check your work on this section only.
Do not turn to any other section in the test.

MATHEMATICS

50 Questions (40 minutes)

Turn to the Mathematics section of your answer sheet to answer the questions in this section.

Directions: Read each question carefully, then solve the problem to find the correct answer.

---

1. The number 0.003 can also be represented by which of the following?

   A. $\dfrac{3}{10,000}$

   B. $\dfrac{3}{1,000}$

   C. $\dfrac{3}{100}$

   D. $\dfrac{3}{10}$

2. Which of the following is the equivalent of 3^3?

   J. 3×3

   K. $3 \times 3 \div 3$

   L. 27

   M. 30

3. What is the sum of $\dfrac{1}{2} + \dfrac{2}{4} + \dfrac{3}{3}$?

   A. 1

   B. 2

   C. $2\dfrac{1}{2}$

   D. 3

4. What is the sum of $(3 \times 3) + (4 \times 4) + (5 \times 5)$?

   J. 24

   K. 50

   L. 60

   M. 345

5. Which of the following represents the reduced form for 1.6?

   A. $1\dfrac{6}{10}$

   B. $1\dfrac{3}{5}$

   C. $\dfrac{16}{10}$

   D. $\dfrac{32}{20}$

6. Which of the following is a prime number?

   J. 27

   K. 28

   L. 29

   M. 30

7. The fraction $\dfrac{8}{4}$ can be reduced to which of the following?

   A. 84

   B. $\dfrac{1}{2}$

   C. $\dfrac{4}{8}$

   D. 2

8. Which of the following is the product of 16 and 4?

   J. 2

   K. 4

   L. 20

   M. 64

9. Which of the following is the equivalent of 6^7?

   A. 6×7

   B. $7 \times 6 \times 6 \times 6 \times 6 \times 6 \times 6$

   C. $6 \times 6 \times 6 \times 6 \times 6 \times 6 \times 6$

   D. $(6 + 6) \times 7$

10. The fraction $2\dfrac{6}{1,000}$ can be expressed as a decimal by which of the following?

   J. 0.0026

   K. 2.006

   L. 26.1000

   M. 26,000.000

11. An accountant's fee for preparing a tax report for a customer is 40% more than his closest competitor. If the competitor charges $300, what is this accountant's fee?

   A. $360

   B. $400

   C. $420

   D. $500

12. Carl has collected 27 of the 32 available Captain Cosmos comic books, 19 of the 24 available Galactic General comic books, and 21 of the 23 available Larry the Laser comic books. If Carl wanted to acquire the missing comics from each series he collects, how many comic books would he need to buy?

   J. 7

   K. 67

   L. 79

   M. Not given

13. The school library recently relocated to a new building on campus. There are many new bookshelves in the new library. Each bookshelf holds 245 books. The library has 12 bookshelves that are 100 percent full and one bookshelf that is $\dfrac{4}{5}$ full. How many books are in the new library?

   A. 2,940

   B. 2,989

   C. 3,136

   D. 294,000

14. Paul's digital camera normally holds 200 images. If Paul sets his camera to take extra-high-quality pictures, his camera holds only 40 pictures. Paul has already saved 100 normal images on his camera, but he wants to take as many pictures as possible of the sunset over the bay. How many extra-high-quality pictures can Paul hold on his camera in addition to the 100 normal images he's already saved?

   J. 10

   K. 20

   L. 30

   M. 40

15. If Paige spends $3\dfrac{1}{4}$ hours per day practicing piano and she practices 4 days per week, how many hours does Paige practice piano each week?

   A. $12\dfrac{1}{4}$

   B. $12\dfrac{3}{4}$

   C. 13

   D. 14

16. A centimeter is what part of a kilometer?

J. $\dfrac{1}{100,000}$

K. $\dfrac{1}{10,000}$

L. $\dfrac{1}{1,000}$

M. $\dfrac{1}{100}$

17. Find the area of a rectangle with a length of 176 feet and a width of 79 feet.

A. 13,304 sq. ft.

B. 13,804 sq. ft.

C. 13,854 sq. ft.

D. 13,904 sq. ft.

18. Mr. Lawson makes a weekly salary of $250 plus 7% commission on his sales. What will his income be for a week in which he made sales totaling $1,250?

J. $87.50

K. $267.50

L. $327.50

M. $337.50

19. Complete the following statement:
$3(\underline{\hspace{1cm}} \times 4) - 20 = 280$.

A. 5

B. 5×2

C. 5^2

D. 5^3

20. Find the area of a triangle whose dimensions are: $b = 14$ inches, $h = 20$ inches.

J. 140 sq. in.

K. 208 sq. in.

L. 280 sq. in.

M. 288 sq. in.

Directions: For questions 21–40, read each problem and find the answer.

---

21. If $x = 2\dfrac{2}{5}$, the reciprocal of x equals

A. $\dfrac{5}{12}$

B. $\dfrac{5}{4}$

C. $\dfrac{12}{5}$

D. $\dfrac{5}{2}$

22. The product of $\dfrac{7}{16}$ and a number x is 1. The number is

J. 1

K. $1\dfrac{7}{16}$

L. $\dfrac{16}{7}$

M. $\dfrac{31}{14}$

23. $\dfrac{\dfrac{1}{x}+1}{1+\dfrac{1}{x}}$ is equivalent to

   A. 1

   B. $\dfrac{1}{x}$

   C. $\dfrac{1}{x}+2$

   D. $1+x$

24. $\dfrac{\dfrac{5}{12}-\dfrac{7}{24}}{\dfrac{1}{2}-\dfrac{3}{8}} =$

   J. $\dfrac{1}{2}$

   K. $\dfrac{3}{8}$

   L. 1

   M. 8

25. In the formula $L = \dfrac{3}{4}bxh$, if $b = 2$, $x = 7$, and $h = \dfrac{1}{2}$, L equals

   A. $\dfrac{21}{8}$

   B. $\dfrac{21}{4}$

   C. $\dfrac{21}{2}$

   D. $\dfrac{7x}{4}$

26.

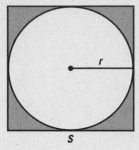

The square above has a side 4" long. The area of the shaded portion is approximately

   J. $\dfrac{22}{7}$ sq. in.

   K. $3\dfrac{3}{7}$ sq. in.

   L. $4\dfrac{3}{7}$ sq. in.

   M. 16 sq. in.

27. The ratio of teachers to students in a certain school is 1:14. If there are fourteen teachers in the school, how many students are there?

   A. 14

   B. 176

   C. 196

   D. 206

28. Evaluate $\dfrac{10^4}{100^5}$.

   J. $\dfrac{1}{10}$

   K. $\dfrac{1}{1,000}$

   L. $\dfrac{1}{100,000}$

   M. $\dfrac{1}{1,000,000}$

29. If x is an odd whole number, which of the following also represents an odd number?

   A. $2x+1$

   B. $x-2$

   C. $4x-3$

   D. All of the above

Practice Test 2: TACHS

30. The sum of 4 hours 17 minutes, 3 hours 58 minutes, 45 minutes, and 7 hours 12 minutes is

    J. 14 hours, 50 minutes

    K. 15 hours, 32 minutes

    L. 16 hours, 12 minutes

    M. 17 hours, 32 minutes

31. If every car that travels along Highway 27 has four wheels, and there are 72 cars driving on Highway 27, how many wheels are touching the road on Highway 27?

    A. 54

    B. 108

    C. 144

    D. 288

32. Ted can text 30 characters in 10 seconds. How many characters can Ted text in 2 minutes?

    J. 300

    K. 360

    L. 600

    M. 3,600

33. Aunt Ethel has 7 dozen antique ornaments for her Christmas tree. She anticipates needing a total of 200 ornaments to finish decorating her tree. How many ornaments should Aunt Ethel purchase at the antique fair to reach her goal of 200 antique ornaments for her tree?

    A. 84

    B. 96

    C. 116

    D. 124

34. Mandie and Mary Beth are planning to paint the concession stand at school. They have four walls to paint. Each wall is exactly the same size. The walls are each 12 feet long and 10 feet high. How many square feet of walls should they plan to paint if they are going to paint all four walls?

    J. 120 sq. ft.

    K. 240 sq. ft.

    L. 480 sq. ft.

    M. 1,200 sq. ft.

35. The penguins at the zoo eat 36,500 pounds of fish each year. How many pounds of fish do the penguins eat each day?

    A. 100

    B. 365

    C. 1,000

    D. Not given

Practice Test 2: TACHS

Use the following chart for Questions 36 and 37:

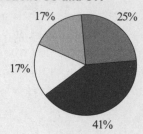

17%   25%

17%

41%

- ■ Cream Filled
- ■ Glazed
- □ Chocolate
- ▨ Jelly Filled

36. At Doodle's Donuts, the most popular item on the menu is Doodle's Dozen. The chart shows the typical distribution of donuts in each Doodle's Dozen that is sold. According to the chart, the single most widely consumed donut in Doodle's Dozen is which of the following?

   J. Cream Filled

   K. Glazed

   L. Chocolate

   M. Jelly Filled

37. Based on the information in the chart, Doodle's Dozen includes three of which type of donut?

   A. Cream Filled

   B. Glazed

   C. Chocolate

   D. Jelly Filled

Use the following graph for Questions 38 and 39:

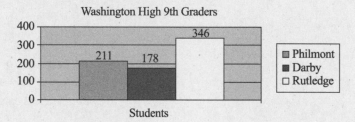

Washington High 9th Graders

400
300
200
100
0

211   178   346

Students

- ■ Philmont
- ■ Darby
- □ Rutledge

38. The chart above shows the feeder schools from which current ninth-graders at Washington High School came. If these are the only feeder schools that sent students to the ninth grade at Washington High School, which school sent the largest percentage of current Washington ninth-graders?

   J. Philmont

   K. Darby

   L. Rutledge

   M. Not given

39. Based on the information in the chart above, Washington High School currently has how many ninth-graders?

   A. 178

   B. 211

   C. 346

   D. 735

40. The pie chart below illustrates the number and types of portraits at the Hudson Museum. Based on the information in the chart, which of the following is true of the number of portraits in the museum?

The Hudson Museum Portraits

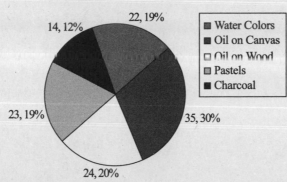

■ Water Colors
■ Oil on Canvas
□ Oil on Wood
□ Pastels
■ Charcoal

J. There are fewer than 100 portraits.

K. There are 100 portraits.

L. There are more than 100 portraits.

M. Not given

Directions: For the following questions, <u>estimate</u> the answer in your head. No scratch work is allowed. Do NOT try to compute exact answers.

---

41. The closest estimate of 46,922 + 32,090 is _____.

A. 70,000

B. 75,000

C. 80,000

D. 85,000

42. The closest estimate of 7,988 ÷ 397 is _____.

J. 20

K. 25

L. 200

M. 220

43. Rick decides to skate along the boardwalk at the local beach. He can skate at 6 miles per hour. If the boardwalk is 15 miles long, how long did it take him to complete the trip?

A. 90 minutes

B. 120 minutes

C. 150 minutes

D. 180 minutes

44. Coach Hollingsworth has a total of 653 wins in her career, and she has coached for 40 years. About how many wins has she averaged per year?

J. 13

K. 16

L. 19

M. 24

Practice Test 2: TACHS

45. The closest estimate of $148 + 153.5 + 146 + 154.1 + 151 + 145.9 + 149 + 153 + 152.5 + 147.75$ is _____ .

A. 1,375

B. 1,400

C. 1,500

D. 1,575

46. $\frac{17}{30}$ is greater than

J. $\frac{7}{8}$

K. $\frac{9}{20}$

L. $\frac{9}{11}$

M. $\frac{22}{25}$

47. One millimeter equals what part of a meter?

A. $\frac{1}{100}$

B. $\frac{1}{1,000}$

C. $\frac{1}{10,000}$

D. $\frac{1}{100,000}$

48. A baseball team won 18 games, which was 40% of its season. How many games did the team lose?

J. 25

K. 27

L. 32

M. 45

49. If $-2 < q < -1$, which of the following is true?

A. $q =$

B. $q > -1$

C. $q > 0$

D. $q > -2$

50. Which pair of values for x and $\square$ will make the following statement true?

$$2x \ \square \ 8$$

J. $(-3, >)$

K. $(0, <)$

L. $(4, >)$

M. $(6, <)$

STOP.

If you finish before time is up, you may check your work on this section only.
Do not turn to any other section in the test.

ABILITY

50 Questions (32 minutes)

Figure Classification

Turn to the Ability section of your answer sheet to answer the questions in this section.

Directions: In questions 1–20, the first three figures are alike in certain ways. Choose the answer choice that corresponds to the first three figures.

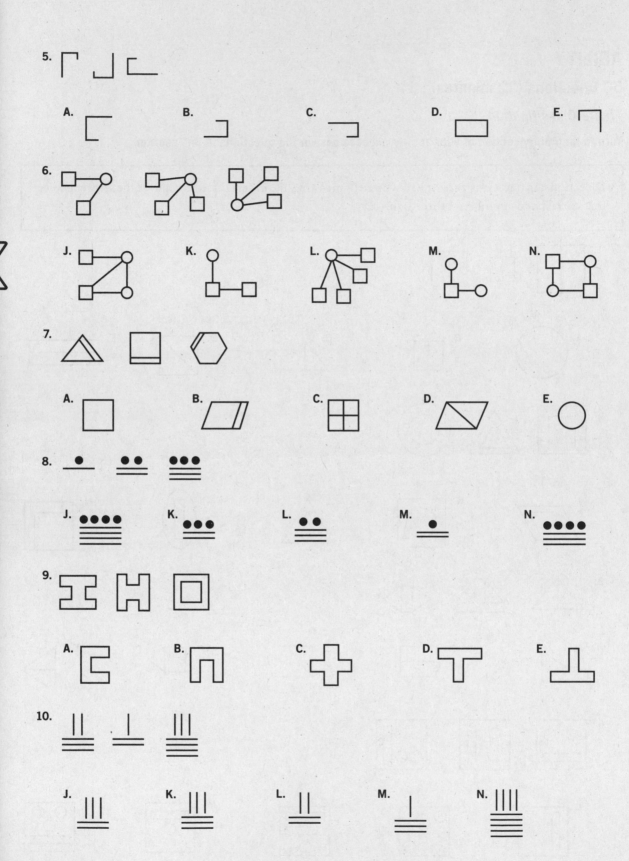

11.

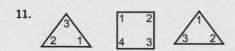

A.   B.   C.   D.   E.

12.

J.   K.   L.   M.   N.

13.

A.    B.   C.   D.    E.

14.

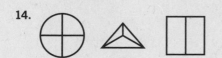

J.   K.   L.   M.   N.

15.

A.   B.   C.   D.   E.

16.

J.   K.   L.   M.   N.

17.

A.   B.   C.   D.   E.

18. ...

J. 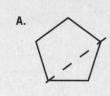   K.   L.   M.   N.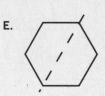

19.

A.   B.   C.   D.   E.

20.

J.   K.   L. 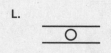   M.   N.

www.petersons.com

Figure Matrices

Directions: In questions 1–20, find the figure that completes the matrix.

1.

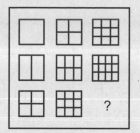

A.   B. ⊞   C. ⊞   D. ⊞   E. ⊞

2.

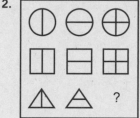

J. ⊞   K. ◁   L. △   M. ⊕   N. △

3.

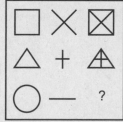

A. △   B. ▭   C. ⊗   D. ⊕   E. ⊖

Practice Test 2: TACHS

4.

?

J.   **K.**   **L.**   **M.**   **N.**

5.

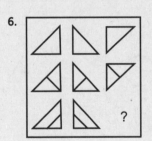

?

A. ← **B.** ↓ **C.** ↑ **D.** → **E.** ↗

6.

?

J. **K.** **L.** **M.** **N.**

7.

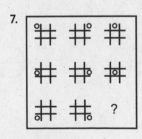

?

A. **B.** **C.** **D.** **E.**

Practice Test 2: TACHS

8.

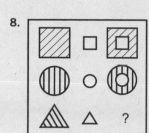

J.   K.   L.   M.   N.

9.

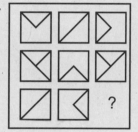

A.   B.   C.   D.   E.

10.

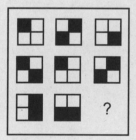

J.   K.   L.   M.   N.

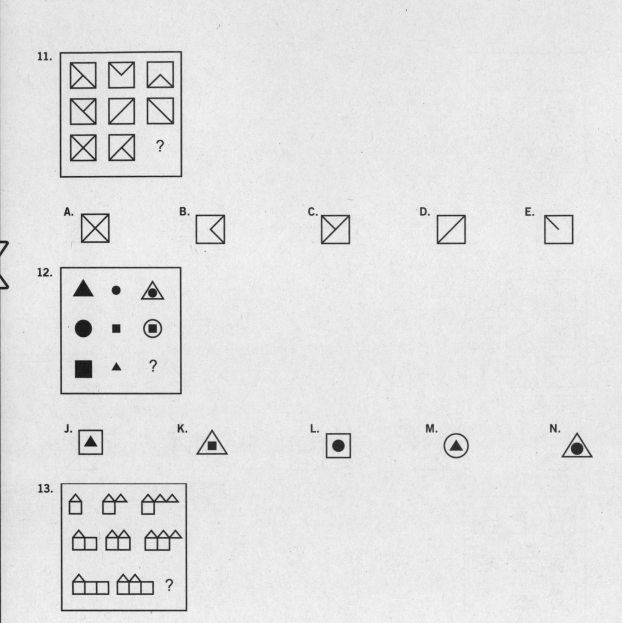

11.

A. B. C. D. E.

12.

J. K. L. M. N.

13.

A. B. C. D. E.

14.

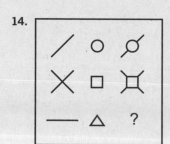

J.   K.   L.   M.   N.

15.

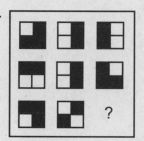

A.   B.   C.   D.   E.

16.

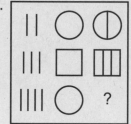

J.   K.   L.   M.   N.

Practice Test 2: TACHS

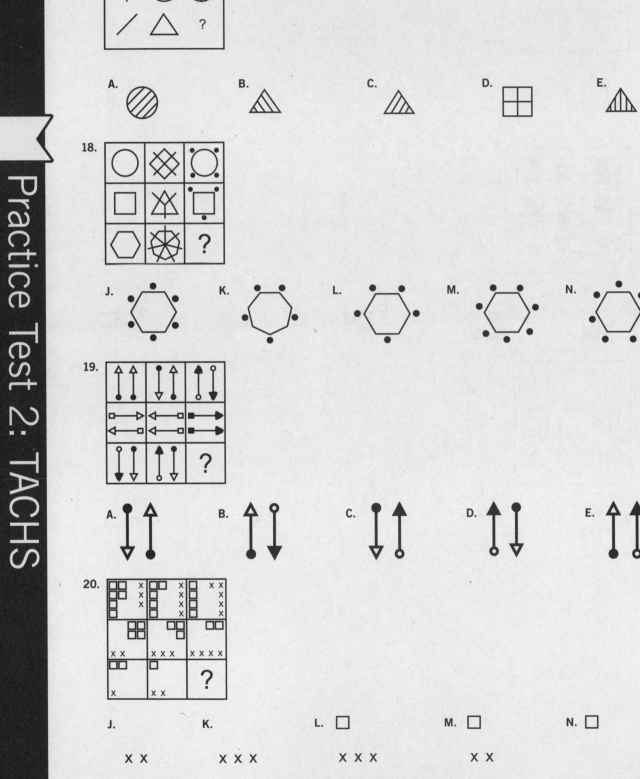

17.

A.

B.

C.

D.

E.

18.

J.

K.

L.

M.

N.

19.

A.

B.

C.

D.

E.

20.

J.

K.

L.

M.

N.

X X

X X X

X X X

X X

Practice Test 2: TACHS

Paper Folding

Directions: In questions 1–10, look at the top row to see how a square piece of paper is folded and where holes are punched into it. Then look at the bottom row to decide which answer choice shows how the paper will look when it is completely unfolded.

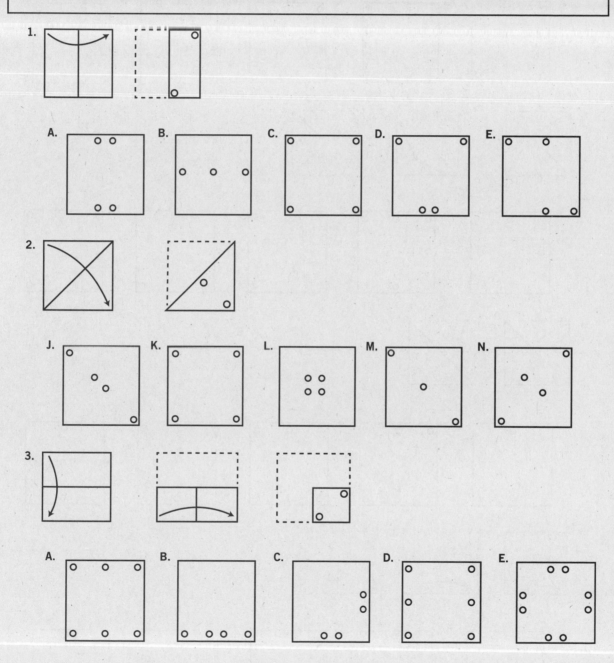

Practice Test 2: TACHS

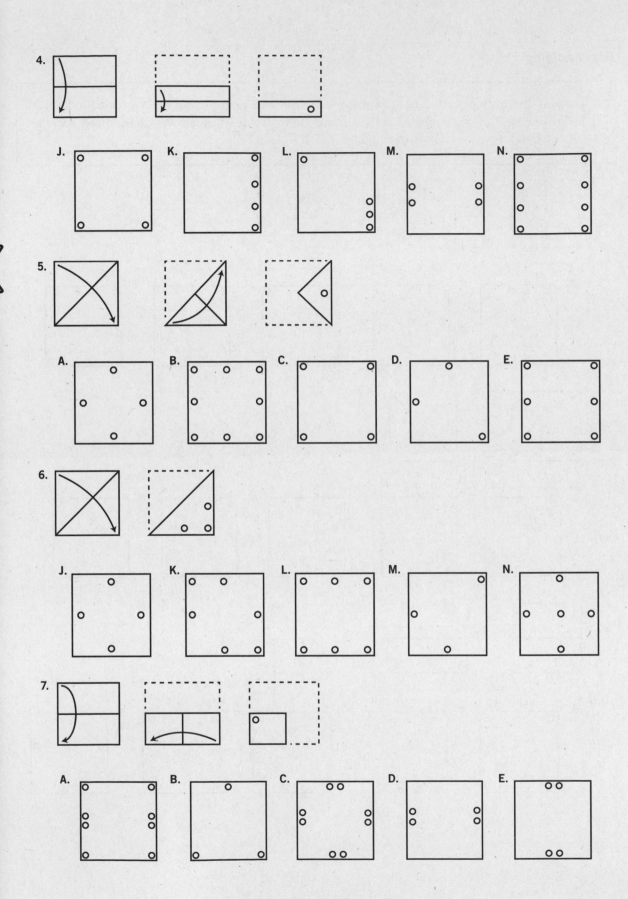

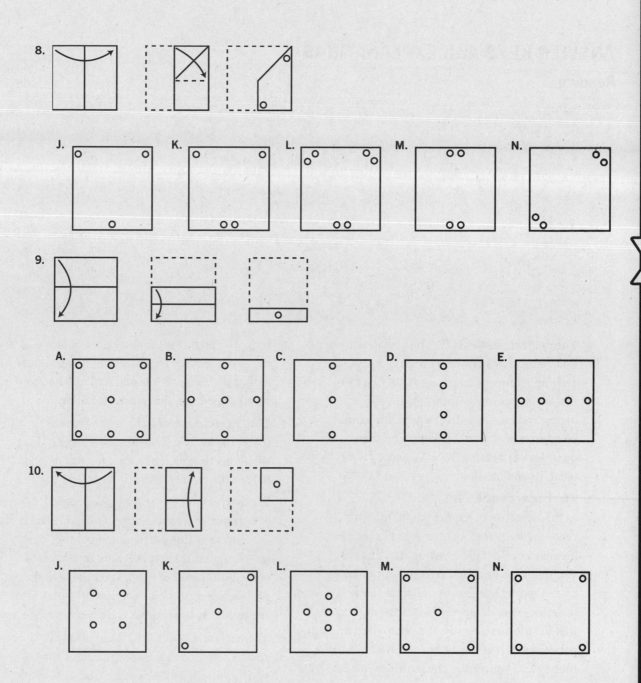

Practice Test 2: TACHS

ANSWER KEYS AND EXPLANATIONS

Reading

1. C	11. C	21. A	31. B	41. A
2. L	12. K	22. L	32. M	42. L
3. B	13. D	23. C	33. C	43. A
4. L	14. L	24. L	34. K	44. L
5. A	15. B	25. B	35. A	45. B
6. K	16. L	26. M	36. L	46. L
7. D	17. C	27. B	37. C	47. D
8. J	18. J	28. K	38. J	48. M
9. C	19. B	29. D	39. B	49. B
10. J	20. J	30. J	40. J	50. J

1. **The correct answer is C.** The passage shows that the author's father is proud of his son's accomplishments. In paragraph 3, the fact that he is "beaming" indicates that he is happy and has a positive expression on his face. Answer choice C best reflects these qualities of the father, who is pleased with what his son has done.

2. **The correct answer is L.** Questions such as this one simply require you to identify certain details that were revealed in the story. To answer a "detail" question like this one, you might go back and refresh your memory by re-reading the part of the passage that describes what happened when the author met his mother's family. We are told in paragraph 4 that the author received gifts of money and yams from the family members as they greeted him.

3. **The correct answer is B.** Because the author does not discuss his relationship with his father before this ceremony, we can't conclude that the father was not proud of his son before this, so choice A is incorrect. Although the passage mentions that the author meets some of his mother's relatives for the first time, we don't know enough about his relationship with his father's line in

order to make this conclusion, so choice C is incorrect. Choice D is incorrect because the author is clearly very proud and honored to be taking part in this family tradition.

4. **The correct answer is L.** In the first sentence, the author identifies the village of Elu, which is the capital of a region (Ohafia) and part of the country Nigeria.

5. **The correct answer is A.** In the second paragraph, the author refers to "many rituals" and calls this particular ritual the "first step," suggesting that there are others yet to come. At the end of the passage, he uses the phrase "emerging into manhood," which also suggests that the process is not yet complete.

6. **The correct answer is K.** The passage is about the process of this particular ritual as one step in the author's path. Choice K is the option that best embraces the main idea of the passage. Choices J and L are too broad, and choice M is too narrow, given that the money and yams are one small part of the ceremony.

7. **The correct answer is D.** The phrase "making ends meet" is a common way of saying that a budget is balanced. In other words, when people make ends meet, they are making their money last long enough to pay

all expenses. The last sentence of the first paragraph gives the context clue about the phrase.

8. **The correct answer is J.** Barrett knew he needed more customers, and the first paragraph indicates that he had just enough customers to balance his budget; it is implied that he was not making much, if any, profit. In order to increase his profit, he needed more paying customers.

9. **The correct answer is C.** *Ambitious* means "having a desire to be successful," and based on the information in the passage that Barrett is making changes to his business so he can be more successful, the reader can infer that he is ambitious. The passage says that he is "making ends meet," so he's not necessarily unsuccessful. There is not enough information to determine whether he's a good photographer or not, so choice D is incorrect.

10. **The correct answer is J.** The passage says that Barrett had put time into researching business strategies, so choices K and M are incorrect. There is nothing in the passage to suggest that his costs will increase, so choice L is not supported by the passage either.

11. **The correct answer is C.** The main idea of the passage is an exploration of accidental inventions—"ingenious advances that were initially unintended but eventually served to benefit mankind." The passage illustrates this topic by providing two examples—the microwave oven and penicillin, both described as inventions that are the direct result of an accident or mistake. Only penicillin is described as an essential invention, so choice A is incorrect. Choices B and D are incorrect because there is no indication that a "professional inventor" was required or that both the microwave and penicillin would have eventually been invented, even if the accidents mentioned in the passage hadn't occurred.

12. **The correct answer is K.** The path, as described in the passage, refers to a line of scientific curiosity by an innovative thinker (like Spencer or Fleming) that is disrupted by an unintended event, but ultimately leads to a new innovation. For Percy Spencer, that led to the creation of the microwave oven. For Alexander Fleming, that led to the development of penicillin.

13. **The correct answer is D.** *Inhibited* can mean "shy," but given the context, it's apparent that *inhibited* is being used as a verb, so choices B and C are incorrect. The best meaning of *inhibited* in this case is "prevented," given that penicillin is referred to as an "antibiotic," meaning it prevents bacteria and disease.

14. **The correct answer is L.** Both penicillin and the microwave are used as examples of accidental inventions. The Petri dish was a tool used in the discovery of penicillin, and there is not enough information in the passage to tell you about its own invention.

15. **The correct answer is B.** A title for this passage should include the idea that some accidents happen to be lucky. Choices A and D are too generically about science to convey what the passage is about, and choice C only tells half of the story.

16. **The correct answer is L.** The passage talks about how some accidents can spark creativity—not necessarily that all accidents are good or will lead to unexpected discoveries, but that they should be embraced when they do.

17. **The correct answer is C.** "The Possible Effects of Electronic Communication on Communication Skills of Computer Users" is the best title because the passage directly addresses the social skills of computer users and the ways that those skills are affected by communicating electronically, via e-mail and instant messaging.

18. **The correct answer is J.** The phrase implies that the more something is practiced by

someone, the better he or she becomes at whatever is practiced. The next-to-last sentence mentions increased communications, so it is implied that "practice makes perfect" refers to that increase in communications.

19. **The correct answer is B.** If someone is hiding his or her communication flaws behind an anonymous name or persona, the passage suggests that they are avoiding working on their own true communication skills.

20. **The correct answer is J.** With the phrase "practice makes perfect," the author is suggesting that the more people interact online, the better they'll get. E-mail and instant messaging are both important, and the passage doesn't say that one is more important than the other. The passage also does not recommend face-to-face conversation as a way to improve digital communication skills.

21. **The correct answer is A.** For this question, you have to rely on the passage itself. Neither choice B nor choice C is mentioned in the passage, so you can eliminate those. The passage also doesn't say that people will forget how to communicate face-to-face (just that these skills may decline), so choice D is incorrect as well.

22. **The correct answer is L.** An adage is a motto, or old saying.

23. **The correct answer is C.** Reality TV actually consists of very little reality. The author of the passage contends that there is little reality in reality TV because the producers and directors still have a huge influence on the things that are filmed and televised, and this prevents reality TV from being real, which theoretically is the defining characteristic of reality.

24. **The correct answer is L.** An author who criticizes and points out flaws or weaknesses is most likely a person who is a critic or opponent of that about which he or she writes.

25. **The correct answer is B.** The entire passage is about how "reality" shows actually

don't have much reality, so that eliminates choice A, and supports choice B. The author states that reality shows are likely here to stay, so choice C is incorrect. And the author is very critical of reality shows, so it would not be in keeping with the passage's tone for the author to say that reality shows are "fantastic."

26. **The correct answer is M.** There is no mention in the passage that some reality shows have scripts, and therefore are not "real." (Remember that your answer must be based on what you've read in the passage, *not* on what you may believe you know from other sources to be true.)

27. **The correct answer is B.** The author debunks reality TV shows by calling them "staged," so it's likely that this is what the two types of shows would have in common.

28. **The correct answer is K.** *Bombarding* can mean "attacking" or "hitting," but in this case it's more likely to mean "presenting," as the author does not seem to be arguing that reality TV is harmful or dangerous to the viewers.

29. **The correct answer is D.** The focus of the passage is the ability of Polynesian navigators to guide their canoes without the benefit of charts or navigational tools. The other choices are too broad.

30. **The correct answer is J.** This is stated in the first sentence of the passage.

31. **The correct answer is B.** *Mariner* means "sailor" or "seaman."

32. **The correct answer is M.** The passage makes it clear that Polynesian navigators used the sun and stars to find their way, meaning they must have studied the movements of the stars.

33. **The correct answer is C.** The steering paddle served an integral part in each journey. So much so, that the steering paddle was always given a personal name.

34. **The correct answer is K.** Dual canoes were often used for transpacific journeys because they could carry cargo such as food, water, and domestic animals, as well as passengers. Nowhere in the passage is fishing, warfare, or leisure mentioned.

35. **The correct answer is A.** Polynesian navigators were skilled in using the sun and stars, as well as tidal trends and seabirds to guide their crafts.

36. **The correct answer is L.** The last sentence in the passage states this information, but does not mention any of the other information listed in choices J, K, or M.

37. **The correct answer is C.** The context words here are *on the contrary* and *lavish*, so you know the correct choice will be the opposite of *lavish*. *Stingy* is the only option that fits this context.

38. **The correct answer is J.** The passage describes Phileas Fogg as avoiding talking to others, even when it comes to his own stories. *Reserved*, or detached, fits the characterization the best out of the options given. *Sociable* (choice L) means the opposite of how Fogg is presented in the passage, so it is incorrect. Choices K and M are not supported by the passage, so they are incorrect.

39. **The correct answer is B.** The passage is concerned with trying to illustrate Phileas Fogg, but it presents conflicting information (he is wealthy but not greedy, he can answer complicated questions but doesn't seem to have left town, etc.), so there aren't many things that can be said definitively about Phileas Fogg. The only fact in these options that can be verified by the passage is that Phileas Fogg is very "familiar" with the world.

40. **The correct answer is J.** The author is humorously suggesting that Phileas Fogg must have special insight or psychic abilities in order to know the things he knows, without having left the city recently.

41. **The correct answer is A.** The author/narrator is presenting information about Phileas Fogg, but doing it in a comic way. The author is not especially critical of or harsh on Phileas Fogg, but instead describes him and adds humorous theories ("second sight") about why he is the way he is, and why he knows what he does.

42. **The correct answer is L.** The passage mentions Phileas Fogg's wealth, but it comes to focus on his travel (or apparent lack thereof). From that context, you can infer that the author will continue talking about Phileas Fogg's travels.

43. **The correct answer is A.** Although the passage describes the popularity of the Brontosaurus (choice D), it is mainly about how our knowledge about the dinosaur has changed since O.C. Marsh's mistake was discovered. As such, choice A is the best answer. The passage does not suggest that all other dinosaur knowledge is untrue or inaccurate, so choices B and C are incorrect.

44. **The correct answer is L.** According to the passage, O.C. Marsh was the person responsible for misidentifying the Brontosaurus. The reference to *The Flintstones* television show merely provided a cultural representation of the Brontosaurus, and the Carnegie Museum helped to correct the mistake, so choices J and K are incorrect.

45. **The correct answer is B.** The passage mentions the Apatosaurus only in passing, so choice A is incorrect. Choice C is too general, so that one is incorrect. Choice D is incorrect because the passage talks about the Brontosaurus disappearing as a result of new information, but there is nothing about the Brontosaurus making a comeback.

46. **The correct answer is L.** According to the second paragraph, a Camarasaurus head was attached to the Apatosaurus body (which means choice M is incorrect as well). The

Brontosaurus has been found not to exist, so choice J is incorrect. The Tyrannosaurus Rex was mentioned only as a fellow dinosaur, so choice K is incorrect as well.

47. **The correct answer is D.** The author is using positive, mild adjectives to describe the "restful" atmosphere, so you can infer that the adjective *balmy* is similarly positive. Because it's summer, choice A is incorrect. *Restful* makes choice B incorrect, and *hostile* (choice C) means "opposed or antagonistic," which does not accurately describe the atmosphere.

48. **The correct answer is M.** Although the author doesn't describe Tom's actual task until the final paragraph, the steps outlined describe painting. "Whitewashing" and "coating and recoating" are the key context words that tell you what Tom has been working on.

49. **The correct answer is B.** That Aunt Polly "would have been content to find twenty percent of Tom's statement true," suggests that she didn't expect any of it to be true. There is no information in the passage to suggest that Tom likes painting, or that he always does what he's asked—and in fact, Aunt Polly's doubt suggests that he does not.

50. **The correct answer is J.** Although the author uses the word *evidence*, he is using it to suggest that to Aunt Polly, Tom's word is the *opposite* of evidence.

Written Expression

1. A	11. A	21. A	31. A	41. A
2. N	12. J	22. L	32. K	42. K
3. B	13. B	23. C	33. B	43. C
4. L	14. K	24. K	34. L	44. J
5. A	15. C	25. D	35. B	45. B
6. M	16. M	26. K	36. M	46. M
7. B	17. B	27. D	37. A	47. C
8. J	18. K	28. K	38. L	48. L
9. B	19. B	29. A	39. C	49. A
10. N	20. J	30. M	40. J	50. K

1. **The correct answer is A.** The correct spelling is *dictionary*.

2. **The correct answer is N.** *(No mistakes)*

3. **The correct answer is B.** The correct spelling is *obtain*.

4. **The correct answer is L.** The correct spelling is *persuade*.

5. **The correct answer is A.** The correct spelling is *discuss*.

6. **The correct answer is M.** The correct spelling is *messenger*.

7. **The correct answer is B.** The correct spelling is *amateur*.

8. **The correct answer is J.** The correct spelling is *cancellation*.

9. **The correct answer is B.** The correct spelling is *migrate*.

10. **The correct answer is N.** *(No mistakes)*

11. **The correct answer is A.** The word *college* is capitalized only when included in a proper noun such as Boston College or Ithaca College.

12. **The correct answer is J.** The word *river* is capitalized when included as part of a proper noun such as "Mississippi River."

13. **The correct answer is B.** Although the name of a country's cuisine is capitalized, the word *restaurant* is not capitalized unless it is used to begin a sentence or is part of a proper name.

14. **The correct answer is K.** Holidays, because they are proper nouns, should be capitalized.

15. **The correct answer is C.** Names of seasons are not proper nouns and do not need capitalization.

16. **The correct answer is M.** *(No mistakes)*

17. **The correct answer is B.** *Space* needs no capitalization because it is a common noun, but related terms such as *Haley's Comet* or *Jupiter* should be capitalized because they are proper nouns.

18. **The correct answer is K.** The word *newspaper* is a common noun and would be capitalized only as part of a proper noun such as the "Baltimore Newspaper Publishing Company."

19. **The correct answer is B.** Words like *father* or *sister* require capitalization when used as part of (or in place of) a person's name, as in the cases of "Father Dowling" or "Sister Wendy."

20. **The correct answer is J.** Names of streets, roads, or avenues are to be capitalized, as in "Abbey Road" or "Penny Lane," but not when used as common nouns like "the dirt road" or "the winding country lane."

21. **The correct answer is A.** Choice A expresses the idea clearly with the correct punctuation, so it is correct. Choice D is incorrect because it contains the unnecessary phrase "where he was" at the end of the sentence.

22. **The correct answer is L.** Choice L most efficiently and effectively expresses the ideas in this sentence, without the unnecessary

wordiness, redundancy, and confusion that makes the other choices incorrect.

23. **The correct answer is C.** As written, the underlined portion of the sentence incorrectly uses the plural pronoun *they* to replace the singular noun, *Cape Hatteras Lighthouse.* Choice C correctly uses the singular pronoun *it* to replace the singular noun.

24. **The correct answer is K.** As written, the passage makes an incorrect assumption that the information about Cape Hatteras Lighthouse not being the original is obvious. This is more of an interesting bit of trivia than something obvious that everyone knows, so choice K would be a more effective way to begin this sentence, given the context of the passage.

25. **The correct answer is D.** *(No change).* Both the words *bold* and *swift* are adjectives modifying the noun *strokes.* Since two adjectives are used together to modify one noun, the two adjectives must be separated with a comma.

26. **The correct answer is K.** Commas are needed to separate the phrase "especially behind-the-scenes glimpses of ballerinas rehearsing or warming up backstage" from the remainder of the sentence, so choice K is correct.

27. **The correct answer is D.** *(No change).* The word *Indeed* signifies that a similar idea to what was presented in the first sentence will follow in the next sentence. Choices A and B both suggest information that opposes what has already been stated, and choice C would indicate a cause-and-effect relationship.

28. **The correct answer is K.** The word *planet* is a common noun and would need capitalization only if used as part of a name, such as "Small Planet Institute."

29. **The correct answer is A.** The word *museum* by itself is a common noun, but it requires capitalization when used as part of a proper

noun naming a specific place. The other answer choices are incorrect since all four words in the name of the Smithsonian Natural History Museum must be capitalized.

30. **The correct answer is M.** *(No change).* No change is necessary to the sentence, since the plural noun *Legends* takes a plural verb. Furthermore, the verb should be in present tense to match the rest of the sentence, ruling out choice K. Choice L contains a noun rather than a verb, which makes no sense in this context.

31. **The correct answer is A.** As written, the sentence contains an incorrect possessive form of *millions*. A possessive form is not required here, so choice A is correct. Choice B fails to capitalize the word, which should be done because it's at the beginning of a sentence. Choice C provides a possessive plural form that's incorrect for this sentence.

32. **The correct answer is K.** The underlined portion of the sentence incorrectly capitalizes these words, and is incorrect. Choice K fixes this problem by using the correct lowercase form of "unemployment rate." Choices J and L also use incorrect capitalization, given the context of this sentence.

33. **The correct answer is B.** The sentence as written contains incorrect internal punctuation. A semicolon should only be used to separate two independent clauses, which we don't have here. No internal punctuation is needed at this part of the sentence, so choice B is correct. Choice A incorrectly creates two sentence fragments by adding a period. Choice C is incorrect, as a comma is not needed here.

34. **The correct answer is L.** This paragraph ends with a statement about "National S'Mores Day" but doesn't provide any information about when it is. Choice L follows up on this thought by providing the date, and is the most logical final sentence for this

paragraph. The other answer choices focus on minor, tangential details and aren't effective final sentences given the context of the paragraph.

35. **The correct answer is B.** New York City is a proper noun, and it should always be capitalized. The other answer choices make incorrect use of lowercase forms.

36. **The correct answer is M.** *(No change).* Items in a simple list should be separated by commas, which the sentence as written does; thus, it is the correct answer. Choice J incorrectly uses a period and creates sentence fragments. Choice K uses no punctuation. Choice L incorrectly uses semicolons, which should be used only for more complex lists.

37. **The correct answer is A.** Book titles, like the *Guinness Book of World Records*, should always be italicized, which choice A does. The other answer choices are incorrect ways to write a book title.

38. **The correct answer is L.** When looking to determine the appropriate word choice, context matters. We're told that the underlined words stand *in contrast* to the main topic of the paragraph—the Roe River, the shortest river in the world. The logical contrast to the shortest river is the longest river, and the fact that we're told the length of the Amazon River is a good indication that choice L is the correct answer.

39. **The correct answer is C.** As written, the sentence incorrectly uses the future tense for an activity that has already been occurring. Choice C corrects this error. The other answer choices utilize incorrect verb forms.

40. **The correct answer is J.** As written, the sentence ends in a question mark, although no question is being posed; therefore, it is incorrect. This simple declarative sentence should end in a period, so choice J is correct. Choice K is incorrect because a semicolon is not appropriate end punctuation for a

sentence. Choice L is incorrect because it completely removes all end punctuation from this sentence.

41. **The correct answer is A.** The sentence as written is illogical. Here, we're looking at two clearly related issues, and *besides* would indicate something "other than," which does not fit, given the context of the sentence. Choice A utilizes the conjunction *and*, which appropriately indicates the connection between "worker safety" and "employer accountability" issues, and is the correct answer. Choice B incorrectly uses the conjunction *or*, which is inappropriate as no alternative or choice between options is being presented here.

42. **The correct answer is K.** As written, the singular noun *worker* is incorrect to refer to a group of women. The plural *workers* is required, so choice K is correct. Choices J and L use incorrect forms of *work*, given the context of the sentence.

43. **The correct answer is C.** As written, the plural form of the word *worlds* is incorrect here; the possessive form is required, so choice C is correct. Choice A utilizes the incorrect possessive plural form, as we're only talking about one world. Choice B incorrectly capitalizes this common noun.

44. **The correct answer is J.** As written, the incorrect verb form of "to be" is being used. The singular *is* does not fit with the plural *scientists*. Choice J corrects the problem and uses the appropriate plural form *are*. Choices K and L also use incorrect verb forms for this sentence.

45. **The correct answer is B.** This paragraph focuses on Harvard University and discusses both its age and its "illustrious graduates." The best option to introduce this topic is choice B, which suggests Harvard is one of

the oldest and most prestigious universities in the United States. The other answer choices focus on inconsequential details of the paragraph and are ineffective options.

46. **The correct answer is M.** (*No change*). Since Harvard University's establishment in 1636 clearly occurred in the past, the correct verb form required here is the past tense, which the sentence as written correctly uses. The other answer choices utilize incorrect verb forms given the context of the sentence.

47. **The correct answer is C.** The items in this list should each be separated by commas, as choice C does. The other answer choices use inappropriate internal and end-of-sentence punctuation for this simple list.

48. **The correct answer is L.** As written, the sentence incorrectly uses an exclamation point as end punctuation, which should be used only when expressing surprise or heightened emotion. A question is being posed here, so the sentence should end in a question mark. Choice J uses a semicolon, which is not appropriate end of sentence punctuation. Choice K uses a period, which is not appropriate to end a question.

49. **The correct answer is A.** Proper nouns like "Washington Monument" should always be capitalized, so choice A is correct. Quotation marks are not needed when referring to a proper noun that isn't part of the name of a poem or short story or piece of dialog, so choice C is incorrect.

50. **The correct answer is K.** As written, the sentence contains inappropriate internal punctuation and creates awkward pauses in this sentence. No punctuation is needed at the underlined portion of this sentence, so choice K is correct.

Mathematics

1. B	**11.** C	**21.** A	**31.** D	**41.** C
2. L	**12.** M	**22.** L	**32.** K	**42.** J
3. B	**13.** C	**23.** A	**33.** C	**43.** C
4. K	**14.** K	**24.** L	**34.** L	**44.** K
5. B	**15.** C	**25.** B	**35.** A	**45.** C
6. L	**16.** J	**26.** K	**36.** K	**46.** K
7. D	**17.** D	**27.** C	**37.** A	**47.** B
8. M	**18.** M	**28.** M	**38.** L	**48.** K
9. C	**19.** C	**29.** D	**39.** D	**49.** D
10. K	**20.** J	**30.** L	**40.** L	**50.** K

1. **The correct answer is B.** The third place to the right of the decimal is thousandths.

2. **The correct answer is L.**

$$3 \times 3 \times 3 = 3 \times 9 = 27$$

3. **The correct answer is B.**

$$\frac{1}{2} + \frac{2}{4} - \frac{3}{3} = \frac{1}{2} + \frac{1}{2} + 1 = 1 + 1 = 2$$

4. **The correct answer is K.** $(3 \times 3) + (4 \times 4) + (5 \times 5) = 9 + 16 + 25 = 50$

5. **The correct answer is B.** $1.6 = 1\frac{6}{10}$, which must be reduced to $1\frac{3}{5}$.

6. **The correct answer is L.** 29 is divisible only by 1 and 29.

7. **The correct answer is D.** $\frac{8}{4}$ can be reduced to $\frac{2}{1}$, or 2.

8. **The correct answer is M.** The term *product* is a clue to multiply.

9. **The correct answer is C.** $6 \times 6 \times 6 \times 6 \times 6 \times 6 \times 6$; 6^7 means that 6 is multiplied by itself 7 times.

10. **The correct answer is K.** The number 2.006 is the same as $2\frac{6}{1,000}$.

11. **The correct answer is C.** 40% of $300 is $120. So, the accountant's fee is $420.

12. **The correct answer is M.** $32 - 27 = 5$, $24 - 19 = 5$, and $23 - 21 = 2$. There are $5 + 5 + 2 = 12$ comic books that Carl needs to buy; 12 is not an answer choice.

13. **The correct answer is C.** $12 \times 245 = 2,940$ books on the 100 percent full book shelves. The fraction $\frac{4}{5}$ is the same as 80%, so 80% of 245, or 0.8×245, equals 196. $2,940 + 196 = 3,136$ books.

14. **The correct answer is K.** 100 normal images is the same as $\frac{1}{2}$, or 50 percent, of the 200 high-quality images. If $\frac{1}{2}$ of the memory is already used, then only $\frac{1}{2}$ of the camera's memory is still available. $\frac{1}{2}$ of 40 high-quality images the camera normally would hold is 20.

15. **The correct answer is C.** $4 \times 3\frac{1}{4} = 13$ hours each week.

16. **The correct answer is J.** There are 100,000 centimeters in a kilometer. Each centimeter is $\frac{1}{100,000}$ of a kilometer.

17. **The correct answer is D.**

$$\text{Area} = \text{length} \times \text{width}$$
$$= 176 \text{ ft.} \times 79 \text{ ft.}$$
$$= 13{,}904 \text{ sq. ft.}$$

18. **The correct answer is M.** Mr. Lawson's total income is equal to 7% of his sales plus $250. 7% of his sales is $1,250 × 0.07 = $87.50 + $250 = $337.50.

19. **The correct answer is C.**

$$3(y \times 4) - 20 = 280$$
$$3(y \times 4) = 280 + 20$$
$$3(y \times 4) = 300$$
$$4y = 100$$
$$y = 25 \text{ or } 5^2$$

You can check your calculations by plugging your answer into the original equation.

$$3(5^2 \times 4) - 20 = 3(25 \times 4) - 20$$
$$= 3(100) - 20$$
$$= 300 - 20$$
$$= 280$$

20. **The correct answer is J.** The area of a triangle is found by using the formula:

$$A = \frac{1}{2}bh$$

Since the base = 14 and the height = 20,

$$A = \frac{1}{2} \times 14 \times 20$$

$$A = 140 \text{ sq. in.}$$

21. **The correct answer is A.** Convert x to an improper fraction and then flip it over to get the reciprocal: $x = 2\frac{2}{5} = \frac{12}{5}$, so the reciprocal is $\frac{5}{12}$.

22. **The correct answer is L.** The product of any number and its reciprocal is 1. Therefore, $\frac{7}{16} \times \frac{16}{7} = 1$, making choice L the correct

answer. Even if you didn't know this rule, you could have examined the answers and eliminated choice K because that product was greater than 1 and choice M because its product was less than 1. Choice J is easily eliminated because any number multiplied by 1 is equal to itself.

23. **The correct answer is A.** This problem looks much harder than it really is. The numerator of this complex fraction is the same as the denominator. When numerator and denominator are equivalent, the fraction is equal to 1.

24. **The correct answer is L.** First, simplify the numerator:

$$\frac{5}{12} - \frac{7}{24} = \frac{10}{24} - \frac{7}{24}$$
$$= \frac{3}{24}$$
$$= \frac{1}{8}$$

Next, simplify the denominator:

$$\frac{1}{2} - \frac{3}{8} = \frac{4}{8} - \frac{3}{8} = \frac{1}{8}$$

So,

$$\frac{\dfrac{5}{12} - \dfrac{7}{24}}{\dfrac{1}{2} - \dfrac{3}{8}} = \frac{\dfrac{1}{8}}{\dfrac{1}{8}} = 1.$$

25. **The correct answer is B.** This is a problem in which you must substitute the values given into the formula. After you do that, it is a simple problem.

$$L = \frac{3}{4} \times 2 \times 7 \times \frac{1}{2}$$

$$\frac{3 \times 2 \times 7 \times 1}{4 \times 2} = \frac{42}{8} = \frac{21}{4}$$

Therefore, choice B is the correct answer. The other answers would have resulted if you had forgotten to multiply one of the numbers in the numerator. Choice D might have been chosen by someone who didn't know what to do but thought the most difficult-looking answer would be the best.

26. **The correct answer is K.** The area of the shaded portion is equal to the area of the square, less the area of the circle. The length of the side of the square is equal to the diameter of the circle. Therefore, using $\frac{22}{7}$ for pi:

$$\left(4"\times 4"\right)-\left(\pi 2^2\right)=16 \text{ sq. in.} -\frac{88}{7} \text{ sq. in.}$$

$$=3\frac{3}{7} \text{ sq. in.}$$

If you selected choice L, $4\frac{3}{7}$, check your skills in subtracting fractions from whole numbers.

27. **The correct answer is C.** For each teacher, there are 14 students. Because there are 14 teachers, there must be $14\times 14=196$ students.

28. **The correct answer is M.**

$$\frac{10^4}{100^5}=\frac{10^4}{\left(10^2\right)^5}$$

$$=\frac{10^4}{10^{10}}$$

$$=\frac{1}{10^6}$$

$$=\frac{1}{1,000,000}$$

29. **The correct answer is D.** In the whole number system, every other number is odd and every other number is even. If x is odd, $x+1$ is even, $x+2$ is odd, $x+3$ is even, and so forth. Also, if x is odd, $x-1$ is even, $x-2$ is odd, and $x-3$ is even. If an even or odd number is doubled, the outcome is even. Therefore, if x is odd, $2x+1$ is odd, $x-2$ is odd, and $4x-3$ is odd.

30. **The correct answer is L.** Arrange the periods of time in columns and add as you would add whole numbers.

$$
\begin{array}{rr}
4 \text{ hr.} & 17 \text{ min.} \\
3 \text{ hr.} & 58 \text{ min.} \\
 & 45 \text{ min.} \\
+7 \text{ hr.} & 12 \text{ min.} \\
\hline
14 \text{ hr.} & 132 \text{ min.}
\end{array}
$$

We know there are 60 minutes in each hour. Therefore, 132 minutes equal 2 hours 12 minutes. The correct answer for this addition is 16 hours 12 minutes. When working with units that measure time, volume, and length, it is usually best to represent the answer using as many larger units as possible. That's why 16 hours 12 minutes is preferable to 14 hours 132 minutes as an answer.

31. **The correct answer is D.** 72 cars with 4 wheels each, or $72\times 4=288$.

32. **The correct answer is K.** Two minutes equals $2\times 60=120$ seconds. In this amount of time, Ted can text $30\times 12=360$ characters.

33. **The correct answer is C.** Seven dozen is $7\times 12=84$ ornaments. Subtract that amount from the desired number of ornaments to get $200-84=116$ ornaments still to be purchased.

34. **The correct answer is L.** Each wall is 12×10, or 120 square feet. Four walls of 120 square feet is $4\times 120=480$ square feet.

35. **The correct answer is A.** $36,500 \div 365$ days in a year is 100 pounds of fish each day.

36. **The correct answer is K.** Forty-one percent of the donuts consumed are glazed.

37. **The correct answer is A.** Twenty-five percent of a dozen, or 12, equals 3. The chart shows that cream-filled donuts represent 25% of the Doodle's Dozen.

38. **The correct answer is L.** Because Rutledge sent more students to Washington High than the other two schools, it represents the largest percentage.

39. **The correct answer is D.** $211 + 178 + 346 = 735$.

40. **The correct answer is L.** There are more than 100 portraits. By adding the values, not the percentages, of each section it can be determined that there are $14 + 22 + 35 + 24 + 23 = 118$ portraits.

41. **The correct answer is C.** $46{,}922 + 32{,}090$ is approximately $47{,}000 + 32{,}000$, which equals $79{,}000$. $79{,}000$ is approximately $80{,}000$, so choice C is the closest estimate among the answer choices.

42. **The correct answer is J.** $7{,}988 \div 397$ is approximately $8{,}000 \div 400 = 20$.

43. **The correct answer is C.** Distance equals rate $\times$ time, so $15 = 6x$. Therefore, it takes him $\frac{15}{6} = 2.5$ hours, which equals $2.5(60) = 150$ minutes.

44. **The correct answer is K.** $40 \times 16 = 640$, which is an approximation of 653.

45. **The correct answer is C.** $148 + 153.5 + 146 + 154.1 + 151 + 145.9 + 149 + 153 + 152.5 +$ 147.75 is approximately 150 added 10 times, or 1,500.

46. **The correct answer is K.** Note that $\frac{17}{30}$ is only slightly larger than $\frac{15}{30}$ or $\frac{1}{2}$. Choices J, L, and M are much closer in value to 1 than to $\frac{1}{2}$.

47. **The correct answer is B.** One thousand millimeters equals 1 meter. So, 1 millimeter is $\frac{1}{1{,}000}$ meter.

48. **The correct answer is K.** If 18 games constituted 40% of the season, the season was $18 \div 0.40$, or 45 games long. If the team won 18 games, it lost $45 - 18$, or 27 games.

49. **The correct answer is D.** The inequality should be conceptualized as "q is between -2 and -1." Because q must be closer to 0 than -2, it is *larger* than -2.

50. **The correct answer is K.** If $x = 0$, then $2x < 8$ because $2(0) = 0$, which is less than 8. None of the other pairs results in a true statement.

Ability

Figure Classification

1. B	5. C	9. C	13. C	17. A
2. J	6. L	10. N	14. J	18. J
3. E	7. B	11. B	15. A	19. E
4. M	8. J	12. J	16. L	20. J

1. **The correct answer is B.** Each figure is a square divided vertically into two equal parts.

2. **The correct answer is J.** Each figure consists of two shapes that differ only in size, with one nested inside the other.

3. **The correct answer is E.** Each figure contains two triangles.

4. **The correct answer is M.** Each square contains a rectangle and two circles.

5. **The correct answer is C.** Each figure consists of three segments, and the figures are arranged so that they rotate in a counterclockwise direction going from left to right. Choice C completes that pattern, and belongs between the first and second figures in the example.

6. **The correct answer is L.** Each figure consists of a single circle connected directly to multiple squares via line segments. Although choice K includes a circle and two squares,

one of the squares is not connected directly to the circle, and therefore the figure does not match the pattern.

7. **The correct answer is B.** Each figure is a polygon with an additional segment inside that is parallel to one of the sides.

8. **The correct answer is J.** The number of circles in each figure is equal to the number of horizontal line segments.

9. **The correct answer is C.** Each figure has both horizontal and vertical lines of symmetry. This means that you can fold the image vertically or horizontally and the two halves will match exactly. For example, the figure in choice A could be folded horizontally and the halves would match; however, folding vertically would not match. The correct choice must fold symmetrically in both directions.

10. **The correct answer is N.** The number of horizontal segments in each figure is one more than the number of vertical segments.

11. **The correct answer is B.** The numbers in each figure are arranged so that they increase in a clockwise direction.

12. **The correct answer is J.** Each figure contains exactly two triangles.

13. **The correct answer is C.** Exactly half of each figure is shaded.

14. **The correct answer is J.** Each figure is split into equal-sized parts.

15. **The correct answer is A.** The bottom-right corner of each shade is shaded.

16. **The correct answer is L.** Each figure is split into equal sized parts. The number of these parts is equal to the number of sides of the outer shape.

17. **The correct answer is A.** The figure rotates clockwise a quarter-turn. Choice A continues the pattern.

18. **The correct answer is J.** Regardless of the how many dots there are, the dots must be equally spaced around the circle's perimeter.

19. **The correct answer is E.** A dashed line divides each shape into two equal parts (the resulting parts must have the same area).

20. **The correct answer is J.** Remove a dot and alternate between shaded and unshaded for each step.

Figure Matrices

1. C	**5.** C	**9.** A	**13.** E	**17.** C
2. K	**6.** N	**10.** L	**14.** L	**18.** J
3. E	**7.** A	**11.** E	**15.** B	**19.** C
4. K	**8.** M	**12.** J	**16.** M	**20.** K

1. **The correct answer is C.** Moving left to right, add one vertical and one horizontal line per step.

2. **The correct answer is K.** The third image in each row is a combination of the first two images in that row.

3. **The correct answer is E.** The third image in each row is a combination of the first two images in that row.

4. **The correct answer is K.** In each row, the first image is split into the second and third

images. The second contains only the circle from the left side, and the third contains only the circle from the right side.

5. **The correct answer is C.** Moving from left to right, the arrows rotate clockwise. Moving top to bottom, the arrows rotate counterclockwise.

6. **The correct answer is N.** Each row has a different internal pattern, while each column has a different orientation of triangle.

7. **The correct answer is A.** In the last row, the circle is always in the bottom row of the image. In the last column, the circle is always in the middle column.

8. **The correct answer is M.** The third image in each row nests the second figure inside the first image. Note also that each row has a specific slant for the internal lines, which makes choice M a better option than choice L.

9. **The correct answer is A.** The last image in each row consists of the segments that are shown in either the first image or second image, but not both.

10. **The correct answer is L.** The third image in each row is shaded as follows: a section is shaded only if it is not shaded in either of the first two images in the row.

11. **The correct answer is E.** The last image in each row consists of the segments shown in the first image but not in the second image.

12. **The correct answer is J.** The third image in each row is the second image set inside a hollow version of the first image.

13. **The correct answer is E.** Moving from top to bottom, each row adds a square. Moving left to right, each figure adds an extra triangle.

14. **The correct answer is L.** The third image in each contains the second image set on top of the first image.

15. **The correct answer is B.** The empty section in the third column is filled in both of the two previous columns.

16. **The correct answer is M.** The third image in each row is the second image split into equal parts. The number of parts is determined by the number of segments in the first column.

17. **The correct answer is C.** The third image in each row consists of the shape from the second image filled using segments parallel to the segment in the first image.

18. **The correct answer is J.** Draw lines extending from the center through all sides of the polygon. Then place a shaded dot at the end of each line and remove the line segments.

19. **The correct answer is C.** From left to right, the second figure rotates one of the arrows 180 degrees; the third figure then rotates both arrows and shades the unshaded parts and vice versa.

20. **The correct answer is K.** From left to right, add an "X" and remove a square block for each step. From top to bottom, remove two square blocks and one "X" for each step.

Paper Folding

1. D	3. E	5. A	7. D	9. D
2. J	4. K	6. K	8. L	10. J

1. **The correct answer is D.** Both holes are reflected across the vertical fold. The one near the center line remains near the center line, while the one in the top corner ends up in the opposite top corner.

2. **The correct answer is J.** Each hole is reflected across the diagonal fold, moving toward the opposite corner a distance that is equal to its original distance from the fold.

3. **The correct answer is E.** Unfolding the second fold reflects both holes across the

vertical fold, resulting in four holes on the bottom half of the paper. Each of these is then reflected across the horizontal fold to the top half of the paper, for a total of eight holes.

4. **The correct answer is K.** All of the folds are horizontal; therefore, when unfolding, the hole in the corner only moves vertically, and remains along the right edge of the page.

5. **The correct answer is A.** The hole on the right edge is first reflected diagonally to the

bottom edge of the page. Both holes are then reflected diagonally again, ending up on the top and left sides of the page.

6. **The correct answer is K.** All three holes are reflected diagonally from the bottom right part of the page to the top left.

7. **The correct answer is D.** The hole is first reflected horizontally to the right edge of the page. Both holes are then reflected vertically just over the horizontal center line.

8. **The correct answer is L.** When the second fold is undone, the hole on the top right is reflected over the diagonal, still remaining in the top right corner. The three holes on the

right side of the page are then reflected over the center vertical line, creating a mirror image of them on the left side of the page.

9. **The correct answer is D.** All of the folds are horizontal; therefore, when unfolding, the hole in the center only moves vertically, and remains in the center of the page.

10. **The correct answer is J.** The hole in the top-right quadrant of the page is first reflected to the bottom-right quadrant, and then these are reflected into the top-left and bottom-left quadrants. They all remain in the center of their respective quadrants.

SCORE SHEET

Although your actual exam scores will not be reported as percentages, it might be helpful to convert your test scores to percentages so that you can see at a glance where your strengths and weaknesses lie. The numbers in parentheses represent the questions that test each skill.

Subject	# Correct ÷ # of questions	× 100 = _____%
Reading		
Vocabulary/Word Relationships (7, 13, 22, 28, 29, 37, 40, 47)	_____ ÷ 8 = _____	× 100 = _____ %
Details/Main Idea/Structure (2, 4, 6, 11, 14, 15, 17, 19, 20, 21, 23, 26, 27, 30, 31, 32, 34, 43, 44, 45, 46, 48)	_____ ÷ 22 = _____	× 100 = _____ %
Inference/Understanding (1, 3, 5, 8, 9, 10, 12, 16, 18, 24, 25, 33, 35, 36, 38, 39, 41, 42, 49, 50)	_____ ÷ 20 = _____	× 100 = _____ %
TOTAL READING SKILLS	_____ ÷ 50 = _____	× 100 = _____ %
Written Expression		
Spelling and Capitalization (1, 2, 3, 4, 5, 6, 7, 8, 9, 10, 11, 12, 13, 14, 15, 16, 17, 18, 19, 20, 29, 32, 35, 49)	_____ ÷ 24 = _____	× 100 = _____ %
Punctuation (25, 26, 31, 33, 36, 40, 43, 47, 48, 50)	_____ ÷ 10 = _____	× 100 = _____ %
Grammar (23, 30, 39, 42, 44, 46)	_____ ÷ 6 = _____	× 100 = _____ %
Usage and Composition (21, 22, 24, 27, 28, 34, 37, 38, 41, 45)	_____ ÷ 10 = _____	× 100 = _____ %
TOTAL WRITTEN EXPRESSION SKILLS	_____ ÷ 50 = _____	× 100 = _____ %
Mathematics		
Arithmetic (1, 2, 3, 4, 5, 6, 7, 8, 9, 10, 11, 12, 13, 14, 15, 18, 24, 27, 28, 30, 31, 32, 33, 35, 41, 42, 43, 44, 45, 46, 48)	_____ ÷ 31 = _____	× 100 = _____ %
Algebra (19, 21, 22, 23, 25, 29, 49, 50)	_____ ÷ 8 = _____	× 100 = _____ %
Data Analysis (36, 37, 38, 39, 40)	_____ ÷ 5 = _____	× 100 = _____ %
Geometry and Measurement (16, 17, 20, 26, 34, 47)	_____ ÷ 6 = _____	× 100 = _____ %
TOTAL MATHEMATICS SKIILS	_____ ÷ 50 = _____	× 100 = _____ %
Ability		
Figure Classification (1, 2, 3, 4, 5, 6, 7, 8, 9, 10, 11, 12, 13, 14, 15, 16, 17, 18, 19, 20)	_____ ÷ 20 = _____	× 100 = _____ %
Figure Matrices (1, 2, 3, 4, 5, 6, 7, 8, 9, 10, 11, 12, 13, 14, 15, 16, 17, 18, 19, 20)	_____ ÷ 20 = _____	× 100 = _____ %
Paper Folding (1, 2, 3, 4, 5, 6, 7, 8, 9, 10)	_____ ÷ 10 = _____	× 100 = _____ %
TOTAL ABILITY SKIILS	_____ ÷ 50 = _____	× 100 = _____ %

Practice Test 2: TACHS

ANSWER SHEET: TACHS PRACTICE TEST 3

Reading

1. Ⓐ Ⓑ Ⓒ Ⓓ   11. Ⓐ Ⓑ Ⓒ Ⓓ   21. Ⓐ Ⓑ Ⓒ Ⓓ   31. Ⓐ Ⓑ Ⓒ Ⓓ   41. Ⓐ Ⓑ Ⓒ Ⓓ

2. Ⓙ Ⓚ Ⓛ Ⓜ   12. Ⓙ Ⓚ Ⓛ Ⓜ   22. Ⓙ Ⓚ Ⓛ Ⓜ   32. Ⓙ Ⓚ Ⓛ Ⓜ   42. Ⓙ Ⓚ Ⓛ Ⓜ

3. Ⓐ Ⓑ Ⓒ Ⓓ   13. Ⓐ Ⓑ Ⓒ Ⓓ   23. Ⓐ Ⓑ Ⓒ Ⓓ   33. Ⓐ Ⓑ Ⓒ Ⓓ   43. Ⓐ Ⓑ Ⓒ Ⓓ

4. Ⓙ Ⓚ Ⓛ Ⓜ   14. Ⓙ Ⓚ Ⓛ Ⓜ   24. Ⓙ Ⓚ Ⓛ Ⓜ   34. Ⓙ Ⓚ Ⓛ Ⓜ   44. Ⓙ Ⓚ Ⓛ Ⓜ

5. Ⓐ Ⓑ Ⓒ Ⓓ   15. Ⓐ Ⓑ Ⓒ Ⓓ   25. Ⓐ Ⓑ Ⓒ Ⓓ   35. Ⓐ Ⓑ Ⓒ Ⓓ   45. Ⓐ Ⓑ Ⓒ Ⓓ

6. Ⓙ Ⓚ Ⓛ Ⓜ   16. Ⓙ Ⓚ Ⓛ Ⓜ   26. Ⓙ Ⓚ Ⓛ Ⓜ   36. Ⓙ Ⓚ Ⓛ Ⓜ   46. Ⓙ Ⓚ Ⓛ Ⓜ

7. Ⓐ Ⓑ Ⓒ Ⓓ   17. Ⓐ Ⓑ Ⓒ Ⓓ   27. Ⓐ Ⓑ Ⓒ Ⓓ   37. Ⓐ Ⓑ Ⓒ Ⓓ   47. Ⓐ Ⓑ Ⓒ Ⓓ

8. Ⓙ Ⓚ Ⓛ Ⓜ   18. Ⓙ Ⓚ Ⓛ Ⓜ   28. Ⓙ Ⓚ Ⓛ Ⓜ   38. Ⓙ Ⓚ Ⓛ Ⓜ   48. Ⓙ Ⓚ Ⓛ Ⓜ

9. Ⓐ Ⓑ Ⓒ Ⓓ   19. Ⓐ Ⓑ Ⓒ Ⓓ   29. Ⓐ Ⓑ Ⓒ Ⓓ   39. Ⓐ Ⓑ Ⓒ Ⓓ   49. Ⓐ Ⓑ Ⓒ Ⓓ

10. Ⓙ Ⓚ Ⓛ Ⓜ   20. Ⓙ Ⓚ Ⓛ Ⓜ   30. Ⓙ Ⓚ Ⓛ Ⓜ   40. Ⓙ Ⓚ Ⓛ Ⓜ   50. Ⓙ Ⓚ Ⓛ Ⓜ

Written Expression

1. Ⓐ Ⓑ Ⓒ Ⓓ Ⓔ   14. Ⓙ Ⓚ Ⓛ Ⓜ   27. Ⓐ Ⓑ Ⓒ Ⓓ   40. Ⓙ Ⓚ Ⓛ Ⓜ

2. Ⓙ Ⓚ Ⓛ Ⓜ Ⓝ   15. Ⓐ Ⓑ Ⓒ Ⓓ   28. Ⓙ Ⓚ Ⓛ Ⓜ   41. Ⓐ Ⓑ Ⓒ Ⓓ

3. Ⓐ Ⓑ Ⓒ Ⓓ Ⓔ   16. Ⓙ Ⓚ Ⓛ Ⓜ   29. Ⓐ Ⓑ Ⓒ Ⓓ   42. Ⓙ Ⓚ Ⓛ Ⓜ

4. Ⓙ Ⓚ Ⓛ Ⓜ Ⓝ   17. Ⓐ Ⓑ Ⓒ Ⓓ   30. Ⓙ Ⓚ Ⓛ Ⓜ   43. Ⓐ Ⓑ Ⓒ Ⓓ

5. Ⓐ Ⓑ Ⓒ Ⓓ Ⓔ   18. Ⓙ Ⓚ Ⓛ Ⓜ   31. Ⓐ Ⓑ Ⓒ Ⓓ   44. Ⓙ Ⓚ Ⓛ Ⓜ

6. Ⓙ Ⓚ Ⓛ Ⓜ Ⓝ   19. Ⓐ Ⓑ Ⓒ Ⓓ   32. Ⓙ Ⓚ Ⓛ Ⓜ   45. Ⓐ Ⓑ Ⓒ Ⓓ

7. Ⓐ Ⓑ Ⓒ Ⓓ Ⓔ   20. Ⓙ Ⓚ Ⓛ Ⓜ   33. Ⓐ Ⓑ Ⓒ Ⓓ   46. Ⓙ Ⓚ Ⓛ Ⓜ

8. Ⓙ Ⓚ Ⓛ Ⓜ Ⓝ   21. Ⓐ Ⓑ Ⓒ Ⓓ   34. Ⓙ Ⓚ Ⓛ Ⓜ   47. Ⓐ Ⓑ Ⓒ Ⓓ

9. Ⓐ Ⓑ Ⓒ Ⓓ Ⓔ   22. Ⓙ Ⓚ Ⓛ Ⓜ   35. Ⓐ Ⓑ Ⓒ Ⓓ   48. Ⓙ Ⓚ Ⓛ Ⓜ

10. Ⓙ Ⓚ Ⓛ Ⓜ Ⓝ   23. Ⓐ Ⓑ Ⓒ Ⓓ   36. Ⓙ Ⓚ Ⓛ Ⓜ   49. Ⓐ Ⓑ Ⓒ Ⓓ

11. Ⓐ Ⓑ Ⓒ Ⓓ   24. Ⓙ Ⓚ Ⓛ Ⓜ   37. Ⓐ Ⓑ Ⓒ Ⓓ   50. Ⓙ Ⓚ Ⓛ Ⓜ

12. Ⓙ Ⓚ Ⓛ Ⓜ   25. Ⓐ Ⓑ Ⓒ Ⓓ   38. Ⓙ Ⓚ Ⓛ Ⓜ

13. Ⓐ Ⓑ Ⓒ Ⓓ   26. Ⓙ Ⓚ Ⓛ Ⓜ   39. Ⓐ Ⓑ Ⓒ Ⓓ

Math

1. Ⓐ Ⓑ Ⓒ Ⓓ	11. Ⓐ Ⓑ Ⓒ Ⓓ	21. Ⓐ Ⓑ Ⓒ Ⓓ	31. Ⓐ Ⓑ Ⓒ Ⓓ	41. Ⓐ Ⓑ Ⓒ Ⓓ
2. Ⓙ Ⓚ Ⓛ Ⓜ	12. Ⓙ Ⓚ Ⓛ Ⓜ	22. Ⓙ Ⓚ Ⓛ Ⓜ	32. Ⓙ Ⓚ Ⓛ Ⓜ	42. Ⓙ Ⓚ Ⓛ Ⓜ
3. Ⓐ Ⓑ Ⓒ Ⓓ	13. Ⓐ Ⓑ Ⓒ Ⓓ	23. Ⓐ Ⓑ Ⓒ Ⓓ	33. Ⓐ Ⓑ Ⓒ Ⓓ	43. Ⓐ Ⓑ Ⓒ Ⓓ
4. Ⓙ Ⓚ Ⓛ Ⓜ	14. Ⓙ Ⓚ Ⓛ Ⓜ	24. Ⓙ Ⓚ Ⓛ Ⓜ	34. Ⓙ Ⓚ Ⓛ Ⓜ	44. Ⓙ Ⓚ Ⓛ Ⓜ
5. Ⓐ Ⓑ Ⓒ Ⓓ	15. Ⓐ Ⓑ Ⓒ Ⓓ	25. Ⓐ Ⓑ Ⓒ Ⓓ	35. Ⓐ Ⓑ Ⓒ Ⓓ	45. Ⓐ Ⓑ Ⓒ Ⓓ
6. Ⓙ Ⓚ Ⓛ Ⓜ	16. Ⓙ Ⓚ Ⓛ Ⓜ	26. Ⓙ Ⓚ Ⓛ Ⓜ	36. Ⓙ Ⓚ Ⓛ Ⓜ	46. Ⓙ Ⓚ Ⓛ Ⓜ
7. Ⓐ Ⓑ Ⓒ Ⓓ	17. Ⓐ Ⓑ Ⓒ Ⓓ	27. Ⓐ Ⓑ Ⓒ Ⓓ	37. Ⓐ Ⓑ Ⓒ Ⓓ	47. Ⓐ Ⓑ Ⓒ Ⓓ
8. Ⓙ Ⓚ Ⓛ Ⓜ	18. Ⓙ Ⓚ Ⓛ Ⓜ	28. Ⓙ Ⓚ Ⓛ Ⓜ	38. Ⓙ Ⓚ Ⓛ Ⓜ	48. Ⓙ Ⓚ Ⓛ Ⓜ
9. Ⓐ Ⓑ Ⓒ Ⓓ	19. Ⓐ Ⓑ Ⓒ Ⓓ	29. Ⓐ Ⓑ Ⓒ Ⓓ	39. Ⓐ Ⓑ Ⓒ Ⓓ	49. Ⓐ Ⓑ Ⓒ Ⓓ
10. Ⓙ Ⓚ Ⓛ Ⓜ	20. Ⓙ Ⓚ Ⓛ Ⓜ	30. Ⓙ Ⓚ Ⓛ Ⓜ	40. Ⓙ Ⓚ Ⓛ Ⓜ	50. Ⓙ Ⓚ Ⓛ Ⓜ

Ability

Figure Classification

1. Ⓐ Ⓑ Ⓒ Ⓓ Ⓔ	6. Ⓙ Ⓚ Ⓛ Ⓜ Ⓝ	11. Ⓐ Ⓑ Ⓒ Ⓓ Ⓔ	16. Ⓙ Ⓚ Ⓛ Ⓜ Ⓝ
2. Ⓙ Ⓚ Ⓛ Ⓜ Ⓝ	7. Ⓐ Ⓑ Ⓒ Ⓓ Ⓔ	12. Ⓙ Ⓚ Ⓛ Ⓜ Ⓝ	17. Ⓐ Ⓑ Ⓒ Ⓓ Ⓔ
3. Ⓐ Ⓑ Ⓒ Ⓓ Ⓔ	8. Ⓙ Ⓚ Ⓛ Ⓜ Ⓝ	13. Ⓐ Ⓑ Ⓒ Ⓓ Ⓔ	18. Ⓙ Ⓚ Ⓛ Ⓜ Ⓝ
4. Ⓙ Ⓚ Ⓛ Ⓜ Ⓝ	9. Ⓐ Ⓑ Ⓒ Ⓓ Ⓔ	14. Ⓙ Ⓚ Ⓛ Ⓜ Ⓝ	19. Ⓐ Ⓑ Ⓒ Ⓓ Ⓔ
5. Ⓐ Ⓑ Ⓒ Ⓓ Ⓔ	10. Ⓙ Ⓚ Ⓛ Ⓜ Ⓝ	15. Ⓐ Ⓑ Ⓒ Ⓓ Ⓔ	20. Ⓙ Ⓚ Ⓛ Ⓜ Ⓝ

Figure Matrices

1. Ⓐ Ⓑ Ⓒ Ⓓ Ⓔ	6. Ⓙ Ⓚ Ⓛ Ⓜ Ⓝ	11. Ⓐ Ⓑ Ⓒ Ⓓ Ⓔ	16. Ⓙ Ⓚ Ⓛ Ⓜ Ⓝ
2. Ⓙ Ⓚ Ⓛ Ⓜ Ⓝ	7. Ⓐ Ⓑ Ⓒ Ⓓ Ⓔ	12. Ⓙ Ⓚ Ⓛ Ⓜ Ⓝ	17. Ⓐ Ⓑ Ⓒ Ⓓ Ⓔ
3. Ⓐ Ⓑ Ⓒ Ⓓ Ⓔ	8. Ⓙ Ⓚ Ⓛ Ⓜ Ⓝ	13. Ⓐ Ⓑ Ⓒ Ⓓ Ⓔ	18. Ⓙ Ⓚ Ⓛ Ⓜ Ⓝ
4. Ⓙ Ⓚ Ⓛ Ⓜ Ⓝ	9. Ⓐ Ⓑ Ⓒ Ⓓ Ⓔ	14. Ⓙ Ⓚ Ⓛ Ⓜ Ⓝ	19. Ⓐ Ⓑ Ⓒ Ⓓ Ⓔ
5. Ⓐ Ⓑ Ⓒ Ⓓ Ⓔ	10. Ⓙ Ⓚ Ⓛ Ⓜ Ⓝ	15. Ⓐ Ⓑ Ⓒ Ⓓ Ⓔ	20. Ⓙ Ⓚ Ⓛ Ⓜ Ⓝ

Paper Folding

1. Ⓐ Ⓑ Ⓒ Ⓓ Ⓔ   4. Ⓙ Ⓚ Ⓛ Ⓜ Ⓝ   7. Ⓐ Ⓑ Ⓒ Ⓓ Ⓔ   10. Ⓙ Ⓚ Ⓛ Ⓜ Ⓝ

2. Ⓙ Ⓚ Ⓛ Ⓜ Ⓝ   5. Ⓐ Ⓑ Ⓒ Ⓓ Ⓔ   8. Ⓙ Ⓚ Ⓛ Ⓜ Ⓝ

3. Ⓐ Ⓑ Ⓒ Ⓓ Ⓔ   6. Ⓙ Ⓚ Ⓛ Ⓜ Ⓝ   9. Ⓐ Ⓑ Ⓒ Ⓓ Ⓔ

Answer Sheet

Practice Test 3: TACHS

Practice Test 3: TACHS

READING

50 Questions (35 minutes)

Turn to the Reading section of your answer sheet to answer the questions in this section.

Directions: This is a test of how well you understand what you read.

- Read the passages below and then answer the questions.

- Four answers are given for each question. You must choose the answer you think is better than the others.

Questions 1–6 are based on the following passage.

PASSAGE 1

Charlie finally decided that he had had enough of city life. He made up his mind that he was tired of riding the subway an hour to work every day, tired of living in a tiny apartment, and tired of not seeing the sunrise and sunset. Charlie gathered his family around the dinner table
Line and informed them of his desire to escape the concrete jungle permanently. After a few hours,
5 Charlie persuaded his wife and two kids to give the country life a try.

   Two weeks after Charlie made his decision, the family moved into a ranch house in rural Texas. On the day the family moved in, Charlie's youngest, Laurie, got stung by a small scorpion. Only a few hours later, Charlie's wife began sneezing uncontrollably and developed red, watery eyes. Charlie's son found a rattlesnake in the shed shortly thereafter. Before the movers unloaded
10 half the furniture from the truck, Charlie was on the phone with a realtor back in New York City.

1. In sentence 1 of paragraph 2, what does the word *rural* mean?

   A. Western
   B. In the country
   C. Primitive
   D. Scenic

2. Why did Charlie call his realtor before he was even unpacked in Texas?

   J. He was upset with the view from his porch.
   K. He wanted to double-check the price of his new house.
   L. The country life wasn't what he hoped for, and he was ready to move back to the city.
   M. He was disappointed in the movers.

3. All of these contributed to Charlie's decision to move back to New York City *except*

   A. a rattlesnake.

   B. a scorpion.

   C. the realtor.

   D. illness.

4. The phrase "concrete jungle" refers to

   J. Texas.

   K. Charlie's job.

   L. the city.

   M. the country.

5. What can we infer about Charlie's family's move to Texas?

   A. They did not consider potential drawbacks of life in Texas.

   B. They did not want to move to Texas in the first place.

   C. They never planned to stay in Texas permanently.

   D. They will move back to New York while Charlie stays in Texas.

6. When did Charlie make the decision to move back to New York City?

   J. Two weeks after moving

   K. The same day they moved in

   L. Before they left New York City

   M. After their furniture was unpacked

Questions 7–12 are based on the following passage.

PASSAGE 2

In the nineteenth century, a wave of liberalism swept across Europe. Liberals—those who advocated liberalism—heavily favored liberty, equality, and natural rights for citizens of European nations. Specifically, liberals hoped to win for citizens such things as voting rights and equal
Line protection under the law. Ironically, the vast majority of liberals sought these rights for men
5 only and not for women.

Standing in the way of liberal reform were the wealthy nobles, aristocrats, and the monarchs seated precariously on the thrones of Europe. The nobility felt threatened by liberalism because nobles held nearly all political power in early nineteenth-century Europe. Because they held all the power, the common man had virtually no say in the government. The nobles knew that
10 their political positions would be in jeopardy if the common citizens could choose government officials. Ultimately, liberalism proved too strong a force for the aristocracy to defeat.

7. What was the nobles' greatest fear about common citizens winning the right to vote?

   A. Citizens didn't know how to vote.

   B. Citizens might not exercise their right to vote.

   C. Nobles may not get the right to vote.

   D. Citizens probably would elect people who had not been the power-holding nobles prior to elections, thus leaving the nobles with little or no power.

8. Based on context clues in paragraph 2, the word *monarchs* probably means which of the following?

   J. Commoners

   K. Kings and queens

   L. Jesters

   M. Judges

9. In sentence 4 of paragraph 1, the word *ironically* is used to show that

   A. nobles would prevent the liberals from getting rights.

   B. liberals did not really want voting rights and equal protection.

   C. nobles wanted the same things as the liberals wanted.

   D. liberals were not fully practicing what they preached.

10. The passage suggests that

    J. the aristocrats had a strong grip on political power in the nineteenth century.

    K. the liberals could be defeated if the aristocrats and monarchs united.

    L. although the nobles had political power, they were still vulnerable.

    M. the common man now holds all political power in Europe.

11. This passage would most likely appear in

    A. a persuasive article.

    B. a history textbook.

    C. both of these.

    D. neither of these.

12. From the last sentence of the passage, we can infer that

    J. Europe eventually embraced voting rights and equal protection under the law.

    K. the nobles would lose power but become powerful again later.

    L. Europe would embrace voting rights for women.

    M. the liberals would become aristocrats after they took power.

Questions 13–18 are based on the following passage.

PASSAGE 3

Among the famous Seven Wonders of the Ancient World, do you know which one is truly the most ancient? It's the Great Pyramid of Giza, and curiously enough, it's also the only one of the Wonders that still exists and remains largely unscathed by the ravages of time. Let's explore
Line this architectural marvel and discover what makes this structure a truly wonderful monument
5 to human capability.

Based on extensive research by Egyptologists, it's believed that the Great Pyramid of Giza was built around 2560 BC, as a tomb for the Egyptian Pharaoh Khufu of the fourth dynasty. Pyramids commonly served as majestic resting places for dead royalty in Ancient Egypt, but the Great Pyramid of Giza is truly in a class all its own. Its initial height is a staggering 481 feet,
10 the world's tallest man-made structure for nearly 4,000 years. The pyramid contains a series of chambers and levels for its "royal residents," and it is just one of several pyramids that make up the Giza pyramid complex in Cairo, which also includes the Great Sphinx, cemeteries, and an industrial complex. This grand structure is estimated to include more than 2.3 million blocks of limestone and granite (some blocks weighing upwards of 50 tons), likely excavated from nearby
15 quarries, and set with nearly half a million tons of mortar. Although there is a great amount of disagreement among experts regarding how the Egyptians built the pyramid so long ago, one thing that is hardly in dispute is that it is truly a magnificent and awe-inspiring piece of human history.

13. Based on the information in the passage, the author refers to the Great Pyramid of Giza as "truly in a class all its own" because

A. there were no other pyramids located anywhere near it.

B. the pyramid is taller than the others created at the time.

C. you'll likely only learn about the pyramid in a classroom.

D. the original designers had a great deal of formal education.

14. As used in sentence 2 of paragraph 1, what does the word *unscathed* likely mean?

J. Gigantic

K. Modern

L. Not new

M. Unharmed

15. The original purpose of the Great Pyramid of Giza was

A. a tourist attraction.

B. a tomb for a pharaoh.

C. a housing complex.

D. an industrial complex.

16. All of the following make up the structure of the Great Pyramid of Giza *except*

J. mortar.

K. limestone.

L. granite.

M. steel.

PART V: Six Practice Tests

Practice Test 3: TACHS

17. Which of the following is true of the Great Pyramid of Giza?

A. It contains the Great Sphinx.

B. It is the last surviving Wonder of the Ancient World.

C. It is a naturally occurring structure.

D. It is clear how the pyramid was built.

18. Which of the following describes how the author feels about the Great Pyramid of Giza?

J. Bored

K. Impressed

L. Surprised

M. Skeptical

Questions 19–24 are based on the following passage.

PASSAGE 4

As Margie strolled through the mall, a muscular young man handed her a pamphlet advertising a brand-new workout facility across town. Margie took the pamphlet; she had been pondering a new fitness routine. She read as she walked past store after store. On her way through the
Line department store at the end of the mall, she stopped and browsed the fitness equipment in the
5 store. Margie was convinced that she needed to do something to help herself feel better, have more energy, and generally lead a healthier life.

After much thought, Margie decided that an expensive exercise apparatus eventually would turn into an expensive clothes rack in her bedroom. Margie also decided that the new workout facility would be better than the exercise equipment. However, she wondered if a facility on
10 the other side of town would actually deter her from working out regularly. Margie ultimately decided to spend a fraction of the money she would have spent otherwise, and she purchased small set of weights and some workout videos.

19. What was Margie's true feeling about purchasing the expensive exercise equipment?

A. She was afraid she wouldn't know how to use the equipment.

B. She wanted to hang clothes somewhere other than in her closet.

C. She feared that she wouldn't use the equipment enough to justify the price.

D. She didn't think the equipment would fit anywhere except in her bedroom.

20. Based on context clues, what does the word *deter* mean in paragraph 2 of the passage?

J. Allow

K. Include

L. Encourage

M. Discourage

21. Based on the passage, we can infer that

A. Margie will go back and buy the expensive apparatus.

B. Margie will likely not stick to her new routine.

C. Margie will join the gym across town.

D. Margie will be more likely to stick to her new routine.

22. Margie's new fitness routine is most inspired by

J. the pamphlet.

K. her health.

L. the department store.

M. the young man.

23. What makes Margie decide against the new workout facility?

    A. She feels intimidated by the young man with the pamphlet.

    B. It is less effective than weights and a workout video.

    C. She lives too far away from the gym.

    D. It costs too much money.

24. Based on the information in the passage, Margie is

    J. impulsive.

    K. frustrated.

    L. thoughtful.

    M. unhappy.

Questions 25–30 are based on the following passage.

PASSAGE 5

The camp director stood in front of the staff late Friday evening to address her camp counselors. The counselors had been working for two weeks without a break and faced another two weeks of the same routine before camp was to be dismissed for the summer. The counselors

Line directed or participated in activities like swimming and arts and crafts with the campers for
5 12 or 14 hours every day. In addition, the counselors made themselves available to the campers for one-on-one attention, including giving advice and just listening. The counselors poured themselves into their jobs.

    The director looked at the face of each counselor and smiled. She knew how much of themselves they invested in making the camp a success. She said, "When my elbows get rough,
10 dry, and cracked from work and exposure, I rub lotion on them. It's amazing how that can relax and refresh. I want to give each of you some proverbial lotion to soothe your souls. You get tomorrow off!"

25. Which of the following most likely describes the counselors?

    A. Unruly

    B. Disinterested

    C. Exhausted

    D. Confused

26. Why did the director tell the counselors that she wanted to give them "some proverbial lotion"?

    J. She wanted to give them real lotion, but she didn't have enough for everyone.

    K. She wanted to help them relax and refresh themselves by giving them a day off.

    L. She wanted to give the counselors the hint that some of them had dry skin.

    M. She wanted to encourage them to use suntan lotion when working with the campers.

27. Why did the director give the counselors a day off?

    A. She doesn't need them for the next day's activities.

    B. They are overworked, and the director knows they need a break.

    C. They are terrible at doing their jobs.

    D. The campers want the counselors to have a day off.

28. The director can be described as

    J. sympathetic.

    K. heartless.

    L. lazy.

    M. energetic.

29. Based on the passage, how long is the camp in session by the end of the summer?

    A. 2 weeks

    B. 4 weeks

    C. 12 weeks

    D. 16 weeks

30. Which of the following is *not* one of the counselors' duties?

    J. Giving advice

    K. Directing activities

    L. Listening to campers

    M. Providing medical care

Questions 31–38 are based on the following passage.

PASSAGE 6

The birth of modern science is usually traced back to the work of an English philosopher named Sir Francis Bacon. Before Bacon's time, scientific theories as we know them did not exist. Instead, the ideas that were considered to be knowledge were based upon faith, and most came from the philosophies of the church. Bacon was very opposed to this approach to knowledge. He disliked
5 the notion that knowledge could be based simply on beliefs or on the ideas of the church. He searched for a way of developing knowledge that he felt was more reliable.

Bacon was very interested in the facts that we could gain from simply observing what goes on around us in the physical world. He believed that observing the physical world would produce much more reliable knowledge than simply making up knowledge based on beliefs. In
10 1620, Bacon published a book containing his ideas on the importance of developing knowledge through observation of nature. This book, called *The New Organon*, created a foundation for what is now known as "empirical" science, or science that comes from observing that which can be perceived through our senses.

Bacon's approach came to be known by the name *inductivism*. Inductivism is the idea that
15 a person can develop theories about science by observing events. In the inductivist approach, the scientist views a series of repeating events and draws a general conclusion from these events. The scientist takes this conclusion to be true because it is based on experience. A scientist using the inductivist approach might conclude, for instance, that "all swans are white," based solely on the fact that all swans that he has previously observed are white.

31. Which of the titles below best captures the main idea of this selection?

    A. "Understanding the Scientific Method"

    B. "Bacon and the Development of Science"

    C. "Testing Hypotheses and Theories"

    D. "The History of Sir Francis Bacon"

32. Why did Sir Francis Bacon search for a way to develop knowledge based on observing the physical world?

    J. He believed that knowledge based on observing similar, repeated events was unreliable.

    K. He believed that knowledge based on the principle of inductivism was unreliable.

    L. He believed that knowledge based on faith, or the ideas of the church, was unreliable.

    M. He believed that knowledge based on the principle of falsification was unreliable.

33. Bacon's approach to science was known as

    A. inductivism.

    B. positivism.

    C. radicalism.

    D. relativism.

34. Before Bacon, scientific knowledge was based on

    J. concepts from astronomy.

    K. rigorous testing.

    L. legal precepts.

    M. the ideas of the church.

35. Bacon's book, *The New Organon*, focused on

    A. refining knowledge that is based on personal beliefs.

    B. developing knowledge perceived through the senses.

    C. revising the ideas of political leaders of Bacon's time.

    D. practicing strict scientific discipline in all research.

36. Which of the following would Bacon be most likely to accept as scientific knowledge?

    J. Ideas based on church doctrine

    K. Untested philosophical concepts

    L. Theories based on empirical facts

    M. A hypothesis based on opinion

37. Inductivist theories are developed from

    A. observing events.

    B. scientific mistakes.

    C. ongoing debates.

    D. experimental competitions.

38. Based on the context clues in paragraph 2, the word *foundation* most likely means

    J. charity.

    K. support.

    L. method.

    M. physical structure.

Questions 39–44 are based on the following passage.

PASSAGE 7

In the not-too-distant past, recycling meant dividing materials into separate containers so that they could be recycled with like materials: cans and bottles with other cans and bottles, paper with paper, etc. Since the 1990s, however, a new and innovative recycling trend has emerged—
Line one that makes the process more manageable for people who want to be environmentally con-
5 scious but want an easier way to do it.

As a solution, single-stream recycling was developed in the late 1990s in California. In it, recyclables stay together in one container—cans, plastic bottles, paper, glass, cardboard—and sent to a facility that parses out each material type and packages them for separate recycling. The recyclable materials are still separated from regular garbage like Styrofoam® and food
10 waste, but the process is simplified. This type of single-stream recycling encourages people to recycle more, because they spend less time separating out recyclables from regular trash. The efficiency has led to many towns and cities across the country adopting single-stream recycling processes to replace the old dual-stream facilities. As of 2013, more than 100 million Americans used single-stream recycling programs.

39. Based on the context clues in the passage, what does *like* (sentence 1) mean?

A. Enjoy
B. Similar
C. As if
D. None of the above

40. Which of the following is the best way to describe single-stream recycling?

J. Unsuccessful
K. Growing
L. Expensive
M. Old-fashioned

41. Which of these titles best expresses the main idea of the selection?

A. "Simplifying the Streams in Recycling"
B. "The Wide World of Recycling"
C. "Living a Sustainable Life in the 21st Century"
D. "Recycling Since 2013"

42. As used in the passage, the word *parses* most likely means

J. decides.
K. understands.
L. separates.
M. finishes.

43. What is the main difference between single-stream recycling and dual-stream recycling?

A. The amount of processing done by the recycling facilities
B. The types of materials that are recyclable
C. The quantity of garbage sent to landfills
D. The amount of work consumers need to do at the start of the process

44. Which of these is not a recyclable material, according to the passage?

J. Glass
K. Cardboard
L. Styrofoam®
M. Plastic bottles

Questions 45–50 are based on the following passage.

PASSAGE 8

There was nothing of the giant in the aspect of the man who was beginning to awaken on the sleeping porch of a Dutch Colonial house in that residential district of Zenith known as Floral Heights.

His name was George F. Babbitt. He was forty-six years old now, in April, 1920, and he made nothing in particular, neither butter nor shoes nor poetry, but he was nimble in the calling of selling houses for more than people could afford to pay.

His large head was pink, his brown hair thin and dry. His face was babyish in slumber, despite his wrinkles and the red spectacle-dents on the slopes of his nose. He was not fat but he was exceedingly well fed; his cheeks were pads, and the unroughened hand which lay helpless upon the khaki-colored blanket was slightly puffy. He seemed prosperous, extremely married and unromantic; and altogether unromantic appeared this sleeping-porch, which looked on one sizable elm, two respectable grass-plots, a cement driveway, and a corrugated iron garage. Yet Babbitt was again dreaming of the fairy child, a dream more romantic than scarlet pagodas by a silver sea.

—from *Babbitt*, by Sinclair Lewis

45. George Babbitt is
   A. a real estate salesman.
   B. a poet.
   C. a shoemaker.
   D. a teacher.

46. The physical description of George Babbitt suggests that he is
   J. very young.
   K. physically fit.
   L. not very fit.
   M. giant.

47. Based on the passage, we can infer that Babbitt
   A. has no interest in imaginary things.
   B. has a richer inner life than one would expect.
   C. has no friends or family.
   D. has a special interest in the sea.

48. The author uses the phrase "unroughened hand" to suggest that Babbitt
   J. is a hard worker.
   K. does not do manual labor.
   L. is healthy.
   M. has a lot of wealth.

49. What common saying best sums up the passage?

    A. Appearances can be deceiving.
    B. Judge not lest you be judged.
    C. Money makes the world go 'round.
    D. When life gives you lemons, make lemonade.

50. The neighborhood that George Babbitt lives in is called

    J. Dutch Colony.
    K. Zenith.
    L. Floral Heights.
    M. None of the above

STOP.

If you finish before time is UP, you may check your work on this section only.
Do not turn to any other section in the test.

Practice Test 3: TACHS

WRITTEN EXPRESSION

50 Questions (30 minutes)

Turn to the Written Expression section of your answer sheet to answer the questions in this section.

Directions: This is a test of how well you can find mistakes in writing.

- For the questions with mistakes in spelling, capitalization, and punctuation, choose the answer with the same letter as the **line** containing the mistake.

- For the questions with mistakes in usage and expression, choose the answer with the same letter as the **line** containing the mistake, or choose the word, phrase, or sentence that is better than the others.

- When there is no mistake or no change needed, choose the last answer choice.

1. **A.** ocean
   B. calculater
   C. trench
   D. minute
   E. *(No mistakes)*

2. **J.** transport
   K. attitude
   L. sinse
   M. evaluate
   N. *(No mistakes)*

3. **A.** receive
   B. fault
   C. liquid
   D. lable
   E. *(No mistakes)*

4. **J.** notebook
   K. famine
   L. zebra
   M. knolledge
   N. *(No mistakes)*

5. **A.** destination
   B. declare
   C. mischief
   D. concquer
   E. *(No mistakes)*

6. **J.** liquid
   K. scrumptious
   L. agregate
   M. conspicuous
   N. *(No mistakes)*

7. **A.** finished
   B. relyable
   C. chrome
   D. disappoint
   E. *(No mistakes)*

8. **J.** credible
   K. starlight
   L. venom
   M. accelerate
   N. *(No mistakes)*

9. **A.** initiate

   B. simply

   C. govenor

   D. decline

   E. *(No mistakes)*

10. **J.** monstrous

   K. protection

   L. fields

   M. decieve

   N. *(No mistakes)*

11. **A.** To find my dog, rover, I

   B. sailed across the ocean

   C. to the Johnson's farm.

   D. *(No mistakes)*

12. **J.** The king's jet flew

   K. over the Andes Mountains

   L. and beyond the river.

   M. *(No mistakes)*

13. **A.** The New York Jets' kicker and

   B. the Dallas cowboys' punter

   C. are actually Atlanta Falcons fans.

   D. *(No mistakes)*

14. **J.** President Jefferson once lived

   K. in the famous Virginia Home

   L. known as Monticello.

   M. *(No mistakes)*

15. **A.** For christmas last year,

   B. mom and dad gave me

   C. a coat just like Jamie's.

   D. *(No mistakes)*

16. **J.** The Basketball Coach sent

   K. the injured basketball player

   L. to see Dr. Moore.

   M. *(No mistakes)*

17. **A.** Dr. Jose Sandoz had never

   B. expect to see his cousin

   C. Jules at his office last Monday.

   D. *(No mistakes)*

18. **J.** How many times did j.j.

   K. take a bite of Buddy's ice cream

   L. when Buddy was talking to Sally?

   M. *(No mistakes)*

19. **A.** The leading candy company,

   B. Sweet Tooth, inc., just announced

   C. a new candy bar called O Yum.

   D. *(No mistakes)*

20. **J.** I can't remember if California

   K. is the biggest State

   L. or if Texas is the biggest.

   M. *(No mistakes)*

Practice Test 3: TACHS

Directions: For questions 21 and 22, choose the best way of expressing the idea.

21. **A.** At Shara's office, with incredible food, there was great music, as well as there being an exciting midnight countdown—the New Year's Eve party was an amazing event.

    B. There was incredible food. There was great music. There was an exciting countdown. At midnight, at Shara's office. There was a New Year's Eve party, an amazing event.

    C. The New Year's Eve party at Shara's office was an amazing event, with incredible food, great music, and an exciting midnight countdown.

    D. What an event, an amazing event. There was a party at Shara's office, a New Year's Eve party. There was lots of stuff that made it a great event. There was food, incredible food. Great music that was really great to listen to. And, there was an exciting countdown, at midnight it happened.

22. **J.** To understand advanced calculus, Mr. Johnson has an uncanny knack for teaching his students.

    K. Mr. Johnson has an uncanny knack for teaching his students to understand advanced calculus.

    L. An uncanny knack for teaching his students, Mr. Johnson has to understand advanced calculus.

    M. For teaching his students to understand advanced calculus, Mr. Johnson has an uncanny knack.

Directions: For questions 23–30, choose the best answer based on the following paragraphs.

(1) Although <u>seventy-one</u> percent of the earth's surface is covered with water, freshwater makes up less than three percent of this total. (2) Access to safe drinking water has improved over the last decade; however, many people around the world still lack a reliable supply. (3) To ensure that clean water is available for current and future <u>populations water</u> conservation strategies and practices are essential. (4) These efforts must consider the sustainability of the water supply so that freshwater is not removed more quickly than it can be replaced by an ecosystem. (5) Water conservation policies must also focus on delivering safe drinking water efficiently and preserving freshwater habitats for local wildlife.

23. What is the best way to write the underlined part of sentence 1?

   A. seventy one

   B. seventyone

   C. seventy, one

   D. (*No change*)

24. What is the best way to write the underlined part of sentence 3?

   J. populations, water

   K. populations—water

   L. populations. Water

   M. (*No change*)

(1) Today's vloggers aren't just aimless and meandering individuals who have more free time on their hands than motivation and ambition. (2) As sources of media entertainment shift from corporate studios and major networks to creative individuals with cameras, vloggers represent burgeoning and evolving media brands. (3) Some of the most popular vlogs and <u>there</u> creators are now multi-million-dollar empires, with legions of loyal fans and followers. (4) The entertainment landscape has truly <u>changed; according</u> to a recent study by the Interactive Advertising Bureau, more people watch original internet video content than primetime network television. (5) This trend, spurred on by lightning-quick advances in technology, could hardly have been predicted just a few decades ago.

25. What is the best way to write the underlined part of sentence 3?

   A. their

   B. they are

   C. they're

   D. (*No change*)

26. What is the best way to write the underlined part of sentence 4?

   J. changed according

   K. changed, according

   L. changed? According

   M. (*No change*)

(1) Located 67 miles west of Key West, Florida, the Dry Tortugas are a remote collection of seven small islands, or keys, encompassing about 143 acres. (2) All of the keys' shorelines are affected by erosion; over the years, islands have disappeared and reappeared following strong storms. (3) Visitors arrive by seaplane or boat to visit Dry Tortugas National Park, which <u>included</u> all the islands and the surrounding waters and is known for its clear blue waters, brilliant coral reefs, varied marine and bird life, and the former military fortress, Fort Jefferson. (4) Some of the keys are larger <u>then</u> others. (5) Loggerhead Key, Garden Key, and Bush Key make up more than ninety percent of the Dry Tortugas, while other keys are merely sand bars rising out of the sea.

27. What is the best way to write the underlined part of sentence 3?

   A. includes

   B. had included

   C. has been including

   D. (*No change*)

28. What is the best way to write the underlined part of sentence 4?

   J. as opposed to

   K. regardless of

   L. than

   M. (*No change*)

(1) For many Commuters, being locked in gridlock traffic on crowded highways is a common frustration. (2) In the not-so-distant future, however, our daily commute to work, school, and other activities might involve flying instead of driving. (3) Developed after years of experimentation, the Skycar is the most promising flying car model to date. (4) Reaching speeds of 400 mph, the Skycar has a range of 900 miles and is fully automated using Global Positioning System (GPS) satellites. (5) Although their high costs now make them impractical, flying cars could cost about $60,000 each if they are eventually mass produced. (6) Flying cars taking to the open skies may finally move from the realm of science fiction to everyday reality.

29. What is the best way to write the underlined part of sentence 1?

   A. commuter

   B. commuters'

   C. commuters

   D. (*No change*)

30. What is the best way to write the underlined part of sentence 5?

   J. their

   K. there

   L. it's

   M. (*No change*)

(1) There aren't many national monuments in the United States as ominously named as Devil's Tower. (2) This unmistakable rock formation, technically a butte, will be located in the Bear Lodge Mountains in northeastern Wyoming. (3) A butte, derived from the French word that means "small hill," is a lone hill that is characterized by steep vertical sides and a flat peak. (4) Devil's Tower is made of Igneous Rock and is approximately 867 feet from its base to its summit. (5) Hundred's of thousands of tourists come to visit Devil's Tower annually, and the tower holds the distinction of being the first declared United States National Monument, having achieved this status in 1906.

31. What is the best way to write the underlined portion of sentence 2?

   A. was located

   B. is located

   C. wasn't located

   D. (*No change*)

32. What is the best way to write the underlined portion of sentence 4?

   J. igneous rock

   K. Igneous rock

   L. igneous Rock

   M. (*No change*)

(1) When people discuss the most memorable presidents in United States history, Millard Fillmore tends not to enter the construction. (2) Fillmore, the 13th President of the United States, entered the office in 1850 as a member of the Whig party. (3) Fillmore became president following the death of his predecessor, Zachary Taylor. (4) Among Fillmore's achievements was their involvement in getting the Compromise of 1850 passed, which helped forge a temporary compromise between slave states and free states. (5) Following his presidency, Fillmore and his wife, whom he married after retiring from politics, devoted themselves to philanthropic and social pursuits.

33. What is the best way to write the underlined portion of sentence 1?

A. conversation
B. combination
C. conservation
D. (*No change*)

34. What is the best way to write the underlined portion of sentence 4?

J. our involvement
K. her involvement
L. his involvement
M. (*No change*)

(1) A variety of artistic <u>movements; have</u> taken the spotlight in the cultural landscape of the United States over the years. (2) Among those is the Hudson River School, which began to rise in popularity and prominence in the mid-19th century. (3) The Hudson River School, whose genesis occurred in the Hudson River Valley of New York, was characterized by stunning landscape designs that were heavily influenced by 18th century European romanticism. (4) Artists who are recognized as prominent members of the Hudson River School include <u>Frederic Edwin Church—Asher Durand—and Thomas Cole</u>. (5) Fine examples of this artistic movement are part of permanent collections in museums and galleries across the country, and many pieces have become highly collectible and exceedingly valuable over the years.

35. What is the best way to write the underlined portion of sentence 1?

A. movements have
B. movements. Have
C. movements—have
D. (*No change*)

36. What is the best way to write the underlined portion of sentence 4?

J. Frederic Edwin Church, Asher Durand, and Thomas Cole
K. Frederic Edwin Church; Asher Durand, and Thomas Cole
L. "Frederic Edwin Church," "Asher Durand," and "Thomas Cole"
M. (*No change*)

(1) Tic-tac-toe is a popular but relatively simple <u>(game)</u>, and it has a long history that includes a valuable life lesson. (2) A game that is traditionally played by children using paper and pencil, versions of this game can be traced back to <u>Ancient Egypt</u>. (3) During a game of tic-tac-toe, one player selects Xs and one player select Os, and they proceed to place markers in a 3x3 grid until one player gets three markers in a row and wins. (4) More often than not, the grid is filled with Xs and Os and neither player gets 3 markers in a row; when this occurs, the game ends in a draw. (5) Some claim that tic-tac-toe is a metaphor for life: some battles between opponents are futile and the best possible outcome is a tie, where no one wins and no one loses.

37. What is the best way to write the underlined portion of sentence 1?

   A. "game"

   B. *game*

   C. game

   D. (*No change*)

38. What is the best way to write the underlined portion of sentence 2?

   J. Ancient egypt

   K. ancient Egypt

   L. ancient egypt

   M. (*No change*)

(1) Many of us are <u>aware of or familiar with</u> the phrase "pug ugly," but how much do you know about this popular dog breed? (2) Pugs are actually one of the world's oldest dog breeds, having originated in ancient China as early as 550 BC. (3) Pugs <u>were originally bred</u> to be companion animals for China's elite ruling families, and were brought to Europe in the 16th century, after which they spread to the entire world and grew in popularity. (4) Despite prominent appearances in movies, television shows, and commercials worldwide, opinion seems to be split between those who find pugs adorable and those who consider them unattractive. (5) Perhaps one of the primary jobs that pugs have today is to remind us of the phrase that "beauty is in the eye of the beholder."

39. What is the best way to write the underlined portion of sentence 1?

   A. familiar with

   B. aware of and familiar with

   C. aware with and familiar of

   D. (*No change*)

40. What is the best way to write the underlined portion of sentence 3?

   J. will be originally bred

   K. is originally bred

   L. will one day originally be bred

   M. (*No change*)

(1) What do you know about the <u>avocado!</u> (2) Interestingly, what we commonly refer to as avocadoes are actually the fruit from an avocado tree, and they are actually big berries that each contain a prominent seed in the middle. (3) Commercially available avocadoes in the United States typically come from Mexico, California, and Peru, and are harvested before they are ripe. (4) Once they are dark and soft to the touch, avocadoes are ready to be eaten, and despite their high fat levels, they actually pack quite a nutritional punch. (5) An average avocado is rich in a wide array of vitamins and minerals, including vitamin B, vitamin K, vitamin C, potassium, and lutein.

41. What is the best way to write the underlined portion of sentence 1?

   A. avocado.

   B. avocado;

   C. avocado?

   D. (*No change*)

42. Choose the best last sentence to add to this paragraph.

   J. That's one healthy vegetable!

   K. That's one nutritious fruit!

   L. You should take a multivitamin every day!

   M. What's your favorite food?

(1) Have you ever said a palindrome out loud? (2) Palindromes are curious creations, and refer to words and phrases that read the same <u>forwards and sideways</u>, like *Anna* or *racecar*. (3) Although the modern word *palindrome* was coined by an English playwright in the 17th century, palindromes <u>unfortunately</u> date back to 79 AD, in ancient Greece. (4) If you're ever on the hunt for an extra long palindrome, the *Guinness Book of World Records* places the Finnish word *saippuakivikauppias* as the world's longest everyday palindromic word.

43. What is the best way to write the underlined portion of sentence 2?

A. forwards and backwards
B. upside down and right-side up
C. diagonally and sideways
D. (*No change*)

44. What is the best way to write the underlined portion of sentence 3?

J. actually
K. accidentally
L. jokingly
M. (*No change*)

(1) If you've ever been to Lancaster County, Pennsylvania, you may have come across a group of <u>Amish person</u>. (2) Amish people, who are popularly characterized by their simple style of clothing and lifestyle as well as rejection of various modern technologies, immigrated to Pennsylvania in the early 18th century. (3) Jakob Ammann, a Swiss leader of the Anabaptist religion, is commonly recognized as the <u>Founder and Namesake</u> of the Amish religious movement. (4) Recent census studies suggest that there are approximately 250,000 Amish people currently living in the United States, and this population is growing at a far faster rate than other demographic groups within the country.

45. What is the best way to write the underlined portion of sentence 1?

A. Amish individual
B. Amish people
C. Amish worker
D. (*No change*)

46. What is the best way to write the underlined portion of sentence 3?

J. founder and Namesake
K. Founder and namesake
L. founder and namesake
M. (*No change*)

(1) Have you ever wondered about the inspiration behind the dark, gothic castle that's featured prominently in *Dracula*? (2) Bran Castle, a national monument and fortress that lies on the border of Wallachia and Transylvania, is popularly referred to as "Dracula's Castle." (3) The castle, perched on top of a hill and <u>designed. In</u> the medieval architectural style, has a wealth of rooms, chambers, and secret passages. (4) Despite its nickname, Bran Castle is just one of many locations that have been linked to the legend of Dracula, and was never described as the home of the character in the book. (5) Today, Bran Castle is <u>an unpopular</u> tourist attraction, and many tourists from all over the world come annually for a visit.

47. What is the best way to write the underlined portion of sentence 3?

   A. designed, in

   B. designed; in

   C. designed in

   D. (*No change*)

48. What is the best way to write the underlined portion of sentence 5?

   J. a confusing

   K. a popular

   L. an aromatic

   M. (*No change*)

(1) If you've ever paid a visit to Buckingham Palace in London, England, you may have noticed the distinctive Queen's Guard, clad in red coats and large fur hats. (2) Many people are familiar with the daily Changing the Guard ceremony, a popular tourist spectacle that includes one regiment of soldiers marching to replace the regiment currently on duty, which lasts approximately <u>45 years</u>. (3) These cavalry and infantry soldiers are charged with protecting the official residences of the royal family in the United Kingdom. (4) Those interested in becoming a member of the Queen's Guard must go through a rigorous <u>application interview and training</u> process.

49. What is the best way to write the underlined portion of sentence 2?

   A. 45 minutes

   B. 45 weeks

   C. 45 months

   D. (*No change*)

50. What is the best way to write the underlined portion of sentence 4?

   J. "application interview and training"

   K. application interview; and training

   L. application, interview, and training

   M. (*No change*)

STOP.

If you finish before time is UP, you may check your work on this section only.
Do not turn to any other section in the test.

Practice Test 3: TACHS

MATHEMATICS

50 Questions (40 minutes)

Turn to the Mathematics section of your answer sheet to answer the questions in this section.

> **Directions:** Four answers are given for each problem. Choose the best answer.

1. According to the bar graph below, what was the approximate income of Southerners in 2013?

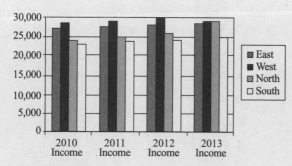

   A. $25,000

   B. $26,000

   C. $27,000

   D. $28,000

2. The pie chart below illustrates the proposed budget for a new company opening soon around the corner. Based on the information in the chart, what will be the most expensive part of running the new company?

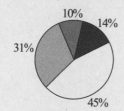

   J. Advertising

   K. Office Supplies

   L. Salaries

   M. Rent & Utilities

3. Which two items in the proposed budget when added together equal the amount spent on salaries?

   A. Advertising and Office Supplies

   B. Rent & Utilities and Office Supplies

   C. Advertising and Salaries

   D. Advertising and Rent & Utilities

Use the following chart for Questions 4 and 5:

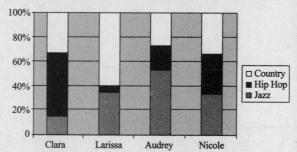

4. The chart above represents the music collections of four high school seniors. Based on the information in the chart, which of the girls has a music collection composed of approximately 60 percent country music?

   J. Clara

   K. Larissa

   L. Audrey

   M. Nicole

5. Based on the information in the chart, if all four collections are the same size, which girl seems to prefer jazz to both hip hop and country music?

   A. Clara

   B. Larissa

   C. Audrey

   D. Nicole

Directions: For the following questions, estimate the answer in your head. No scratch work is allowed. Do *not* try to compute exact answers.

6. According to the chart, if 100 seniors were surveyed, about how many seniors prefer pizza?

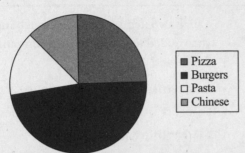

Favorite Foods of New York High School Seniors

J. 10

K. 15

L. 25

M. Not given

7. Most half-hour television shows are actually 23 minutes long once commercial time is deducted. If this is true, approximately how many seconds of commercials do viewers see in one half-hour show?

A. 300

B. 400

C. 500

D. 600

8. The closest estimate of 43 + 71 + 19 + 68 + 11 + 29 is _____ .

J. 200

K. 210

L. 240

M. 300

9. The closest estimate of 63,977 ÷ 7,991 is _____ .

A. 8

B. 80

C. 256

D. Not given

10. The closest estimate of 414 − 289 − 106 + 89 + 277 is _____ .

J. 300

K. 400

L. 500

M. 600

Directions: Four answers are given for each problem. Choose the best answer.

11. The combination of which two portrait types make up half of the entire collection?

The Hudson Museum Portraits

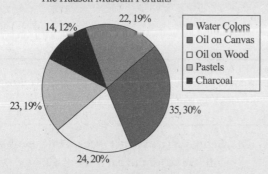

Legend:
- Water Colors
- Oil on Canvas
- Oil on Wood
- Pastels
- Charcoal

- 22, 19%
- 14, 12%
- 23, 19%
- 35, 30%
- 24, 20%

A. Oil on Canvas and Oil on Wood

B. Water Colors and Oil on Canvas

C. Charcoal and Pastels

D. Pastels and Water Colors

Use the following chart for Questions 12 and 13:

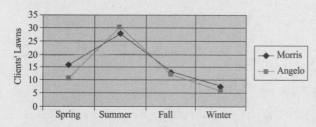

12. The chart above shows the number of yards serviced by Morris and Angelo, each of whom runs a small lawn-care business. Based on the information in the chart, what is the busiest season for lawn care?

J. Spring

K. Summer

L. Fall

M. Winter

13. Based on the information in the chart, which of the following statements is true?

A. Morris experienced a bigger decline in business from the summer to the winter than did Angelo.

B. Angelo experienced a bigger decline in business from the summer to the winter than did Morris.

C. Angelo and Morris experienced the same decline in business from the summer to the winter.

D. Neither Morris nor Angelo experienced a decline in business from the summer to the winter.

Use the following chart for Questions 14 and 15:

Kensington Athletic Club Members

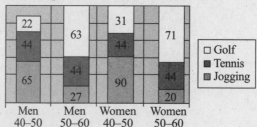

Legend:
- Golf
- Tennis
- Jogging

| Men 40–50 | Men 50–60 | Women 40–50 | Women 50–60 |

14. The chart above illustrates the members of the Kensington Athletic Club between the ages of 40 and 60 and the sports in which they currently participate. Based on the information in the chart, which sport becomes the most popular as both men and women grow older?

J. Golf

K. Tennis

L. Jogging

M. Not enough information available

Practice Test 3: TACHS

15. Based on the information in the chart, which sport currently has the most total members participating in it?

   A. Golf

   B. Tennis

   C. Jogging

   D. Not enough information available

Directions: For the following questions, estimate the answer in your head. No scratch work is allowed. Do *not* try to compute exact answers.

---

16. A typical plain bagel has about 250 calories, and a typical glass of orange juice has about 160 calories. A jelly donut with chocolate icing and sprinkles has about 740 calories, and a large soda has about 255 calories. About how many bagel–juice combos would it take to equal the number of calories in the jelly donut and a large soda?

   J. $1\frac{1}{2}$

   K. 2

   L. $2\frac{1}{2}$

   M. 3

17. The closest estimate of $385 - (2.9 \times 15.8)$ is _____ .

   A. 337

   B. 355

   C. 360

   D. 415

18. George earns $10 per week. How many weeks will it take him to earn about $255?

   J. 25

   K. 52

   L. 144

   M. Not given

19. The closest estimate of 7.1×7.9 is _____ .

   A. 49

   B. 56

   C. 63

   D. 70

20. The closest estimate of $221.8 \div 9.989$ is _____ .

   J. 11

   K. 12

   L. 20

   M. 22

Directions: For questions 21–50, read each problem and find the answer.

21. $(6 \times 2) + (7 \times 3) =$

- **A.** $(6 \times 7) + (2 \times 3)$
- **B.** $(7 - 6) + (3 - 2)$
- **C.** $(7 \times 3) + (6 \times 2)$
- **D.** $(7 \times 3) \times (6 \times 2)$

22. Which of the following will substitute for x and make the statement below true?

$$56 - (7 - x) = 53$$

- **J.** 1
- **K.** 2
- **L.** 3
- **M.** 4

23. An angle that is greater than 90° and less than 180° is a(n)

- **A.** acute angle.
- **B.** right angle.
- **C.** reflex angle.
- **D.** obtuse angle.

24.

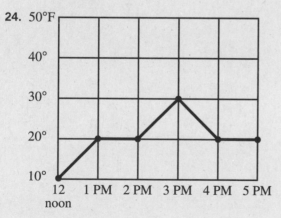

What was the average temperature on the afternoon shown on the above graph?

- **J.** 20°
- **K.** 24°
- **L.** 25°
- **M.** 30°

25. Mr. Jones has agreed to borrow $3,500 for one year at 10% interest. What is the total amount he will pay back to the bank?

- **A.** $350
- **B.** $3,675
- **C.** $3,700
- **D.** $3,850

26. Which of the following statements is true?

- **J.** $4 \times 5 < 4 \times 1 + 6$
- **K.** $87 \div 3 < 30$
- **L.** $2^5 = 2 \times 5$
- **M.** $\frac{1}{4} < \frac{1}{5}$

27. If one angle of a triangle measures 115°, then the sum of the other two angles is

- **A.** 65°
- **B.** 75°
- **C.** 195°
- **D.** 245°

28. At 20 miles per hour, how long does it take to travel 1 mile?

- **J.** 1 min.
- **K.** 2 min.
- **L.** 3 min.
- **M.** 4 min.

29. Approximate the circumference of a circle whose radius is 21 feet. (Use $\pi = \frac{22}{7}$.)

- **A.** 65.94 feet
- **B.** 132 feet
- **C.** 153 feet
- **D.** 1,769.4 feet

30. If $x > -4$, and $x < 2$, then $\{x\}$ includes

J. $-4, 0, 1, 2$

K. $-2, -1, 1, 2$

L. $1, 2, 3, 4$

M. $-3, -2, -1, 0, 1$

31.

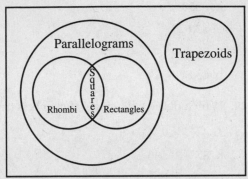

From the diagram above, we know that

A. all trapezoids are parallelograms.

B. some rhombi are parallelograms.

C. some rectangles are rhombi.

D. all parallelograms are rectangles.

32. How many 2-inch tiles would have to be put around the outside edge of a 4-foot × 12-foot rectangle to completely frame the rectangle?

J. 32

K. 36

L. 192

M. 196

33. A certain highway intersection has had A accidents over a ten-year period, resulting in B deaths. What is the yearly average death rate for the intersection?

A. $A + B - 10$

B. $\dfrac{B}{10}$

C. $10 - \dfrac{A}{B}$

D. $\dfrac{AB}{12}$

34. Which point is named by the ordered pair $(-4, 4)$?

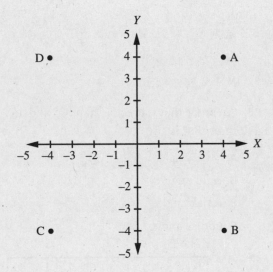

J. A

K. B

L. C

M. D

35. What are the coordinates of point P on the graph?

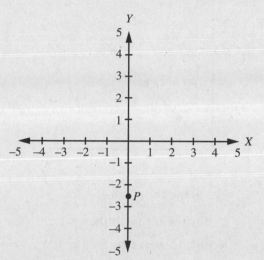

A. $\left(-2\frac{1}{2}, 0\right)$

B. $\left(0, -3\frac{1}{2}\right)$

C. $\left(0, -2\frac{1}{2}\right)$

D. $\left(-1, -2\frac{1}{2}\right)$

36. On a blueprint, 2 inches represents 24 feet. How long must a line be to represent 72 feet?

J. 4 inches

K. 6 inches

L. 12 inches

M. 36 inches

37. A store puts a pair of $14 jeans on sale at a 25% discount. What is the new selling price?

A. $3.50

B. $10.50

C. $13.65

D. $13.75

38.

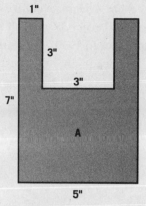

The area of figure A is

J. 19 sq. in.

K. 26 sq. in.

L. 30 sq. in.

M. 44 sq. in.

39. A boy of M years old has a brother six years older and a sister four years younger. The combined age of the three is

A. $M + 10$

B. $3M + 2$

C. $3M - 2$

D. $2M - 6$

40. Event A occurs every 14 minutes and event B every 12 minutes. If they both occur at 1:00 p.m., when will be the next time that both occur together?

J. 1:48 p.m.

K. 2:12 p.m.

L. 2:24 p.m.

M. 3:48 p.m.

41. The ratio of the six inches to six feet is

A. 1:6

B. 12:1

C. 1:12

D. 24:1

Practice Test 3: TACHS

42. Event A occurs every 4 years, event B every 11 years, and event C every 33 years. If they last occurred together in 1950, what is the next year they will occur simultaneously?

J. 1983

K. 2082

L. 3402

M. 6804

43.

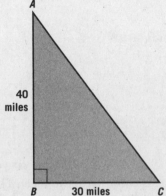

Two drivers begin at point *C* simultaneously. One drives from *C* to *B* to *A*. The other drives directly to *A* at 50 mph. How fast must the first person drive to get to *A* first?

A. Less than 50 mph

B. Less than 60 mph

C. Less than 70 mph

D. More than 70 mph

44.

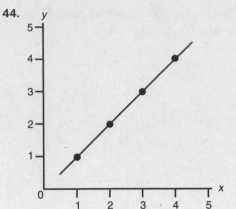

The graph above shows

J. *x* increasing faster than *y*.

K. *y* increasing faster than *x*.

L. *x* increasing as fast as *y*.

M. no relationship between *x* and *y*.

45. In the number 6,000,600,000, there are

A. 6 billions and 6 hundred thousands.

B. 6 millions and 6 thousands.

C. 6 billions and 6 millions.

D. 6 millions and 60 thousands.

46. One of the scales used in drawing topographic maps is 1:24,000. On a scale of this sort, 1 inch on the map would equal how much distance on the ground?

J. 1 inch

K. 2,000 feet

L. 24,000 feet

M. 1 mile

47. If 'A' number of people each make 'L' things, the total number of things made is

A. A/L

B. $A + L$

C. $A - L$

D. AL

48.

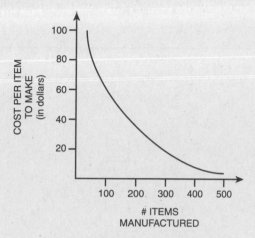

Based upon the graph above, what is the cost per item if 300 items are manufactured?

J. < $20

K. $20

L. $28

M. $40

49.

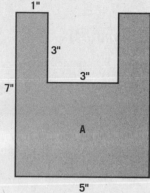

Note: In the figure above, assume that any angle which appears to be a right angle *is* a right angle.

The perimeter of figure A is

A. 19 in.

B. 23 in.

C. 24 in.

D. 30 in.

50. Of 27 people in a certain group, 15 are men and 12 are women. In simplest form, what is the ratio of men to women?

J. 15:12

K. 12:15

L. 5:4

M. 27:12

STOP.

If you finish before time is up, you may check your work on this section only.
Do not turn to any other section in the test.

Practice Test 3: TACHS

ABILITY

50 Questions (32 minutes)

Figure Classification

Turn to the Ability section of your answer sheet to answer the questions in this section.

> **Directions:** In questions 1–20, the first three figures are alike in certain ways. Choose the answer choice that corresponds to the first three figures.

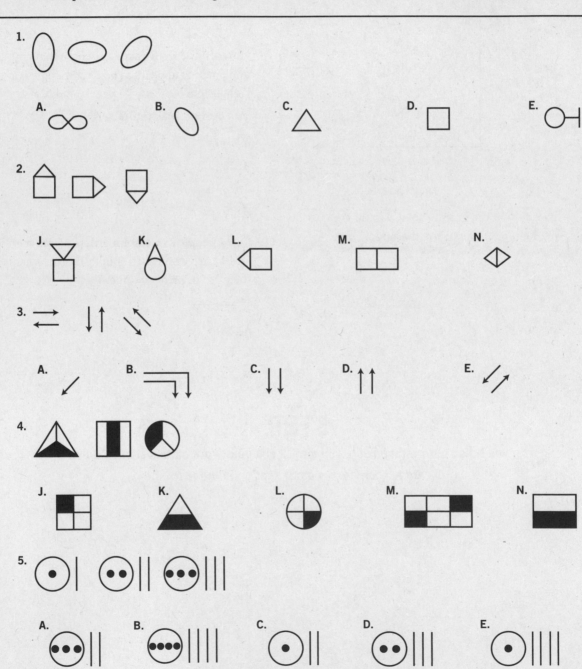

6.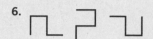

J.   K.   L.   M.   N.

7.

A.   B.   C.   D.   E.

8.

J.   K.   L.   M.   N.

9.

A.   B.   C.   D.   E.

10.

J.   K.   L.   M.   N.

11.

A.   B.   C.   D.   E.

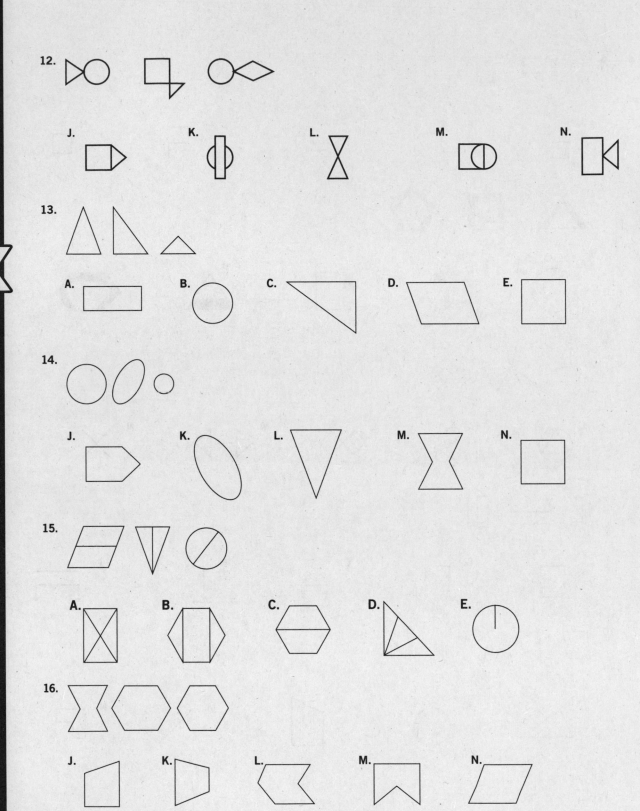

Practice Test 3: TACHS

17.

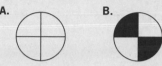

A.   **B.**   **C.**   **D.**   **E.**

18.

J.   **K.**   **L.**   **M.**   **N.**

19.

A. **B.** **C.** **D.** **E.**

20.

J.   **K.** 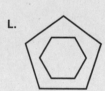 **L.**   **M.**   **N.**

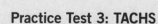

Figure Matrices

Directions: In questions 1–20, find the figure that completes the matrix.

1.

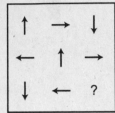

A. →

B. ↑

C. ←

D. ↓

E. ↗

2.

J. ⊙⊙

K. (vertical circles)

L. ○○○

M. ─○─

N. ||

3.

A. △ ○

B. ○

C. △

D. □

E. △ □

4.

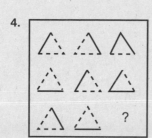

J. K. L. M. N.

5.

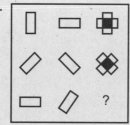

A. B. C. D. E.

6.

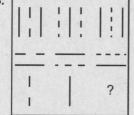

J. K. L. M. N.

7.

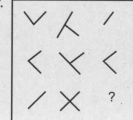

A. B. C. D. E.

8.

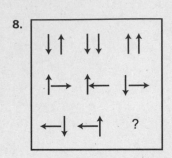

J.   K.   L. ↑↑   M. →↑   N. ←↑

9.

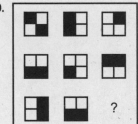

A. ○—■   B. □—●   C. ■—●   D. ●—■   E. ○—□

10.

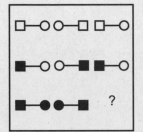

J.   K.   L.   M.   N.

11.

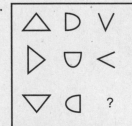

A.   B. △   C. ∧   D. ⊕   E. >

12.

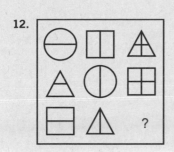

J.   K.   L.   M.   N.

13.

A.   B.   C.   D.   E.

14.

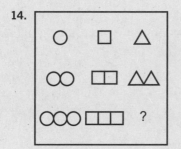

J.   K.   L.   M.   N.

15.

A.   B.   C.   D.   E.

16.

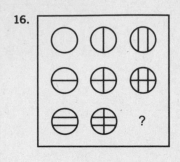

J.   K.   L.   M.   N.

17.

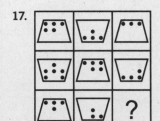

A.   B.   C.

18.

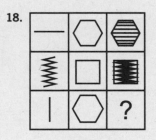

J.   K.   L.   M.   N.

19.

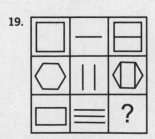

A.   B.   C.   D.   E.

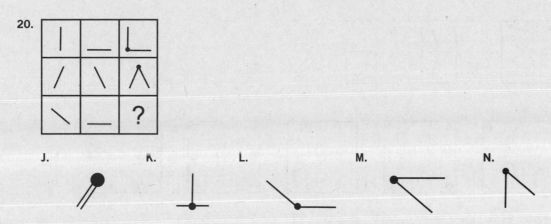

20.

J. K. L. M. N.

Paper Folding

Directions: In questions 1–10, look at the top row to see how a square piece of paper is folded and where holes are punched into it. Then look at the bottom row to decide which answer choice shows how the paper will look when it is completely unfolded.

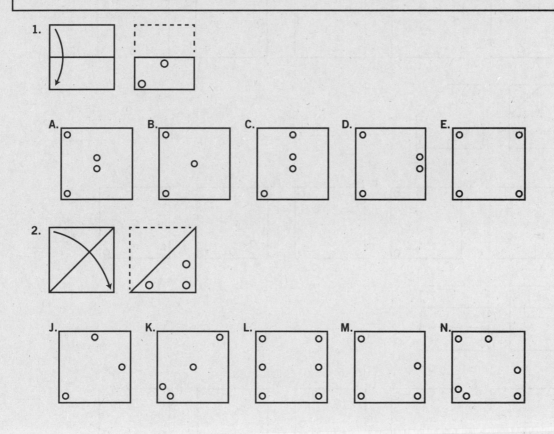

1.

A. B. C. D. E.

2.

J. K. L. M. N.

Practice Test 3: TACHS

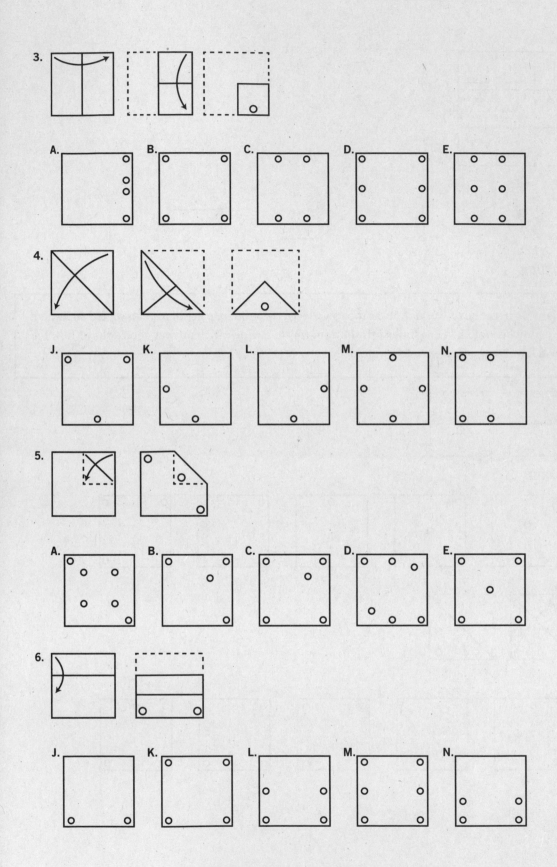

Practice Test 3: TACHS

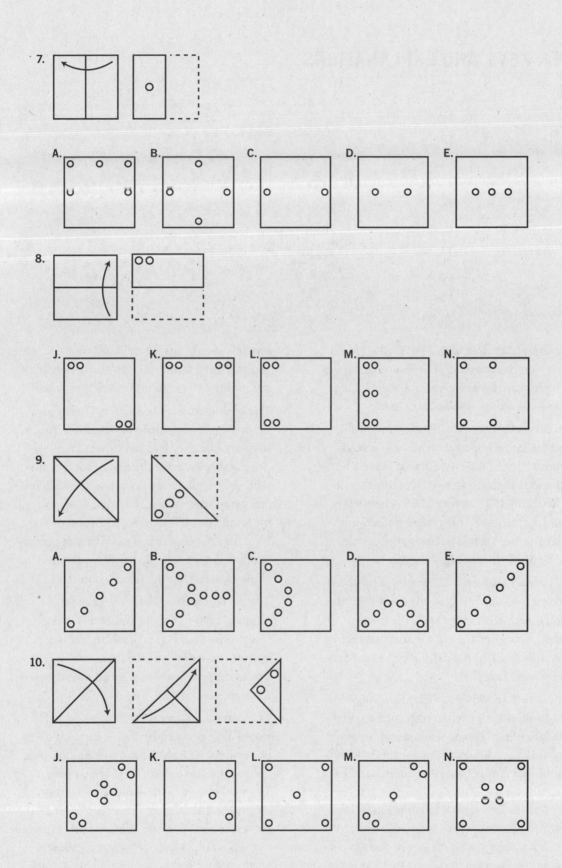

Practice Test 3: TACHS

ANSWER KEYS AND EXPLANATIONS
Reading

1. B	11. B	21. D	31. B	41. A
2. L	12. J	22. K	32. L	42. L
3. C	13. B	23. C	33. A	43. D
4. L	14. M	24. L	34. M	44. L
5. A	15. B	25. C	35. B	45. A
6. K	16. M	26. K	36. L	46. L
7. D	17. B	27. B	37. A	47. B
8. K	18. K	28. J	38. L	48. K
9. D	19. C	29. B	39. B	49. A
10. L	20. M	30. M	40. K	50. L

1. **The correct answer is B.** The word *rural* means "in the country." The last sentence of the first paragraph gives the context clue when it mentions "the country life."

2. **The correct answer is L.** The country life wasn't what he hoped for, and he was ready to move back to the city. Charlie made a hurried and rash decision to move from the city to the country. Therefore, it was characteristic of Charlie to call his realtor quickly and make another rushed decision, the decision that he didn't like life in the country.

3. **The correct answer is C.** Finding a rattlesnake, a scorpion stinging his child, and his wife's illness all convince Charlie to move back to New York City. The realtor (choice C) is someone Charlie calls *after* he has made the decision to leave.

4. **The correct answer is L.** "Concrete jungle" is a common term used to refer to cities, and here the author is using it as a stand-in for New York City, which Charlie wants to leave behind. His family has not yet moved to Texas when this phrase is used, so choice J is incorrect. The reader knows Charlie wants to leave New York City, but there is no indication that he's unhappy with his job, so there is not enough information to suggest that "concrete

jungle" refers to his job, making choice K incorrect. His family goes to Texas, not out of the country, so choice M is incorrect as well.

5. **The correct answer is A.** That Charlie and his family want to move back to New York suggests that they had not expected things like poisonous snakes and scorpions, or his wife's allergies. The story is told from Charlie's perspective, so we don't know whether his family wanted to move to Texas (choice B), if they never planned to stay there permanently (choice C), or that they would move while Charlie stays in Texas (choice D).

6. **The correct answer is K.** The context phrases "on the day the family moved in," "only a few hours later," and "before the movers unloaded half the furniture" all suggest that the decision happened quickly, on the same day.

7. **The correct answer is D.** Citizens probably would elect people who had not been the power-holding nobles prior to elections, thus leaving the nobles with little or no power. The nobles were people whose power didn't depend on the favor of those they controlled and exploited. The nobles knew that common citizens would most likely elect candidates with whom they had something in common.

8. **The correct answer is K.** The reference to thrones in the first sentence of the second paragraph is the context clue that *monarchs* is synonymous with "kings and queens."

9. **The correct answer is D.** This sentence is meant to show that the liberals were calling for rights but would not apply those rights to everybody.

10. **The correct answer is L.** The first sentence of paragraph 2 uses the word *precarious*, or fragile, to describe the nobles' collective hold on political power, so choices J and K are incorrect. The passage focuses on the nineteenth century so, based on the passage, we have no way to know that the common man holds the most power in Europe now, so choice M is incorrect.

11. **The correct answer is B.** The author presents factual information without taking a specific stand or offering his or her own personal opinions, so this text would fit in a textbook, but not a persuasive article.

12. **The correct answer is J.** The last sentence of the passage tells the reader that the aristocracy could not defeat liberalism, suggesting that the liberals' ideals became the law of the land. There is not enough information to determine whether the nobles would eventually regain power (choice K), whether Europe would allow women to vote as well as men (choice L), or that liberals would eventually turn into aristocrats themselves (choice M).

13. **The correct answer is B.** The passage mentions that there were other pyramids in Egypt, and it then goes on to say that the Great Pyramid of Giza was different from the others because it was the tallest, setting it apart from all other structures at the time. Therefore, choice B is the best answer.

14. **The correct answer is M.** The passage mentions that the Great Pyramid of Giza is the only one of the Seven Wonders that still exists, despite the ravages of time, which

tends to harm or decay things. Choice M, *unharmed*, is the correct answer.

15. **The correct answer is B.** Sentence 2 of paragraph 2 states that pyramids were resting places for dead royalty, so choice B is the answer best supported by the passage.

16. **The correct answer is M.** Paragraph 2 describes the limestone and granite blocks that make up the pyramid, as well as the mortar that held them together as part of the architecture. Steel is not mentioned anywhere in the passage.

17. **The correct answer is B.** Sentence 2 of the passage states that the Great Pyramid is the only one of the Seven Wonders of the Ancient World that still exists. The Sphinx is part of the pyramid complex, but not the Great Pyramid itself, so choice A is incorrect. The pyramid was constructed by people, so choice C is incorrect. And the last sentence of the passage says that the pyramid's construction is under dispute among experts, so choice D is incorrect as well.

18. **The correct answer is K.** In the passage, the author describes the pyramid as a "marvel," a truly wonderful monument to human capability," and a "magnificent and awe-inspiring piece of human history." From these context clues, you can figure out that he or she is not bored (choice J) or skeptical (choice M). He or she also doesn't seem very surprised that the pyramid is still standing, so choice L doesn't fit either.

19. **The correct answer is C.** Margie had a feeling that after a while, she would stop using the equipment for exercise. The line about the "expensive clothes rack" is a metaphor for exercise equipment that is not used for exercising. The passage does not support any of the other answer choices.

20. **The correct answer is M.** Based on context clues, the word *deter* means "discourage." The use of the word *however* at the

beginning of the sentence indicates a shift in thought. Margie initially considered the new workout facility (as noted in the sentence before), but she wondered if the location on the other side of town would give her an excuse to not go—in other words, she thought it might deter or discourage her from working out regularly.

21. **The correct answer is D.** In the passage, Margie gives careful thought to the fitness routine that will work best for her, taking the reader through a series of options, as well as the pros and cons for each. Based on her logic, we can infer that she has made the choice that is most likely to result in sticking to her new fitness routine (buying small weights and videos that she can do at home).

22. **The correct answer is K.** Although Margie uses the pamphlet as a factor in her decision about a new fitness routine, she had already been thinking about taking up a new fitness routine before she met the young man at the mall, so choices J and M are incorrect. The last sentence of paragraph 1 says that Margie wants a new fitness routine to feel better and have more energy, suggesting that this is what is driving her to pick a new fitness routine.

23. **The correct answer is C.** Margie doesn't display any feeling (positive or negative) about the young man, so choice A is incorrect. The passage does not compare the effectiveness of each possible solution, so choice B is incorrect. Paragraph 2 says that the distance could deter Margie from working out, so choice C is correct. The passage does not say how much the gym membership costs or how much the weights cost, so there is not enough information to conclude that the gym costs too much money.

24. **The correct answer is L.** Margie shows throughout the passage that she is putting a lot of thought and consideration into her decision. If she were impulsive, she would

likely have joined the gym or bought the equipment right away, so choice J is incorrect. We don't have enough information in the passage to conclude that she is frustrated by her process of finding a new fitness routine, or that she is unhappy, so choices K and M are incorrect as well.

25. **The correct answer is C.** The entire first paragraph describes the grueling and demanding schedule of the counselors. It is reasonable to expect people to be tired, or exhausted, after a schedule like the one described in paragraph 1. There is nothing in the passage to suggest the counselors are unruly; in fact, the director's appreciation of "how much of themselves they invested" suggests the opposite. The entire passage deals with the dedication of the counselors under trying circumstances, so choice B is certainly incorrect. The passage does not mention that the counselors are confused, so choice D is incorrect.

26. **The correct answer is K.** She wanted to help them be relaxed and refreshed by giving them a day off. The director was using "proverbial lotion" as a metaphor for something that would relax and refresh—in this case, a day off. A metaphor is symbolic and representative, and should not be interpreted literally.

27. **The correct answer is B.** Paragraph 1 of the passage describes how good the counselors are at their jobs, so choice A is unlikely. Although the counselors' individual levels of success are not addressed, the tone of the passage is positive and appreciative, so we can infer that choice C is not true. The feelings of the campers are not mentioned in the passage, so choice D is incorrect.

28. **The correct answer is J.** The director understands what the counselors are doing, and sees that they need "lotion," or a break, so she is acting sympathetically, making choice J the best option.

29. **The correct answer is B.** Paragraph 1 says that the counselors have been working for two weeks already, and that there are two more weeks before the camp is dismissed for the summer, so that's four total weeks.

30. **The correct answer is M.** The passage does not make any mention of the counselors providing medical care to the campers, but giving advice (choice J), directing activities (choice K), and listening to campers (choice L) are all included in paragraph 1.

31. **The correct answer is B.** The passage discusses the development of science and Sir Francis Bacon's contributions to it. Choice B best reflects this content. Choice D is incorrect, because it is too narrow. Choice C is outside the scope of the passage.

32. **The correct answer is L.** To answer this "cause and effect" question, you must identify the reason why Francis Bacon chose to look for a new approach to knowledge. Why did he wish to develop an approach based on the observation of physical events? The answer to this question is revealed for us in paragraph 1 of the passage, which tells us that before Bacon's time, knowledge was based on the beliefs of the church. Bacon did not like the idea of basing knowledge only on faith or belief. The last sentence of the paragraph tells us that Bacon "searched for a way of developing knowledge that he felt was more reliable." This sentence suggests that Bacon felt that knowledge based on the beliefs of the church was not very reliable, so choice L is correct.

33. **The correct answer is A.** Paragraph 3 of the passage tells us that Bacon's approach came to be known by the name *inductivism*, so choice A is correct.

34. **The correct answer is M.** According to paragraph 1, scientific knowledge before Bacon's time was based on religious ideas and the doctrine of the church. The ideas that were considered to be knowledge were based upon faith, so M is correct.

35. **The correct answer is B.** The answer to this question is found in paragraph 2. *The New Organon*, published in 1620, became the foundation for what we know today as the "empirical" sciences. It addressed how to develop knowledge gained from observing that which can be perceived through the senses. Choice D is incorrect, because the passage does not mention that the book emphasized practicing strict scientific discipline in all research.

36. **The correct answer is L.** To answer this inference question, you must draw on information given in the passage to make a logical deduction. Bacon did not support scientific ideas based on church doctrine (choice J). He advocated that science should be based on empirical research, or what could be observed through the senses.

37. **The correct answer is A.** The second sentence of paragraph 3 tells us that inductivism is the idea that theories about science can be developed from observing events. Choices B, C, and D are incorrect, because these factors are not mentioned as important for inductivism.

38. **The correct answer is L.** Although *foundation* can have multiple meanings, like a physical structure underneath a building, a charitable organization, or support for an idea, because the author is talking about a concept, *method* is the most likely meaning of the word intended in the passage.

39. **The correct answer is B.** While *like* has several meanings, in this context it is comparing different types of materials, so *similar* (choice B) is the correct answer.

40. **The correct answer is K.** Since this type of recycling was developed in the 1990s, more than 100 million people have started using it. This suggests the opposite of *unsuccessful* (choice J). There is no information about the costs associated with single-stream recycling, so the passage does not support choice L. And the passage calls this recycling "innovative," so *old-fashioned* (choice M) does not describe the recycling, based on what is stated in the passage.

41. **The correct answer is A.** The passage is about how single-stream recycling is replacing a dual-stream process, and choice A is the option that describes that main idea most fully. Choices B and D are too broad, and choice C is misleading because the passage talks about changes in recycling since the 1990s.

42. **The correct answer is L.** *Parse* means to "pull apart" or "analyze," and choice L is the closest choice to that definition.

43. **The correct answer is D.** The difference between single-stream recycling and dual-stream recycling, as outlined in the passage, is that the materials are packaged differently before the recyclable materials even get to the facility. While it may be true that single-stream recycling changes the amount of processing done at the recycling facilities (choice A), the main focus of the passage is that decreasing the effort for consumers results in higher overall levels of recycling. Since that is the author's main theme, he or she clearly sees this as the main difference between the two types of recycling, making choice D the best option.

44. **The correct answer is L.** Styrofoam® is mentioned in the passage as an item in regular garbage, while glass (choice J), cardboard (choice K), and plastic bottles (choice M) are all mentioned as recyclable materials.

45. **The correct answer is A.** The passage states that Babbitt sells houses to people for more than they can afford to pay. The passage specifically says that he does not make "butter nor shoes nor poetry," so choices B and C are incorrect. Choice D isn't mentioned (or alluded to) at all.

46. **The correct answer is L.** Although he is described as "babyish," he is also described as having wrinkles and spectacles, so choice J is incorrect. The first sentence of the passage states that there is "nothing of the giant" in Babbitt, so choice M is clearly incorrect. He is also described as "extremely well fed" and "puffy," so choice K becomes unlikely as well. Of the options available, choice L is the one that best fits the given description.

47. **The correct answer is B.** The author presents a specific physical picture of what Babbitt is like, and then uses that to contrast with the "fairy child" in his dreams. This contrast between the ordinary (Babbitt and his surroundings) and the extraordinary (his "romantic" dream) is best matched by choice B. His dream disproves choice A. The passage suggests that Babbitt is "extremely married," so there is not enough evidence to suggest that he has no loved ones, which means choice C is incorrect. Choice D is incorrect because, while his dream is compared to "scarlet pagodas by a silver sea," he is not actually dreaming about the sea.

48. **The correct answer is K.** The image of rough hands is frequently associated with hard physical labor, and the author is trying to show that Babbitt does not have a physically taxing job.

49. **The correct answer is A.** Much of the passage is spent describing the reality of how Babbitt looks, including an observation that he seems "unromantic." Yet his dreams are "more romantic than scarlet pagodas by a

silver sea." This contrast is best described by choice A. The passage makes its observations objectively and without judgement, so choice B is incorrect. Although wealth is mentioned, it is not central to the passage, so choice C is not the best choice. Based only on the passage, we don't know enough to say whether Babbitt has experienced misfortunes in life, so choice D is incorrect.

50. **The correct answer is L.** The first sentence states that Floral Heights is a district (or neighborhood) of the town of Zenith. The phrase "Dutch Colonial" describes the house where George is sleeping.

Written Expression

1. B	11. A	21. C	31. B	41. C
2. L	12. M	22. K	32. J	42. K
3. D	13. B	23. D	33. A	43. A
4. M	14. K	24. J	34. L	44. J
5. D	15. A	25. A	35. A	45. B
6. L	16. J	26. M	36. J	46. L
7. B	17. B	27. A	37. C	47. C
8. N	18. J	28. L	38. K	48. K
9. C	19. B	29. C	39. A	49. A
10. M	20. K	30. M	40. M	50. L

1. **The correct answer is B.** The correct spelling is *calculator*.

2. **The correct answer is L.** The correct spelling is either *sense* or *since*.

3. **The correct answer is D.** The correct spelling is *label*.

4. **The correct answer is M.** The correct spelling is *knowledge*.

5. **The correct answer is D.** The correct spelling is *conquer*.

6. **The correct answer is L.** The correct spelling is *aggregate*.

7. **The correct answer is B.** The correct spelling is *reliable*.

8. **The correct answer is N.** *No mistakes*

9. **The correct answer is C.** The correct spelling is *governor*.

10. **The correct answer is M.** The correct spelling is *deceive*.

11. **The correct answer is A.** The name "Rover" should be capitalized because a name is a proper noun.

12. **The correct answer is M.** *No mistakes*

13. **The correct answer is B.** The Dallas Cowboys is the name of a professional team and, as with names of other professional organizations (including the New York Jets and the Atlanta Falcons), *Cowboys* should be capitalized because it is a proper noun.

14. **The correct answer is K.** In this sentence, *home* simply means a house and is not part of a title. Therefore, *home* is a common noun and needs no capitalization.

15. **The correct answer is A.** Holidays are proper nouns and should be capitalized.

16. **The correct answer is J.** As used in this sentence, *basketball coach* is a common noun. If "coach" were included in a title like "Coach Van Gundy" or "Coach Parcells," then it would be capitalized.

17. **The correct answer is B.** Because the action in the sentence occurred in the past, the correct form of the verb in choice B is the past tense *expected*.

18. **The correct answer is J.** Even though these initials are an abbreviation, they should be capitalized because they are a person's name, a proper noun.

19. **The correct answer is B.** The abbreviation "Inc." is short for "Incorporated," which is part of the official name of a business organization and must be capitalized as a proper noun.

20. **The correct answer is K.** The word *state* is a common noun; the names of states—Texas or New York, for example—are proper nouns and should be capitalized.

21. **The correct answer is C.** Choice C most efficiently and effectively expresses the ideas in this sentence without the unnecessary wordiness, redundancy, and confusion that makes the other choices incorrect.

22. **The correct answer is K.** Although some of the alternate answer choices come close to expressing the main idea of the sentence, choices J and L lead us to the incorrect conclusion that Mr. Johnson needs to learn advanced calculus instead of teaching the subject to his students. Choice M is simply a rearranged version of choice K, but K is nevertheless more understandable, and therefore the best choice.

23. **The correct answer is D.** *No change.* No change is needed in the way the number "seventy-one" is written since the hyphenated form is correct.

24. **The correct answer is J.** In this sentence, the subject "water conservation strategies and practices" and the verb *are* follow a long introductory phrase. The introductory phrase, or dependent clause, must be set off with a comma to link it to the main part of the sentence that follows.

25. **The correct answer is A.** As written, the underlined portion of the sentence incorrectly uses the adverb *there*. The adjective *their* is required here to refer to the vlog creators.

26. **The correct answer is M.** *No change.* As written, the sentence correctly uses a semicolon to join these two independent clauses. The other choices introduce errors into the sentence.

27. **The correct answer is A.** Since the passage is written in present tense, the verb *include* must be in agreement with the rest of the passage.

28. **The correct answer is L.** The word *then* should be replaced with the word *than* in this sentence. Using *then* indicates a sequence of events, but *than* introduces a comparison of unequal items.

29. **The correct answer is C.** The word *commuter* is not a proper noun, so it does not need capitalization. Choice A is incorrect since a plural form of the noun is needed, and choice B shows the plural possessive version of the word *commuter*, which is not needed in this sentence.

30. **The correct answer is M.** *No change.* No change is needed, because the phrase "they are" refers back to the subject of the sentence, *flying cars. Their* and *there* are commonly confused with the correct answer because they sound very similar, and *it's* is a singular pronoun form, so choices J, K, and L are incorrect.

31. **The correct answer is B.** As written, the sentence contains the incorrect future tense of the underlined verbs. Since Devil's Tower is currently in this location, it should be written in the present tense, so the phrase, "is located" is correct. Choices A and C are also incorrect verb tenses given the context of the sentence.

32. The correct answer is J. Common nouns and the adjectives used to describe them should be lowercased unless they appear at the beginning of a sentence. Choice J correctly lowercases these words. Choices K and L make incorrect use of capitalization given the context of this sentence.

33. The correct answer is A. When trying to select the appropriate word choice in a sentence, we need to understand the context. Here, we are looking for a word that refers to people discussing memorable presidents. *Conversation* is the word that best fits this activity. The words provided in the other answer choices don't describe a discussion between people, which is what is needed here.

34. The correct answer is L. As written, the sentence contains an incorrect pronoun. *Their* is a plural pronoun that's being used to replace the singular antecedent "Millard Fillmore." A singular, masculine pronoun is needed here, so "his involvement" is correct. Choices J and K also provide incorrect pronouns given the context of the sentence.

35. The correct answer is A. As written, the semicolon in the sentence is incorrectly placed. Semicolons should be used to separate connected independent clauses, which we do not have here. No internal sentence punctuation is needed here, so Choice A is correct. Choice B incorrectly creates a sentence fragment by inserting a period. Choice C incorrectly adds an em dash, which is used to create a long pause in a sentence and is not needed here.

36. The correct answer is J. This simple list of names should be separated by commas, as choice J correctly does. Choice K includes an unnecessary mix of semicolons and commas. Choice L includes quotation marks, which aren't used to separate list items.

37. The correct answer is C. As written, the underlined portion of the sentence incorrectly includes parentheses. Parentheses are reserved for additional information or asides, which is not what we have here. This information is part of the regular narrative flow of the sentence and requires no special treatment, so choice C is correct. Quotation marks (choice A) and italics (choice B) are incorrect here.

38. The correct answer is K. As used in the sentence, *ancient* is an adjective and should be lowercased, while *Egypt* is a proper noun and should be capitalized. Choice K correctly handles this. The other choices make incorrect use of capitalization and lowercase.

39. The correct answer is A. The phrases, "aware of," and, "familiar with," are close enough in meaning that they would be redundant. Choice A selects just one of the two options. Choice B merely replaces the conjunction *or* with *and*, which does not solve the problem of redundancy. Choice C jumbles the words so that the prepositions are incorrect.

40. The correct answer is M. *No change.* Since the original breeding of pugs is something that had occurred in the past, the correct verb form here is the past plural, and Choice M is correct. Choices J, K, and L use incorrect verb forms given the context of the sentence.

41. The correct answer is C. Here, we have a question—the question-word *what* at the beginning of the sentence is a good clue. Choice C correctly punctuates the sentence with a question mark. Choices A and B use incorrect punctuation for this sentence.

42. The correct answer is K. The primary topic of this paragraph is the avocado, which we are told is a fruit that contains a variety of healthy properties. Therefore, the best sentence to sum these ideas up is Choice

Answers | Practice Test 3: TACHS

K. Choice J is incorrect, as we are told that avocadoes are fruits, not vegetables. Choice L is incorrect, as taking multivitamins is not mentioned at all in this paragraph. Choice M is incorrect, as it is out of context in this paragraph.

43. **The correct answer is A.** There are context clues available in this sentence to help us determine what the right word choices are here. We are looking to determine the directions that palindromes can be read that match. The examples provided (*Anna* and *racecar*) tell us that they are the same forwards and backwards, so Choice A is correct. The other answer choices provide incorrect directions for reading palindromes.

44. **The correct answer is J.** As written, there's no logical justification for using the adverb *unfortunately*, as there's nothing unfortunate going on in this sentence. There's also no justification for using *accidentally* (choice K), since nothing accidental is being referred to. Since no jokes are being made, choice L is also incorrect. The only logical choice here is *actually* (choice J).

45. **The correct answer is B.** The sentence as written contains a logical error—you can't have a group consisting of one Amish "person." "Amish people" corrects this error. Choices A and C also incorrectly use singular nouns.

46. **The correct answer is L.** Despite referring to a specific person, these two underlined words are common nouns and should be

lowercase, which choice L does. Choices J and K both contain incorrect capitalization.

47. **The correct answer is C.** As written, the two sentences separated by a period are fragments. These two fragments should be joined into one cohesive sentence with no internal punctuation, which choice C does. Choice A incorrectly adds a comma, and choice B incorrectly adds a semicolon, neither of which is needed here.

48. **The correct answer is K.** The sentence as written is illogical—an "unpopular" tourist attraction does not get "many tourists from all over the world," as Bran Castle does. A better adjective to describe a well-visited tourist attraction is *popular* (choice K). Calling Bran Castle "confusing" (choice J) doesn't make sense here, and neither does *aromatic* (choice L).

49. **The correct answer is A.** The Changing the Guard ceremony cannot take 45 years if it's a daily ceremony, as we are told in sentence 2, so choice D is incorrect. The only answer choice that contains a time period that can occur daily is choice A, 45 minutes.

50. **The correct answer is L.** This list of process steps for applying to become a member of the Queen's Guard should be separated by commas, so choice L is correct. The list items should not be set in quotation marks, so choice J is incorrect. Choice K incorrectly uses one semicolon to separate the three list items.

Mathematics

1. A	11. A	21. C	31. C	41. C
2. L	12. K	22. M	32. M	42. K
3. B	13. B	23. D	33. B	43. D
4. K	14. J	24. J	34. M	44. L
5. C	15. C	25. D	35. C	45. A
6. L	16. L	26. K	36. K	46. K
7. B	17. A	27. A	37. B	47. D
8. L	18. J	28. L	38. K	48. K
9. A	19. B	29. B	39. B	49. D
10. K	20. M	30. M	40. L	50. L

1. **The correct answer is A.** According to the bar graph, the approximate income of Southerners (the white bar) in 2013 was $25,000.

2. **The correct answer is L.** The money that will be spent on salaries represents 45% of the entire budget—more than any other single category of expenditure.

3. **The correct answer is B.** When added together, Rent & Utilities plus Office Supplies (31% + 14% = 45%) equals Salaries (45%).

4. **The correct answer is K.** Each horizontal band on the chart equals 20%. Even though the white portion (country music) of Larissa's column starts at the 40% mark, it is easy to see that it occupies 3 bands. Since 3 times 20 equals 60, Larissa's collection includes 60% country.

5. **The correct answer is C.** Audrey's collection consists of approximately 50% jazz, 20% hip hop, and 30% country.

6. **The correct answer is L.** About one fourth, or 25 percent, chose pizza; $100 \times 25\% = 25$.

7. **The correct answer is B.** Subtract 23 minutes from 30 to determine how many minutes of commercials are seen; $30 - 23 = 7$. Seven minutes is 7×60 seconds $= 420$ seconds, which is about 400.

8. **The correct answer is L.** The original addition problem of $43 + 71 + 19 + 68 + 11 + 29$ can be approximated to $40 + 70 + 20 + 70 + 10 + 30$, which is 240.

9. **The correct answer is A.** $63,977 \div 7,991$ is approximately $64,000 \div 8,000$, which is 8. Since this is a division problem, you could drop the zeros from the estimates on both figures, and you would still arrive at the correct answer; $64 \div 8 = 8$.

10. **The correct answer is K.** $414 - 289 - 106 + 89 + 277$ is approximately $400 - 300 - 100 + 100 + 300 = 400$.

11. **The correct answer is A.** Oil on Wood and Oil on Canvas make up 59 of the 118 portraits, or 50 percent of the portraits.

12. **The correct answer is K.** Morris had 28 lawns in the summer, and Angelo had 30 lawns in the summer.

13. **The correct answer is B.** Angelo experienced a bigger decline in business from the summer to the winter than Morris did; Angelo's business went from 30 lawns in the summer to 6 lawns in the winter, a difference of 24, whereas Morris' business went from 28 to 7 in the same period, a difference of only 21.

14. **The correct answer is J.** The number of members who play golf in the older-age category is much more than the number of members who play golf in the younger-age

category. This holds true for both men and women.

15. **The correct answer is C.** A total of 202 members currently participate in jogging, whereas 187 members participate in golf and 176 members participate in tennis.

16. **The correct answer is L.** It would take $2\frac{1}{2}$ combos of about 400 calories to equal the approximately 1,000 calories of the donut-soda combo.

17. **The correct answer is A.** $385 - (2.9 \times 15.8)$ is approximately equal to $385 - (3 \times 16) = 385 - 48 = 337$.

18. **The correct answer is J.** If you revised the $255 to $250, it is easy to recognize that 10 goes into 250 exactly 25 times. It would take about 25 weeks to earn $255.

19. **The correct answer is B.** 7.1×7.9 is approximately 7×8, which is 56.

20. **The correct answer is M.** $221.8 \div 9.989$ is approximately $222 \div 10$, and $222 \div 10$ is 22.2, or about 22.

21. **The correct answer is C.** The order in which numbers are added does not affect the sum; changing the signs does. Choice A has the operational symbols correct, but has transposed the numbers in parenthesis, so it is incorrect. Choice B changes the signs within the parenthesis from multiplication to subtraction, and choice D changes the operator between the two sets of parenthesis from addition to multiplication. As such, both choices B and D are incorrect.

22. **The correct answer is M.** We want the amount in the parentheses to be equal to 3. This can only be accomplished if the value of x is equal to 4.

23. **The correct answer is D.** An angle that is greater than 90° and less than 180° is an obtuse angle.

24. **The correct answer is J.** The temperature over the 6 hours graphed was $10° + 20° + 20° + 30° + 20° + 20° = 120° \div 6 = 20°$.

25. **The correct answer is D.** He will pay back $3,500 plus 10% interest. Ten percent of $3,500 is $350; when added to the original amount borrowed, the result is $3,500 + $350 = $3,850.

26. **The correct answer is K.** Each option must be examined. Choice K is true because 87 divided by 3 equals 29, and 29 is less than 30. Choice J is untrue because 4 times 5 is 20, which is not less than $4 \times 1 + 6$, which equals 10. Choice L is incorrect because 2^5 equals 32, which does not equal 2×5, or 10. Choice M is incorrect because $\frac{1}{4}$ is greater than (not less than) $\frac{1}{5}$.

27. **The correct answer is A.** The sum of the angles of a triangle is 180°. Therefore, the sum of the other two angles must be $180° - 115° = 65°$.

28. **The correct answer is L.** Because Distance = Rate × Time, it follows that Time = Distance ÷ Rate. Therefore, Time = $\frac{1}{20}$ of an hour = 3 minutes. Or, because 60 mph is 1 mile per minute, 20 mph is 1 mile every 3 minutes.

29. **The correct answer is B.** Use the formula circumference = π × diameter. We are told the radius is 21 feet, so the diameter is twice that, or 42 feet.

Circumference = $\pi \times 21 \times 2$

Circumference = $\pi \times 42$

Circumference = $\frac{22}{7} \times 42$

Circumference = 132 feet

30. **The correct answer is M.** The set $\{x\}$ includes all those numbers larger than −4 and smaller than 2. Considering only whole numbers, this set includes −3, −2, −1, 0, and 1. Choice J includes -4, but all numbers

in the set must be greater than −4. Choice L includes 2, 3, and 4, all of which are beyond the range of the set. Choice K omits −3 and 0, and also includes 2, which is beyond the acceptable range for the set.

31. **The correct answer is C.** Careful study of the Venn diagram shows overlap of the circles enclosing rectangles and rhombi, so some rectangles are rhombi as those same rhombi are rectangles. The other statements should read as follows: No trapezoids are parallelograms; all rhombi are parallelograms; and some parallelograms are rectangles, or all rectangles are parallelograms.

32. **The correct answer is M.** Each tile is 2 inches wide, so there are 6 tiles per foot. 12 feet × 6 = 72 tiles across each length. Each width equals 4 feet × 6, or 24 tiles. Each corner needs 1 extra tile, so add 4 more tiles.

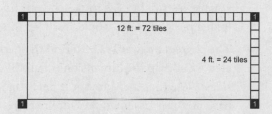

$$(2 \times 72) + (2 \times 24) + 4 = 144 + 48 + 4$$
$$= 196$$

Hence, 196 tiles is the correct answer.

33. **The correct answer is B.** The number of accidents is irrelevant to the question. B deaths occurred in 10 years, so each year, an average of one tenth of B deaths occurred.

34. **The correct answer is M.** Point D is in the upper-left quadrant. First read to the left along the negative x-axis, then read up on the y-axis.

35. **The correct answer is C.** Because point P has not moved along the x-axis, the x coordinate is 0. Moving down on the y-axis, point P is located at $-2\frac{1}{2}$. As such, the coordinates for point P are expressed as $\left(0, -2\frac{1}{2}\right)$.

36. **The correct answer is K.** If 2 inches equals 24 feet, 1 inch equals 12 feet. A line representing 72 feet, therefore, must be 6 inches long ($72 \div 12 = 6$).

37. **The correct answer is B.** Start by determining the amount of the price reduction:

$$25\% \text{ of } \$14 = \$14 \times 0.25 = \$3.50$$

Next, subtract the reduction from the original price to obtain the reduced price:

$$\$14 - \$3.50 = \$10.50 \text{ (new price)}$$

Choice C indicates a reduction of only 35 cents, and choice D is a reduction of only 25 cents; both options can be quickly eliminated. Choice A represents the amount of the reduction to the original price.

38. **The correct answer is K.** The area is most easily found by multiplying the length of the figure by its width, and then subtracting the area of the small 3" × 3" square.

$$(7" \times 5") - (3" \times 3") = \text{area}$$
$$35 \text{ sq. in} - 9 \text{ sq. in.} = 26 \text{ sq. in.}$$

Shapes such as this are often used for irregular pieces of carpeting or covering.

39. **The correct answer is B.** The boy's age is M years. His older brother is $M + 6$ years old, and his younger sister is $M - 4$ years old. Adding the three ages together:

$$M + (M + 6) + (M - 4) = 3M + 2$$

40. **The correct answer is L.** This problem requires two steps. First, find the smallest number divisible by both 14 and 12 (the least common multiple, or LCM). Second, add the number to 1:00 and rename it as time of day. The LCM of 14 and 12 is 84. Both events will occur simultaneously 84 minutes (1 hour 24 minutes) past 1:00, or 2:24 p.m.

41. **The correct answer is C.**

Step 1. To find the correct ratio, write it as:

$$\frac{6 \text{ inches}}{6 \text{ feet}}$$

Step 2. Rewrite each quantity in inches.

$$\frac{6 \text{ inches}}{72 \text{ inches}}$$

Step 3. Simplify the ratio.

$$\frac{6}{72} = \frac{1}{12} = 1:12$$

42. **The correct answer is K.** Here, three events occur periodically, so we must find the LCM of 4, 11, and 33 and add that number to 1950. That year will be the next common occurrence. The LCM of 4, 11, and 33 is 132, so $1,950 + 132 = 2,082$.

43. **The correct answer is D.** This is a two-step problem. First, find the length of the hypotenuse, so you know how far the other person is driving.

$$\begin{aligned}(AC)^2 &= (AB)^2 + (BC)^2 \\ &= (40)^2 + (30)^2 \\ &= 1,600 + 900 \\ (AC) &= \sqrt{2,500} = 50 \text{ miles}\end{aligned}$$

This tells you that the person driving directly from *C* to *A* is driving 50 miles at 50 miles per hour (mph). He or she will get there in 1 hour. The other driver going from *C* to *B* to *A* is driving 70 miles. To get there first, he or she must drive faster than 70 miles per hour, choice D.

44. **The correct answer is L.** This graph contains a line that has points with coordinates (1, 1), (2, 2), (3, 3), and (4, 4). From one point to another, the value of the *x*-coordinate changes just as much as the value of the *y*-coordinate. This line is at a 45° angle from the *x*-axis and will be created whenever the *x*- and *y*-coordinates are equal.

45. **The correct answer is A.** The first 6 is in the billions place; the second, in the hundred-thousands place. If you had trouble with this problem, review the sections on how to read numbers and determine place values in your math textbook.

46. **The correct answer is K.** A scale of 1:24,000 means that 1 inch on the map equals 24,000 inches on the ground. 24,000 inches equals 2,000 feet (24,000 ÷ 12 = 2,000).

47. **The correct answer is D.** This is a *literal problem* requiring you to "think without numbers." Creating mental pictures might help you solve this type of problem. If each person in a group makes *L* number of things, the group's output will be the product of the number of people in the group and the number of things each makes. Choice D represents the product and is the correct answer.

48. **The correct answer is K.** Find 300 on the horizontal axis. Draw a vertical line upward until you touch the line. Move horizontally from this point on the line to the vertical axis. Note that you touch the vertical axis at a point roughly equivalent to $20. We suggest you use a straight edge to sketch your line. A folded piece of paper would work for this.

49. **The correct answer is D.** To find the perimeter, we add up the dimensions of all the sides. Note that there are some parts that have not been assigned measurements, so we should infer that they are the same as those corresponding parts whose measurements have been designated because we are told to assume that there are right angles in the figure. Beginning at the bottom and moving clockwise, the dimensions are:

$$5" + 7" + 1" + 3" + 3" + 3" + 1" + 7"$$

The sum of these lengths is 30 inches. If you selected choices A, C, or D, you failed to add up all the segments.

50. **The correct answer is L.** The ratio of men to women is 15:12, but this ratio must be expressed in simplest form. Because 15 and 12 have 3 as a common factor, divide both figures by 3 to obtain the ratio expressed correctly as 5:4. The ratio of women to men would be 12:15 or 4:5.

Ability

Figure Classification

1. B	5. B	9. E	13. C	17. B
2. L	6. J	10. L	14. K	18. L
3. E	7. E	11. A	15. C	19. D
4. M	8. K	12. N	16. L	20. N

1. **The correct answer is B.** Each of the figures is an oval.

2. **The correct answer is L.** Each figure consists of a triangle and a square conjoined along one full side of the square.

3. **The correct answer is E.** Each figure contains two parallel arrows pointing in opposite directions.

4. **The correct answer is M.** Each figure has exactly one-third of its area shaded.

5. **The correct answer is B.** The number of dots in the circle is equal to the number of vertical segments.

6. **The correct answer is J.** Each figure can be transformed to any of the others by rotating it.

7. **The correct answer is E.** Each figure is regular polygon where all but one side has been made thicker.

8. **The correct answer is K.** Each figure consists of three copies of the same shape joined at a single point.

9. **The correct answer is E.** In each figure, there are two arrows pointing away from a pair of parallel segments.

10. **The correct answer is L.** Each figure is a quadrilateral (it has four sides).

11. **The correct answer is A.** Each figure consists of an *S*-shaped part along with a straight segment.

12. **The correct answer is N.** Each figure contains two different shapes joined by a single point.

13. **The correct answer is C.** The three given figures are all triangles.

14. **The correct answer is K.** The three given figures are all ovals.

15. **The correct answer is C.** Each of the three given figures is bisected by a line segment.

16. **The correct answer is L.** The first three figures each have six sides, as does choice L.

17. **The correct answer is B.** Each of the given figures has half its area shaded in black, as does choice B.

18. **The correct answer is L.** The example figures are all identical, apart from being rotated in 90 degree increments. The second figure has been rotated 90 degrees from the first figure. The third figure has been rotated 270 degrees from the first figure. The only rotation missing is 180 degrees, choice L, which would logically be placed between the second and third figures.

19. **The correct answer is D.** The number of dots equals the number of sides to each shape, minus one.

20. **The correct answer is N.** Each figure features a smaller version of itself nested inside its outer shape. The other answer choices all feature non-identical shape combinations.

Figure Matrices

1. B	5. A	9. C	13. D	17. A
2. L	6. L	10. K	14. J	18. M
3. D	7. D	11. C	15. E	19. B
4. N	8. J	12. N	16. L	20. L

1. **The correct answer is B.** Moving from left to right rotates the arrow clockwise. Moving from top to bottom rotates the arrow counterclockwise.

2. **The correct answer is L.** The third image in each row is created as follows: rotate the second image in the row, and line up three copies of the first image from the row alongside it. The example figures reverse the direction of the second image, making choice K incorrect and choice L correct.

3. **The correct answer is D.** The first image in a row is made up of both a small and large shape. The second image in the row is the small one by itself, and the third image in the row is the large one by itself. It could also be said, more simply, that the larger shape from the first figure appears as the third figure.

4. **The correct answer is N.** The third triangle in each row has sides that obey the following rule: a side is solid if the corresponding side is solid in either the first or second image in the row.

5. **The correct answer is A.** The third image in each row consists of the first two images in the row placed atop one another, with their intersection shaded in. The third image in each row preserves the angle of the first two images, making choice E incorrect and making choice A correct.

6. **The correct answer is L.** Moving from column to column changes dashed segments to solid and vice versa, and also changes the number of dashes that make up each dashed segment. For the third column, that number is four.

7. **The correct answer is D.** The last image in each column consists of those segments that the first and second images in the row both have in common.

8. **The correct answer is J.** Moving from the first to second image in each row, the first arrow remains the same, while the second arrow is reversed. Moving from the second to the third image in each row, both arrows are reversed.

9. **The correct answer is C.** Images that are horizontally adjacent to each other are horizontal reflections of each other, so the third image in each row is identical to the first image in the row. Which row an image is in determines whether neither end is shaded (first row), only the square is shaded (second row), or both the square and the circle are shaded (third row).

10. **The correct answer is K.** In the third square in each row, a corner is shaded only if it is not shaded in either of the first two squares in the row.

11. **The correct answer is C.** The images in each column rotate by 90 degrees clockwise as you move from top to bottom.

12. **The correct answer is N.** The columns differ in the pattern inside each shape; for the third column, the pattern includes both horizontal and vertical segments. Each row consists of a square, a triangle, and a circle, so the missing image must be a circle.

13. **The correct answer is D.** Starting with the first image in a row, obtain the third image in the row by mentally erasing any parts that appear in the second image.

14. **The correct answer is J.** The third column consists of triangles, and the third row consists of three copies of a shape put together.

15. **The correct answer is E.** The third image in a row is formed by moving the first two images in the row towards each other just until they touch.

16. **The correct answer is L.** Moving from top to bottom adds a horizontal stripe, while moving from left to right adds a vertical stripe.

17. **The correct answer is A.** Moving left to right, the rule is to subtract one dot and rotate the shape 180 degrees for each step.

18. **The correct answer is M.** Multiply the figure from the first box and use it to fill the second box to get the figure for box three.

19. **The correct answer is B.** Center the lines from the second figure inside the first figure to get the figure for box three.

20. **The correct answer is L.** Use a dot to join the line segments from figures one and two to get the figure for box three.

Paper Folding

1. A	3. C	5. B	7. D	9. E
2. N	4. M	6. J	8. L	10. J

1. **The correct answer is A.** Both holes reflect upward across the horizontal. The one near the center line remains near the center line, while the one in the bottom-left corner ends up in the top-left corner.

2. **The correct answer is N.** Each hole reflects across the diagonal fold. The hole in the bottom-right corner ends up in the top-left corner, while the one on the right edge ends up on the top edge.

3. **The correct answer is C.** The single hole is punched near the bottom edge, in the middle of its quadrant. Unfolding the second fold reflects the hole to the top of the paper, also along the edge and in the middle of its quadrant. Unfolding the first fold results in the two holes reflecting to the left side of the sheet, resulting in a total of four holes.

4. **The correct answer is M.** The hole reflects along the second diagonal fold onto the center of the left edge of the page, and then the two holes reflect onto the centers of the right and top edges, respectively.

5. **The correct answer is B.** The holes in the corners are unaffected by the unfolding. The hole near the center of the page reflects up and to the right towards the top-right corner of the page.

6. **The correct answer is J.** Both holes are on the bottom edge, an area which is not involved in the fold.

7. **The correct answer is D.** The hole is centered in the left half of the page. When reflected across the vertical fold, it ends up in the center of the right half of the page.

8. **The correct answer is L.** From the top-left corner, the two holes reflect onto the bottom-left corner.

9. **The correct answer is E.** The holes extending from the bottom-left corner to the center of the page reflect across the diagonal fold. They form the other half of the line that continues from the center of the page to the top-right corner.

10. **The correct answer is J.** After unfolding the second fold, the two holes reflect towards the bottom-left of the page, remaining below the long diagonal fold. They then reflect just across the long diagonal, forming two parallel lines of four holes each.

SCORE SHEET

Although your actual exam scores will not be reported as percentages, it might be helpful to convert your test scores to percentages so that you can see at a glance where your strengths and weaknesses lie. The numbers in parentheses represent the questions that test each skill.

Subject	# Correct ÷ # of questions	× 100 = _____ %
Reading		
Vocabulary/Word Relationships (1, 4, 8, 14, 20, 38, 39, 42, 48)	_____ ÷ 9 = _____	× 100 = _____ %
Details/Main Idea/Structure (3, 6, 7, 11, 15, 16, 17, 29, 30, 31, 33, 34, 35, 37, 41, 43, 44, 45, 49, 50)	_____ ÷ 20 = _____	× 100 = _____ %
Inference/Understanding (2, 5, 9, 10, 12, 13, 18, 19, 21, 22, 23, 24, 25, 26, 27, 28, 32, 36, 40, 46, 47)	_____ ÷ 21 = _____	× 100 = _____ %
TOTAL READING SKILLS	_____ ÷ 50 = _____	× 100 = _____ %
Written Expression		
Spelling and Capitalization (1, 2, 3, 4, 5, 6, 7, 8, 9, 10, 11, 12, 13, 14, 15, 16, 18, 19, 20, 25, 29, 30, 32, 38, 46)	_____ ÷ 25 = _____	× 100 = _____ %
Punctuation (23, 24, 26, 35, 36, 37, 41, 47, 50)	_____ ÷ 9 = _____	× 100 = _____ %
Grammar (17, 27, 31, 34, 40)	_____ ÷ 5 = _____	× 100 = _____ %
Usage and Composition (21, 22, 28, 33, 39, 42, 43, 44, 45, 48, 49)	_____ ÷ 11 = _____	× 100 = _____ %
TOTAL WRITTEN EXPRESSION SKILLS	_____ ÷ 50 = _____	× 100 = _____ %
Mathematics		
Arithmetic (8, 9, 10, 16, 17, 18, 19, 20, 21, 25, 26, 36, 37, 45, 50)	_____ ÷ 15 = _____	× 100 = _____ %
Algebra (22, 30, 33, 34, 35, 39, 40, 42, 44, 47)	_____ ÷ 10 = _____	× 100 = _____ %
Data Analysis (1, 2, 3, 4, 5, 6, 7, 11, 12, 13, 14, 15, 24, 48)	_____ ÷ 14 = _____	× 100 = _____ %
Geometry and Measurement (23, 27, 28, 29, 31, 32, 38, 41, 43, 46, 49)	_____ ÷ 11 = _____	× 100 = _____ %
TOTAL MATHEMATICS SKILLS	_____ ÷ 50 = _____	× 100 = _____ %
Ability		
Figure Classification (1, 2, 3, 4, 5, 6, 7, 8, 9, 10, 11, 12, 13, 14, 15, 16, 17, 18, 19, 20)	_____ ÷ 20 = _____	× 100 = _____ %
Figure Matrices (1, 2, 3, 4, 5, 6, 7, 8, 9, 10, 11, 12, 13, 14, 15, 16, 17, 18, 19, 20)	_____ ÷ 20 = _____	× 100 = _____ %
Paper Folding (1, 2, 3, 4, 5, 6, 7, 8, 9, 10)	_____ ÷ 10 = _____	× 100 = _____ %
TOTAL ABILITY SKILLS	_____ ÷ 50 = _____	× 100 = _____ %

Practice Test 3: TACHS

ANSWER SHEET: HSPT® PRACTICE TEST 4

Verbal Skills

1. Ⓐ Ⓑ Ⓒ Ⓓ	13. Ⓐ Ⓑ Ⓒ	25. Ⓐ Ⓑ Ⓒ Ⓓ	37. Ⓐ Ⓑ Ⓒ Ⓓ	49. Ⓐ Ⓑ Ⓒ Ⓓ
2. Ⓐ Ⓑ Ⓒ Ⓓ	14. Ⓐ Ⓑ Ⓒ	26. Ⓐ Ⓑ Ⓒ Ⓓ	38. Ⓐ Ⓑ Ⓒ Ⓓ	50. Ⓐ Ⓑ Ⓒ Ⓓ
3. Ⓐ Ⓑ Ⓒ Ⓓ	15. Ⓐ Ⓑ Ⓒ	27. Ⓐ Ⓑ Ⓒ Ⓓ	39. Ⓐ Ⓑ Ⓒ Ⓓ	51. Ⓐ Ⓑ Ⓒ Ⓓ
4. Ⓐ Ⓑ Ⓒ Ⓓ	16. Ⓐ Ⓑ Ⓒ	28. Ⓐ Ⓑ Ⓒ Ⓓ	40. Ⓐ Ⓑ Ⓒ Ⓓ	52. Ⓐ Ⓑ Ⓒ Ⓓ
5. Ⓐ Ⓑ Ⓒ Ⓓ	17. Ⓐ Ⓑ Ⓒ	29. Ⓐ Ⓑ Ⓒ Ⓓ	41. Ⓐ Ⓑ Ⓒ Ⓓ	53. Ⓐ Ⓑ Ⓒ Ⓓ
6. Ⓐ Ⓑ Ⓒ Ⓓ	18. Ⓐ Ⓑ Ⓒ	30. Ⓐ Ⓑ Ⓒ Ⓓ	42. Ⓐ Ⓑ Ⓒ Ⓓ	54. Ⓐ Ⓑ Ⓒ Ⓓ
7. Ⓐ Ⓑ Ⓒ Ⓓ	19. Ⓐ Ⓑ Ⓒ	31. Ⓐ Ⓑ Ⓒ Ⓓ	43. Ⓐ Ⓑ Ⓒ Ⓓ	55. Ⓐ Ⓑ Ⓒ Ⓓ
8. Ⓐ Ⓑ Ⓒ Ⓓ	20. Ⓐ Ⓑ Ⓒ	32. Ⓐ Ⓑ Ⓒ Ⓓ	44. Ⓐ Ⓑ Ⓒ Ⓓ	56. Ⓐ Ⓑ Ⓒ Ⓓ
9. Ⓐ Ⓑ Ⓒ Ⓓ	21. Ⓐ Ⓑ Ⓒ Ⓓ	33. Ⓐ Ⓑ Ⓒ Ⓓ	45. Ⓐ Ⓑ Ⓒ Ⓓ	57. Ⓐ Ⓑ Ⓒ Ⓓ
10. Ⓐ Ⓑ Ⓒ Ⓓ	22. Ⓐ Ⓑ Ⓒ Ⓓ	34. Ⓐ Ⓑ Ⓒ Ⓓ	46. Ⓐ Ⓑ Ⓒ Ⓓ	58. Ⓐ Ⓑ Ⓒ Ⓓ
11. Ⓐ Ⓑ Ⓒ	23. Ⓐ Ⓑ Ⓒ Ⓓ	35. Ⓐ Ⓑ Ⓒ Ⓓ	47. Ⓐ Ⓑ Ⓒ Ⓓ	59. Ⓐ Ⓑ Ⓒ Ⓓ
12. Ⓐ Ⓑ Ⓒ	24. Ⓐ Ⓑ Ⓒ Ⓓ	36. Ⓐ Ⓑ Ⓒ Ⓓ	48. Ⓐ Ⓑ Ⓒ Ⓓ	60. Ⓐ Ⓑ Ⓒ Ⓓ

Quantitative Skills

61. Ⓐ Ⓑ Ⓒ Ⓓ	73. Ⓐ Ⓑ Ⓒ Ⓓ	85. Ⓐ Ⓑ Ⓒ Ⓓ	97. Ⓐ Ⓑ Ⓒ Ⓓ	109. Ⓐ Ⓑ Ⓒ Ⓓ
62. Ⓐ Ⓑ Ⓒ Ⓓ	74. Ⓐ Ⓑ Ⓒ Ⓓ	86. Ⓐ Ⓑ Ⓒ Ⓓ	98. Ⓐ Ⓑ Ⓒ Ⓓ	110. Ⓐ Ⓑ Ⓒ Ⓓ
63. Ⓐ Ⓑ Ⓒ Ⓓ	75. Ⓐ Ⓑ Ⓒ Ⓓ	87. Ⓐ Ⓑ Ⓒ Ⓓ	99. Ⓐ Ⓑ Ⓒ Ⓓ	111. Ⓐ Ⓑ Ⓒ Ⓓ
64. Ⓐ Ⓑ Ⓒ Ⓓ	76. Ⓐ Ⓑ Ⓒ Ⓓ	88. Ⓐ Ⓑ Ⓒ Ⓓ	100. Ⓐ Ⓑ Ⓒ Ⓓ	112. Ⓐ Ⓑ Ⓒ Ⓓ
65. Ⓐ Ⓑ Ⓒ Ⓓ	77. Ⓐ Ⓑ Ⓒ Ⓓ	89. Ⓐ Ⓑ Ⓒ Ⓓ	101. Ⓐ Ⓑ Ⓒ Ⓓ	
66. Ⓐ Ⓑ Ⓒ Ⓓ	78. Ⓐ Ⓑ Ⓒ Ⓓ	90. Ⓐ Ⓑ Ⓒ Ⓓ	102. Ⓐ Ⓑ Ⓒ Ⓓ	
67. Ⓐ Ⓑ Ⓒ Ⓓ	79. Ⓐ Ⓑ Ⓒ Ⓓ	91. Ⓐ Ⓑ Ⓒ Ⓓ	103. Ⓐ Ⓑ Ⓒ Ⓓ	
68. Ⓐ Ⓑ Ⓒ Ⓓ	80. Ⓐ Ⓑ Ⓒ Ⓓ	92. Ⓐ Ⓑ Ⓒ Ⓓ	104. Ⓐ Ⓑ Ⓒ Ⓓ	
69. Ⓐ Ⓑ Ⓒ Ⓓ	81. Ⓐ Ⓑ Ⓒ Ⓓ	93. Ⓐ Ⓑ Ⓒ Ⓓ	105. Ⓐ Ⓑ Ⓒ Ⓓ	
70. Ⓐ Ⓑ Ⓒ Ⓓ	82. Ⓐ Ⓑ Ⓒ Ⓓ	94. Ⓐ Ⓑ Ⓒ Ⓓ	106. Ⓐ Ⓑ Ⓒ Ⓓ	
71. Ⓐ Ⓑ Ⓒ Ⓓ	83. Ⓐ Ⓑ Ⓒ Ⓓ	95. Ⓐ Ⓑ Ⓒ Ⓓ	107. Ⓐ Ⓑ Ⓒ Ⓓ	
72. Ⓐ Ⓑ Ⓒ Ⓓ	84. Ⓐ Ⓑ Ⓒ Ⓓ	96. Ⓐ Ⓑ Ⓒ Ⓓ	108. Ⓐ Ⓑ Ⓒ Ⓓ	

Answer Sheet ▷ **Practice Test 4: HSPT®**

Reading
Comprehension

113. Ⓐ Ⓑ Ⓒ Ⓓ   121. Ⓐ Ⓑ Ⓒ Ⓓ   129. Ⓐ Ⓑ Ⓒ Ⓓ   137. Ⓐ Ⓑ Ⓒ Ⓓ   145. Ⓐ Ⓑ Ⓒ Ⓓ

114. Ⓐ Ⓑ Ⓒ Ⓓ   122. Ⓐ Ⓑ Ⓒ Ⓓ   130. Ⓐ Ⓑ Ⓒ Ⓓ   138. Ⓐ Ⓑ Ⓒ Ⓓ   146. Ⓐ Ⓑ Ⓒ Ⓓ

115. Ⓐ Ⓑ Ⓒ Ⓓ   123. Ⓐ Ⓑ Ⓒ Ⓓ   131. Ⓐ Ⓑ Ⓒ Ⓓ   139. Ⓐ Ⓑ Ⓒ Ⓓ   147. Ⓐ Ⓑ Ⓒ Ⓓ

116. Ⓐ Ⓑ Ⓒ Ⓓ   124. Ⓐ Ⓑ Ⓒ Ⓓ   132. Ⓐ Ⓑ Ⓒ Ⓓ   140. Ⓐ Ⓑ Ⓒ Ⓓ   148. Ⓐ Ⓑ Ⓒ Ⓓ

117. Ⓐ Ⓑ Ⓒ Ⓓ   125. Ⓐ Ⓑ Ⓒ Ⓓ   133. Ⓐ Ⓑ Ⓒ Ⓓ   141. Ⓐ Ⓑ Ⓒ Ⓓ   149. Ⓐ Ⓑ Ⓒ Ⓓ

118. Ⓐ Ⓑ Ⓒ Ⓓ   126. Ⓐ Ⓑ Ⓒ Ⓓ   134. Ⓐ Ⓑ Ⓒ Ⓓ   142. Ⓐ Ⓑ Ⓒ Ⓓ   150. Ⓐ Ⓑ Ⓒ Ⓓ

119. Ⓐ Ⓑ Ⓒ Ⓓ   127. Ⓐ Ⓑ Ⓒ Ⓓ   135. Ⓐ Ⓑ Ⓒ Ⓓ   143. Ⓐ Ⓑ Ⓒ Ⓓ   151. Ⓐ Ⓑ Ⓒ Ⓓ

120. Ⓐ Ⓑ Ⓒ Ⓓ   128. Ⓐ Ⓑ Ⓒ Ⓓ   136. Ⓐ Ⓑ Ⓒ Ⓓ   144. Ⓐ Ⓑ Ⓒ Ⓓ   152. Ⓐ Ⓑ Ⓒ Ⓓ

Vocabulary

153. Ⓐ Ⓑ Ⓒ Ⓓ   158. Ⓐ Ⓑ Ⓒ Ⓓ   163. Ⓐ Ⓑ Ⓒ Ⓓ   168. Ⓐ Ⓑ Ⓒ Ⓓ   173. Ⓐ Ⓑ Ⓒ Ⓓ

154. Ⓐ Ⓑ Ⓒ Ⓓ   159. Ⓐ Ⓑ Ⓒ Ⓓ   164. Ⓐ Ⓑ Ⓒ Ⓓ   169. Ⓐ Ⓑ Ⓒ Ⓓ   174. Ⓐ Ⓑ Ⓒ Ⓓ

155. Ⓐ Ⓑ Ⓒ Ⓓ   160. Ⓐ Ⓑ Ⓒ Ⓓ   165. Ⓐ Ⓑ Ⓒ Ⓓ   170. Ⓐ Ⓑ Ⓒ Ⓓ

156. Ⓐ Ⓑ Ⓒ Ⓓ   161. Ⓐ Ⓑ Ⓒ Ⓓ   166. Ⓐ Ⓑ Ⓒ Ⓓ   171. Ⓐ Ⓑ Ⓒ Ⓓ

157. Ⓐ Ⓑ Ⓒ Ⓓ   162. Ⓐ Ⓑ Ⓒ Ⓓ   167. Ⓐ Ⓑ Ⓒ Ⓓ   172. Ⓐ Ⓑ Ⓒ Ⓓ

Mathematics

Concepts

175. Ⓐ Ⓑ Ⓒ Ⓓ   180. Ⓐ Ⓑ Ⓒ Ⓓ   185. Ⓐ Ⓑ Ⓒ Ⓓ   190. Ⓐ Ⓑ Ⓒ Ⓓ   195. Ⓐ Ⓑ Ⓒ Ⓓ

176. Ⓐ Ⓑ Ⓒ Ⓓ   181. Ⓐ Ⓑ Ⓒ Ⓓ   186. Ⓐ Ⓑ Ⓒ Ⓓ   191. Ⓐ Ⓑ Ⓒ Ⓓ   196. Ⓐ Ⓑ Ⓒ Ⓓ

177. Ⓐ Ⓑ Ⓒ Ⓓ   182. Ⓐ Ⓑ Ⓒ Ⓓ   187. Ⓐ Ⓑ Ⓒ Ⓓ   192. Ⓐ Ⓑ Ⓒ Ⓓ   197. Ⓐ Ⓑ Ⓒ Ⓓ

178. Ⓐ Ⓑ Ⓒ Ⓓ   183. Ⓐ Ⓑ Ⓒ Ⓓ   188. Ⓐ Ⓑ Ⓒ Ⓓ   193. Ⓐ Ⓑ Ⓒ Ⓓ   198. Ⓐ Ⓑ Ⓒ Ⓓ

179. Ⓐ Ⓑ Ⓒ Ⓓ   184. Ⓐ Ⓑ Ⓒ Ⓓ   189. Ⓐ Ⓑ Ⓒ Ⓓ   194. Ⓐ Ⓑ Ⓒ Ⓓ

Problem Solving

199. Ⓐ Ⓑ Ⓒ Ⓓ   207. Ⓐ Ⓑ Ⓒ Ⓓ   215. Ⓐ Ⓑ Ⓒ Ⓓ   223. Ⓐ Ⓑ Ⓒ Ⓓ   231. Ⓐ Ⓑ Ⓒ Ⓓ

200. Ⓐ Ⓑ Ⓒ Ⓓ   208. Ⓐ Ⓑ Ⓒ Ⓓ   216. Ⓐ Ⓑ Ⓒ Ⓓ   224. Ⓐ Ⓑ Ⓒ Ⓓ   232. Ⓐ Ⓑ Ⓒ Ⓓ

201. Ⓐ Ⓑ Ⓒ Ⓓ   209. Ⓐ Ⓑ Ⓒ Ⓓ   217. Ⓐ Ⓑ Ⓒ Ⓓ   225. Ⓐ Ⓑ Ⓒ Ⓓ   233. Ⓐ Ⓑ Ⓒ Ⓓ

202. Ⓐ Ⓑ Ⓒ Ⓓ   210. Ⓐ Ⓑ Ⓒ Ⓓ   218. Ⓐ Ⓑ Ⓒ Ⓓ   226. Ⓐ Ⓑ Ⓒ Ⓓ   234. Ⓐ Ⓑ Ⓒ Ⓓ

203. Ⓐ Ⓑ Ⓒ Ⓓ   211. Ⓐ Ⓑ Ⓒ Ⓓ   219. Ⓐ Ⓑ Ⓒ Ⓓ   227. Ⓐ Ⓑ Ⓒ Ⓓ   235. Ⓐ Ⓑ Ⓒ Ⓓ

204. Ⓐ Ⓑ Ⓒ Ⓓ   212. Ⓐ Ⓑ Ⓒ Ⓓ   220. Ⓐ Ⓑ Ⓒ Ⓓ   228. Ⓐ Ⓑ Ⓒ Ⓓ   236. Ⓐ Ⓑ Ⓒ Ⓓ

205. Ⓐ Ⓑ Ⓒ Ⓓ   213. Ⓐ Ⓑ Ⓒ Ⓓ   221. Ⓐ Ⓑ Ⓒ Ⓓ   229. Ⓐ Ⓑ Ⓒ Ⓓ   237. Ⓐ Ⓑ Ⓒ Ⓓ

206. Ⓐ Ⓑ Ⓒ Ⓓ   214. Ⓐ Ⓑ Ⓒ Ⓓ   222. Ⓐ Ⓑ Ⓒ Ⓓ   230. Ⓐ Ⓑ Ⓒ Ⓓ   238. Ⓐ Ⓑ Ⓒ Ⓓ

Language

239. Ⓐ Ⓑ Ⓒ Ⓓ	251. Ⓐ Ⓑ Ⓒ Ⓓ	263. Ⓐ Ⓑ Ⓒ Ⓓ	275. Ⓐ Ⓑ Ⓒ Ⓓ	287. Ⓐ Ⓑ Ⓒ Ⓓ
240. Ⓐ Ⓑ Ⓒ Ⓓ	252. Ⓐ Ⓑ Ⓒ Ⓓ	264. Ⓐ Ⓑ Ⓒ Ⓓ	276. Ⓐ Ⓑ Ⓒ Ⓓ	288. Ⓐ Ⓑ Ⓒ Ⓓ
241. Ⓐ Ⓑ Ⓒ Ⓓ	253. Ⓐ Ⓑ Ⓒ Ⓓ	265. Ⓐ Ⓑ Ⓒ Ⓓ	277. Ⓐ Ⓑ Ⓒ Ⓓ	289. Ⓐ Ⓑ Ⓒ Ⓓ
242. Ⓐ Ⓑ Ⓒ Ⓓ	254. Ⓐ Ⓑ Ⓒ Ⓓ	266. Ⓐ Ⓑ Ⓒ Ⓓ	278. Ⓐ Ⓑ Ⓒ Ⓓ	290. Ⓐ Ⓑ Ⓒ Ⓓ
243. Ⓐ Ⓑ Ⓒ Ⓓ	255. Ⓐ Ⓑ Ⓒ Ⓓ	267. Ⓐ Ⓑ Ⓒ Ⓓ	279. Ⓐ Ⓑ Ⓒ Ⓓ	291. Ⓐ Ⓑ Ⓒ Ⓓ
244. Ⓐ Ⓑ Ⓒ Ⓓ	256. Ⓐ Ⓑ Ⓒ Ⓓ	268. Ⓐ Ⓑ Ⓒ Ⓓ	280. Ⓐ Ⓑ Ⓒ Ⓓ	292. Ⓐ Ⓑ Ⓒ Ⓓ
245. Ⓐ Ⓑ Ⓒ Ⓓ	257. Ⓐ Ⓑ Ⓒ Ⓓ	269. Ⓐ Ⓑ Ⓒ Ⓓ	281. Ⓐ Ⓑ Ⓒ Ⓓ	293. Ⓐ Ⓑ Ⓒ Ⓓ
246. Ⓐ Ⓑ Ⓒ Ⓓ	258. Ⓐ Ⓑ Ⓒ Ⓓ	270. Ⓐ Ⓑ Ⓒ Ⓓ	282. Ⓐ Ⓑ Ⓒ Ⓓ	294. Ⓐ Ⓑ Ⓒ Ⓓ
247. Ⓐ Ⓑ Ⓒ Ⓓ	259. Ⓐ Ⓑ Ⓒ Ⓓ	271. Ⓐ Ⓑ Ⓒ Ⓓ	283. Ⓐ Ⓑ Ⓒ Ⓓ	295. Ⓐ Ⓑ Ⓒ Ⓓ
248. Ⓐ Ⓑ Ⓒ Ⓓ	260. Ⓐ Ⓑ Ⓒ Ⓓ	272. Ⓐ Ⓑ Ⓒ Ⓓ	284. Ⓐ Ⓑ Ⓒ Ⓓ	296. Ⓐ Ⓑ Ⓒ Ⓓ
249. Ⓐ Ⓑ Ⓒ Ⓓ	261. Ⓐ Ⓑ Ⓒ Ⓓ	273. Ⓐ Ⓑ Ⓒ Ⓓ	285. Ⓐ Ⓑ Ⓒ Ⓓ	297. Ⓐ Ⓑ Ⓒ Ⓓ
250. Ⓐ Ⓑ Ⓒ Ⓓ	262. Ⓐ Ⓑ Ⓒ Ⓓ	274. Ⓐ Ⓑ Ⓒ Ⓓ	286. Ⓐ Ⓑ Ⓒ Ⓓ	298. Ⓐ Ⓑ Ⓒ Ⓓ

Answer Sheet

Practice Test 4: HSPT®

Practice Test 4: HSPT®

VERBAL SKILLS

60 Questions (16 minutes)

Turn to the verbal skills section of your answer sheet to answer the questions in this section.

Directions: Mark one answer—the answer you think is best—for each problem.

1. Lobster is to ocean as scorpion is to
   A. zoo.
   B. desert.
   C. sting.
   D. animal.

2. Tea is to leaves as coffee is to
   A. caffeine.
   B. hot.
   C. drink.
   D. beans.

3. Sombrero is to hat as poodle is to
   A. furry.
   B. obedient.
   C. dog.
   D. white.

4. Dozen is to gross as inch is to
   A. foot.
   B. meter.
   C. measurement.
   D. ruler.

5. Tall is to short as quick is to
   A. athlete.
   B. speedy.
   C. slow.
   D. race.

6. Slice is to pie as piece is to
   A. water.
   B. air.
   C. pudding.
   D. puzzle.

7. Mold is to clay as carve is to
   A. bag.
   B. wood.
   C. slice.
   D. artist.

8. Bee is to falcon as trout is to
   A. shark.
   B. gerbil.
   C. aquarium.
   D. fisherman.

9. Monkey is to mouse as rhinoceros is to

   A. ram.

   B. snake.

   C. turtle.

   D. goose.

10. Snail is to slimy as rabbit is to

   A. carrot.

   B. hop.

   C. furry.

   D. smart.

11. Syrah is younger than Myriam. Radja is younger than Syrah. Myriam is younger than Radja. If the first two statements are true, the third is

   A. true.

   B. false.

   C. uncertain.

12. Last week, Antonio ate more nachos than Kevin. Kevin ate fewer nachos than Patricia. Patricia ate more nachos than Antonio. If the first two statements are true, the third is

   A. true.

   B. false.

   C. uncertain.

13. Frieda is thirstier than Paulo. Gus is thirstier than Freida. Paulo drank more water than Gus. If the first two statements are true, the third is

   A. true.

   B. false.

   C. uncertain.

14. Nareen did better than Tariq in the school-wide spelling bee. Tariq did not win the school-wide spelling bee. Nareen came in last place in the school-wide spelling bee. If the first two statements are true, the third is

   A. true.

   B. false.

   C. uncertain.

15. Poplar trees grow faster than myrtle trees. Willow trees grow faster than poplar trees. Myrtle trees grow faster than willow trees. If the first two statements are true, the third is

   A. true.

   B. false.

   C. uncertain.

16. Iron costs more than aluminum. Iron costs less than copper. Copper costs more than aluminum and iron. If the first two statements are true, the third is

   A. true.

   B. false.

   C. uncertain.

17. Eric swims faster than Marco. Carrie swims faster than Eric. Marco swims faster than Carrie. If the first two statements are true, the third is

   A. true.

   B. false.

   C. uncertain.

18. All the carrots in Bob's garden are orange. All the tomatoes in Bob's garden are red. All the vegetables in Bob's garden are either orange or red. If the first two statements are true, the third is

   A. true.

   B. false.

   C. uncertain.

19. Arianna is the tallest child in the orange classroom. Jake is the shortest child in the green classroom. Jake is shorter than Arianna. If the first two statements are true, the third is

    A. true.

    B. false.

    C. uncertain.

20. During the past month, Sadie downloaded more songs than Roxy. Roxy downloaded more songs than Henry. Henry downloaded more songs than Sadie. If the first two statements are true, the third is

    A. true.

    B. false.

    C. uncertain.

21. Which word does *not* belong with the others?

    A. Kettle

    B. Pot

    C. Spoon

    D. Pan

22. Which word does *not* belong with the others?

    A. Baseball

    B. Archery

    C. Football

    D. Soccer

23. Which word does *not* belong with the others?

    A. Scissor

    B. Knife

    C. Wrench

    D. Saw

24. Which word does *not* belong with the others?

    A. Glass

    B. Cement

    C. Construction worker

    D. Brick

25. Which word does *not* belong with the others?

    A. Pencil

    B. Book

    C. Newspaper

    D. Website

26. Which word does *not* belong with the others?

    A. Dragon

    B. Harmful

    C. Lion

    D. Tiger

27. Which word does *not* belong with the others?

    A. Throw

    B. Catch

    C. Ball

    D. Pitch

28. Which word does *not* belong with the others?

    A. Firefighter

    B. Police officer

    C. Comedian

    D. Problem solver

29. Which word does *not* belong with the others?

    A. Biscuit

    B. Calzone

    C. Taco

    D. Pizza

Practice Test 4: HSPT®

30. Which word does *not* belong with the others?

A. Eel

B. Pony

C. Seahorse

D. Whale

31. Which word does *not* belong with the others?

A. Chisel

B. Shovel

C. Spoon

D. Spatula

32. Which word does *not* belong with the others?

A. Ladder

B. Stairs

C. Mountain

D. Waterfall

33. Which word does *not* belong with the others?

A. Winning

B. Sorrow

C. Fear

D. Joy

34. Which word does *not* belong with the others?

A. Cosmetics

B. Groceries

C. Fulfillment

D. Clothing

35. Which word does *not* belong with the others?

A. Contemporary

B. List

C. Enjoyable

D. Extend

36. Which word does *not* belong with the others?

A. Eggs

B. Oysters

C. Walnuts

D. Tomatoes

37. An *anomalous* event is

A. disgraceful

B. formless

C. irregular

D. threatening

38. A *courteous* gentleman is

A. quiet

B. sleeping

C. energetic

D. polite

39. A *spacious* environment is

A. ugly.

B. roomy.

C. loud.

D. confusing.

40. A *loquacious* speaker is

A. talkative.

B. confident.

C. humorous.

D. quiet.

41. A *deft* performer is

A. clumsy.

B. bashful.

C. untalented.

D. skillful.

42. A *venerable* judge is
    A. angry.
    B. tired.
    C. honored.
    D. untrustworthy.

43. A *fecund* cornfield is
    A. barren.
    B. delicious.
    C. fruitful.
    D. spare.

44. A *cantankerous* voter is
    A. disagreeable.
    B. thoughtful.
    C. pleasant.
    D. informed.

45. A *caustic* remark is
    A. scathing.
    B. comical.
    C. meaningful.
    D. clever.

46. A *collaborative* effort is
    A. exclusive.
    B. cooperative.
    C. individual.
    D. difficult.

47. A *bombastic* speech is
    A. boring.
    B. destructive.
    C. grandiose.
    D. plain.

48. A *rancorous* employee is
    A. tall.
    B. loyal.
    C. swift.
    D. resentful.

49. A *contentious* meeting is
    A. crowded.
    B. wistful.
    C. wasteful.
    D. combative.

50. An *erudite* professor is
    A. confused.
    B. educated.
    C. loud.
    D. tough.

51. A *prominent* leader is
    A. noticeable.
    B. intelligent.
    C. effective.
    D. hidden.

52. Diligent means the *opposite* of
    A. generous.
    B. focused.
    C. passive.
    D. mournful.

53. Industrious means the *opposite* of
    A. idle.
    B. excessive.
    C. annoying.
    D. reasonable.

54. Intelligible means the *opposite* of

    A. agreeable.
    B. fluent.
    C. cheerful.
    D. inarticulate.

55. Denigrate means the *opposite* of

    A. ruminate.
    B. decorate.
    C. approve.
    D. dismiss.

56. Frugal means the *opposite* of

    A. odorous.
    B. wasteful.
    C. colorful.
    D. silly.

57. Altruistic means the *opposite* of

    A. extended.
    B. truthful.
    C. charitable.
    D. selfish.

58. Oblivious means the *opposite* of

    A. aware.
    B. ignorant.
    C. overweight.
    D. comical.

59. Beguile means the *opposite* of

    A. connect.
    B. adorn.
    C. repel.
    D. improvise.

60. Mollify means the *opposite* of

    A. gladden.
    B. aggravate.
    C. shrink.
    D. soften.

STOP.

If you finish before time is up, you may check your work on this section only.
Do not turn to any other section in the test.

PART V: Six Practice Tests

QUANTITATIVE SKILLS

52 Questions (30 minutes)

Turn to the Quantitative skills section of your answer sheet to answer the questions in this section.

> **Directions:** Mark one answer—the answer you think is best—for each problem.

61. What number is 3 more than 20% of 40?

    A. 11
    B. 9
    C. 8
    D. 5

62. Look at this series: 32, 39, 46, 53, ... What number should come next?

    A. 68
    B. 61
    C. 59
    D. 60

63. What number is $\frac{3}{4}$ of $\sqrt{256}$?

    A. 6
    B. 12
    C. 15
    D. 20

64. Examine A, B, and C and find the best answer.

    A.   B.   C.

    A. A plus C is less than B.
    B. C is equal to A.
    C. A is greater than C.
    D. C is less than B and greater than A.

65. Examine A, B, and C and find the best answer.

    A. 0.625
    B. $\frac{4}{7}$
    C. 0.297×2.1

    A. B is less than A but greater than C.
    B. A and C are equal and greater than B.
    C. C is greater than A and B.
    D. B is less than A and C.

66. What number is 5 cubed divided by 5?

    A. 15
    B. 25
    C. 75
    D. 125

67. Look at this series: 10, 12, 6, __, 4, 6, 3. What number should fill in the blank in the middle of the series?

    A. 5
    B. 8
    C. 9
    D. 10

68. Examine A, B, and C and find the best answer.

A.   B.   C.

A. A is more shaded than B.

B. B and C are equally shaded.

C. C is less shaded than either A or B.

D. A and C are both less shaded than B.

69. Look at this series: 1, 4, 11, _____, 21, 24, 31. What number should fill the blank in the middle of the series?

A. 3

B. 14

C. 20

D. 22

70. Examine A, B, and C and find the best answer.

    A. 10% of 80

    B. 80% of 10

    C. 10% of 80%

A. B is greater than A or C.

B. A, B, and C are equal.

C. A is equal to B and smaller than C.

D. A is greater than C.

71. What number is 4 more than $\frac{2}{3}$ of 39?

A. 30

B. 26

C. 15

D. 12

72. Look at this series: 56, 51, 47, 48, 43, 39, 40, ... What three numbers come next?

A. 36, 37, 32

B. 36, 31, 32

C. 35, 31, 32

D. 34, 30, 31

73. What number subtracted from 30 leaves 7 more than $\frac{3}{5}$ of 25?

A. 8

B. 15

C. 22

D. 23

74. What number is 7 less than $\frac{1}{4}$ of 64?

A. 4

B. 9

C. 18

D. 23

75. Elliot bought 23 party hats and paid $14.95. How much was each hat?

A. $0.89

B. $0.45

C. $0.65

D. $0.54

76. Look at this series: 821, 812, 804, 797, ... What number should come next?

A. 791

B. 788

C. 787

D. 778

77. Examine A, B, and C and find the best answer.

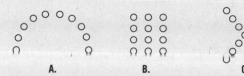

A.   B.   C.

A. A has more circles than B.

B. B and C have the same number of circles.

C. B and C each have more circles than A.

D. A and C each have fewer circles than B.

78. Examine A, B, and C and find the best answer.

A.   B.   C.

A. C is more shaded than B.

B. A and C are equally shaded, and both are more shaded than B.

C. B is more shaded than A and less shaded than C.

D. A, B, and C are equally shaded.

79. Look at this series: 95, 99, _____, 107, 111. What number should fill the blank in the middle of the series?

A. 98

B. 103

C. 104

D. 106

80. What number divided by 4 is $\frac{1}{5}$ of 100?

A. 400

B. 200

C. 80

D. 20

81. Look at this series: 1, V, 6, X, ... What number should come next?

A. XV

B. 11

C. 10

D. IX

82. Examine A, B, and C and find the best answer.

A.   B.   C.

A. A and B are each shaded more than C.

B. A, B, and C are equally shaded.

C. C is more shaded than A.

D. B is shaded less than C, which is shaded less than A.

83. $\frac{1}{2}$ of what number is 7 times 3?

A. 49

B. 42

C. 21

D. 5

84. Examine A, B, and C and find the best answer.

A.   B.   C.

A. A, B, and C are equally shaded.

B. B is less shaded than C and more shaded than A.

C. A is more shaded than B or C.

D. C is more shaded than A.

85. What number added to 6 is 3 times the product of 5 and 2?

A. 4

B. 16

C. 24

D. 30

86. Look at this series: 50, 48, 52, 50, 54, 52, ... What number should come next?

A. 50

B. 54

C. 56

D. 58

87. Examine A, B, and C and find the best answer.

   A. 125%

   B. 1.25

   C. $\dfrac{25}{2}$

A. A is greater than C, and C is greater than B.

B. A and B are equal, and both are less than C.

C. A and C are equal, and both are greater than B.

D. A, B, and C are all equal.

88. Six factorial (6!) falls between which two numbers?

A. 700 and 725

B. 580 and 625

C. 340 and 560

D. 335 and 380

89. Look at this series: 12, 14, 28, _____, 60. What number should fill the blank in this series?

A. 16

B. 19

C. 30

D. 40

90. Alexei's father got a $33 discount on a new trumpet that normally sells for $150. What percentage was the discount?

A. 31%

B. 22%

C. 18%

D. 13%

91. Examine the triangle and find the best answer.

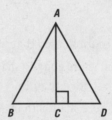

A. *AD* is greater than *CD*.

B. *BA* and *AD* are each less than *BC*.

C. *AB* is equal to *BC*.

D. *AB* is equal to *AC* plus *BC*.

92. What number multiplied by 3 is 5 less than 29?

A. 24

B. 14

C. 8

D. 6

93. Look at this series: 23, 29, 32, 38, 41, _____, 50. What number should fill the blank in this series?

A. 42

B. 47

C. 48

D. 51

94. Examine A, B, and C and find the best answer.

A. $(10 \div 5) \times 10$

B. $(5 \div 1) \times 4$

C. $(20 \div 5) \times 5$

A. A is equal to B, which is equal to C.

B. A is equal to B and less than C.

C. B is equal to C and less than A.

D. C is greater than A and B.

95. Look at this series: 100, 101, 91, 92, 82, …. What two numbers should come next?

A. 72, 74

B. 72, 73

C. 83, 73

D. 84, 74

96. Examine the cube and find the best answer.

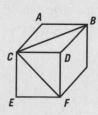

A. CF is greater than CB.

B. EF is less than AB.

C. CB is equal to CE.

D. CF is greater than AB.

97. Examine A, B, and C, and choose the best answer.

A. $\frac{1}{2}$ of $\frac{2}{3}$

B. $\frac{3}{4}$ of 1

C. $\frac{1}{2}$ of $\frac{3}{2}$

A. $A < B < C$

B. $A = B < C$

C. $A = B = C$

D. $A < B = C$

98. Examine A, B, and C. Choose the best answer if $1 < x < y$ and x and y are whole numbers.

A. xy

B. y^2

C. x^2

A. A is less than B and B is less than C.

B. C is less than A and A is less than B.

C. B is less than A and A is less than C.

D. C is less than B and B is less than A.

99. Look at this series: 14, 28, 32, 64, 68, …. What number should come next?

A. 136

B. 132

C. 78

D. 76

100. Look at this series: 1, 3, 7, 13, 21, …. What number comes next?

A. 22

B. 29

C. 31

D. 42

101. Look at this series: A24, C28, E18, G22, ...
What term comes next?

A. H26

B. J14

C. I12

D. F20

102. Examine the graph and find the best answer.

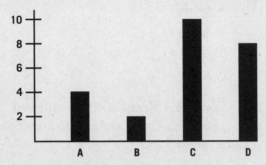

A. B plus C minus A equals D.

B. C minus A minus B equals D.

C. C plus D equals A plus B.

D. D minus B equals A plus C.

103. What number is 2 less than $\frac{3}{5}$ of 10?

A. 8

B. 6

C. 4

D. 2

104. Look at this series: 4, 16, 5, 25, 6, ... What number should come next?

A. 36

B. 30

C. 20

D. 6

105. Examine A, B, and C and find the best answer.

A. 5^2

B. 4^3

C. 2^4

A. A > B > C

B. B > A > C

C. A = B = C

D. B > A = C

106. Look at this series: 10, $7\frac{1}{2}$, 5, $2\frac{1}{2}$, ... What number should come next?

A. 2

B. $1\frac{1}{2}$

C. $\frac{1}{2}$

D. 0

107. Look at this series: AA, A1, BA, B1, CA, ... What term should come next?

A. CB

B. C1

C. DA

D. D1

108. Look at this series: 26, 30, 28, 27, 31, 29, 28, ... What three numbers should come next?

A. 32, 38, 24

B. 32, 30, 25

C. 32, 30, 29

D. 24, 26, 27

109. $\frac{1}{3}$ of what number added to 6 is 2 times 9?

A. 38

B. 36

C. 18

D. 3

110. Examine the parallelogram and find the best answer.

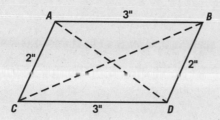

A. The perimeter of the parallelogram is 10 inches.

B. The area of the parallelogram is 5 square inches.

C. The area of triangle *ABD* is greater than the area of triangle *ACD*.

D. The perimeter of triangle *BAC* is equal to the perimeter of the parallelogram.

111. What number is 10 more than $\frac{4}{9}$ of 27?

A. 2

B. 12

C. 22

D. 37

112. What number is 11 more than 5 squared?

A. 36

B. 21

C. 14

D. 1

STOP.

If you finish before time is up, you may check your work on this section only.
Do not turn to any other section in the test.

Practice Test 4: HSPT®

READING

62 Questions (25 minutes)

Comprehension

Turn to the Reading Comprehension section of your answer sheet to answer the questions in this section.

> **Directions:** This is a test of how well you understand what you read.
>
> • Read the passages below and answer the questions.
>
> • Four answers are given for each question. You must choose the answer that you think is better than the others.

Questions 113–122 refer to the following passage.

Contrary to what we may have heard, not all fats we eat are bad for our health. It is certainly wise to be cautious about how much fat we eat: many nutritionists recommend that we restrict our fat intake to about 30 percent of our total daily calories. Research now shows, however, that

Line it is also important to be sure that we consume enough of the good fats in our diets, so that we
5 can provide ourselves with optimal nutrition.

The fats that are particularly important for us belong to a group of fats that scientists call "essential fatty acids." These fats are termed "essential" because they are so vital to our health. Scientists have determined that there are two types of essential fatty acids that we humans must get from our diets: these are known as omega-3 and omega-6 fatty acids.

10 According to nutrition author Clara Felix, scientists now believe that we should consume at least one gram of omega-3 fatty acids for every 3 grams of omega-6 fatty acids that we eat. Although we tend to eat enough omega-6 fats, the American diet falls short when it comes to omega-3 fats. The best way to balance out our diets, Felix recommends, is to reduce the amount of omega-6 oils we are eating while at the same time increasing the amount of omega-3 fat.

15 We can do this by first limiting the amounts of salad dressing and margarine that we eat, as well as baked goods such as breads, muffins, cakes, and donuts. Next, to increase our omega-3 fats, we can add flaxseed oil and olive oil into our diets, as well as more walnuts and fish. The fish that provide the greatest sources of omega-3 fats, according to Felix, are herring, mackerel, salmon, sardines, trout, tuna, and whitefish.

113. Which of the following is true about Clara Felix?

A. She has conducted experiments on dietary fat.

B. She is a medical doctor.

C. She has written works about nutrition.

D. She has a degree in biology.

114. What is the author's opinion about omega-6 fatty acids?

A. We should consume more of them.

B. We get plenty of them in our diets already.

C. We should not consume them in our diets.

D. They are difficult to find in common foods.

115. This passage mainly focuses on how to

    A. lose weight by consuming less dietary fat.

    B. eliminate bad fats from our diet.

    C. improve nutrition by consuming more Omega-3.

    D. analyze the importance of fat in the diet.

116. According to the passage, nutritionists recommend that we limit our consumption of fats to

    A. around 30 calories a day.

    B. a little more than 30 ounces a day.

    C. about 30 percent of total ounces of food consumed every day.

    D. about 30 percent of total calories consumed every day.

117. According to the passage, good sources of omega-3 fats include

    A. bread, salmon, and walnuts.

    B. olive oil, margarine, and sardines.

    C. salads, sardines, and white fish.

    D. olive oil, walnuts, and sardines.

118. As used in the passage, the word *optimal* in paragraph 1 most nearly means

    A. disadvantageous.

    B. ideal.

    C. expensive.

    D. limiting.

119. We can infer from the information provided in the passage that the author would most likely characterize the average American diet as

    A. falling short on the consumption of good fats.

    B. falling short on the consumption of bad fats.

    C. ideally balanced compared to other countries.

    D. balanced in terms of consumption of good versus bad fats.

120. Which of the following pieces of information would make the results of Clara Felix's research clearer and more focused?

    A. The school at which Clara Felix studied

    B. How far the American diet falls short on omega-6 fats

    C. How far the American diet falls short on omega-3 fats

    D. Recipes for incorporating more good fats into our diets

121. Based on the information provided in the passage, we can predict that readers who follow the author's advice will

    A. eat more margarine.

    B. increase their consumption of bad fats.

    C. increase their consumption of good fats.

    D. eat an average amount of muffins and cakes.

122. According to the passage, compared to omega-3 fatty acids, the average American should

    A. decrease their consumption of omega-6 fatty acids.

    B. eliminate their consumption of omega-6 fatty acids.

    C. increase their consumption of omega-6 fatty acids.

    D. not change their consumption of omega-6 fatty acids.

Practice Test 4: HSPT®

Questions 123–132 refer to the following passage.

Few people have seen the world from the vantage point of John Amatt. Some of those who have didn't live to tell about it.

Amatt was a leader and climber on a 1982 Canadian expedition to Mount Everest, which
Line is the tallest mountain in the world at 29,028 feet. This was the first Canadian expedition to
5   Mount Everest. In the end, it was successful in placing two Canadian climbers on the summit of the great mountain. The journey to that goal, however, was extremely challenging.

The trip started with 16 Canadian climbers and 24 Sherpas, expert mountain guides who live in the Himalayas in Nepal. By the end of the trip, ten weeks later, only two Canadians and four Sherpas made it to the top of the mountain. One Canadian and three Sherpas had lost their
10 lives in avalanche accidents during the early part of the trip. The accidents almost caused the climb to be called off, but the team chose to press on.

In his book, *Straight to the Top and Beyond*, Amatt describes how his experiences during the Everest expedition helped his team to learn from their setbacks. In Amatt's view, the experience of loss helped the team to strengthen their perspective on the reality of what they were
15 up against. It also inspired them to approach their challenges with clarity and humbleness. He believes that the team learned from the accidents to take the risks that they faced more seriously. This lesson ultimately helped make the Everest expedition a success.

123. The main contrast in the article is between
   A. the work of the Canadians and the work of the Sherpas.
   B. those who have seen the world from Mount Everest and those who have not.
   C. the success of the expedition and the losses it faced.
   D. John Amatt and less successful climbers.

124. According to the passage, how many Sherpas reached the top of Mount Everest with the Canadian expedition?
   A. 2
   B. 4
   C. 6
   D. 24

125. The passage states that the expedition led by John Amatt was the
   A. first expedition to scale Mount Everest.
   B. only successful expedition to scale Mount Everest.
   C. first Canadian expedition to scale Mount Everest.
   D. last expedition that Amatt led up Mount Everest.

126. In his book, Amatt states that his team learned several lessons from their setbacks and challenges, including how to approach their efforts with
   A. indifference.
   B. pride.
   C. ambition.
   D. humility.

127. In the following sentence in the last paragraph, "It also inspired them to approach their challenges with clarity and humbleness," the word *it* refers to the

  A. experience of loss cited in sentence 2 of the last paragraph.

  B. experiences of Amatt's expedition cited in sentence 1 of the last paragraph.

  C. book written by Amatt cited in sentence 1 of the last paragraph.

  D. accidents cited in sentence 4 of the last paragraph.

128. As used in the passage, the word *summit* in paragraph 2 most nearly means

  A. peak.

  B. success.

  C. climb.

  D. step.

129. Based on the information provided in the passage, we can infer that the author would most likely compare John Amatt to

  A. a professional athlete who attempts to cheat if she thinks she can get away with it.

  B. a runner who had to stop mid race due to a severely swollen ankle.

  C. a restaurant owner who hired a manager to run the daily business for him.

  D. a swimmer who overcame treacherous conditions to successfully swim the English Channel.

130. Based on the information provided in the passage, what is the most likely explanation why Amatt titled his book *Straight to the Top and Beyond*?

  A. Because Amatt climbed higher than any other climber had done before in history

  B. Because Amatt did not climb Mount Everest alone; instead, he went with other Canadian climbers and Sherpas

  C. Because the book describes both his climb to the top of Mount Everest and the lessons he learned from the adversity he faced

  D. Because Amatt was flown by helicopter straight to the top of Mount Everest and beyond

131. Based on the information provided in the passage, the "experience of loss" mentioned in paragraph 4 most likely refers to:

  A. time wasted while climbing Mount Everest.

  B. lives lost during the climb up Mount Everest.

  C. the equipment the climbers lost during the treacherous storm that hit Mount Everest.

  D. the fact that Amatt failed to reach the top of Mount Everest.

132. The main idea of the passage is to

  A. tell the story of John Amatt's experience and lessons learned through his success and adversity as a climber.

  B. warn readers against mountain climbing due to the potential dangers and perils of the activity.

  C. tell the history of mountain climbing in Canada in the 20th century.

  D. provide the history of attempts to climb Mount Everest, one of the most famous mountains in the entire world.

Practice Test 4: HSPT®

Questions 133–142 refer to the following passage.

The dark and the sea are full of dangers to the fishermen of Norway. A whale might come and destroy the floating chain of corks that edges the nets, break it, and carry it off. Or a storm might come suddenly, unexpectedly, out of the night. The sea seems to turn somersaults. It opens and
Line closes immense caverns with terrible clashes, chasing boats and fishermen who must flee from
5 their nets and the expected catch. Then the fishermen might lift their nets as empty as they set them. At other times, the herring might come in such masses that the lines break from the weight when lifted, and the fishermen must return home empty-handed, without line, nets, or herring.

But often the nets are full of herring that shine and glisten like silver. Once in a while, a couple of fishermen will venture in their boats along the net lines to see whether the herring
10 are coming, and when the corks begin to bob and jerk as if something were hitting the nets to which they are attached, they then know that the herring are there. The nets are being filled, and all the fishermen sit in quiet excitement. They dare only to whisper to each other, afraid to disturb, and quite overcome by the overwhelming generosity of the sea. Eyes shine with happy anticipation; hands folded in thanks. Then muscles strain with power. It is as though the strength
15 of the body doubled. They can work day-and-night without thoughts of weariness. They need neither food nor rest; the thought of success keeps their vigor up almost endlessly. They will take food and rest when it is all over.

133. Which is the best title for this passage?

A. "Hard Work in Norway"

B. "The Perils and Rewards of Fishing"

C. "Risky Business"

D. "The Generosity of the Sea"

134. The difficulties faced by the Norwegian fishermen include

A. the eating of the herring by whales.

B. the difficulty of being very calm.

C. interference by rough seas.

D. the jerking of the corks.

135. At the first indication that herring are entering the nets, the fishermen

A. try not to frighten the fish away.

B. strain every muscle to haul in the catch.

C. collect the nets quickly.

D. row quickly along the edge of the nets.

136. When the article says that the sea "opens and closes immense caverns," it is referring to

A. caves along the shoreline.

B. deep holes in the ocean floor.

C. dangerous large boulders that get rolled around.

D. hollow pockets beneath very high waves.

137. The fishermen are described as

A. strong, angry, and excitable.

B. skillful, religious, and impatient.

C. patient, brave, and grateful.

D. surly, hardworking, and cautious.

138. Of the following, the one that is not mentioned as posing a problem to the fishermen is

A. destruction of the nets.

B. theft of the nets by other fishermen.

C. too large a catch.

D. whales.

139. The author of the passage would most likely compare the sea in Norway mentioned in the passage to

   A. a peaceful and tranquil pond.

   B. a fun-filled car ride.

   C. a dark and dangerous storm.

   D. an informative historical trip through nature.

140. Based on the information provided in the passage, we can conclude that the life of a fisherman is

   A. filled with danger and hard work, with peaks of satisfying success.

   B. lucrative and fun, with occasional moments of quiet solitude.

   C. serious and hilarious, with temporary moments of enjoyable weather.

   D. rapidly disappearing in today's technology-focused modern society.

141. We can infer from the information provided in the passage that a net without herring to a Norwegian fisherman is like

   A. a lost baseball.

   B. a store without a manager.

   C. a salesman without a sale.

   D. lightning striking a tree.

142. According to the passage, which of the following items might *not* be found on a Norwegian fishing boat?

   A. Lines

   B. Lantern

   C. Nets

   D. Fisherman

Questions 143–152 refer to the following passage.

In caffeine-fueled cultures across the globe, it has never been easier to enjoy a great cup of coffee, regardless of where you may find yourself. Coffee has become one of the most profitable—and revered—businesses in the world, with ever-increasing numbers of coffee house openings, some
Line of which proclaim to make and serve the best cup of coffee around. While individual coffee
5 tastes and preferences are as varied as the number of bean varieties that exist, it would be hard to find a coffee more interesting—or expensive—than kopi luwak.

Kopi luwak is also referred to as civet coffee, and for good reason. These prized beans are harvested from the digested remains of coffee cherries that have been eaten by Asian palm civets, small squirrel-like creatures that inhabit Southeast Asia. The vast majority of kopi luwak is
10 produced in the islands of Java, Bali, Sumatra, Sulawesi, and the Philippines. Many coffee experts proclaim that civets naturally select only the best, most fleshy coffee cherries to consume—and ultimately eliminate—and that during the digestion process, a process of fermentation occurs within the civets that diminishes the coffee bean's natural acidity, reduces bitterness, and ultimately leads to a smoother and more satisfying beverage.

15 After the fruity pulp of the coffee cherries are consumed by the civets, the remains are excreted and collected for cleaning and roasting. Because of the unique conditions in which the beans are obtained, their limited supply, and its prized taste, kopi luwak is widely recognized as one of the most expensive and rare coffees in the world. Prices have been known to go as high as several hundred dollars or more for a pound of beans. As a result, farmers and harvesters,
20 keen on profiting from the prized droppings, have taken to extreme methods to increase supply, including trapping and caging these creatures in overcrowded civet farms, which have raised concerns regarding the welfare and safety of these animals. Unsavory merchants have also taken to selling inferior beans under the kopi luwak name in an effort to turn a profit.

While kopi luwak has its critics, and not everyone believes this process yields a superior
25 cup of coffee, there are certainly enough people who either greatly enjoy the beans or are at least curious enough to try it to ensure that the harvesting of kopi luwak remains a profitable enterprise. One could argue that when it comes to kopi luwak the old adage, "there's no accounting for taste," is on full display.

143. Which title best expresses the main idea of this passage?

A. "Kopi Luwak: A Prized Cup of Coffee"
B. "Exploring the Life of the Civet"
C. "Discover How Coffee is Made"
D. "What's Your Favorite Beverage?"

144. What bodily process helps kopi luwak achieve its distinct flavor?

A. Respiration
B. Digestion
C. Perspiration
D. Circulation

145. Based on the final sentence of the passage, the word *adage* most nearly means a

    A. warning.

    B. saying.

    C. joke.

    D. secret code.

146. According to the passage, kopi luwak can most likely be found in all the following places *except*

    A. Java.

    B. Sumatra.

    C. Bali.

    D. Nicaragua.

147. Which of the following happens to coffee beans during the fermentation process within civets?

    A. The color is changed.

    B. The thickness is diminished.

    C. The bitterness is reduced.

    D. The sweetness is increased.

148. Based on how they're described in the passage, unsavory kopi luwak merchants can best be compared to

    A. a restaurant accidentally serving you a hamburger when you really ordered a pizza.

    B. a contractor finishing a building project three weeks ahead of schedule.

    C. a salesman selling cheaply made smart phones and pretending they're more expensive iPhones.

    D. a science teacher helping his student earn a passing score on the midterm exam.

149. Based on the passage, we can say that the source for creating kopi luwak, the Asian palm civet, is

    A. unnecessary.

    B. essential.

    C. uneventful.

    D. disagreeable.

150. What is the author's purpose for including the adage "there's no accounting for taste" at the end of the passage?

    A. To highlight the notion that it's hard to explain why different people like different things, even if they're unappealing

    B. To discuss the fact that most people enjoy the taste of coffee and are willing to pay almost anything to have it

    C. To highlight the fact that coffee growing is a business, and that an accounting department is required to run the business

    D. To assert the notion that everyone enjoys the taste of kopi luwak coffee, which explains its high price

151. As used in the passage, the word *revered* in paragraph 1 most nearly means

    A. unpopular.

    B. admired.

    C. unethical.

    D. combined.

152. Based on the information in the passage, we can infer that compared to the kopi luwak, the process of collecting traditional coffee beans is more

    A. time consuming.

    B. expensive.

    C. uncommon.

    D. common.

Practice Test 4: HSPT®

Vocabulary

Turn to the Vocabulary section of your answer sheet to answer the questions in this section.

> **Directions:** Choose the word closest in meaning to the underlined word in the question.

153. a pioneer in her industry

    A. expert

    B. last person

    C. first person

    D. novice

154. a plausible explanation

    A. phony

    B. truthful

    C. easy

    D. reasonable

155. gave sage advice

    A. wise

    B. optimistic

    C. angry

    D. strange

156. a plaque commemorating the war

    A. describing

    B. honoring

    C. depicting

    D. ending

157. decipher the code

    A. cover up

    B. discover

    C. read

    D. translate

158. his blasé attitude

    A. unconcerned

    B. unusual

    C. uninformed

    D. unhappy

159. apprehended the suspect

    A. interrogated

    B. arrested

    C. arranged

    D. released

160. to forfeit the game

    A. win

    B. lose

    C. surrender

    D. complete

161. need to build stamina

    A. skills

    B. patience

    C. immunity

    D. endurance

162. a lucrative business

    A. failing

    B. profitable

    C. brand new

    D. long term

163. a standing <u>ovation</u>

   A. review
   B. applause
   C. appointment
   D. idea

164. a mountain <u>panorama</u>

   A. view
   B. photograph
   C. trail
   D. terrain

165. a <u>conscientious</u> worker

   A. indiscreet
   B. quick
   C. careful
   D. experienced

166. a <u>voracious</u> eater

   A. picky
   B. tasteful
   C. indiscriminate
   D. insatiable

167. a <u>haven</u> for like-minded people

   A. vacation
   B. sanctuary
   C. house
   D. trap

168. a purely <u>mercenary</u> decision

   A. academic
   B. scientific
   C. financial
   D. emotional

169. the regional <u>dialect</u>

   A. cuisine
   B. language
   C. history
   D. geography

170. an <u>eccentric</u> millionaire

   A. cruel
   B. shrewd
   C. strange
   D. reputable

171. at the <u>pivotal</u> moment

   A. incorrect
   B. essential
   C. last
   D. worst

172. a sense of <u>foreboding</u>

   A. contentment
   B. optimism
   C. agony
   D. dread

173. an <u>elite</u> squad

   A. exclusive
   B. experienced
   C. large
   D. diverse

174. she acted <u>aloof</u>

   A. foolish
   B. alone
   C. unfriendly
   D. excited

STOP.

If you finish before time is up, you may check your work on this section only.
Do not turn to any other section in the test.

MATHEMATICS

64 Questions (45 minutes)

Concepts

Turn to the Mathematics concepts section of your answer sheet to answer the questions in this section.

Directions: Read each question carefully, then solve the problem to find the correct answer.

---

175. 19 inches is closest to

   A. 1 foot

   B. 2 feet

   C. 3 feet

   D. 4 feet

176. There are 3 feet in 1 yard. Therefore, to convert from feet to yards, you would

   A. add 3.

   B. subtract 3.

   C. multiply by 3.

   D. divide by 3.

177. If x and y are two different numbers, then their average will always be

   A. greater than both x and y.

   B. smaller than both x and y.

   C. between x and y.

   D. equal to either x or y.

178. 1 inch is equal to 2.54 centimeters. Which answer best describes the number of centimeters in 7 inches?

   A. Exactly 7

   B. More than 7

   C. Less than 7

   D. Exactly 14

179. If the measures of all the angles in a triangle are added, what is the sum?

   A. 540°

   B. 360°

   C. 200°

   D. 180°

180. How many centimeters are in 1 meter?

   A. 0.1

   B. 1

   C. 10

   D. 100

181. If there are 16 cups in 1 gallon, which expression shows the number of cups in x gallons?

   A. $\dfrac{x}{16}$

   B. $x + 16$

   C. $x \times 16$

   D. $x - 16$

182. Which of the following is *not* a quadrilateral?

   A. Square

   B. Trapezoid

   C. Triangle

   D. Rectangle

183. To the nearest tenth, 63.594 is written

   A. 63.6

   B. 64

   C. 63.59

   D. 63.5

184. As a fraction, 0.24 is

    A. $\dfrac{24}{1,000}$

    B. $\dfrac{6}{25}$

    C. $\dfrac{1}{4}$

    D. $\dfrac{100}{24}$

185. How many integers are between $\dfrac{33}{7}$ and 8.001?

    A. 3

    B. 6

    C. 5

    D. 4

186. Which of the following is true?

    A. $a \div (b + c) = \dfrac{a}{b} + \dfrac{a}{c}$

    B. $a(x + b) = ax + b$

    C. $a(x + b) = a(x) + ab$

    D. $a \div b = b\left(\dfrac{1}{a}\right)$

187. It is possible to have a right triangle that is also

    A. equilateral.

    B. equiangular.

    C. obtuse.

    D. isosceles.

188. The perimeter of the rectangle is

    A. 2

    B. 7

    C. 14

    D. 18

189. Find the median of the following list:
1, 2, 3, 9, 10

    A. 3

    B. 4

    C. 5

    D. 6

190. If there is a 20% chance of rain on a certain day, what is the percent chance that it will NOT rain that day?

    A. 90%

    B. 80%

    C. 40%

    D. 20%

191. The average of –2, 0, 2, and 4 is

    A. A. 0

    B. B. 1

    C. C. 2

    D. D. 4

192. $\{4, 7, 9\} \cup \{4, 9, 12, 15\} =$

    A. {4, 9}

    B. {4, 7, 9}

    C. {4, 7, 9, 12, 15}

    D. { }

193. Simplify: $3(-2)^3 =$

    A. –216

    B. –18

    C. 1

    D. –24

194. The measure of angle A is

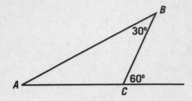

A. 15°

B. 20°

C. 30°

D. 35°

195. Which of the following is a pair of reciprocals?

A. $(3, -3)$

B. $\left(3\frac{1}{3}, \frac{3}{10}\right)$

C. $(2^3, 3^2)$

D. $(0, 1)$

196. The circumference of this circle is

A. 32π

B. 16

C. 8π

D. 4

197. The ratio of 3 yards to 18 inches is

A. 3 to 18

B. 1 to 6

C. 3 to 2

D. 6 to 1

198. The square root of 198 is between

A. 98 and 100

B. 90 and 100

C. 19 and 20

D. 14 and 15

Problem Solving

199. Which fraction shows the greatest value?

A. $\frac{5}{9}$

B. $\frac{2}{3}$

C. $\frac{6}{7}$

D. $\frac{7}{8}$

200. $\triangle ABC$ is similar to $\triangle DBE$. The length of AB is

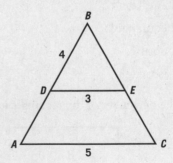

A. $6\frac{1}{3}$

B. $6\frac{2}{3}$

C. $8\frac{1}{3}$

D. $8\frac{2}{3}$

201. Mr. Allen paid $542.40 for his telephone bills last year. How much did he pay, on average, per month?

    A. $55.20

    B. $54.20

    C. $46.20

    D. $45.20

202. Simplify: $(-2) \cdot (-4) \cdot (3) \cdot (-1)$

    A. -24

    B. -4

    C. 12

    D. 24

203. Solve: $4\frac{1}{8} - 2\frac{2}{3} =$

    A. $2\frac{13}{24}$

    B. $2\frac{11}{24}$

    C. $1\frac{13}{24}$

    D. $1\frac{11}{24}$

204. If $-5 + 4x = 21$, $x =$

    A. 4

    B. 5.75

    C. 6.5

    D. 8.5

205. Solve: $3\frac{1}{3} \times 3\frac{3}{4} \times \frac{2}{5} =$

    A. $9\frac{1}{4}$

    B. 6

    C. 5

    D. $4\frac{2}{5}$

206. If $A = 6$ and $B = 3$, then $7A - 3B =$

    A. 7

    B. 9

    C. 32

    D. 33

207. If $N\%$ of 60 is 24, $N =$

    A. 40

    B. 84

    C. 125

    D. 150

208. If $10x - 3 = 2x + 4$, then x equals

    A. $\frac{9}{8}$

    B. $\frac{7}{8}$

    C. $\frac{8}{7}$

    D. $\frac{6}{7}$

209. The ratio of $\frac{3}{4}$ to $\frac{5}{2}$ is

    A. 10 to 3

    B. 15 to 8

    C. 3 to 10

    D. 8 to 15

210. Solve: 65.14×0.093

    A. 6.05802

    B. 6.06502

    C. 605.602

    D. 605.802

211. 26.80, 26.86, 26.92, 26.98, ... What number should come next in this sequence?

    A. 27.04

    B. 27.02

    C. 26.04

    D. 26.02

212. Solve: $72,528 \times 109$

    A. 1,377,032

    B. 1,378,032

    C. 7,805,452

    D. 7,905,552

213. How many boards $1\frac{1}{3}$ feet long can be cut from a board $9\frac{1}{2}$ feet long?

    A. 9

    B. 8

    C. 7

    D. 6

214. Solve for x: $3x + 3 < 9 + x$

    A. $x = 6$

    B. $x > 3$

    C. $x < 3$

    D. $x > 6$

215. Solve: $0.602 + 4.2 + 5.03 =$

    A. 9.644

    B. 9.802

    C. 9.832

    D. 10.441

216. Solve: $28\overline{)54,900}$

    A. 1,960 R20

    B. 1,868 R20

    C. 1,858 R12

    D. 1,642 R16

217. Solve: If $\sqrt{x + 36} = 10$, then $x =$

    A. 64

    B. 56

    C. −16

    D. −4

218. A basket contains 2 red balls and 3 green balls. If a person reaches in without looking and randomly chooses one of the balls, what is the probability that the ball chosen is red?

    A. $\frac{1}{5}$

    B. $\frac{1}{4}$

    C. $\frac{2}{5}$

    D. $\frac{3}{4}$

219. If Katie is half of her brother's age, and her brother is 10 years old, in how many years will Katie be 12 years old?

    A. 12

    B. 10

    C. 7

    D. 5

220. A movie ticket normally costs $12, but there is a 25% discount on Wednesday afternoons. How much do 3 movie tickets cost on Wednesday afternoon?

    A. 12

    B. 27

    C. 31

    D. 48

221. If Caleb has the option between 2 pairs of pants and 3 shirts, how many different outfits can he create?

    A. 2

    B. 3

    C. 5

    D. 6

222. A TV that normally costs $600 is advertised as being on sale for 50% off. You also have a 10% off coupon that will be applied to the sale price. What will be the final price of the TV?

    A. $240

    B. $270

    C. $300

    D. $540

223. The average of 10 and what other number is equal to 18?

    A. 10

    B. 18

    C. 20

    D. 26

224. Each square foot of a sheet of rubber weighs 17 ounces. If you cut out a rectangle from this sheet that is 16 inches long and 18 inches wide, how much would it weigh?

    A. 17 ounces

    B. 22 ounces

    C. 29 ounces

    D. 34 ounces

225. If Kai is 7 months older than Hunter, and Hunter is 3 months younger than Paul, then Kai is how much older than Paul?

    A. 2 months

    B. 3 months

    C. 4 months

    D. 10 months

226. If Bill can mow a lawn in x hours, what part of the lawn can he mow in 2 hours?

    A. $\dfrac{2}{x}$

    B. $\dfrac{x}{2}$

    C. $\dfrac{1}{2}$

    D. $\dfrac{1}{x}$

227. A movie theater sold 130 student tickets at $1.25 each and 340 adult tickets at $1.90 each. How much was collected?

    A. $708.50

    B. $798.50

    C. $808.50

    D. $818.50

228. Bob has $10 less than four times the amount Tim has. If Bob has $88, how much does Tim have?

    A. $48

    B. $24.50

    C. $22

    D. $16

229. The formula $F = \dfrac{9}{5}C + 32$ converts temperature from Centigrade to Fahrenheit. What is the Fahrenheit temperature for 85° Centigrade?

    A. 192°

    B. 185°

    C. 175°

    D. 130°

Practice Test 4: HSPT®

230. If the 5% sales tax on a snowmobile was $42, what was the price of the snowmobile not including the tax?

A. $840

B. $820

C. $680

D. $640

231. Mr. Symon paid $58.50 interest on a loan that had a 6% simple interest rate. How much did he borrow?

A. $975

B. $951

C. $898

D. $410

232. If a flagpole has a shadow 56 feet long when a 6-foot man's shadow is 14 feet long, what is the height of the flagpole?

A. 20 feet

B. 24 feet

C. 28 feet

D. 32 feet

233. If the perimeter of a rectangular region is 50 units, and the length of one side is 7 units, what is the area of the rectangular region?

A. 291 square units

B. 252 square units

C. 126 square units

D. 124 square units

234. If 18 is added to an integer, and the result is $\frac{5}{4}$ of the integer, what is the integer?

A. 72

B. 36

C. 24

D. −18

235. Four years ago, Jim's father was 5 times as old as Jim. How old is Jim's father now if Jim is 12?

A. 56

B. 44

C. 40

D. 36

236. What is the cost of carpeting a square room that is 27 feet by 27 feet if the carpet costs $11 per square yard?

A. $594

B. $729

C. $891

D. $8,019

237. What is the volume of this rectangular solid?

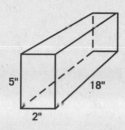

5" 18"

2"

A. 90 cu. in.

B. 160 cu. in.

C. 140 cu. in.

D. 180 cu. in.

238. If the tax rate is $3.62 per $100, how much tax must be paid on a home assessed at $25,000?

A. $80.50

B. $90.50

C. $805

D. $905

STOP.

If you finish before time is up, you may check your work on this section only.

Do not turn to any other section in the test.

Practice Test 4: HSPT®

LANGUAGE

60 Questions (25 minutes)

Turn to the Language section of your answer sheet to answer the questions in this section.

> **Directions:** In questions 239-267, look for errors in capitalization, punctuation, or usage. Mark the answer choice that contains the error. If you find no mistake, mark D on your answer sheet.

239. **A.** Gus couldn't swim to the end of the lake and back without stopping.
   B. What time are you going to the chess club meeting today!
   C. Can you please make me pancakes for breakfast tomorrow morning?
   D. *(No mistakes)*

240. **A.** Nareen watched her favorite movie, star wars, with her cousin.
   B. Kareef just finished reading his new favorite novel, *To the End and Back.*
   C. The *Hammondville Tribune* just published an article on national tax reform.
   D. *(No mistakes)*

241. **A.** Raymond took their overdue book back to the library.
   B. Carmine had a new set of art supplies to work with at home.
   C. The bookstore had a new shipment of novels to organize.
   D. *(No mistakes)*

242. **A.** The thunderbolt struck with tremendous force!
   B. What is the best route to get to the courthouse?
   C. How tall is the giraffe in the Cincinnati Zoo?
   D. *(No mistakes)*

243. **A.** Were you surprised by how difficult the exam questions were?
   B. Blaine was surprised by how difficult the exam questions were?
   C. Do you know where the final science exam is taking place today?
   D. *(No mistakes)*

244. **A.** The watchmaker's items for sale were displayed in his case.
   B. Silence filled the club as the singer jumped onto the stage.
   C. Alison took its new dog for a walk around the block.
   D. *(No mistakes)*

245. **A.** However, we couldn't predict that the rainstorm would be as bad as it was.
   B. Sharee was by far the tallest student in her homeroom;
   C. The clown completed an impressive juggling display for the kids.
   D. *(No mistakes)*

246. **A.** My favorite uncle lives in Jackson Hole, Wyoming.
   B. Our class took a trip to the Lincoln Memorial in Washington, DC.
   C. The statue of Liberty is one of the most famous tourist attractions in New York City.
   D. *(No mistakes)*

247. **A.** Jane walked cautious down the slippery staircase.

B. Did you see the way Harriet ran through the hallway?

C. The tiger cage at the zoo was full of lurking animals.

D. (*No mistakes*)

248. **A.** Trevor had a notebook headphones and a sandwich in his backpack.

B. The biggest dog in the dog park, Sherman, scared the other dogs.

C. We took a wrong turn at the edge of the woods and needed to look at a map.

D. (*No mistakes*)

249. **A.** Do you think Janelle should lend her friend Myriam his jacket?

B. The roar of the crowd, louder than the band's playing, was tremendous.

C. Myriam asked her friend Janelle, "Can I please borrow a jacket?"

D. (*No mistakes*)

250. **A.** Lebron was excited to see the new action movie; at his neighborhood theater.

B. Cameron met his first cousin, Lebron, at the movie theater on Tuesday.

C. Can Sheila join her friends for an afternoon at the movies on Tuesday?

D. (*No mistakes*)

251. **A.** Beverly couldn't remember the combination to her locker.

B. There was a mysterious sound coming from Daphnes closet.

C. Doug accidentally left his phone on his desk at work.

D. (*No mistakes*)

252. **A.** Simon always gets nervous when he drives across the Golden Gate Bridge.

B. If you could visit any country in the world, which one would you choose?

C. Darnelle couldn't, believe, his luck as he, listened to the lotto numbers being called.

D. (*No mistakes*)

253. **A.** Does anyone know what's being served for lunch in the cafeteria today?

B. Jarett was the first to finish the marathon; Shana was the runner-up.

C. The nearest gas station, in Pinedale, also sells coffee and hot dogs.

D. (*No mistakes*)

254. **A.** Lou had always wondering why cookies never lasted long in his house.

B. Parrots are an expensive but rewarding type of pet.

C. Susan couldn't decide what type of dress to wear to work today.

D. (*No mistakes*)

255. **A.** Carissa's new blog received a surprising amount of traffic.

B. No one was ever able to pass Mrs. Hudson's easy final exam.

C. This is possibly the longest elevator ride in history.

D. (*No mistakes*)

256. **A.** People often wonder how they can lose weight as quickly as possible?

B. The final exam, which covered geometry, was the hardest exam this year.

C. Cecille won the 8th grade science fair this year; Sharon won an honorable mention.

D. (*No mistakes*)

257. **A.** Cindy has always dreamed of visiting the Louvre Museum in Paris.
B. Mika's favorite painting in the museum was create by Renoir.
C. Harold purchased a new laptop from the computer store on Airedale Road.
D. *(No mistakes)*

258. **A.** Have you ever visited the Guggenheim Museum in New York City?
B. Freida asked Archie, *Are you certain you can't make it to my party?*
C. Can anyone pick up Jerry from the airport this evening?
D. *(No mistakes)*

259. **A.** Can Lawrence finish his chores and make it to work on time?
B. Francine got two toppings on her yogurt—strawberries and sprinkles.
C. Crystal had to decide whether she wanted to eat either chicken and steak.
D. *(No mistakes)*

260. **A.** Patrice has never enjoyed lying out on a hot beach.
B. Melissa has decided to ride her bicycle to work today.
C. Tomorrow, Caroline went to the senior prom at her school.
D. *(No mistakes)*

261. **A.** Janice purchased a magazine, two cans of soda, and a bagel from the store.
B. Shirelle went to the post office to purchase some stamps!
C. Francine manages the pet store where Cheryl purchased her iguana.
D. *(No mistakes)*

262. **A.** Joey couldn't tell which spices were in his mother's chili.
B. Do you know that woman who is standing in the stage?
C. Arnelle's new phone was faster and thinner than her old one.
D. *(No mistakes)*

263. **A.** The new bridge was built over the sprawling lake.
B. Vincent had to duck under the table to retrieve his pencil.
C. Larissa arrived before breakfast was over and missed her chance to eat.
D. *(No mistakes)*

264. **A.** I think that peanut butter or chocolate make an excellent combination.
B. The French toast was just too burnt to eat and was thrown away.
C. Harrison couldn't wait to get home and check his email.
D. *(No mistakes)*

265. **A.** Jovan kept his head below water so he wouldn't get his hair wet.
B. If there are any onions on the plate, I won't be eating them.
C. The gym was too crowded for Andy to work out comfortably.
D. *(No mistakes)*

266. **A.** The picnic basket was closed, but the ants had found their way into it.
B. Lilith can only go to the baseball game tomorrow but she finishes her homework first.
C. There was no space in the lot for Juan to park his new car.
D. *(No mistakes)*

267. **A.** The electric drill is an indispensable tool in Fiona's tool kit.

B. Hassan wondered if he had the discipline needed to compete on the wrestle team.

C. Jacqui went to the mall to purchase some new jewelry.

D. *(No mistakes)*

Directions: For questions 268–277, look for mistakes in spelling only.

---

268. **A.** Damon thought the long wait for a table was unacceptable.

B. Claire was well aware of the affect of exhaustion on her daily routine.

C. Daniel helped his good friend through a challenging dilemma.

D. *(No mistakes)*

269. **A.** Johann asked his tutor for some advise on studying for the midterm exam.

B. The debate team got into a heated argument about the debate rules.

C. Amy was a conscientious worker who could always be counted on by others.

D. *(No mistakes)*

270. **A.** Kiernan tripped while going up the auditorium stairs and was embarrassed.

B. Cyril considered himself to be the best skateboarder in existence.

C. Hikers were not aloud to go to the top of the steep mountain.

D. *(No mistakes)*

271. **A.** Her mentor's presents in the classroom made Lisa nervous during her presentation.

B. The keys to success in life are different for everyone.

C. The carnival workers had to stay at the fairgrounds late.

D. *(No mistakes)*

272. **A.** Charles always considered himself someone with good judgment.

B. Jann always remembered to seperate the recyclables from the trash.

C. Marcia couldn't wait to get her new driver's license.

D. *(No mistakes)*

273. **A.** Sherman was intrigued but afraid to visit a foreign country.

B. Larissa was grateful for the help she got while building her tree house.

C. Casey was dissapointed by his score during the bowling team competition.

D. *(No mistakes)*

274. A. Stu occasionally felt the need to call his aunt on the phone.

    B. Alison didn't find the plot of the television show beleivable.

    C. Ellen knew that being on the elite chess team was a privilege.

    D. *(No mistakes)*

275. A. The comic book store on Vantage Road sold a variety of colectible items.

    B. Sydney took a humorous approach to his award acceptance speech.

    C. Myrna took some aspirin and felt an immediate effect.

    D. *(No mistakes)*

276. A. Matt was two tired to go to the concert after work on Friday.

    B. Lorraine almost fell asleep during the committee meeting.

    C. Corey took a yacht ride during her vacation in Greece.

    D. *(No mistakes)*

277. A. Gemma's family had an adorable miniature poodle for a pet.

    B. The work crew took their lunch brake in the nearby park.

    C. Our neighbor never seemed to take care of his lawn.

    D. *(No mistakes)*

Directions: In questions 278–288, look for errors and mark the sentence that demonstrates correct usage.

---

278. A. Will the hockey team beat her high score during today's game?

    B. Kendra lent her new earmuffs to her best friend, Natasha.

    C. Everyone is waiting to get his copy of the new suspense novel.

    D. Janice wore the new earrings it got at the mall last Thursday.

279. A. The faculty at Eden View High School have their annual meeting this afternoon.

    B. The members of the chorus left her instruments in the concert hall during the break.

    C. Darian teased our sister until they laughed uncontrollably during dinner.

    D. The golden retriever pulled off our collar and ran across the empty field.

280. A. Lawrence decided to eating dinner at the Thai restaurant.

    B. The new hybrid car was released for sale next year.

    C. We decided to go hiking through the woods on our vacation.

    D. The deer frolicked through the meadow and stop by the river.

281. A. Barb worked on her science project day and night, by the time her life depended on it.

    B. Only if Arielle is the best lacrosse player on the team, she never brags.

    C. Before Lisa discovered the spider under her bed, she ran out of the room.

    D. Jimmy completed as much of his homework on his own as possible before asking for help.

282. A. We all went together to the end-of-summer party at Sharons house.

   B. The table's had a wobbly leg and shook horribly.

   C. Clarice checked out the selection of skirt's at the department store.

   D. The parade of cars honked loudly in the rush hour traffic.

283. A. Louis hates it when people talk beyond the movie and cause a disruption.

   B. Darren layered the roast beef and mustard between two pieces of bread.

   C. Sylvia leaned her umbrella among the coat rack in the hallway.

   D. The new chairs had to be returned because they didn't fit about the table.

284. A. The Robinson family took her family photo every Thanksgiving.

   B. The bookcase fell on her side when Diego leaned against it.

   C. Chiara's classmates sent her a beautiful get-well-soon card.

   D. The leaves made a beautiful display when he fell to the ground.

285. A. Boris always handles his job responsibilities capable.

   B. The snail slow slithered across the freshly mown lawn.

   C. The French vanilla wedding cake was decorated beautiful.

   D. Gianna was greeted coolly by the strangers at the art gallery.

286. A. Can you meet Fabian at his house during the presentation starts?

   B. Derek wasn't allowed to eat his dessert because after he finished dinner.

   C. Sam will breathe a huge sigh of relief after the final exam is over.

   D. David won the debate competition because he was more convincing because anyone else.

287. A. Mandy approached the edge of the slippery diving board very carefully.

   B. Tamryn absentminded left her water bottle at the gym last night.

   C. Phillip tiptoed quiet through the crowded library and went to the water fountain.

   D. The athletes hungry devoured the pizza after today's practice.

288. A. I'd never been to a lecture at the university and was excited to go.

   B. She wanted to get a ice cream cone after dinner tonight.

   C. Bonnie bought her daughter an new purse for her birthday.

   D. Can someone lend Fiona a umbrella so she doesn't get wet on her way home?

Directions: For questions 289–298, follow the individual directions.

289. Choose the pair of sentences that best develops this topic sentence:

   "A healthy diet and exercise can improve your brain function."

   A. Folks who eat a lot of lean protein and low-fat meals tend to live longer. Working out makes people look better and improves their self-confidence.

   B. Do you maintain a healthy diet and get regular exercise? If so, then you're part of a growing group of health-conscious people.

   C. Individuals who eat a diet rich in vitamins do better on tests of intelligence. People who work out more than twice a week have been shown to have a better memory than people who don't.

   D. There is no reason not to try and improve your diet and get some regular exercise. There's no better time than now to live a healthier and more active life!

290. Choose the word that best completes this sentence.

   Sharrod, who was late for his meeting, moved _____ through the train station in order to get to his office.

   A. briskly

   B. slowly

   C. casually

   D. jokingly

291. Which of the following sentences offers the *least* support for the topic "Why the town of Willowbrook Needs a Library"?

   A. Every town surrounding Willowbrook has its own library.

   B. The children of Willowbrook need a place to borrow books.

   C. There's a retail bookstore located in the town's mall.

   D. Towns with libraries have a better educated citizenry.

292. Choose the word that best completes this sentence.

   Phineas had to carefully parallel park his car _____ an SUV and a pickup truck.

   A. beneath

   B. between

   C. beyond

   D. but

293. Which of these expresses the idea most clearly?

A. Who were packing for a weekend getaway in the country, put their camping gear and picnic basket, Tim and Sylvia into the back of their car.

B. Put their camping gear and picnic basket, Tim and Sylvia, who were packing for a weekend getaway in the country into the back of their car.

C. Into the back of their car for a weekend getaway in the country, who were Tim and Sylvia packing for? Put their camping gear and picnic basket.

D. Tim and Sylvia, who were packing for a weekend getaway in the country, put their camping gear and picnic basket into the back of their car.

294. Choose the best word to join the thoughts together.

The cleaning crew had the unfortunate task of cleaning up the street _____ the busy parade was finished.

A. since
B. while
C. until
D. after

295. Which of these expresses the idea most clearly?

A. Many pastry chefs feel that it's best to use room temperature eggs when baking, as it creates a fluffier, lighter, and more flavorful final product.

B. A fluffier, lighter, and more flavorful final product, when baking, as it creates—many pastry chefs feel that room temperature eggs it's best to use.

C. That it's best to use room temperature eggs when baking, many pastry chefs create a fluffier, lighter, and more flavorful final product as it creates.

D. When baking as it creates, many pastry chefs create a fluffier, lighter, and more flavorful final product and feel that it's best to use room temperature eggs.

296. Which sentence does *not* belong in the paragraph?

(1) Snakes are fascinating and diverse creatures that also move in interesting ways. (2) Without legs, they utilize their muscles and scales to help them get around. (3) Earthworms move in a similar way. (4) Snakes push off of whatever surface they are laying upon to propel themselves forward.

A. Sentence 1
B. Sentence 2
C. Sentence 3
D. Sentence 4

297. Which of the following sentences would best fit at the end of this paragraph?

(1) Giraffes are tall, herbivorous mammals that typically live in savannahs and open woodlands. (2) They tend to avoid contact with other animals and use their immense height to feed in places where other animals can't. (3) Fully grown giraffes tend to range between 14 and 18 feet in height.

A. Giraffes are often found in zoos.

B. Giraffes truly are gentle giants.

C. Few get the change to ride a giraffe.

D. Who doesn't love a funny giraffe?

298. Which of the following sentences offers the *least* support to the topic "College Should be Free for Everybody"?

A. Too many students deal with excessive student loans after graduating from college.

B. College tuition helps to fund a variety of campus upgrades, innovations, and events.

C. Some people feel that choosing a major while in college is too limiting and unfair.

D. More students than ever before are deciding to skip going to college and start their own businesses.

ANSWER KEYS AND EXPLANATIONS

Verbal Skills

1. B	13. C	25. A	37. C	49. D
2. D	14. B	26. B	38. D	50. B
3. C	15. B	27. C	39. B	51. A
4. A	16. A	28. D	40. A	52. C
5. C	17. B	29. A	41. D	53. A
6. D	18. C	30. B	42. C	54. D
7. B	19. C	31. A	43. C	55. C
8. A	20. B	32. D	44. A	56. B
9. A	21. C	33. A	45. A	57. D
10. C	22. B	34. C	46. B	58. A
11. B	23. C	35. B	47. C	59. C
12. C	24. C	36. D	48. D	60. B

1. **The correct answer is B.** This analogy shows a creature-habitat relationship. Lobsters live in the ocean, and scorpions live in the desert.

2. **The correct answer is D.** This is a product-source relationship. Tea is made from tea leaves, and coffee is made from coffee beans.

3. **The correct answer is C.** This is an example-object relationship. A sombrero is a type of hat, and a poodle is a type of dog.

4. **The correct answer is A.** This analogy is a measurement-range relationship. Twelve dozens make up a gross, and twelve inches make up a foot.

5. **The correct answer is C.** This is an opposite relationship. The opposite of tall is short, and the opposite of quick is slow.

6. **The correct answer is D.** This is a part-whole relationship. A slice is a part of a pie, and a piece is part of a puzzle.

7. **The correct answer is B.** This is an object-process relationship. Molding is a process to shape and transform clay, and carving is a process to shape and transform wood.

8. **The correct answer is A.** This is a move-ment/transportation relationship. Bees and falcons both fly to get around. Trout and sharks both swim to get around.

9. **The correct answer is A.** This is a common characteristic relationship. Monkeys and mice both have tails. Rhinoceroses and rams both have distinctive horns.

10. **The correct answer is C.** This is a tactile characteristic relationship. Snails are slimy to the touch, and rabbits are furry to the touch.

11. **The correct answer is B.** Based on the infor-mation we're told, Myriam *must* be older than Radja, since we know that Myriam is older than Syrah and Syrah is older than Radja. Therefore, statement three is false.

12. **The correct answer is C.** Although we know that both Antonio and Patricia ate more nachos than Kevin, we don't know by *how much* more, and therefore cannot determine if Antonio or Patricia ate more nachos. Therefore, choice C is correct.

13. **The correct answer is C.** Although we are told how thirsty these individuals are, we are given no information regarding how much water they may or may not have drank, so choice C is correct.

14. **The correct answer is B.** We know that there's no way that Nareen could have come in last place in the school-wide spelling bee because we're told that he did better than Tariq. Therefore, choice B is correct.

15. **The correct answer is B.** If the first two statements are true, myrtle trees grow the least fast of the three types of trees. Therefore, the third statement must be false.

16. **The correct answer is A.** If the first two statements are true, copper is the most expensive of the three metals.

17. **The correct answer is B.** We know from the first two statements that Carrie swims the fastest, so the third statement must be false.

18. **The correct answer is C.** The first two statements give information about Bob's carrots and tomatoes. Information about any other vegetables in Bob's garden cannot be determined.

19. **The correct answer is C.** Despite the fact that Jake is the shortest child in the green classroom, he could *still* be taller than Arianna (and everyone else in the orange classroom). Therefore, choice C is correct.

20. **The correct answer is B.** If the first two statements are true, both Sadie and Roxy downloaded more music than Henry, so the third statement is false.

21. **The correct answer is C.** Choices A, B, and D are all kitchen tools that are designed to be heated on the stove. Choice C is not meant to be heated on the stove.

22. **The correct answer is B.** Choices A, C, and D are all team sports. Archery (choice B) is a solo sport.

23. **The correct answer is C.** The common feature among choices A, B, and D is that they are all tools designed to cut. A wrench (choice C) is not designed to cut.

24. **The correct answer is C.** Choices A, B, and D are all types of building equipment. A construction worker (choice C) may work in building but does not share the characteristic of being a type of building equipment.

25. **The correct answer is A.** Choices B, C, and D are all things that can be read. A pencil (choice A) is something that can be written with, not read.

26. **The correct answer is B.** *Dragon*, *lion*, and *tiger* are all nouns. Although they may all be harmful, *harmful* (choice B) is an adjective, not a noun.

27. **The correct answer is C.** *Catch*, *throw*, and *pitch* are all verbs. Although you can throw, catch, and pitch a ball, *ball* (choice C) does not belong with the others because it is a noun, not a verb.

28. **The correct answer is D.** The common feature among a firefighter, police officer, and comedian is that they are all types of jobs. Someone may be a problem solver while they're solving a specific problem, but it's not a job type.

29. **The correct answer is A.** Although they are all types of food, *calzone*, *taco*, and *pizza* all end with vowels; *biscuit* (choice A) ends with a consonant.

30. **The correct answer is B.** Although they are all living creatures, an eel, seahorse, and whale are all found in the water, while a pony (choice B) is found on the land.

31. **The correct answer is A.** The common feature among a shovel, spoon, and spatula is that they are all designed to scoop or pick up things, while a chisel (choice A) is designed to chip away at things.

32. **The correct answer is D.** Ladders, stairs, and mountains are all things that you climb, while a waterfall (choice D) is not.

33. **The correct answer is A.** Sorrow, fear, and joy are all types of emotions. Winning (choice A) may bring positive emotions, but it itself is not a type of emotion.

34. **The correct answer is C.** The common feature among cosmetics, groceries, and clothing is that they are all things that can be directly purchased; fulfillment (choice C) cannot be directly purchased.

35. **The correct answer is B.** *Contemporary*, *enjoyable*, and *extend* are all multi-syllabic words, which means that they have more than one syllable. *List* is a one-syllable word.

36. **The correct answer is D.** Eggs, oysters, and walnuts are all types of foods that have a shell that's discarded before eating. Tomatoes do not have a shell that is thrown away before eating.

37. **The correct answer is C.** An *anomalous* event is irregular.

38. **The correct answer is D.** A *courteous* gentleman is polite.

39. **The correct answer is B.** A *spacious* environment is roomy.

40. **The correct answer is A.** A *loquacious* speaker is talkative.

41. **The correct answer is D.** A *deft* performer is skillful.

42. **The correct answer is C.** A *venerable* judge is honored.

43. **The correct answer is C.** A *fecund* cornfield is fruitful.

44. **The correct answer is A.** A *cantankerous* voter is disagreeable.

45. **The correct answer is A.** A *caustic* remark is scathing.

46. **The correct answer is B.** A *collaborative* effort is cooperative.

47. **The correct answer is C.** A *bombastic* speech is grandiose.

48. **The correct answer is D.** A *rancorous* employee is resentful.

49. **The correct answer is D.** A *contentious* meeting is combative.

50. **The correct answer is B.** An *erudite* professor is educated.

51. **The correct answer is A.** A *prominent* leader is noticeable.

52. **The correct answer is C.** *Diligent* means the opposite of *passive*.

53. **The correct answer is A.** *Industrious* means the opposite of *idle*.

54. **The correct answer is D.** *Intelligible* means the opposite of *inarticulate*.

55. **The correct answer is C.** *Denigrate* means the opposite of *approve*.

56. **The correct answer is B.** *Frugal* means the opposite of *wasteful*.

57. **The correct answer is D.** *Altruistic* means the opposite of *selfish*.

58. **The correct answer is A.** *Oblivious* means the opposite of *aware*.

59. **The correct answer is C.** *Beguile* means the opposite of *repel*.

60. **The correct answer is B.** *Mollify* means the opposite of *aggravate*.

Quantitative Skills

61. A	72. C	83. B	93. B	103. C
62. D	73. A	84. A	94. A	104. A
63. B	74. B	85. C	95. C	105. B
64. C	75. C	86. C	96. D	106. D
65. D	76. A	87. B	97. D	107. B
66. B	77. C	88. A	98. B	108. C
67. B	78. D	89. C	99. A	109. B
68. D	79. B	90. B	100. C	110. A
69. B	80. C	91. A	101. C	111. C
70. D	81. B	92. C	102. A	112. A
71. A	82. C			

61. **The correct answer is A.** Start by finding 20% of 40; $0.20 \times 40 = 8$. Then add 3 to get $8 + 3 = 11$.

62. **The correct answer is D.** The pattern in this series is created by adding 7 to each number.

63. **The correct answer is B.** The square root of 256 is 16. Multiply by $\frac{3}{4} \times 16 = 12$.

64. **The correct answer is C.** Determine the amount of money for A, B, and C. Then test the alternatives given to see which is correct.

65. **The correct answer is D.** A is 0.625; B is 0.571; and C is 0.6237. Clearly B is less than both A and C, which are not equal.

66. **The correct answer is B.** The cube of 5 is 125. 125 divided by $5 = 25$.

67. **The correct answer is B.** The pattern in this series is +2, ÷2, +2, ÷2, and so on. Since $6 + 2 = 8$, and $8 \div 2 = 4$, the missing term is 8.

68. **The correct answer is D.** Determine how much of each box is shaded. Then test each alternative to see which is correct.

69. **The correct answer is B.** The pattern in this series is +3, +7, +3, +7, and so on.

70. **The correct answer is D.** Determine the amounts for A, B, and C. Here, A = 8, B = 8,

and C = 0.08. When you test each alternative to see which is correct, you see that choice D is the correct answer: A is greater than C.

71. **The correct answer is A.** Start by finding $\frac{2}{3}$ of 39; $\frac{2}{3} \times 39 = 26$

Then add 4 to find your answer; $26 + 4 = 30$.

72. **The correct answer is C.** The pattern in this series is −5, −4, +1, −5, −4, +1, ... So, the next three numbers in the series are 35, 31, 32.

73. **The correct answer is A.** Start this problem from the end and work backward:

$$\frac{3}{5} \times \frac{25}{1} = 15$$
$$15 + 7 = 22$$

The number you're looking for is found by setting up an equation.

$$30 - x = 22$$
$$x = 30 - 22$$
$$x = 8$$

74. **The correct answer is B.** $\frac{1}{4}$ of 64 is 16, and 7 less than 16 is 9.

75. **The correct answer is C.** Finding the answer is as simple as dividing the total cost by the number of hats.

$$\begin{array}{r} 0.65 \\ 23)\overline{\$14.95} \\ -13.80 \\ \hline 1.15 \\ -1.15 \\ \hline .00 \end{array}$$

76. **The correct answer is A.** The pattern in this series is –9, –8, –7, –6, and so on.

77. **The correct answer is C.** Count the circles in A, B, and C. Test each alternative to find the one that is true. You will see that B has 12 circles and C has 13 circles—both of which are more than A, which has only 10 circles.

78. **The correct answer is D.** Determine how much of each figure is shaded. Then test each alternative to find the one that is true. In this case, A, B, and C each have 3 parts shaded, so they're equally shaded.

79. **The correct answer is B.** The pattern in this series is created by adding 4 to each number. $99 + 4 = 103$.

80. **The correct answer is C.** Determine $\frac{1}{5}$ of 100: $\frac{1}{5} \times \frac{100}{1} = 20$. Multiply this result by 4 to find the answer; $20 \times 4 = 80$.

81. **The correct answer is B.** The pattern in this series is +4, +1, +4, +1, and so on. Also, whenever 1 is added, the result is expressed as an Arabic numeral; whenever 4 is added, the result is expressed as a Roman numeral.

82. **The correct answer is C.** Each circle is divided into five equal parts. Circle B has the fewest shaded wedges, while figure C has the most.

83. **The correct answer is B.** First find 7 times 3; $7 \times 3 = 21$. Double this result to find the answer: $2 \times 21 = 42$.

84. **The correct answer is A.** Each box is shaded by $\frac{1}{2}$. Therefore, only A can be true.

85. **The correct answer is C.** Figure this problem from the end and work forward:

$$5 \times 2 = 10$$
$$3 \times 10 = 30$$
$$6 + x = 30$$
$$x = 30 - 6 = 24$$

86. **The correct answer is C.** The pattern in this series is –2, +4, –2, +4, and so on.

87. **The correct answer is B.** 125% = 1.25, so A and B are equal. But $\frac{25}{2} = 12.5$, which is greater than A and B. So, A and B are both less than C.

88. **The correct answer is A.** With factorials, you multiply whole numbers from 1 to the given number. In this case, $1 \times 2 \times 3 \times 4 \times 5 \times 6$.

89. **The correct answer is C.** The pattern in this series is +2, ×2, +2, ×2, and so on.

90. **The correct answer is B.** To find the answer, you need to enter the information you have into the percent change formula.

$$\frac{\% \ change}{100} = \frac{33}{150}$$

Then cross-multiply and solve for the percent change (p).

$$\frac{p \times 150}{100 \times 33} = \frac{150p}{3,300} \ \text{or} \ 150p = 3,300$$

$$\frac{150p}{150} = \frac{3,300}{150}$$
$$p = 22$$

91. **The correct answer is A.** The line drawn from point A to the base of triangle ABD divides this triangle into two right triangles, one of which is ACD. AD is the hypotenuse of this right triangle whose length must be greater than the length CD, a leg of ACD.

92. **The correct answer is C.** Begin by subtracting 5 from 29. This number divided by 3 will provide the answer:

$$29 - 5 = 24$$
$$24 \div 3 = 8$$

93. **The correct answer is B.** The pattern in this series is +6, +3, +6, +3, and so on.

94. **The correct answer is A.** Determine the amounts for A, B, and C. Then choose the best alternative. Be sure to do the operations in the parentheses first when figuring.

95. **The correct answer is C.** The pattern in this series is +1, −10, +1, −10, and so on.

96. **The correct answer is D.** Because the figure is a cube, all edges and sides are equal. When a diagonal line is drawn across one side, like $\overline{CE}$, it forms a hypotenuse of a right triangle whose length is longer than the length of either of its sides ($\overline{CE}$ and $\overline{EF}$). Because the sides of the cube are all equal, $\overline{CF}$ must also be longer than $\overline{AB}$.

97. **The correct answer is D.** The value of A is $\frac{1}{2} \times \frac{2}{3} = \frac{1}{3}$, B is $\frac{3}{4} \times 1 = \frac{3}{4}$, and C is $\frac{1}{2} \times \frac{2}{3} = \frac{3}{4}$. B and C are equal, and A is less than these.

98. **The correct answer is B.** Since $x < y$, multiplying both sides by x gives $x^2 < xy$. So, C is less than A. Likewise, since $x < y$, multiplying both sides by y gives $xy < y^2$. A is less than B.

99. **The correct answer is A.** The pattern in this series is ×2, +4, ×2, +4, and so on.

100. **The correct answer is C.** The pattern here is +2, +4, +6, +8, and so on. The next term should be 21 + 10 = 31.

101. **The correct answer is C.** The pattern for the letters in this series is made by using every other letter starting with A. The pattern for the numbers is +4, −10, +4, −10, and so on.

102. **The correct answer is A.** Determine the values for each bar in the graph by using the number scale to the left. Then choose the correct alternative. Choice A is correct because 2 + 10 − 4 = 8 or 12 − 4 = 8.

103. **The correct answer is C.** This can be set up as an algebraic equation to solve for x:

$$x = \frac{3}{5}(10) - 2$$
$$x = 6 - 2$$
$$x = 4$$

104. **The correct answer is A.** The pattern in this series is created by taking numbers in sequential order (4, 5, 6, and so on) and following each number with its square. The last number in the series is 6, so $6^2 = 36$, choice A.

105. **The correct answer is B.** Determine the amounts for A, B, and C. Then, decide which alternative is true.

A. $5^2 = 25$

B. $4^3 = 64$

C. $2^4 = 16$

So, B is greater than A, which is greater than C.

106. **The correct answer is D.** The pattern in this series is created by subtracting $2\frac{1}{2}$ from each number.

107. **The correct answer is B.** Each letter is paired with A, and then with 1. C has already been paired with A, so the next term should be C1.

108. **The correct answer is C.** The pattern in this series is +4, −2, −1, +4, −2, −1, and so on.

109. **The correct answer is B.** This can be set up as an algebraic equation if you're solving for x:

$$6 + \frac{1}{3}x = 2 \times 9$$
$$6 + \frac{1}{3}x = 18$$
$$\frac{1}{3}x = 12$$
$$x = 36$$

110. **The correct answer is A.** Test each of the alternatives to find the true one. To find the perimeter, add the length of all four sides together: 2 + 3 + 2 + 3 = 10.

111. **The correct answer is C.** This can be set up as an algebraic equation if you're solving for *x*:

$$x = \frac{4}{9}(27) + 10$$
$$x = 12 + 10$$
$$x = 22$$

112. **The correct answer is A.** 5 squared is 25, and 11 more than 25 is 36.

Reading

Comprehension

113. C	121. C	129. D	137. C	145. B
114. B	122. A	130. C	138. B	146. D
115. C	123. C	131. B	139. C	147. C
116. D	124. B	132. A	140. A	148. C
117. D	125. C	133. B	141. C	149. B
118. B	126. D	134. C	142. B	150. A
119. A	127. A	135. A	143. A	151. B
120. C	128. A	136. D	144. B	152. D

113. **The correct answer is C.** In paragraph 3, we are told that Felix is a "nutrition author," which means that she has written works on the subject of nutrition. The passage never tells us that Felix has conducted experiments on fats (choice A), that she is a medical doctor (choice B), or that she has a degree in biology (choice D). We cannot draw these conclusions without specific information from the passage, so each of these choices can be eliminated.

114. **The correct answer is B.** The author tells us in paragraph 2 of the article that both omega-3 and omega-6 fats are essential for our health, so choice C is incorrect. We are then told in the next paragraph that "Americans tend to get plenty of omega-6 oils in their diets already." Therefore, choice B is correct.

115. **The correct answer is C.** The second and third paragraphs of the passage, in particular, focus on the need for more omega-3 fats in the diet and which foods are good sources for omega-3 fats. Choice D is incorrect

because, although the first two paragraphs mention the overall needs for fats in the diet, the passage deals specifically with reducing omega-6 and increasing omega-3, making this answer too general.

116. **The correct answer is D.** We are told in paragraph 1 that we should restrict our intake of fats to 30 percent of the total number of calories we consume every day.

117. **The correct answer is D.** Olive oil, walnuts, and sardines are three of the foods specifically mentioned in the last paragraph as good sources of omega-3 fats. Choice C is incorrect because, although salads in general are considered good for health, the passage does not say that they are good sources of omega-3 fats. Choices A and B are incorrect because the passage specifically states we should limit our consumption of salad dressing, margarine, bread, and other baked goods.

118. **The correct answer is B.** The author of the passage is advocating for an increase in the

amount of good fats consumed in the average diet, as this would help improve nutrition levels. Thus, the best adjective to describe the positive influence that an increased consumption of good fats would have on the American diet is *ideal*. The author of the passage does not mention the cost or any disadvantageous or limiting effect an increased consumption of good fats would have on one's diet, so choices A, C, and D don't fit given the context of the passage.

119. **The correct answer is A.** The passage mentions that "the American diet falls short when it comes to omega-3 fats." Since omega-3 is an essential fatty acid (good fat), we can infer from the information provided in the passage that the author would most likely characterize the average American diet as falling short on the consumption of good fats.

120. **The correct answer is C.** Clara Felix's research mentions that the American diet falls short on omega-3 fats but does not mention how far short. Providing this information will help readers to understand how critical and drastic this issue is, and how much effort would be required in order to fully balance their consumption of good fats.

121. **The correct answer is C.** The primary purpose of the passage is to educate readers on the value of increasing their consumption of good fats as part of a healthy, nutritionally optimal diet. Therefore, readers who follow the author's advice will increase their consumption of good fats.

122. **The correct answer is A.** According to the information in the passage, the average American is consuming more than enough omega-6 fatty acids as compared to omega-3 fatty acids. According to Felix, the best way to balance our diets "is to reduce the amount of omega-6 oils we are eating while at the same time increasing the amount of omega-3 fat," so choice A is correct.

123. **The correct answer is C.** We are told in paragraph 2 that though the expedition was successful in placing six climbers at the summit of Mount Everest, it had to overcome many challenges and setbacks. The next two paragraphs describe those challenges and their effect on the climbers.

124. **The correct answer is B.** The passage states in paragraph 3 that two Canadians and four Sherpas made it to the top of Mount Everest. Choice C is incorrect, as it refers to the total number of climbers who made it to the top, including both Canadians and Sherpas.

125. **The correct answer is C.** Paragraph 2 states that this was the first Canadian expedition to Mount Everest, making choice C the correct answer. Choice D is incorrect, because the passage does not give us any information on whether this was the last expedition that Amatt led up Mount Everest.

126. **The correct answer is D.** The last paragraph mentions that the expedition inspired Amatt's team to approach their challenges with humbleness, so choice D is the correct answer. Choice A is incorrect, because indifference would indicate that the team did not care about the accidents. Choice B is incorrect, because humbleness is the opposite of pride.

127. **The correct answer is A.** The *it* refers back to the second sentence of the paragraph, which cites the experience of loss that Amatt and his team encountered. The noun *experience* is singular, so it agrees with the singular pronoun *it*. Choice B is incorrect because the noun *experiences* in the first sentence is plural, and it would not use the singular pronoun *it*.

128. **The correct answer is A.** The passage recounts John Amatt's successful climb to the top—or peak—of the great mountain, so choice A is correct. The other answer choices don't fit given the context of the paragraph and passage.

129. The correct answer is D. According to the information provided in the passage, John Amatt overcame great adversity to successfully complete a physical challenge. The scenario that most closely compares to this is a swimmer who overcame treacherous conditions to successfully swim the English Channel.

130. The correct answer is C. Based on the information provided in the passage, the most likely explanation why Amatt titled his book *Straight to the Top and Beyond* is because the book describes both his climb to the top of Mount Everest and the lessons he learned from the adversity he faced during the experience.

131. The correct answer is B. The experience of loss referenced in paragraph 4 most likely refers to the climbers and sherpas who lost their lives during the climb, as mentioned in paragraph 3. There is no mention of wasted time (choice A) or lost equipment (choice C). Amatt successfully made it to the top of Mount Everest, so choice D is incorrect.

132. The correct answer is A. This passage focuses on John Amatt, a Canadian climber; his 1982 expedition to the top of Mount Everest; and the lessons he learned through overcoming adversity and loss as a climber. The passage does not attempt to warn readers against mountain climbing (choice B) or tell the history of mountain climbing in Canada in the 20th century (choice C). The passage also does not provide the history of attempts to climb Mount Everest (choice D).

133. The correct answer is B. The first paragraph speaks of the perils of fishing; the second speaks about its rewards.

134. The correct answer is C. The middle of the first paragraph discusses the problems created by rough seas. None of the other choices is mentioned as a difficulty.

135. The correct answer is A. In the middle of the second paragraph, we learn that when fishermen note that herring are entering the nets, they sit in quiet excitement so as not to frighten the fish away. They row along the net earlier in order to find out if the net is filling and haul in the nets later, when they are full.

136. The correct answer is D. This phrase represents a powerful metaphor. Picture huge waves rising over empty space and crashing down upon fishermen and boats.

137. The correct answer is C. All the other choices include at least one trait that is not ascribed to these fishermen.

138. The correct answer is B. One might add honesty to the traits of the fishermen. Theft is not mentioned as a problem. If you had forgotten about the whales, reread the first sentence.

139. The correct answer is C. The first paragraph of the passage describes the sea as dark and dangerous, unpredictable and unexpected. The answer choice that most resembles this description is a dark and dangerous storm (choice C).

140. The correct answer is A. The author of the passage paints a specific portrait of life as a fisherman in Norway, one "full of dangers" on the high seas, with fisherman constantly working, muscles straining, working "day-and-night without thoughts of weariness" to handle the bounty of herring. The choice that best captures this portrait is choice A. There is no mention of fun or quiet solitude (choice B) and no talk of life being hilarious or the weather being enjoyable (choice C). Also, the passage doesn't discuss the idea that fisherman are rapidly disappearing in today's technology-focused modern society (choice D).

141. The correct answer is C. A net without herring to a Norwegian fisherman is disappointing and an unfortunate occurrence for a fisherman's professional livelihood. Similarly, a salesman without a sale is also disappointing and an unfortunate occurrence for a salesman's professional livelihood, so this is the correct answer. The other choices are not effective comparisons.

142. **The correct answer is B.** All of the items listed among the answer choices are mentioned as being a part of a fisherman's life on a Norwegian fishing boat except a lantern (choice B).

143. **The correct answer is A.** This passage is about kopi luwak coffee, the process it undergoes to be created, and why it's such a prized and expensive beverage. The title that best expresses the main idea of this passage is "Kopi Luwak: A Prized Cup of Coffee."

144. **The correct answer is B.** The passage explicitly mentions that "these prized beans are harvested from the digested remains of coffee cherries that have been eaten by Asian palm civets," so choice B is correct.

145. **The correct answer is B.** The word *adage*, which appears in the final sentence of the passage, appears right before the following quoted material: "'there's no accounting for taste' is on full display." Scanning the answer choices, this is most closely a saying. This isn't a warning (choice A), joke (choice C), or secret code (choice D).

146. **The correct answer is D.** The passage mentions that "the vast majority of kopi luwak is produced in the islands of Java, Bali, Sumatra, Sulawesi, and the Philippines." The only choice not mentioned in the passage is Nicaragua (choice D).

147. **The correct answer is C.** The passage discusses some of the properties of the fermentation process, and how the coffee beans are changed. This includes a reduction in the bitterness of the coffee beans (choice C). The other choices are not mentioned in the passage.

148. **The correct answer is C.** In the passage, we are told that some unsavory coffee merchants have "taken to selling inferior beans under the kopi luwak name in an effort to turn a profit." The comparison among the answer choices that most closely resembles this unethical behavior is a salesman selling cheaply made smart phones and pretending they're more expensive iPhones.

149. **The correct answer is B.** According to the passage, in order to create kopi luwak coffee beans, they're "harvested from the digested remains of coffee cherries that have been eaten by Asian palm civets, small squirrel-like creatures that inhabit Southeast Asia." Therefore, we can conclude that the Asian palm civet is *essential* to the process.

150. **The correct answer is A.** The author of the passage is making the point that even though kopi luwak beans are made through a possibly strange and unique process that some people would find unappetizing, the beans are still highly prized by some and are expensive—which highlights the notion that it's hard to explain why different people like different things, even if they're unappealing.

151. **The correct answer is B.** Paragraph 1 discusses how profitable and successful the coffee industry has been in recent years, with new businesses opening all around the globe. The answer choice that best highlights the fact that this is a revered business is *admired* (choice B). Choices A and C would indicate that the business is not thriving or healthy, so they are incorrect. Choice D does not make sense given the context of the passage.

152. **The correct answer is D.** We are told in the passage that the process of creating kopi luwak coffee beans is a "unique" process that yields a "limited supply" of beans—therefore, we can infer that compared to the kopi luwak, the process of collecting traditional coffee beans is more common.

Vocabulary

153. C	158. A	163. B	167. B	171. B
154. D	159. B	164. A	168. C	172. D
155. A	160. C	165. C	169. B	173. A
156. B	161. D	166. D	170. C	174. C
157. D	162. B			

153. **The correct answer is C.** A pioneer is a person who is the first (or among the first) to do or accomplish something. Although it is possible to be an expert (choice A) in an industry, or even a novice (choice D), this is not the same as being a pioneer. A person who is the last person (choice B) in an industry would be the opposite of a pioneer.

154. **The correct answer is D.** *Plausible* means "reasonable" or "possible." It doesn't tell the reader anything about whether an explanation is truthful (choice B) or phony (choice A). It is unusual to say an explanation is "easy" (choice C).

155. **The correct answer is A.** *Sage* means "wise" or "knowledgeable."

156. **The correct answer is B.** *Commemorate* means "to honor something or someone."

157. **The correct answer is D.** To decipher something is to translate it into an understandable format. *Discover* (choice B) is close because it's similar in meaning to *understanding*, but *translate* (choice D) is a better answer.

158. **The correct answer is A.** *Blasé* means "nonchalant," "carefree," or "unconcerned."

159. **The correct answer is B.** To apprehend someone is to arrest or detain them. A suspect can certainly be interrogated (choice A) or even released (choice D), but that does not mean the same thing. It makes no sense to say the suspect was arranged, so choice C is incorrect.

160. **The correct answer is C.** To forfeit means to surrender (as in a sports game) or to submit to a penalty. *Lose* (choice B) is close, because a forfeit can be a type of loss, but *surrender* is a more direct meaning of the word.

161. **The correct answer is D.** *Stamina* can mean "endurance," "strength," or "resilience."

162. **The correct answer is B.** *Lucrative* means "profitable," "rewarding," or "well-compensated."

163. **The correct answer is B.** An ovation is a round of applause after a performance.

164. **The correct answer is A.** A panorama describes a broad physical view, usually an outdoor landscape.

165. **The correct answer is C.** To be conscientious about something means to work diligently or carefully at it.

166. **The correct answer is D.** To be voracious means that you consume things (often eating food or reading books) in a "greedy," "hungry," or "insatiable" way.

167. **The correct answer is B.** A haven is a place of "refuge," or "sanctuary," where someone is safe or happy. It is possible you may go to a house (choice C) that is a haven for your vacation (choice A), but *sanctuary* is a far more accurate choice. A haven should not be a trap (choice D).

168. **The correct answer is C.** If someone is making a mercenary decision, they are making it based on monetary needs or financial concerns. An emotional decision (choice D) is the opposite of a mercenary decision.

169. **The correct answer is B.** A dialect is a specific variety of a language. For example, Mandarin is a dialect of the Chinese language.

170. The correct answer is C. *Eccentric* describes someone or something that is "unusual," "strange," or "unconventional."

171. The correct answer is B. *Pivotal* means "essential" or "crucial." It does not tell the reader anything about when a moment occurs but rather, how important it is, so choice C is incorrect. *Pivotal* also does not indicate whether the moment was good or bad, so choices A and D are incorrect.

172. The correct answer is D. If something is foreboding, it brings with it a sense of "dread" or something bad to come. *Agony* is too strong of a word to fit with *foreboding*.

173. The correct answer is A. *Elite* means "exclusive," "top," or "privileged." It's a subset chosen from a larger group.

174. The correct answer is C. *Aloof* can mean "standoffish" or "distant." It doesn't always have negative connotations, but it can mean "unfriendly." *Aloof* does not mean "foolish" (choice A) or "excited" (choice D). *Aloof* implies exclusivity, which can be connected to being alone (choice B). But one does not say someone "acted alone" (choice B) as a way of describing a person's manner.

Mathematics

Concepts

175. B	**180.** D	**185.** D	**190.** B	**195.** B
176. D	**181.** C	**186.** C	**191.** B	**196.** C
177. C	**182.** C	**187.** D	**192.** C	**197.** D
178. B	**183.** A	**188.** D	**193.** D	**198.** D
179. D	**184.** B	**189.** A	**194.** C	

175. The correct answer is B. 19 inches is between 1 and 2 feet, but it is closer to 2 feet (24 inches) than to 1 foot (12 inches).

176. The correct answer is D. Since each group of 3 feet only counts for 1 yard, you need to figure out how many groups of 3 feet you can make. This is the same as dividing by 3.

177. The correct answer is C. The average of two different numbers is the number that falls exactly halfway between the two on a number line.

178. The correct answer is B. To convert from inches to centimeters, multiply the number of inches by 2.54. The product of 7×2.54 must be more than 14, so the only possible correct answer is choice B.

179. The correct answer is D. The angles in any triangle always add up to 180°.

180. The correct answer is D. A meter contains 100 centimeters.

181. The correct answer is C. Each gallon contains 16 cups, so the number of gallons needs to be multiplied by 16 to obtain the number of cups.

182. The correct answer is C. A quadrilateral is defined as a figure with four sides. A triangle has only three sides.

183. The correct answer is A. This problem requires you to "round off" the given number to the place one digit to the right of the decimal point, which immediately eliminates choices B and C. Since the digits in the hundredths place are more than 5, the figure must be rounded upward. Choice D would be the result if you erroneously rounded down.

184. **The correct answer is B.** The digits 2 and 4 end in the hundredths place. This means $0.24 = \frac{24}{100}$. When simplified to simplest form, $\frac{24}{100} = \frac{6}{25}$.

185. **The correct answer is D.** $\frac{33}{7}$ is about 4.7; so, 5, 6, 7, and 8 are between $\frac{33}{7}$ and 8.001.

186. **The correct answer is C.** The distributive property makes choice C true.

187. **The correct answer is D.** By definition, an isosceles triangle is any triangle with two equal sides. Therefore, it is the only possible answer.

188. **The correct answer is D.** The perimeter of a rectangle is the sum of all four sides: $7 + 7 + 2 + 2 = 18$.

189. **The correct answer is A.** If there are an odd number of values in a sorted list, the median is the value that is exactly in the middle. In this case, the 3 is in the middle.

190. **The correct answer is B.** The percent chance of something not happening is always 100 minus the chance of it happening. Since there is a 20% chance of rain, the chance that it will not rain is 100 – 20, or 80%.

191. **The correct answer is B.** The average of a list of numbers is the sum of the numbers divided by how many there are. $-2 + 0 + 2 + 4 = 4$, and $4 \div 4 = 1$.

192. **The correct answer is C.** The union of two sets is the set containing all the elements that are in *at least one* of the sets.
$\{4,7,9\} \cup \{4,9,12,15\} = \{4, 7, 9, 12, 15\}$

193. **The correct answer is D.** Always start with the operations in the parentheses first:

$$(-2)^3 = (-2) \times (-2) \times (-2)$$
$$(-2)^3 = -8$$

Then continue with the operations outside the parentheses:

$$3 \times (-8) = -24$$

Remember, multiplying a negative by a positive results in a negative, but a negative times a negative equals a positive number.

194. **The correct answer is C.** A straight line represents a "straight angle" of 180°. An angle of 60° is given, so $m\angle C$ must be 120° to complete the line. All the angles in a triangle added together equal 180°, therefore:

$$m\angle A + m\angle B + m\angle C = 180°$$
$$m\angle A + 30° + 120° = 180°$$
$$m\angle A = 180° - 150°$$
$$m\angle A = 30°$$

195. **The correct answer is B.** The reciprocal of a fraction is the fraction "reversed." To find the answer, you would have to rename $3\frac{1}{3}$ as an improper fraction: $3\frac{1}{3} = \frac{10}{3}; \frac{10}{3}$ is the reciprocal of $\frac{3}{10}$.

196. **The correct answer is C.** The formula for finding the circumference of a circle is π times the diameter. The diameter is 2 times the radius. In this case, $2 \times 4 = 8$ is the diameter. Therefore:

$$C = d\pi$$
$$C = 8\pi$$

197. **The correct answer is D.** The components of this problem must be stated in the same units. Therefore, 3 yards = 108 inches. The ratio of 108 to 18 is simplified to 6 to 1.

198. **The correct answer is D.** First, determine the value of the squared numbers: $14^2 = 196$; $15^2 = 225$. This shows us that the square root of 198 must fall between 14 and 15.

Problem Solving

199. D	207. A	215. C	223. D	231. A
200. B	208. B	216. A	224. D	232. B
201. D	209. C	217. A	225. C	233. C
202. A	210. A	218. C	226. A	234. A
203. D	211. A	219. C	227. C	235. B
204. C	212. D	220. B	228. B	236. C
205. C	213. C	221. D	229. B	237. D
206. D	214. C	222. B	230. A	238. D

199. **The correct answer is D.** This problem may be done without computation. The larger the denominator, the smaller the parts of the whole have been divided. The larger the numerator, the more parts are being considered. An alternative to this method is to find a common denominator and compare numerators. The largest numerator in this case shows the greatest value.

200. **The correct answer is B.** Figures are "similar" when their corresponding angles are equal, and their corresponding sides are in proportion.

$$\frac{4}{AB} = \frac{3}{5}$$
$$3AB = 20$$
$$AB = \frac{20}{3} = 6\frac{2}{3}$$

201. **The correct answer is D.** There are 12 months in 1 year. If $542.40 is the total amount paid in a year, the average amount paid per month is $542.40 ÷ 12 = $45.20.

202. **The correct answer is A.** Multiply the numbers as you would whole numbers. Then, since there are an odd number of negative signs, affix a negative sign to the product. Doing so yields $(-2) \cdot (-4) \cdot (3) \cdot (-1) = -24$.

203. **The correct answer is D.** Rename the fractions of the equation with a common denominator.

$$4\frac{1}{8} - 2\frac{2}{3} = \frac{33}{8} - \frac{8}{3}$$
$$= \frac{99}{24} - \frac{64}{24}$$
$$= \frac{35}{24}$$
$$= 1\frac{11}{24}$$

204. **The correct answer is C.** Solve for x:

$$-5 + 4x = 21$$
$$4x = 21 + 5$$
$$4x = 26$$
$$x = \frac{26}{4}$$
$$x = 6.5$$

205. **The correct answer is C.** Before multiplying, rename the mixed numbers as improper fractions:

$$3\frac{1}{3} \times 3\frac{3}{4} \times \frac{2}{5} = \frac{10}{3} \times \frac{15}{4} \times \frac{2}{5}$$
$$= \frac{300}{60} = 5$$

206. **The correct answer is D.** Replace the letters with the given numbers and solve:

$$7A - 3B =$$
$$7(6) - 3(3) =$$
$$42 - 9 = 33$$

Answers Practice Test 4: HSPT®

207. The correct answer is A.

$$N\% \times 60 = 24$$

$$N\% = \frac{24}{60}$$

$$N\% = \frac{2}{5}$$

$$N\% = 0.4$$

$$N\% = 40$$

208. The correct answer is B. Solve for x:

$$10x - 3 = 2x + 4$$

$$10x - 2x = 4 + 3$$

$$8x = 7$$

$$x = \frac{7}{8}$$

209. The correct answer is C. To determine ratios, multiply the first numerator by the second denominator and the first denominator by the second numerator. Then reduce:

$$\frac{3}{4} \text{ to } \frac{5}{2}$$

$$6 \text{ to } 20$$

$$3 \text{ to } 10$$

210. The correct answer is A. When solving this problem, remember that the number of decimal places to the right of the decimal point in the answer should equal the total number of places to the right of the decimal points in the two factors being multiplied.

$$
\begin{array}{r}
65.14 \\
\times 0.093 \\
\hline
19542 \\
586260 \\
\hline
6.05802
\end{array}
$$

211. The correct answer is A. The pattern in this sequence is formed by adding 0.06 to each number.

212. The correct answer is D.

$$
\begin{array}{r}
72,528 \\
\times\ 109 \\
\hline
652\ 752 \\
000\ 00 \\
7\ 252\ 8 \\
\hline
7,905,552
\end{array}
$$

213. The correct answer is C. Convert the mixed numbers into improper fractions. Reduce, then divide the total length of the board by the length into which it will be cut.

$$9\frac{1}{2} \div 1\frac{1}{3} = \frac{19}{2} \div \frac{4}{3}$$

$$= \frac{19}{2} \times \frac{3}{4}$$

$$= \frac{57}{8}$$

$$= 7\frac{1}{8}$$

Though $\frac{1}{8}$ of a board is left, only 7 full-size boards can be made.

214. The correct answer is C.

$$3x + 3 < 9 + x$$

$$3x - x < 9 - 3$$

$$2x < 6$$

$$x < \frac{6}{2}$$

$$x < 3$$

215. The correct answer is C. When adding decimal numbers, line up the decimal points.

$$
\begin{array}{r}
0.602 \\
4.200 \\
+5.030 \\
\hline
9.832
\end{array}
$$

216. The correct answer is A.

$$
\begin{array}{r}
1{,}960 \\
28\overline{)54{,}900} \\
\underline{28} \\
269 \\
\underline{252} \\
170 \\
\underline{168} \\
20
\end{array}
$$

217. The correct answer is A.

$$\sqrt{x+36} = 10$$
$$x + 36 = 10^2$$
$$x + 36 = 100$$
$$x = 100 - 36$$
$$x = 64$$

218. The correct answer is C. The probability is the number of red balls over the total number of balls in the basket.

219. The correct answer is C. Since her brother is 10, Katie herself is half of 10, or 5 years old. She will be 12 in 7 years, since $5 + 7 = 12$.

220. The correct answer is B. 25% of \$12 is \$3, so each ticket will cost \$9. Three tickets will cost $\$9 \times 3 = \$27$.

221. The correct answer is D. Each pair of pants can be matched up with 3 different shirts, so there are $2 \times 3 = 6$ different outfits.

222. The correct answer is B. 50% of \$600 is \$300, so the sale price is $\$600 - \$300 = \$300$. The coupon is for 10% of \$300, or \$30. The final price will be \$300 - \$30 = \$270.

223. The correct answer is D. The average of two numbers is half their sum. If the average is 18, their sum must be 36. The second number must then be $36 - 10 = 26$.

224. The correct answer is D. There are $16 \times 18 = 288$ square inches of rubber. Each square foot is 144 square inches, so that is $288 \div 144 = 2$ square feet. Since each square foot weighs 17 ounces, the total weight is $17 \times 2 = 34$ ounces.

225. The correct answer is C. Since Paul is 3 months older than Hunter, Paul is 3 months closer to Kai than Hunter is, and $7 - 3 = 4$.

226. The correct answer is A. This problem is solved by using ratios. The relationship between part of the lawn and the whole lawn is the same as the relationship between the time it takes to mow part of the lawn and the time it takes to mow the whole lawn.

227. The correct answer is C. This involves multiplication and addition.

Student
tickets 130 × \$1.25 =   \$162.50
Adult
tickets 340 × \$1.90 =+ \$646.00
Total =   \$808.50

228. The correct answer is B.
First, add \$10 to Bob's \$88:

$$\$88 + \$10 = \$98$$

Then, divide by 4:

$$\$98 \div 4 = \$24.50$$

229. The correct answer is B. Replace the C in the formula with 85 and solve:

$$F = \frac{9}{5}(85) + 32 = 153 + 32$$
$$= 185$$

230. The correct answer is A. This can be set up as an algebraic equation. If n equals the price of the snowmobile, 5% of n equals \$42, or

$$0.05n = \$42$$
$$n = \$42 \div 0.05$$
$$n = \$840$$

231. The correct answer is A. This can be set up as an algebraic equation. If n is the amount Mr. Symon borrowed:

$$6\%(n) = 58.50$$
$$n = \frac{58.50}{6\%}$$
$$= \frac{58.50}{0.06}$$
$$= 975$$

232. The correct answer is B. This problem is solved using ratios:

$$\frac{n}{6} = \frac{56}{14}$$
$$336 = 14n$$
$$\frac{336}{14} = n$$
$$24 = n$$

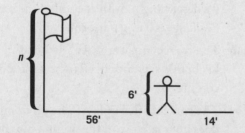

233. The correct answer is C. By definition, opposite sides of a rectangle are equal to each other. Because of this, if one side is 7 units, the opposite side is also 7 units. Consequently, 14 units account for two sides $(7 + 7)$. The other two sides are each equal to $(50 - 14) \div 2$, or 18 units. Area is length times width—in this case: $7 \times 18 = 126$ square units.

234. The correct answer is A. Solve this as an algebraic equation with n as the unknown integer:

$$n + 18 = \frac{5}{4}n$$
$$18 = \frac{5}{4}n - n$$
$$18 = \frac{1}{4}n$$
$$72 = n$$

235. The correct answer is B. Because Jim is now 12, four years ago he was 8. His father was then 5 times older, or 40. Now, 4 years later, Jim's father is 44.

236. The correct answer is C. The area to be carpeted is $(27 \times 27) = 729$ square feet. Since there are 9 square feet in one yard, this is equivalent to 81 square yards, and since it costs $11 per square yard, the total cost is $(81 \times 11) = \$891$.

237. The correct answer is D.

$$V = lwh$$
$$V = 18 \times 2 \times 5$$
$$V = 180 \text{ cu. in.}$$

238. The correct answer is D. First determine how many times 25,000 can be divided by 100: $25,000 \div 100 = 250$.

For *every* $100 in 25,000, $3.62 must be paid in taxes: $250 \times 3.62 = \$905.00$.

Answers | Practice Test 4: HSPT®

Language

Answers

239. B	251. B	263. C	275. A	287. A
240. A	252. C	264. A	276. A	288. A
241. A	253. D	265. A	277. B	289. C
242. D	254. A	266. B	278. B	290. A
243. B	255. B	267. B	279. A	291. C
244. C	256. A	268. B	280. C	292. B
245. B	257. B	269. A	281. D	293. D
246. C	258. B	270. C	282. D	294. D
247. A	259. C	271. A	283. B	295. A
248. A	260. C	272. B	284. C	296. C
249. A	261. B	273. C	285. D	297. B
250. A	262. B	274. B	286. C	298. B

239. **The correct answer is B.** This is a question and should thus end in a question mark (the word *what* at the beginning is a clue).

240. **The correct answer is A.** The names of movies, like *Star Wars*, should be capitalized.

241. **The correct answer is A.** The pronoun *their* is incorrect, as *Raymond* is a singular noun and should be replaced by the singular, masculine *his*.

242. **The correct answer is D.** *No Mistakes.* All the sentences are punctuated correctly.

243. **The correct answer is B.** This simple, declarative statement, which is not a question, should end with a period, not a question mark.

244. **The correct answer is C.** The possessive pronoun *its* is incorrect. There is no "it" that owns the dog. Alison could own the dog (and in that case we could use *her*), or her family could own the dog (in which case we could use *their*).

245. **The correct answer is B.** This sentence incorrectly ends with a semicolon, which is internal sentence punctuation, not end-of-sentence punctuation.

246. **The correct answer is C.** The Statue of Liberty is a proper noun and should be capitalized.

247. **The correct answer is A.** The adjective *cautious* should be an adverb (*cautiously*) since it's describing how the action of the sentence (*walking*) is being performed.

248. **The correct answer is A.** The items in the list in this sentence need to be separated by commas.

249. **The correct answer is A.** The pronoun his does not match with the noun it modifies, *Janelle*.

250. **The correct answer is A.** This sentence contains a semicolon, which creates an awkward pause. Semicolons should be used to connect independent clauses, which we do not have here.

251. **The correct answer is B.** The noun *Daphnes* should be in the possessive form (*Daphne's*), as ownership of the closet is being shown here.

252. **The correct answer is C.** This sentence contains inappropriate commas, which create awkward pauses in the sentence. The sentence does not need internal punctuation as written.

253. **The correct answer is D.** *No mistakes.* All the sentences are punctuated correctly.

254. **The correct answer is A.** The verb *wondering* should be *wondered* as the action began in the past.

255. **The correct answer is B.** The adjective *easy* in this sentence is illogical, as we are told that no one has ever been able to pass the test. A more appropriate adjective would be *difficult* or *challenging*.

256. **The correct answer is A.** This simple declarative statement, which is not a question, should end with a period, not a question mark.

257. **The correct answer is B.** In this sentence, the verb *create* does not agree with the adverb *was*, and should be in the past-tense, *created*.

258. **The correct answer is B.** The dialogue in this sentence should be set in quotation marks, not italicized: "Are you certain you can't make it to my party?"

259. **The correct answer is C.** The sentence as written is illogical—a choice between two items, and the use of the word *either*, indicates that the correct article to use is *or*, not *and*.

260. **The correct answer is C.** Since we are told that the action in this sentence will occur in the future ("tomorrow"), the verb should be set in the future tense: "will be going."

261. **The correct answer is B.** This simple sentence does not contain any pointed emotion or surprise, so it should end in a period, not an exclamation point.

262. **The correct answer is B.** The preposition *in* does not make sense in this sentence, as you can't stand inside of a stage. The correct preposition here is *on*.

263. **The correct answer is C.** The sentence as written is illogical—if Larissa arrived "before" breakfast was over, she shouldn't have missed her chance to eat. A more appropriate preposition here would be *after*.

264. **The correct answer is A.** When two things are described as an excellent "combination," they should be joined by the conjunction *and*, not *or*.

265. **The correct answer is A.** The incorrect preposition is used in this sentence. If Jovan didn't want to get his hair wet, he must have kept his hair "above" the water, not "below."

266. **The correct answer is B.** This sentence contains an error in preposition choice. Since a conditional activity (going to the baseball game) is dependent on the completion of another activity (finishing her homework), the preposition *if* is a more appropriate choice: Lilith can only go to the baseball game tomorrow if she finishes her homework first.

267. **The correct answer is B.** The sentence contains an error in adjective usage. *Wrestle* should be changed to *wrestling*.

268. **The correct answer is B.** The correct spelling is *effect*.

269. **The correct answer is A.** The correct spelling is *advice*.

270. **The correct answer is C.** The correct spelling is *allowed*.

271. **The correct answer is A.** The correct spelling is *presence*.

272. **The correct answer is B.** The correct spelling is *separate*.

273. **The correct answer is C.** The correct spelling is *disappointed*.

274. **The correct answer is B.** The correct spelling is *believable*.

275. **The correct answer is A.** The correct spelling is *collectible*.

276. **The correct answer is A.** The correct spelling is *too*.

277. **The correct answer is B.** The correct spelling is *break*.

278. **The correct answer is B.** This sentence demonstrates correct usage. The other answer choices contain incorrect pronoun choices.

279. **The correct answer is A.** This sentence demonstrates correct usage. The other answer choices contain incorrect pronoun choices.

280. **The correct answer is C.** This sentence demonstrates correct usage. The other answer choices contain incorrect verb forms.

281. **The correct answer is D.** This sentence demonstrates correct usage. The other answer choices contain conjunction errors. Choice A should use *as if*, rather than *by the time*. Choice B should use *Although* instead of *Only if*, and choice C should use *When* in place of *Before*.

282. **The correct answer is D.** This sentence demonstrates correct usage. The other answer choices contain incorrect possessive noun forms.

283. **The correct answer is B.** This sentence demonstrates correct usage. The other answer choices contain incorrect preposition choices. Choice A should use *about* rather than *beyond*; choice C should use *on* rather than *among*, and Choice D should use *around* rather than *about*.

284. **The correct answer is C.** This sentence demonstrates correct usage. The other answer choices contain incorrect pronoun choices.

285. **The correct answer is D.** This sentence demonstrates correct usage. The other answer choices contain adverb errors. Proper adverb choices would have been *capably* (choice A), *slowly* (choice B), and *beautifully* (choice C).

286. **The correct answer is C.** This sentence demonstrates correct usage. The other answer choices contain conjunction or preposition errors. Choice A should use *when* instead of *during*; choice B should eliminate the word *because*; and Choice D should use *than* rather than *because*.

287. **The correct answer is A.** This sentence demonstrates correct usage. The other answer choices contain adverb errors. The correct adverb choices would have been

absentmindedly (choice B), *quietly* (choice C), and *hungrily* (choice D).

288. **The correct answer is A.** This sentence demonstrates correct usage. The other answer choices contain incorrect articles (*a* versus *an*).

289. **The correct answer is C.** These two sentences best support the topic sentence that a healthy diet and exercise can improve your brain functioning.

290. **The correct answer is A.** We are told in the sentence that Sharrod is late for a meeting, so it follows that he would move briskly through the train station.

291. **The correct answer is C.** Mentioning that there's a retail bookstore located in the town's mall offers the least support for why the town of Willowbrook needs a library.

292. **The correct answer is B.** This is the best word choice to complete this sentence: "Phineas had to carefully parallel park his car *between* an SUV and a pickup truck."

293. **The correct answer is D.** This version of the sentences expresses the ideas most clearly.

294. **The correct answer is D.** This is the best word choice to complete this thought: "The cleaning crew had the unfortunate task of cleaning up the street *after* the busy parade was finished."

295. **The correct answer is A.** This version of the sentence expresses the ideas most clearly.

296. **The correct answer is C.** This sentence veers off topic from the main subject of the paragraph (snakes) and does not belong.

297. **The correct answer is B.** This sentence best captures the two main ideas of the paragraph, that giraffes are gentle and quite tall creatures.

298. **The correct answer is B.** This sentence provides no direct support for the idea that college should be free for everybody, and could be used to argue against the topic.

SCORE SHEET

Although your actual exam scores will not be reported as percentages, it might be helpful to convert them so you can better visualize your strengths and weaknesses. The numbers in parentheses represent the question numbers testing each skill.

Subject	# Correct ÷ # of questions	× 100 = _____ %
Verbal Analogies (1-10)	_____ ÷ 10 = _____	× 100 = _____ %
Synonyms (37-51)	_____ ÷ 15 = _____	× 100 = _____ %
Logic (11-20)	_____ ÷ 10 = _____	× 100 = _____ %
Verbal Classification (21-36)	_____ ÷ 16 = _____	× 100 = _____ %
Antonyms (52-60)	_____ ÷ 9 = _____	× 100 = _____ %
TOTAL VERBAL SKILLS	_____ ÷ 60 = _____	× 100 = _____ %
Number Series (62, 67, 69, 72, 76, 79, 81, 86, 89, 93, 95, 99, 100, 101, 104, 106, 107, 108)	_____ ÷ 18 = _____	× 100 = _____ %
Geometric Comparisons (68, 77, 78, 82, 84, 91, 96, 102, 110)	_____ ÷ 9 = _____	× 100 = _____ %
Nongeometric Comparisons (64, 65, 70, 87, 94, 97, 98, 105)	_____ ÷ 8 = _____	× 100 = _____ %
Number Manipulation (61, 63, 66, 71, 73, 74, 75, 80, 83, 85, 88, 90, 92, 103, 109, 111, 112)	_____ ÷ 17 = _____	× 100 = _____ %
TOTAL QUANTITATIVE SKILLS	_____ ÷ 52 = _____	× 100 = _____ %
Reading—Comprehension (113–152)	_____ ÷ 40 = _____	× 100 = _____ %
Reading—Vocabulary (153–174)	_____ ÷ 22 = _____	× 100 = _____ %
TOTAL READING SKILLS	_____ ÷ 62 = _____	× 100 = _____ %
Mathematics—Concepts (175–198)	_____ ÷ 24 = _____	× 100 = _____ %
Mathematics—Problem Solving (199–238)	_____ ÷ 40 = _____	× 100 = _____ %
TOTAL MATHEMATICS SKILLS	_____ ÷ 64 = _____	× 100 = _____ %
Punctuation and Capitalization (239, 240, 242, 243, 245, 246, 248, 250, 252, 253, 256, 261)	_____ ÷ 12 = _____	× 100 = _____ %
Usage (241, 244, 247, 249, 251, 254, 255, 257, 258, 259, 260, 262–267, 278–288)	_____ ÷ 28 = _____	× 100 = _____ %
Spelling (268–277)	_____ ÷ 10 = _____	× 100 = _____ %
Composition (289–298)	_____ ÷ 10 = _____	× 100 = _____ %
TOTAL LANGUAGE SKILLS	_____ ÷ 60 = _____	× 100 = _____ %

Practice Test 4: HSPT®

ANSWER SHEET: HSPT® PRACTICE TEST 5

Verbal Skills

1. Ⓐ Ⓑ Ⓒ Ⓓ   13. Ⓐ Ⓑ Ⓒ Ⓓ   25. Ⓐ Ⓑ Ⓒ Ⓓ   37. Ⓐ Ⓑ Ⓒ Ⓓ   49. Ⓐ Ⓑ Ⓒ
2. Ⓐ Ⓑ Ⓒ Ⓓ   14. Ⓐ Ⓑ Ⓒ Ⓓ   26. Ⓐ Ⓑ Ⓒ Ⓓ   38. Ⓐ Ⓑ Ⓒ   50. Ⓐ Ⓑ Ⓒ Ⓓ
3. Ⓐ Ⓑ Ⓒ Ⓓ   15. Ⓐ Ⓑ Ⓒ   27. Ⓐ Ⓑ Ⓒ Ⓓ   39. Ⓐ Ⓑ Ⓒ Ⓓ   51. Ⓐ Ⓑ Ⓒ Ⓓ
4. Ⓐ Ⓑ Ⓒ   16. Ⓐ Ⓑ Ⓒ Ⓓ   28. Ⓐ Ⓑ Ⓒ Ⓓ   40. Ⓐ Ⓑ Ⓒ Ⓓ   52. Ⓐ Ⓑ Ⓒ
5. Ⓐ Ⓑ Ⓒ Ⓓ   17. Ⓐ Ⓑ Ⓒ Ⓓ   29. Ⓐ Ⓑ Ⓒ Ⓓ   41. Ⓐ Ⓑ Ⓒ Ⓓ   53. Ⓐ Ⓑ Ⓒ Ⓓ
6. Ⓐ Ⓑ Ⓒ Ⓓ   18. Ⓐ Ⓑ Ⓒ Ⓓ   30. Ⓐ Ⓑ Ⓒ Ⓓ   42. Ⓐ Ⓑ Ⓒ Ⓓ   54. Ⓐ Ⓑ Ⓒ Ⓓ
7. Ⓐ Ⓑ Ⓒ Ⓓ   19. Ⓐ Ⓑ Ⓒ Ⓓ   31. Ⓐ Ⓑ Ⓒ Ⓓ   43. Ⓐ Ⓑ Ⓒ Ⓓ   55. Ⓐ Ⓑ Ⓒ
8. Ⓐ Ⓑ Ⓒ Ⓓ   20. Ⓐ Ⓑ Ⓒ Ⓓ   32. Ⓐ Ⓑ Ⓒ Ⓓ   44. Ⓐ Ⓑ Ⓒ Ⓓ   56. Ⓐ Ⓑ Ⓒ Ⓓ
9. Ⓐ Ⓑ Ⓒ Ⓓ   21. Ⓐ Ⓑ Ⓒ Ⓓ   33. Ⓐ Ⓑ Ⓒ   45. Ⓐ Ⓑ Ⓒ Ⓓ   57. Ⓐ Ⓑ Ⓒ Ⓓ
10. Ⓐ Ⓑ Ⓒ Ⓓ   22. Ⓐ Ⓑ Ⓒ   34. Ⓐ Ⓑ Ⓒ Ⓓ   46. Ⓐ Ⓑ Ⓒ Ⓓ   58. Ⓐ Ⓑ Ⓒ Ⓓ
11. Ⓐ Ⓑ Ⓒ Ⓓ   23. Ⓐ Ⓑ Ⓒ Ⓓ   35. Ⓐ Ⓑ Ⓒ Ⓓ   47. Ⓐ Ⓑ Ⓒ Ⓓ   59. Ⓐ Ⓑ Ⓒ Ⓓ
12. Ⓐ Ⓑ Ⓒ Ⓓ   24. Ⓐ Ⓑ Ⓒ   36. Ⓐ Ⓑ Ⓒ Ⓓ   48. Ⓐ Ⓑ Ⓒ Ⓓ   60. Ⓐ Ⓑ Ⓒ

Quantitative Skills

61. Ⓐ Ⓑ Ⓒ Ⓓ   73. Ⓐ Ⓑ Ⓒ Ⓓ   85. Ⓐ Ⓑ Ⓒ Ⓓ   97. Ⓐ Ⓑ Ⓒ Ⓓ   109. Ⓐ Ⓑ Ⓒ Ⓓ
62. Ⓐ Ⓑ Ⓒ Ⓓ   74. Ⓐ Ⓑ Ⓒ Ⓓ   86. Ⓐ Ⓑ Ⓒ Ⓓ   98. Ⓐ Ⓑ Ⓒ Ⓓ   110. Ⓐ Ⓑ Ⓒ Ⓓ
63. Ⓐ Ⓑ Ⓒ Ⓓ   75. Ⓐ Ⓑ Ⓒ Ⓓ   87. Ⓐ Ⓑ Ⓒ Ⓓ   99. Ⓐ Ⓑ Ⓒ Ⓓ   111. Ⓐ Ⓑ Ⓒ Ⓓ
64. Ⓐ Ⓑ Ⓒ Ⓓ   76. Ⓐ Ⓑ Ⓒ Ⓓ   88. Ⓐ Ⓑ Ⓒ Ⓓ   100. Ⓐ Ⓑ Ⓒ Ⓓ   112. Ⓐ Ⓑ Ⓒ Ⓓ
65. Ⓐ Ⓑ Ⓒ Ⓓ   77. Ⓐ Ⓑ Ⓒ Ⓓ   89. Ⓐ Ⓑ Ⓒ Ⓓ   101. Ⓐ Ⓑ Ⓒ Ⓓ
66. Ⓐ Ⓑ Ⓒ Ⓓ   78. Ⓐ Ⓑ Ⓒ Ⓓ   90. Ⓐ Ⓑ Ⓒ Ⓓ   102. Ⓐ Ⓑ Ⓒ Ⓓ
67. Ⓐ Ⓑ Ⓒ Ⓓ   79. Ⓐ Ⓑ Ⓒ Ⓓ   91. Ⓐ Ⓑ Ⓒ Ⓓ   103. Ⓐ Ⓑ Ⓒ Ⓓ
68. Ⓐ Ⓑ Ⓒ Ⓓ   80. Ⓐ Ⓑ Ⓒ Ⓓ   92. Ⓐ Ⓑ Ⓒ Ⓓ   104. Ⓐ Ⓑ Ⓒ Ⓓ
69. Ⓐ Ⓑ Ⓒ Ⓓ   81. Ⓐ Ⓑ Ⓒ Ⓓ   93. Ⓐ Ⓑ Ⓒ Ⓓ   105. Ⓐ Ⓑ Ⓒ Ⓓ
70. Ⓐ Ⓑ Ⓒ Ⓓ   82. Ⓐ Ⓑ Ⓒ Ⓓ   94. Ⓐ Ⓑ Ⓒ Ⓓ   106. Ⓐ Ⓑ Ⓒ Ⓓ
71. Ⓐ Ⓑ Ⓒ Ⓓ   83. Ⓐ Ⓑ Ⓒ Ⓓ   95. Ⓐ Ⓑ Ⓒ Ⓓ   107. Ⓐ Ⓑ Ⓒ Ⓓ
72. Ⓐ Ⓑ Ⓒ Ⓓ   84. Ⓐ Ⓑ Ⓒ Ⓓ   96. Ⓐ Ⓑ Ⓒ Ⓓ   108. Ⓐ Ⓑ Ⓒ Ⓓ

Reading

Comprehension

113. Ⓐ Ⓑ Ⓒ Ⓓ   121. Ⓐ Ⓑ Ⓒ Ⓓ   129. Ⓐ Ⓑ Ⓒ Ⓓ   137. Ⓐ Ⓑ Ⓒ Ⓓ   145. Ⓐ Ⓑ Ⓒ Ⓓ

114. Ⓐ Ⓑ Ⓒ Ⓓ   122. Ⓐ Ⓑ Ⓒ Ⓓ   130. Ⓐ Ⓑ Ⓒ Ⓓ   138. Ⓐ Ⓑ Ⓒ Ⓓ   146. Ⓐ Ⓑ Ⓒ Ⓓ

115. Ⓐ Ⓑ Ⓒ Ⓓ   123. Ⓐ Ⓑ Ⓒ Ⓓ   131. Ⓐ Ⓑ Ⓒ Ⓓ   139. Ⓐ Ⓑ Ⓒ Ⓓ   147. Ⓐ Ⓑ Ⓒ Ⓓ

116. Ⓐ Ⓑ Ⓒ Ⓓ   124. Ⓐ Ⓑ Ⓒ Ⓓ   132. Ⓐ Ⓑ Ⓒ Ⓓ   140. Ⓐ Ⓑ Ⓒ Ⓓ   148. Ⓐ Ⓑ Ⓒ Ⓓ

117. Ⓐ Ⓑ Ⓒ Ⓓ   125. Ⓐ Ⓑ Ⓒ Ⓓ   133. Ⓐ Ⓑ Ⓒ Ⓓ   141. Ⓐ Ⓑ Ⓒ Ⓓ   149. Ⓐ Ⓑ Ⓒ Ⓓ

118. Ⓐ Ⓑ Ⓒ Ⓓ   126. Ⓐ Ⓑ Ⓒ Ⓓ   134. Ⓐ Ⓑ Ⓒ Ⓓ   142. Ⓐ Ⓑ Ⓒ Ⓓ   150. Ⓐ Ⓑ Ⓒ Ⓓ

119. Ⓐ Ⓑ Ⓒ Ⓓ   127. Ⓐ Ⓑ Ⓒ Ⓓ   135. Ⓐ Ⓑ Ⓒ Ⓓ   143. Ⓐ Ⓑ Ⓒ Ⓓ   151. Ⓐ Ⓑ Ⓒ Ⓓ

120. Ⓐ Ⓑ Ⓒ Ⓓ   128. Ⓐ Ⓑ Ⓒ Ⓓ   136. Ⓐ Ⓑ Ⓒ Ⓓ   144. Ⓐ Ⓑ Ⓒ Ⓓ   152. Ⓐ Ⓑ Ⓒ Ⓓ

Vocabulary

153. Ⓐ Ⓑ Ⓒ Ⓓ   158. Ⓐ Ⓑ Ⓒ Ⓓ   163. Ⓐ Ⓑ Ⓒ Ⓓ   168. Ⓐ Ⓑ Ⓒ Ⓓ   173. Ⓐ Ⓑ Ⓒ Ⓓ

154. Ⓐ Ⓑ Ⓒ Ⓓ   159. Ⓐ Ⓑ Ⓒ Ⓓ   164. Ⓐ Ⓑ Ⓒ Ⓓ   169. Ⓐ Ⓑ Ⓒ Ⓓ   174. Ⓐ Ⓑ Ⓒ Ⓓ

155. Ⓐ Ⓑ Ⓒ Ⓓ   160. Ⓐ Ⓑ Ⓒ Ⓓ   165. Ⓐ Ⓑ Ⓒ Ⓓ   170. Ⓐ Ⓑ Ⓒ Ⓓ

156. Ⓐ Ⓑ Ⓒ Ⓓ   161. Ⓐ Ⓑ Ⓒ Ⓓ   166. Ⓐ Ⓑ Ⓒ Ⓓ   171. Ⓐ Ⓑ Ⓒ Ⓓ

157. Ⓐ Ⓑ Ⓒ Ⓓ   162. Ⓐ Ⓑ Ⓒ Ⓓ   167. Ⓐ Ⓑ Ⓒ Ⓓ   172. Ⓐ Ⓑ Ⓒ Ⓓ

Mathematics

Concepts

175. Ⓐ Ⓑ Ⓒ Ⓓ   180. Ⓐ Ⓑ Ⓒ Ⓓ   185. Ⓐ Ⓑ Ⓒ Ⓓ   190. Ⓐ Ⓑ Ⓒ Ⓓ   195. Ⓐ Ⓑ Ⓒ Ⓓ
176. Ⓐ Ⓑ Ⓒ Ⓓ   181. Ⓐ Ⓑ Ⓒ Ⓓ   186. Ⓐ Ⓑ Ⓒ Ⓓ   191. Ⓐ Ⓑ Ⓒ Ⓓ   196. Ⓐ Ⓑ Ⓒ Ⓓ
177. Ⓐ Ⓑ Ⓒ Ⓓ   182. Ⓐ Ⓑ Ⓒ Ⓓ   187. Ⓐ Ⓑ Ⓒ Ⓓ   192. Ⓐ Ⓑ Ⓒ Ⓓ   197. Ⓐ Ⓑ Ⓒ Ⓓ
178. Ⓐ Ⓑ Ⓒ Ⓓ   183. Ⓐ Ⓑ Ⓒ Ⓓ   188. Ⓐ Ⓑ Ⓒ Ⓓ   193. Ⓐ Ⓑ Ⓒ Ⓓ   198. Ⓐ Ⓑ Ⓒ Ⓓ
179. Ⓐ Ⓑ Ⓒ Ⓓ   184. Ⓐ Ⓑ Ⓒ Ⓓ   189. Ⓐ Ⓑ Ⓒ Ⓓ   194. Ⓐ Ⓑ Ⓒ Ⓓ

Problem Solving

199. Ⓐ Ⓑ Ⓒ Ⓓ   207. Ⓐ Ⓑ Ⓒ Ⓓ   215. Ⓐ Ⓑ Ⓒ Ⓓ   223. Ⓐ Ⓑ Ⓒ Ⓓ   231. Ⓐ Ⓑ Ⓒ Ⓓ
200. Ⓐ Ⓑ Ⓒ Ⓓ   208. Ⓐ Ⓑ Ⓒ Ⓓ   216. Ⓐ Ⓑ Ⓒ Ⓓ   224. Ⓐ Ⓑ Ⓒ Ⓓ   232. Ⓐ Ⓑ Ⓒ Ⓓ
201. Ⓐ Ⓑ Ⓒ Ⓓ   209. Ⓐ Ⓑ Ⓒ Ⓓ   217. Ⓐ Ⓑ Ⓒ Ⓓ   225. Ⓐ Ⓑ Ⓒ Ⓓ   233. Ⓐ Ⓑ Ⓒ Ⓓ
202. Ⓐ Ⓑ Ⓒ Ⓓ   210. Ⓐ Ⓑ Ⓒ Ⓓ   218. Ⓐ Ⓑ Ⓒ Ⓓ   226. Ⓐ Ⓑ Ⓒ Ⓓ   234. Ⓐ Ⓑ Ⓒ Ⓓ
203. Ⓐ Ⓑ Ⓒ Ⓓ   211. Ⓐ Ⓑ Ⓒ Ⓓ   219. Ⓐ Ⓑ Ⓒ Ⓓ   227. Ⓐ Ⓑ Ⓒ Ⓓ   235. Ⓐ Ⓑ Ⓒ Ⓓ
204. Ⓐ Ⓑ Ⓒ Ⓓ   212. Ⓐ Ⓑ Ⓒ Ⓓ   220. Ⓐ Ⓑ Ⓒ Ⓓ   228. Ⓐ Ⓑ Ⓒ Ⓓ   236. Ⓐ Ⓑ Ⓒ Ⓓ
205. Ⓐ Ⓑ Ⓒ Ⓓ   213. Ⓐ Ⓑ Ⓒ Ⓓ   221. Ⓐ Ⓑ Ⓒ Ⓓ   229. Ⓐ Ⓑ Ⓒ Ⓓ   237. Ⓐ Ⓑ Ⓒ Ⓓ
206. Ⓐ Ⓑ Ⓒ Ⓓ   214. Ⓐ Ⓑ Ⓒ Ⓓ   222. Ⓐ Ⓑ Ⓒ Ⓓ   230. Ⓐ Ⓑ Ⓒ Ⓓ   238. Ⓐ Ⓑ Ⓒ Ⓓ

✂

Language

239. Ⓐ Ⓑ Ⓒ Ⓓ	251. Ⓐ Ⓑ Ⓒ Ⓓ	263. Ⓐ Ⓑ Ⓒ Ⓓ	275. Ⓐ Ⓑ Ⓒ Ⓓ	287. Ⓐ Ⓑ Ⓒ Ⓓ
240. Ⓐ Ⓑ Ⓒ Ⓓ	252. Ⓐ Ⓑ Ⓒ Ⓓ	264. Ⓐ Ⓑ Ⓒ Ⓓ	276. Ⓐ Ⓑ Ⓒ Ⓓ	288. Ⓐ Ⓑ Ⓒ Ⓓ
241. Ⓐ Ⓑ Ⓒ Ⓓ	253. Ⓐ Ⓑ Ⓒ Ⓓ	265. Ⓐ Ⓑ Ⓒ Ⓓ	277. Ⓐ Ⓑ Ⓒ Ⓓ	289. Ⓐ Ⓑ Ⓒ Ⓓ
242. Ⓐ Ⓑ Ⓒ Ⓓ	254. Ⓐ Ⓑ Ⓒ Ⓓ	266. Ⓐ Ⓑ Ⓒ Ⓓ	278. Ⓐ Ⓑ Ⓒ Ⓓ	290. Ⓐ Ⓑ Ⓒ Ⓓ
243. Ⓐ Ⓑ Ⓒ Ⓓ	255. Ⓐ Ⓑ Ⓒ Ⓓ	267. Ⓐ Ⓑ Ⓒ Ⓓ	279. Ⓐ Ⓑ Ⓒ Ⓓ	291. Ⓐ Ⓑ Ⓒ Ⓓ
244. Ⓐ Ⓑ Ⓒ Ⓓ	256. Ⓐ Ⓑ Ⓒ Ⓓ	268. Ⓐ Ⓑ Ⓒ Ⓓ	280. Ⓐ Ⓑ Ⓒ Ⓓ	292. Ⓐ Ⓑ Ⓒ Ⓓ
245. Ⓐ Ⓑ Ⓒ Ⓓ	257. Ⓐ Ⓑ Ⓒ Ⓓ	269. Ⓐ Ⓑ Ⓒ Ⓓ	281. Ⓐ Ⓑ Ⓒ Ⓓ	293. Ⓐ Ⓑ Ⓒ Ⓓ
246. Ⓐ Ⓑ Ⓒ Ⓓ	258. Ⓐ Ⓑ Ⓒ Ⓓ	270. Ⓐ Ⓑ Ⓒ Ⓓ	282. Ⓐ Ⓑ Ⓒ Ⓓ	294. Ⓐ Ⓑ Ⓒ Ⓓ
247. Ⓐ Ⓑ Ⓒ Ⓓ	259. Ⓐ Ⓑ Ⓒ Ⓓ	271. Ⓐ Ⓑ Ⓒ Ⓓ	283. Ⓐ Ⓑ Ⓒ Ⓓ	295. Ⓐ Ⓑ Ⓒ Ⓓ
248. Ⓐ Ⓑ Ⓒ Ⓓ	260. Ⓐ Ⓑ Ⓒ Ⓓ	272. Ⓐ Ⓑ Ⓒ Ⓓ	284. Ⓐ Ⓑ Ⓒ Ⓓ	296. Ⓐ Ⓑ Ⓒ Ⓓ
249. Ⓐ Ⓑ Ⓒ Ⓓ	261. Ⓐ Ⓑ Ⓒ Ⓓ	273. Ⓐ Ⓑ Ⓒ Ⓓ	285. Ⓐ Ⓑ Ⓒ Ⓓ	297. Ⓐ Ⓑ Ⓒ Ⓓ
250. Ⓐ Ⓑ Ⓒ Ⓓ	262. Ⓐ Ⓑ Ⓒ Ⓓ	274. Ⓐ Ⓑ Ⓒ Ⓓ	286. Ⓐ Ⓑ Ⓒ Ⓓ	298. Ⓐ Ⓑ Ⓒ Ⓓ

Practice Test 5: HSPT®

VERBAL SKILLS (16 MINUTES)

60 Questions

Turn to the Verbal Skills section of your answer sheet to answer the questions in this section.

Directions: Read each question carefully, then consider all options and mark the correct answer.

---

1. Which word does *not* belong with the others?

   A. Oven
   B. Toaster
   C. Cook
   D. Microwave

2. Which word does *not* belong with the others?

   A. Run
   B. Walk
   C. Jog
   D. Sneaker

3. Red is to pink as black is to

   A. beige.
   B. white.
   C. dark.
   D. gray.

4. Ann reads faster than Sue. Karen reads faster than Ann. Karen reads more slowly than Sue. If the first two statements are true, the third is

   A. true.
   B. false.
   C. uncertain.

5. *Create* most nearly means

   A. destroy.
   B. despise.
   C. discover.
   D. invent.

6. Youth is to young as age is to

   A. people.
   B. parents.
   C. grandmother.
   D. old.

7. Which word does *not* belong with the others?

   A. Quality
   B. Honesty
   C. Sincerity
   D. Integrity

8. Sand is to beach as black dirt is to

   A. earth.
   B. plants.
   C. water.
   D. farm.

9. Which word does *not* belong with the others?

   A. Day

   B. Time

   C. Month

   D. Hour

10. A *salamander* is a(n)

    A. amphibian.

    B. hammock.

    C. spice.

    D. fish.

11. *Arrogant* most nearly means

    A. poised.

    B. superior.

    C. fragrant.

    D. haughty.

12. North is to south as left is to

    A. west.

    B. down.

    C. right.

    D. sideways.

13. One is to two as three is to

    A. two.

    B. five.

    C. thirty.

    D. six.

14. Which word does *not* belong with the others?

    A. Figure

    B. Number

    C. Add

    D. Letter

15. Paul is taller than Peter. Peter is shorter than John. Paul is taller than John. If the first two statements are true, the third is

    A. true.

    B. false.

    C. uncertain.

16. A *mature* peach is

    A. ripe.

    B. rotten.

    C. yellow.

    D. green.

17. *Gossamer* most nearly means

    A. beautiful.

    B. flimsy.

    C. eerie.

    D. supernatural.

18. *Coddle* most nearly means

    A. handle.

    B. embrace.

    C. pamper.

    D. love.

19. Books are to libraries as rides are to

    A. carnivals.

    B. fun.

    C. roller coaster.

    D. bookstore.

20. Choir is to director as team is to

    A. sport.

    B. coach.

    C. player.

    D. athlete.

21. *Diversify* most nearly means

    A. vary.

    B. oppose.

    C. change.

    D. strengthen.

22. Harry is more intelligent than George. Sam is more intelligent than Ralph. Harry is more intelligent than Ralph. If the first two statements are true, the third is

    A. true.

    B. false.

    C. uncertain.

23. A *superficial* wound is

    A. serious.

    B. deep.

    C. facial.

    D. shallow.

24. Jackie can throw a javelin farther than Elsa. Liandra can throw a javelin farther than Shelley but not as far as Jackie. Shelley won the javelin-throwing contest. If the first two sentences are true, the third is

    A. true.

    B. false.

    C. uncertain.

25. A *bellicose* general is

    A. peaceful.

    B. combative.

    C. understanding.

    D. weak.

26. A *sadistic* remark is

    A. sad.

    B. silly.

    C. hurtful.

    D. sudden.

27. Which word does *not* belong with the others?

    A. College

    B. University

    C. School

    D. Dormitory

28. *Truncate* most nearly means

    A. pack.

    B. cut.

    C. sound.

    D. transport.

29. A *facetious* game show host is

    A. serious.

    B. intelligent.

    C. humorous.

    D. boring.

30. An *indigent* person is

    A. delicate.

    B. intelligent.

    C. indignant.

    D. needy.

31. Table is to leg as automobile is to

    A. wheel.

    B. axle.

    C. door.

    D. fuel.

32. Which word does *not* belong with the others?

    A. Dungeon

    B. Residence

    C. Dwelling

    D. Domicile

Practice Test 5: HSPT®

33. Bishop's house is the largest on his street. Terrence and Arianna both live on Oakville Lane, but Arianna's house is much larger than Terrence's house. Arianna and Bishop live on the same street. Arianna's house is the largest on Oakville Lane. If the first three sentences are true, the fourth is

    A. true.
    B. false.
    C. uncertain.

34. Which word does *not* belong with the others?

    A. Prison
    B. Jail
    C. Reformatory
    D. Punishment

35. Refuse means the *opposite* of

    A. reheat.
    B. accept.
    C. reveal.
    D. tidy.

36. Ink is to pen as paint is to

    A. canvas.
    B. bucket.
    C. wall.
    D. brush.

37. Acquire means the *opposite* of

    A. solo.
    B. buy.
    C. release.
    D. collect.

38. River A is wider than River B. River B is narrower than River C. River A is wider than River C. If the first two statements are true, the third is

    A. true.
    B. false.
    C. uncertain.

39. Scant means the *opposite* of

    A. sparse.
    B. scoundrel.
    C. abundant.
    D. straight.

40. Pinnacle means the *opposite* of

    A. bridge.
    B. base.
    C. wall.
    D. rummy.

41. Team is to captain as office is to

    A. secretary.
    B. accountant.
    C. staff.
    D. manager.

42. Which word does *not* belong with the others?

    A. Window
    B. Drape
    C. Shade
    D. Curtain

43. Corpulent means the *opposite* of

    A. bulky.
    B. singular.
    C. company.
    D. slender.

44. Naive means the *opposite* of

    A. rural.

    B. dull.

    C. sophisticated.

    D. funny.

45. Which word does *not* belong with the others?

    A. Fez

    B. Turban

    C. Glove

    D. Derby

46. Which word does *not* belong with the others?

    A. Gallery

    B. Audience

    C. Congregation

    D. Podium

47. *Pledge* most nearly means

    A. promise.

    B. beg.

    C. join.

    D. obey.

48. Depression is the *opposite* of

    A. incline.

    B. valley.

    C. hill.

    D. oppression.

49. Grapes cost more than apples but less than pineapples. Oranges cost more than apples but less than lemons. Apples cost the least of the fruits. If the first two statements are true, the third is

    A. true.

    B. false.

    C. uncertain.

50. Which word does *not* belong with the others?

    A. Oak

    B. Elm

    C. Maple

    D. Fir

51. Diminish is the *opposite* of

    A. trim.

    B. augment.

    C. decorate.

    D. decrease.

52. Jay's batting average is better than Michael's. Michael's batting average is higher than Tom's. Jay's batting average is lower than Tom's. If the first two statements are true, the third is

    A. true.

    B. false.

    C. uncertain.

53. Abandon is the *opposite* of

    A. abdicate.

    B. keep.

    C. maintain.

    D. encourage.

54. Which word does *not* belong with the others?

    A. Flexible

    B. Feasible

    C. Supple

    D. Malleable

55. A is northeast of B. C is southwest of D, but northwest of A. C is north of B. If the first two statements are true, the third is

    A. true.

    B. false.

    C. uncertain.

56. Which word does *not* belong with the others?

    A. Leather

    B. Cotton

    C. Wool

    D. Fur

57. Which word does *not* belong with the others?

    A. Zipper

    B. Button

    C. Snap

    D. Seam

58. *Dwindle* most nearly means

    A. shrink.

    B. ooze.

    C. leak.

    D. spoil.

59. Which word does *not* belong with the others?

    A. Oxygen

    B. Water

    C. Helium

    D. Gold

60. Jon ran faster than Carl. Ron ran faster than George but not as fast as Jon. Carl was the fastest runner. If the first two statements are true, the third is

    A. true.

    B. false.

    C. uncertain.

STOP.

If you finish before time is UP, you may check your work on this section only.
Do not turn to any other section in the test.

Quantitative Skills

52 Questions (30 minutes)

Turn to the Quantitative Skills section of your answer sheet to answer the questions in this section.

> **Directions:** Read each question carefully, then solve the problem to find the correct answer.

61. Look at this series: 23, 22, 20, 19, 16, 15, 11, ... What number should come next?

    A. 13

    B. 10

    C. 7

    D. 6

62. Examine A, B, C, and D, then find the best answer.

    A. A is longer than C but shorter than D.

    B. C is shorter than A minus D.

    C. B and D together are longer than A.

    D. C plus D is longer than A plus B.

63. Examine A, B, and C and find the best answer.

    A. $(5 + 8)^2$

    B. $5^2 + 8^2$

    C. $2(5) + 2(8)$

    A. A equals B, and C is less than A.

    B. A equals B, and B equals C.

    C. B is less than C, and C is less than A.

    D. C is less than B, and B is less than A.

64. What number is 5 less than 60% of 40?

    A. 19

    B. 20

    C. 24

    D. 29

65. Look at this series: 50, 52, 48, 50, 46, 48, 44, ... What number should come next?

    A. 38

    B. 40

    C. 46

    D. 48

66. Look at this series: A+, B−, C+, D−, E+, ... What are the next three terms?

    A. F−, G+, H−

    B. F+, G+, H+

    C. G, H+, H

    D. F, G, H

67. What number is 2 times the average of {6, 12, 4, 41, 7}?

    A. 12

    B. 14

    C. 28

    D. 30

68. Look at this series: 42, 40, 38, 35, 32, 28, 24, ... What two numbers should come next?

    A. 21, 18

    B. 20, 14

    C. 19, 14

    D. 18, 16

Practice Test 5: HSPT®

69. Look at this series: 34, 41, 43, 50, 52, ... What is the next number in the series?

   A. 54

   B. 59

   C. 61

   D. 68

70. Examine the triangle and find the best answer.

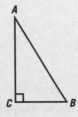

   A. *AB* is equal to *AC.*

   B. *m∠B* is greater than *m∠C.*

   C. *AB* minus *AC* is equal to *BC.*

   D. *m∠A* + *m∠B* = *m∠C.*

71. What number times $\frac{2}{3}$ equals 6 times 4?

   A. 16

   B. 36

   C. 48

   D. 52

72. What number divided by $\frac{1}{4}$ is 3 less than 79?

   A. 304

   B. 298

   C. 20.5

   D. 19

73. Examine A, B, and C and find the best answer.

   A.   B.   C.

   A. B is less shaded than A.

   B. B and C are equally shaded.

   C. A and B are both less shaded than C.

   D. A and C are both more shaded than B.

74. What is the reciprocal of $3\frac{5}{8}$?

   A. $5\frac{8}{3}$

   B. $\frac{64}{16}$

   C. $\frac{8}{15}$

   D. $\frac{8}{29}$

75. Examine A, B, and C and find the best answer.

   A. 0.875

   B. 0.33 × 2.6

   C. $\frac{7}{8}$

   A. A, B, and C are all equal.

   B. B is greater than C.

   C. B is less than A.

   D. A is greater than C.

76. The number that is 6 less than 69 is the product of 7 and what other number?

   A. 10

   B. 9

   C. 8

   D. 6

77. Examine A, B, and C and find the best answer.

      A. $\frac{1}{5}$ of 20

      B. $\frac{1}{4}$ of 24

      C. $\frac{1}{8}$ of 32

  A. B is equal to C.

  B. A is less than B and equal to C.

  C. A plus C equals B.

  D. B minus A equals C.

78. Examine A, B, and C and find the best answer.

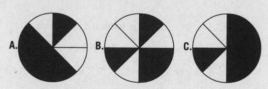

  A. Figure A is less shaded than both figures B and C.

  B. Figures A and C are equally shaded, and are more shaded than figure B.

  C. Figure B is more shaded than figure A, but not as shaded as figure C.

  D. All three figures are shaded equally.

79. Look at this series: 8, 16, 9, 18, 11, _____, 15, 30. What number should fill the blank in this series?

  A. 32

  B. 22

  C. 19

  D. 7

80. Find the greatest common factor for (42, 39)

  A. 13

  B. 6

  C. 5

  D. 3

81. Look at this series: A1, B1, B2, C1, C2, C3, D1, D2, ... What term should come next?

  A. E1

  B. E3

  C. D3

  D. D4

82. By how much does the average of 12, 87, 72, and 41 exceed 25?

  A. 78

  B. 53

  C. 28

  D. 25

83. Look at this series: 24, 25, 23, 24, 21, 22, 18, ... What number should come next?

  A. 27

  B. 23

  C. 21

  D. 19

84. Examine A, B, C, and D and find the best answer.

    A.   **B.**   **C.**   **D.**

  A. A has fewer paddles than B but more than D.

  B. A and D together are equal to B and C together.

  C. B has fewer paddles than A and C together.

  D. B has more paddles than C and D together.

85. Look at this series: 1, 3, 7, 15, 31, ... What number comes next?

   A. 32
   B. 42
   C. 54
   D. 63

86. How many pints in 17 quarts? How many gallons is 17 quarts?

   A. 8.5 pts., 6 gal.
   B. 34 pts., 5.75 gal.
   C. 34 pts., 6.25 gal.
   D. 68 pts., 8.5 gal.

87. Examine A, B, and C and find the best answer.

   A. 62
   B. 26
   C. $(2 \times 6)(6 \times 2)$

   A. $A + B = C$
   B. $C - B = A$
   C. A = B and both are smaller than C.
   D. C is greater than either A or B.

88. Examine A, B, C, and D and find the best answer.

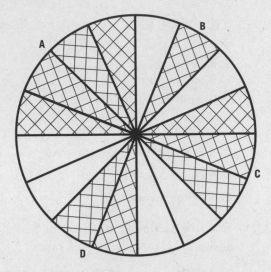

   A. A is equal to C, which is smaller than D.
   B. C is greater than B but equal to A.
   C. A is greater than B, which is less than C.
   D. D is greater than A.

89. What number added to 30 is 3 times the product of 8 and 4?

   A. 39
   B. 63
   C. 66
   D. 93

90. Examine A, B, and C, and choose the best answer.

   A. 4 more than the square of 3
   B. 4 less than the square of 4
   C. 4 more than the cube of 2

   A. $A < B < C$
   B. $A = B > C$
   C. $A = B = C$
   D. $A > B = C$

91. Look at this series: 0.125, 0.250, 0.375, 0.500, ... What number should come next?

A. 0.620

B. 0.625

C. 0.728

D. 0.875

92. Examine A, B, and C and find the best answer.

   A.   B.   C.

A. C is more shaded than A.

B. A and B are equally shaded and are more shaded than C.

C. A is less shaded than B and more shaded than C.

D. A and C are equally shaded.

93. Look at this series: $\frac{1}{1}, \frac{1}{2}, \frac{1}{4}, \frac{1}{7}, \frac{1}{11}, \ldots$ What term should come next?

A. $\frac{1}{13}$

B. $\frac{1}{14}$

C. $\frac{1}{15}$

D. $\frac{1}{16}$

94. What number divided by $\frac{3}{4}$ yields a quotient that is equal to the divisor?

A. $\frac{9}{16}$

B. $\frac{5}{8}$

C. $\frac{7}{16}$

D. $\frac{3}{4}$

95. Examine A, B, and C and find the best answer.

A. 0.8

B. 80%

C. $\frac{8}{10}$ %

A. B is greater than A or C.

B. A is greater than B plus C.

C. A, B, and C are equal.

D. C is smaller than both A and B.

96. Examine the figure and find the best answer.

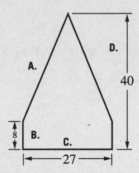

A. Line segment A is shorter than line segment D, which is longer than line segment C.

B. Line segment B is shorter than line segment A, which is longer than line segment D.

C. Line segment C is longer than line segment D, which is longer than line segment B.

D. Line segment B plus line segment C together equal the length of line segment D.

97. Look at this series: 81, 9, 64, 8, _____, 7, 36. What number should fill the blank in this series?

A. 9

B. 49

C. 56

D. 63

98. Find the mean, median, and mode for {2, 7, 4, 5, 9, 32, 25, 17, 3, 9, 28}

   A. Mean = 12.8, median = 9, mode = 9

   B. Mean = 14.6, median = 21, mode = 2

   C. Mean = 15.75, median = 7, mode = 5

   D. Mean = 23.5, median = 32, mode = 18

99. Look at this series: 1, 3, 3, 9, 9, 27, 27, ... What three numbers should come next?

   A. 81, 81, 729

   B. 81, 81, 243

   C. 27, 81, 81

   D. 27, 36, 36

100. If $\frac{3}{8}$ of a number is 9, then $83\frac{1}{3}\%$ of the number is

   A. 20

   B. 27

   C. 32

   D. 54

101. Examine the figure and choose the best answer.

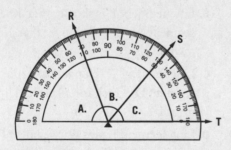

   A. Angle B plus angle C equals a right angle.

   B. Angle A is greater than angle C, which is smaller than angle B.

   C. Angle B minus angle C equals angle A.

   D. Angle A is equal to angle C.

102. Convert 27,840,000,000 to scientific notation.

   A. $2,784 \times 10^7$

   B. 278.4×10^8

   C. 27.84×10^9

   D. 2.784×10^{10}

103. Look at this series: −19, −14, −12, −7, −5, ... What number should come next?

   A. 0

   B. 5

   C. 1

   D. −1

104. What number when subtracted from 75 is twice the sum of 9 and 3?

   A. 24

   B. 51

   C. 61

   D. 99

105. Look at this series: 0.2, 0.1, 0.05, 0.025, ... What number should come next?

   A. 0.00625

   B. 0.0025

   C. 0.0125

   D. 0.055

106. What number is 12 less than $\frac{5}{8}$ of 96?

   A. 48

   B. 56

   C. 60

   D. 65

107. Examine A, B, and C and find the best answer.

A.   **B.**   **C.**

A. A is equal to C.

B. B is greater than A and less than C.

C. A is not greater than C, which is not greater than B.

D. A plus B is not greater than C.

108. Look at this series: VI, IX, 12, 15, XVIII, ... What term should come next?

A. XXI

B. 21

C. XXII

D. 22

109. Look at this series: $\frac{16}{2}, \frac{8}{2}, \frac{8}{4}, \frac{8}{8}, \frac{8}{16}, ...$ What number should come next?

A. $\frac{16}{16}$

B. $\frac{4}{8}$

C. $\frac{16}{32}$

D. $\frac{8}{32}$

110. Examine A, B, and C and find the best answer.

A. 100% of 95

B. 100% of 195%

C. 95% of 100

A. B is greater than A.

B. C is greater than A plus B.

C. A and C are equal and are greater than B.

D. A and C are equal and are smaller than B.

111. What number decreased by 40% of itself is 90?

A. 150

B. 36

C. 60

D. 145

112. Look at this series: 26, 18, 18, 12, 12, 8, 8, ... What two numbers should come next?

A. 7, 7

B. 8, 6

C. 6, 6

D. 6, 4

STOP.

If you finish before time is UP, you may check your work on this section only.

Do not turn to any other section in the test.

READING

62 Questions (25 minutes)

Comprehension

Turn to the Reading Comprehension section of your answer sheet to answer the questions in this section.

> **Directions:** Read each passage and review the associated questions, then re-read—if necessary—to find the correct answer.

Questions 113–122 refer to the following passage.

Our planet Earth is divided into seven separate layers. The outer layer is called the crust and appears to be approximately twenty miles thick. Next in line are the four layers of the mantle. These layers <u>vary</u> in thickness from 250 to 1,000 miles. The <u>remaining</u> two layers are divided
Line into the outer core and inner core. The thickness of the outer core has been determined to be
5 <u>slightly</u> more than 1,200 miles, while that of the inner core is slightly less than 800 miles. Scientists calculate the location and depth of these layers by measuring and studying the speed and direction of earthquake waves. They have also determined that both temperature and pressure are much greater at the core than at the crust.

113. The thickest portion of the earth is its

A. crust.

B. outer core.

C. mantle.

D. inner core.

114. The earth has how many separate layers?

A. Two

B. Four

C. Seven

D. Twenty

115. Which of the following is correct?

A. No two sets of earthquake waves ever travel in the same direction.

B. Earthquakes usually travel in the same direction.

C. Earthquake waves travel at different speeds.

D. Earthquake waves travel at the same speed but in different directions.

116. You would expect to find the kind of information in this passage in

A. an encyclopedia.

B. a science book.

C. neither an encyclopedia nor a science book.

D. both an encyclopedia and a science book.

117. In going from the surface to the center of the earth, in which order would you pass through the layers?

A. Crust, outer core, mantle, inner core

B. Outer core, inner core, crust, mantle

C. Outer core, crust, inner core, mantle

D. Crust, mantle, outer core, inner core

118. The word *vary*, as underlined and used in this passage, most nearly means

A. stabilize.

B. increase.

C. range.

D. arbitrate.

119. Which of the following is correct?

   A. Scientists know the exact thickness of the crust.

   B. Scientists believe they know the thickness of the crust.

   C. The thickness of the crust cannot be determined.

   D. Scientists cannot agree on the thickness of the crust.

120. In comparing the core with the crust, you would find that at the core,

   A. temperature and pressure are less.

   B. pressure is greater, temperature is less.

   C. temperature is greater, pressure is less.

   D. temperature and pressure are greater.

121. The word *slightly*, as underlined and used in this passage, most nearly means

   A. scarcely.

   B. considerably.

   C. a little.

   D. at least.

122. The word *remaining*, as underlined and used in this passage, most nearly means

   A. previous.

   B. outer.

   C. last.

   D. prior.

Questions 123–132 refer to the following passage.

The man is in <u>utter</u> darkness. Only the <u>wavering</u> beam of light from his flashlight pierces the blackness. The air, damp and cold, smells of dank, unseen, decaying material.

The man stumbles over stones and splashes into a hidden puddle. He bangs into a cold rocky
Line wall. The flashlight cocks upward, and suddenly, the air is filled with the flutter of thousands
5 of wings and the piping of tiny animal wails. He ducks, startled, then grins. He's found what he's looking for—bats!

This man is a spelunker, another name for someone who explores caves for the fun of it. Spelunkers enjoy crawling on their stomachs in narrow, rocky tunnels far below the surface of the earth.

10 Spelunkers have discovered new caves. Some have formed clubs, sharing safety knowledge, developing new techniques, and teaching novices.

Spelunkers believe that Earth's inner spaces are as exciting as the universe's outer spaces.

123. The first two paragraphs of this passage describe a cave's

   A. rocks.

   B. depth.

   C. atmosphere.

   D. streams.

124. What effect does the first paragraph have on the passage?

   A. It emphasizes that spelunking is full of unknowns.

   B. It shows that the spelunker is terrified of bats.

   C. It contrasts bats and spelunkers.

   D. It sets up a persuasive argument.

125. The author of this passage is most likely a

    A. spelunker.

    B. cave scientist.

    C. medical doctor.

    D. magazine writer.

126. The cave the man was exploring was probably

    A. large and dry.

    B. deep underground.

    C. near the surface.

    D. dangerous.

127. According to this passage, what made the bats start flying about?

    A. The spelunker

    B. The damp and cold air

    C. The flashlight

    D. The sudden noise

128. The man ducked when the bats flew because he was

    A. angry.

    B. afraid.

    C. surprised.

    D. hurt.

129. The word <u>utter</u>, as underlined and used in this passage, most nearly means

    A. bovine.

    B. unspeakable.

    C. oppressive.

    D. great.

130. According to this passage, spelunkers ignore

    A. safety rules.

    B. light.

    C. discomfort.

    D. other spelunkers.

131. Which title is best for this passage?

    A. "Batty about Bats"

    B. "Spelunkers—Underground Explorers"

    C. "Inner Space"

    D. "The Life of a Spelunker"

132. According to this passage, which word would most nearly describe spelunkers?

    A. Experimental

    B. Cautious

    C. Antisocial

    D. Adventurous

Questions 133–142 refer to the following passage.

Even adventurous eaters may have very little experience encountering the kohlrabi, also known as the turnip cabbage or German turnip. Often misidentified as a root vegetable because of its bulbous, root-like appearance, kohlrabi is both a resilient crop and a <u>protean</u> menu ingredient—it
Line   can be eaten raw or cooked and serves as an excellent addition to a wide array of recipes. Many
5   of its fans insist that it deserves a wider audience and more attention than it currently receives.

This versatile—but largely unknown—vegetable is a member of the *Brassica oleracea* species, which also includes broccoli, kale, cauliflower, and Brussels sprouts. This may not come as a surprise to those who have eaten kohlrabi, as the taste is similar to these other vegetables. Kohlrabi grows above ground and comes in both green and purple colors. Among the many
10   currently available <u>varietals</u> are the White Danube, Purple Danube, White Vienna, and Purple Vienna, perhaps a reflection of the vegetable's popularity in Germany.

Need a few more reasons to give kohlrabi a try? This hearty vegetable is a great addition to salads, stews, and slaws, and also packs a nutrient-rich punch—it's an excellent source of vitamin C, vitamin B, potassium, and fiber and helps promote good muscle and nerve function, vision
15   and digestive health, bone strength, and more. The next time you're doing some meal planning, think beyond the usual ingredients and consider adding kohlrabi.

133. The author's opinion on kohlrabi as a food is most likely

A. pessimistic.

B. cautious.

C. enthusiastic.

D. curious.

134. Which is the best title for this passage?

A. "Consider Kohlrabi"

B. "Exploring German Foods"

C. "Mix Up Your Menu"

D. "A Brand New Vegetable"

135. The word <u>protean</u>, as underlined and used in this passage, most nearly means

A. delicious.

B. versatile.

C. expensive.

D. nutritious.

136. According to the passage, kohlrabi is a good source of

A. calories.

B. energy.

C. spice.

D. potassium.

137. What is the most logical explanation for the author's statement regarding kohlrabi's popularity in Germany?

A. The Danube and Vienna are of German origin.

B. The author of the passage is from Germany.

C. Germany often leads the world in new food trends.

D. It's well known that Germans love eating vegetables.

Practice Test 5: HSPT®

138. The word *varietal*, as underlined and used in this passage, most nearly means the

    A. flavor of kohlrabi.

    B. price of kohlrabi.

    C. use of kohlrabi.

    D. type of kohlrabi.

139. According to the passage, what is the main reason why kohlrabi is often mistaken as a root vegetable?

    A. Its taste

    B. Its color

    C. Its appearance

    D. Its name

140. Kohlrabi is *not* in the same vegetable species as

    A. turnips.

    B. broccoli.

    C. kale.

    D. cauliflower.

141. All the following are mentioned in the passage as benefits of kohlrabi *except*

    A. muscle and nerve function.

    B. heart health.

    C. vision and digestive health.

    D. bone strength.

142. What is most likely the author's purpose in writing this passage?

    A. To compare kohlrabi with other vegetables

    B. To get people interested in trying kohlrabi

    C. To convince individuals to cook more

    D. To promote a healthy vegetarian lifestyle

Questions 143–152 refer to the following passage.

Belief in witchcraft, which goes back many hundreds of years, is today nonetheless still shrouded in unresolved mystery, speculation, and superstition. Many people today would laugh at a belief in witches, magic spells, and the like.

Line
5   Hundreds of thousands of people in Europe who were accused of being witches were executed during the Middle Ages and even as late as the early eighteenth century. Their deaths probably resulted from hysterical fears. Yet the judges undoubtedly were sincere in their desire to eliminate what they thought was a real danger. Some modern psychologists have theorized that so-called witches were dangerous. In essence, they say a person who believes in the powers of witchcraft can be affected emotionally or physically—and may even die—because of a
10 "witch's spell."

European immigrants brought their beliefs with them when they came to America. Witchcraft trials were hosted in Massachusetts during the 1600s; however, after the execution of twenty Salem "witches" in 1692, prosecution for witchcraft didn't survive long in the New World.

Most people in the civilized world no longer believe in the sort of witchcraft encountered
15 in Salem. Nonetheless, the subject is fascinating for many people. As an example, the TV show *Bewitched* was a very popular program for more than five years.

143. This passage was probably printed in a(n)

    A. history book.

    B. magazine.

    C. psychology book.

    D. encyclopedia.

144. According to this passage, the mystery of the Salem witches and trials, and beliefs in witchcraft in general, are

    A. a major problem for psychologists.

    B. of very little interest today.

    C. still not fully understood.

    D. a major problem for sincere judges.

145. One reminder of the impact of beliefs in witchcraft is

    A. Halloween.

    B. April Fools' Day.

    C. the use of brooms.

    D. the death penalty for certain crimes.

146. Which group can we be sure has at one time had members who believed in witchcraft?

    A. Judges

    B. TV producers

    C. Psychologists

    D. Newspaper reporters

147. This passage notes that witchcraft has been shrouded in "mystery and superstition." Which of these would also be a superstition?

    A. "Many hands make light work."

    B. "Breaking a mirror brings bad luck."

    C. "Eating sweets causes pimples."

    D. "Great oaks from little acorns grow."

148. According to some psychologists, persons who *do* believe in witchcraft

    A. can be harmed by it.

    B. tend to laugh at it today.

    C. are crazy.

    D. tend to be dangerous.

149. The underlined phrase "in essence," as used in this passage, most nearly means

    A. probably.

    B. basically.

    C. briefly.

    D. finally.

150. The word *fascinating*, as used in this passage, most nearly means

    A. frightening.

    B. enjoyable.

    C. frustrating.

    D. interesting.

151. This passage suggests that what you believe

    A. can hurt you.

    B. should be based on facts.

    C. does not affect you.

    D. changes as you grow older.

152. Which is the best title for this passage?

    A. "Witchcraft—Fact or Fiction?"

    B. "The End of Witchcraft"

    C. "Witchcraft in the New World"

    D. "The Powers of Witchcraft"

Vocabulary

Turn to the Vocabulary section of your answer sheet to answer the questions in this section.

Directions: Choose the answer that's closest in meaning to the underlined word in the question.

---

153. a new <u>perspective</u>

    A. receptacle

    B. sight

    C. picture

    D. view

154. <u>impair</u> his vision

    A. test

    B. weaken

    C. improve

    D. destroy

155. strong business <u>acumen</u>

    A. intelligence

    B. speed

    C. flexibility

    D. confusion

156. <u>subjugate</u> the enemy

    A. confront

    B. bargain with

    C. trick

    D. overpower

157. to <u>reproach</u>

    A. approach

    B. praise

    C. blame

    D. steal

158. to be <u>elated</u>

    A. happy

    B. akin

    C. moved

    D. upset

159. his <u>brusque</u> manner

    A. foreign

    B. subtle

    C. soft

    D. abrupt

160. <u>depress</u> the key

    A. put away

    B. insert

    C. turn

    D. push down

161. <u>quench</u> your thirst

    A. end

    B. increase

    C. continue

    D. decrease

162. a famous <u>exploit</u>

    A. crime

    B. deed

    C. reputation

    D. game

163. a <u>precipitous</u> incline

    A. gradual
    B. steep
    C. unavoidable
    D. delicate

164. an interesting <u>chronicle</u>

    A. fairy tale
    B. record
    C. time
    D. item

165. that <u>amiable</u> soul

    A. casual
    B. honest
    C. fine
    D. likable

166. her <u>astute</u> mind

    A. shrewd
    B. careful
    C. stupid
    D. astounding

167. to <u>sever</u> contact

    A. cut
    B. maintain
    C. seek
    D. establish

168. the <u>eminent</u> man

    A. wicked
    B. destitute
    C. ancient
    D. outstanding

169. to <u>terminate</u> a contract

    A. end
    B. enter
    C. make
    D. determine

170. to <u>hinder</u> someone

    A. assist
    B. follow
    C. impede
    D. slight

171. a spirit of <u>contention</u>

    A. debate
    B. content
    C. inquiry
    D. calm

172. to <u>concede</u> defeat

    A. suspect
    B. admit
    C. realize
    D. refuse

173. to <u>forego</u> his rights

    A. usurp
    B. insure
    C. insist on
    D. give up

174. your <u>canny</u> guess

    A. uncertain
    B. mistaken
    C. clever
    D. insincere

STOP.

If you finish before time is UP, you may check your work on this section only.
Do not turn to any other section in the test.

MATHEMATICS

64 Questions (45 minutes)

Concepts

Turn to the Mathematics Concepts section of your answer sheet to answer the questions in this section.

Directions: Read each question carefully, then solve the problem to find the correct answer.

---

175. Which of these is the longest length?

  A. 17 inches

  B. 2 feet

  C. 0.5 yards

  D. 14 centimeters

176. Which of the following is *not* a parallelogram?

  A. Rhombus

  B. Square

  C. Rectangle

  D. Triangle

177. Three numbers are added together, and the sum is divided by three. What is the result called?

  A. Mean

  B. Median

  C. Mode

  D. Probability

178. Two objects are weighed on a scale at the same time. One object has a weight of x pounds, and the other has a weight of y pounds. What is their combined weight, in pounds?

  A. $x + y$

  B. xy

  C. $\dfrac{x}{y}$

  D. $2x + 2y$

179. What is the sum of the measures of the angles in a square?

  A. 90

  B. 180

  C. 270

  D. 360

180. How many variables are there in the equation $\dfrac{m}{n} + 2p = 5$?

  A. 0

  B. 1

  C. 3

  D. 5

181. In which of the following types of triangles are all the sides the same length?

  A. Equilateral

  B. Isosceles

  C. Scalene

  D. Right

182. How many centimeters are in 2 meters?

  A. 2

  B. 50

  C. 100

  D. 200

183. There are 8 ounces in a cup, and 2 cups in a pint. How many ounces are in a pint?

    A. 16

    B. 10

    C. 8

    D. 6

184. Three hundred twenty-six million, nine hundred thousand, six hundred nineteen can be expressed numerically as

    A. 3,269,619

    B. 32,690,619

    C. 326,900,619

    D. 326,960,019

185. A number is changed if

    A. 0 is added to it.

    B. 1 is subtracted from it.

    C. it is divided by 1.

    D. it is multiplied by 1.

186. In the number 4,000,400,000, there are

    A. 4 billions and 4 hundred thousands.

    B. 4 millions and 4 thousands.

    C. 4 billions and 4 millions.

    D. 4 millions and 40 thousands.

187. Which is the longest time?

    A. 1,440 minutes

    B. 25 hours

    C. $\frac{1}{2}$ day

    D. 3,600 seconds

188. Find the average of 3, 5, 1, 2, and 9.

    A. 1

    B. 3

    C. 4

    D. 9

189. Find the median of 3, 5, 1, 2, and 9.

    A. 1

    B. 3

    C. 4

    D. 9

190. A contest is held in which two winners are chosen. If 8 people enter the contest, what is each person's probability of being one of the winners?

    A. $\frac{4}{2}$

    B. $\frac{8}{8}$

    C. $\frac{1}{2}$

    D. $\frac{1}{4}$

191. Which of the following has the same value as $1\frac{3}{4}\%$?

    A. 1.75

    B. 0.0175

    C. $\frac{7}{4}$

    D. $\frac{7}{40}$

192. What is the total number of degrees found in angles A and C in the triangle below?

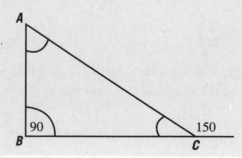

    A. 180°

    B. 100°

    C. 90°

    D. 60°

193. If $x > 9$, then

   A. $x^2 > 80$

   B. $x^2 - 2 = 47$

   C. $x^2 < 65$

   D. $x^2 - 2 < 90$

194. Any number that is divisible by both 3 and 4 is also divisible by

   A. 8

   B. 9

   C. 12

   D. 16

195. Which symbol belongs in the circle? 0.023 O 0.0086

   A. >

   B. <

   C. =

   D. ≅

196. The greatest common factor of 50 and 10 is

   A. 1

   B. 5

   C. 10

   D. 25

197. What number belongs in the box?

$$+ 5 + \square = -3$$

   A. $+8$

   B. $+3$

   C. -3

   D. -8

198. The area of the circle is

   A. 3π sq. cm.

   B. 6π sq. cm.

   C. 9π sq. cm.

   D. 36π sq. cm.

Problem Solving

199. The ratio of 3 quarts to 3 gallons is

   A. 3:1

   B. 1:4

   C. 6:3

   D. 4:1

200. Which pair of values for x and $\square$ will make the following statement true?

$$2x \; \square \; 8$$

   A. $(6, <)$

   B. $(4, >)$

   C. $(0, <)$

   D. $(-3, >)$

201. How many fifths are there in $4\frac{1}{4}$?

   A. $21\frac{1}{4}$

   B. 20

   C. $\frac{17}{20}$

   D. $\frac{4}{85}$

202. Set M = {1,2,3,4}; Set N = {2,5,6}. The intersection of the two sets is

   A. {2}

   B. {1,2,3,4,5}

   C. {3}

   D. {26}

Practice Test 5: HSPT®

203. If Mary is x years old now and her sister is 3 years younger, then what age will her sister be 5 years from now?

A. $x + 5$ years

B. $x + 3$ years

C. $x + 2$ years

D. 8 years

204. Which of the following statements is true?

A. $7 \times 11 > 78$

B. $6 + 4 < 10.5$

C. $8 - 3 = 7 + 4$

D. $16 \div 2 > 9$

205.

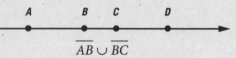

$$\overline{AB} \cup \overline{BC}$$

A. $\overline{BD}$

B. $\overline{BC}$

C. $\overline{AD}$

D. $\overline{AC}$

206. Solve: $2.01 \div 1.02 =$

A. 0.507

B. 1.97

C. 2.0001

D. 3.03

207. Simplify: $-2[3 - 2(1 - 5) - 6]$

A. -10

B. -6

C. 22

D. 34

208. What is 140% of 70?

A. 9.8

B. 98

C. 150

D. 9,800

209. Solve: $6 \div \frac{1}{3} + \frac{2}{3} \times 9 =$

A. $\frac{2}{3}$

B. 24

C. 54

D. 168

210. If $x = -3$, $y = 5$, and $z = -2$, the value of $x(y - z)^2$ is

A. 147

B. 27

C. -27

D. -147

211. Seven is to 21 as $\frac{2}{3}$ is to

A. 3

B. 2

C. $\frac{4}{3}$

D. 1

212. The mean of -10, 6, 0, -3, and 22 is

A. -6

B. -3

C. 2

D. 3

213. Solve for x: $x^2 + 5 = 41$

A. ± 6

B. ± 7

C. ± 8

D. ± 9

214. Find the area of a rectangle with a length of 168 feet and a width of 82 feet.

   A. 13,306 sq. ft.

   B. 13,706 sq. ft.

   C. 13,776 sq. ft.

   D. 13,856 sq. ft.

215. Solve: $63 \div \frac{1}{9} =$

   A. 7

   B. 56

   C. 67

   D. 567

216. Solve: $72.61 \div 0.05 =$

   A. 1.45220

   B. 14.522

   C. 145.220

   D. 1,452.20

217. Increased by 150%, the number 72 becomes

   A. 206

   B. 188

   C. 180

   D. 170

218. Consider this list of numbers: 2, 5, 5, 6, 7. Which of the following is true?

   A. The mean is greater than the median.

   B. The mode is greater than the mean.

   C. The mean, median, and mode are all equal.

   D. The median is greater than the mode and the mean.

219. A class is voting for a class president and a class vice president. If there are 10 students running for president, and 7 students running for vice president, how many different combinations of president and vice president are possible?

   A. 17

   B. 70

   C. 77

   D. 170

220. A rectangle has a length of $x + 3$, and a width of $x - 1$. If $x = 2$, what is the perimeter of the rectangle?

   A. 10

   B. 12

   C. 18

   D. 21

221. If John studies for his math test, there is an 80% chance he will get an A. If he studies, what is the probability that he will not get an A?

   A. 10%

   B. 20%

   C. 50%

   D. 80%

222. The ratio of teachers to students in a certain school is 1:12. If there are 16 teachers in the school, how many students are there?

   A. 16

   B. 176

   C. 192

   D. 202

223. The legend on a trail map indicates that 1.2 inches represents 50 feet. How many feet does 6 inches represent?

   A. 200
   B. 250
   C. 360
   D. 400

224. A department store marks up its clothing 75% over cost. If it sells khaki pants for $17, how much did the store pay for them?

   A. $1.12
   B. $9.71
   C. $11.20
   D. $17.50

225.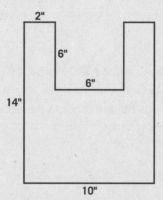

   Note: In the figure above, assume that any angle which appears to be a right angle *is* a right angle.

   The perimeter of the figure above is

   A. 38 in.
   B. 38 sq. in.
   C. 46 sq. in.
   D. 60 in.

226. The area of the figure above is

   A. 104 sq. in.
   B. 120 sq. in.
   C. 240 sq. in.
   D. 276 sq. in.

227. The charge for a long-distance call was $1.56 for the first 3 minutes and $0.22 for each additional minute. What was the total charge for a 16-minute call?

   A. $5.80
   B. $5.08
   C. $4.42
   D. $2.86

228. The winner of a race received $\frac{1}{3}$ of the total purse. The third-place finisher received $\frac{1}{3}$ of the winner's share. If the winner's share was $2,700, what was the total purse?

   A. $8,100
   B. $2,700
   C. $1,800
   D. $900

229. As a train departs from station A, it has 12 empty seats, 14 seated passengers, and 4 standing passengers. At the next stop, 8 passengers get off, 13 passengers get on, and everyone on the train takes a seat. How many empty seats are there?

   A. 1
   B. 2
   C. 3
   D. 4

230. In order to increase revenues, a municipality considers raising its sales tax from 5% to 8%. How much more will it cost to buy a $250 television set if the 8% sales tax is approved?

   A. $7.50
   B. $10
   C. $12.50
   D. $15.50

231.   5 gallons 2 quarts 1 pint
     −1 gallon 3 quarts
     ─────────────────────

     A. 4 gallons 9 quarts 1 pint
     B. 4 gallons 2 quarts 1 pint
     C. 3 gallons 3 quarts 1 pint
     D. 2 gallons 6 quarts 2 pints

232. The number of phones in Adelaide, Australia, is 48,000. If this represents 12.8 phones per 100 persons, the population of Adelaide to the nearest thousand is

     A. 128,000
     B. 375,000
     C. 378,000
     D. 556,000

233. A carpenter needs four boards, each 2 feet 9 inches long. If wood is sold only by the foot, how many feet must he buy?

     A. 9
     B. 10
     C. 11
     D. 12

234. A square has an area of 49 sq. in. The number of inches in its perimeter is

     A. 7
     B. 28
     C. 35
     D. 98

235. Aluminum bronze consists of copper and aluminum, usually in the ratio of 10:1 by weight. If an object made of this alloy weighs 77 pounds, how many pounds of aluminum does it contain?

     A. 7
     B. 7.7
     C. 10
     D. 70

236. Mr. Wilson makes a weekly salary of $175 plus 8% commission on his sales. What will his income be for a week in which he makes sales totaling $1,025?

     A. $247
     B. $257
     C. $260.50
     D. $267

237. A house was valued at $83,000 and insured for 80% of that amount. Find the yearly premium if it is figured at $0.45 per $100 of value.

     A. $83.80
     B. $252.63
     C. $298.80
     D. $664

238. A group left on a trip at 8:50 a.m. and reached its destination at 3:30 p.m. How long, in hours and minutes, did the trip take?

     A. 3 hours 10 minutes
     B. 4 hours 40 minutes
     C. 5 hours 10 minutes
     D. 6 hours 40 minutes

STOP.

If you finish before time is UP, you may check your work on this section only.
Do not turn to any other section in the test.

LANGUAGE

60 Questions (25 minutes)

Turn to the Language section of your answer sheet to answer the questions in this section.

> **Directions:** In questions 239–267, look for errors in capitalization, punctuation, or usage. Mark the answer choice that contains the error. If there are no mistakes, mark D on your answer sheet

239. **A.** Alexis hit a home run "her tenth one this year" to win the championship game.
   B. Rhianna spent all of her savings on a new couch for her living room.
   C. When should people start thinking about college and the future?
   D. *(No mistakes)*

240. **A.** Joris read the *daily cryer* newspaper each morning.
   B. Mr. Judson prepared the annual quarterly report for his presentation.
   C. Gemma ordered the cod entrée from the restaurant's expansive menu options.
   D. *(No mistakes)*

241. **A.** This year's corn maze was extremely difficult to figure out.
   B. Have you ever seen someone run as fast as Caryn can!
   C. There were not enough pockets to hold Harry's stuff.
   D. *(No mistakes)*

242. **A.** The greedy lion ate an entire sirloin steak in just a few seconds.
   B. Sari yearned to travel to America and see the grand canyon.
   C. Have you ever cooked a turkey for Thanksgiving?
   D. *(No mistakes)*

243. **A.** Where in the world did you leave your gloves?
   B. The dog licked its chops after the meal.
   C. "Oh, that's terrible!" Sally cried.
   D. *(No mistakes)*

244. **A.** Detroit is the center of the automobile industry.
   B. Governor Jones was an officer in the Navy.
   C. Their making a terrible mistake.
   D. *(No mistakes)*

245. **A.** How is your cold?
   B. The rabbit got sick and died.
   C. Who's book is this?
   D. *(No mistakes)*

246. **A.** That is a pretty dress, isn't it, Sheila?
   B. How old is your pet, Alfie?
   C. Why are you so tired?
   D. *(No mistakes)*

247. **A.** Katie's final exam grade was the highest in her geometry class.
   B. Anderson's favorite movie of all time is *Star Wars*.
   C. Sherman thinks the Bronx Zoo were his favorite place to visit.
   D. *(No mistakes)*

248. **A.** Don told us where he'd bought his coat.

    B. What's your name, little girl?

    C. Yellowstone is run by the National Park Service.

    D. *(No mistakes)*

249. **A.** How are you, Jim?

    B. I'm fine, thank you.

    C. Did you notice that John left early?

    D. *(No mistakes)*

250. **A.** Ross felt butterflies in his stomach before the interview.

    B. A trip to Chicago in the spring is an absolutely wonderful idea.

    C. Jocelyn purchased; a gigantic piñata for; her birthday party on Sunday.

    D. *(No mistakes)*

251. **A.** Will, you're parents are very nice.

    B. Ted's family is buying a boat.

    C. My father is a textbook publisher.

    D. *(No mistakes)*

252. **A.** What is the matter with Sam's leg?

    B. The first show is at 2:30, isn't it?

    C. How much is your plane ticket?

    D. *(No mistakes)*

253. **A.** The award was given jointly to Deirdre and I.

    B. John asked if he might go home early.

    C. Cats and dogs sometimes play well together.

    D. *(No mistakes)*

254. **A.** The explosion at the "fireworks factory" was unbelievably loud.

    B. Frederico has basil and cilantro growing on his kitchen windowsill.

    C. Kevin knew it was time to change the water in the aquarium tank.

    D. *(No mistakes)*

255. **A.** She and I consider ourselves to be best friends.

    B. Do you know which of the spellings of *too* means *also*?

    C. There is a narrow path beside the railroad track.

    D. *(No mistakes)*

256. **A.** We would have called you if we'd known.

    B. May I open my eyes now?

    C. My brother-in-law lives in Butte, Montana.

    D. *(No mistakes)*

257. **A.** Actually, ice hockey is exciting to watch.

    B. Janet plays guitar almost as well like Tom.

    C. Does Dave like to talk to Debby Ann?

    D. *(No mistakes)*

258. **A.** Ken will graduate from Stanford this June.

    B. Jack is learning Kay to draw.

    C. Before we knew it, the class was over.

    D. *(No mistakes)*

259. **A.** When will you know what the assignment is?

    B. You should of seen the crowd at Paul's yesterday.

    C. Joe will be stationed at Fort Benning, Georgia.

    D. *(No mistakes)*

260. A. Unfortunately, the rug delivery was delayed by six days.

 B. The bright lights in the auditorium gave Yasmine a headache.

 C. Please include your (complete name) on the application form.

 D. *(No mistakes)*

261. A. We have already sold too many tickets.

 B. If I knew the answer, I would be rich now.

 C. The artist works less hours than the carpenter.

 D. *(No mistakes)*

262. A. Everyone must sign their name on the register.

 B. I am all ready, but the taxi is not here yet.

 C. I do not believe that I have only two choices.

 D. *(No mistakes)*

263. A. If you don't know the answer, don't raise your hand.

 B. The baby is playing in her crib.

 C. Jeff is the taller of my three sons.

 D. *(No mistakes)*

264. A. Neither Lisa nor Liz has made the honor roll.

 B. I have much more free time than you.

 C. Everyone wants to have his own way.

 D. *(No mistakes)*

265. A. Piper loved all the natural light that flooded into her new apartment.

 B. Marianna has packed her, favorite novel, for a day at the beach.

 C. Jessica happily ordered coffee and pecan pie for dessert.

 D. *(No mistakes)*

266. A. The sun set at 5:15 this afternoon.

 B. Mary set the table for dinner yesterday.

 C. Please set those books over there, Jim.

 D. *(No mistakes)*

267. A. The horse ran swiftly and won the race.

 B. I feel badly that I cannot attend your wedding.

 C. Most birds and some people fly south for the winter.

 D. *(No mistakes)*

Directions: In questions 268–278, mark the sentence that demonstrates <u>correct</u> usage.

---

268. A. Perry stacked the bundle of envelopes on the desk in his office.

 B. There was an empty parking spot next to supermarket entrance.

 C. Painting that hung on Regina's bedroom wall fell to the floor.

 D. Shawn did not make single noise for fear of waking up his brother

269. A. Brendan placed his new bowling trophy on his bedroom dresser.

 B. Have our ever seen a comet race across the night sky?

 C. What is the best time for they to pick you up for the dance?

 D. Sharlene couldn't wait for its book to arrive in the mail.

270. A. The newborn puppy scampered timid through the house.

    B. Bevyn waited nervously for the midterm exam to begin.

    C. Hannah sat anxious in traffic, late for her first day of work.

    D. I will happy take that last slice of chocolate cream cake.

271. A. Matthew didn't think it was fair when our parents took away his skateboard.

    B. Harvey was never able to improve our grade in chemistry this year.

    C. The squirmy pile of puppies jumped excitedly from its bed.

    D. Have you seen the way Carrie had her hair styled yesterday?

272. A. He decided to wear leather jacket to his first day of school.

    B. Dan went to store and purchased a bag of peanuts.

    C. The New York City is my favorite place to visit.

    D. I wanted to get a pizza for dinner, but I had no money.

273. A. Can you believed how tired Heidi was during her speech in class?

    B. Will you be gone to the antique fair at the church this weekend?

    C. Celeste is determined to finish reading her mystery novel today.

    D. The store having a sale on light bulbs and cooking utensils today.

274. A. The lightning bolt crackled and shot across the rain-filled sky?

    B. Nadine was really nervous about her upcoming dental appointment?

    C. Will Douglas rally and come from behind to win the game?

    D. Did you pick up the mail yet.

275. A. Michael was short on time, yet he decided to skip a visit to the mall.

    B. Chuck was a real connoisseur of both vintage automobiles or motorcycles.

    C. Peggy really wanted to go to the hair salon today, but she was too busy.

    D. Melissa wanted either sushi and tacos for dinner after work.

276. A. The happy crowd booed their favorite band as they took the stage.

    B. Congrats on your big win today!

    C. The boring beige dress had plenty of zing!

    D. The guest speaker yelled "oops!" when he walked effortlessly to the podium.

277. A. Tanisha went outside of the library to get out of the rain.

    B. Brianna sat in the chair and put her feet carefully beyond the desk.

    C. Oliver climbed the ladder and stood on top of the roof.

    D. Fabian reclined on the ground and looked down at the night sky.

278. A. Belle didn't not borrow the library book, as she didn't have her library card.

    B. Lucas couldn't go to the movies tonight, so he binge-watched his favorite sci-fi series.

    C. Angelina was grounded for her poor grades, so she couldn't not got to the party.

    D. Did you see the parrot that Eddie didn't have on his shoulder at the park?

Directions: For questions 279–288, look for mistakes in spelling only.

279. A. Clarence Darrow was a distinguished trial lawyer.
  B. Apparantly, Suzy couldn't find her umbrella.
  C. Alice will be married next Wednesday.
  D. (No mistakes)

280. A. Are you sure you can complete the assignment on time?
  B. The entire crew worked very efficently.
  C. Mary went to the library yesterday.
  D. (No mistakes)

281. A. It occured to me that I should write home.
  B. "What a dreadful comparison," Ida remarked.
  C. Bob's temperature was back to normal yesterday.
  D. (No mistakes)

282. A. Mary Lou is eligible for the committee.
  B. Discussion and argument are not the same thing.
  C. The chemist anayzed the solution in his laboratory.
  D. (No mistakes)

283. A. My brother's going out for athletics next year.
  B. "This is a small token of my esteem," he told his teacher.
  C. Mary dropped her handkerchief in the corridor.
  D. (No mistakes)

284. A. Tyler noticed a mispelled word in the book he just purchased.
  B. The steering committee couldn't wait to vote on the new referendum.
  C. The inn was unable to accommodate the large group of tourists.
  D. (No mistakes)

285. A. The schedule is posted on the bulletin board in the hall.
  B. Don discribed the play with sweeping gestures.
  C. Occasionally our class runs over into the next period.
  D. (No mistakes)

286. A. Pete perfers to sit by the door.
  B. Joy has a very agreeable personality.
  C. We struggle with ourselves to overcome our faults.
  D. (No mistakes)

287. A. Did you hear the announcement about the picnic?
  B. While the initial cost is high, the maintenance is low.
  C. Jan's coat is similar to mine.
  D. (No mistakes)

288. A. Al said it was not neccessary to read all of the plays.
  B. It's disappointing to have missed the picture.
  C. The original order was difficult to decipher.
  D. (No mistakes)

Directions: For questions 289–298, review the text and look for errors in composition.

289. Choose the best word or words to join the thoughts together.

I left my books at school; _____ I won't be able to do my homework.

- **A.** therefore,
- **B.** nevertheless,
- **C.** however,
- **D.** None of these

290. Choose the best word or words to join the thoughts together.

That area is experiencing great economic hardship; _____ its unemployment rate is very high.

- **A.** for example,
- **B.** in contrast,
- **C.** suprisingly,
- **D.** None of these

291. Choose the group of words that best completes this sentence.

After a hard day at work, _____

- **A.** sleep was something Mary did very well.
- **B.** Mary slept very well.
- **C.** Mary slept well afterwards.
- **D.** sleeping was what Mary did.

292. Which of these sentences expresses the idea most clearly?

- **A.** Tom, every morning at breakfast, the paper he liked to read.
- **B.** At breakfast every morning it was the paper that Tom liked to read.
- **C.** At breakfast, reading the paper was what Tom liked to do every morning.
- **D.** Tom liked to read the paper every morning at breakfast.

293. Which of these expresses the idea most clearly?

- **A.** In order to hear her favorite musician perform, 50 miles it was that she drove.
- **B.** She drove 50 miles in order to hear her favorite musician perform.
- **C.** She drove, in order to hear her favorite musician perform, 50 miles.
- **D.** Her favorite musician performed, and she drove 50 miles in order to hear him perform.

294. Which of these best fits under the topic "History of the Automobile"?

- **A.** Cars require a great deal of attention and care in order to prevent problems from developing.
- **B.** The legal driving age varies from one state to another.
- **C.** The invention of the automobile cannot be credited to any one person.
- **D.** None of these

295. Which of these sentences expresses the idea most clearly?

- **A.** His brother, and Stuart, were eager to experience—never on an airplane voyaging in the skies.
- **B.** Stuart and his brother had never been on an airplane, and they were eager to experience their first voyage in the skies.
- **C.** Voyage in the skies? Eager Stuart and his brother haven't. They've never been on an airplane.
- **D.** Never on an airplane, never voyaging—in the skies—Stuart or his brother have never had this eager experience.

296. Which sentence does *not* belong in the paragraph?

(1) Everyone in the class was looking forward to the Halloween party. (2) Five students had difficulty with their math homework from the previous day. (3) Each student had prepared a snack to bring. (4) The costumes included four ghosts, five space creatures, and two pumpkins.

A. Sentence 1

B. Sentence 2

C. Sentence 3

D. Sentence 4

297. Which topic is best for a one-paragraph theme?

A. How to Open Your Own Business

B. Child Psychology

C. The Geography of Asia and Africa

D. None of these

298. Where should the sentence, "The government has set up laws restricting or forbidding the hunting of certain animals," be placed in the paragraph below?

(1) Many animal species are now becoming or have recently become extinct. (2) Both government and private efforts are being made to protect those species currently in danger. (3) It has also attempted to educate the public about the problem.

A. Between sentences 1 and 2

B. Between sentences 2 and 3

C. After sentence 3

D. The sentence does not fit in this paragraph.

ANSWER KEYS AND EXPLANATIONS

Verbal Skills

1. C	13. D	25. B	37. C	49. A
2. D	14. C	26. C	38. C	50. D
3. D	15. C	27. D	39. C	51. B
4. B	16. A	28. B	40. B	52. B
5. D	17. B	29. C	41. D	53. B
6. D	18. C	30. D	42. A	54. B
7. A	19. A	31. A	43. D	55. A
8. D	20. B	32. A	44. C	56. B
9. B	21. A	33. B	45. C	57. D
10. A	22. C	34. D	46. D	58. A
11. D	23. D	35. B	47. A	59. B
12. C	24. C	36. D	48. C	60. B

1. **The correct answer is C.** Ovens, toasters, and microwave ovens are all types of appliances that are used for cooking. *Cook* (choice C) does not share this common characteristic with the other words.

2. **The correct answer is D.** The common feature among three of the answer choices is that they're all verbs—*run*, *walk*, and *jog*. *Sneaker* (choice D) is a noun, not a verb.

3. **The correct answer is D.** This is a cause-effect relationship. The effect of lightening red is pink; the effect of lightening black is gray.

4. **The correct answer is B.** Because the first two statements are true, and Karen reads faster than Ann, she must also read faster than Sue.

5. **The correct answer is D.** *Create* means "to bring into existence" or to "invent."

6. **The correct answer is D.** The analogy illustrates a noun-adjective relationship.

7. **The correct answer is A.** *Quality* is a general classification. The other choices are examples of good qualities.

8. **The correct answer is D.** The analogy establishes a part-whole relationship. Sand is part of the beach; black dirt is part of a farm.

9. **The correct answer is B.** *Time* is a general classification. The other choices are measures of time.

10. **The correct answer is A.** A *salamander* is an amphibian resembling a lizard.

11. **The correct answer is D.** *Arrogant* means "proud" or "haughty."

12. **The correct answer is C.** The first part of the analogy establishes opposite directions. The opposite direction of left is right (choice C).

13. **The correct answer is D.** The analogy establishes a part-whole relationship. One is half of two; three is half of six.

14. **The correct answer is C.** *Add* is a function. The others are general classifications of symbols.

15. **The correct answer is C.** From the first two statements, it is only certain that Peter is the shortest of the three boys. The relationship between Paul and John cannot be determined.

16. **The correct answer is A.** A mature fruit is one that is tender and sweet, or ripe.

17. **The correct answer is B.** Other synonyms for *gossamer* are *insubstantial*, *delicate*, or *tenuous*.

18. **The correct answer is C.** *Coddle* means "to treat with extreme care," or "pamper."

19. **The correct answer is A.** The first part of the analogy establishes a type of item (books) and a place where they're usually found (libraries). Rides are usually found in carnivals.

20. **The correct answer is B.** The analogy establishes an object-purpose relationship. The purpose of a director is to lead a choir; the purpose of a coach is to lead a team.

21. **The correct answer is A.** *Diversify* means "to make or become more varied."

22. **The correct answer is C.** The first two statements indicate no relationship between Harry and Ralph; therefore, the third statement is uncertain.

23. **The correct answer is D.** A superficial wound is a surface wound, or "shallow."

24. **The correct answer is C.** Although Shelley cannot throw a javelin farther than Liandra, we are not told who took part in the javelin-throwing contest, so we cannot be certain who won.

25. **The correct answer is B.** Someone who is bellicose is eager to fight, or "combative."

26. **The correct answer is C.** A sadistic remark is intended to inflict pain, or to be hurtful.

27. **The correct answer is D.** A dormitory is only one part of a school, university, or college.

28. **The correct answer is B.** *Truncate* means "to shorten or to cut off."

29. **The correct answer is C.** Someone who is facetious is clever and humorous.

30. **The correct answer is D.** An indigent person is impoverished, or needy.

31. **The correct answer is A.** The analogy establishes a part-whole relationship. A leg is a part of a table on which the table rests; a wheel is a part of a car on which the car rests.

32. **The correct answer is A.** A dungeon is a place where people may be forced to stay. The other choices are places in which people choose to live.

33. **The correct answer is B.** We are told early on that "Bishop's house is the largest on his street." We are also told that "Arianna and Bishop live on the same street." Therefore, even though Arianna's house is much larger than Terrence's house, it is false that Arianna's house is the largest on Oakville Lane, since Bishop's house is the largest on his street, and he lives on the same street as Arianna.

34. **The correct answer is D.** *Punishment* is a general classification. The other choices describe specific types or places of punishment.

35. **The correct answer is B.** *Refuse* means to decline; the opposite is *accept*.

36. **The correct answer is D.** The analogy establishes an object-user relationship. Ink is used in a pen when applied; paint is used on a brush when applied.

37. **The correct answer is C.** *Acquire* means "to gain possession of," which is the opposite of *release*.

38. **The correct answer is C.** Though the first two statements are considered true, they do not provide any information as to the direct relationship between rivers A and C.

39. **The correct answer is C.** *Scant* means "meager," which is the opposite of *abundant*.

40. **The correct answer is B.** *Pinnacle* means "peak," which is the opposite of *base*.

41. **The correct answer is D.** The analogy establishes a part-whole relationship. The captain is the part of a team that guides the team; the

manager is the part of an office that guides the office.

42. **The correct answer is A.** A window may be covered by the other three choices.

43. **The correct answer is D.** *Corpulent* means "obese," which is the opposite of *slender.*

44. **The correct answer is C.** *Naive* means "lacking experience or knowledge," which is the opposite of *sophisticated.*

45. **The correct answer is C.** A glove is a hand covering; all the other choices are head coverings.

46. **The correct answer is D.** A podium is positioned at the front of an auditorium or theater. The other choices represent those who face the podium.

47. **The correct answer is A.** To pledge is to promise.

48. **The correct answer is C.** A depression is a low spot or a hollow; the opposite is a hill.

49. **The correct answer is A.** Because the first two statements are true, and all the fruits cost more than apples, apples must cost the least.

50. **The correct answer is D.** A fir tree is an evergreen; all of the other trees are deciduous, which means they lose their leaves.

51. **The correct answer is B.** *Diminish* means "to decrease," which is the opposite of *augment.*

52. **The correct answer is B.** Because the first two statements are true, Jay's batting average must be higher than Tom's.

53. **The correct answer is B.** *Abandon* means "to give up," which is the opposite of *keep.*

54. **The correct answer is B.** *Feasible* is an attribute of abstract things or ideas. The other choices are generally attributes applied to concrete objects regarding texture or firmness.

55. **The correct answer is A.** Because the first two statements are true and C is north of A, it must also be north of B.

56. **The correct answer is B.** Cotton is a vegetable product; leather, wool, and fur are animal products.

57. **The correct answer is D.** A seam is a type of closing. The other choices are things for opening and closing.

58. **The correct answer is A.** *Dwindle* means "to grow smaller."

59. **The correct answer is B.** Oxygen, helium, and gold are elements; water is a compound of hydrogen and oxygen.

60. **The correct answer is B.** Because the first two statements are true, and the third statement is in direct opposition to the first, it cannot be true.

Quantitative Skills

61. B	72. D	83. D	93. D	103. A
62. C	73. C	84. B	94. A	104. B
63. D	74. D	85. D	95. D	105. C
64. A	75. C	86. C	96. A	106. A
65. C	76. B	87. D	97. B	107. C
66. A	77. B	88. C	98. A	108. A
67. C	78. B	89. C	99. B	109. D
68. C	79. B	90. D	100. A	110. C
69. B	80. D	91. B	101. B	111. A
70. D	81. C	92. D	102. D	112. C
71. B	82. C			

61. **The correct answer is B.** If you write the direction and amount of change between the numbers of the series, you see that the pattern of the series is −1, −2, −1, −3, −1, −4, …. The next step is −1; 11 − 1 = 10.

62. **The correct answer is C.** The relationships are clearly visible. Just read and examine carefully.

63. **The correct answer is D.** Evaluate each separately:

    A. = $(5 + 8)^2 = 13^2 = 169$

    B. = $5^2 + 8^2 = 25 + 64 = 89$

    C. = $2(5) + 2(8) = 10 + 16 = 26$

    So, C is less than B, and B is less than A.

64. **The correct answer is A.** Start by calculating 60% of 40, which equals 24. Then subtract five, to get 24 − 5 = 19.

65. **The correct answer is C.** The pattern is +2, −4, +2, −4, and so on. The next step is 44 + 2 = 46.

66. **The correct answer is A.** The letters in each term move forward by one, and the + and − alternate. The next three terms are F−, G+, H−.

67. **The correct answer is C.** Add the numbers within the brackets and divide by 5 to get the average; 6 + 12 + 4 + 41 + 7 = 70 ÷ 5 = 14.

The question asks for twice that amount, so multiply to get the final answer; 14 × 2 = 28.

68. **The correct answer is C.** The series so far is: −2, −2, −3, −3, −4, −4. Next should come −5, −5, which, when applied to the last number in the series, results in 24 − 5 = 19, and 19 − 5 = 14.

69. **The correct answer is B.** The pattern is to add 7, then add 2, add 7, then add 2. So, the next number is 52 + 7 = 59.

70. **The correct answer is D.** Angle C is a right angle (90°). The three angles of a triangle must add up to 180°. Therefore, the sum of the other two angles is equal to 90°.

71. **The correct answer is B.**

$$6 \times 4 = 24$$
$$\frac{2}{3}x = 24$$
$$x = 24\left(\frac{3}{2}\right)$$
$$x = 36$$

72. **The correct answer is D.** Let x denote the number. Then, translate the number sentence into the equation $\frac{x}{\frac{1}{4}} = 79 - 3$.

Solve as follows:

$$\frac{x}{\frac{1}{4}} = 79 - 3$$

$$4x = 76$$

$$x = 19$$

73. **The correct answer is C.** Count the shaded areas, taking note of the fact that some areas are larger than others. Then choose your answer by inspection and careful reading. If it is visually easier, you could also count the non-shaded areas, noting that fewer non-shaded area means more shaded areas.

74. **The correct answer is D.** The first thing to do with this question is to convert $3\frac{5}{8}$ to an improper fraction. $(3 \times 8) + 5 = 29$, so we get the improper fraction $\frac{29}{8}$. The reciprocal of $\frac{29}{8}$ is $\frac{8}{29}$.

75. **The correct answer is C.** Doing the math, B = 0.858. The decimal form of C = 0.875, which makes it equal to A. Now you can see that there is only one true statement.

76. **The correct answer is B.** First perform the subtraction, and then divide by 7; $69 - 6 = 63 \div 7 = 9$.

77. **The correct answer is B.** Start by calculating the three fraction problems; A is 4, B is 6, and C is 4. Now just be careful when reviewing the answer options.

78. **The correct answer is B.** Each of the figures is divided into eight equal wedges. By counting the shaded wedges, we see that figure A and figure C both have five wedges shaded, while figure B has only four.

79. **The correct answer is B.** Sometimes you must shift gears. Most series are based upon addition and subtraction but not all. You cannot make sense of this series if you stick to the + 8 with which you probably started

out. The relationship between 9 and 18 and between 15 and 30 should make you think of multiplication.

The series reads: ×2, –7, ×2, –7, ×2, –7, ... The next step would be $11 \times 2 = 22$. Since we are provided with the next term in the series, we can confirm the answer; $22 - 7 = 15$.

80. **The correct answer is D.** Find the factors for both numbers.

42: 1, 2, 3, 6, 7, 14, 21   39: 1, 3, 13

The only shared factor besides 1 is 3.

81. **The correct answer is C.** Each letter is repeated a number of times that increases by one for each letter. A is repeated once, B is repeated twice, C is repeated three times. D should be repeated four times, so the next term is D3.

82. **The correct answer is C.** First find the average; $12 + 87 + 72 + 41 = 212 \div 4 = 53$. Next, determine how much this figure exceeds 25 by subtracting; $53 - 25 = 28$.

83. **The correct answer is D.** The series +1, –2, +1, –3, +1, –4 now continues with +1, so add $18 + 1 = 19$.

84. **The correct answer is B.** Read each answer choice, and then count and reason carefully. There is no special trick for this kind of question, apart from being alert and following the question closely.

85. **The correct answer is D.** Each term is double the previous term, plus 1. Since $2 \times 31 = 62$, the next term is $62 + 1 = 63$.

86. **The correct answer is C.** There are two pints in a quart, and four quarts in a gallon. To find the number of pints, multiply $17 \times 2 = 34$. To find the number of gallons, divide $17 \div 4 = 6.25$. Be certain that both terms in your answer choice are correct.

87. **The correct answer is D.** By completing the last of the three options, $(2 \times 6)(6 \times 2)$, we are left with $12 \times 12 = 144$. Since 144 is

greater than the other numbers, the only correct answer is choice D.

88. **The correct answer is C.** By counting the shaded wedges corresponding to each letter, you can see that section A has four wedges, while section C has three, D has two, and B has one.

89. **The correct answer is C.** First, find the product of $8 \times 4 = 32$. Multiply this product by 3 and then subtract 30 to get the result; $32 \times 3 = 96$, and $96 - 30 = 66$.

90. **The correct answer is D.** The values of each expression are A = $3^2 + 4 = 13$, B = $4^2 - 4 = 12$, C = $2^3 + 4 = 12$. A is greater than B and C, which are equal.

91. **The correct answer is B.** The series may be interpreted as a repetition of +0.125 or as increasing decimals of $\frac{1}{8}, \frac{2}{8}, \frac{3}{8}$, and so on. Taking the figure from the end of the series, we find that $0.500 + 0.125 = 0.625$.

92. **The correct answer is D.** Count, then read carefully. If you find it visually confusing to count the dark squares, it may be easier to count the white squares and subtract from the total number of squares, which is 15.

93. **The correct answer is D.** The denominator increases by 1, then 2, then 3, then 4. For the next term, the denominator should increase by 5, resulting in $11 + 5 = 16$.

94. **The correct answer is A.** The easiest way to find the solution is to try out each of the answers.

$$\frac{9}{16} \div \frac{3}{4} = \frac{9}{16} \times \frac{4}{3} = \frac{3}{4}; \frac{5}{8} \div \frac{3}{4} = \frac{5}{6};$$
$$\frac{7}{16} \div \frac{3}{4} = \frac{7}{12}; \frac{3}{4} \div \frac{3}{4} = 1.$$

95. **The correct answer is D.** 0.8 and 80% are equal, but $\frac{8}{10}$% is only 0.008. Now it's easy.

96. **The correct answer is A.** The order of the lengths of the line segments, shortest to longest, is B, C, A, D. Only choice D requires more information, but the sum of both sides is $8 + 17 = 25$, which is not equal to the length of line segment D, so choice D is incorrect.

97. **The correct answer is B.** You should see quite readily that the series is based on squares followed by their positive number square roots in descending order. The missing number is the square of 7, which is 49.

98. **The correct answer is A.** The mean is also the average; combine the data points, then divide the sum by the number of data points to get an average, or mean, of 12.8. For the median, put the data points in order and identify the data point in the middle of the set, which is 9. For mode, find the data point that appears most often within the set, which is also 9.

99. **The correct answer is B.** After you look beyond the first two numbers, you can see that the progression is ×3, repeat the number, ×3, repeat the number, ×3, repeat the number. We pick up the series at $27 \times 3 = 81$. Then repeat the number 81. Then, $81 \times 3 = 243$.

100. **The correct answer is A.** If $\frac{3}{8}x = 9$, then $3x = 72$ and $x = \frac{72}{3}$. So, $x = 24$.

$$83\frac{1}{3}\% , \text{ or } \frac{5}{6}, \text{ of } 24 = 20.$$

101. **The correct answer is B.** The size of the angle is easily read on the arc of the protractor. A = 70°, B = 60°, and C = 50°. A right angle is 90°. Now, plug the angle sizes into the statements to find the answer.

102. **The correct answer is D.** To convert a number to scientific notation, move the decimal point to the left until you have a number between 1 and 10; for 27,840,000,000 we get

2.784. Count how many spaces you move to the decimal point (ignoring the commas), and that becomes your exponent; in this case it's 10. Then multiply your first number by 10 raised to your exponent.

$$2.784 \times 10^{10} = 27,840,000,000$$

103. **The correct answer is A.** Don't be thrown by the negative numbers. The series is: +5, +2, +5, +2. Next comes +5, so $-5 + 5 = 0$.

104. **The correct answer is B.** Let x represent the number. We translate the number sentence into the following equation:

$75 - x = 2(9 + 3)$. Solve for x, as follows:

$$
\begin{aligned}
75 - x &= 2(12) \\
75 - x &= 24 \\
75 - 24 &= x \\
51 &= x
\end{aligned}
$$

105. **The correct answer is C.** This is a simple ÷ 2 series. The decimals make it a bit confusing. The next number in the series would be $.0025 \div 2 = 0.0125$

106. **The correct answer is A.** First, calculate $\frac{5}{8}$ of 96, which equals 60. Then subtract 12 to get the final answer; $60 - 12 = 48$.

107. **The correct answer is C.** A is 21¢, B is 28¢, and C is 25¢. Replace letters with money amounts and you will see that choice C is the only true statement.

108. **The correct answer is A.** The progress of the series is +3, so the next value is $18 + 3 = 21$. However, in the small segment that we see, the series alternates two Roman numerals and two Arabic numbers. Having no reason to suppose that this alternation will change later in the series, we must assume that the next entry will be a Roman numeral. Hence, XXI is the correct form for the next number in the series.

109. **The correct answer is D.** This is a ÷2 series, which you might find somewhat hard to visualize in the fraction form. Rename the improper fractions as whole numbers to make this clear:

$$\frac{16}{2} = 8; \frac{8}{2} = 4; \frac{8}{4} = 2; \frac{8}{8} = 1; \frac{8}{16} = \frac{1}{2}$$

Picking up the series where it leaves off, the correct answer is $\frac{8}{16} \div 2$, or $\frac{8}{32}$.

$$\frac{8}{16} \div 2 = \frac{8}{16} \times \frac{1}{2} = \frac{8}{32}$$

110. **The correct answer is C.** A is 95, B is 1.95, and C is 95. Work with the numbers instead of the letters to find the answer.

111. **The correct answer is A.** This is another instance in which it is easiest to try out the answers. Multiply each answer choice by 40%. In this case, however, 40% of 150 is 60, and when we decrease 150 by 40%, we arrive at the desired answer, $150 - 60 = 90$. Because the first choice works, there is no reason to continue. Choices B and C, being less than 90, could not possibly be correct. If you wanted to be doubly sure (and if you had spare time), you could try 40% of $145 = 58$, and continue with $145 - 58 = 87$, which is not 90.

112. **The correct answer is C.** The pattern being established is as follows: −8, repeat the number, −6, repeat the number, −4, repeat the number. Logically, the next step is −2, repeat the number; $8 - 2 = 6$. Then repeat the 6.

Reading

Comprehension

113. C	121. C	129. D	137. A	145. A
114. C	122. C	130. C	138. D	146. A
115. C	123. C	131. B	139. C	147. B
116. D	124. A	132. D	140. A	148. A
117. D	125. D	133. C	141. B	149. B
118. C	126. B	134. A	142. B	150. D
119. B	127. C	135. B	143. B	151. A
120. D	128. C	136. D	144. C	152. A

113. **The correct answer is C.** Sentences 3 and 4 say the mantle has four layers, all of which are between 250 and 1,000 miles thick, so the combined layers of the mantle, at minimum, would be 1,750 miles thick. This minimum is larger than the other layers. Sentence 6 says the outer core (choice B) is a little over 1,200 miles thick, and the inner core (choice D) is slightly less than 800 miles. The crust (choice A) is only about 20 miles thick.

114. **The correct answer is C.** The answer is in sentence 1: "Our planet Earth is divided into seven separate layers."

115. **The correct answer is C.** This is an inference question. Based on sentence 7, we know that both the speed and direction of earthquake waves vary. We do not know from this information if choice A is true, so we must assume that C is the best answer.

116. **The correct answer is D.** Because of the nature of the information, it would be found in both an encyclopedia and a science book.

117. **The correct answer is D.** This answer is determined by the entire passage, which describes the layers in order. The answer can be verified by eliminating choices A, B, and C.

118. **The correct answer is C.** *Vary* most closely means "range." *Stabilize* means "to steady," so choice A is incorrect. Choice B may

be tempting because the thickness does increase, but *increase* is not a synonym for *vary.* Choice D is incorrect because to arbitrate means "to judge."

119. **The correct answer is B.** This is an inference question. Though not specifically stated, the answer can be assumed based on sentence 2 and the phrase "appears to be."

120. **The correct answer is D.** The last sentence of the paragraph states that "both temperature and pressure are much greater at the core than at the crust."

121. **The correct answer is C.** In this passage, *slightly* most nearly means "a little."

122. **The correct answer is C.** *Remaining* most closely means "last."

123. **The correct answer is C.** This answer may be verified by eliminating choices A, B, and D. Though rocks are mentioned, they are only a part of the entire description.

124. **The correct choice is A.** The author uses specific imagery—a dark, scary cave—to show what kind of environment spelunkers face. There is no mention of bats in the first paragraph, so there is no indication that the man is afraid of bats (choice B), and there is no information to compare bats with spelunkers (choice C). This is an informative passage, so choice D is incorrect as well.

125. **The correct answer is D.** This answer may be verified by eliminating choices A, B, and C. One clue to the answer is in the way the passage is written—without technical terms and in the third person.

126. **The correct answer is B.** The cave the man was exploring was probably deep underground. This is an inference question. The answer may be verified by eliminating the other choices.

127. **The correct answer is C.** This is the most specific, direct answer, though the other choices may have been indirectly related. The answer is found in paragraph 2, where the flashlight is mentioned immediately before the bats suddenly begin to fly about.

128. **The correct answer is C.** In paragraph 2, sentence 4 states: "He ducks, startled, then grins." The key context word is *startled*, which is a synonym for "surprised," so choice C is the best option. The passage does not suggest that he is angry, afraid, or hurt by the bats, so these options are incorrect.

129. **The correct answer is D.** *Utter* most nearly means "great."

130. **The correct answer is C.** Spelunkers ignore discomfort. In the course of the passage, the author refers to "decaying" smells, banging into a "cold rocky wall," and crawling through narrow passage "on their stomachs." Yet the author also describes these spelunking activities as fun and exciting. In paragraph 4, the author specifically refers to spelunkers forming clubs, which makes choice D incorrect. In the same paragraph, he mentions that spelunkers share safety tips, which eliminates choice A. Although the author does mention the darkness as a major feature of spelunking, he does not ignore it, but rather brings a light with him, making choice B incorrect.

131. **The correct answer is B.** A good title for this passage would be "Spelunkers—Underground

Explorers." Though the author mentions bats, the passage concentrates on the more general topic of spelunkers, so choice A is not the best option. Choices C and D are too broad.

132. **The correct answer is D.** According to this passage, *adventurous* is the word that would most nearly describe spelunkers. The answer may be verified by eliminating the other choices.

133. **The correct answer is C.** This passage provides positive information about kohlrabi, and based on the optimistic tone, readers can determine that the author's opinion on kohlrabi as a food is most likely enthusiastic, choice C.

134. **The correct answer is A.** This passage is a persuasive piece that highlights the many merits of this vegetable in an effort to get readers to try it. Therefore, "Consider Kohlrabi" (choice A) would be the best title for this passage.

135. **The correct answer is B.** *Protean* means "mutable and adaptable." As used in the passage, *protean* is used to describe the type of menu ingredient that "can be eaten raw or cooked and is an excellent addition to a wide array of recipes." This description attempts to portray kohlrabi as a versatile ingredient, making choice B the correct answer.

136. **The correct answer is D.** According to the passage, kohlrabi is a good source of vitamin C, vitamin B, fiber, and potassium. There is no mention of kohlrabi being a source of calories, energy, or spice, so choices A, B, and C are incorrect.

137. **The correct answer is A.** The author mentions "the vegetable's popularity in Germany" in the same sentence as the types of kohlrabi (White Danube, Purple Danube, White Vienna, and Purple Vienna). The most likely scenario is that these names are of German origin, making choice A the correct answer.

138. **The correct answer is D.** Within the passage, the word *varietal* is used to introduce the White Danube, Purple Danube, White Vienna, and Purple Vienna—each a type of kohlrabi. Therefore, choice D is correct.

139. **The correct answer is C.** According to the passage, the main reason why kohlrabi is often mistaken as a root vegetable is its bulbous, root-like appearance (choice C). The kohlrabi's taste (choice A), color (choice B), and name (choice D) have nothing to do with its being mistaken for a root vegetable.

140. **The correct answer is A.** Kohlrabi is a member of the *Brassica oleracea* species, which also includes broccoli (choice B), kale (choice C), cauliflower (choice D), and Brussels sprouts. There is no mention of it being in the same species as turnips, so choice A is correct.

141. **The correct answer is B.** In the passage, the only item among the answer choices that's *not* mentioned as a benefit of kohlrabi is heart health, making choice B the correct answer.

142. **The correct answer is B.** This passage is an enthusiastic piece of writing that is in full support of giving kohlrabi a try. It discusses a wide array of kohlrabi's benefits and positive characteristics, and it suggests trying kohlrabi "the next time you're doing some meal planning." Therefore, choice B is correct.

143. **The correct answer is B.** The passage was probably printed in a magazine. This answer may be verified by eliminating the other three choices. The passage covers several aspects of the topic—more than would be contained in just one type of book.

144. **The correct answer is C.** See paragraph 1. According to this passage, the mystery of witchcraft is "unresolved."

145. **The correct answer is A.** This is a question based on your general knowledge. One remnant of beliefs in witches and in witchcraft can be found in modern Halloween celebrations, which often include witches, ghosts, goblins, and other such creatures.

146. **The correct answer is A.** Judges, according to the passage, are the group that has had members who believed in witchcraft. In paragraph 2, it states, "...the judges undoubtedly were sincere in their desire to eliminate what they thought was a real danger."

147. **The correct answer is B.** Another superstition is "Breaking a mirror brings bad luck." This question is actually testing your vocabulary.

148. **The correct answer is A.** As stated in paragraph 2, according to some psychologists, persons who do believe in witchcraft can be harmed by it.

149. **The correct answer is B.** As it is used in the passage, "in essence" most closely means "basically."

150. **The correct answer is D.** *Interesting* is the best answer; it could be substituted for *fascinating*.

151. **The correct answer is A.** This is an inference question. The answer is implied in paragraph 2. This passage suggests that what you believe can hurt you.

152. **The correct answer is A.** A good title for this passage might be "Witchcraft—Fact or Fiction?" This theme occurs throughout the passage, and this answer may be verified by eliminating the other choices.

Vocabulary

153. D	158. A	163. B	167. A	171. A
154. B	159. D	164. B	168. D	172. B
155. A	160. D	165. D	169. A	173. D
156. D	161. A	166. A	170. C	174. C
157. C	162. B			

153. **The correct answer is D.** *Perspective* means "aspect," "attitude," or "view."

154. **The correct answer is B.** To impair is to spoil, damage, or weaken.

155. **The correct answer is A.** *Acumen* refers to a "keen intelligence."

156. **The correct answer is D.** To subjugate means to dominate or overpower.

157. **The correct answer is C.** *Reproach* means to condemn, chide, or blame.

158. **The correct answer is A.** To be elated is to be jubilant, exhilarated, or happy.

159. **The correct answer is D.** *Brusque* means to be curt, blunt, or abrupt.

160. **The correct answer is D.** To depress something is to squash, flatten, or push down.

161. **The correct answer is A.** To quench is to allay, stifle, or end.

162. **The correct answer is B.** An exploit is an escapade, deed, or venture.

163. **The correct answer is B.** A precipitous incline is steep.

164. **The correct answer is B.** A chronicle is an account, a history, or a record of something.

165. **The correct answer is D.** To be an amiable person means to be likeable.

166. **The correct answer is A.** The meaning of the word *astute* is "to be keen, shrewd, or clever."

167. **The correct answer is A.** *Sever* means "divide," "split," or "cut."

168. **The correct answer is D.** *Eminent* means "distinguished," "important," or "outstanding."

169. **The correct answer is A.** To terminate is to end, cancel, or stop something.

170. **The correct answer is C.** To hinder means to obstruct, interfere, or impede something.

171. **The correct answer is A.** To be in contention means to be in strife, discord, or debate.

172. **The correct answer is B.** To concede means to admit, allow, or acknowledge.

173. **The correct answer is D.** The word *forego* means "concede," "give up," or "relinquish."

174. **The correct answer is C.** For something to be canny means to be clever.

Mathematics

Concepts

175. B	**180.** C	**185.** B	**190.** D	**195.** A
176. D	**181.** A	**186.** A	**191.** B	**196.** C
177. A	**182.** D	**187.** B	**192.** C	**197.** D
178. A	**183.** A	**188.** C	**193.** A	**198.** C
179. D	**184.** C	**189.** B	**194.** C	

175. **The correct answer is B.** You don't have to do any deep calculating to find the answer here; just note that 2 feet is 24 inches, 0.5 yards is 1.5 feet or 18 inches, and, since a centimeter is smaller than an inch, 14 centimeters is certainly smaller than 17 inches. Therefore, 2 feet (choice B) is the largest.

176. **The correct answer is D.** A parallelogram has four sides, with each pair of opposite sides being parallel. A rhombus, square, and rectangle all satisfy these conditions. A triangle, however, only has three sides.

177. **The correct answer is A.** The mean, or average, of a set of numbers is their sum divided by how many numbers are in the set.

178. **The correct answer is A.** The weight of a set of objects will always be the sum of the weights of the individual objects.

179. **The correct answer is D.** Each angle in a square is a right angle, or 90 degrees. Four of these add up to 360 degrees.

180. **The correct answer is C.** The variables are the unknown values represented as letters. There are three variables in this equation: m, n, and p.

181. **The correct answer is A.** An equilateral triangle is one in which all the sides are the same length, and all the angles are the same size (think "equal").

182. **The correct answer is D.** Each meter is 100 centimeters, so 2 meters is 200 centimeters.

183. **The correct answer is A.** A pint is 2 cups, so it contains $8 + 8 = 16$ ounces.

184. **The correct answer is C.** The millions begin with the seventh digit to the left of the decimal place. Because you need 326 million, you can immediately eliminate choices A and B. Read on to the thousands place, and you will see it is 900 thousand. You need look no further for the correct answer.

185. **The correct answer is B.** A number is changed if 1 is subtracted from it. You should know this answer instantly. If you do not, try out each option.

186. **The correct answer is A.** The first 4 is in the billion's place; the second, in the hundred-thousand's place. If you had trouble with this problem, review the sections on how to read numbers and determine place values in your math textbook.

187. **The correct answer is B.** You should recognize immediately that $\frac{1}{2}$ day is shorter than 25 hours and that 3,600 seconds is far shorter than 1,440 minutes. Narrowing down to the first two choices, you probably know that there are 1,440 minutes in a day. If you do not know this, multiply 24 by 60 to see for yourself.

188. **The correct answer is C.** To find the average, or mean, add the digits in the set, then divide by the number of digits. So, $3 + 5 + 1 + 2 + 9 = 20$, and $20 \div 5 = 4$.

189. **The correct answer is B.** In order, the numbers are 1, 2, 3, 5, 9. The median is the middle number.

190. **The correct answer is D.** The probability is the number of winners divided by the total number of contestants. In this case, that is the fraction $\frac{2}{8}$ which reduces to $\frac{1}{4}$.

191. **The correct answer is B.**

$$1\frac{3}{4}\% = 1.75\% = 0.0175$$

192. **The correct answer is C.** Since the sum of the angles of a triangle always equals 180° and $m\angle B = 90°$, angles A and C together must equal 90°. Do not allow yourself to be diverted by extra information. $m\angle C$ of the triangle is equal to 30°, so $m\angle A = 60°$, but this knowledge is irrelevant to the question being asked. Do not waste time on unnecessary calculations.

193. **The correct answer is A.** $9^2 = 81$. Because x is greater than 9, x^2 would have to be greater than 81, which also makes it greater than 80. As such, choice A is the correct option.

194. **The correct answer is C.** Many numbers are divisible by either 3 or 4 but not by both. All numbers that are divisible by both 3 and 4 are also divisible by their multiple, 12.

195. **The correct answer is A.** Compare the digit in the hundredths place; 0.023 is greater than 0.0086.

196. **The correct answer is C.** The *greatest* common factor of 50 and 10 is 10 itself. 1 and 5 are also common factors, but they are smaller.

197. **The correct answer is D.** For the sum to be smaller than the given number of an addition problem, the missing number must be negative.

198. **The correct answer is C.** The formula for determining the area of a circle is πr^2. Since $r = 3$, the formula can be expressed as $3^2\pi = 9\pi$ sq. cm.

Problem Solving

199. B	207. A	215. D	223. B	231. C
200. C	208. B	216. D	224. B	232. B
201. A	209. B	217. C	225. D	233. C
202. A	210. D	218. C	226. A	234. B
203. C	211. B	219. B	227. C	235. A
204. B	212. D	220. B	228. A	236. B
205. D	213. A	221. B	229. C	237. C
206. B	214. C	222. C	230. A	238. D

199. **The correct answer is B.** Three gallons contain 12 quarts. The ratio is 3:12, or, in simplest form, 1:4.

200. **The correct answer is C.** For this question, you must try out all of the answer options. If $x = 0$, then $2x < 8$ because $2(0) < 8$. None of the other pairs results in a true statement.

201. **The correct answer is A.**

$$4\frac{1}{4} \div \frac{1}{5} = \frac{17}{4} \div \frac{1}{5}$$
$$= \frac{17}{4} \times 5$$
$$= \frac{85}{4}$$
$$= 21\frac{1}{4}$$

202. The correct answer is A. The intersection ($\cap$) of two sets has as its elements only those numbers that are in both original sets. In this case, only the number 2 is found in both sets.

203. The correct answer is C. Mary's age now = x. Her sister's age now $x - 3$. In 5 years, her sister's age will be $x - 3 + 5$, or, in simplest form, $x + 2$.

204. The correct answer is B. For this question, you must perform the calculation for each answer option. However, this is a good problem to do in your head. For example, in the correct answer, choice B, you can quickly see that $6 + 4 < 10.5$ is the same as $10 < 10.5$.

205. The correct answer is D. The union of the two adjacent line segments creates one continuous line segment.

206. The correct answer is B.

$$
\begin{array}{r}
1.970 \\
1.02\overline{)2.01000} \\
\underline{1\ 02} \\
99\ 0 \\
\underline{91\ 8} \\
7\ 20 \\
\underline{7\ 14} \\
60
\end{array}
$$

207. The correct answer is A. Use the order of operations:

$$
\begin{aligned}
-2\big[3 - 2(1 - 5) - 6\big] &= -2\big[3 - 2(-4) - 6\big] \\
&= -2\big[3 + 8 - 6\big] \\
&= -2\big[11 - 6\big] \\
&= -2[5] \\
&= -10
\end{aligned}
$$

208. The correct answer is B. This is a good problem to do in your head. Note that 10% of 70 is 7. It then follows that 140% is 14×7, or 98.

209. The correct answer is B. Bracket the multiplication and division first, then solve the problem.

$$
\begin{aligned}
\left(6 \div \frac{1}{3}\right) + \left(\frac{2}{3} \times 9\right) \\
= 18 + 6 \\
= 24
\end{aligned}
$$

210. The correct answer is D. Substitute in the values of x, y, and z and simplify using the order of operations:

$$
\begin{aligned}
x(y - z)^2 &= -3(5 - (-2))^2 \\
&= -3(7)^2 \\
&= -3(49) \\
&= -147
\end{aligned}
$$

211. The correct answer is B. Seven is one-third of 21, and $\frac{2}{3}$ is one-third of 2.

212. The correct answer is D. To find the average, find the sum of the addends and divide that sum by the number of addends.

$$
\begin{aligned}
-10 + 6 + 0 - 3 + 22 &= 15 \\
15 \div 5 &= 3
\end{aligned}
$$

213. The correct answer is A.

$$
\begin{aligned}
x^2 + 5 &= 41 \\
x^2 &= 41 - 5 \\
x^2 &= 36 \\
x &= \pm 6
\end{aligned}
$$

214. The correct answer is C.

$$
\begin{aligned}
\text{Area} &= \text{length} \times \text{width} \\
\text{Area} &= 168 \text{ ft.} \times 82 \text{ ft.} \\
\text{Area} &= 13{,}776 \text{ sq. ft.}
\end{aligned}
$$

215. The correct answer is D.

$$
63 \div \frac{1}{9} = 63 \times \frac{9}{1} = 567
$$

This is a good answer to estimate. By dividing a number by $\frac{1}{9}$, you are, in effect, multiplying it by 9. Only one of the suggested answers is close.

216. **The correct answer is D.** Move the decimal point of the divisor two places to the right; do the same for the dividend. Then divide by 0.5. Since $0.5 = \frac{1}{2}$, you could choose to divide by $\frac{1}{2}$ or multiply by 2.

217. **The correct answer is C.** This is a tricky question. It doesn't ask for 150% of 72, but rather to increase 72 by 150%. Because 150% of 72 = 108, we add 72 and 108 for the correct answer. Careful reading is an important factor in test success.

218. **The correct answer is C.** The mean is $(2 + 5 + 5 + 6 + 7) \div 5 = 5$. The median is the number in the middle, which is 5. The mode is the number that appears most often, which is also 5.

219. **The correct answer is B.** For each of the 10 possible presidents, there are 7 possible vice presidents. Therefore, the total number of combinations is $10 \times 7 = 70$.

220. **The correct answer is B.** Since $x = 2$, the length is $2 + 3 = 5$, and the width is $2 - 1 = 1$. The perimeter is $5 + 5 + 1 + 1 = 12$. We are not told what units are being used.

221. **The correct answer is B.** The probability that he will not get an A is 100% minus the probability that he will get an A. That is, $100\% - 80\% = 20\%$.

222. **The correct answer is C.** For each teacher, there are 12 students. Because there are 16 teachers, there must be 12×16, or 192, students.

223. **The correct answer is B.**

Set up a proportion:

$$\frac{1.2 \text{ inches}}{50 \text{ feet}} = \frac{6 \text{ inches}}{x \text{ feet}}$$

Solve for x, as follows:

$$1.2x = (6)(50)$$
$$1.2x = 300$$

$$x = \frac{300}{1.2} = 250$$

224. **The correct answer is B.** A store markup of 100% would exactly double the price. A 75% markup almost doubles the price. The $17 pants are priced at almost double their cost to the store. By estimation, the best answer is A. To figure precisely, remember that a 75% markup is the equivalent of multiplying the cost by 175%, or 1.75.

$$\text{cost} \times 1.75 = 17.00$$
$$\text{cost} = 17.00 \div 1.75$$
$$\text{cost} = \$9.71$$

225. **The correct answer is D.** To find the perimeter, we add up the dimensions of all the sides. Note that there are some parts that have not been assigned measurements, so we should infer that they are the same as those corresponding parts whose measurements have been designated because we are told to assume that there are right angles in the figure. Beginning at the bottom and moving clockwise, the dimensions are:

$$10" + 14" + 2" + 6" + 6" + 6" + 2" + 14"$$

These equal 60 inches. If you selected choice A, C, or D, you failed to add up all the segments. Also, you should have rejected choices C and D because a perimeter is a linear measurement, and would not be expressed in square inches.

226. **The correct answer is A.** The area is most easily found by multiplying the length of the figure by its width, and then subtracting the area of the small 6" × 6" square.

$$(14" \times 10") - (6" \times 6") = \text{area}$$
$$140 \text{ sq. in.} - 36 \text{ sq. in.} = 104 \text{ sq. in.}$$

227. The correct answer is C. A 16-minute call would cost $1.56 for the first 3 minutes, plus 22¢ for each of the 13 additional minutes. The total cost is found as follows: $1.56 + 13(0.22) = $1.56 + $2.86 = $4.42.

228. The correct answer is A. You only need to read the first and third sentences to solve this problem. The information in the second sentence is not relevant to the problem. The winner received $\frac{1}{3}$ of the total, or $2,700. Thus, the total purse was $2,700 × 3 = $8,100.

229. The correct answer is C. Number of seats = 12 + 14 = 26

Number of passengers at station A = 14 + 4 = 18

Number of passengers at next stop = 18 − 8 + 13 = 23

Number of empty seats = 26 − 23 = 3

230. The correct answer is A. Raising the sales tax from 5% to 8% is a raise of 3%. The dollar amount is found by calculating 3% of $250 = 0.03 × $250 = $7.50.

231. The correct answer is C. Borrow a gallon and add it to 2 quarts. Rewrite the problem.

```
   4 gallons 6 quarts 1 pint
−  1 gallon  3 quarts 0 pints
   3 gallons 3 quarts 1 pint
```

232. The correct answer is B. By knowing how many phones are in Adelaide (48,000) and how many serve each group of 100 in the population (12.8), we can find how many groups of 100 are in the population. 48,000 phones ÷ 12.8 phones per 100 of population = 3,750 groups of 100 in the population. Therefore, 3,750 × 100 = 375,000 people.

233. The correct answer is C. Four boards, each 2'9" long, total 11 feet. The carpenter must buy 11 feet of wood.

234. The correct answer is B.

Area of a square = s^2

$49 = 7^2$

one side = 7 inches

$P = 4s$

$P = 4 \times 7" = 28$ inches

235. The correct answer is A. Copper and aluminum in the ratio of 10:1 means 10 parts copper to 1 part aluminum.

Let x = weight of aluminum, then $10x$ = weight of copper

$$10x + x = 77$$
$$11x = 77$$
$$x = 7$$

236. The correct answer is B. His total income is equal to 8% of his sales plus $175. First, calculate 8% of his sales; $1,025 × 0.08 = $82. This commission must be added to his weekly salary, so $82 + $175 = $257.

237. The correct answer is C. The amount for which the house was insured is 80% of $83,000, or $66,400. The insurance is calculated at 45¢ per hundred, or $4.50 per thousand of value. Because we are insuring 66.4 thousands in value, 66.4 × $4.50 per thousand equals the yearly premium of $298.80.

238. The correct answer is D. First convert to a 24-hour clock.

3:30 p.m. = 15:30

15:30	14:90		
− 8:50	− 8:50		
	6:40	=	6 hours 40 minutes

To subtract a greater number of minutes from a lesser number of minutes, "borrow" 60 minutes from the hour to enlarge the lesser number, as shown in the second column.

Answers Practice Test 5: HSPT®

Language

239. A	251. A	263. C	275. C	287. D
240. A	252. D	264. D	276. B	288. A
241. B	253. A	265. B	277. C	289. A
242. B	254. A	266. D	278. B	290. A
243. D	255. D	267. B	279. B	291. B
244. C	256. D	268. A	280. B	292. D
245. C	257. B	269. A	281. A	293. B
246. D	258. B	270. B	282. C	294. C
247. C	259. B	271. D	283. D	295. B
248. D	260. C	272. D	284. A	296. B
249. D	261. C	273. C	285. B	297. D
250. C	262. A	274. C	286. A	298. B

239. **The correct answer is A.** The part of the sentence that is set in quotation marks is done so incorrectly. This additional piece of information about Alexis should be set in parentheses.

240. **The correct answer is A.** The names of newspapers are both capitalized and italicized: *Daily Cryer.*

241. **The correct answer is B.** This sentence is a question and should end with a question mark.

242. **The correct answer is B.** The proper names of places are capitalized: Grand Canyon.

243. **The correct answer is D.** *No mistakes*

244. **The correct answer is C.** The word *Their* is incorrect in this context. The word should be *They're* (they are).

245. **The correct answer is C.** The word *Who's* (who is) is incorrect in this context. The word should be *Whose.*

246. **The correct answer is D.** *No mistakes*

247. **The correct answer is C.** The adjective *were* is plural, and does not agree with the singular subject of the sentence, *Sherman.*

248. **The correct answer is D.** *No mistakes*

249. **The correct answer is D.** *No mistakes*

250. **The correct answer is C.** The semicolons in this sentence are incorrect and create awkward pauses. Semicolons should be used for joining related independent clauses, which we do not have here.

251. **The correct answer is A.** The word *you're* (you are) is incorrect in this context. The word should be *your.*

252. **The correct answer is D.** *No mistakes*

253. **The correct answer is A.** The object of the preposition *to* is Deirdre and *me.*

254. **The correct answer is A.** There is no need to set *fireworks factory* in quotes, and they should be removed from this sentence.

255. **The correct answer is D.** *No mistakes*

256. **The correct answer is D.** *No mistakes*

257. **The correct answer is B.** The word *like* relates two or more things, while *as well as* compares two or more things. In this sentence, we are comparing Janet's ability to Tom's, so *as well as* is correct.

258. **The correct answer is B.** The word *learning* is incorrect in this context. The word should be *teaching.*

259. **The correct answer is B.** The word *of* is incorrect in this context. The word should be *have*.

260. **The correct answer is C.** There is no need to set *complete name* in parentheses, as it's a primary and essential component of the sentence, and not an aside or tangential information.

261. **The correct answer is C.** The number of hours can be counted—therefore, *fewer* is the correct word.

262. **The correct answer is A.** *Everyone* is singular. The pronoun must be singular as well. Either *his* or *her* would be correct.

263. **The correct answer is C.** There are three, so the comparative term must be *tallest*.

264. **The correct answer is D.** *No mistakes*

265. **The correct answer is B.** As written, the commas create unnecessary pauses in the sentence and should be removed.

266. **The correct answer is D.** *No mistakes*

267. **The correct answer is B.** "I feel bad" is the correct usage. "I feel badly" would be correct if something were wrong with the speaker's hands.

268. **The correct answer is A.** This sentence demonstrates correct usage. The other answer choices are missing articles, which result in awkward sentences.

269. **The correct answer is A.** This sentence demonstrates correct usage. The other answer choices contain incorrect pronouns.

270. **The correct answer is B.** This sentence demonstrates correct usage. The other answer choices contain incorrect adverbs.

271. **The correct answer is D.** This sentence demonstrates correct usage. The other answer choices contain pronoun errors.

272. **The correct answer is D.** This sentence demonstrates correct usage. The other answer choices are either missing articles or they have too many.

273. **The correct answer is C.** This sentence demonstrates correct usage. The other answer choices contain errors in verb tense.

274. **The correct answer is C.** This sentence demonstrates correct usage. The other answer choices use incorrect end punctuation.

275. **The correct answer is C.** This sentence demonstrates correct usage. The other answer choices contain incorrect conjunction choices.

276. **The correct answer is B.** This sentence demonstrates correct usage. The other answer choices contain incorrect choices of interjections.

277. **The correct answer is C.** This sentence demonstrates correct usage. The other answer choices contain incorrect preposition choices.

278. **The correct answer is B.** This sentence demonstrates correct usage. The other answer choices contain incorrect negatives or double negatives, which lead to illogical sentences.

279. **The correct answer is B.** The correct spelling is *apparently*.

280. **The correct answer is B.** The correct spelling is *efficiently*.

281. **The correct answer is A.** The correct spelling is *occurred*. (See Spelling—Rule 9.)

282. **The correct answer is C.** The correct spelling is *analyzed*.

283. **The correct answer is D.** *No mistakes*

284. **The correct answer is A.** The correct spelling of the word is *misspelled*.

285. **The correct answer is B.** The correct spelling is *described*.

286. **The correct answer is A.** The correct spelling is *prefers*.

287. **The correct answer is D.** *No mistakes*

288. **The correct answer is A.** The correct spelling is *necessary*.

289. **The correct answer is A.** *Therefore* indicates the cause-and-effect relationship of the two clauses.

290. **The correct answer is A.** The second clause provides an example.

291. **The correct answer is B.** The subject (*Mary*) must follow the introductory phrase. The use of *afterward* makes choice C redundant.

292. **The correct answer is D.** This sentence expresses the idea most clearly.

293. **The correct answer is B.** The second clause offers the reason she drove 50 miles.

294. **The correct answer is C.** The invention of the automobile belongs in a discussion of the automobile's history.

295. **The correct answer is B.** This choice most clearly and succinctly presents the ideas provided here.

296. **The correct answer is B.** Sentences 1, 3, and 4 all concern preparation for the Halloween party.

297. **The correct answer is D.** All these topics are too broad for a one-paragraph theme.

298. **The correct answer is B.** The given sentence should be placed before sentence 3, because it refers to a singular noun, and sentence 2 contains a plural noun. By placing this sentence between sentences 2 and 3, the paragraph makes sense.

SCORE SHEET

Although your actual exam scores will not be reported as percentages, it might be helpful to convert them so you can better visualize your strengths and weaknesses. The numbers in parentheses represent the question numbers testing each skill.

Subject	# Correct ÷ # of questions	× 100 = _____ %
Verbal Analogies (3, 6, 8, 12, 13, 19, 20, 31, 36, 41)	_____ ÷ 10 = _____	× 100 = _____ %
Synonyms (5, 10, 11, 16, 17, 18, 21, 23, 25, 26, 28, 29, 30, 47, 58)	_____ ÷ 15 = _____	× 100 = _____ %
Logic (4, 15, 22, 24, 33, 38, 49, 52, 55, 60)	_____ ÷ 10 = _____	× 100 = _____ %
Verbal Classification (1, 2, 7, 9, 14, 27, 32, 34, 42, 45, 46, 50, 54, 56, 57, 59)	_____ ÷ 16 = _____	× 100 = _____ %
Antonyms (35, 37, 39, 40, 43, 44, 47, 48, 51, 53)	_____ ÷ 9 = _____	× 100 = _____ %
TOTAL VERBAL SKILLS	_____ ÷ 60 = _____	× 100 = _____ %
Number Series (61, 65, 66, 68, 69, 79, 81, 83, 85, 91, 93, 97, 99, 103, 105, 108, 109, 112)	_____ ÷ 18 = _____	× 100 = _____ %
Geometric Comparisons (62, 70, 73, 78, 84, 88, 92, 96, 101)	_____ ÷ 9 = _____	× 100 = _____ %
Nongeometric Comparisons (63, 75, 77, 87, 90, 95, 107, 110)	_____ ÷ 8 = _____	× 100 = _____ %
Number Manipulation (64, 67, 71, 72, 74, 76, 80, 82, 86, 89, 94, 98, 100, 102, 104, 106, 111)	_____ ÷ 17 = _____	× 100 = _____ %
TOTAL QUANTITATIVE SKILLS	_____ ÷ 52 = _____	× 100 = _____ %
Reading—Comprehension (113–152)	_____ ÷ 40 = _____	× 100 = _____ %
Reading—Vocabulary (153–174)	_____ ÷ 22 = _____	× 100 = _____ %
TOTAL READING SKILLS	_____ ÷ 62 = _____	× 100 = _____ %
Mathematics—Concepts (175-198)	_____ ÷ 24 = _____	× 100 = _____ %
Mathematics—Problem Solving (199–238)	_____ ÷ 40 = _____	× 100 = _____ %
TOTAL MATHEMATICS SKILLS	_____ ÷ 64 = _____	× 100 = _____ %
Punctuation and Capitalization (239, 240, 241, 242, 243, 246, 248, 249, 252, 256, 265, 256)	_____ ÷ 12 = _____	× 100 = _____ %
Usage (244, 245, 247, 250, 251, 253, 254, 255, 257–264, 267–278)	_____ ÷ 28 = _____	× 100 = _____ %
Spelling (279–288)	_____ ÷ 10 = _____	× 100 = _____ %
Composition (289–298)	_____ ÷ 10 = _____	× 100 = _____ %
TOTAL LANGUAGE SKILLS	_____ ÷ 60 = _____	× 100 = _____ %

Practice Test 5: HSPT®

ANSWER SHEET: HSPT® PRACTICE TEST 6

Verbal Skills

1. Ⓐ Ⓑ Ⓒ Ⓓ   13. Ⓐ Ⓑ Ⓒ Ⓓ   25. Ⓐ Ⓑ Ⓒ Ⓓ   37. Ⓐ Ⓑ Ⓒ Ⓓ   49. Ⓐ Ⓑ Ⓒ Ⓓ
2. Ⓐ Ⓑ Ⓒ Ⓓ   14. Ⓐ Ⓑ Ⓒ Ⓓ   26. Ⓐ Ⓑ Ⓒ Ⓓ   38. Ⓐ Ⓑ Ⓒ Ⓓ   50. Ⓐ Ⓑ Ⓒ Ⓓ
3. Ⓐ Ⓑ Ⓒ   15. Ⓐ Ⓑ Ⓒ   27. Ⓐ Ⓑ Ⓒ   39. Ⓐ Ⓑ Ⓒ Ⓓ   51. Ⓐ Ⓑ Ⓒ
4. Ⓐ Ⓑ Ⓒ Ⓓ   16. Ⓐ Ⓑ Ⓒ Ⓓ   28. Ⓐ Ⓑ Ⓒ Ⓓ   40. Ⓐ Ⓑ Ⓒ Ⓓ   52. Ⓐ Ⓑ Ⓒ Ⓓ
5. Ⓐ Ⓑ Ⓒ Ⓓ   17. Ⓐ Ⓑ Ⓒ Ⓓ   29. Ⓐ Ⓑ Ⓒ Ⓓ   41. Ⓐ Ⓑ Ⓒ Ⓓ   53. Ⓐ Ⓑ Ⓒ Ⓓ
6. Ⓐ Ⓑ Ⓒ Ⓓ   18. Ⓐ Ⓑ Ⓒ Ⓓ   30. Ⓐ Ⓑ Ⓒ   42. Ⓐ Ⓑ Ⓒ Ⓓ   54. Ⓐ Ⓑ Ⓒ Ⓓ
7. Ⓐ Ⓑ Ⓒ Ⓓ   19. Ⓐ Ⓑ Ⓒ Ⓓ   31. Ⓐ Ⓑ Ⓒ Ⓓ   43. Ⓐ Ⓑ Ⓒ Ⓓ   55. Ⓐ Ⓑ Ⓒ Ⓓ
8. Ⓐ Ⓑ Ⓒ Ⓓ   20. Ⓐ Ⓑ Ⓒ   32. Ⓐ Ⓑ Ⓒ Ⓓ   44. Ⓐ Ⓑ Ⓒ   56. Ⓐ Ⓑ Ⓒ Ⓓ
9. Ⓐ Ⓑ Ⓒ Ⓓ   21. Ⓐ Ⓑ Ⓒ Ⓓ   33. Ⓐ Ⓑ Ⓒ Ⓓ   45. Ⓐ Ⓑ Ⓒ Ⓓ   57. Ⓐ Ⓑ Ⓒ Ⓓ
10. Ⓐ Ⓑ Ⓒ   22. Ⓐ Ⓑ Ⓒ Ⓓ   34. Ⓐ Ⓑ Ⓒ Ⓓ   46. Ⓐ Ⓑ Ⓒ Ⓓ   58. Ⓐ Ⓑ Ⓒ
11. Ⓐ Ⓑ Ⓒ Ⓓ   23. Ⓐ Ⓑ Ⓒ Ⓓ   35. Ⓐ Ⓑ Ⓒ Ⓓ   47. Ⓐ Ⓑ Ⓒ Ⓓ   59. Ⓐ Ⓑ Ⓒ Ⓓ
12. Ⓐ Ⓑ Ⓒ Ⓓ   24. Ⓐ Ⓑ Ⓒ Ⓓ   36. Ⓐ Ⓑ Ⓒ   48. Ⓐ Ⓑ Ⓒ Ⓓ   60. Ⓐ Ⓑ Ⓒ Ⓓ

Quantitative Skills

61. Ⓐ Ⓑ Ⓒ Ⓓ   73. Ⓐ Ⓑ Ⓒ Ⓓ   85. Ⓐ Ⓑ Ⓒ Ⓓ   97. Ⓐ Ⓑ Ⓒ Ⓓ   109. Ⓐ Ⓑ Ⓒ Ⓓ
62. Ⓐ Ⓑ Ⓒ Ⓓ   74. Ⓐ Ⓑ Ⓒ Ⓓ   86. Ⓐ Ⓑ Ⓒ Ⓓ   98. Ⓐ Ⓑ Ⓒ Ⓓ   110. Ⓐ Ⓑ Ⓒ Ⓓ
63. Ⓐ Ⓑ Ⓒ Ⓓ   75. Ⓐ Ⓑ Ⓒ Ⓓ   87. Ⓐ Ⓑ Ⓒ Ⓓ   99. Ⓐ Ⓑ Ⓒ Ⓓ   111. Ⓐ Ⓑ Ⓒ Ⓓ
64. Ⓐ Ⓑ Ⓒ Ⓓ   76. Ⓐ Ⓑ Ⓒ Ⓓ   88. Ⓐ Ⓑ Ⓒ Ⓓ   100. Ⓐ Ⓑ Ⓒ Ⓓ   112. Ⓐ Ⓑ Ⓒ Ⓓ
65. Ⓐ Ⓑ Ⓒ Ⓓ   77. Ⓐ Ⓑ Ⓒ Ⓓ   89. Ⓐ Ⓑ Ⓒ Ⓓ   101. Ⓐ Ⓑ Ⓒ Ⓓ
66. Ⓐ Ⓑ Ⓒ Ⓓ   78. Ⓐ Ⓑ Ⓒ Ⓓ   90. Ⓐ Ⓑ Ⓒ Ⓓ   102. Ⓐ Ⓑ Ⓒ Ⓓ
67. Ⓐ Ⓑ Ⓒ Ⓓ   79. Ⓐ Ⓑ Ⓒ Ⓓ   91. Ⓐ Ⓑ Ⓒ Ⓓ   103. Ⓐ Ⓑ Ⓒ Ⓓ
68. Ⓐ Ⓑ Ⓒ Ⓓ   80. Ⓐ Ⓑ Ⓒ Ⓓ   92. Ⓐ Ⓑ Ⓒ Ⓓ   104. Ⓐ Ⓑ Ⓒ Ⓓ
69. Ⓐ Ⓑ Ⓒ Ⓓ   81. Ⓐ Ⓑ Ⓒ Ⓓ   93. Ⓐ Ⓑ Ⓒ Ⓓ   105. Ⓐ Ⓑ Ⓒ Ⓓ
70. Ⓐ Ⓑ Ⓒ Ⓓ   82. Ⓐ Ⓑ Ⓒ Ⓓ   94. Ⓐ Ⓑ Ⓒ Ⓓ   106. Ⓐ Ⓑ Ⓒ Ⓓ
71. Ⓐ Ⓑ Ⓒ Ⓓ   83. Ⓐ Ⓑ Ⓒ Ⓓ   95. Ⓐ Ⓑ Ⓒ Ⓓ   107. Ⓐ Ⓑ Ⓒ Ⓓ
72. Ⓐ Ⓑ Ⓒ Ⓓ   84. Ⓐ Ⓑ Ⓒ Ⓓ   96. Ⓐ Ⓑ Ⓒ Ⓓ   108. Ⓐ Ⓑ Ⓒ Ⓓ

Answer Sheet

Practice Test 6: HSPT®

Reading
Comprehension

113. Ⓐ Ⓑ Ⓒ Ⓓ
114. Ⓐ Ⓑ Ⓒ Ⓓ
115. Ⓐ Ⓑ Ⓒ Ⓓ
116. Ⓐ Ⓑ Ⓒ Ⓓ
117. Ⓐ Ⓑ Ⓒ Ⓓ
118. Ⓐ Ⓑ Ⓒ Ⓓ
119. Ⓐ Ⓑ Ⓒ Ⓓ
120. Ⓐ Ⓑ Ⓒ Ⓓ

121. Ⓐ Ⓑ Ⓒ Ⓓ
122. Ⓐ Ⓑ Ⓒ Ⓓ
123. Ⓐ Ⓑ Ⓒ Ⓓ
124. Ⓐ Ⓑ Ⓒ Ⓓ
125. Ⓐ Ⓑ Ⓒ Ⓓ
126. Ⓐ Ⓑ Ⓒ Ⓓ
127. Ⓐ Ⓑ Ⓒ Ⓓ
128. Ⓐ Ⓑ Ⓒ Ⓓ

129. Ⓐ Ⓑ Ⓒ Ⓓ
130. Ⓐ Ⓑ Ⓒ Ⓓ
131. Ⓐ Ⓑ Ⓒ Ⓓ
132. Ⓐ Ⓑ Ⓒ Ⓓ
133. Ⓐ Ⓑ Ⓒ Ⓓ
134. Ⓐ Ⓑ Ⓒ Ⓓ
135. Ⓐ Ⓑ Ⓒ Ⓓ
136. Ⓐ Ⓑ Ⓒ Ⓓ

137. Ⓐ Ⓑ Ⓒ Ⓓ
138. Ⓐ Ⓑ Ⓒ Ⓓ
139. Ⓐ Ⓑ Ⓒ Ⓓ
140. Ⓐ Ⓑ Ⓒ Ⓓ
141. Ⓐ Ⓑ Ⓒ Ⓓ
142. Ⓐ Ⓑ Ⓒ Ⓓ
143. Ⓐ Ⓑ Ⓒ Ⓓ
144. Ⓐ Ⓑ Ⓒ Ⓓ

145. Ⓐ Ⓑ Ⓒ Ⓓ
146. Ⓐ Ⓑ Ⓒ Ⓓ
147. Ⓐ Ⓑ Ⓒ Ⓓ
148. Ⓐ Ⓑ Ⓒ Ⓓ
149. Ⓐ Ⓑ Ⓒ Ⓓ
150. Ⓐ Ⓑ Ⓒ Ⓓ
151. Ⓐ Ⓑ Ⓒ Ⓓ
152. Ⓐ Ⓑ Ⓒ Ⓓ

Vocabulary

153. Ⓐ Ⓑ Ⓒ Ⓓ
154. Ⓐ Ⓑ Ⓒ Ⓓ
155. Ⓐ Ⓑ Ⓒ Ⓓ
156. Ⓐ Ⓑ Ⓒ Ⓓ
157. Ⓐ Ⓑ Ⓒ Ⓓ

158. Ⓐ Ⓑ Ⓒ Ⓓ
159. Ⓐ Ⓑ Ⓒ Ⓓ
160. Ⓐ Ⓑ Ⓒ Ⓓ
161. Ⓐ Ⓑ Ⓒ Ⓓ
162. Ⓐ Ⓑ Ⓒ Ⓓ

163. Ⓐ Ⓑ Ⓒ Ⓓ
164. Ⓐ Ⓑ Ⓒ Ⓓ
165. Ⓐ Ⓑ Ⓒ Ⓓ
166. Ⓐ Ⓑ Ⓒ Ⓓ
167. Ⓐ Ⓑ Ⓒ Ⓓ

168. Ⓐ Ⓑ Ⓒ Ⓓ
169. Ⓐ Ⓑ Ⓒ Ⓓ
170. Ⓐ Ⓑ Ⓒ Ⓓ
171. Ⓐ Ⓑ Ⓒ Ⓓ
172. Ⓐ Ⓑ Ⓒ Ⓓ

173. Ⓐ Ⓑ Ⓒ Ⓓ
174. Ⓐ Ⓑ Ⓒ Ⓓ

Mathematics

Concepts

175. Ⓐ Ⓑ Ⓒ Ⓓ   180. Ⓐ Ⓑ Ⓒ Ⓓ   185. Ⓐ Ⓑ Ⓒ Ⓓ   190. Ⓐ Ⓑ Ⓒ Ⓓ   195. Ⓐ Ⓑ Ⓒ Ⓓ
176. Ⓐ Ⓑ Ⓒ Ⓓ   181. Ⓐ Ⓑ Ⓒ Ⓓ   186. Ⓐ Ⓑ Ⓒ Ⓓ   191. Ⓐ Ⓑ Ⓒ Ⓓ   196. Ⓐ Ⓑ Ⓒ Ⓓ
177. Ⓐ Ⓑ Ⓒ Ⓓ   182. Ⓐ Ⓑ Ⓒ Ⓓ   187. Ⓐ Ⓑ Ⓒ Ⓓ   192. Ⓐ Ⓑ Ⓒ Ⓓ   197. Ⓐ Ⓑ Ⓒ Ⓓ
178. Ⓐ Ⓑ Ⓒ Ⓓ   183. Ⓐ Ⓑ Ⓒ Ⓓ   188. Ⓐ Ⓑ Ⓒ Ⓓ   193. Ⓐ Ⓑ Ⓒ Ⓓ   198. Ⓐ Ⓑ Ⓒ Ⓓ
179. Ⓐ Ⓑ Ⓒ Ⓓ   184. Ⓐ Ⓑ Ⓒ Ⓓ   189. Ⓐ Ⓑ Ⓒ Ⓓ   194. Ⓐ Ⓑ Ⓒ Ⓓ

Problem Solving

199. Ⓐ Ⓑ Ⓒ Ⓓ   207. Ⓐ Ⓑ Ⓒ Ⓓ   215. Ⓐ Ⓑ Ⓒ Ⓓ   223. Ⓐ Ⓑ Ⓒ Ⓓ   231. Ⓐ Ⓑ Ⓒ Ⓓ
200. Ⓐ Ⓑ Ⓒ Ⓓ   208. Ⓐ Ⓑ Ⓒ Ⓓ   216. Ⓐ Ⓑ Ⓒ Ⓓ   224. Ⓐ Ⓑ Ⓒ Ⓓ   232. Ⓐ Ⓑ Ⓒ Ⓓ
201. Ⓐ Ⓑ Ⓒ Ⓓ   209. Ⓐ Ⓑ Ⓒ Ⓓ   217. Ⓐ Ⓑ Ⓒ Ⓓ   225. Ⓐ Ⓑ Ⓒ Ⓓ   233. Ⓐ Ⓑ Ⓒ Ⓓ
202. Ⓐ Ⓑ Ⓒ Ⓓ   210. Ⓐ Ⓑ Ⓒ Ⓓ   218. Ⓐ Ⓑ Ⓒ Ⓓ   226. Ⓐ Ⓑ Ⓒ Ⓓ   234. Ⓐ Ⓑ Ⓒ Ⓓ
203. Ⓐ Ⓑ Ⓒ Ⓓ   211. Ⓐ Ⓑ Ⓒ Ⓓ   219. Ⓐ Ⓑ Ⓒ Ⓓ   227. Ⓐ Ⓑ Ⓒ Ⓓ   235. Ⓐ Ⓑ Ⓒ Ⓓ
204. Ⓐ Ⓑ Ⓒ Ⓓ   212. Ⓐ Ⓑ Ⓒ Ⓓ   220. Ⓐ Ⓑ Ⓒ Ⓓ   228. Ⓐ Ⓑ Ⓒ Ⓓ   236. Ⓐ Ⓑ Ⓒ Ⓓ
205. Ⓐ Ⓑ Ⓒ Ⓓ   213. Ⓐ Ⓑ Ⓒ Ⓓ   221. Ⓐ Ⓑ Ⓒ Ⓓ   229. Ⓐ Ⓑ Ⓒ Ⓓ   237. Ⓐ Ⓑ Ⓒ Ⓓ
206. Ⓐ Ⓑ Ⓒ Ⓓ   214. Ⓐ Ⓑ Ⓒ Ⓓ   222. Ⓐ Ⓑ Ⓒ Ⓓ   230. Ⓐ Ⓑ Ⓒ Ⓓ   238. Ⓐ Ⓑ Ⓒ Ⓓ

Language

239. Ⓐ Ⓑ Ⓒ Ⓓ	251. Ⓐ Ⓑ Ⓒ Ⓓ	263. Ⓐ Ⓑ Ⓒ Ⓓ	275. Ⓐ Ⓑ Ⓒ Ⓓ	287. Ⓐ Ⓑ Ⓒ Ⓓ
240. Ⓐ Ⓑ Ⓒ Ⓓ	252. Ⓐ Ⓑ Ⓒ Ⓓ	264. Ⓐ Ⓑ Ⓒ Ⓓ	276. Ⓐ Ⓑ Ⓒ Ⓓ	288. Ⓐ Ⓑ Ⓒ Ⓓ
241. Ⓐ Ⓑ Ⓒ Ⓓ	253. Ⓐ Ⓑ Ⓒ Ⓓ	265. Ⓐ Ⓑ Ⓒ Ⓓ	277. Ⓐ Ⓑ Ⓒ Ⓓ	289. Ⓐ Ⓑ Ⓒ Ⓓ
242. Ⓐ Ⓑ Ⓒ Ⓓ	254. Ⓐ Ⓑ Ⓒ Ⓓ	266. Ⓐ Ⓑ Ⓒ Ⓓ	278. Ⓐ Ⓑ Ⓒ Ⓓ	290. Ⓐ Ⓑ Ⓒ Ⓓ
243. Ⓐ Ⓑ Ⓒ Ⓓ	255. Ⓐ Ⓑ Ⓒ Ⓓ	267. Ⓐ Ⓑ Ⓒ Ⓓ	279. Ⓐ Ⓑ Ⓒ Ⓓ	291. Ⓐ Ⓑ Ⓒ Ⓓ
244. Ⓐ Ⓑ Ⓒ Ⓓ	256. Ⓐ Ⓑ Ⓒ Ⓓ	268. Ⓐ Ⓑ Ⓒ Ⓓ	280. Ⓐ Ⓑ Ⓒ Ⓓ	292. Ⓐ Ⓑ Ⓒ Ⓓ
245. Ⓐ Ⓑ Ⓒ Ⓓ	257. Ⓐ Ⓑ Ⓒ Ⓓ	269. Ⓐ Ⓑ Ⓒ Ⓓ	281. Ⓐ Ⓑ Ⓒ Ⓓ	293. Ⓐ Ⓑ Ⓒ Ⓓ
246. Ⓐ Ⓑ Ⓒ Ⓓ	258. Ⓐ Ⓑ Ⓒ Ⓓ	270. Ⓐ Ⓑ Ⓒ Ⓓ	282. Ⓐ Ⓑ Ⓒ Ⓓ	294. Ⓐ Ⓑ Ⓒ Ⓓ
247. Ⓐ Ⓑ Ⓒ Ⓓ	259. Ⓐ Ⓑ Ⓒ Ⓓ	271. Ⓐ Ⓑ Ⓒ Ⓓ	283. Ⓐ Ⓑ Ⓒ Ⓓ	295. Ⓐ Ⓑ Ⓒ Ⓓ
248. Ⓐ Ⓑ Ⓒ Ⓓ	260. Ⓐ Ⓑ Ⓒ Ⓓ	272. Ⓐ Ⓑ Ⓒ Ⓓ	284. Ⓐ Ⓑ Ⓒ Ⓓ	296. Ⓐ Ⓑ Ⓒ Ⓓ
249. Ⓐ Ⓑ Ⓒ Ⓓ	261. Ⓐ Ⓑ Ⓒ Ⓓ	273. Ⓐ Ⓑ Ⓒ Ⓓ	285. Ⓐ Ⓑ Ⓒ Ⓓ	297. Ⓐ Ⓑ Ⓒ Ⓓ
250. Ⓐ Ⓑ Ⓒ Ⓓ	262. Ⓐ Ⓑ Ⓒ Ⓓ	274. Ⓐ Ⓑ Ⓒ Ⓓ	286. Ⓐ Ⓑ Ⓒ Ⓓ	298. Ⓐ Ⓑ Ⓒ Ⓓ

Practice Test 6: HSPT®

VERBAL SKILLS (16 MINUTES)

60 Questions

Turn to the Verbal Skills section of your answer sheet to answer the questions in this section.

> **Directions:** Read each question carefully, then consider all options and mark the correct answer.

1. Which word does *not* belong with the others?

   A. One
   B. Three
   C. Fourth
   D. Nine

2. Arouse is to pacify as agitate is to

   A. smooth.
   B. ruffle.
   C. understand.
   D. ignore.

3. Henri is a much better juggler than Jerome. Francine is a better juggler than Jerome. Francine is a better juggler than Henri. If the first two statements are true, the third is

   A. true.
   B. false.
   C. uncertain.

4. Query means the *opposite* of

   A. argument.
   B. answer.
   C. square.
   D. loner.

5. *Impair* most nearly means

   A. direct.
   B. improve.
   C. stimulate.
   D. weaken.

6. Which word does *not* belong with the others?

   A. Rotate
   B. Revolve
   C. Spin
   D. Planet

7. If the wind is *variable*, it is

   A. shifting.
   B. mild.
   C. chilling.
   D. steady.

8. Egg is to beat as potato is to

   A. yam.
   B. bake.
   C. eye.
   D. mash.

9. If you *obstruct* the entrance to a building, you

   A. block it.

   B. enter it.

   C. leave it.

   D. cross it.

10. The red balloon is higher in the sky than the green balloon. The yellow balloon is higher in the sky than the red balloon. The green balloon is higher in the sky than the yellow balloon. If the first two statements are true, the third is

    A. true.

    B. false.

    C. uncertain.

11. Which word does *not* belong with the others?

    A. Blended

    B. Stirred

    C. Mixing

    D. Whisked

12. Cause means the *opposite* of

    A. affect.

    B. result.

    C. question.

    D. accident.

13. Weight is to gain as lemonade is to

    A. blast.

    B. drink.

    C. tart.

    D. cold.

14. Which word does *not* belong with the others?

    A. Tent

    B. Igloo

    C. Cabin

    D. Cave

15. Pepper is the shaggiest dog in the obedience school class. Pretzel is a dachshund. Pepper and Pretzel are in the same obedience school class. If the first two statements are true, the third is

    A. true.

    B. false.

    C. uncertain.

16. Camera is to lens as lightbulb is to

    A. filament.

    B. lamp.

    C. bright.

    D. watts.

17. *Revenue* most nearly means

    A. taxes.

    B. income.

    C. expenses.

    D. produce.

18. Which word does *not* belong with the others?

    A. Trapeze

    B. Wedge

    C. Lever

    D. Pulley

19. Which word does *not* belong with the others?

    A. Joy

    B. Sadness

    C. Tears

    D. Glee

20. Linda jumps rope faster than Mary but slower than Inez. Lori jumps faster than Inez but slower than Cleo. Mary is the slowest jumper in the group. If the first two statements are true, the third is

    A. true.

    B. false.

    C. uncertain.

21. If a machine has *manual* controls, it is

    A. self-acting.

    B. simple.

    C. hand-operated.

    D. handmade.

22. *Marshy* most nearly means

    A. swampy.

    B. sandy.

    C. wooded.

    D. rocky.

23. Seal is to fish as bird is to

    A. wing.

    B. minnow.

    C. worm.

    D. snail.

24. Profit means the *opposite* of

    A. ratio.

    B. gross.

    C. net.

    D. loss.

25. Rest means the *opposite* of

    A. sleep.

    B. activity.

    C. wake.

    D. speak.

26. Which word does *not* belong with the others?

    A. Wind

    B. Gale

    C. Hurricane

    D. Zephyr

27. All people eaters are purple. No cyclops eat people. No cyclops are purple. If the first two statements are true, the third is

    A. true.

    B. false.

    C. uncertain.

28. A *churlish* old cat is

    A. small.

    B. tired.

    C. surly.

    D. energetic.

29. The judge who rules evidence to be *immaterial* means it is

    A. unclear.

    B. unimportant.

    C. unpredictable.

    D. missing.

30. Green books are heavier than red books but not as heavy as orange books. Orange books are lighter than blue books, but not as light as yellow books. Yellow books are heavier than green books. If the first two statements are true, the third is

    A. true.

    B. false.

    C. uncertain.

31. Shoe is to leather as highway is to

    A. passage.

    B. road.

    C. trail.

    D. asphalt.

32. Mend means the *opposite* of

    A. give back.
    B. change.
    C. destroy.
    D. clean.

33. Abstract means the *opposite* of

    A. art.
    B. absurd.
    C. sculpture.
    D. concrete.

34. A computer that does not *function* does not

    A. operate.
    B. finish.
    C. stop.
    D. overheat.

35. Which word does *not* belong with the others?

    A. Vitamin E
    B. Protein
    C. Meat
    D. Calcium

36. All Ts are either green-eyed Ys or blue-tailed Gs. All blue-tailed Gs have brown eyes and red noses. Some Ts have red noses. If the first two statements are true, the third is

    A. true.
    B. false.
    C. uncertain.

37. A *cacophony* of sirens is

    A. loud.
    B. pleasant.
    C. melodic.
    D. helpful.

38. Which word does *not* belong with the others?

    A. Stag
    B. Monkey
    C. Bull
    D. Ram

39. Taste is to tongue as touch is to

    A. finger.
    B. eye.
    C. feeling.
    D. borrow.

40. Discord means the *opposite* of

    A. reward.
    B. record.
    C. harmony.
    D. music.

41. Which word does *not* belong with the others?

    A. Aroma
    B. Odor
    C. Scent
    D. Fumes

42. Which word does *not* belong with the others?

    A. Ride
    B. Creep
    C. Shuffle
    D. Run

43. *Fatal* most nearly means

    A. accidental.
    B. deadly.
    C. dangerous.
    D. beautiful.

44. Terry has won more races than Bill. Bill has won more races than Luis. Terry has won fewer races than Luis. If the first two statements are true, the third is

    A. true.
    B. false.
    C. uncertain.

45. Which word does *not* belong with the others?

    A. Glass
    B. Screen
    C. Brick
    D. Lattice

46. If the packages were kept in a *secure* place, the place was

    A. distant.
    B. safe.
    C. convenient.
    D. secret.

47. Garish means the *opposite* of

    A. dull.
    B. damp.
    C. nice.
    D. closed.

48. Horse is to foal as mother is to

    A. mare.
    B. son.
    C. stallion.
    D. father.

49. Which word does *not* belong with the others?

    A. Gelatin
    B. Tofu
    C. Gum
    D. Cracker

50. *Counterfeit* most nearly means

    A. mysterious.
    B. false.
    C. unreadable.
    D. priceless.

51. The thruway has more lanes than the parkway. The parkway has fewer lanes than the highway. The thruway has more lanes than the highway. If the first two statements are true, the third is

    A. true.
    B. false.
    C. uncertain.

52. Dog is to flea as horse is to

    A. rider.
    B. mane.
    C. fly.
    D. shoe.

53. The foghorn that sounded *intermittently* sounded

    A. constantly.
    B. annually.
    C. using intermediaries.
    D. at intervals.

54. Which word does *not* belong with the others?

    A. Greek
    B. Acrylic
    C. Latin
    D. Arabic

55. Diverse means the *opposite* of

    A. definite.
    B. understandable.
    C. similar.
    D. boring.

Practice Test 6: HSPT®

56. Finder is to reward as repenter is to

    A. religion.

    B. sin.

    C. absolution.

    D. contrition.

57. Which word does *not* belong with the others?

    A. Bend

    B. Explode

    C. Shatter

    D. Burst

58. The grocery store is south of the drugstore, which is between the gas station and the dry cleaner. The bookstore is north of the gas station. The grocery store is north of the dry cleaner. If the first two statements are true, the third is

    A. true.

    B. false.

    C. uncertain.

59. *Deception* most nearly means

    A. secrets.

    B. fraud.

    C. mistrust.

    D. hatred.

60. Which word does *not* belong with the others?

    A. Cotton

    B. Linen

    C. Silk

    D. Nylon

STOP.

If you finish before time is up, you may check your work on this section only.
Do not turn to any other section in the test.

QUANTITATIVE SKILLS

52 Questions (30 minutes)

Turn to the Quantitative Skills section of your answer sheet to answer the questions in this section.

Directions: Read each question carefully, then solve the problem to find the correct answer.

---

61. Look at this series: 2, 4, __, 16, 32. What number should fill in the blank in the middle of the series?

    A. 12
    B. 8
    C. 6
    D. 5

62. What number is double the average of 4, 9, and 17?

    A. 6
    B. 8
    C. 10
    D. 20

63. What number is 20 more than $\frac{1}{4}$ of 48?

    A. 20
    B. 32
    C. 48
    D. 68

64. Look at this series: 3, 4, 8, 9, 13, 14, ... What number comes next?

    A. 15
    B. 16
    C. 18
    D. 20

65. Examine A, B, and C and find the best answer.

    A. 50% of 20
    B. 20% of 50
    C. 5% of 200

    A. A, B, and C are equal
    B. A is greater than B and less than C.
    C. A is greater than C.
    D. A is less than B.

66. Examine A, B, and C, and find the best answer.

    A   B   C

    A. A, B, and C are equally shaded.
    B. A is more shaded than B.
    C. C is shaded more than A or B.
    D. C is shaded less than A.

67. What number is 5 less than 9^2?

    A. 5
    B. 13
    C. 76
    D. 86

68. Examine A, B, and C and find the best answer.

    A. $4 + (3 \times 2)$

    B. $(4 + 3) \times 2$

    C. $(3 + 2) \times 4$

    A. A is greater than B and C.

    B. B is greater than A and C.

    C. C is less than A and B.

    D. C is greater than A and B.

69. What number subtracted from 22 leaves 3 more than half of 26?

    A. 6

    B. 13

    C. 16

    D. 19

70. Examine the square and find the best answer.

    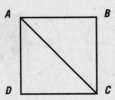

    A. *AB*, *BC*, and *AC* are all equal.

    B. *AC* is greater than *CD*.

    C. *AC* and *AB* are equal.

    D. *BC* is greater than *AD*.

71. Look at this series: 3, 6, 8, 16, 18, ... What number should come next?

    A. 18

    B. 20

    C. 36

    D. 38

72. What number is 7 more than half of 14?

    A. 0

    B. 7

    C. 14

    D. 21

73. Look at this series: A, B, B, A, B, B, A, B, ... What should the next three terms of this series be?

    A. B, A, B

    B. A, A, A

    C. B, B, A

    D. A, A, B

74. Examine A, B, and C and find the best answer.

    A. 6^2

    B. 5^2

    C. 3^2

    A. $A < B < C$

    B. $A = B < C$

    C. $A > B > C$

    D. $A = B = C$

75. Look at this series: $2\frac{1}{2}$, 4, $5\frac{1}{2}$, 7, ... What number should come next?

    A. $7\frac{1}{2}$

    B. 8

    C. $8\frac{1}{2}$

    D. 9

76. Look at this series: 67, 73, __, 85, 91. What number should fill in the blank?

    A. 78

    B. 79

    C. 80

    D. 81

77. Examine the triangle and find the best answer.

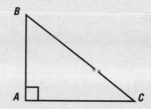

A. *AB* is equal to *BC*.

B. *AC* is equal to *BC*.

C. *BC* is greater than *AB*.

D. *BC* is less than *AC*.

78. Look at this series: Z5, Y7, X9, W11, ... What term should come next?

A. T12

B. S12

C. U13

D. V13

79. What number can be averaged with 10 to get 12?

A. 10

B. 12

C. 14

D. 16

80. How many nickels are equal to three quarters and two dimes?

A. 5

B. 18

C. 20

D. 19

81. Look at this series: 2, 0, 2, 0, 0, 2, 0, 0, 0, 2, ... What should the next four terms be?

A. 0, 0, 0, 0

B. 0, 0, 0, 2

C. 0, 2, 0, 2

D. 2, 2, 2, 2

82. What number is seven more than $\frac{1}{3}$ of 12^2?

A. 42

B. 48

C. 55

D. 57

83. Look at this series: 9, 7, 8, 6, 7, 5, 6, ... What number should come next?

A. 4

B. 5

C. 6

D. 7

84. How many millimeters are in 335 meters?

A. 3,550

B. 35,000

C. 355,000

D. 3,550,000

85. Look at this series: A, BB, CCC, DDDD, ... What term should come next?

A. EEEE

B. EEEEE

C. E

D. EEE

86. Examine A, B, and C and choose the best answer.

    A. 50% of 30

    B. 25% of 60

    C. 10% of 100

A. A = B = C

B. A = B > C

C. A < B = C

D. A < B < C

87. Look at this series: __, 5, 9, 12, 16, 19. What number should fill in the blank?

    A. 1
    B. 2
    C. 3
    D. 4

88. What is half of a quarter of six squared?

    A. 1.5
    B. 3
    C. 4.5
    D. 6

89. Look at this series: 1, 4, 7, 10, 13, ... If the pattern continues, what number will *not* eventually appear?

    A. 16
    B. 18
    C. 19
    D. 22

90. Examine the square and the rectangle and find the best answer.

    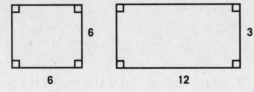

    A. The area of the square is greater than the area of the rectangle.
    B. The perimeter of the square is greater than the perimeter of the rectangle.
    C. The area of the square is equal to the area of the rectangle.
    D. The perimeter of the square is equal to the perimeter of the rectangle.

91. Look at this series: 1, 2, 4, 8, 16, 32, ... Which term of this series will be the first to exceed 100?

    A. 7th
    B. 8th
    C. 9th
    D. 10th

92. What number is 75% of the median of {1, 2, 3, 3, 4, 5, 6, 9, 9, 14, 17, 20}?

    A. $\frac{11}{3}$
    B. $\frac{13}{4}$
    C. $\frac{28}{6}$
    D. $\frac{33}{8}$

93. Examine the parallelogram and choose the best answer.

    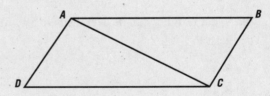

    A. *AD* is greater than *BC*.
    B. *CD* is less than *AB*.
    C. The area of the parallelogram is equal to the area of triangle *ABC*.
    D. The perimeter of triangle *ABC* is equal to the perimeter of triangle *ADC*.

94. Look at this series: ABC, CDE, EFG, GHI, ... What term should come next?

    A. IJK
    B. JKL
    C. HIJ
    D. GIJ

95. What is the reciprocal of $\frac{18}{5} \div 3$?

    A. $\frac{5}{6}$

    B. $\frac{12}{10}$

    C. $\frac{18}{15}$

    D. $\frac{4}{7}$

96. Examine A, B, and C and choose the best answer.

    A. $(3 + 2) \div 5$

    B. $(3 + 1) \div 4$

    C. $(2 + 4) \div 3$

    A. A is equal to B and less than C.

    B. A is equal to C.

    C. B is equal to C.

    D. C is less than A and B.

97. The square of what number is equal to 7 more than the square of 3?

    A. 3

    B. 4

    C. 9

    D. 16

98. Look at this series: 13, 24, 35, 46, ... What number comes next?

    A. 52

    B. 53

    C. 56

    D. 57

99. What number is 5 less than half the average of 7, 9, and 26?

    A. 1

    B. 2

    C. 3

    D. 4

100. Examine the rectangles A, B, and C and choose the best answer.

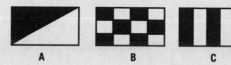

    A. The shading in A is greater than the shading in B.

    B. The shading is the same in all three rectangles.

    C. The shading in C is more than the shading in A and B.

    D. The shading in B is less than the shading in C.

101. Look at this series: 0, –2, –4, –6, –12, –14, –28, ... What number should come next?

    A. –30

    B. –26

    C. –20

    D. 26

102. There are on average 27.5 students for every teacher, and eight teachers per principal. How many students are there if the district has 14 principals?

    A. 3,020.5

    B. 3,080

    C. 3,120

    D. 3,200.5

103. Examine the cube and choose the best answer.

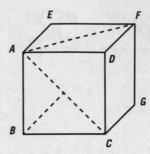

A. *AC* is equal to *DF*.

B. *AC* is equal to *AF*.

C. *CG* is equal to *AF*.

D. *AE* is equal to *AC*.

104. Examine A, B, and C, and find the best answer.

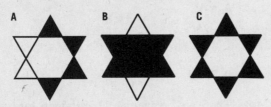

A. A > B < C

B. A < B > C

C. A < B < C

D. A > B > C

105. Examine A, B, and C and choose the best answer.

　A. $\frac{3}{4}$

　B. $\frac{5}{8}$

　C. $\frac{3}{8}$

A. A < B < C

B. B < C < A

C. C < A < B

D. C < B < A

106. What is $\frac{1}{3}$ of the largest two-digit number?

A. 3

B. 9

C. 33

D. 99

107. Look at this series: 4, __, 10, __, 16. If the pattern is to add the same number for each step, what two numbers are missing?

A. 6 and 13

B. 6 and 12

C. 7 and 12

D. 7 and 13

108. Which series has a pattern that uses both addition and multiplication?

A. 2, 3, 6, 7, 14, 15, 30

B. 1, 2, 4, 8, 16, 32, 64

C. 2, 4, 6, 8, 10, 12, 14

D. 8, 7, 6, 5, 4, 3, 2

109. Examine the circle, square, and triangle, and choose the best answer.

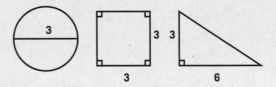

A. All the shapes have an equal area.

B. The area of the square is equal to the area of the triangle, and greater than the area of the circle.

C. The area of the triangle is equal to the area of the circle.

D. The area of the square is greater than the area of the triangle.

110. Examine A, B, and C and choose the best answer.

    A. 6 more than $\frac{1}{3}$ of 21

    B. 2 less than $\frac{1}{2}$ of 26

    C. 5 more than $\frac{1}{4}$ of 100

    A. $C > A > B$

    B. $A > B = C$

    C. $A = B = C$

    D. $A > B > C$

111. The variable x is the average of 10, 10, and 11. Choose the best answer.

    A. x is less than 10.

    B. x is between 10 and 11.

    C. x is between 11 and 12.

    D. x is greater than 12.

112. Examine A, B, and C and choose the best answer.

    A. 3 dimes and 17 pennies

    B. 4 dimes and 2 nickels

    C. 2 quarters

    A. $A < B = C$

    B. $A = B < C$

    C. $A < B < C$

    D. $A = B = C$

STOP.

If you finish before time is up, you may check your work on this section only.
Do not turn to any other section in the test.

Practice Test 6: HSPT®

READING

62 Questions (25 minutes)

Comprehension

Turn to the Reading Comprehension section of your answer sheet to answer the questions in this section.

> **Directions:** Read each passage and review the associated questions, then re-read—if necessary—to find the correct answer.

Questions 113–122 refer to the following passage.

Early in the nineteenth century, American youth were playing a game, somewhat like the English game of rounders, that contained all the elements of modern baseball. It was neither scientifically planned nor skillfully played, but it furnished considerable excitement for players and spectators
Line alike. The playing field was a sixty-foot square with goals, or bases, at each of its four corners. A
5 pitcher stationed himself at the center of the square, and a catcher and an indefinite number of fielders supported the pitcher and completed the team. None of these players, usually between 8 and 20 on a side, covered the bases. The batter was ruled out for balls caught on the fly or on the first bounce, and a base runner was out if he was hit by a thrown ball while off base. The bat was nothing more than a <u>stout</u> paddle with a two-inch-thick handle. The ball was apt to be
10 an <u>impromptu</u> affair composed of a bullet, cork, or metal slug tightly wound with wool yarn and string. With its simple equipment and only a few rules, this game steadily increased in popularity during the first half of the century.

113. Which of the following titles best expresses the main idea of the selection?

 A. "Baseball Rules"

 B. "An English Game"

 C. "Baseball's Predecessor"

 D. "American Pastimes"

114. The rules of this game required

 A. 8 fielders.

 B. a pitcher, a catcher, and one fielder for each base.

 C. 20 fielders.

 D. no specific number of players.

115. The shape of the playing field was

 A. oblong.

 B. irregular.

 C. square.

 D. subject to no rules.

116. The game was

 A. scientifically planned.

 B. exciting for the players but boring to watch.

 C. boring for the players but exciting to watch.

 D. like an English game called "rounders."

117. The word <u>impromptu</u>, as used in this passage, most nearly means

  A. proven.

  B. unavoidable.

  C. improvised.

  D. argued about.

118. This passage roughly places the playing of this game between the years of

  A. 1900 to 1950.

  B. 1800 to 1850.

  C. 1700 to 1750.

  D. 1760 to 1790.

119. This selection suggests that

  A. the game continued growing in its popularity.

  B. the game was dangerous.

  C. baseball originated in the United States.

  D. the game required skilled players.

120. According to the author, the popularity of this game was based largely upon

  A. the excitement of watching skillful players.

  B. the low cost of equipment.

  C. the fact that none of the players covered the bases.

  D. it being a new, strictly American game.

121. Based on the passage, we can infer that the game is different from modern baseball in that

  A. the game in the passage includes four bases.

  B. the game in the passage is more like rounders.

  C. baseball is nothing like the game in the passage.

  D. baseball is more organized and has more official rules.

122. The writer of this selection

  A. disdains this game because of its unprofessional aspects.

  B. is nostalgic for days when games were simpler.

  C. presents a factual report.

  D. admires the ingenuity of American youth.

Practice Test 6: HSPT®

Questions 123–132 refer to the following passage.

Nuclear power is generated is through a process known as nuclear fission. The term *fission* means "to split," as nuclear fission occurs when an atom absorbs an extra neutron, or an atomic particle that has no electrical charge. If an atom is hit by a neutron traveling at high speed, the atom will
Line split into two or more parts. Two types of atoms that release considerable energy when split are
5   uranium and plutonium. When uranium or plutonium atoms are split, they release a great deal of energy. They also release more neutrons, which causes the splitting process to continue. This continued splitting process is known as a nuclear chain reaction. It is the process that enables nuclear fission to create power.

   Most nuclear reactors today use uranium as the main element in the fission process. Ura-
10 nium is found naturally in the earth and is <u>extracted</u> through mining. When natural uranium is first mined, it contains two components known as Uranium-235 and Uranium-238. The first component, Uranium-235, creates large amounts of energy in a nuclear reaction and can there-fore be used for the fission process. The second component, Uranium-238, cannot be used in the fission process and must be discarded. However, most natural uranium is made up of 99.3
15 percent U-238 and only 0.07 percent U-235. Before the uranium is used in nuclear reactions, then, it first goes through a process known as enrichment. The <u>enriched</u> uranium contains much more of the usable U-235 than natural uranium—about 4 or 5 percent.

123. When natural uranium is first mined, how much of it is usable in a nuclear reactor?

A. 0.07 percent

B. 4 percent

C. 96 percent

D. 99. 3 percent

124. In a nuclear chain reaction, what causes the nuclear splitting process to continue?

A. The neutrons released when uranium or plutonium atoms are split

B. The energy released when uranium or plutonium atoms are split

C. The radioactive waste produced when uranium or plutonium atoms are split

D. The fuel rods used to house the fission process, during which uranium atoms are split

125. All the following statements are true according to the passage, *except*

A. plutonium atoms release a lot of energy when split.

B. natural uranium does not contain enough usable U-235.

C. nuclear fission is an entirely natural process.

D. power is created by a nuclear chain reaction.

126. The word *enriched*, as used in this passage, most nearly means

A. weakened.

B. strengthened.

C. wealthier.

D. lightened.

127. A neutron is a particle that has

A. a negative electrical charge.

B. a positive electrical charge.

C. no electrical charge.

D. an alternating electrical charge.

128. What do the elements uranium and pluto-nium have in common?

    A. They both contain atoms that split very easily.

    B. They do not possess any neutrons.

    C. They both are enriched by one another.

    D. They both have a positive electrical charge.

129. A nuclear chain reaction is the process that creates

    A. enriched uranium.

    B. nuclear reactors.

    C. an electrical charge.

    D. nuclear power.

130. How many uranium components are found in uranium in its natural state?

    A. None

    B. One

    C. Two

    D. Four

131. The author's purpose in writing this selection was most probably to

    A. warn people of the dangers of nuclear power.

    B. explain how nuclear power is created.

    C. promote the benefits of nuclear power.

    D. explore alternatives to fossil fuels.

132. Which of the following titles best expresses the main idea of this passage?

    A. "The Discovery of Nuclear Fission"

    B. "The Uses of Nuclear Fission"

    C. "The Process of Nuclear Fission"

    D. "The Varieties of Nuclear Fission"

Practice Test 6: HSPT®

Questions 133–142 refer to the following passage.

Have you ever wondered about the origins of the humble and unassuming fortune cookie? Many people have been introduced to these curious little treats at the <u>cessation</u> of a meal at a Chinese restaurant—after eating, your waiter or waitress brought you a small plate with fortune cookies for your table on it. You'd then carefully select a cookie, crack it open, and read your fortune on the small slip of paper inside while eating the cookie. These intriguing slips of paper may contain a wise saying, a prophecy, or even a good luck phrase and numbers. Whether or not that slip of paper truly holds your fortune is best left to fate to decide. For many, their first experience with fortune cookies left an <u>indelible</u> mark on their memories. But where do these cookies come from?

Believe it or not, the origins of the fortune cookie are as mysterious as the messages found inside of them. Traditional fortune cookies were handmade, and claims as to who invented it are varied and far-reaching, spanning countries across the globe—folks in the United States, Japan, and China all claim to have invented the fortune cookie. Variations of the fortune cookie go back at least as far as 19th-century Japan, although they didn't resemble the modern cookies many people recognize today. Some even claim that the roots of the fortune cookie go back as far as the late 17th century in Romania, where "note pies" were commonly served as part of elegant royal feasts. Others declare that Japanese mooncakes from the Ming revolution, which contained hidden messages, are the direct ancestors of modern fortune cookies. Regarding the origins of the fortune cookie, only one thing seems certain—the dispute as to who invented them may never be definitively settled.

Today's fortune cookies, typically made with vanilla, butter, flour, sugar, and sesame oil, are often manufactured by huge machines—a big change from traditional cookies. Approximately 3 billion fortune cookies are made worldwide every year, and they are always a welcome sight at meals, gatherings, and special events. We may not always be able to predict the future, but hopefully we'll always have fortune cookies around to help us get a glimpse of what's in store for us.

Line 5

10

15

20

25

133. Which of the following titles best expresses the main idea of this passage?

   A. "Fortune Cookies: A Mysterious Treat with Mysterious Origins"

   B. "What is Your Favorite Treat after a Good Meal?"

   C. "An Exploration of Hidden Messages and Secret Codes"

   D. "A History of the World's Most Popular and Beloved Cookie"

134. The word *cessation*, as used in this passage, most nearly means

   A. ending.

   B. beginning.

   C. climax.

   D. middle.

135. The best word to sum up the author's beliefs regarding the origins of the fortune cookie is

   A. obvious.

   B. unclear.

   C. traceable.

   D. humorous.

136. Why does the author refer to modern, machine-made fortune cookies as "a big change from traditional cookies"?

    A. Because no one knows who invented traditional fortune cookies

    B. Because traditional fortune cookies were larger and had different ingredients

    C. Because traditional fortune cookies were made by hand

    D. Because traditional fortune cookies tasted better

137. The word *indelible*, as used in this passage, most nearly means

    A. inedible.

    B. brief.

    C. unimaginable.

    D. unforgettable.

138. Based on the information in the passage, can we conclude that fortune cookies are the author's favorite cookie?

    A. Yes, the author says that this is his or her favorite type of cookie.

    B. Yes, that's the only reason the author would write this passage.

    C. No, there's not enough information in the passage to determine this.

    D. No, the author most likely prefers another type of cookie.

139. According to the information in the passage, all the following ingredients make up the modern fortune cookie *except*

    A. vanilla.

    B. cinnamon.

    C. butter.

    D. flour.

140. According to the information in the passage, all the following are possible things you'd find in a fortune cookie fortune *except* a

    A. funny riddle.

    B. wise saying.

    C. prophecy.

    D. good luck phrase.

141. What is the author's most likely purpose for writing this passage?

    A. To practice writing an investigative essay

    B. To confess his or her obsession with fortune cookies

    C. To inform readers about the origin of fortune cookies

    D. To persuade readers to eat more fortune cookies

142. According to the information in the passage, fortune cookies were potentially invented in which of the following places?

    A. Thailand

    B. Brazil

    C. Bali

    D. Japan

Questions 143–152 refer to the following passage.

By the mere age of 25, Orson Welles had already distinguished himself in multiple areas of the entertainment field. He'd founded his own theater group called the Mercury Theatre that not only produced dramas for the stage but also crafted celebrated radio plays. He'd inadvertently
Line executed one of history's most noteworthy hoaxes when many people mistook his radio produc-
5 tion of H.G. Welles's novel *The War of the Worlds*, a thrilling tale about a Martian invasion, for an actual news report. However, despite his multiple achievements and <u>claims to fame</u>, even Welles must have been surprised by the outcome of his very first foray into the world of cinema. When the 25-year old wrote, directed, and starred in *Citizen Kane* for RKO Pictures, he made what is often considered to be the greatest film of all time because of its innovative storytell-
10 ing, superb acting, and experimental filmmaking techniques. Perhaps most incredible of all is the fact that audiences did not embrace *Citizen Kane* eagerly when it was first released. In fact, the film ultimately lost money for RKO. Of course, for the man who once said, "I have always been more interested in experiment than in accomplishment," such financial failure could not have mattered much.

143. Orson Welles was a

A. filmmaker.

B. film critic.

C. film studio chief.

D. film teacher.

144. Orson Welles's version of *The War of the Worlds* is a

A. novel.

B. radio play.

C. stage play.

D. film.

145. By his statement, "I have always been more interested in experiment, than in accomplishment," Orson Welles implies that he

A. thought that every artist should be mainly focused on trying new things.

B. was afraid that people might find out how little money *Citizen Kane* made.

C. preferred making original art to being thought of as successful.

D. knew that his work was too experimental but did not care.

146. The phrase "claims to fame," as used in the passage, most nearly means

A. arguments for success.

B. noteworthy achievements.

C. statements about popularity.

D. maintains celebrity.

147. Orson Welles formed the Mercury Theatre

A. when he was 25-years old.

B. in order to perform *The War of the Worlds*.

C. for RKO Pictures.

D. before he made *Citizen Kane*.

148. Orson Welles

A. was extremely creative.

B. was the greatest artist ever.

C. produced more successful work than failures.

D. respected everyone who made great art.

149. Critics who praised *Citizen Kane* did not

    A. think Orson Welles deserved so much credit for making the film.
    B. give any other film as much praise as they showered on *Citizen Kane*.
    C. care that few people went to see the film.
    D. convince many people to see the film when it was released.

150. Based on this passage, Orson Welles would probably *not* choose to

    A. act in a stage play.
    B. write a movie script.
    C. direct a radio play.
    D. paint a picture.

151. In the first sentence, the writer uses "mere" to describe Orson Welles's age because

    A. Welles was very inexperienced when he made *Citizen Kane*.
    B. most people thought Welles was too old to make *Citizen Kane*.
    C. 25 is a relatively young age at which to make such an important film.
    D. Welles had just turned 25 when he made his first film.

152. *Citizen Kane* was probably popular with film critics because they

    A. always appreciated films like *Citizen Kane*.
    B. appreciated its many impressive qualities.
    C. liked the other films Orson Welles had made.
    D. thought Orson Welles was a good actor.

Vocabulary

Turn to the Vocabulary section of your answer sheet to answer the questions in this section.

Directions: Choose the answer that's closest in meaning to the underlined word in the question.

153. tedious work

    A. technical
    B. interesting
    C. tiresome
    D. confidential

154. to rescind an order

    A. revise
    B. cancel
    C. misinterpret
    D. confirm

155. a histrionic reaction

    A. confusing
    B. impressive
    C. dramatic
    D. productive

156. the problem of indigence

    A. poverty
    B. corruption
    C. intolerance
    D. laziness

157. a <u>vindictive</u> person

   A. prejudiced
   B. unpopular
   C. petty
   D. revengeful

158. unsatisfactory <u>remuneration</u>

   A. payment
   B. summary
   C. explanation
   D. estimate

159. a <u>deficient</u> program

   A. excellent
   B. inadequate
   C. demanding
   D. interrupted

160. a <u>detrimental</u> influence

   A. favorable
   B. lasting
   C. harmful
   D. restraining

161. <u>accurate</u> information

   A. correct
   B. good
   C. ample
   D. useful

162. to <u>amplify</u> one's remarks

   A. soften
   B. simplify
   C. enlarge
   D. repeat

163. to be legally <u>competent</u>

   A. expert
   B. ineligible
   C. accused
   D. able

164. a <u>shrewd</u> comment

   A. clever
   B. boring
   C. tired
   D. meaningless

165. a <u>relevant</u> article

   A. applicable
   B. controversial
   C. miscellaneous
   D. recent

166. an office <u>manual</u>

   A. laborer
   B. handbook
   C. typewriter
   D. handle

167. a computational <u>device</u>

   A. calculator
   B. adder
   C. mathematician
   D. machine

168. a <u>conventional</u> test

   A. agreeable
   B. public
   C. large-scale
   D. ordinary

169. the subject of <u>controversy</u>

    A. annoyance

    B. debate

    C. envy

    D. review

170. a <u>diplomatic</u> person

    A. well-dressed

    B. tactful

    C. domineering

    D. tricky

171. an <u>irate</u> student

    A. irresponsible

    B. untidy

    C. insubordinate

    D. angry

172. <u>durable</u> paint

    A. cheap

    B. long-lasting

    C. easily applied

    D. quick-drying

173. an intense <u>skirmish</u>

    A. conversation

    B. conflict

    C. meal

    D. package

174. the <u>inception</u> of the program

    A. beginning

    B. discussion

    C. rejection

    D. purpose

STOP.

If you finish before time is up, you may check your work on this section only.

Do not turn to any other section in the test.

MATHEMATICS

64 Questions (45 minutes)

Concepts

Turn to the Mathematics Concepts section of your answer sheet to answer the questions in this section.

Directions: Read each question carefully, then solve the problem to find the correct answer.

175. Which of the following could be a valid measurement for the speed at which a car is moving?

   A. 6 minutes

   B. 5 miles per hour

   C. 17 kilometers

   D. 14 pounds per inch

176. If there are five numbers, all of which are between 4 and 9, which of the following *cannot* be the average of these numbers?

   A. 3

   B. 4

   C. 5

   D. 6

177. It is possible for a scalene triangle to also be

   A. right.

   B. equilateral.

   C. isosceles.

   D. equiangular.

178. Which of the following is true?

   A. $a(b + c) = ab + c$

   B. $a + (b + c) = ab + ac$

   C. $(a + b) + c = a + (b + c)$

   D. $ab + ac = a + bc$

179. Which of these is a unit of volume?

   A. Square inches

   B. Seconds

   C. Pounds

   D. Cubic centimeters

180. If the radius of a circle is 3, what is its diameter?

   A. 1.5

   B. 3

   C. 6

   D. 9

181. Which of the following is the best unit of measure to use for the weight of a pencil?

   A. Ounces

   B. Pounds

   C. Tons

   D. Kilometers

182. Which of the following is a quadrilateral?

   A. Circle

   B. Pentagon

   C. Triangle

   D. Rhombus

183. If there are 2.54 centimeters in an inch, which of the following is closest to the number of centimeters in 10 inches?

    A. 20

    B. 25

    C. 30

    D. 35

184. If there are y kilometers in a mile, which expression represents the number of kilometers in k miles?

    A. ky

    B. $k + y$

    C. $y \div k$

    D. $k \div y$

185. To multiply a number by 100, move the decimal point

    A. one place to the right.

    B. two places to the left.

    C. three places to the right.

    D. two places to the right.

186. Which of these is a correctly written scientific notation?

    A. $0.038 = 3.8 \times 10^{-2}$

    B. $0.38 = 3.8 \times 10^{-2}$

    C. $380 = 3.8 \times 10^{3}$

    D. $3,800 = 3.8 \times 10^{2}$

187. Which of the following is true?

    A. $8 \leq 6$

    B. $6 \geq 6$

    C. $0.080 > 0.08$

    D. $15 < 8$

188. If two angles in a triangle are measured at 48° and 92°, what is the size of the third angle?

    A. 30°

    B. 40°

    C. 140°

    D. 180°

189. Evaluate: $3\frac{1}{2} + 2\frac{1}{4} - 1\frac{3}{4}$

    A. 4

    B. $3\frac{3}{4}$

    C. $2\frac{1}{2}$

    D. $1\frac{3}{5}$

190. A squirrel collected 165 acorns over the course of a 30-day month. On average, how many acorns did it collect per day?

    A. 3.9

    B. 4.1

    C. 5.5

    D. 6.2

191. A book was sold for $14.70, which was 30% off its regular price. What is its regular price?

    A. $16

    B. $17

    C. $19

    D. $21

192. There are 5,280 feet in a mile, and 3 feet in a yard. How many yards are in half a mile?

    A. 750

    B. 770

    C. 800

    D. 880

193. Consider this list of numbers: 3, 5, 9, 9, 2, 7, 1. Find the median and mode of the list. What is the average of the median and mode?

    A. 4

    B. 5

    C. 6

    D. 7

194. Simplify: $2\frac{2}{3} \times 4\frac{1}{4}$

    A. $10\frac{1}{3}$

    B. $10\frac{3}{4}$

    C. $11\frac{1}{3}$

    D. $11\frac{2}{3}$

195. What is the greatest common factor of 24 and 40?

    A. 4

    B. 8

    C. 10

    D. 16

196. The square root of 60 is between

    A. 5 and 6.

    B. 6 and 7.

    C. 7 and 8.

    D. 8 and 9.

197. Using a standard 6-sided number cube, what is the probability of rolling an even number?

    A. 25%

    B. 50%

    C. 75%

    D. 100%

198. What is the length of the hypotenuse in the triangle?

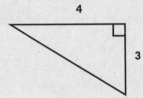

    A. 4

    B. 5

    C. 6

    D. 7

Problem Solving

Turn to the Mathematics Problem Solving section of your answer sheet to answer the questions in this section.

Directions: Read each question carefully, then solve the problem to find the correct answer.

199. Which set of numbers has a median of 13?

    A. 10, 12, 14, 15

    B. 12, 13, 14, 15, 16

    C. 10, 12, 12, 13, 13

    D. 9, 10, 15, 16

200. The perimeter of this shape is

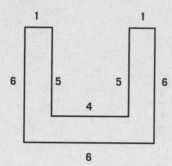

    A. 34

    B. 36

    C. 37

    D. 39

201. In a base-five system of numeration, what are the next three counting numbers after $43_{(5)}$?

    A. $44_{(5)}, 45_{(5)}, 50_{(5)}$

    B. $44_{(5)}, 45_{(5)}, 46_{(5)}$

    C. $44_{(5)}, 50_{(5)}, 52_{(5)}$

    D. $44_{(5)}, 100_{(5)}, 101_{(5)}$

202. Which one of the following is *not* equal to $62\frac{1}{2}\%$?

    A. $\frac{10}{16}$

    B. $\frac{5}{8}$

    C. 0.625

    D. 62.5

203. Solve: $12 - 2\frac{3}{16} =$

    A. $10\frac{13}{16}$

    B. $10\frac{3}{16}$

    C. $9\frac{13}{16}$

    D. $9\frac{3}{16}$

204. If $5(1 - 2x) + 25 = 0$, then $x =$ _____.

    A. 20

    B. 15

    C. 3

    D. −3

205. Solve: $2\frac{1}{2} + 7\frac{2}{3} + \frac{3}{4} =$

    A. $11\frac{7}{12}$

    B. $11\frac{1}{2}$

    C. $10\frac{11}{12}$

    D. $10\frac{1}{4}$

206. Solve: $6.41\overline{)3.6537}$

    A. 67

    B. 57

    C. 0.57

    D. 0.47

207. If $A = 3$, $B = 2$, and $C = 6$, find $\dfrac{3ABC}{2A}$.

    A. 18

    B. 16

    C. $4\dfrac{1}{2}$

    D. $4\dfrac{1}{6}$

208. Simplify: $4\dfrac{2}{5} \times 2\dfrac{3}{11}$

    A. $1\dfrac{117}{125}$

    B. $6\dfrac{1}{2}$

    C. $8\dfrac{6}{55}$

    D. 10

209. If $\dfrac{5}{6}x = 30$, then $x =$

    A. 42

    B. 36

    C. 25

    D. 20

210. The product of 11 and 12 is 3 more than N. What is N?

    A. 135

    B. 132

    C. 129

    D. 126

211. Solve for x: $2.5x + 12.5 = 30$

    A. 7

    B. 9

    C. 17

    D. 70

212. Add in base 5:

$$\begin{array}{r} 143_{(5)} \\ +\quad 33_{(5)} \\ \hline \end{array}$$

    A. $131_{(5)}$

    B. $221_{(5)}$

    C. $231_{(5)}$

    D. $241_{(5)}$

213. $\dfrac{3 \times 8}{6 \times 5} =$

    A. $\dfrac{1}{6}$

    B. $\dfrac{2}{3}$

    C. $\dfrac{3}{4}$

    D. $\dfrac{4}{5}$

214. What does 493 look like written out in expanded form using exponents?

    A. $(4 \times 10^2) + (9 \times 10) + 3$

    B. $(4 \times 10^3) + (9 \times 10^2) + (3 \times 10)$

    C. $(4 \times 10^1) + (9 \times 10) + 3$

    D. None of the above

215. Solve: $\dfrac{1\dfrac{3}{4} - \dfrac{1}{8}}{\dfrac{1}{8}} =$

    A. 12

    B. 13

    C. 14

    D. 15

216. $(3+4)^3 =$

   A. 21

   B. 91

   C. 343

   D. 490

217. Find the area of a triangle with the dimensions $b = 12'$, $h = 14'$.

   A. 168 sq. ft.

   B. 84 sq. ft.

   C. 42 sq. ft.

   D. 24 sq. ft.

218. If the average of 10, x, and 20 is equal to 30, what is the value of x?

   A. 10

   B. 20

   C. 60

   D. 80

219. If the three sides of a triangle have lengths $x + 1$, $2x$, and $3x - 2$, what is the perimeter of the triangle in terms of x?

   A. $6x - 1$

   B. $6x$

   C. $5x + 3$

   D. $x + 7$

220. Sally is 3 years older than Jim, and Jim is 2 years younger than Kate. Sally is 12 years old. How old is Kate?

   A. 9

   B. 10

   C. 11

   D. 12

221. The ratio of boys to girls in the class is 2:3. If there are 12 girls in the class, how many boys are there?

   A. 4

   B. 6

   C. 8

   D. 10

222. A $35 shirt is on sale for 20% off. How much is the sale price?

   A. $35

   B. $28

   C. $20

   D. $14

223. If the square has a perimeter of 40, what is the area of the circle?

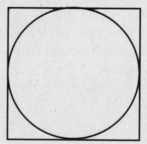

   A. 2π

   B. 15π

   C. 20π

   D. 25π

224. A board is 7 feet 8 inches long. A piece measuring 2 feet 10 inches is cut from one end. What is the remaining length of the board?

   A. 4 feet 10 inches

   B. 5 feet

   C. 5 feet 2 inches

   D. 5 feet 3 inches

225. Mary bought 3 boxes of pencils for $2.50 each, and 2 large erasers for $1.75 each. How much did she spend altogether?

    A. $4.25
    B. $9.80
    C. $10.75
    D. $11.00

226. A bag contains both cherry and lemon-flavored candies. If the bag contains 50 candies altogether, and the ratio of cherry to lemon candies is 4:1, how many lemon candies are in the bag?

    A. 10
    B. 20
    C. 30
    D. 40

227. A bag contains 3 blue chips, 5 green chips, and 6 red chips. If a chip is chosen at random from this bag, what is the probability that it is *not* green?

    A. $\dfrac{9}{14}$
    B. $\dfrac{5}{14}$
    C. $\dfrac{1}{3}$
    D. $\dfrac{3}{7}$

228. The perimeter of a rectangular garden is 120 feet. The length of the garden is 20 feet. What is the area of the garden, in square feet?

    A. 140
    B. 700
    C. 800
    D. 2,400

229. Two thirds of a number added to half the same number equals 14. What is the number?

    A. 6
    B. 9
    C. 10
    D. 12

230. Silver costs $17 per ounce. What is the cost of 3 pounds of silver?

    A. $792
    B. $794
    C. $816
    D. $1,078

231. Charles is $x + 3$ years old, and his sister Jenna is $2x + 1$ years old. If Jenna is 13, how old is Charles?

    A. 6
    B. 7
    C. 8
    D. 9

232. The population of a certain sample of bacteria doubles every 3 days. If there are 126 bacteria on a Monday morning, how many will there be on Wednesday morning of the following week?

    A. 936
    B. 1,008
    C. 1,134
    D. 1,200

233. On a certain day, there is a 25% chance of rain and a 30% chance of snow. What is the probability that it neither rains nor snows?

    A. 45%
    B. 55%
    C. 65%
    D. 75%

Practice Test 6: HSPT®

234. Admission to a museum is $3 for children and $7 for adults. On a certain day, the museum had 80 adult visitors. If they earned a total of $851 that day, how many children visitors did they have?

    A. 61

    B. 80

    C. 97

    D. 102

235. Christopher has $40, and he wants to buy a game that costs $38.50 before a 6% sales tax. How much more money does he need?

    A. $0.81

    B. $1.20

    C. $1.55

    D. $1.98

236. A store puts $17 pants on sale at a 20% discount. What is the new selling price?

    A. $16.80

    B. $13.60

    C. $12.65

    D. $3.40

237. What is the difference between $(4 \times 10^3) + 6$ and $(2 \times 10^3) + (3 \times 10) + 8$?

    A. 55,968

    B. 10,213

    C. 3,765

    D. 1,968

238.

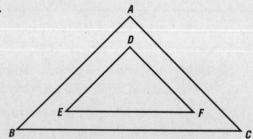

In the figure above, the sides of $\triangle ABC$ are respectively parallel to the sides of $\triangle DEF$. If the complement of $\angle A$ is 40°, then the complement of $\angle D$ is

    A. 20°

    B. 40°

    C. 50°

    D. 60°

STOP.

If you finish before time is up, you may check your work on this section only.

Do not turn to any other section in the test.

LANGUAGE

60 Questions (25 minutes)

Turn to the Language section of your answer sheet to answer the questions in this section.

Directions: In questions 239–267, look for errors in capitalization, punctuation, or usage. Then mark the answer choice containing that error. If there is no error, mark D on your answer sheet.

---

239. **A.** We had swum across the lake before the sun rose.

B. Clearly visible on the desk were those letters he claimed to have mailed yesterday.

C. John Kennedy effected many executive reforms during the tragically few years that he served as president of the United States.

D. *(No mistakes)*

240. **A.** The waiter brought a salad two steaks and a glass of iced tea to the corner table.

B. Everyone looked forward to the circus; each year, a new venue was chosen to host the spectacle.

C. Can we please stop making such a big deal about leaving the sleeping bag in the car?

D. *(No mistakes)*

241. **A.** Rather than go with John, he decided to stay at home.

B. Each of the nurses were scrupulous about personal cleanliness.

C. His education had filled him with anger against those who he believed had hurt or humiliated him.

D. *(No mistakes)*

242. **A.** Neither tears nor protests effected their parents' decision.

B. Being able to trust one's sources is indispensable for the investigative reporter.

C. When you go to the library tomorrow, please take this book to the librarian who sits in the reference room.

D. *(No mistakes)*

243. **A.** It's not good to have too much cholesterol in your diet.

B. Jack waited for his favorite newspaper, *The Haverford Courier*, to be delivered.

C. Frieda ate Muriel's signature dish, Eggplant Lasagna, on Sunday night.

D. *(No mistakes)*

244. **A.** If you prepare systematically and diligently for the examination, one can be confident of passing it.

B. Mary was so uninterested in the baseball game that she yawned unashamedly.

C. If he had thought to arrange an appointment, his reception might have been more friendly.

D. *(No mistakes)*

245. **A.** Carlie, Gracie, and Sammie are members of the swim team.

B. Sheila and Margie are the school's best pitchers.

C. My favorite zoo exhibit is the snake house.

D. *(No mistakes)*

246. A. Are you familiar with the benefits of own-ing life insurance.

B. What can you say about such a decorated soccer player?

C. The steam from the subway grate made the entire platform hazy.

D. (No mistakes)

247. A. Do not make a choice that changed the meaning of the original sentence.

B. I would appreciate your treating me as if I were your sister.

C. The contract should not have been awarded to the secretary's nephew.

D. (No mistakes)

248. A. There is a fantastic miniature golf course in Ocean City, Maryland.

B. At the time, the titanic was the largest pas-senger liner ever built.

C. Emily must have her wisdom teeth removed by a dentist.

D. (No mistakes)

249. A. You must explain that, in the United States, there is no government interference with the arts.

B. Failure to pay back loans is a major issue for banks.

C. The former Soviet Union was unsuccess-ful in curbing youth's "addiction" to hard rock and heavy metal music.

D. (No mistakes)

250. A. The driver was fined for driving more than 200 miles per hour.

B. The lady looked well in her new boots.

C. Neither the manager nor the employees want to work overtime.

D. (No mistakes)

251. A. The *Santa Maria* was the larger of Chris-topher Columbus's three ships.

B. His speech is so precise that it seems affected.

C. The door opens and in walk John and Mary.

D. (No mistakes)

252. A. His testimony today is different from that of yesterday.

B. If you had studied the problem carefully, you would have found the solution more quickly.

C. The flowers smelled so sweet that the whole house was perfumed.

D. (No mistakes)

253. A. Band practice is every other Tuesday.

B. Charlotte and Kelly are planning a Memo-rial Day tribute with the local Firefighters.

C. The deadline for signing up for soccer is next Friday.

D. (No mistakes)

254. A. Thanking someone in advance is an unac-ceptable modern practice.

B. I like Burns's poem, "To a Mountain Daisy."

C. Venetian blinds—called that even though they probably did not originate in Venice, are no longer used in most homes.

D. (No mistakes)

255. A. You see, you did mail the letter to yourself!

B. Your introduction to your new classmates has been a pleasant experience, has it not.

C. During the broadcast, you are expected to stand, to salute, and to sing the fourth stanza of "America the Beautiful."

D. (No mistakes)

Practice Test 6: HSPT®

256. A. Participation in active sports produces both release from tension as well as physical well-being.

B. One of those clerks is responsible for these errors.

C. None of the rocks that form the solid crust of our planet is more than two billion years old.

D. *(No mistakes)*

257. A. We all prefer those other kinds of candy.

B. The law prescribes when, where, and to whom the tax should be paid.

C. Everything would have turned out well if only she had waited.

D. *(No mistakes)*

258. A. Yesterday they laid their uniforms aside with the usual end-of-season regret.

B. John told William that he were sure he had seen it.

C. He decided to be guided by the opinion of whoever spoke first.

D. *(No mistakes)*

259. A. While driving through the mountain pass, the breathtaking scenes awed the travelers.

B. I do not understand why Mother should object to my playing the piano at the party.

C. My experience in South Africa taught me that the climate there is quite different from ours.

D. *(No mistakes)*

260. A. Learning to speak a foreign language fluently requires practice.

B. Buzzing around the picnic basket, a bumblebee flew into Sam's open mouth.

C. It would be interesting to compare the interior of one of the pyramids in Mexico with that of one in Egypt.

D. *(No mistakes)*

261. A. "Complaints from the public," reports a government official, "are no longer considered to be a mere nuisance."

B. Statistics tell us, "that heart disease kills more people than any other illness."

C. According to a report released by the Department of Agriculture, the labor required to produce a bushel of wheat in 1830 was three hours.

D. *(No mistakes)*

262. A. His written work has been done in so careless a manner that I refuse to read it.

B. I never feel badly if, after trying hard, I fail to win a prize; the effort gives me satisfaction.

C. Neither the United States nor any other country has seriously regretted having joined the United Nations.

D. *(No mistakes)*

263. A. My landlord does not approve of my sending that letter to the local rent control agency.

B. My artist friend and myself were the only guests in the gallery to truly appreciate the abstract paintings on display.

C. The messenger will have gone to the airport before the package arrives at the shipping room.

D. *(No mistakes)*

264. A. Due to the impending snowstorm, we will go directly home instead of stopping for ice cream.

B. The eraser was lost after it had lain alongside the typewriter for weeks.

C. Please distribute these newly arrived booklets among all the teachers in the building.

D. *(No mistakes)*

265. **A.** The lecture was interrupted by the whir-ring sound of the street-repair machinery right outside the window.

B. Mandated school courses include mathematics, literature, history, and science; optional subjects include drama, marching band, and weaving.

C. The pupil's account of his lateness is incredible, I will not give him a classroom pass.

D. *(No mistakes)*

266. **A.** Winter came before the archaeologists could do anything more than mark out the burial site.

B. Since her concentration was disrupted by the loud noise, she decided to wash her hair.

C. Let's you and me settle the matter between ourselves.

D. *(No mistakes)*

267. **A.** I recommend that you participate in all the discussions and heed the council of your elders.

B. Upon graduation from the training course, my friend will be assigned to a permanent position.

C. He finally realized that the extra practice had had a visible effect on his accuracy at the foul line.

D. *(No mistakes)*

Directions: For questions 268–277, look for mistakes in spelling only.

---

268. **A.** A novocaine shot promises only transient pain in place of agony from prolonged drilling.

B. I will join the theater party next week if I am able to locate a responseble babysitter.

C. That painting is so valuable that it is described as priceless.

D. *(No mistakes)*

269. **A.** Zach thinks downhill skiing is absolutely exhilarating.

B. Nala understood that being successful on the gymnastic team would require great disipline.

C. Gloria knew she wanted a red convertible immediately after getting her license.

D. *(No mistakes)*

270. **A.** Mary and Tom listened to the announcer on the radio as they drove back from the party.

B. The first game of the year was marred by what appeared to be unprofessional refereeing.

C. I went to the museum, but remained unimpressed throughout the tour.

D. *(No mistakes)*

271. **A.** The eager young politician stood at the street corner handing out political pamphlets.

B. If you do not watch your eating habits in a foreign country, you may return with an intestinal paresite.

C. My childhood heroes were mainly cartoon characters.

D. *(No mistakes)*

272. **A.** Begin to descend into the cave by way of the staircase just beyond the huge copper beech tree.
   B. Admissible evidence is evidence that has been collected in entirely legal ways.
   C. Since our army is so outnumbered, we might as well conceed defeat and limit our casualties.
   D. *(No mistakes)*

273. **A.** The scavengers desecrated many native graves.
   B. Be sure you enter your figures in a straight column.
   C. Even an exorbitant charge does not guarantee that the doctor will perform a thorough examination.
   D. *(No mistakes)*

274. **A.** The prologue to the play greatly enhanced its meaning.
   B. All students in attendance today will join together for an assembly program and a physical education class.
   C. The error on the scoreboard was immediately noticable to all.
   D. *(No mistakes)*

275. **A.** The union and management agreed that the reccomendation of the arbitrator would be binding.
   B. Parallel lines never meet.
   C. Drinking and driving often combine to conclude with a tragic accident.
   D. *(No mistakes)*

276. **A.** The hospital issued a daily bulletin regarding the movie star's medical condition.
   B. Please do not interrup my telephone conversation.
   C. The newest soft contact lenses allow for extended wear.
   D. *(No mistakes)*

277. **A.** The manufacturer's reply was terse but cordial.
   B. Every student who was questioned gave a similar explanation.
   C. The writer has created a clever psuedonym for himself.
   D. *(No mistakes)*

Directions: In questions 278-288, choose the sentence that demonstrates <u>correct</u> usage.

---

278. **A.** We all hope there are no onions on our pizzas when it arrive.
   B. All the tables in the furniture showroom have our tops dusted daily.
   C. Mohammed has an amazing collection of books displayed in its bookshelf.
   D. Will Diane remember to bring her famous pie to the reception dinner?

279. **A.** Derrick placed his new pair of scissor's in the kitchen drawer.
   B. Amelia's new cat ran nervously under her living room couch.
   C. Will we ever get to finally see Richards new play?
   D. I want to buy the same headphone's that Leland has.

280. A. Ethan knows that he'll need a great grade on the final to pass the class.

B. The chess team is facing an opponent that he'll never faced before.

C. The cleaning crew said that it'll be willing to work late this weekend.

D. Can we ask Aya how she'll knew that it would rain yesterday?

281. A. Little bit of patience can go a long way when working with a team.

B. What are the benefits to eating healthy diet every day?

C. I rented umbrella to keep us out of the sun this afternoon.

D. I just couldn't believe how long the movie was.

282. A. All of Wilma's video games were alphabetized in her entertainment unit.

B. Victor gathered all the cupcakes and put sprinkles on his tops.

C. Edwin set the antique globe upon their newly varnished wooden desk.

D. Will we ever see lasting improvements in their environment?

283. A. Chris has a surprising number of room's in his new house.

B. Lucy went to the flower shop's in search of a new orchid.

C. Will Ed's prediction about the outcome of the game come true?

D. We have yet to see Daphne's reach her full potential in class.

284. A. Hildy purchased too lavender vases from the florist shop.

B. Lucas spent to years working on earning his degree.

C. Kimmie is looking forward too her gymnastics meet tomorrow.

D. There were way too many people in the crowded elevator.

285. A. The millionaire lavish flaunted his incredible wealth.

B. Chenille careful diced two carrots for the salad.

C. Our new house cat sat lazy on the back of the sofa.

D. The player took a really long time to make the free throw.

286. A. Would you like to add an onion to the pot of chili?

B. Will there be opening act at the concert this weekend?

C. Keys hung on the hook by the front door.

D. Nearest highway rest stop was about five miles away.

287. A. Shea knows that she isn't eat the cake, but she did anyway.

B. Terence sprained his ankle and don't be able to run on Friday.

C. Unfortunately, Kira can't make it to the charity auction.

D. Let's make a list of who they're coming to the gala in March.

288. A. The paw's of the alley cat had extremely sharp claws.

B. Martin's treadmill was used only a handful of times.

C. Margot tablet ran out of battery power at the worst time.

D. Kirsten's placed the boxes in her basement for storage

Practice Test 6: HSPT®

Directions: For questions 289–298, follow the individual instructions.

---

289. Choose the best word or words to join the thoughts together.

    The soldiers will not come home _____ the war is over.

    A. while

    B. since

    C. before

    D. None of these

290. Choose the best word or words to join the thoughts together.

    We enjoyed the movie _____ the long wait in line.

    A. during

    B. despite

    C. because of

    D. None of these

291. Choose the word that best completes this sentence.

    Darren, a responsible security guard, could not leave his post _____ his shift replacement arrived each night.

    A. however

    B. because

    C. until

    D. but

292. Which of these expresses the idea most clearly?

    A. In tropical waters you can swim and see colorful fish in glass-bottomed boats.

    B. You can see glass-bottomed fish swimming among coral reefs and colorful boats in tropical waters.

    C. In tropical waters you often can see glass-bottomed boats, colorful fish, and coral reefs swimming.

    D. From glass-bottomed boats you can see colorful fish swimming in tropical waters among the coral reefs.

293. Which of these expresses the idea most clearly?

    A. Backgammon is a complex game, and you must change strategies often to learn it well.

    B. Though backgammon is easy to learn, it's a complex game that requires frequent shifts in strategy at the highest levels.

    C. To learn to play backgammon, you must shift complex strategies easily.

    D. You must easily learn to shift strategies to play the complex game of backgammon well.

294. Choose the pair of sentences that best develops this topic sentence.

"For cities, computers came along at just the right moment."

A. Cities were growing larger and spreading farther. People found they couldn't gather facts fast enough to make needed decisions.

B. The computer is a mass of complex parts and flashing lights. However, it is still just a machine made by humans to serve humans.

C. The most unusual use for computers lately has been in the supermarket. At the wave of a wand, the computer can read what a person has bought.

D. The computer aids business by storing information. It is able to provide this information almost as soon as a problem comes up.

295. Which of the following sentences offers *least* support to the topic "The Need to Protect the Bald Eagle"?

A. In flight, the bald eagle is beautiful.

B. Today, it enjoys the full protection of the law and seems to be slowly increasing.

C. It is so plentiful that it is seen as a dangerous rival to the fishing industry.

D. The game laws of Alaska are under local jurisdiction.

296. Which of these best fits under the topic "The Squid—A Master of Disguise"?

A. Because the squid is shy, it is often misunderstood.

B. Little sacs of pigment enable the squid to change its color and evade predators.

C. In reality they're adaptable, intelligent, and, oftentimes, even beautiful.

D. They propel themselves backward by squirting water out of a nozzle located near their heads.

297. Which sentence does *not* belong in the paragraph?

(1) Intense religious zeal was the main reason for the Crusades, but it was not the only reason. (2) The Crusades weakened feudalism. (3) Businessmen saw good opportunities to set up new markets in the East. (4) Some knights hoped to win military glory, and many just sought adventure.

A. Sentence 1

B. Sentence 2

C. Sentence 3

D. Sentence 4

298. Where should the sentence "Man is learning." be placed in the paragraph below?

(1) His past experiences have taught him well. (2) He imports ladybugs to destroy aphids. (3) He irrigates, fertilizes, and rotates his crops.

A. Before sentence 1

B. Between sentences 1 and 2

C. Between sentences 2 and 3

D. The sentence does not fit in this paragraph.

Practice Test 6: HSPT®

ANSWER KEYS AND EXPLANATIONS

Verbal Skills

1. C	13. B	25. B	37. A	49. D
2. A	14. D	26. A	38. B	50. B
3. C	15. C	27. C	39. A	51. C
4. B	16. A	28. C	40. C	52. C
5. D	17. B	29. B	41. D	53. D
6. D	18. A	30. C	42. A	54. B
7. A	19. C	31. D	43. B	55. C
8. D	20. A	32. C	44. B	56. C
9. A	21. C	33. D	45. C	57. A
10. B	22. A	34. A	46. B	58. C
11. C	23. C	35. C	47. A	59. B
12. B	24. D	36. A	48. B	60. D

1. **The correct answer is C.** *Fourth* is an ordinal number. The other three are cardinal numbers.

2. **The correct answer is A.** *Arouse* and *pacify* are antonyms, as are *agitate* and *smooth*. *Ruffle* is a synonym for *agitate*.

3. **The correct answer is C.** If the first two statements are true, then the only thing we can be certain of is that both Francine and Henri are better jugglers than Jerome. It is uncertain if Francine is a better juggler than Henri, or vice versa.

4. **The correct answer is B.** A query is a question, which is the opposite of *answer*.

5. **The correct answer is D.** To impair is to damage or to weaken.

6. **The correct answer is D.** All other choices are synonyms of the word *spin*. A planet (choice D) is something that spins, but it is not a synonym for the word.

7. **The correct answer is A.** That which is variable is changeable, fluctuating, or shifting.

8. **The correct answer is D.** The relationship is that of object to an action. When one beats an egg, one performs a violent act upon the substance of the egg in preparation for eating. When one mashes a potato, one performs an analogous act upon the potato. Baking a potato (choice B) prepares it for eating, but the act of baking is not analogous to the act of beating. If *mash* were not offered as a choice, *bake* might have served as the answer. You must always choose the best answer available.

9. **The correct answer is A.** To obstruct is to clog or to block.

10. **The correct answer is B.** The green balloon is lower in the sky than the red balloon. Since the yellow balloon is higher in the sky than the red balloon, the green balloon cannot be higher than the yellow balloon, so the third statement must be false.

11. **The correct answer is C.** The common feature among three of the answer choices is that they're all in the past tense. *Mixing* (choice C) is in the present tense.

12. **The correct answer is B.** The result is the product of a cause. A synonym for *result* is *effect*. Do not confuse *effect* with *affect*, which means "to influence."

13. **The correct answer is B.** The first part of the analogy establishes a noun (*weight*) and a verb that is typically used with it (*gain*). Lemonade is a beverage that one typically drinks (choice B).

14. **The correct answer is D.** A cave is a naturally occurring shelter that might be used as a dwelling place. All the other choices are man-made.

15. **The correct answer is C.** Pretzel, the dachshund, is clearly less shaggy than Pepper and so could be in the same dog obedience class, but there is no information to suggest that Pretzel even goes to obedience school.

16. **The correct answer is A.** The first part of the analogy establishes an item (camera) and a part that it comprises (lens). A lightbulb is an item and a filament (choice A) is part of it.

17. **The correct answer is B.** *Revenue* means "income." Taxes produce revenue, but they are not in themselves revenue.

18. **The correct answer is A.** A trapeze is a short horizontal bar that gymnasts and aerialists swing from and upon which they perform. All the other choices are tools that make work easier.

19. **The correct answer is C.** Tears may well come as a sign of emotion. All the other choices are emotions themselves.

20. **The correct answer is A.** From fastest to slowest jumper we have: Cleo—Lori—Inez—Linda—Mary.

21. **The correct answer is C.** *Manual*, as opposed to *automatic* or *mechanical*, means "hand-operated."

22. **The correct answer is A.** *Marshy* means "boggy" or "swampy."

23. **The correct answer is C.** The relationship is that of actor to object or, if you like, eater to eaten. A seal eats fish; a bird eats worms.

24. **The correct answer is D.** *Loss* is the opposite of *profit*.

25. **The correct answer is B.** Activity is motion. Rest is the absence of activity.

26. **The correct answer is A.** *Wind* is the general term for air in motion. All the other choices are descriptions of winds based upon wind speed.

27. **The correct answer is C.** All people eaters are purple, but it does not necessarily follow that all things purple eat people. We cannot tell whether there are some cyclops that are purple even though they do not eat people.

28. **The correct answer is C.** *Churlish* most nearly means "surly."

29. **The correct answer is B.** The word *immaterial* means "unimportant."

30. **The correct answer is C.** From the heaviest to the lightest books, we are told the order is: blue, orange, green, and red. Although we are told that orange books are not as light as yellow books, we cannot tell whether yellow books are heavier or lighter than the green books.

31. **The correct answer is D.** A shoe is made of leather; a highway is made of asphalt.

32. **The correct answer is C.** To mend is to repair, which is the opposite of *destroy*.

33. **The correct answer is D.** *Concrete* means "specific" or "particular." *Abstract* means "general" or "theoretical."

34. **The correct answer is A.** To function is to operate or to work.

35. **The correct answer is C.** Meat is food. All the other choices are nutrients found in food.

36. **The correct answer is A.** Because all Ts are either green-eyed Ys or blue-tailed Gs, it is reasonable to assume that some are blue-tailed Gs. Because all blue-tailed Gs have red noses, we can safely assume that some Ts, at least those that are blue-tailed Gs, have red noses.

37. **The correct answer is A.** A cacophony is a collection of loud or harsh noises.

Answers

Practice Test 6: HSPT®

38. **The correct answer is B.** *Monkey* is the general term describing a whole class of primates, regardless of gender. All the other choices are specifically male animals.

39. **The correct answer is A.** You taste with your tongue, but touch with your finger.

40. **The correct answer is C.** *Discord* means "deep disagreement." Music may be either harmonious (when the notes complement one another) or discordant (when the notes "disagree").

41. **The correct answer is D.** Fumes are gas, smoke, or vapor emanations. The other choices describe the smell of fumes.

42. **The correct answer is A.** Riding is a passive act; an animal or machine does the transporting. All the other choices are active ways to move from one place to another.

43. **The correct answer is B.** *Fatal* means "causing death" or "deadly."

44. **The correct answer is B.** Terry has won the most races of all.

45. **The correct answer is C.** A brick is opaque. All the other choices are translucent.

46. **The correct answer is B.** *Secure* means "safe," as in "not exposed to danger."

47. **The correct answer is A.** *Garish* means "gaudy" and "glaring," the opposite of *dull*.

48. **The correct answer is B.** This is a sequential relationship. A foal is the child of a horse, just as a son is the child of a mother.

49. **The correct answer is D.** Crackers are hard and crunchy in their texture, while all of the other foods listed are soft.

50. **The correct answer is B.** That which is counterfeit is an "imitation made with intent to defraud," and is therefore false.

51. **The correct answer is C.** All you know is that the thruway and the highway have more lanes than the parkway.

52. **The correct answer is C.** In this actor-and-object relationship, the actor serves as an irritant to the object. Thus, a flea irritates a dog; a fly irritates a horse.

53. **The correct answer is D.** The word *intermittently* means "recurring from time to time."

54. **The correct answer is B.** *Acrylic* means a type of paint, and is not a language like the other choices.

55. **The correct answer is C.** *Diverse* means "different," so its antonym would be *similar*.

56. **The correct answer is C.** The finder seeks and receives a reward; the repenter seeks and receives absolution (from sin, choice B). Contrition (choice D) is the feeling the repenter must have in order to repent. *Religion* (choice A) may be associated with *repentance* but without the same essential actor-to-object relationship.

57. **The correct answer is A.** When an object bends, it changes shape or orientation but remains intact. All other choices imply the breaking apart of an object.

58. **The correct answer is C.** We are told only relative positions regarding north and south, with no information about the concrete positions of these establishments. We cannot tell from this information exactly where the grocery store is in relation to the dry cleaner.

59. **The correct answer is B.** *Deception* means "fraud" or "subterfuge."

60. **The correct answer is D.** Nylon is a synthetic fiber; all other choices are natural.

Quantitative Skills

61. B	**72.** C	**83.** A	**93.** D	**103.** B
62. D	**73.** A	**84.** C	**94.** A	**104.** C
63. B	**74.** C	**85.** B	**95.** A	**105.** D
64. C	**75.** C	**86.** B	**96.** A	**106.** C
65. A	**76.** B	**87.** B	**97.** B	**107.** D
66. C	**77.** C	**88.** C	**98.** D	**108.** A
67. C	**78.** D	**89.** B	**99.** B	**109.** B
68. D	**79.** C	**90.** C	**100.** C	**110.** A
69. A	**80.** D	**91.** B	**101.** A	**111.** B
70. B	**81.** A	**92.** D	**102.** B	**112.** A
71. C	**82.** C			

61. The correct answer is B. The pattern in this series is made by multiplying each number by 2, and $2 \times 4 = 8$.

62. The correct answer is D. To find the average, add the numbers and divide the total by 3: $\frac{4+9+17}{3} = 10$. So, double the average is 20.

63. The correct answer is B. Start by finding $\frac{1}{4}$ of 48: $\frac{1}{4} \times 48 = 12$. Add 20 to this to get $12 + 20 = 32$.

64. The correct answer is C. The pattern here is $+1, +4, +1, +4$, and so on; $14 + 4 = 18$.

65. The correct answer is A. First find each number. $A = 10$, $B = 10$, and $C = 10$. All three are equal, so choice A is correct.

66. The correct answer is C. Examine the shading in each circle: A is $\frac{1}{4}$ shaded, B is $\frac{3}{8}$ shaded, and C is $\frac{1}{2}$ shaded. Now examine the answers. Only C is true, since $\frac{1}{4} < \frac{3}{8} < \frac{1}{2}$.

67. The correct answer is C. Since $9^2 = 81$, subtract 5 to get $81 - 5 = 76$.

68. The correct answer is D. Find each value. A is $4 + (3 \times 2) = 10$, B is $(4 + 3) \times 2 = 14$, and

C is $(3 + 2) \times 4 = 20$. C is the largest, so the answer is D.

69. The correct answer is A. Half of 26 is 13, and 3 more than that is 16. The number that leaves 16 when subtracted from 22 is 6.

70. The correct answer is B. *AB*, *BC*, *CD*, and *AD* are all equal since they are the sides of a square. *AC* is greater than any of these, since it is the hypotenuse of a right triangle whose legs are the sides of the square.

71. The correct answer is C. The pattern in this series is $\times 2, +2, \times 2, +2$, and so on. Apply this pattern to the series to get $18 \times 2 = 36$.

72. The correct answer is C. First find half of 14; $\frac{1}{2} \times 14 = 7$. Then add 7 to get the answer to the question; $7 + 7 = 14$.

73. The correct answer is A. The pattern in the series is one A, followed by two B's. To continue this pattern, the next three terms need to be B, A, B.

74. The correct answer is C. Find each value: A is $6^2 = 36$, B is $5^2 = 25$, and C is $3^2 = 9$. They are in order from largest to smallest, so A > B > C.

75. **The correct answer is C.** Each number is $1\frac{1}{2}$ more than the previous number. The next number is $7 + 1\frac{1}{2} = 8\frac{1}{2}$.

76. **The correct answer is B.** Each number in the series is 6 more than the previous number, so the missing number must be $73 + 6 = 79$. To check your answer, see if the next number matches the series; $79 + 6 = 85$.

77. **The correct answer is C.** This is a right triangle, and *BC* is the hypotenuse. The hypotenuse is the longest side of any right triangle, so *BC* is greater than both other sides.

78. **The correct answer is D.** The letter in each term is one place in the alphabet earlier than the letter in the previous term. The number is two more than the number in the previous term. The next term that follows this pattern is V13.

79. **The correct answer is C.** The average of two numbers is their sum divided by 2. If the answer is 12, that means the sum of the two numbers must be 24, since $24 \div 2 = 12$. To get a sum of 24 from 10, you need to add 14.

80. **The correct answer is D.** Each quarter is worth 5 nickels, so three quarters is worth $3 \times 5 = 15$ nickels. Each dime is worth 2 nickels, so two dimes is worth $2 \times 2 = 4$ nickels. The total is $15 + 4 = 19$ nickels.

81. **The correct answer is A.** The number of zeros following each "2" increases by one for each step. Next there should be four zeros.

82. **The correct answer is C.** The square of 12 is 144. One third of 144 is 48, so add 7 to get 55.

83. **The correct answer is A.** The pattern is −2, +1, −2, +1, and so on. The next term is $6 - 2 = 4$.

84. **The correct answer is C.** There are 1,000 millimeters in one meter. Multiply 1,000 by 355 to get your answer.

85. **The correct answer is B.** Each term in the series advances by one letter and increases the number of times that letter is repeated by one. The next term is the letter E repeated 5 times.

86. **The correct answer is B.** Find each value. A is 15, B is 15, and C is 10, so A = B > C.

87. **The correct answer is B.** The pattern is +4, +3, +4, +3, and so on. Since the first increase shown (from 5 to 9) is +4, the one before that should have been +3, and $2 + 3 = 5$.

88. **The correct answer is C.** $6^2 = 36$, a quarter of that is $36 \div 4 = 9$, and half of that is $9 \div 2 = 4.5$.

89. **The correct answer is B.** The pattern is +3, +3, +3, and so on. The series continues with 16, 19, 22, skipping over 18.

90. **The correct answer is C.** The square has a perimeter of $6 + 6 + 6 + 6 = 24$, and an area of $6 \times 6 = 36$. The rectangle has a perimeter of $2 \times 3 + 2 \times 12 = 30$, and an area of $3 \times 12 = 36$. Both figures have an area of 36, making choice C the correct answer.

91. **The correct answer is B.** The pattern is ×2, ×2, ×2, and so on. After 32, the series continues with 64, 128, and 256, so the first term to exceed 100 would be 128, the 8th term.

92. **The correct answer is D.** When you have an even number of data points in a set, you will find the median between the two center data points. In this case, it falls between 5 and 6, so 5.5 is the median. Multiply that by 75% to get 4.125, which converts to $4\frac{1}{8}$, or $\frac{33}{8}$.

93. **The correct answer is D.** The parallelogram is split into two identical triangles by the diagonal *AC*. Since these triangles are identical, they have the same perimeter.

94. **The correct answer is A.** Each term starts with the last letter of the previous term, and also includes the next two letters. The next term should start with I, and also include J and K.

95. **The correct answer is A.** Remember to flip the divisor; $\frac{18}{5} \times \frac{1}{3} = \frac{18}{15} = \frac{6}{5}$. Then, flip your result to get the reciprocal.

96. **The correct answer is A.** Start by finding the values of the 3 expressions; A is $(3 + 2) \div 5 = 1$, B is $(3 + 1) \div 4 = 1$, and C is $(2 + 4) \div 3 = 2$. So, A and B are equal, but they are less than C.

97. **The correct answer is B.** The square of 3 is $3^2 = 9$, and 7 more than this is $9 + 7 = 16$. The question asks for "the square of what number," so you need to find the square root of 16; $4^2 = 16$, so the answer is 4 (choice B). It is important to read carefully to provide the answer the question asks.

98. **The correct answer is D.** The pattern is +11, +11, +11, and so on. The next term is $46 + 11 = 57$.

99. **The correct answer is B.** The average of 7, 9, and 26 is $(7 + 9 + 26) \div 3 = 14$. Half of this average is $14 \div 2 = 7$, and 5 less than 7 is 2.

100. **The correct answer is C.** In A, half the rectangle is shaded. In B, 6 of the 12 squares are shaded, equal to one half. In C, $\frac{3}{5}$ of the rectangle is shaded, which is greater than one half, so C is the correct answer.

101. **The correct answer is A.** The pattern is -2, $\times2$, -2, $\times2$, and so on. The next term is $-28 - 2 = -30$.

102. **The correct answer is B.** For this, we use order of operations, starting within the parentheses: $(27.5 \times 8) \times 14 = 220 \times 14 = 3,080$.

103. **The correct answer is B.** All sides of a cube are the same. This means that the diagonals shown, *AF* and *AC*, are equal.

104. **The correct answer is C.** Each image is divided into seven parts: the center, and six point sections. Count the shaded portions of each figure, ignoring the size differences. Figure A is less shaded than figure B, which is less shaded than figure C.

105. **The correct answer is D.** Since B and C have the same denominator, and B has a larger numerator, you can immediately see that C < B. The fraction in A is $\frac{3}{4} = \frac{6}{8}$, and therefore B < A, meaning choice D is correct.

106. **The correct answer is C.** The largest two-digit number is 99 (the next number, 100, has three digits). Take $\frac{1}{3}$ of 99 to get 33, choice C.

107. **The correct answer is D.** The jump from 4 to 10 is 6, and this must be equal to adding the same number twice. Therefore, the pattern must be +3, +3, +3, and so on. The same logic can be used observing the second gap in the series. The missing terms are $4 + 3 = 7$, and $10 + 3 = 13$.

108. **The correct answer is A.** The pattern in choice A is +1, ×2, +1, ×2. The pattern in choice B is ×2, ×2, ×2. The pattern in choice C is +2, +2, +2. The pattern in choice D is −1, −1, −1. Only choice A involves both addition and multiplication.

109. **The correct answer is B.** Since the answer options all deal with areas, first calculate the area of each figure. The area of the square is $3 \times 3 = 9$, and the area of the triangle is $\frac{1}{2} \times 6 \times 3 = 9$. Since the circle fits inside the square, we know it has a smaller area, so there is no need to calculate the circle's actual area. Reading each of the answer options, choice B is the only one that fits the conditions.

110. **The correct answer is A.** Start by calculating values; $\frac{1}{3}$ of 21 is 7, and 6 more than 7 is 13. Similarly, B is 2 less than 13, or 11, and C is 5 more than 25, or 30. Once you have the values, plug them into the answer options, and you will find that C (30) is greater than A (13), which is greater than 11, as stated in choice A.

111. The correct answer is B. You might be able to do this one in your head. An average of 10, 10, and 11 is going to be more than 10, its lowest term, and less than 11, its highest term. As such, it is logical that the average would be between 10 and 11. In fact, the average of 10, 10, and 11 is $(10 + 10 + 11) \div 3$, or $31 \div 3$. This equals $10\frac{1}{3}$, which is indeed between 10 and 11.

112. The correct answer is A. The value of A is 30 cents + 17 cents = 47 cents, B is 40 cents + 10 cents = 50 cents, and C is 50 cents. Plugging these values into the answer choices shows that A (47 cents) is less than B (50 cents), which is equal to C (also 50 cents), making choice A correct.

Reading

Comprehension

113. C	121. D	129. D	137. D	145. C
114. D	122. C	130. C	138. C	146. B
115. C	123. A	131. B	139. B	147. D
116. D	124. A	132. C	140. A	148. A
117. C	125. C	133. A	141. C	149. D
118. B	126. B	134. A	142. D	150. D
119. A	127. C	135. B	143. A	151. C
120. B	128. A	136. C	144. B	152. B

113. The correct answer is C. The selection is about a game that appears to be an early version of modern baseball, so choice C is the best option. The paragraph is not actually about baseball, so choices A and D are incorrect. The article also mentions that the game is "somewhat like" the English game of rounders, but calling it "An English Game" would be misleading, making choice B incorrect.

114. The correct answer is D. There were "usually between 8 and 20 players." The number of players was not fixed by rule. In fact, according to the last sentence, there were very few rules.

115. The correct answer is C. One of the few rules defined the playing field as a 60-foot square.

116. The correct answer is D. Sentence 1 tells us that the game was similar to the English game of rounders. Sentence 2 assures us that the game was exciting for both players and spectators.

117. The correct answer is C. *Impromptu* means "improvised" or "made up on the spot." The ball is described as a bullet, cork, or metal slug wound with yarn and string, which matches the meaning of *impromptu* very well.

118. The correct answer is B. The nineteenth century consists of the years in the 1800s. The game is placed in the early nineteenth century, from 1800 on. Its popularity increased throughout the first half of the century, so it clearly was played at least until 1850—and probably beyond.

119. The correct answer is A. See the last sentence of the passage, in which the author specifically says the game "steadily increased in popularity." None of the other choices are supported in the selection.

120. The correct answer is B. The simple, improvised equipment made this a low-cost pastime. The players were not exceptionally skillful, and the game was only an American adaptation of an English game, so choices A and D are incorrect. Choice C is not singled out as an attraction of the game, so it not a good choice.

121. **The correct answer is D.** Sentence 1 says that the game had "all the elements of modern baseball," but then sentence 2 says that this game was not "scientifically planned nor skillfully played." Modern baseball is an organized sport, so this suggests the main difference between the two. Choice A is incorrect because modern baseball also includes four bases. Choice B is incorrect because we don't know enough about round-ers from the passage to make this determi-nation. Choice C is incorrect because the passage explicitly says that many elements are similar between this game and baseball.

122. **The correct answer is C.** The writer of the passage expresses no feeling whatsoever. This is nothing more than a clear, factual report. There are no specific opinions about this game or baseball, about whether this time period was better than now, or about the people who invented this game.

123. **The correct answer is A.** The answer to this detail question can be found by re-reading paragraph 2 of the passage, which discusses the percentage of usable uranium found in natural uranium when it is first mined. The passage tells us that most natural uranium contains only 0.07 percent of the usable type of uranium, which is known as U-235. Therefore, choice A is correct.

124. **The correct answer is A.** This question is a cause and effect question. In this case, you're asked to identify what causes the nuclear splitting process to continue in a chain reaction. The answer to this question can be found in paragraph 1 of the passage. Here, we are told that the release of neu-trons that occurs during fission causes the nuclear splitting process to continue. Choice

A pinpoints the cause as "the neutrons released" when uranium and plutonium atoms are split.

125. **The correct answer is C.** According to the passage, nuclear fission occurs after ura-nium is enriched and atoms are split—not as a natural process. Choices A, B, and D are all specifically mentioned as facts in the passage.

126. **The correct answer is B.** The passage states that the process of enrichment makes the uranium contain a higher percentage of U-235. Enriched uranium is therefore a more powerful type of uranium, so the word *strengthened* is the correct answer.

127. **The correct answer is C.** Paragraph 1 states that a neutron is an atomic particle with no electrical charge.

128. **The correct answer is A.** Paragraph 1 states that two types of atoms that split very easily are found in uranium and plutonium.

129. **The correct answer is D.** Paragraph 1 states that a nuclear chain reaction is the process that creates power, making choice D the cor-rect answer. Choice B is incorrect, because a nuclear reactor is a device in which nuclear power is created. Nuclear chain reactions do not create reactors, but instead take place *within* nuclear reactors.

130. **The correct answer is C.** Paragraph 2 states that natural uranium contains two compo-nents, Uranium-235 and Uranium-238.

131. **The correct answer is B.** The author explains the process of nuclear fission and uranium's role in that process. Choices A and C are incorrect, because the author doesn't offer any personal opinions regarding the dangers or benefits of nuclear power. Choice D is incorrect because the author does not discuss nuclear power as an alternative to fossil fuels.

132. **The correct answer is C.** The passage focuses almost entirely on the process of nuclear fission and how it creates nuclear

power. The passage does not explore or expand upon the ways in which nuclear power may be employed, so choice B is incorrect. Choices A and D imply information that is not addressed in the passage.

133. **The correct answer is A.** The purpose of the passage is to inform readers about the history of the fortune cookie, and the mystery that surrounds its origins. Therefore, the most appropriate title for this passage would be: "Fortune Cookies: A Mysterious Treat with Mysterious Origins." The other choices are too general for this passage.

134. **The correct answer is A.** The word *cessation* is used to describe the point at which fortune cookies come during the meal, and the author mentions that the cookies are served "after eating." Therefore, it most nearly means "ending."

135. **The correct answer is B.** The author states that "regarding the origins of the fortune cookie, only one thing seems certain—the dispute as to who invented them may never be definitively settled." Therefore, *unclear* is the best word to sum up the author's beliefs regarding the origins of the fortune cookie.

136. **The correct answer is C.** The author refers to modern, machine-made fortune cookies as "a big change from traditional cookies" because traditional cookies were made by hand, as mentioned in paragraph 2.

137. **The correct answer is D.** The word *indelible* is used in the passage to describe the lasting memory one's first experience with a fortune cookie can provide.

138. **The correct answer is C.** It may be true that the fortune cookie is the author's favorite cookie, but there's not enough information in the passage to determine this.

139. **The correct answer is B.** The only ingredient among the answer choices that is not explicitly mentioned in the passage is cinnamon.

140. **The correct answer is A.** The only choice among the answer choices that is not explicitly stated in the passage as something you could potentially find in a fortune cookie is a funny riddle.

141. **The correct answer is C.** This is an informative piece of writing regarding the fortune cookie and its origins, and the author's most likely purpose in writing this passage is to inform readers about the origin of the fortune cookie.

142. **The correct answer is D.** The passage explicitly states that Japan is one of the places where individuals claim the fortune cookie was invented.

143. **The correct answer is A.** According to the passage, Orson Welles wrote and directed films, which means he was a filmmaker. Film critics offer educated opinions on films, and this isn't among the numerous jobs mentioned in the passage. Therefore, choice B is incorrect. While Welles worked for the film studio RKO Pictures, the passage offers no evidence that he ran that studio, so choice C is incorrect. There is no evidence in the passage that Welles taught film either, so choice D is wrong as well.

144. **The correct answer is B.** According to the passage, Orson Welles's version of *The War of the Worlds* was a radio play. Although H.G. Welles's original version of the story was a novel, Orson Welles's version was not, so choice A is incorrect. While Welles did produce plays for the stage, there is no evidence in the passage to support the idea that he made a version of *The War of the Worlds* for the stage, so choice C is incorrect too. There have been film versions of *The War of the Worlds*, but the passage never suggests that Orson Welles made any of them, so choice D is incorrect.

145. **The correct answer is C.** Experimentation is often an important element of original art. In addition, the passage uses the words

innovative and *experimental* to describe Welles's work, making choice C the most logical interpretation of Welles's statement. Welles was only talking about himself when he made this statement; he was not talking about *all* artists, so choice A lacks support. While it is true that *Citizen Kane* did not make much money, Welles's statement does not seem to support the idea that he was afraid that people would find this out, so choice B is not a strong answer. Choice D implies that Welles was uncomfortable with how experimental his work was, but nothing in the statement supports that conclusion.

146. **The correct answer is B.** The idiom "claims to fame" means "noteworthy achievements," and the fact that this phrase follows mention of Welles's noteworthy achievements supports this interpretation of the phrase. While a claim can be an argument, and fame can signify success, the phrase "claims to fame" does not mean "arguments for success" in this context, as choice A suggests. Choices C and D make similar misinterpretations.

147. **The correct answer is D.** The passage suggests that Welles formed the Mercury Theatre before making *Citizen Kane*. However, it only mentions making *Citizen Kane* as something Welles did when he was 25, so choice A lacks support. While the Mercury Theatre did perform *The War of the Worlds*, choice B implies that performing that play was the specific reason Welles started the theater in the first place, and the passage does not support that conclusion. RKO Pictures made movies, not radio plays for the Mercury Theatre, so choice C is wrong.

148. **The correct answer is A.** Welles's ability to act in, write, and direct films—including stage radio and theater plays—is sufficient evidence of his extreme creativity. However, not everyone may agree with the extreme statement in choice B, so this answer is not as strong as choice A is. There is simply not enough evidence in the passage to support the conclusion in choice C. There is no evidence that supports choice D either.

149. **The correct answer is D.** The passage suggests that while most critics loved *Citizen Kane*, relatively few people actually went to see the movie, and this supports the conclusion in choice D, since it is a critic's job to either convince people to see a film or dissuade them from seeing a film. There is no evidence in the passage that supports choices A or B. And it's a critics job to persuade readers to see a movie or stay home, so choice C is incorrect.

150. **The correct answer is D.** While the passage provides ample evidence that Orson Welles worked in stage, film, and radio, there is no evidence that he was also a painter, so choice D is the likeliest answer.

151. **The correct answer is C.** The word *mere* means "basic," and the author uses it to indicate that 25 was a relatively young age at which to make a film as important as *Citizen Kane*. However, the fact that Welles had so much success in radio or on the stage by the time he was 25 makes choice A an unlikely answer. Choice B mistakes the meaning of the word *mere* for its opposite. And *mere* does not mean "recent," as assumed in choice D.

152. **The correct answer is B.** The passage discusses *Citizen Kane's* impressive qualities directly, mentioning its "innovative storytelling, superb acting, and experimental filmmaking techniques." The innovative and experimental nature of the film suggests that there were no others like *Citizen Kane*, so choice A is incorrect. *Citizen Kane* was Welles's first film, so choice C cannot be true. Choice D describes only one quality of *Citizen Kane* that may have impressed film critics, so it is not as strong an answer as choice B.

Vocabulary

153. C	**158.** A	**163.** D	**167.** D	**171.** D
154. B	**159.** B	**164.** A	**168.** D	**172.** B
155. C	**160.** C	**165.** A	**169.** B	**173.** B
156. A	**161.** A	**166.** B	**170.** B	**174.** A
157. D	**162.** C			

153. **The correct answer is C.** *Tedious* means "monotonous," "boring," or 'tiresome."

154. **The correct answer is B.** *Rescind* means "to take back," "to revoke," or "to cancel."

155. **The correct answer is C.** *Histrionic* refers to something or someone who is "dramatic."

156. **The correct answer is A.** Indigence is destitution or poverty. The word that means "laziness" is *indolence*.

157. **The correct answer is D.** *Vindictive* means "eager to get even," or "revengeful."

158. **The correct answer is A.** *Remuneration* means "compensation," "reward," or "payment."

159. **The correct answer is B.** *Deficient* means "lacking," "incomplete," or "inadequate."

160. **The correct answer is C.** *Detrimental* means "causing damage," or "harmful."

161. **The correct answer is A.** *Accurate* means "precise," or "correct."

162. **The correct answer is C.** To amplify is "to make larger or stronger," "to develop more fully," or "enlarge upon, as with details and examples."

163. **The correct answer is D.** To be competent is to be able, sufficient, permissible, or authorized.

164. **The correct answer is A.** *Shrewd* refers to something or someone that is "clever."

165. **The correct answer is A.** *Relevant* means "related to the matter at hand," or "applicable."

166. **The correct answer is B.** A manual is a book of instructions, or a handbook.

167. **The correct answer is D.** A device is a machine devised for a specific purpose. Be careful to define *only* the underscored word. A calculator (choice A) is a "computational device," but that is not the correct answer to the question.

168. **The correct answer is D.** *Conventional* means "customary," "usual," or "ordinary."

169. **The correct answer is B.** *Controversy* is "difference of opinion," "argument," or "debate."

170. **The correct answer is B.** *Diplomatic* means "tactful when dealing with people."

171. **The correct answer is D.** *Irate* means "angry."

172. **The correct answer is B.** *Durable* means "long-lasting, even under conditions of hard use."

173. **The correct answer is B.** *Skirmish* refers to a conflict.

174. **The correct answer is A.** *Inception* means "the beginning."

Mathematics

Concepts

175. B	180. C	185. D	190. C	195. B
176. A	181. A	186. A	191. D	196. C
177. A	182. D	187. B	192. D	197. B
178. C	183. B	188. B	193. D	198. B
179. D	184. A	189. A	194. C	

175. **The correct answer is B.** Units of speed are of the form x per y, where x is distance, and y is time. In choice B, x is miles and y is one hour.

176. **The correct answer is A.** The average of a set of numbers can never be outside of the range of values of the original numbers.

177. **The correct answer is A.** A scalene triangle has 3 sides that are all different. It is possible to also have a right angle in such a triangle. On the other hand, it is not possible for the triangle to be equilateral (choice B) since that means all 3 sides are the same. It cannot be isosceles (choice C) because that means that 2 sides are the same. Nor can it be equiangular (choice D) since that means all 3 angles are the same, which can only happen in an equilateral triangle.

178. **The correct answer is C.** This is the associative property of addition.

179. **The correct answer is D.** Volume units are cubed measurements of space occupied (or enclosed) by a substance or object.

180. **The correct answer is C.** The diameter of a circle is double its radius, so $2 \times 3 = 6$.

181. **The correct answer is A.** A pencil weighs much less than a pound (choice B) or a ton (choice C), so ounces are the most appropriate unit of measure from among the choices we are given. Kilometers (choice D) measure distance, not weight.

182. **The correct answer is D.** A quadrilateral must have 4 sides. A circle (choice A) does not have any sides, a pentagon (choice B)

has 5, and a triangle (choice C) has 3. Only the rhombus has 4 sides, making it a quadrilateral.

183. **The correct answer is B.** The number of centimeters in 10 inches is $2.54 \times 10 = 25.4$, which is closest to 25.

184. **The correct answer is A.** If each mile is equal to y kilometers, then k miles consists of y kilometers added to itself k times, or ky kilometers.

185. **The correct answer is D.** When multiplying by 10, 100, 1,000, etc., move the decimal point one place to the right for each zero in the multiplier. For this example, 100 has two zeros, so the decimal point would be moved two places to the right.

186. **The correct answer is A.** When working with scientific notation, the exponent represents the number of places the decimal point moves in the multiplier. If the exponent of 10 is positive, the decimal point moves to the right; if negative, it moves to the left.

187. **The correct answer is B.** The symbol $\geq$ means "greater than or equal to," and 6 is equal to 6.

188. **The correct answer is B.** The sum of the two angles given is $48° + 92° = 140°$. The angles in a triangle always add up to $180°$, so the third angle must be $180° - 140° = 40°$.

189. **The correct answer is A.** Converting each mixed number to a fraction makes the expression $\frac{7}{2} + \frac{9}{4} - \frac{7}{4}$. The

common denominator is 4, so this turns into $\frac{14}{4} + \frac{9}{4} - \frac{7}{4} = \frac{16}{4} = 4$.

190. **The correct answer is C.** If the total is 165, and the number of days is 30, the average per day is $165 \div 30 = 5.5$ acorns collected per day.

191. **The correct answer is D.** The sale price, \$14.70, is 30% off the regular price, so it is equal to 70% of the regular price. To compute the number that 14.70 is 70% of, calculate $14.70 \div 0.7 = 21$. The regular price is \$21.

192. **The correct answer is D.** To find the number of yards in a mile, divide by 3 to get $5,280 \div 3 = 1,760$ yards. The question asks for the yards in half a mile, so $1,760 \div 2 = 880$ yards. Be sure to review each answer to verify you have included all the steps the question asks for.

193. **The correct answer is D.** To find the median, put the list in order: 1, 2, 3, 5, 7, 9, 9. The median is 5, since it is in the middle of the list. The mode is the number that appears most often, which is 9. The average of 5 and 9 is $(5 + 9) \div 2 = 7$.

194. **The correct answer is C.** First, convert the mixed numbers into improper fractions;

$2\frac{2}{3} = \frac{8}{3}$, and $4\frac{1}{4} = \frac{17}{4}$. The product is $\frac{8}{3} \times \frac{17}{4} = \frac{136}{12}$. Dividing the top and bottom by 4 reduces this fraction to $\frac{34}{3}$, which is equal to $11\frac{1}{3}$.

195. **The correct answer is B.** The prime factorization of 24 is $2 \times 2 \times 2 \times 3$, and the prime factorization of 40 is $2 \times 2 \times 2 \times 5$. They have $2 \times 2 \times 2$ in common, so the greatest common factor is 8.

196. **The correct answer is C.** $7^2 = 49$, and $8^2 = 64$. 60 is between 49 and 64, so the square root of 60 is greater than 7 and less than 8.

197. **The correct answer is B.** The numbers on a standard number cube are 1, 2, 3, 4, 5, and 6. Three of these (2, 4, 6) are even, and there are six numbers altogether. Therefore, the probability of rolling an even number is $\frac{3}{6} = \frac{1}{2}$, or 50%.

198. **The correct answer is B.** By the Pythagorean Theorem, the square of the hypotenuse must be equal to $3^2 + 4^2 = 9 + 16 = 25$. Therefore, the hypotenuse itself must be 5.

Problem Solving

199. A	207. A	215. B	223. D	231. D
200. A	208. D	216. C	224. A	232. B
201. D	209. B	217. B	225. D	233. A
202. D	210. C	218. C	226. A	234. C
203. C	211. A	219. A	227. A	235. A
204. C	212. C	220. C	228. C	236. B
205. C	213. D	221. C	229. D	237. D
206. C	214. A	222. B	230. C	238. B

199. **The correct answer is A.** When there are an even number of terms, the median of a list is the average of the two middle numbers. In answer A, the two middle numbers are 12 and 14, and the median of these is 13. Answer B has a average of 14, answer C has a median of 12, and answer D has a median of 12.5 (the average of 10 and 15).

200. **The correct answer is A.** The perimeter is the sum of the lengths of all the sides. The lengths of all sides are included in the figure, so they only need to be added. There are three sides of length 6, two of length 5, two of length 1, and one of length 4. These numbers have a sum of 34.

201. **The correct answer is D.** The base-five system uses only five symbols: 1, 2, 3, 4, and 0. Because of this, the other three alternatives are eliminated.

202. **The correct answer is D.** For choice D to be equal, it would need the percent symbol after it. $62\frac{1}{2}\%$ is actually equal to 0.625 (choice C).

203. **The correct answer is C.** When subtracting fractional numbers, you must first rename the numbers with a common denominator.

$$12 - 2\frac{3}{16} = \frac{192}{16} - \frac{35}{16}$$
$$= \frac{157}{16}$$
$$= 9\frac{13}{16}$$

204. **The correct answer is C.** Solve for x:

$$5(1 - 2x) + 25 = 0$$
$$5 - 10x + 25 = 0$$
$$30 - 10x = 0$$
$$30 = 10x$$
$$3 = x$$

205. **The correct answer is C.** Convert the mixed numbers into improper fractions, then find the common denominator and add:

$$2\frac{1}{2} + 7\frac{2}{3} + \frac{3}{4} = \frac{5}{2} + \frac{23}{3} + \frac{3}{4}$$
$$= \frac{30}{12} + \frac{92}{12} + \frac{9}{12}$$
$$= \frac{131}{12}$$
$$= 10\frac{11}{12}$$

206. **The correct answer is C.**

$$
\begin{array}{r}
0.57 \\
6.41{\overline{)3.6537}} \\
3205 \\
\hline
4487 \\
4487 \\
\hline
0
\end{array}
$$

Answers | Practice Test 6: HSPT®

207. The correct answer is A. Replace the letters in the problem with the given numbers.

$$\frac{3ABC}{2A} = \frac{3 \times 3 \times 2 \times 6}{2 \times 3}$$
$$= \frac{108}{6}$$
$$= 18$$

208. The correct answer is D. Convert the mixed numbers to improper fractions and then multiply:

$$4\frac{2}{5} \times 2\frac{3}{11} = \frac{22}{5} \times \frac{25}{11}$$
$$= \frac{550}{55}$$
$$= 10$$

209. The correct answer is B.

$$\frac{5}{6}x = 30$$
$$x = \frac{30}{1} \cdot \frac{6}{5}$$
$$x = \frac{180}{5}$$
$$x = 36$$

210. The correct answer is C. Set this problem up as an algebraic equation.

$$11 \times 12 = N + 3$$
$$132 = N + 3$$
$$132 - 3 = N$$
$$129 = N$$

211. The correct answer is A.

$$2.5x + 12.5 = 30$$
$$2.5x = 30 - 12.5$$
$$2.5x = 17.5$$
$$x = \frac{17.5}{2.5}$$
$$x = 7$$

212. The correct answer is C.

$$\begin{array}{r} 143_{(5)} \\ +33_{(5)} \\ \hline 231_{(5)} \end{array}$$

213. The correct answer is D. Multiply and simplify:

$$\frac{3 \times 8}{6 \times 5} = \frac{24}{30} = \frac{4}{5}$$

214. The correct answer is A. Choice B is 4,930, and choice C is 133.

215. The correct answer is B. Simplify the numerator of the fraction, then divide.

$$\frac{1\frac{3}{4} - \frac{1}{8}}{\frac{1}{8}} = \frac{1\frac{6}{8} - \frac{1}{8}}{\frac{1}{8}}$$
$$= \frac{1\frac{5}{8}}{\frac{1}{8}} = 1\frac{5}{8} \cdot \frac{8}{1}$$
$$= \frac{13}{8} \cdot \frac{8}{1} = 13$$

216. The correct answer is C. First perform the operation within the parentheses. To cube a number, multiply it by itself two times.

$$(3 + 4)^3 = (7)^3 = 7 \times 7 \times 7 = 343$$

217. The correct answer is B. The formula for the area of a triangle is $A = \frac{1}{2}bh$. Plug in the numbers:

$$A = \frac{1}{2} \times 12 \times 14$$
$$A = 84 \text{ sq. ft.}$$

218. The correct answer is C. If the average of 3 numbers is 30, the sum of the numbers must be $3 \times 30 = 90$. Since the two numbers given, 10 and 20, have a sum of 30, the remaining number must be $90 - 30 = 60$.

219. **The correct answer is A.** The perimeter of a triangle is the sum of the lengths of its sides. Here, the sum is $(x + 1) + (2x) + (3x - 2) = 6x - 1$.

220. **The correct answer is C.** Sally is 12, and that is 3 years older than Jim, so Jim is $12 - 3 = 9$. Jim is 2 years younger than Kate, so Kate is $9 + 2 = 11$.

221. **The correct answer is C.** Since the ratio of boys to girls is 2:3, there are $\frac{2}{3}$ as many boys as girls, and $\frac{2}{3} \times 12 = 8$.

222. **The correct answer is B.** Start by calculating the amount of the discount; 20% of \$35 is \$7. Then subtract the discount from the regular price to get the final answer; \$35 - \$7 = \$28.

223. **The correct answer is D.** If the perimeter of the square is 40, each side must have a length of 10. From the placement of the circle within the square, we can assume that the circle's diameter is equal to the length of a side of the square, or 10. The radius of the circle is equal to half of the diameter, so it is 5. The area of the circle is therefore $\pi \times 5^2$, or 25π.

224. **The correct answer is A.** Starting with 7 feet 8 inches and subtracting 2 feet leaves 5 feet 8 inches. Subtracting an additional 10 inches means that the remaining length is 2 inches less than 5 feet, which is 4 feet 10 inches.

225. **The correct answer is D.** The pencils cost $3 \times \$2.50 = \$7.50$. The erasers cost $2 \times \$1.75 = \$3.50$. In total, Mary spent $\$7.50 + \$3.50 = \$11$.

226. **The correct answer is A.** The ratio of cherry to lemon candies being 4:1 means that for each group of 5 candies, 4 of them are cherry and 1 is lemon. There are 10 groups of 5 in the bag, since $50 \div 5 = 10$. Each of these groups contains only a single lemon candy, so there are 10 lemon candies.

227. **The correct answer is A.** There are total of $3 + 5 + 6 = 14$ chips, and $3 + 6 = 9$ of them are not green. The probability of a randomly chosen chip not being green is $\frac{9}{14}$. Choice B is the probability that it *will* be green.

228. **The correct answer is C.** The length is 20 feet, so the two 20-foot sides make up 40 feet of the 120 foot perimeter. This leaves 80 feet, which must come from the other two sides. These other two sides must each be 40 feet. So, the dimensions of the garden are 20 feet by 40 feet. Therefore, its area is $20 \times 40 = 800$ square feet.

229. **The correct answer is D.** The description given can be translated into the equation $\frac{2}{3}x + \frac{1}{2}x = 14$, where x is the unknown number. Using a common denominator of 6, the left side of the equation is equal to $\frac{7}{6}x$. Multiplying both sides of the equation by $\frac{6}{7}$ gives $x = 12$.

230. **The correct answer is C.** There are 16 ounces in a pound, so 3 pounds is $16 \times 3 = 48$ ounces. Each ounce costs \$17, so 48 ounces costs $\$17 \times 48 = \$816$.

231. **The correct answer is D.** Since Jenna's age is given as both $2x + 1$ and 13, the equation $2x + 1 = 13$ must hold. The solution to this equation is $x = 6$. Charles is then $x + 3 = 6 + 3 = 9$ years old.

232. **The correct answer is B.** Nine days pass between Monday morning and the Wednesday morning of the following week. In other words, there are three 3-day periods in that time, so the population will double 3 times. $2 \times 126 = 252$, $2 \times 252 = 504$, and $2 \times 504 = 1{,}008$.

233. **The correct answer is A.** Rain and snow have a combined $25\% + 30\% = 55\%$ chance of happening. All the probabilities must add up to 100%, so the chance of neither happening is $100\% - 55\% = 45\%$ (choice A).

234. The correct answer is C. The 80 adults account for $80 \times \$7 = \$560$. Since $\$851 - \$560 = \$291$, the children must account for $291. Each child admission is $3, so the number of children must have been $\$291 \div 3 = 97$.

235. The correct answer is A. Start by calculating the amount of sales tax; 6% of $38.50 is $2.31. This means the total cost will be $38.50 + $2.31 = $40.81. Christopher already has $40, so he needs $0.81 more.

236. The correct answer is B. Reduce the $17 price by 20%.

20% of $17 = $17 × 0.20 = $3.40

$17.00 − 3.40 = $13.60 (new price)

Choice A indicates a reduction of only 20 cents, when it should be 20%. Choice C is a reduction of $4.35, which is not correct. Choice D is the amount of the 20% reduction, which needs to be subtracted from the original price.

237. The correct answer is D.

$(4 \times 10^3) + 6 = 4{,}006$

$(2 \times 10^3) + (3 \times 10) + 8 = 2{,}038$

The difference is 1,968.

238. The correct answer is B. If the sides are parallel, the angles are congruent, and would both have a complement of 40°.

Language

239. D	251. A	263. B	275. A	287. C
240. A	252. D	264. A	276. B	288. B
241. B	253. B	265. C	277. C	289. C
242. A	254. C	266. D	278. D	290. B
243. C	255. B	267. A	279. B	291. C
244. A	256. A	268. B	280. A	292. D
245. D	257. D	269. B	281. D	293. B
246. A	258. B	270. D	282. A	294. A
247. A	259. A	271. B	283. C	295. C
248. B	260. D	272. C	284. D	296. B
249. D	261. B	273. D	285. D	297. B
250. B	262. B	274. C	286. A	298. A

239. The correct answer is D. *No mistakes*

240. The correct answer is A. This sentence contains a list of items that need to be separated by commas: " ... a salad, two steaks, and a glass of iced tea to the corner table."

241. The correct answer is B. Each of the nurses, one at a time, *was* careful. If you selected choice C, you may not have realized that *who,* rather than *whom,* is correctly the subject of the clause "who had hurt or humiliated him."

242. The correct answer is A. *Effect* is a noun meaning "result," while *affect* is a verb meaning "to influence."

243. The correct answer is C. *Eggplant lasagna* is not a proper noun and shouldn't be capitalized unless it's at the beginning of a sentence—even then, only the first word would be capitalized.

244. The correct answer is A. Maintain a consistent voice and point of view throughout a sentence. "If *you* prepare, *you* can be confident." The statement, "If *one* prepares, *one* can be confident" would also be correct.

245. **The correct answer is D.** *No mistakes*

246. **The correct answer is A.** This sentence is a question and therefore needs to be punctuated with a question mark.

247. **The correct answer is A.** In this sentence, there is a change in verb tense that renders it nonsensical. The choice that you have not yet made (future tense) cannot have already changed (past tense) the meaning of the sentence.

248. **The correct answer is B.** The name of a ship, such as the Titanic, is a proper noun and should be capitalized.

249. **The correct answer is D.** *No mistakes*

250. **The correct answer is B.** It is unlikely that the new boots made the lady look healthy; they made her look *good,* that is, attractive.

251. **The correct answer is A.** Three ships are being compared, so the superlative, *largest,* must be used. Choice C might sound awkward, but both verbs are in the present tense, and the sentence is correct.

252. **The correct answer is D.** *No mistakes*

253. **The correct answer is B.** *Firefighters* isn't a proper noun and thus should not be capitalized.

254. **The correct answer is C.** Long dashes—used to set apart amplifying but extraneous information—must be used in pairs (the comma after *Venice* should be replaced by a dash).

255. **The correct answer is B.** This direct question should end with a question mark.

256. **The correct answer is A.** *Both* requires two objects connected by *and*: "Sports produce both release from tension *and* physical well-being."

257. **The correct answer is D.** *No mistakes*

258. **The correct answer is B.** *Were* is the past tense plural form of *was.* Since *he* is singular, *were* is incorrect.

259. **The correct answer is A.** The breathtaking scenes did not drive, but that is what the sentence implies. The "travelers" must be cast as the subject of the sentence. "While driving, the travelers were awed by ...." In answer B, the upper-case M in *Mother* is correct because in this case, *mother* is used as a proper noun.

260. **The correct answer is D.** *No mistakes*

261. **The correct answer is B.** There is no direct quote here, so quotation marks are inappropriate, as is the comma following *us.*

262. **The correct answer is B.** Feeling "badly" refers to one's sense of touch. When referring to health or emotions, one feels "bad."

263. **The correct answer is B.** The correct subject of the sentence is "my artist friend and *I.*" The reflexive *myself* is used only when someone reflects back on themselves, for instance, "I was beside myself with grief."

264. **The correct answer is A.** It is poor form to begin a sentence with "due to." The correct introduction to such an explanatory statement is "because of." In choice B, the past participle of the verb *to lie* is *lain,* so this sentence is correct.

265. **The correct answer is C.** This error is called a comma splice. The cure is to create two sentences with a period at the end of the first, or to join the two independent clauses with a semicolon or conjunction.

266. **The correct answer is D.** *No mistakes*

267. **The correct answer is A.** A council is a group; *counsel,* the required word, means "advice."

268. **The correct answer is B.** The correct spelling is *responsible.*

269. **The correct answer is B.** The correct spelling is *discipline.*

270. **The correct answer is D.** *No mistakes*

271. **The correct answer is B.** The correct spelling is *parasite.*

272. **The correct answer is C.** The correct spelling is *concede.*

273. **The correct answer is D.** *No mistakes*

274. **The correct answer is C.** The correct spelling is *noticeable*. (See Spelling—Rule 4.)

275. **The correct answer is A.** The correct spelling is *recommendation*.

276. **The correct answer is B.** The correct spelling is *interrupt*.

277. **The correct answer is C.** The correct spelling is *pseudonym*.

278. **The correct answer is D.** This sentence demonstrates correct usage. The other answer choices contain incorrect pronouns.

279. **The correct answer is B.** This sentence demonstrates correct usage. The other answer choices contain incorrect possessive noun forms.

280. **The correct answer is A.** This sentence demonstrates correct usage. The other answer choices contain incorrect contractions that don't fit, given the context of the sentence.

281. **The correct answer is D.** This sentence demonstrates correct usage. The other answer choices have missing articles, which result in awkward sentences.

282. **The correct answer is A.** This sentence demonstrates correct usage. The other answer choices contain incorrect pronouns.

283. **The correct answer is C.** This sentence demonstrates correct usage. The other answer choices contain incorrect possessive noun forms.

284. **The correct answer is D.** This sentence demonstrates correct usage. The other answer choices contain incorrect forms of the homonyms *too*, *two*, and *to*.

285. **The correct answer is D.** This sentence demonstrates correct usage. The other answer choices are missing correct adverb forms.

286. **The correct answer is A.** This sentence demonstrates correct usage. The other answer choices have missing articles, which result in awkward sentences.

287. **The correct answer is C.** This sentence demonstrates correct usage. The other answer choices contain incorrect contractions.

288. **The correct answer is B.** All other choices exhibit incorrect use of the possessive apostrophe.

289. **The correct answer is C.** The point is that the soldiers are busy fighting a war and won't return until it's over.

290. **The correct answer is B.** Choice A represents an impossibility, and choice C is highly improbable. If the movie is very good, one might consider it to have been worth the wait.

291. **The correct answer is C.** *Until* is the correct choice: "Darren, a responsible security guard, could not leave his post until his shift replacement arrived each night."

292. **The correct answer is D.** "Glass-bottomed fish" and "coral reefs swimming" make no sense at all, so choices B and C are incorrect. Choice A has a misplaced modifier—the *fish* are not in the glass-bottom boats; readers would be watching the fish from the boats.

293. **The correct answer is B.** Choices A and C are incorrect, as they suggest that changing strategies is part of the learning process. Choice D is totally garbled, and contradicts itself by stating that one "must easily learn" a "complex game." The statement made by choice B is more reasonable.

294. **The correct answer is A.** The growth of cities and the information explosion define the moment at which computers were needed.

295. **The correct answer is C.** The threat that the bald eagle poses to the fishing industry counters (i.e., argues against) the need to protect the bird.

296. **The correct answer is B.** Changing one's color is a means for disguise. None of the other choices address the squid's ability to hide itself in this manner.

297. The correct answer is B. Sentences 1, 3, and 4 present reasons for the Crusades. Sentence 2, however, presents an effect of the Crusades, rather than a reason for their existence.

298. The correct answer is A. This sentence serves as a topic sentence and provides a subject. All the other sentences begin with pronouns referring to "man" and offer examples to bolster the topic sentence.

SCORE SHEET

Although your actual exam scores will not be reported as percentages, it might be helpful to convert them so you can better visualize your strengths and weaknesses. The numbers in parentheses represent the question numbers testing each skill.

Subject	# Correct ÷ # of questions	× 100 = _____ %
Analogies (2, 8, 13, 16, 23, 31, 39, 48, 52, 56)	_____ ÷ 10 = _____	× 100 = _____ %
Synonyms (5, 7, 9, 17, 21, 22, 28, 29, 34, 37, 43, 46, 50, 53, 59)	_____ ÷ 15 = _____	× 100 = _____ %
Logic (3, 10, 15, 20, 27, 30, 36, 44, 51, 58)	_____ ÷ 10 = _____	× 100 = _____ %
Verbal Classification (1, 6, 11, 14, 18, 19, 26, 35, 38, 41, 42, 45, 49, 54, 57, 60)	_____ ÷ 16 = _____	× 100 = _____ %
Antonyms (4, 12, 24, 25, 32, 33, 40, 47, 55)	_____ ÷ 9 = _____	× 100 = _____ %
TOTAL VERBAL SKILLS	_____ ÷ 60 = _____	× 100 = _____ %
Number Series (61, 64, 71, 73, 75, 76, 78, 81, 83, 85, 87, 89, 91, 94, 98, 101, 107, 108)	_____ ÷ 18 = _____	× 100 = _____ %
Geometric Comparisons (66, 70, 77, 90, 93, 100, 103, 104, 109)	_____ ÷ 9 = _____	× 100 = _____ %
Nongeometric Comparisons (65, 68, 74, 86, 96, 105, 110, 112)	_____ ÷ 8 = _____	× 100 = _____ %
Number Manipulation (62, 63, 67, 69, 72, 79, 80, 82, 84, 88, 92, 95, 97, 99, 102, 106, 111)	_____ ÷ 17 = _____	× 100 = _____ %
TOTAL QUANTITATIVE SKILLS	_____ ÷ 52 = _____	× 100 = _____ %
Reading—Comprehension (113–152)	_____ ÷ 40 = _____	× 100 = _____ %
Reading—Vocabulary (153–174)	_____ ÷ 22 = _____	× 100 = _____ %
TOTAL READING SKILLS	_____ ÷ 62 = _____	× 100 = _____ %
Mathematics—Concepts (175–198)	_____ ÷ 24 = _____	× 100 = _____ %
Mathematics—Problem Solving (199–238)	_____ ÷ 40 = _____	× 100 = _____ %
TOTAL MATHEMATICS SKILLS	_____ ÷ 64 = _____	× 100 = _____ %
Punctuation and Capitalization (239, 240, 243, 245, 246, 248, 249, 253, 254, 255, 261, 265)	_____ ÷ 12 = _____	× 100 = _____ %
Usage (241, 242, 244, 247, 250, 251, 252, 256, 257, 258, 259, 260, 262, 263, 264, 266, 267, 278–288)	_____ ÷ 28 = _____	× 100 = _____ %
Spelling (268–277)	_____ ÷ 10 = _____	× 100 = _____ %
Composition (289–298)	_____ ÷ 10 = _____	× 100 = _____ %
TOTAL LANGUAGE SKILLS	_____ ÷ 60 = _____	× 100 = _____ %

APPENDIXES

Word List

A

abbreviate (verb) to make briefer, to shorten. *Because time was running out, the speaker had to abbreviate his remarks.* **abbreviation** (noun).

abrasive (adjective) irritating, grinding, rough. *The manager's rude, abrasive way of criticizing the workers was bad for morale.* **abrasion** (noun).

abridge (verb) to shorten, to reduce. *The Bill of Rights is designed to prevent Congress from abridging the rights of Americans.* **abridgment** (noun).

absolve (verb) to free from guilt, to exonerate. *The criminal jury absolved Mr. Callahan of the murder of his neighbor.* **absolution** (noun).

abstain (verb) to refrain, to hold back. *After his heart attack, William was warned by his doctor to abstain from smoking, drinking, and overeating.* **abstinence** (noun), **abstemious** (adjective).

accentuate (verb) to emphasize, to stress. *The overcast skies and chill winds only accentuate our gloomy mood.* **accentuation** (noun).

acrimonious (adjective) biting, harsh, caustic. *The election campaign became acrimonious, as the candidates traded insults and accusations.* **acrimony** (noun).

adaptable (adjective) able to be changed to be suitable for a new purpose. *Some scientists say that the mammals outlived the dinosaurs because they were more adaptable to a changing climate.* **adapt** (verb), **adaptation** (noun).

adulation (noun) extreme admiration. *The young actress received great adulation from critics and fans following her performance on Broadway.* **adulate** (verb), **adulatory** (adjective).

adversary (noun) an enemy or opponent. *When Germany became an American ally, the United States lost a major adversary.* **adversarial** (adjective).

adversity (noun) misfortune. *It's easy to be patient and generous when things are going well, but true character is revealed in times of adversity.* **adverse** (adjective).

aesthetic (adjective) relating to art or beauty. *Mapplethorpe's photos have been attacked on moral grounds, but no one questions their aesthetic value—they are beautiful.* **aestheticism** (noun).

aggressive (adjective) forceful, energetic, and attacking. *Some believe that a football player needs a more aggressive style of play than a soccer player.* **aggression** (noun).

alacrity (noun) promptness, speed. *The alacrity of her arrival caught him entirely by surprise—he still hadn't gotten dinner ready.* **alacritous** (adjective).

allege (verb) to state without proof. *Some have alleged that Foster was murdered, but all the evidence points to suicide.* **allegation** (noun).

alleviate (verb) to make lighter or more bearable. *Although no cure for AIDS has been found, doctors are able to alleviate the suffering of those with the disease.* **alleviation** (noun).

ambiguous (adjective) having two or more possible meanings. *The phrase, "Let's table that discussion" is ambiguous; some think it means, "Let's discuss it now," while others think it means, "Let's save it for later."* **ambiguity** (noun).

ambivalent (adjective) having two or more contradictory feelings or attitudes; uncertain. *She was ambivalent toward her impending marriage; at times she was eager to go ahead, while at other times she wanted to call it off.* **ambivalence** (noun).

amiable (adjective) likable, agreeable, friendly. *He was an amiable lab partner, always smiling, on time, and ready to work.* **amiability** (noun).

amicable (adjective) friendly, peaceable. *They remained amicable despite their divorce.*

amplify (verb) to enlarge, expand, increase, or make louder. *The students asked the teacher to amplify his explanation.* **amplification** (noun).

anachronistic (adjective) outside the proper time. *Shakespeare's reference in Julius Caesar to "the clock striking twelve" is anachronistic, since there were no striking timepieces in ancient Rome.* **anachronism** (noun).

anarchy (noun) absence of law or order. *For several months after the Nazi government collapsed, anarchy ruled Germany.* **anarchic** (adjective).

anomaly (noun) something different or irregular. *Tiny Pluto, orbiting next to the giants Jupiter, Saturn, and Neptune, had long appeared to be an anomaly.* **anomalous** (adjective).

antagonism (noun) hostility, conflict, opposition. *As more and more reporters investigated the Watergate scandal, antagonism between Nixon and the press increased.* **antagonistic** (adjective), **antagonize** (verb).

antiseptic (adjective) fighting infection; extremely clean. *Open wounds should be washed with an antiseptic solution.*

apathy (noun) lack of interest, concern, or emotion. *Tom's apathy toward his job could be seen in his lateness, his sloppy work, and his overall poor attitude.* **apathetic** (adjective).

arable (adjective) able to be cultivated for growing crops. *Rocky New England has relatively little arable farmland.*

arbiter (noun) someone able to settle disputes; a judge or referee. *The public is the ultimate arbiter of financial value; it decides what sells and what doesn't.*

arbitrary (adjective) based on random or merely personal preference. *Both computers cost the same and had the same features, so in the end my decision was arbitrary.*

arcane (adjective) little-known, mysterious, obscure. *Eliot's Waste Land is filled with arcane lore, including quotations in Latin, Greek, French, German, and Sanskrit.* **arcana** (noun, plural).

ardor (noun) a strong feeling of passion, energy, or zeal. *The young revolutionary proclaimed his convictions with an ardor that excited the crowd.* **ardent** (adjective).

arid (adjective) very dry; boring and meaningless. *The arid climate of Arizona makes farming difficult. Some find the law a fascinating, but for me it's an arid subject.* **aridity** (noun).

ascetic (adjective) practicing strict self-discipline for moral or spiritual reasons. *The so-called Desert Fathers were hermits who lived an ascetic life of fasting, study, and prayer.* **asceticism** (verb).

assiduous (adjective) working with care, attention, and diligence. *Although Karen is not a naturally gifted math student, by assiduous study she earned an A in trigonometry.* **assiduity** (noun).

astute (adjective) observant, intelligent, and shrewd. *The reporter's years of experience in Washington and his personal acquaintance with many political insiders made him an astute commentator on politics.*

atypical (adjective) not typical; unusual. *In* Hyde Park on Hudson, *Bill Murray, best known as a comic actor, gave an atypical dramatic performance.*

audacious (adjective) bold, daring, adventurous. *Her plan to cross the Atlantic single-handed in a 12-foot sailboat was audacious, if not reckless.* **audacity** (noun).

audible (adjective) able to be heard. *Although she whispered, her voice was picked up by the microphone and her words were audible throughout the theater.* **audibility** (noun).

auspicious (adjective) promising good fortune; propitious. *The news that a team of British climbers had reached the summit of Everest seemed an auspicious sign for the reign of newly crowned Queen Elizabeth II.* **auspice** (noun).

authoritarian (adjective) favoring or demanding blind obedience to leaders. *Despite Americans' belief in democracy, the American government has supported authoritarian regimes in other countries.* **authoritarianism** (noun).

B

belated (adjective) delayed past the proper time. *She called her mother on January 5th to offer a belated "Happy New Year."*

belie (verb) to present a false or contradictory appearance. *Lena Horne's youthful appearance belied her long, distinguished career in show business.*

benevolent (adjective) wishing or doing good. *In old age, Carnegie used his wealth for benevolent purposes, donating large sums to found schools and libraries.* **benevolence** (noun).

berate (verb) to scold or criticize harshly. *The judge angrily berated the two lawyers for their unprofessional behavior.*

bereft (adjective) lacking or deprived of something. *Bereft of parental love, orphans sometimes grow up insecure.*

bombastic (adjective) inflated or pompous in style. *Old-fashioned bombastic political speeches don't work on television, which demands a more intimate style of communication.* **bombast** (noun).

bourgeois (adjective) middle class or reflecting middle-class values. *The Dadaists of the 1920s produced art deliberately designed to offend bourgeois art collectors, with their taste for respectable, refined, uncontroversial pictures.* **bourgeois** (noun).

buttress (noun) something that supports or strengthens; a projecting structure of masonry or wood. *The endorsement of the American Medical Association is a powerful buttress for the claims made about this new medicine. The buttress on the south wall of the Medieval castle was crumbling.* **buttress** (verb).

C

camaraderie (noun) a spirit of friendship. *Spending long days and nights together on the road, the members of a traveling theater group develop a strong sense of camaraderie.*

candor (noun) openness, honesty, frankness. *In his memoir about the Vietnam War, former defense secretary McNamara described his mistakes with remarkable candor.* **candid** (adjective).

capricious (adjective) unpredictable, whimsical. *The pop star has changed her image so many times that each*

Word List

new transformation now appears capricious rather than purposeful. **caprice** (noun).

carnivorous (adjective) meat-eating. *The long, dagger-like teeth of the Tyrannosaurus make it obvious that it was a carnivorous dinosaur.* **carnivore** (noun).

carping (adjective) unfairly or excessively critical; querulous. *New York is famous for its demanding critics, but none is harder to please than the carping John Simon, said to have single-handedly destroyed many acting careers.* **carp** (verb).

catalytic (adjective) bringing about, causing, or producing some result. *The conditions for revolution existed in America by 1765; the disputes about taxation that arose later were the catalytic events that sparked the rebellion.* **catalyze** (verb), catalyst (noun).

caustic (adjective) burning, corrosive. *No one was safe when the satirist H. L. Mencken unleashed his caustic wit.*

censure (noun) blame, condemnation. *The news that the senator had harassed several women brought censure from feminists around the world.* **censure** (verb).

chaos (noun) disorder, confusion, chance. *The first moments after the explosion were chaos: no one was sure what happened, and the area was filled with people screaming.* **chaotic** (adjective).

circuitous (adjective) winding or indirect. *We drove to the cottage by a circuitous route so we could see as much of the surrounding countryside as possible.*

circumlocution (noun) speaking in a roundabout way; wordiness. *Legal documents often contain circumlocutions that make them difficult to understand.*

circumscribe (verb) to define by a limit or boundary. *The original role of the executive branch was clearly circumscribed, but that role has greatly expanded over time.* **circumscription** (noun).

circumvent (verb) to get around. *When James was caught speeding, he tried to circumvent the law by offering the police officer a bribe.*

clandestine (adjective) secret, surreptitious. *As a member of the underground, Balas took part in clandestine meetings to discuss ways of sabotaging the Nazi forces.*

cloying (adjective) overly sweet or sentimental. *The death-bed scenes in the novels of Dickens are famously cloying; as Oscar Wilde said, "One would need a heart of stone to read the death of Little Nell without dissolving into tears . . . of laughter."*

cogent (adjective) forceful and convincing. *The committee members were won over to the project by the cogent arguments of the chairman.* **cogency** (noun).

cognizant (adjective) aware, mindful. *Cognizant of the fact that it was getting late, the master of ceremonies decided to cut part of his speech.* **cognizance** (noun).

cohesive (adjective) sticking together, unified. *An effective military unit must be a cohesive team with all its members working together for a common goal.* **cohere** (verb), **cohesion** (noun).

collaborate (verb) to work together. *To create a truly successful movie, the director, writers, and actors must collaborate closely.* **collaboration** (noun), **collaborative** (adjective).

colloquial (adjective) informal in language; conversational. *Some of Shakespeare's expressions—such as his use of thou and thee—sound overly formal today, but they were colloquial English in his time.*

competent (adjective) having the skill and knowledge needed for a specific task; capable. *Any competent lawyer can draw up a will.* **competence** (noun).

complacent (adjective) smug, self-satisfied. *Until recently, American automakers were complacent, believing that they would continue to be successful with little effort.* **complacency** (noun).

composure (noun) calm, self-assurance. *The company's president managed to keep his composure during his speech even when the teleprompter broke down, leaving him without a script.* **composed** (adjective).

conciliatory (adjective) seeking agreement, compromise, or reconciliation. *As a conciliatory gesture, the union leaders agreed to postpone a strike and to continue negotiations with management.* **conciliate** (verb), **conciliation** (noun).

concise (adjective) expressed briefly and simply; succinct. *Less than a page long, the Bill of Rights is a concise statement of the freedoms enjoyed by all Americans.* **concision** (noun).

condescending (adjective) having an attitude of superiority toward another; patronizing. *"What a cute little car," she remarked in a condescending tone, "I suppose it's the nicest one someone like you could afford!"* **condescension** (noun), condescend (verb).

condolence (noun) pity for someone else's sorrow or loss; sympathy. *After the sudden death of Princess Diana, thousands of condolences were sent to her family by mail.* **condole** (verb).

confidant (noun) someone entrusted with another's secrets. *No one knew about Jane's engagement, except Sarah, her confidant.* **confide** (verb), **confidential** (adjective).

conformity (noun) agreement with or adherence to custom or rule. *Conformity was common in my high school: everyone dressed the same, talked the same, and listened to the same music.* **conform** (verb), **conformist** (noun, adjective).

consensus (noun) general agreement among a group. *Traditional voting isn't used among Quakers; instead, discussion continues until a consensus is formed among the entire group.*

consolation (noun) relief or comfort in sorrow or suffering. *Although we miss our dog very much, it is a consolation to know that she died quickly and without suffering.* **console** (verb).

consternation (noun) shock, amazement, dismay. *When a voice in the back of the church shouted out, "I know why they shouldn't be married!" the entire gathering was thrown into consternation.*

consummate (verb) to complete, finish, or perfect. *The deal was consummated with a handshake and the payment of the agreed-upon fee.* **consummate** (adjective), **consummation** (noun).

contaminate (verb) to make impure. *Chemicals dumped in a nearby forest had seeped into the soil and contaminated the local water supply.* **contamination** (noun).

contemporary (adjective) modern, current; from the same time. *I prefer old-fashioned furniture rather than contemporary styles. The composer Vivaldi was practically Bach's contemporary.* **contemporary** (noun).

contrite (adjective) sorry for past misdeeds. *The public is often willing to forgive celebrities involved in scandal so long as they appear contrite.* **contrition** (noun).

conundrum (noun) a riddle, puzzle, or problem. *The question of why an all-powerful, all-loving God allows evil to exist is a conundrum pondered by philosophers since the beginning of time.*

convergence (noun) the act of coming together or becoming more like one another. *A remarkable example of evolutionary convergence can be seen in the shark and dolphin, two sea creatures that developed from different origins to become very similar in form.* **converge** (verb).

convoluted (adjective) twisting, complicated, intricate. *Tax law has become so convoluted that it's easy to accidentally violate it.* **convolute** (verb), **convolution** (noun).

corroborating (adjective) supporting with evidence; confirming. *A passerby who witnessed the crime gave corroborating testimony about the presence of the accused.* **corroborate** (verb), **corroboration** (noun).

corrosive (adjective) eating away, gnawing, or destroying. *Years of poverty and hard work had a corrosive effect on her beauty.* **corrode** (verb), **corrosion** (noun).

credulity (noun) willingness to believe, even with little evidence. *Con artists fool people by taking advantage of their credulity.* **credulous** (adjective).

criterion (noun) a standard of measurement or judgment. *In choosing a design for the new taxicabs, reliability will be our main criterion.* **criteria** (plural).

critique (noun) a critical evaluation. *The editor gave a detailed critique of the manuscript, explaining its strengths and weaknesses.* **critique** (verb).

culpable (adjective) deserving blame, guilty. *Although he committed the crime, because he was mentally ill, he* should not be considered culpable for his actions. **culpability** (noun).

cumulative (adjective) made up of successive additions. *Smallpox was eliminated only through the cumulative efforts of several generations.* **accumulation** (noun), **accumulate** (verb).

curtail (verb) to shorten. *The opening round of the golf tournament was curtailed by thunderstorms.*

D

debased (adjective) lowered in quality, character, esteem, or value. *The quality of TV journalism has been debased by the popularity of tabloid-style talk shows.* **debase** (verb).

debunk (verb) to expose as false or worthless. *Magician James Randi loves to debunk psychics, mediums, clairvoyants, and others who claim supernatural powers.*

decorous (adjective) having good taste; proper, appropriate. *Prior to her visit to Buckingham Palace, the young woman was instructed to demonstrate the most decorous behavior.* **decorum** (noun).

decry (verb) to criticize or condemn. *The workers continued to decry the lack of safety in their factory.*

deduction (noun) a logical conclusion based on a process of elimination. *Given what's known about the effects of greenhouse gases on atmospheric temperature, scientists have made several deductions about the likelihood of their contribution to global warming.* **deduce** (verb).

delegate (verb) to give authority or responsibility. *The president delegated the vice president to represent the administration at the peace talks.* **delegate, delegation** (noun).

deleterious (adjective) harmful. *More than 50 years ago, scientists proved that working with asbestos could be deleterious to one's health by causing cancer and other diseases.*

delineate (verb) to outline or describe. *Naturalists had long theorized about evolution, but Darwin was the first to delineate a process—natural selection—by which evolution occurred.* **delineation** (noun)

demagogue (noun) a leader who plays dishonestly on the prejudices and emotions of his followers. *Senator Joseph McCarthy was a demagogue who used the paranoia of the anti-Communist 1950s as a means for seizing fame and power in Washington.* **demagoguery** (noun).

demure (adjective) modest or shy. *The demure heroines of Victorian fiction have given way to today's stronger, more opinionated, and more independent female characters.*

denigrate (verb) to criticize or belittle. *The firm's new president tried to explain his plans for improving the company without appearing to denigrate the work of his predecessor.* **denigration** (noun).

depose (verb) to remove from office, especially from a throne. *Iran was once ruled by a monarch called the Shah who was deposed in 1979.*

derelict (adjective) neglecting one's duty. *The train crash was blamed on a derelict switchman who fell asleep on-the-job.* **dereliction** (noun).

derivative (adjective) taken from or inspired by another source. *When a person first writes poetry, their poems are often derivative of whatever poet they enjoy reading most.* **derivation** (noun), **derive** (verb).

desolate (adjective) empty, lifeless, and deserted; hopeless, gloomy. *Robinson Crusoe was shipwrecked and had to survive alone on a desolate island. Mary Todd Lincoln was left desolate after the murder of her husband.* **desolation** (noun).

destitute (adjective) very poor. *Years of rule by a dictator who stole the wealth of the country left the people of the Philippines destitute.* **destitution** (noun).

deter (verb) to discourage from acting. *The best way to deter crime is to ensure that criminals will receive swift and certain punishment.* **deterrence** (noun), **deterrent** (adjective).

detractor (noun) someone who belittles or disparages. *Neil Diamond has many detractors who consider his music boring, inane, and melodramatic.* **detract** (verb).

deviate (verb) to depart from a standard or norm. *Having agreed upon a spending budget for the company, we mustn't deviate from it; if we do, we may run out of money.* **deviation** (noun).

devious (adjective) tricky, deceptive. *The CEO's devious financial tactics were designed to enrich his firm while confusing or misleading government regulators.*

didactic (adjective) intended to teach; instructive. *The children's TV show Sesame Street is designed to be both entertaining and didactic.* **didacticism** (noun).

diffident (adjective) hesitant, reserved, shy. *Someone with a diffident personality should pursue a career that requires little public contact.* **diffidence** (noun).

diffuse (verb) to spread out, to scatter. *The red dye quickly became diffused through the water, turning it a very pale pink.* **diffusion** (noun).

digress (verb) to wander from the main path or the main topic. *My high school biology teacher loved to digress from science lectures into personal anecdotes about his college adventures.* **digression** (noun), **digressive** (adjective).

dilatory (adjective) delaying, procrastinating. *The lawyer used various dilatory tactics, hoping that his opponent would get tired of waiting for a trial and drop the case.*

diligent (adjective) working hard and steadily. *Through diligent efforts, the townspeople were able to clear the debris from the disaster site in a matter of days.* **diligence** (noun).

diminutive (adjective) unusually small, tiny. *Children are fond of Shetland ponies because their diminutive size makes them easy to ride.* **diminution** (noun).

discern (verb) to detect, notice, or observe. *I could discern the shape of a whale off the starboard bow, but it was too far away to determine its size or species.* **discernment** (noun).

disclose (verb) to make known; to reveal. *Election laws require candidates to disclose the names of those who contribute large sums of money to their campaigns.* **disclosure** (noun).

discomfit (verb) to frustrate, thwart, or embarrass. *Discomfited by the interviewer's unexpected question, Peter could only stammer in reply.* **discomfiture** (noun).

disconcert (verb) to confuse or embarrass. *When the hallway bells began to ring halfway through her lecture, the speaker was disconcerted and didn't know what to do.* **disconcerted** (noun).

discredit (verb) to cause disbelief in the accuracy of some statement or the reliability of a person. *Many believe in extraterrestrials life, even though reports of "alien encounters" have been thoroughly discredited among scientists.*

discreet (adjective) showing good judgment in speech and behavior. *Be discreet when discussing confidential business matters; for example, don't talk among strangers in an elevator.* **discretion** (noun).

discrepancy (noun) a difference or variance between two or more things. *The discrepancies between the two witnesses' stories show that one of them must be lying.* **discrepant** (adjective).

disdain (noun) contempt, scorn. *The professor could not hide his disdain for students who were perpetually late to class.* **disdain** (verb), **disdainful** (adjective).

disingenuous (adjective) pretending to be candid, simple, and frank. *When Texas billionaire H. Ross Perot ran for president, many considered his downhome style disingenuous.*

disparage (verb) to speak disrespectfully about, to belittle. *Many political ads today both praise their own candidate and disparage their opponent.* **disparagement** (noun), **disparaging** (adjective).

disparity (noun) difference in quality or kind. *There's often a disparity in the types of assets held by the rich and the poor.* **disparate** (adjective).

disregard (verb) to ignore, to neglect. *If you don't write a will, when you die your survivors may disregard your wishes about how your property should be handled.* **disregard** (noun).

disruptive (adjective) causing disorder, interrupting. *When the senator spoke at our college, angry demonstrators picketed, heckled, and engaged in other disruptive activities.* **disrupt** (verb), **disruption** (noun).

Word List

dissemble (verb) to pretend, to simulate. *When the police questioned her about the crime, she dissembled innocence.*

dissipate (verb) to spread out or scatter. *The windows and doors were opened, allowing the smoke that filled the room to dissipate.* **dissipation** (noun).

dissonance (noun) lack of music harmony; lack of agreement between ideas. *Much modern music is characterized by dissonance, which many listeners find hard to enjoy.* **dissonant** (adjective).

diverge (verb) to move in different directions. *Be careful not to diverge too far from the marked path.* **divergence** (noun), **divergent** (adjective).

diversion (noun) a distraction or pastime. *The game on his phone was a welcome diversion during the two hours he spent in the waiting room.* **divert** (verb).

divination (noun) the art of predicting the future. *In ancient Greece, people wanting to know their fate would visit the Oracle at Delphi, supposedly skilled at divination.* **divine** (verb).

divisive (adjective) causing disagreement or disunity. *Throughout history, race has been the most divisive issue in American society.*

divulge (verb) to reveal. *The people who count the votes for the Oscar awards are under strict orders not to divulge the names of the winners.*

dogmatic (adjective) holding firmly to a set of beliefs with little or no basis. *Believers in Marxist doctrine tend to be dogmatic and ignore evidence that contradicts their beliefs.* **dogmatism** (noun).

dominant (adjective) greatest in importance or power. *Television quickly became a dominant influence in American culture.* **dominate** (verb), **domination** (noun).

dubious (adjective) doubtful, uncertain. *Despite the chairman's attempts to convince the committee members that his plan would succeed, most of them remained dubious.* **dubiety** (noun).

durable (adjective) long lasting. *Denim is a popular material for work clothes because it's strong and durable.* **durability** (noun).

duress (noun) compulsion or restraint. *Fearing the police might beat him, he confessed to the crime under duress.*

E

eclectic (adjective) drawn from many sources; varied, heterogeneous. *The Mellon family art collection is an eclectic one, including works from ancient Greek and Mesopotamia.* **eclecticism** (noun).

efficacious (adjective) able to produce a desired effect. *Though thousands of people today are taking herbal supplements to treat depression, researchers haven't yet proved them efficacious.* **efficacy** (noun).

effrontery (noun) shameless boldness. *The sports world was shocked when a professional basketball player had the effrontery to choke his head coach during practice.*

effusive (adjective) pouring forth one's emotions freely. *Having won the Oscar for Best Actress, Sally Field gave an effusive acceptance speech.* **effusion** (noun).

egotism (noun) excessive concern with oneself; conceit. *Robert's egotism was so great that all he could talk about was the importance—and brilliance—of his own opinions.* **egotistic** (adjective).

egregious (adjective) obvious, conspicuous, flagrant. *It's hard to imagine how the editor could allow such an egregious error to go to print.*

elated (adjective) excited and happy; exultant. *When the Washington Redskins' last, desperate pass was intercepted, elated Philadelphia Eagle's fans began to celebrate.* **elate** (verb), **elation** (noun).

elliptical (adjective) very terse or concise in writing or speech; difficult to understand. *Rather than speak plainly, she hinted at her meaning through a series of nods, gestures, and elliptical half sentences.*

elusive (adjective) hard to capture, grasp, or understand. *Though everyone thinks they know what "justice" is, it's a concept that proves quite elusive to definition.*

embezzle (verb) to steal money or property that has been entrusted to your care. *The treasurer embezzled thousands of dollars by writing phony checks on the company bank account.* **embezzlement** (noun).

emend (verb) to correct. *Before the letter is mailed, please emend the two spelling errors.* **emendation** (noun).

emigrate (verb) to leave one's place or country to settle elsewhere. *Millions of Irish emigrated to the New World in the wake of the great Irish famines of the 1840s.* **emigrant** (noun), **emigration** (noun).

eminent (adjective) noteworthy, famous. *Vaclav Havel was an eminent author before he was elected president of the Czech Republic.* **eminence** (noun).

emissary (noun) someone who represents another. *To avoid a military showdown, former President Jimmy Carter was sent as an emissary to Korea to negotiate a settlement.*

emollient (noun) something that softens or soothes. *She used a soothing cream as an emollient for her dry, work-roughened hands.* **emollient** (adjective).

empathy (noun) imaginative sharing of the feelings, thoughts, or experiences of another. *It's easy for a parent to have empathy for their own children.* **empathetic** (adjective).

empirical (adjective) based on experience or personal observation. *Although many people believe in ESP, scientists have found no empirical evidence of its existence.* **empiricism** (noun).

emulate (verb) to imitate or copy. *The British band Oasis admitted their desire to emulate their idols, the Beatles.* **emulation** (noun).

encroach (verb) to go beyond acceptable limits; to trespass. *Robert Moses continually encroached on the powers of other government leaders by seizing undue authority.* **encroachment** (noun).

enervate (verb) to reduce the energy or strength of someone or something. *Extended exposure to the sun enervated the shipwrecked crew, leaving them too weak to spot the passing vessel.*

engender (verb) to produce, to cause. *Countless disagreements over the proper use of national forests have engendered feelings of hostility between ranchers and environmentalists.*

enhance (verb) to improve in value or quality. *New kitchen appliances will enhance your house and increase the amount of money you'll make when you sell it.* **enhancement** (noun).

enmity (noun) hatred, hostility, ill will. *Long-standing enmity, like that between the Protestants and Catholics in Northern Ireland, is difficult to overcome.*

enthrall (verb) to enchant or charm. *The Swedish singer Jenny Lind enthralled American audiences in the nineteenth century with her beauty and talent.*

ephemeral (adjective) quickly disappearing; transient. *Stardom in pop music is ephemeral; many of the top acts of ten years ago have been forgotten about today.*

equanimity (noun) calmness of mind, especially under stress. *Franklin Roosevelt faced the great crises of his presidency—the Depression and the Second World War—with equanimity and humor.*

eradicate (verb) to destroy completely. *American society has failed to eradicate racism despite decades of effort.*

espouse (verb) to take up as a cause; to adopt. *No politician in America today will openly espouse racism, although some behave and speak in racially prejudiced ways.*

euphoric (adjective) a feeling of extreme happiness and well-being; elation. *One often feels euphoric during the early days of a love affair.* **euphoria** (noun).

evanescent (adjective) vanishing like a vapor; fragile and transient. *As she walked by, the evanescent fragrance of her perfume hit me only for an instant.*

exacerbate (verb) to make worse or more severe. *The roads in our town already have too much traffic; building a new shopping mall will exacerbate the problem.*

exasperate (verb) to irritate or annoy. *Sharon was exasperated by the yelling of her neighbors' children while trying to study.*

exculpate (verb) to free from blame or guilt. *When someone else confessed to the crime, the previous suspect was exculpated.* **exculpation** (noun), **exculpatory** (adjective).

exemplary (adjective) worthy to serve as a model. *The Baldrige Award is given to a company with exemplary standards of excellence in products and service.* **exemplar** (noun), **exemplify** (verb).

exonerate (verb) to free from blame. *Although the truck driver was at first a suspect in the bombing, later evidence exonerated him.* **exoneration** (noun), **exonerative** (adjective).

expansive (adjective) broad and large; to speak openly and freely. *It was a large tract of land on an expansive ranch in Texas.* **expand** (verb), **expansion** (noun).

expedite (verb) to carry out promptly. *As the flood waters rose, the governor ordered state agencies to expedite their rescue efforts.*

expertise (noun) skill, mastery. *The software company was eager to hire new graduates with programming expertise.*

expiate (verb) to atone for. *The president's apology to the survivors of the notorious Tuskegee experiments was an attempt to expiate the nation's guilt over their mistreatment.* **expiation** (noun).

expropriate (verb) to seize ownership of. *When the Communists came to power in China, they expropriated most businesses and turned them over to government-appointed managers.* **expropriation** (noun).

extant (adjective) currently in existence. *Of the seven ancient Wonders of the World, only the pyramids of Egypt are still extant.*

extenuate (verb) to make less serious. *Jeanine's guilt is extenuated by the fact that she was only twelve when she committed the theft.* **extenuating** (adjective), **extenuation** (noun).

extol (verb) to greatly praise. *At the party convention, speaker after speaker rose to extol the virtues of their candidate for the presidency.*

extricate (verb) to free from a difficult or complicated situation. *Much of the humor in the TV show I Love Lucy comes in watching Lucy try to extricate herself from her own problems.* **extricable** (adjective).

extrinsic (adjective) not an innate part or aspect of something; external. *The high price of old baseball cards is due to extrinsic factors like the nostalgia felt by baseball fans for the stars of their youth rather than the inherent beauty or value of the cards themselves.*

exuberant (adjective) wildly joyous and enthusiastic. *As the final seconds of the game ticked away, the fans of the winning team began an exuberant celebration.* **exuberance** (noun).

F

facile (adjective) easy; shallow or superficial. *One-minute political commercials favor candidates with facile opinions rather than serious, thoughtful solutions.* **facilitate** (verb), **facility** (noun).

Word List

fallacy (noun) an error in fact or logic. *It's a fallacy to think that "natural" means "healthy"; after all, the deadly poison arsenic is a completely natural compound.* **fallacious** (adjective).

felicitous (adjective) pleasing, fortunate, apt. *The sudden blossoming of the dogwood trees on the morning of Matt's wedding seemed a felicitous sign of good luck.* **felicity** (noun).

feral (adjective) wild. *The dump was inhabited by a pack of feral dogs that escaped from their owners.*

fervent (adjective) full of intense feeling; ardent, zealous. *In the days just after his religious conversion, his piety was at its most fervent.* **fervid** (adjective), **fervor** (noun).

flagrant (adjective) obviously wrong; offensive. *Nixon was forced to resign the presidency after a series of flagrant crimes against the U.S. Constitution.* **flagrancy** (noun).

flamboyant (adjective) colorful, showy, or elaborate. *At Mardi Gras, partygoers compete in a display of the most wild and flamboyant outfits.*

florid (adjective) flowery, fancy; reddish. *The ballroom looked magnificent with its florid decoration.*

foppish (adjective) one who is foolishly vain in dress or appearance. *The foppish character of the 1890s wore bright-colored spats and a top hat; in the 1980s, he wore fancy suspenders and a shirt with a contrasting collar.* **fop** (noun).

formidable (adjective) awesome, impressive, or frightening. *According to his plaque in the Baseball Hall of Fame, pitcher Tom Seaver turned the New York Mets "from lovable losers into formidable foes."*

fortuitous (adjective) lucky, fortunate. *Although the mayor claimed credit for the falling crime rate, there were several fortuitous trends behind it.*

fractious (adjective) troublesome, unruly. *Members of the British Parliament are often fractious, shouting insults and sarcastic questions during debates.*

fragility (noun) easily broken; delicacy, weakness. *Because of their fragility, few stained-glass windows from the early Middle Ages have survived.* **fragile** (adjective).

fraternize (verb) to associate with on friendly terms. *Although baseball players aren't supposed to fraternize with opponents, players from opposing teams often chat before games.* **fraternization** (noun).

frenetic (adjective) chaotic, frantic. *The floor of the stock exchange, filled with traders shouting and gesturing, is a scene of frenetic activity.*

frivolity (noun) lack of seriousness; levity. *The frivolity of the Mardi Gras carnival contrasts with the seriousness of the religious season that follows.* **frivolous** (adjective).

frugal (adjective) spending little. *We bought a frugal dinner with our last few dollars: a loaf of bread and some slices of cheese.* **frugality** (noun).

fugitive (noun) someone trying to escape. *When two prisoners broke out of the local jail, police were warned to keep an eye out for the fugitives.* **fugitive** (adjective).

G

gargantuan (adjective) huge, colossal. *The Great Wall of China was one of the most gargantuan building projects ever undertaken.*

genial (adjective) friendly, gracious. *A good host welcomes all visitors in a warm and genial fashion.*

grandiose (adjective) overly large, pretentious, or showy. *Among Hitler's grandiose plans for Berlin was a gigantic building with a dome several times larger than any ever built.* **grandiosity** (noun).

gratuitous (adjective) given freely or without cause. *Since her opinion was not requested, her harsh criticism of his singing seemed a gratuitous insult.*

gregarious (adjective) one who enjoys the company of others; sociable. *Naturally gregarious, Emily is a popular member of several clubs and a sought-after lunch companion.*

guileless (adjective) without cunning; innocent or naïve. *Deborah's guileless personality and total honesty made it hard for her to survive in the harsh world of politics.*

gullible (adjective) easily fooled. *When the sweepstakes entry form arrived bearing the message, "You may be a winner!" my gullible neighbor tried to claim a prize.* **gullibility** (noun).

H

hackneyed (adjective) without originality, trite. *The phrase "no pain, no gain" used to be clever, but now it's so overused that it seems hackneyed.*

haughty (adjective) overly proud. *The fashion model strode down the runway, her hips thrust forward and a haughty expression on her face.* **haughtiness** (noun).

hedonist (noun) one who pursues pleasure as their chief purpose. *Having inherited great wealth, he chose to live the life of a hedonist, traveling the world in luxury.* **hedonism** (noun), **hedonistic** (adjective).

heinous (adjective) evil, hateful. *The massacre by Pol Pot of more than a million Cambodians is one of the twentieth century's most heinous crimes.*

hierarchy (noun) an ordered ranking of people, ideas, or things. *A cabinet secretary ranks just below the president and vice president in the hierarchy of the executive branch.* **hierarchical** (adjective).

hypocrisy (noun) a false pretense of virtue. *When the sexual misconduct of the television preacher was exposed, his followers were shocked by his hypocrisy.* **hypocritical** (adjective).

I

iconoclast (noun) someone who attacks traditional beliefs or institutions. *Comedian Stephen Colbert enjoys his reputation as an iconoclast, though people in power often resent his satirical jabs.* **iconoclasm** (noun), **iconoclastic** (adjective).

idiosyncratic (adjective) peculiar to an individual; eccentric. *Cyndi Lauper sings pop music in an idiosyncratic style, mingling high-pitched whoops and squeals with throaty gurgles.* **idiosyncrasy** (noun).

idolatry (noun) the worship of a person, thing, or institution as a god. *In Communist China, Chairman Mao was the subject of widespread praise and idolatry.* **idolatrous** (adjective).

impartial (adjective) fair, equal, unbiased. *If a judge is not impartial, then all her rulings are questionable.* **impartiality** (noun).

impeccable (adjective) flawless. *The crooks printed impeccable counterfeit tickets that were impossible to distinguish from the real thing.*

impetuous (adjective) acting hastily or impulsively. *Stuart's resignation was an impetuous act; he did it without thinking, and soon regretted the decision.* **impetuosity** (noun).

impinge (verb) to encroach upon, touch, or affect. *You have a right to do whatever you want, so long as your actions don't impinge on the rights of others.*

implicit (adjective) understood without being openly expressed; implied. *Although most clubs had no rules excluding minorities, there was an implicit understanding that no blacks were allowed inside.*

impute (verb) to attribute; to pass onto someone else. *Although Helena's comments embarrassed me, I don't impute her with any ill; I don't think she realized what she was saying.* **imputation** (noun).

inarticulate (adjective) unable to speak or express oneself clearly and understandably. *A skilled athlete may be an inarticulate public speaker, as demonstrated by many post-game interviews.*

incisive (adjective) clear and direct expression. *Franklin settled the debate with a few incisive remarks that perfectly summarized the issue at hand.*

incompatible (adjective) unable to exist together; conflicting. *The Bluetooth speaker was incompatible with my phone, so we had to use an old radio.* **incompatibility** (noun).

inconsequential (adjective) of little importance. *When the flat screen TV was delivered, it was a slightly different shade of gray than expected, but the difference was inconsequential.*

incontrovertible (adjective) impossible to question. *The fact that Alexandra's fingerprints were the only ones on the murder weapon made her guilt seem incontrovertible.*

incorrigible (adjective) impossible to manage or reform. *Lou is an incorrigible trickster, constantly playing practical jokes despite frequent complaints.*

incremental (adjective) increasing gradually by small amounts. *Although the initial cost of the program was small, the incremental expenses have been relentless.* **increment** (noun).

incriminate (verb) to give evidence of guilt. *The fifth amendment to the Constitution says no one is required to reveal information that would incriminate themselves.* **incriminating** (adjective).

incumbent (noun) someone who occupies an office or position. *It is often difficult for a challenger to win a seat from an incumbent member of Congress.* **incumbency** (noun), **incumbent** (adjective).

indeterminate (adjective) not definitely known. *The college plans to enroll an indeterminate number of students; class sizes will depend on the number of applicants who accept their offers.* **determine** (verb).

indifferent (adjective) unconcerned, apathetic. *The mayor's small proposed budget for education suggests his indifference to the needs of our school system.* **indifference** (noun).

indistinct (adjective) unclear, uncertain. *We could see boats on the water, but in the thick morning fog their shapes were indistinct.*

indomitable (adjective) unable to be conquered or controlled. *The world admired the indomitable spirit of Nelson Mandela, who remained courageous despite years of imprisonment.*

induce (verb) to cause. *The doctor prescribed a medicine that was supposed to induce a lowering of the blood pressure.* **induction** (noun).

ineffable (adjective) difficult to describe or express. *He gazed in silence at the sunrise over the Taj Mahal, his eyes reflecting an ineffable sense of wonder.*

inevitable (adjective) impossible to avoid. *Once the Japanese attacked Pearl Harbor, American involvement in World War II was inevitable.* **inevitability** (noun).

inexorable (adjective) unable to be deterred; relentless. *It's difficult to imagine how the mythic character of Oedipus could have avoided his evil destiny; his fate appears inexorable.*

ingenious (adjective) showing cleverness and originality. *The Post-it note is an ingenious solution to a common problem—how to mark papers without spoiling them.* **ingenuity** (noun).

inherent (adjective) naturally part of something. *Compromise is inherent to democracy, since not everyone gets his or her way.* **inhere** (verb), **inherence** (noun).

Word List

innate (adjective) inborn, native. *Not everyone who takes lessons becomes a fine musician, which shows that music requires some innate talent as well as training.*

innocuous (adjective) harmless, inoffensive. *I'm surprised Melissa was offended by my innocuous joke.*

inoculate (verb) to prevent a disease by infusing a host with a disease-causing organism. *Pasteur found he could prevent rabies by inoculating patients with the virus itself.* **inoculation** (noun).

insipid (adjective) flavorless, uninteresting. *Some TV shows are so insipid that you can watch them while reading and not miss a thing.* **insipidity** (noun).

insolence (noun) an attitude or behavior that is bold and disrespectful. *Some feel that news reporters who shout questions at the president are behaving with insolence.* **insolent** (adjective).

insular (adjective) narrow or isolated in attitude or viewpoint. *Americans are famous for their insular beliefs that nothing important has ever happened outside of their country.* **insularity** (noun).

insurgency (noun) uprising, rebellion. *The insurgency of angry townspeople bordered on revolution as they flooded the streets in protest.* **insurgent** (adjective).

integrity (noun) honesty, uprightness; soundness, completeness. *"Honest Abe" Lincoln was a model of political integrity. Inspectors examined the building and found no reason to doubt its structural integrity.*

interlocutor (noun) someone taking part in a dialogue or conversation. *Annoyed by constant questions from the crowd, the speaker challenged his interlocutor directly.* **interlocutory** (adjective).

interlude (noun) a break or interruption. *The two most dramatic scenes in* King Lear *are separated, ironically, by comic interludes starring the king's jester.*

interminable (adjective) endless or seemingly endless. *Addressing the United Nations, Castro announced "we will be brief" before delivering an interminable four-hour speech.*

intransigent (adjective) unwilling to compromise. *Despite the mediator's attempts to suggest a fair solution, the two parties were intransigent and wanted a showdown.* **intransigence** (noun).

intrepid (adjective) fearless and resolute. *Only an intrepid traveler is willing to undertake the long and dangerous trip by sled to the South Pole.* **intrepidity** (noun).

intrusive (adjective) forcing a way in; unwelcome. *The legal requirement of a search warrant is supposed to protect Americans from intrusive searches by police.* **intrude** (verb), **intrusion** (noun).

intuitive (adjective) known directly, without apparent thought or effort. *An experienced chess player has an intuitive sense of the best move, even if they can't explain it.* **intuit** (verb), **intuition** (noun).

inundate (verb) to flood; to overwhelm. *As soon as the playoff tickets went on sale, eager fans inundated the box office with orders.*

invariable (adjective) unchanging, constant. *When writing a book, it was her invariable habit to rise at 6 a.m. and work at her desk from 7 to 12.* **invariability** (noun).

inversion (noun) turned backward, inside-out, or upside-down; reversed. *Latin poetry often features an inversion of word order; like the first line of Virgil's* Aeneid: *"Arms and the man I sing."* **invert** (verb), **inverted** (adjective).

inveterate (adjective) persistent, habitual. *It's notoriously difficult for an inveterate gambler to stop on their own accord.* **inveteracy** (noun).

invigorate (verb) to give energy to, to stimulate. *As her car climbed the mountain road, Lucinda felt invigorated by the clear air and cool breezes.*

invincible (adjective) impossible to conquer or overcome. *For three years, at the height of his career, boxer Mike Tyson seemed invincible.*

inviolable (adjective) impossible to undo or trespass upon. *In the President's remote hideaway at Camp David guarded by the Secret Service, his privacy is inviolable.*

irrational (adjective) unreasonable. *Richard knew that his fear of insects was irrational, but he was unable to overcome it.* **irrationality** (noun).

irresolute (adjective) uncertain how to act, indecisive. *The line in the ice cream shop grew as the irresolute child wavered between her two favorite flavors.* **irresolution** (noun).

J

jeopardize (verb) to put in danger. *Terrorist attacks jeopardize fragile peace not just in the Middle East, but also right here at home.* **jeopardy** (noun).

juxtapose (verb) to compare side by side. *Juxtaposing the two editorials revealed the enormous differences in the writers' opinions.* **juxtaposition** (noun).

L

languid (adjective) without energy; slow, sluggish, listless. *The hot, humid weather of late August can make anyone feel languid.* **languish** (verb), **languor** (noun).

latent (adjective) not currently obvious or active; hidden. *Although he only committed a minor crime, the psychiatrist said it's likely he's always had a latent potential for violence.* **latency** (noun).

laudatory (adjective) giving praise. *The movie ads were filled with laudatory comments from critics.*

lenient (adjective) mild, soothing, or forgiving. *The judge was known for his lenient disposition and he rarely imposed long jail sentences.* **leniency** (noun).

lethargic (adjective) lacking energy; sluggish. *Visitors to the zoo are often surprised that the lions appear so lethargic; in the wild, however, lions sleep up to 18 hours a day.* **lethargy** (noun).

liability (noun) an obligation or debt; a weakness or drawback. *The insurance company had a liability of millions of dollars after the town was destroyed by a tornado.* **liable** (adjective).

lithe (adjective) flexible and graceful. *The ballet dancer was lithe as a cat.*

longevity (noun) length of life; durability. *The reduction in early deaths from infectious diseases is responsible for most of the increase in human longevity over the past two centuries.*

lucid (adjective) clear and understandable. *Hawking's A Short History of the Universe is a lucid explanation of modern scientific theories about the origin of the universe.* **lucidity** (noun).

lurid (adjective) shocking, gruesome. *The newspapers were filled with lurid stories about his crimes.*

M

malediction (noun) a curse. *In the fairy tale "Sleeping Beauty," the princess is trapped in a death-like sleep because of the malediction uttered by an angry witch.*

malevolence (noun) hatred, ill will. *Critics say that Iago, the villain in Shakespeare's Othello, seems to exhibit malevolence with no understandable motivation.* **malevolent** (adjective).

malinger (verb) to pretend incapacity or illness to avoid a duty or work. *During the labor dispute, hundreds of employees malingered and forced the company to slow production.*

malleable (adjective) susceptible to change from outside pressures. *Gold is useful because it's so malleable. A child's personality is malleable and deeply influenced by their upbringing.* **malleability** (noun).

mandate (noun) order, command. *The new policy of using only organic produce in the restaurant went into effect as soon as the manager issued the mandate.* **mandate** (verb), **mandatory** (adjective).

maturation (noun) the process of becoming fully grown or developed. *Free markets in former Communist nations are likely to operate smoothly only after a long period of maturation.* **mature** (adjective and verb), **maturity** (noun).

mediate (verb) to reconcile differences between two parties. *During the baseball strike, both the players and club owners were willing to have the president mediate the dispute.* **mediation** (noun).

mediocrity (noun) the state of being middling or poor in quality. *The New York Mets finished in ninth place in 1968, but won the World Championship in 1969, going from horrible to great in a single year and skipping mediocrity.* **mediocre** (adjective).

mercurial (adjective) changing quickly and unpredictably. *The mercurial personality of Robin Williams made him perfect for the role of the ever-changing genie in Aladdin.*

meticulous (adjective) careful with details. *Repairing an old watch requires a meticulous craftsman.*

mimicry (noun) imitation, aping. *The continued popularity of Elvis Presley has given rise to a class of entertainers who make a living through mimicry of "The King."* **mimic** (noun and verb).

misconception (noun) a mistaken idea; misunderstanding. *Columbus sailed west with the misconception that he would reach the shores of Asia.* **misconceive** (verb).

mitigate (verb) to make less severe; to relieve. *Wallace certainly committed the assault, but the verbal abuse he'd received helps explain his behavior and mitigate his guilt.* **mitigation** (noun).

modicum (noun) a small amount. *The plan for your new business is well-designed; with a modicum of luck, you should be successful.*

mollify (verb) to soothe or calm; to appease. *Sam tried to mollify the angry customer with a full refund.*

morose (adjective) gloomy, sullen. *After Chuck's girlfriend dumped him, he laid around the house for days feeling morose.*

mundane (adjective) everyday, ordinary, commonplace. *Moviegoers in the 1930s liked the glamorous films of Fred Astaire as they provided an escape from the mundane problems of the Great Depression.*

munificent (adjective) very generous; lavish. *Ted Turner's billion-dollar donation to the United Nations was one of the most munificent acts of charity in history.* **munificence** (noun).

mutable (adjective) likely to change. *A politician's reputation can be highly mutable, as seen in the case of Harry Truman, who was mocked during his lifetime, but revered after his death.*

N

narcissistic (adjective) showing excessive love for oneself; egoistic. *Andre's room, decorated with photos of himself and sports trophies he's won, suggests a narcissistic personality.* **narcissism** (noun).

nocturnal (adjective) of the night; active at night. *Travelers on the Underground Railroad escaped from slavery to the North with a series of nocturnal flights.*

nonchalant (adjective) appearing to be unconcerned. *Unlike other players who pumped their fists when announced, John took the field with a nonchalant wave of his hand.* **nonchalance** (noun).

Word List

nondescript (adjective) without distinctive qualities; drab. *The bank robber's clothes were nondescript; none of the witnesses could remember their color or style.*

notorious (adjective) famous, especially for evil actions or qualities. *Warner Brothers produced a series of movies about notorious gangsters such as John Dillinger and Al Capone.* **notoriety** (noun).

novice (noun) beginner. *Lifting your head before finishing your swing is a typical novice golf mistake.*

nuance (noun) a subtle difference or quality. *At first glance, Monet's paintings of waterlilies all look alike; the closer one looks, however, the more nuance one sees.*

nurture (verb) to nourish or help to grow. *The money given by the National Endowment for the Arts helps nurture local arts organizations throughout the country.* **nurture** (noun).

O

obdurate (adjective) unwilling to change; stubborn, inflexible. *Despite many pleas, the governor was obdurate in his refusal to grant clemency to the convicted murderer.*

objective (adjective) dealing with observable facts rather than opinions or interpretations. *When a legal case involves a shocking crime, it may be hard for a judge to remain objective in his ruling.*

oblivious (adjective) unaware, unconscious. *Karen practiced her oboe with complete concentration, oblivious to the noise and activity around her.* **oblivion** (noun), **obliviousness** (noun).

obscure (adjective) little known; hard to understand. *Mendel was an obscure monk until his scientific work was finally discovered decades after his death.* **obscure** (verb), **obscurity** (noun).

obsessive (adjective) haunted or preoccupied by an idea or feeling. *His concern with cleanliness became so obsessive that he washed his hands twenty times a day.* **obsess** (verb), **obsession** (noun).

obsolete (adjective) no longer current; old-fashioned. *W. H. Auden said that his ideal landscape would include water wheels, wooden grain mills, and other forms of obsolete machinery.* **obsolescence** (noun).

obstinate (adjective) stubborn, unyielding. *Drug abuse remains as obstinate as ever.* **obstinacy** (noun).

obtrusive (adjective) overly prominent, in the way. *Philip should sing more softly; his voice is so obtrusive that the other singers can barely be heard over him.* **obtrude** (verb), **obtrusion** (noun).

ominous (adjective) foretelling evil. *Ominous black clouds gathered on the horizon.* **omen** (noun).

onerous (adjective) heavy, burdensome. *The hero Hercules was ordered to clean the Augean Stables, one of several onerous tasks now known as "the labors of Hercules."* **onus** (noun).

opportunistic (adjective) eagerly seizing chances as they arise. *When Princess Diana died suddenly, opportunistic publishers were quick to release books about her life and death.* **opportunism** (noun).

opulent (adjective) rich, lavish. *The mansion of newspaper tycoon William Randolph Hearst is famous for its opulent decor.* **opulence** (noun).

ornate (adjective) highly decorated, elaborate. *Baroque architecture is often highly ornate, featuring surfaces covered with detailed carvings, sinuous curves, and painted scenes.*

ostentatious (adjective) overly showy, pretentious. *To show off his wealth, the millionaire threw an ostentatious party featuring a full orchestra and famous singer.*

ostracize (verb) to exclude from a group. *In Biblical times, those who suffered from the disease of leprosy were ostracized from the community and forced to live alone.* **ostracism** (noun).

P

pallid (adjective) pale; dull. *Working all day in the coal mine had given him a pallid complexion. The new musical offers only pallid entertainment; it's lifeless, the acting is dull, the story is beyond absurd.*

parched (adjective) very dry; thirsty. *After two months without rain, the crops were shriveled and parched by the sun.* **parch** (verb).

pariah (noun) outcast. *Accused of robbery, he became a pariah; his neighbors stopped talking to him, and people he'd considered friends no longer called.*

partisan (adjective) reflecting strong allegiance to a specific political party or cause. *The vote on the president's budget was strictly partisan: every member of his party voted yes.* **partisan** (noun).

pathology (noun) disease or the study of disease; extreme abnormality. *Some people believe that high rates of crime are symptoms of an underlying social pathology.* **pathological** (adjective).

pellucid (adjective) very clear; transparent; easy to understand. *The water in the mountain stream was cold and pellucid. Thanks to the professor's pellucid explanation, I finally understand relativity theory.*

penitent (adjective) feeling sorry for past sins or crimes. *Having grown penitent, he wrote a long letter of apology asking forgiveness.*

penurious (adjective) extremely frugal; stingy. *Haunted by memories of poverty, he lived in penurious fashion, driving a 12-year-old car and wearing only the cheapest clothes.* **penury** (noun).

perceptive (adjective) quick to notice, observant. *With his perceptive intelligence, Holmes was the first to notice the importance of this clue.* **perceptible** (adjective), **perception** (noun).

perfidious (adjective) disloyal, treacherous. *Although one of the most talented generals of the American Revolution, Benedict Arnold is remembered as a perfidious betrayer of his country.* **perfidy** (noun).

perfunctory (adjective) unenthusiastic, routine, or mechanical. *When the play opened, the actors sparkled, but by the thousandth night their performance had become perfunctory.*

permeate (verb) to spread through or penetrate. *Little by little, the smell of gas from the broken pipe permeated the house.*

persevere (adjective) to continue despite difficulties. *Although several of her teammates dropped out of the marathon, Gail persevered.* **perseverance** (noun).

perspicacity (noun) keenness of observation or understanding. *Journalist Murray Kempton was famous for the perspicacity of his comments on social and political issues.* **perspicacious** (adjective).

peruse (verb) to examine or study. *Carol perused the contract carefully before signing.* **perusal** (noun).

pervasive (adjective) spreading throughout. *As news of the disaster reached the town, a pervasive sense of gloom could be felt.* **pervade** (verb).

phlegmatic (adjective) sluggish and unemotional in temperament. *It was surprising to see Tom, who's normally so phlegmatic, acting upbeat and excited.*

placate (verb) to soothe or appease. *The waiter tried to placate the angry customer with the offer of a free dessert.* **placatory** (adjective).

plastic (adjective) able to be molded or reshaped. *Because it is highly plastic, clay is an easy material for beginning sculptors to use.*

plausible (adjective) apparently believable. *According to the judge, the defense attorney's argument was both powerful and plausible.* **plausibility** (noun).

polarize (verb) to separate into opposing groups or forces. *The abortion debate has polarized the American people for years, with extreme views being voiced on both sides.* **polarization** (noun).

portend (verb) to indicate a future event; to forebode. *According to folklore, a red sky at dawn portends a day of stormy weather.*

potentate (noun) a powerful ruler. *The Tsar of Russia was one of the last hereditary potentates of Europe.*

pragmatism (noun) a belief in approaching problems through practical rather than theoretical means. *Roosevelt's approach to the Great Depression was based on pragmatism: "Try something," he said, and "if it doesn't work, try something else."* **pragmatic** (adjective).

preamble (noun) an introductory statement. *The preamble to the Constitution begins with the famous line, "We the people of the United States of America..."*

precocious (adjective) mature at an unusually early age. *Picasso was so precocious as an artist that, at nine, he is said to have painted better than his teacher.* **precocity** (noun).

predatory (adjective) living by killing and eating other animals; exploiting others for personal gain. *The tiger is the largest predatory animal native to Asia. Microsoft has been accused of predatory business practices.* **predation** (noun), **predator** (noun).

predilection (noun) a liking or preference. *Kennedy had a predilection for spy novels that helped him escape from his presidential duties.*

predominant (adjective) greatest in numbers or influence. *Although hundreds of religions are practiced in India, the predominant faith is Hinduism.* **predominance** (noun), **predominate** (verb).

prepossessing (adjective) attractive. *Smart, lovely, and talented, she has all the prepossessing qualities that mark a potential movie star.*

presumptuous (adjective) going beyond the limits of courtesy or appropriateness. *The senator winced when the presumptuous young staffer addressed him as "Chuck."* **presume** (verb), **presumption** (noun).

pretentious (adjective) claiming excessive value or importance. *For a shoe salesman to call himself a "Personal Foot Apparel Consultant" seems awfully pretentious.* **pretension** (noun).

procrastinate (verb) to put off, to delay. *If you habitually procrastinate, try never touching a piece of paper without either filing it, responding to it, or throwing it out immediately.* **procrastination** (noun).

profane (adjective) impure, unholy. *It is inappropriate and rude to use profane language in a church.* **profane** (verb), **profanity** (noun).

proficient (adjective) skillful, adept. *Only a proficient artist could sketch a scene of such complexity.* **proficiency** (noun).

proliferate (verb) to increase or multiply. *Over the past twenty-five years, tech companies have proliferated in northern California, Massachusetts, and Seattle.* **proliferation** (noun), **prolific** (adjective).

prominence (noun) the quality of standing out; fame. *Barack Obama rose to political prominence after his keynote address at the 2004 Democratic National Convention.* **prominent** (adjective).

promulgate (verb) to make public, to declare. *Lincoln signed the proclamation that freed the slaves in 1862, but he waited several months to promulgate it.*

Word List

propagate (verb) to cause to grow; to foster. *The school was propagated by its original founder and continues to grow even after his death.* **propagation** (noun).

propriety (noun) appropriateness. *The principal questioned the propriety of the discussion the teacher had with her students about another instructor's gambling addiction.*

prosaic (adjective) everyday, ordinary, unremarkable. *"Paul's Case" tells the story of a boy who longs to escape from the prosaic life of a clerk into a world of wealth, glamour, and beauty.*

protagonist (noun) the main character in a story or play; the main supporter of an idea. *Leopold Bloom is the protagonist of James Joyce's great novel* Ulysses.

provocative (adjective) likely to stimulate emotions, ideas, or controversy. *The demonstrators began the provocative act of chanting obscenities at police.* **provoke** (verb), **provocation** (noun).

proximity (noun) closeness, nearness. *Neighborhood residents were angry over the proximity of the sewage plant to the local school.* **proximate** (adjective).

prudent (adjective) wise, cautious, and practical. *A prudent investor will avoid putting all their money into a single investment.* **prudence** (noun), **prudential** (adjective).

pugnacious (adjective) combative, bellicose, truculent; ready to fight. *Ty Cobb, the pugnacious Detroit Tiger's outfielder, got into his fair share of brawls both on and off the field.* **pugnacity** (noun).

punctilious (adjective) concerned with proper forms of behavior and manners. *A punctilious dresser like James would rather skip the party altogether than wear the wrong color tie.* **punctilio** (noun).

pundit (noun) someone who offers opinions in an authoritative style. *The Sunday morning talk shows are filled with pundits, each with his or her own theory about the week's political news.*

punitive (adjective) inflicting punishment. *The jury awarded the plaintiff one million dollars in punitive damages, hoping to teach the defendant a lesson.*

purify (verb) to make pure, clean, or perfect. *The new plant is supposed to purify the drinking water provided to everyone in the nearby towns.* **purification** (noun).

Q

quell (verb) to quiet, to suppress. *It took a huge number of police officers to quell the rioting.*

querulous (adjective) complaining, whining. *The nursing home attendant needed a lot of patience to care for the three querulous, unpleasant residents on his floor.*

R

rancorous (adjective) expressing bitter hostility. *Many Americans are disgusted by recent political campaigns, which seem more rancorous than ever before.* **rancor** (noun).

rationale (noun) an underlying reason or explanation. *Looking at the sad faces of his employees, it was hard for the company president to explain the rationale for closing the business.* **rational** (adjective).

raze (verb) to destroy; demolish. *The old coliseum will soon be razed to make room for a new hotel.*

reciprocate (verb) to give and take mutually. *If you'll watch my children tonight, I'll reciprocate by taking care of yours tomorrow.* **reciprocity** (noun).

reclusive (adjective) withdrawn from society. *During the last years of her life, actress Greta Garbo led a reclusive existence, rarely appearing in public.* **recluse** (noun).

reconcile (verb) to make consistent or harmonious. *It's always wise to reconcile individual differences before starting a group project.* **reconciliation** (noun).

recrimination (noun) a retaliatory accusation. *After the governor called his opponent unethical, he was met with recriminations of his own guilt.* **recriminate** (verb), **recriminatory** (adjective).

recuperate (verb) to regain health after an illness. *Although Marie left the hospital two days after her operation, it took her a few weeks to fully recuperate.* **recuperation** (noun), **recuperative** (adjective).

redoubtable (adjective) inspiring respect, awe, or fear. *Johnson's knowledge, experience, and personal clout made him a redoubtable political opponent.*

refurbish (verb) to fix up; renovate. *It took three days' work by a team of carpenters, painters, and decorators to completely refurbish the apartment.* **refurbished** (adjective).

refute (verb) to prove false. *The company invited reporters to visit their plant to refute charges of unsafe working conditions.* **refutation** (noun).

relevance (noun) connection to the matter at hand; pertinence. *Testimony in a criminal trial may be admitted only if it has clear relevance to the question of guilt or innocence.* **relevant** (adjective).

remedial (adjective) serving to remedy, cure, or correct some condition. *Affirmative action is a remedial step to help minority members overcome past discrimination.* **remediation** (noun), **remedy** (verb).

remorse (noun) a painful sense of guilt over wrongdoing. *In Poe's story* The Tell-Tale Heart, *a murderer is driven insane by remorse over his crime.* **remorseful** (adjective).

remuneration (noun) pay. *In a civil lawsuit, the attorney often receives part of the financial settlement as his or her remuneration.* **remunerate** (verb), **remunerative** (adjective).

renovate (verb) to renew by repairing or rebuilding. *The television program* This Old House *shows how skilled craftspeople renovate houses.* **renovation** (noun).

renunciation (noun) the act of rejecting or refusing something. *King Edward VII's renunciation of the throne was driven by his taboo desire to marry an American divorcee.* **renounce** (verb).

replete (adjective) filled abundantly. *Graham's book is replete with wonderful stories and deep insights.*

reprehensible (adjective) deserving criticism or censure. *Pete Rose's misdeeds were reprehensible, but not all fans agree he should be banned from the Hall of Fame.* **reprehend** (verb), **reprehension** (noun).

repudiate (verb) to reject, to renounce. *After it became known that Duke had been a leader of the Ku Klux Klan, most Republican leaders repudiated him.* **repudiation** (noun).

reputable (adjective) having a good reputation; respected. *Find a reputable auto mechanic by asking your friends for recommendations based on their own experiences.* **reputation** (noun), **repute** (noun).

resilient (adjective) able to recover from difficulty. *A professional athlete must be resilient, able to lose a game one day and come back the next with confidence and enthusiasm.* **resilience** (noun).

resplendent (adjective) glowing, shining. *In late December, midtown New York is resplendent with holiday lights and decorations.* **resplendence** (noun).

responsive (adjective) reacting quickly and appropriately. *The new director of the Internal Revenue Service has promised to make the agency more responsive to public complaints.* **respond** (verb), **response** (noun).

restitution (noun) return of something to its original owner; repayment. *Some Native American leaders are demanding that the U.S. government make restitution for the lands taken from them.*

revere (verb) to admire deeply, to honor. *Millions of people around the world revered Mother Teresa for her saintly generosity.* **reverence** (noun), **reverent** (adjective).

rhapsodize (verb) to praise in a wildly emotional way. *That critic is such a huge fan of Toni Morrison that she will surely rhapsodize over the writer's next novel.* **rhapsodic** (adjective).

S

sagacious (adjective) discerning, wise. *Only a leader as sagacious as Nelson Mandela could have united South Africa so successfully and peacefully.* **sagacity** (noun).

salvage (verb) to save from wreck or ruin. *After the hurricane destroyed her home, she was able to salvage only a few of her belongings.* **salvage** (noun), **salvageable** (adjective).

sanctimonious (adjective) showing false or excessive piety. *The sanctimonious prayers of the TV preacher were interspersed with requests that the viewers send him money.* **sanctimony** (noun).

scapegoat (noun) someone who bears the blame for others' acts; someone hated for no apparent reason. *Although Buckner's error was only one reason the Red Sox lost, many fans made him the scapegoat, booing him mercilessly.*

scrupulous (adjective) acting with extreme care; painstaking. *Disney theme parks are famous for their scrupulous attention to small details.* **scruple** (noun).

scrutinize (verb) to study closely. *The lawyer scrutinized the contract, searching for any sentence that could pose a risk for her client.* **scrutiny** (noun).

secrete (verb) to emit; to hide. *Glands in the mouth secrete saliva when eating to aid digestion.*

sedentary (adjective) static; unmoving. *When Officer Samson was given a desk job, she had trouble getting used to sedentary work after years on the street.*

sequential (adjective) arranged in an order or series. *The courses for the chemistry major are sequential; you must take them in order, since each course builds on the previous ones.* **sequence** (noun).

serendipity (noun) the act of lucky, accidental discoveries. *Great inventions sometimes come through deliberate research and hard work, and others through pure serendipity.* **serendipitous** (adjective).

servile (adjective) like a slave or servant; submissive. *The tycoon demanded that his underlings behave in a servile manner, agreeing quickly with everything he said.* **servility** (noun).

simulated (adjective) imitating something else; artificial. *High-quality simulated gems must be examined under a magnifying glass to be distinguished from real ones.* **simulate** (verb), **simulation** (noun).

solace (verb) to comfort or console. *There was little the rabbi could say to solace the husband after his wife's death.* **solace** (noun).

spontaneous (adjective) happening without plan. *When the news of Kennedy's assassination broke, people everywhere gathered in a spontaneous effort to share their shock and grief.* **spontaneity** (noun).

spurious (adjective) false, fake. *The so-called Piltdown Man, supposed to be the fossil of a primitive human, turned out to be spurious, although who created the hoax is still uncertain.*

squander (verb) to use up carelessly, to waste. *Those who had made donations to the charity were outraged to learn that its director had squandered millions on fancy dinners and first-class travel.*

stagnate (verb) to become stale through lack of movement or change. *Having had no contact with the outside world for generations, Japan's culture gradually stagnated.* **stagnant** (adjective), **stagnation** (noun).

Word List

staid (adjective) sedate, serious, and grave. *This college is not a "party school"; the students work hard, and the campus has a staid reputation.*

stimulus (noun) something that excites a response or provokes an action. *The arrival of merchants and missionaries from the West provided a stimulus for change in Japanese society.* **stimulate** (verb).

stoic (adjective) showing little feeling, even in response to pain or sorrow. *A soldier must respond to the death of his comrades in stoic fashion, since the fighting will not stop for his grief.* **stoicism** (noun).

strenuous (adjective) requiring energy and strength. *Hiking the foothills of the Rockies may be easy, but climbing higher peaks is strenuous exercise.*

submissive (adjective) accepting the will of others; humble, compliant. *At the end of* A Doll's House, *Nora leaves her husband and abandons her role as a submissive housewife.*

substantiate (verb) to verify or support with evidence. *The charge that Nixon had helped to cover up crimes was substantiated by his comments about it on a series of audio tapes.* **substantiated** (adjective), **substantiation** (noun).

sully (verb) to soil, stain, or defile. *Nixon's misdeeds as president did much to sully the reputation of the American government.*

superficial (adjective) on the surface only; without depth or substance. *Her wound was superficial and required only a light bandage.* **superficiality** (noun).

superfluous (adjective) more than is needed, excessive. *Once you've won the debate, don't keep talking; superfluous arguments will only bore and annoy the audience.*

suppress (verb) to put down or restrain. *As soon as the unrest began, thousands of helmeted police were sent into the streets to suppress the riots.* **suppression** (noun).

surfeit (noun) an excess. *Most Americans have a surfeit of food on Thanksgiving Day.* **surfeit** (verb).

surreptitious (adjective) done in secret. *Because Iraq avoided weapons inspections, many believed it had a surreptitious weapons development program.*

surrogate (noun) a substitute. *When the congressman died in office, his wife was named to serve the rest of his term as a surrogate.* **surrogate** (adjective).

sustain (verb) to keep up, to continue; to support. *Because of fatigue, he was unable to sustain the effort needed to finish the marathon.*

T

tactile (adjective) relating to the sense of touch. *The thick brush strokes and gobs of color give the paintings of van Gogh a strongly tactile quality.* **tactility** (noun).

talisman (noun) an object supposed to have magical effects or qualities. *Superstitious people sometimes carry a rabbit's foot, a lucky coin, or some other talisman.*

tangential (adjective) touching lightly; only slightly connected or related. *My travels to South America were of only tangential interest to the students in my African-American history class.* **tangent** (noun).

tedium (noun) boredom. *For most people, watching the Weather Channel for 24 hours would be sheer tedium.* **tedious** (adjective).

temerity (noun) boldness, rashness, excessive daring. *Only someone who didn't understand the danger would have the temerity to try to climb Everest without a guide.* **temerarious** (adjective).

temperance (noun) moderation or restraint in feelings and behavior. *Most professional athletes practice temperance in their personal habits; too much eating or drinking, they know, can harm their performance.* **temperate** (adjective).

tenacious (adjective) clinging, sticky, or persistent. *Tenacious in pursuit of her goal, she applied for the grant unsuccessfully four times before it was finally approved.* **tenacity** (noun).

tentative (adjective) subject to change; uncertain. *A firm schedule has not been established, but the Super Bowl in 2019 has been given the tentative date of February 3.*

terminate (verb) to end, to close. *The Olympic Games terminate with a grand ceremony attended by athletes from every participating country.* **terminal** (noun), **termination** (noun).

terrestrial (adjective) of the Earth. *The movie* Close Encounters of the Third Kind *tells the story of the first contact between beings from outer space and terrestrial humans.*

therapeutic (adjective) curing or helping to cure. *Hot-water spas were popular in the nineteenth century among the sickly, who believed that soaking in the water had therapeutic effects.* **therapy** (noun).

timorous (adjective) fearful, timid. *The cowardly lion approached the throne of the wizard with a timorous look on his face.*

toady (noun) someone who flatters a superior in hopes of gaining favor; a sycophant. *"I can't stand a toady!" declared the movie mogul. "Give me someone who'll tell me the truth—even if it costs him his job!"* **toady** (verb).

tolerant (adjective) accepting, enduring. *San Franciscans have a tolerant attitude about lifestyles: "Live and let live" seems to be their motto.* **tolerate** (verb), **toleration** (noun).

toxin (noun) poison. *Insecticides are powerful toxins used to kill insects, but many are now banned in the United States because of the risk they pose to human health.* **toxic** (adjective).

tranquility (noun) freedom from disturbance or turmoil; calm. *She moved from New York City to rural Vermont seeking the tranquility of country life.* **tranquil** (adjective).

transgress (verb) to go past limits; to violate. *No one could fathom why the honor student transgressed by shoplifting hundreds of dollars of merchandise from his favorite clothing store.* **transgression** (noun).

transient (adjective) passing quickly. *Long-term visitors to this hotel pay a different rate than transient guests who stay for just a day or two.* **transience** (noun).

transitory (adjective) quickly passing. *Public moods tend to be transitory; people may be anxious and angry one month but relatively content and optimistic the next.* **transition** (noun).

translucent (adjective) letting some light pass through. *Panels of translucent glass let daylight into the room while maintaining privacy.*

transmute (verb) to change in form or substance. *In the Middle Ages, the alchemists tried to discover ways to transmute metals such as iron into gold.* **transmutation** (noun).

treacherous (adjective) untrustworthy or disloyal; dangerous or unreliable. *Nazi Germany proved to be a treacherous ally, first signing a peace pact with the Soviet Union, then invading. Be careful crossing the rope bridge; parts are badly frayed and treacherous.* **treachery** (noun).

tremulous (adjective) trembling or shaking; timid or fearful. *Never having spoken in public before, he began his speech in a tremulous, hesitant voice.*

trite (adjective) boring because of over-familiarity; hackneyed. *Her letters were filled with trite expressions, like "all's well that ends well" and "so far so good."*

truculent (adjective) aggressive, hostile, belligerent. *Hitler's truculent behavior in demanding more territory for Germany made it clear that war was inevitable.* **truculence** (noun).

truncate (verb) to cut off. *The poor copying job truncated the playwright's manuscript: the last page ended in the middle of a scene, halfway through the first act.*

turbulent (adjective) agitated or disturbed. *The night before the championship match, Serena Williams was unable to sleep, her mind turbulent with fears and hopes.* **turbulence** (noun).

U

unheralded (adjective) little known, unexpected. *In a year of big-budget, much-hyped, mega-movies, this unheralded foreign film has surprised everyone with its popularity.*

unpalatable (adjective) distasteful, unpleasant. *Although I agree with the candidate on many issues, I can't vote for her because I find her position on capital punishment unpalatable.*

unparalleled (adjective) with no equal; unique. *Tiger Woods's victory in the Masters golf tournament by a full twelve strokes was an unparalleled accomplishment.*

unstinting (adjective) giving freely and generously. *Eleanor Roosevelt was much admired for her unstinting efforts on behalf of the poor.*

untenable (adjective) impossible to defend. *The theory that this painting is a genuine van Gogh became untenable when the artist who painted it came forth.*

untimely (adjective) out of the natural or proper time. *The untimely death of a youthful Princess Diana seemed far more tragic than Mother Teresa's death of old age.*

unyielding (adjective) firm, resolute, obdurate. *Despite criticism, former governor Mario Cuomo was unyielding in his opposition to capital punishment as he vetoed several death-penalty bills.*

usurper (noun) someone who takes a place or possession without the right to do so. *Kennedy's most devoted followers tended to regard later presidents as usurpers, holding the office they felt he or his brothers should have held.* **usurp** (verb), **usurpation** (noun).

utilitarian (adjective) purely of practical benefit. *The design of the Model T car was simple and utilitarian, lacking the luxuries found in later models.*

utopia (noun) an imaginary, perfect society. *Those who founded the Oneida community dreamed that it could be a kind of utopia—a prosperous state of freedom and harmony.* **utopian** (adjective).

V

validate (verb) to officially approve or confirm. *The election of the president is validated when the members of the Electoral College meet to confirm the choice of the voters.* **valid** (adjective), **validity** (noun).

variegated (adjective) spotted with different colors. *The brilliant, variegated appearance of butterflies makes them popular among collectors.* **variegation** (noun).

venerate (verb) to admire or honor. *In Communist China, Chairman Mao Zedong was venerated as an almost god-like figure.* **venerable** (adjective), **veneration** (noun).

verdant (adjective) green with plant life. *Southern England is famous for its verdant countryside filled with gardens and small farms.*

vestige (noun) a trace or remainder. *Today's tiny Sherwood Forest is the last vestige of a woodland that once covered most of England.* **vestigial** (adjective).

Word List

vex (verb) to irritate, annoy, or trouble. *It vexes me that she never helps with any chores around the house.* **vexation** (noun).

vicarious (adjective) experienced through someone else's actions by way of the imagination. *Great literature broadens our minds by giving us vicarious participation in the lives of other people.*

vindicate (verb) to confirm, justify, or defend. *Lincoln's Gettysburg Address was intended to vindicate the objectives of the Union in the Civil War.* **vindication** (noun), **vindictive** (adjective).

virtuoso (noun) someone very skilled, especially in an art. *Vladimir Horowitz was one of the great piano virtuosos of the twentieth century.* **virtuosity** (noun).

vivacious (adjective) lively, sprightly. *The role of Maria in* The Sound of Music *is usually played by a charming, vivacious young actress.* **vivacity** (noun).

volatile (adjective) quickly changing; fleeting, transitory; prone to violence. *Public opinion is notoriously volatile; a politician who is very popular one month may be voted out of office the next.* **volatility** (noun).

W

whimsical (adjective) based on a capricious, carefree impulse or idea; fanciful, playful. *Dave Barry's* Book of Bad Songs *is filled with goofy jokes typical of his whimsical sense of humor.* **whim** (noun).

Z

zealous (adjective) filled with eagerness, fervor, or passion. *A crowd of the candidate's most zealous supporters greeted her at the airport with banners, signs, and a marching band.* **zeal** (noun), **zealot** (noun), **zealotry** (noun).

Word List

List of Synonyms and Antonyms

A

abbreviate
Synonyms—shorten, make concise
Antonyms—lengthen, elongate (to make longer)

abrasive
Synonyms—harsh, rough, irritating
Antonyms—smooth, soft, soothing

abstain
Synonyms—refrain, give up, hold back
Antonyms—give in, indulge (to allow oneself to partake or participate)

acclaim
Synonyms—praise, approve, applaud
Antonyms—blame, condemn, censure (to criticize)

accumulate
Synonyms—acquire, gain, hoard
Antonyms—diminish, give away, squander (to waste)

accuse
Synonyms—challenge, blame, incriminate (to attribute responsibility)
Antonyms—forgive, exonerate (to free from guilt)

adaptable
Synonyms—flexible, changeable
Antonyms—inflexible, rigid

adept
Synonyms—skillful, proficient, competent
Antonyms—inexperienced, incompetent, unskillful

adhere
Synonyms—attach, stick, follow, uphold
Antonyms—detach, disengage, reject

adversary
Synonyms—enemy, opponent, foe, nemesis (an arch enemy)
Antonyms—friend, collaborator, ally (one who collaborates)

adverse
Synonyms—bad, negative
Antonyms—good, positive

aggressive
Synonyms—combative, belligerent (hostile)
Antonyms—peaceful, conciliatory (easily makes amends)

agitate
Synonyms—irritate, anger, upset, stir
Antonyms—soothe, calm, pacify (to calm)

agreeable
Synonyms—pleasant, likeable, delightful
Antonyms—mean, unkind, unpleasant

ambiguous
Synonyms—unclear, vague
Antonyms—clear, straightforward

ambitious
Synonyms—determined, driven, motivated
Antonyms—lazy, unmotivated, unenthusiastic

ambivalent
Synonyms—indecisive, wishy-washy, unsure
Antonyms—decided, determined, sure

amplify
Synonyms—expand, heighten, enlarge
Antonyms—decrease, minimize, diminish

animated
Synonyms—energetic, lively, spirited
Antonyms—lazy, sluggish, depressed

animosity
Synonyms—hostility, resentment, hatred
Antonyms—kindness, friendliness, warmth, compassion (caring)

anomalous
Synonyms—odd, inconsistent, irregular, unusual
Antonyms—commonplace, ordinary, normal, regular

anonymous
Synonyms—nameless, unknown, unidentified
Antonyms—identified, known, recognized

antagonize
Synonyms—irritate, bother, annoy
Antonyms—help, aid, soothe

apathy
Synonyms—indifference, unconcern, disregard (lack of interest)
Antonyms—interest, concern

arbitrary
Synonyms—random, chance, inconsistent
Antonyms—steady, unchanging, reliable, predictable

arid
Synonyms—dry, barren, parched (lacking water)
Antonyms—humid, soaked, well-watered

attentive
Synonyms—interested, observant, aware
Antonyms—unaware, unconcerned, neglectful

astute
Synonyms—quick-witted, intelligent, smart
Antonyms—inept, foolish, slow-witted

atypical
Synonyms—not normal, uncommon, unnatural
Antonyms—normal, regular, common, typical

audacious
Synonyms—outrageous, bold, daring
Antonyms—meek, mild, quiet

audible
Synonyms—perceptible, discernible, distinct (able to be heard)
Antonyms—silent, indistinct (quiet or not able to be heard)

authentic
Synonyms—original, trustworthy, credible
Antonyms—corrupt, untrustworthy, fake

autonomous
Synonyms—independent, self-governing
Antonyms—dependent, helpless, subjugated (controlled by others)

B

baffle
Synonyms—confuse, stump, puzzle
Antonyms—clarify, elucidate (to make clear)

banal
Synonyms—usual, common, ordinary
Antonyms—unusual, different, special

barren
Synonyms—lifeless, empty, unfruitful (not able to support life)
Antonyms—productive, fruitful (able to support life)

belated
Synonyms—late, overdue
Antonyms—prompt, punctual (on time)

benevolent
Synonyms—kind, good-hearted
Antonyms—cruel, evil, malevolent (willing to cause harm)

benign
Synonyms—mild, peaceable, harmless
Antonyms—deadly, dangerous, harmful

berate
Synonyms—scold, criticize, reprimand (to scold or blame)
Antonyms—praise, encourage, uplift

bleak
Synonyms—grim, hopeless, desolate (deserted and empty)
Antonyms—hopeful, cheerful, encouraging

boisterous
Synonyms—noisy, loud, rambunctious (uncontrolled)
Antonyms—quiet, orderly, subdued (calm and under control)

bombastic
Synonyms—boastful, ostentatious (showy), pompous (full of oneself)
Antonyms—restrained, quiet, humble, reserved (private)

buttress
Synonyms—bolster, reinforce, support
Antonyms—weaken

C

cajole
Synonyms—coax, persuade, wheedle (to convince by asking nicely)
Antonyms—order, force, compel

camaraderie
Synonyms—friendship, companionship, togetherness
Antonyms—animosity, isolation

candid
Synonyms—truthful, straightforward, unrehearsed
Antonyms—dishonest, staged, set up

candor
Synonyms—honesty, directness, veracity (truthfulness)
Antonyms—insincerity, deceit, lying

capricious
Synonyms—willful, arbitrary, impulsive (acting without thought)
Antonyms—predictable, steady, sensible

captivate
Synonyms—dazzle, enchant, fascinate
Antonyms—bore, offend, repulse

caustic
Synonyms—burning, hurtful, sarcastic (cutting or mocking)
Antonyms—soothing, mild, innocuous (harmless)

chaos
Synonyms—disorder, confusion, pandemonium (an uproar or hubbub)
Antonyms—harmony, order, tranquility (peace)

circumvent
Synonyms—go around, avoid, elude (to get away from)
Antonyms—take on, confront, face

clandestine
Synonyms—secret, undercover, covert, surreptitious (hidden)
Antonyms—public, open, aboveboard, overt (open)

cloying
Synonyms—sticky, sentimental, clingy
Antonyms—independent, detached, cool

coerce
Synonyms—force, bully, pressure
Antonyms—coax, cajole, encourage

cogent
Synonyms—powerful, logical, persuasive
Antonyms—unconvincing, ineffective, illogical

cognizant
Synonyms—aware, informed, sentient (conscious)
Antonyms—ignorant, oblivious (not attentive)

coherent
Synonyms—understandable, clear
Antonyms—confused, meaningless

cohesive
Synonyms—close-knit, unified, interconnected
Antonyms—scattered, disorganized, fragmented

collaborate
Synonyms—work together, cooperate, join forces
Antonyms—separate, part ways, conflict

commend
Synonyms—praise, applaud, honor
Antonyms—criticize, put down, disapprove

compatible
Synonyms—harmonious, well-suited, congenial (friendly)
Antonyms—mismatched, clashing, incompatible

compel
Synonyms—force, require, pressure
Antonyms—discourage, prevent, dissuade (to advise against)

competent
Synonyms—skilled, qualified, proficient (good at)
Antonyms—inept, useless, bungling (prone to making mistakes)

complacent
Synonyms—self-satisfied, comfortable, smug (self-satisfied)
Antonyms—restless, dissatisfied, discontent

comply
Synonyms—obey, conform, follow
Antonyms—rebel, resist, defy

comprehensive
Synonyms—thorough, inclusive, complete
Antonyms—limited, partial, restricted

concise
Synonyms—short, to the point, succinct (brief)
Antonyms—rambling, long-winded, wordy

condescending
Synonyms—rude, snobbish
Antonyms—down-to-earth, friendly, kind

confident
Synonyms—sure, convinced, positive
Antonyms—insecure, shy, fearful

conform
Synonyms—comply, submit, follow
Antonyms—defy, disobey, flout (to go against or disregard)

conformity
Synonyms—compliance, submission
Antonyms—defiance, disobedience

congested
Synonyms—packed, jammed, blocked
Antonyms—empty, free, wide-open

congruent
Synonyms—alike, matching, harmonious (goes well together)
Antonyms—incompatible, mismatched, dissimilar

consensus
Synonyms—agreement, compromise, harmony
Antonyms—difference, disparity, confrontation

consequential
Synonyms—important, major, meaningful
Antonyms—trivial, insignificant

conservative
Synonyms—traditional, old-fashioned, conventional
Antonyms—progressive, adventurous, avant-garde (extremely modern)

constant
Synonyms—steady, persistent, incessant (unceasing)
Antonyms—irregular, occasional

constrain
Synonyms—hold back, restrict, inhibit (to slow down or prevent)
Antonyms—expand, develop, increase

consummate
Synonyms—ideal, perfect, superlative (the best)
Antonyms—inferior, awful, abysmal (very bad)

List of Synonyms and Antonyms

contaminate
Synonyms—pollute, spoil, taint (to spoil or damage)
Antonyms—purify, cleanse

contemporary
Synonyms—modern, up to date, new
Antonyms—old-fashioned, antique

contradict
Synonyms—disagree, oppose, challenge
Antonyms—support, concur (to agree)

conventional
Synonyms—usual, established, typical
Antonyms—uncommon, odd, original

converge
Synonyms—meet, come together, join
Antonyms—diverge, separate

convey
Synonyms—tell, express, communicate
Antonyms—hold back, contain

convoluted
Synonyms—complex, difficult
Antonyms—simple, uncomplicated, straightforward

corroborate
Synonyms—confirm, support, substantiate (to back up with evidence)
Antonyms—contradict, deny, challenge, refute

corrupt
Synonyms—dishonest, shady, crooked
Antonyms—truthful, honest, moral, upstanding

covert
Synonyms—secret, hidden, underground
Antonyms—open, public, exposed

criticize
Synonyms—disparage (to cut down), denigrate (to put down)
Antonyms—praise, commend

culpable
Synonyms—responsible, guilty, at fault
Antonyms—innocent, blameless

curtail
Synonyms—cut back, limit, shorten, restrict
Antonyms—increase, expand, lengthen

D

debased
Synonyms—corrupted, depraved (wicked)
Antonyms—upright, noble, dignified

decisive
Synonyms—determined, conclusive, sure
Antonyms—undetermined, indecisive, irresolute (unsure)

decorous
Synonyms—polite, proper, suitable
Antonyms—indecent, wrong, unsuitable

decry
Synonyms—devalue, disparage (to criticize), demean (to put down)
Antonyms—respect, approve, praise

deficient
Synonyms—lacking, insufficient, not enough
Antonyms—ample, adequate, enough

deficit
Synonyms—deficiency, loss, shortage
Antonyms—excess, surplus, extra

definite
Synonyms—certain, explicit, indubitable (not questionable)
Antonyms—uncertain, questionable, refutable

defy
Synonyms—disregard, flout (to go against)
Antonyms—obey, respect, follow

delete
Synonyms—remove, take away, expunge (to get rid of)
Antonyms—add, build up, create

deleterious
Synonyms—damaging, hurtful, injurious (harmful)
Antonyms—helpful, good for the health, beneficial, harmless

denigrate
Synonyms—malign, impugn, slander (to put down)
Antonyms—encourage, boost, celebrate

deplete
Synonyms—diminish, reduce, use up
Antonyms—fill, increase, enhance

deplore
Synonyms—despise, hate, undervalue
Antonyms—appreciate, accept, value

deprecate
Synonyms—ridicule, disparage (to criticize), denigrate (to put down)
Antonyms—commend, approve, bolster, support

deprive
Synonyms—take away, rob, remove
Antonyms—give, confer, bestow (to give)

desire
Synonyms—want, longing, craving
Antonyms—disinterest, apathy (lack of interest), repulsion (extreme dislike)

desolate
Synonyms—barren, lifeless, devoid (empty)
Antonyms—inhabited, lively, fruitful (productive)

destitute
Synonyms—poor, indigent (without money)
Antonyms—wealthy, secure, prosperous

destroy
Synonyms—eliminate, obliterate (to wipe out), raze (to completely destroy)
Antonyms—build, fix, improve

detach
Synonyms—remove, segregate, separate
Antonyms—join, put together, assemble

deter
Synonyms—stop, halt, hinder
Antonyms—aid, inspire, incite (to promote)

detractor
Synonyms—critic, enemy
Antonyms—supporter, benefactor, friend

detrimental
Synonyms—bad, harmful, unfavorable
Antonyms—positive, helpful, useful

devastate
Synonyms—destroy, wreck, annihilate (to demolish)
Antonyms—save, protect, expand, augment (to add to)

devious
Synonyms—dishonest, evil, duplicitous (scheming)
Antonyms—honest, forthright, righteous

diffuse
Synonyms—spread out, expanded, propagated (spread out)
Antonyms—condensed, confined, succinct (brief)

digress
Synonyms—stray, ramble, deviate (to go off in another direction)
Antonyms—focus, be direct, stay on course

diligent
Synonyms—hard-working, earnest, persistent
Antonyms—thoughtless, careless, lazy

diminish
Synonyms—decrease, dwindle, reduce
Antonyms—prolong, increase, enhance, extend

diminutive
Synonyms—petite, small, short
Antonyms—big, enormous, huge

dire
Synonyms—critical, very important, desperate, grave (serious)
Antonyms—trivial, unimportant, silly

disagree
Synonyms—conflict, go against, dissent (to differ in opinion)
Antonyms—agree, concur (to have the same opinion), acquiesce (to accept without protesting)

discern
Synonyms—recognize, distinguish, perceive
Antonyms—confuse, misunderstand, discombobulate (to confuse)

disclose
Synonyms—tell, expose, reveal, make known
Antonyms—suppress, hide, disavow (to deny)

discomfort
Synonyms—unpleasantness, irritation, pain, anguish (great pain)
Antonyms—comfort, peacefulness, ease

disconcerting
Synonyms—disturbing, unbalancing, upsetting
Antonyms—quieting, calming, comforting

discord
Synonyms—disharmony, conflict
Antonyms—harmony, peacefulness

discrepancy
Synonyms—variation, difference, incongruity (difference)
Antonyms—consistency, sameness, reliability

dismal
Synonyms—bleak, sad, horrible
Antonyms—bright, hopeful, encouraging

dismay
Synonyms—disappointment, discouragement, trepidation (anxiety or fear)
Antonyms—encouragement, security, confidence

dismiss
Synonyms—send away, discard, push aside
Antonyms—permit, allow, keep, maintain

disparage
Synonyms—mock, criticize, belittle (to put down)
Antonyms—lift up, support, encourage, sanction (to support)

disparate
Synonyms—at variance, contrasting, different
Antonyms—similar, invariable, like

disparity
Synonyms—imbalance, gap, inequity
Antonyms—equity, likeness, sameness

dispute
Synonyms—bicker, argue, contend
Antonyms—harmonize, agree, go along with

disruptive
Synonyms—disorderly, disturbing
Antonyms—unifying, peaceful, calming

disseminate
Synonyms—publicize, scatter, radiate, disperse
Antonyms—condense, conceal, hide

List of Synonyms and Antonyms

dissipate
Synonyms—deplete, use up, squander (to waste)
Antonyms—save, preserve, conserve (to save)

distinct
Synonyms—separate, clearly defined, explicit (obvious)
Antonyms—vague, unsure, ambiguous (poorly defined)

distorted
Synonyms—warped, bent out of shape, perverted
Antonyms—straight, pure, invariable

diverge
Synonyms—separate, deviate (to go off course)
Antonyms—converge, join

diverse
Synonyms—dissimilar, different, varied
Antonyms—conforming, uniform, similar

divide
Synonyms—split up, disjoin, partition (to cut up)
Antonyms—join, add, combine

divulge
Synonyms—bring to light, confess, tell
Antonyms—protect, suppress, hide, conceal

dominant
Synonyms—superior, controlling, main
Antonyms—subordinate, inferior, auxiliary (additional)

dominate
Synonyms—rule over, influence, overshadow
Antonyms—follow, submit, acquiesce (to go along with)

dubious
Synonyms—suspicious, doubtful, disputable
Antonyms—reliable, true, unambiguous

duplicitous
Synonyms—two-faced, shady, dishonest
Antonyms—trustworthy, reliable, truthful, honest

durable
Synonyms—rugged, tough, tenacious (persistent)
Antonyms—flimsy, fragile, weak

duress
Synonyms—hardship, suffering, threat
Antonyms—ease, support, peace

E

endure
Synonyms—bear, withstand, suffer, tolerate, cope with
Antonyms—give up, surrender, cave in

effusive
Synonyms—expressive, gushing, unrestrained
Antonyms—reserved, restrained, aloof

egotism
Synonyms—narcissism, self-absorption (focusing only on one's self and one's own desires)
Antonyms—selflessness, compassion, thoughtfulness

elaborate
Synonyms—ornate, refined, complicated
Antonyms—plain, simple, uncomplicated

elated
Synonyms—thrilled, joyful, euphoric (extremely happy)
Antonyms—deflated, melancholy, disappointed

elusive
Synonyms—mysterious, puzzling, baffling (difficult to understand)
Antonyms—clear, understandable, concise (brief and clear)

eminent
Synonyms—prestigious, well-known, illustrious (well-known in a positive manner)
Antonyms—unimportant, ordinary, unknown

emulate
Synonyms—copy, mimic, act like
Antonyms—act independently

encompass
Synonyms—include, circumscribe, encircle
Antonyms—exclude, leave out, remove

enervate
Synonyms—weaken, incapacitate, drain
Antonyms—animate, empower, strengthen

engage
Synonyms—deal with, undertake, employ
Antonyms—avoid, repulse, ignore, fire

engender
Synonyms—incite, provoke, rouse (to move to action)
Antonyms—calm, discourage, hinder (to block or stop), dissuade (to advise against)

enhance
Synonyms—heighten, improve, increase
Antonyms—devalue, weaken, reduce, lessen, undermine (to weaken)

enrich
Synonyms—improve, enhance, aggrandize (to make bigger)
Antonyms—decrease, impoverish (to make poorer)

enthrall
Synonyms—charm, captivate, mesmerize (to capture the attention of)
Antonyms—bore, disgust, repel

eradicate
Synonyms—eliminate, destroy, get rid of
Antonyms—maintain, protect

erratic
Synonyms—irregular, unpredictable, volatile (explosive)
Antonyms—steadfast, predictable, regular

espouse
Synonyms—advocate, defend, support
Antonyms—disallow, reject, forsake (to abandon)

essential
Synonyms—necessary, requisite (required), indispensable (very much needed)
Antonyms—trivial, unnecessary, extra

euphoric
Synonyms—excited, thrilled, very happy
Antonyms—depressed, grieving, sorrowful

exacerbate
Synonyms—embitter, intensify, irritate
Antonyms—calm down, alleviate (to lesson), placate (to please)

exasperate
Synonyms—provoke, rile up, infuriate (to make angry)
Antonyms—mollify (to soothe), tranquilize (to calm down)

exclude
Synonyms—keep out, omit, ostracize (to ban someone from a group)
Antonyms—include, welcome, allow in

exculpate
Synonyms—forgive, excuse, acquit (to free from guilt)
Antonyms—punish, accuse, incriminate (to make appear responsible for a crime)

exempt
Synonyms—not required to, immune
Antonyms—responsible, required to

exonerate
Synonyms—hold blameless, vindicate (to free from guilt), exculpate (to free from guilt)
Antonyms—condemn, convict, hold accountable

expand
Synonyms—enlarge, increase, swell
Antonyms—decrease, minimize, reduce

expansive
Synonyms—all-inclusive, broad, widespread
Antonyms—exclusive, narrow, limited

expedite
Synonyms—quicken, hurry, hasten
Antonyms—delay, slow down, retard

expert
Synonyms—skilled, knowledgeable, experienced
Antonyms—amateur, inept (unskilled), novice (new at something)

extenuate
Synonyms—diminish, lessen
Antonyms—increase, worsen, exacerbate (to make worse)

extol
Synonyms—praise, exalt, acclaim (to rave about)
Antonyms—disapprove, condemn, disparage (to complain about)

extraneous
Synonyms—extra, not needed, unnecessary, irrelevant
Antonyms—vital, relevant

extricate
Synonyms—liberate, free
Antonyms—restrain, involve, constrain (to limit)

extrinsic
Synonyms—foreign, alien, external (outside)
Antonyms—native, natural, inherent (originating from within)

exuberant
Synonyms—cheerful, buoyant (high-spirited), ebullient (full of positive energy)
Antonyms—unenthusiastic, dull, lethargic (slow)

F

fabricate
Synonyms—manufacture, make up, formulate
Antonyms—disassemble, break apart

fallacy
Synonyms—falsehood, lie, deception
Antonyms—truth, fact, reality

fanatic
Synonyms—lunatic, zealot, radical (extremist)
Antonyms—conservative, disinterested party, unbeliever, infidel (non-believer)

fecund
Synonyms—propagating, fertile, fruitful (able to reproduce)
Antonyms—infertile, sterile, barren (unable to have children)

felicitous
Synonyms—appropriate, suitable, apropos (appropriate)
Antonyms—inopportune, poorly-timed, irrelevant

feral
Synonyms—wild, savage, untamed
Antonyms—tamed, mild-mannered, civilized

fervent
Synonyms—sincere, impassioned
Antonyms—unenthusiastic, unfeeling, dispassionate (unmoved)

flagrant
Synonyms—shameless, undisguised, brazen (brash)
Antonyms—obscure, contained, camouflaged (hidden)

List of Synonyms and Antonyms

flamboyant
Synonyms—glamorous, over-the-top, pretentious (showy)
Antonyms—refined, dull, common

forbid
Synonyms—prohibit, disallow, ban
Antonyms—facilitate, advance, admit (to allow)

formal
Synonyms—official, established, conventional
Antonyms—casual, informal, unofficial

forthright
Synonyms—sincere, honest, candid (open and direct)
Antonyms—dishonest, sneaky, lying

fortitude
Synonyms—courage, endurance, tenacity (persistence)
Antonyms—cowardice, laziness

foster
Synonyms—champion, support, nurture
Antonyms—neglect, halt, starve, deprive (to withhold
   support)

fragile
Synonyms—breakable, weak, frail
Antonyms—strong, durable, sturdy, rugged

frenetic
Synonyms—obsessive, overwrought (very upset), maniacal
   (frenzied, like a madman)
Antonyms—normal, balanced, calm

frivolity
Synonyms—whimsicality, silliness, childishness,
   playfulness
Antonyms—seriousness, sternness

frugal
Synonyms—economical, penny-pinching, thrifty
Antonyms—wasteful, spendthrift, lavish

furtive
Synonyms—secretive, clandestine (hidden), stealthy (done
   in a sneaky way)
Antonyms—candid, straightforward, overt (done in an
   obvious way)

futile
Synonyms—pointless, purposeless, trifling (having no
   value)
Antonyms—useful, worthwhile, efficacious (effective)

G

gargantuan
Synonyms—huge, gigantic, enormous
Antonyms—tiny, infinitesimal (infinitely small), minute
   (really small or insignificant)

generate
Synonyms—make, create, produce
Antonyms—end, terminate, destroy

genial
Synonyms—cordial, amiable, kindly (likeable)
Antonyms—disagreeable, unfriendly, surly (gruff)

grandiose
Synonyms—exaggerating, pompous (full of oneself), osten-
   tatious (acting like a "show-off")
Antonyms—humble, lowly, unimposing (humble)

gratuitous
Synonyms—excessive, uncalled for, unnecessary
Antonyms—warranted, necessary, vital

greedy
Synonyms—gluttonous, insatiable (strong desire for selfish
   gain)
Antonyms—generous, giving, satisfied, metered
   (controlled)

gregarious
Synonyms—sociable, outgoing, good-natured
Antonyms—shy, introverted (turning inward to oneself),
   antisocial (unfriendly or aloof)

guileless
Synonyms—truthful, honest, straightforward
Antonyms—cunning, deceitful, tricky

gullible
Synonyms—simple, credulous (easily fooled)
Antonyms—sophisticated, skeptical, incredulous
   (unbelieving)

H

hackneyed
Synonyms—stale, common, trite (something overdone or
   constantly repeated)
Antonyms—original, fresh, authentic

haughty
Synonyms—snotty, narcissistic (focused on the self), arro-
   gant (feeling superior to others)
Antonyms—humble, polite, self-effacing (humble)

heinous
Synonyms—wicked, repugnant (very bad), atrocious (awful)
Antonyms—honorable, wonderful, pleasing

heretic
Synonyms—pagan, unbeliever, iconoclast (one who goes
   against a belief system)
Antonyms—believer, loyalist, adherent (one who follows a
   belief system)

hesitate
Synonyms—pause, defer (to put off), balk (to refuse to move forward)
Antonyms—charge into, perform, hasten (to speed up)

honorable
Synonyms—well-regarded, law-abiding, esteemed (well-respected)
Antonyms—unethical, unjust, corrupt, dishonorable, base (lowly)

hypocrisy
Synonyms—phoniness, fraudulence (fakeness), duplicity (lying)
Antonyms—honesty, sincerity, genuineness

hypothetical
Synonyms—supposed, presumed, guessed
Antonyms—factual, actual, real

I

imitate
Synonyms—copy, mimic (copy), impersonate (to act like someone), emulate (to strive to be like)
Antonyms—differ from, diverge from (to differ from)

immature
Synonyms—childish, infantile (like an infant)
Antonyms—experienced, mature, adult, seasoned (experienced)

impede
Synonyms—block, hinder, stymie (thwart)
Antonyms—facilitate, accelerate, bolster (to support), expedite (to speed up)

impersonate
Synonyms—mimic, copy, imitate (to act like)
Antonyms—differ from

impetuous
Synonyms—hasty, rash (acting with little thought)
Antonyms—cautious, thoughtful, planned

impulsive
Synonyms—unpredictable, erratic (irregular), hasty (acting quickly, without thought)
Antonyms—deliberate, planned, designed (well-thought-out)

inarticulate
Synonyms—stammering, incomprehensible, tongue-tied (not well-spoken)
Antonyms—intelligible, clear, understandable, eloquent (well-spoken)

incisive
Synonyms—clever, acute, sharp (quick-witted)
Antonyms—dull, half-witted, incompetent (not capable)

incompatible
Synonyms—opposite, clashing (conflicting), disparate (different)
Antonyms—suitable, harmonious, simpatico (compatible)

incongruent
Synonyms—unlike, conflicting, inconsistent
Antonyms—alike, equal, analogous (similar)

incontrovertible
Synonyms—irrefutable, unquestionable, sure
Antonyms—questionable, inconclusive, unconvincing

incorporate
Synonyms—include, join, merge, mix
Antonyms—exclude, divide, separate

incriminate
Synonyms—accuse, involve, blame
Antonyms—free, exonerate (to remove from guilt)

indecision
Synonyms—ambivalence, hesitancy, tentativeness
Antonyms—certainty, assurance, decisiveness

independent
Synonyms—self-determining, free, self-sufficient, liberated
Antonyms—dependent

indeterminate
Synonyms—inexact, inconclusive, imprecise (not accurate)
Antonyms—conclusive, definite, irrefutable (certain)

indict
Synonyms—accuse, condemn, blame
Antonyms—hold blameless, exonerate (to excuse), acquit (to find not guilty)

indifference
Synonyms—disinterest, apathy (lack of interest)
Antonyms—concern, involvement, interest

indistinct
Synonyms—poorly defined, murky (unclear), ambiguous (not clearly marked or understood)
Antonyms—obvious, well-defined, discernible (distinct)

induce
Synonyms—motivate, cause, instigate (to set in motion)
Antonyms—hinder, block, impede (to slow or stop), dissuade (to advise against)

inept
Synonyms—unskillful, clumsy, incompetent (not capable), bungling (prone to making mistakes)
Antonyms—skillful, masterful, competent (capable), dexterous (demonstrating skill)

inevitable
Synonyms—unavoidable, impending (happening soon), destined (bound by destiny to happen)
Antonyms—avoidable, unlikely, uncertain

infamous
Synonyms—disreputable (having a bad reputation), notorious (well-known in a negative way)
Antonyms—righteous, noble, goodly

informal
Synonyms—casual, unofficial, unfussy
Antonyms—fussy, formal, stiff (acting in a strict manner)

ingenious
Synonyms—gifted, intelligent, resourceful (clever)
Antonyms—foolish, dumb, dull-witted

inherent
Synonyms—built-in, natural, innate (found naturally within)
Antonyms—acquired, unnatural, learned

inhibit
Synonyms—constrain, suppress, restrain, prevent
Antonyms—assist, encourage, support

inhibited
Synonyms—shy, subdued, reserved (quiet or timid in manner)
Antonyms—outrageous, loud, boisterous (noisy)

initiate
Synonyms—start, begin, inaugurate (to implement)
Antonyms—end, finish, cease (to stop)

initiative
Synonyms—drive, motivation, gumption
Antonyms—idleness, laziness

innocuous
Synonyms—inoffensive, mild, harmless
Antonyms—offensive, shocking, wild

insipid
Synonyms—dull, tedious, boring
Antonyms—exciting, interesting, fun

insolence
Synonyms—crudeness, disrespect, impertinence (lack of respect)
Antonyms—respect, obedience, humility

instigate
Synonyms—start, initiate (to begin), foment (to stimulate to action)
Antonyms—suppress, not allow, dissuade (to advise against)

integrate
Synonyms—put together, merge, harmonize
Antonyms—separate, leave out, cast aside

intimidating
Synonyms—coercive, threatening, compelling
Antonyms—easy-going, non-threatening

intrepid
Synonyms—fearless, courageous, undaunted (unafraid)
Antonyms—cautious, fearful, afraid

inundate
Synonyms—overload, flood, overwhelm
Antonyms—relieve, lessen

invariable
Synonyms—unchanging, consistent, constant, steady
Antonyms—variable, changing, inconsistent, wavering

invigorate
Synonyms—energize, stimulate, enliven
Antonyms—drain, discourage, deflate

invincible
Synonyms—strong, unbeatable, indomitable (unable to be conquered)
Antonyms—weak, downtrodden, conquerable

irate
Synonyms—angry, furious, enraged
Antonyms—calm, peaceful, pacified (soothed)

irrational
Synonyms—illogical, nonsensical
Antonyms—rational, logical, sensible

irregular
Synonyms—variable, unsteady, inconsistent, unusual, variegated (full of variety)
Antonyms—regular, steady, predictable, consistent, normal, uniform

irresolute
Synonyms—uncertain, undecided, indecisive
Antonyms—resolute, certain, decisive

irritate
Synonyms—annoy, upset, aggravate
Antonyms—please, soothe, placate (to make happy)

J

jeopardize
Synonyms—endanger, threaten
Antonyms—protect, support, empower

jovial
Synonyms—happy, upbeat, good-natured
Antonyms—cranky, grumpy, glum (sullen)

judicious
Synonyms—thoughtful, cautious, prudent (wise)
Antonyms—reckless, ill-considered, imprudent (unwise)

K

keen
Synonyms—sharp, quick, astute (smart)
Antonyms—dull, slow, unintelligent

L

laborious
Synonyms—difficult, hard, demanding
Antonyms—easy, relaxed, undemanding

lackluster
Synonyms—dull, boring, uninteresting
Antonyms—brilliant, captivating, interesting

lament
Synonyms—mourn, regret, grieve
Antonyms—celebrate

languid
Synonyms—slow, sluggish, weak
Antonyms—energetic, vital, strong

languish
Synonyms—droop, decline, suffer
Antonyms—thrive, grow, flourish (to grow)

latent
Synonyms—unexpressed, inactive, hidden, undeveloped
Antonyms—expressed, active, actualized, developed

lavish
Synonyms—extravagant, posh, opulent (abundant)
Antonyms—poor, bare, understated, low-key

lax
Synonyms—relaxed, loose, permissive, lenient (not strict)
Antonyms—strict, tight, rigid

lazy
Synonyms—unmotivated, unenergetic, indolent (avoiding work)
Antonyms—driven, energetic, hardworking, industrious

legitimate
Synonyms—actual, real, verified (shown to be true)
Antonyms—illegitimate, false, fake, unreal

lenient
Synonyms—allowing, permissive, forgiving, lax (not strict)
Antonyms—strict, rigid, restrictive, punishing

lethargic
Synonyms—slow, lazy, sluggish, inactive
Antonyms—quick, energetic, vital, active

liability
Synonyms—obligation, debt, weakness, disadvantage
Antonyms—asset, strength, advantage

linger
Synonyms—stay, loiter, delay
Antonyms—leave, flee, rush, expedite (to hurry)

livid
Synonyms—angry, irate, furious
Antonyms—calm, pleased, contented

lofty
Synonyms—high, ambitious, pretentious (showy)
Antonyms—low, lowly, meager (very poor or not enough)

loquacious
Synonyms—talkative, chatty, wordy, garrulous (talkative)
Antonyms—silent, unresponsive, concise (brief), taciturn (unexpressive), terse (short)

lucid
Synonyms—clear, understandable, rational
Antonyms—unclear, muddled, confusing

M

malevolence
Synonyms—hatred, ill will, malice (intent to harm)
Antonyms—goodness, kindness, benevolence (good will)

malingering
Synonyms—lazy, shirking (avoiding duties)
Antonyms—hardworking, industrious

malignant
Synonyms—harmful, dangerous
Antonyms—beneficial, harmless, benign (not harmful)

malleable
Synonyms—changeable, bendable, pliable (easy to bend)
Antonyms—unchangeable, inflexible, rigid

mature
Synonyms—full-grown, developed, ripe
Antonyms—immature, undeveloped, underdeveloped

mediocre
Synonyms—unimpressive, ordinary, average, so-so
Antonyms—impressive, extraordinary, excellent, stellar (outstanding)

mercurial
Synonyms—ever-changing, unpredictable, fickle (not loyal), capricious (quick to change)
Antonyms—steady, constant, predictable

meticulous
Synonyms—neat, careful, detailed, precise (accurate)
Antonyms—messy, sloppy, imprecise (lacking accuracy)

misconception
Synonyms—misunderstanding, misperception, false belief
Antonyms—fact, truth

mitigate
Synonyms—reduce, lessen, relieve
Antonyms—worsen, exacerbate (to make more severe)

moderate
Synonyms—mild, medium, average
Antonyms—extreme, excessive, intense

List of Synonyms and Antonyms

modicum
Synonyms—bit, tidbit, morsel (a tiny amount)
Antonyms—load, large amount

mollify
Synonyms—soothe, calm, pacify (to calm)
Antonyms—enrage, aggravate, irritate, anger

moribund
Synonyms—dying, ending, declining, terminal (at the end)
Antonyms—vital, thriving, alive, living

morose
Synonyms—negative, dark, sullen (gloomy)
Antonyms—positive, happy, cheerful

mundane
Synonyms—ordinary, commonplace, everyday
Antonyms—extraordinary, unique, original

munificent
Synonyms—generous, lavish, liberal (giving freely)
Antonyms—stingy, miserly, withholding

mutable
Synonyms—changeable, flexible, malleable (able to be changed)
Antonyms—inflexible, rigid, steadfast

N

naive
Synonyms—innocent, trusting, newcomer
Antonyms—experienced, sophisticated

narcissistic
Synonyms—self-absorbed, conceited, selfish
Antonyms—generous, altruistic (helping others)

nebulous
Synonyms—vague, unclear
Antonyms—precise, specific, well-defined

neglect
Synonyms—forget, abandon, overlook
Antonyms—nurture, care for, foster

nemesis
Synonyms—arch enemy, opponent, adversary
Antonyms—best friend, collaborator, ally (friend)

nocturnal
Synonyms—nighttime, vampirish
Antonyms—daytime, diurnal (during the day)

nonchalant
Synonyms—casual, relaxed, laid-back
Antonyms—formal, stiff, uptight

notorious
Synonyms—disreputable (having a bad reputation), infamous (well-known for a bad reason)
Antonyms—unknown, unfamiliar, unheard of

novel
Synonyms—new, unique, imaginative
Antonyms—ordinary, everyday, unoriginal

novice
Synonyms—beginner, trainee, neophyte (new learner)
Antonyms—expert, authority, professional

nurture
Synonyms—care for, foster, protect
Antonyms—neglect, abandon, ignore, harm

O

objective
Synonyms—fair, unbiased, open-minded
Antonyms—prejudiced, partial, subjective (biased)

obliterate
Synonyms—demolish, eliminate, eradicate (wipe out)
Antonyms—assemble, build, create

oblivious
Synonyms—unresponsive, unaware, forgetting
Antonyms—mindful, conscious, alert

obscure
Synonyms—unknown, minor, unseen
Antonyms—famous, prominent, recognized

obsolete
Synonyms—outdated, irrelevant, archaic (old)
Antonyms—contemporary, current, trendy, modern

obstinate
Synonyms—stubborn, headstrong, obdurate (stubborn), tenacious (determined)
Antonyms—obedient, yielding (giving in), accommodating (eager to please others)

obtrusive
Synonyms—obvious, prominent, blatant (highly noticeable)
Antonyms—ordinary, unremarkable, inconspicuous (unnoticeable)

occlude
Synonyms—block, obstruct, impede (to hold back)
Antonyms—assist, facilitate, ease

omnipotent
Synonyms—supreme, invincible (unstoppable)
Antonyms—powerless, weak, helpless

onerous
Synonyms—burdensome, tedious (repetitive and boring), arduous (difficult and demanding)
Antonyms—easy, effortless, trouble-free

opinionated
Synonyms—inflexible, unbending, dogmatic (having rigid opinions)
Antonyms—mellow, easygoing, laid-back

opponent
Synonyms—rival, foe, challenger
Antonyms—friend, colleague, teammate, ally (friend)

opportune
Synonyms—well-timed, advantageous (helpful)
Antonyms—inconvenient, unfortunate

optimistic
Synonyms—hopeful, positive, sanguine (confident)
Antonyms—pessimistic, gloomy

opulent
Synonyms—lavish, luxurious, sumptuous (expensive)
Antonyms—inadequate, meager (very poor or not enough), impoverished (poor)

ordinary
Synonyms—common, usual, regular, normal
Antonyms—extraordinary, exceptional, unique

ornate
Synonyms—lavish, bejeweled, adorned (decorated)
Antonyms—plain, simple, basic

orthodox
Synonyms—conventional, mainstream, usual
Antonyms—innovative, pioneering, ground-breaking

ostentatious
Synonyms—flashy, flamboyant, pretentious (showy)
Antonyms—modest, down-to-earth, humble

ostracize
Synonyms—banish, ignore, cast out
Antonyms—welcome, include, embrace

overt
Synonyms—open, unconcealed, blatant (obvious)
Antonyms—hidden, covert (concealed), clandestine (secret)

P

parched
Synonyms—dry, dehydrated, waterless
Antonyms—wet, saturated, drenched

pariah
Synonyms—outcast, untouchable, exile
Antonyms—insider, hero, idol

passion
Synonyms—enthusiasm, zeal, delight
Antonyms—indifference, apathy (lack of interest)

passive
Synonyms—sluggish, lifeless, inert (inactive)
Antonyms—active, lively, energetic

pathetic
Synonyms—pitiful, wretched, lame
Antonyms—admirable, excellent, worthy

penitent
Synonyms—sorry, apologetic, contrite (sorry)
Antonyms—unrepentant, shameless, unremorseful

perceptive
Synonyms—insightful, observant
Antonyms—insensitive, oblivious (unaware)

perish
Synonyms—die, pass away, expire
Antonyms—live, survive, endure

perplexing
Synonyms—puzzling, bewildering, mystifying
Antonyms—simple, effortless, trouble-free, clear, understandable

persevere
Synonyms—persist, continue, keep on
Antonyms—quit, surrender, give up

perturb
Synonyms—annoy, disturb, bother
Antonyms—please, delight, gratify (make happy)

pervasive
Synonyms—omnipresent, all-encompassing (found everywhere)
Antonyms—contained, limited

pessimistic
Synonyms—gloomy, negative
Antonyms—optimistic, hopeful

pious
Synonyms—religious, reverent
Antonyms—disrespectful, heretical (going against established beliefs)

placate
Synonyms—soothe, pacify, appease (to calm down)
Antonyms—enrage, anger, infuriate (to anger)

placid
Synonyms—calm, peaceful, easygoing
Antonyms—anxious, stressed, agitated (upset)

plausible
Synonyms—believable, possible, likely
Antonyms—improbable, far-fetched, questionable

popular
Synonyms—appealing, well-liked, admired
Antonyms—disliked, ill-favored, unpopular

potent
Synonyms—powerful, strong, effective
Antonyms—weak, unsuccessful, incapable

practical
Synonyms—useful, sensible, no-nonsense
Antonyms—unrealistic, unreasonable, impractical

List of Synonyms and Antonyms

precede
Synonyms—lead, go before
Antonyms—follow, trail

predatory
Synonyms—aggressive, rapacious (out to kill)
Antonyms—harmless, passive (inactive)

predominant
Synonyms—major, principal, most common
Antonyms—secondary, insignificant

pretentious
Synonyms—showy, conceited, self-important
Antonyms—practical, down-to-earth, humble

privilege
Synonyms—advantage, benefit
Antonyms—disadvantage, drawback, shortcoming

procrastinate
Synonyms—postpone, delay
Antonyms—advance, proceed, progress, hurry

proficient
Synonyms—skilled, talented, capable
Antonyms—incompetent, clumsy, inept (unskilled)

proliferate
Synonyms—increase, flourish, spread, thrive (to do well)
Antonyms—reduce, diminish, dwindle

propagate
Synonyms—spread, transmit, publicize
Antonyms—suppress, hold back

propensity
Synonyms—tendency, inclination, penchant (tendency)
Antonyms—reluctance, aversion (dislike)

proponent
Synonyms—supporter, advocate, fan
Antonyms—opponent, foe, antagonist (enemy)

propriety
Synonyms—respectability, politeness
Antonyms—rudeness, discourtesy

prosaic
Synonyms—dull, ordinary, commonplace
Antonyms—inspiring, stirring, exciting

prosperous
Synonyms—wealthy, affluent, abundant
Antonyms—unsuccessful, disadvantaged

proximity
Synonyms—closeness, convenience, nearness
Antonyms—distance, remoteness

prudent
Synonyms—wise, cautious, practical
Antonyms—foolish, risky, reckless

punitive
Synonyms—penalizing, disciplinary, retaliatory (punishing)
Antonyms—rewarding, incentivizing, inducing (encouraging), enticing (tempting)

purify
Synonyms—cleanse, distill, filter, sanitize
Antonyms—soil, pollute, muddy

Q

quell
Synonyms—crush, defeat, conquer, suppress
Antonyms—incite, provoke, inflame, encourage

querulous
Synonyms—difficult, irritable, argumentative, cantankerous (argumentative)
Antonyms—amiable, friendly, good-natured, genial (likeable)

quarrelsome
Synonyms—querulous, cranky, grouchy, bad-tempered
Antonyms—affable, likable, good-humored, kind

quiescent
Synonyms—quiet, sluggish, passive (inactive), dormant (inactive)
Antonyms—active, lively, energetic, vigorous

R

random
Synonyms—accidental, haphazard, chance, casual
Antonyms—predictable, intentional, planned, on purpose

rational
Synonyms—sane, normal, coherent (makes sense)
Antonyms—unreasonable, absurd, illogical

rebut
Synonyms—deny, disprove, invalidate
Antonyms—accept, believe, recognize, support

recede
Synonyms—ebb, diminish, draw back
Antonyms—advance, press forward, progress

reclusive
Synonyms—isolated, solitary, withdrawn
Antonyms—outgoing, friendly, sociable

reconcile
Synonyms—reunite, resolve, bring together
Antonyms—separate, split, break up

recuperate
Synonyms—recover, get well, improve
Antonyms—decline, weaken, deteriorate (to get worse)

refined
Synonyms—polished, developed, cultivated
Antonyms—coarse, crude, rough

remedy
Synonyms—cure, restore, fix
Antonyms—worsen, aggravate, exacerbate (make worse)

remorse
Synonyms—guilt, sorrow, regret, shame
Antonyms—indifference, hard-heartedness, pride

remote
Synonyms—distant, isolated, far
Antonyms—close, nearby

renovate
Synonyms—renew, refresh, repair
Antonyms—demolish, destroy

renounce
Synonyms—reject, abandon, deny
Antonyms—accept, embrace

replete
Synonyms—full, stuffed, plentiful
Antonyms—hungry, empty, bare

reprehensible
Synonyms—criminal, wicked, disgraceful
Antonyms—honorable, noble, praiseworthy

repress
Synonyms—restrain, control, suppress, stifle (to hold back)
Antonyms—express, release, free (to let go)

reputable
Synonyms—trustworthy, dependable, respectable, legitimate
Antonyms—questionable, shady, dishonest

resilient
Synonyms—flexible, elastic, rebounding
Antonyms—rigid, unyielding, stiff

resplendent
Synonyms—dazzling, magnificent, glorious, stunning
Antonyms—unimpressive, ordinary, forgettable

restrain
Synonyms—control, confine, hold back
Antonyms—free, release, liberate

retain
Synonyms—keep, save, preserve
Antonyms—discard, throw away, let go

revere
Synonyms—admire, respect, esteem (to regard highly)
Antonyms—disapprove, dislike, object to

robust
Synonyms—healthy, strong, vigorous
Antonyms—weak, feeble, frail

routine
Synonyms—usual, ordinary, normal
Antonyms—exceptional, uncommon

rupture
Synonyms—break, burst, rip open
Antonyms—heal, mend, repair

S

sagacious
Synonyms—wise, shrewd, learned, perceptive
Antonyms—foolish, thoughtless, irrational

saturate
Synonyms—soak, flood, inundate (to overwhelm)
Antonyms—dehydrate, desiccate (to dry)

scrutinize
Synonyms—examine, inspect, analyze
Antonyms—ignore, disregard, overlook

secrete
Synonyms—conceal, hide, stash
Antonyms—reveal, disclose, divulge (to reveal)

sedentary
Synonyms—inactive, immobile, lethargic (slow)
Antonyms—active, lively, energetic

sequential
Synonyms—in order, chronological (sorted by time)
Antonyms—disordered, chaotic, random

serene
Synonyms—calm, peaceful, tranquil
Antonyms—busy, lively, hectic

skeptical
Synonyms—doubtful, unconvinced, disbelieving
Antonyms—persuaded, converted, won over

solace
Synonyms—comfort, support, relief
Antonyms—irritation, annoyance, hurt

soporific
Synonyms—dull, sleep-inducing, monotonous (boring)
Antonyms—stimulating, exciting, lively, energizing

sparse
Synonyms—limited, scarce, inadequate, scant (a small amount)
Antonyms—abundant, plentiful, profuse (in good supply)

spontaneous
Synonyms—unplanned, spur-of-the-moment, impromptu (unplanned)
Antonyms—structured, deliberate, premeditated (planned)

squander
Synonyms—waste, spend, misuse
Antonyms—save, keep, conserve (to save)

List of Synonyms and Antonyms

stagnant
Synonyms—still, inactive, inert (not active)
Antonyms—moving, mobile, dynamic

sterile
Synonyms—antiseptic, disinfected, sanitary
Antonyms—contaminated, dirty, soiled

stimulate
Synonyms—encourage, motivate, inspire
Antonyms—discourage, dampen, stifle (to hold back)

strenuous
Synonyms—taxing, straining, demanding, arduous (difficult)
Antonyms—easy, effortless, painless

strict
Synonyms—firm, exacting, rigorous
Antonyms—lenient, relaxed, easygoing

submissive
Synonyms—obedient, passive (inactive), compliant (willing to obey)
Antonyms—assertive, pushy, aggressive

substantial
Synonyms—considerable, extensive, sizeable, significant
Antonyms—minor, insignificant, limited

substantiate
Synonyms—verify, prove, corroborate (to prove)
Antonyms—disprove, refute, invalidate

subtle
Synonyms—slight, understated, delicate
Antonyms—obvious, noticeable, apparent

sullen
Synonyms—brooding, grim, gloomy
Antonyms—cheerful, smiling, joyful

summon
Synonyms—call, beckon, gather
Antonyms—dismiss, release

superficial
Synonyms—shallow, surface
Antonyms—deep, profound, meaningful

superfluous
Synonyms—extra, surplus (more than is needed)
Antonyms—indispensable, necessary, vital, essential

supply
Synonyms—provide, give, contribute
Antonyms—remove, take away, deprive (to withhold from)

support
Synonyms—maintain, encourage, sustain (to keep going)
Antonyms—abandon, ignore, forsake (to abandon)

suppress
Synonyms—prevent, repress (to hold down), stifle (to hold back), constrain (to limit)
Antonyms—spread, express, distribute

surge
Synonyms—rush, flow, pour, gush
Antonyms—stagnate, stand still, pool (to gather in one place)

surplus
Synonyms—extra, spare, leftover
Antonyms—basic, essential

surreptitious
Synonyms—secret, sneaky, stealthy (sneaky), covert (hidden)
Antonyms—open, honest, direct

surrogate
Synonyms—substitute, replacement, stand-in
Antonyms—real, permanent, genuine

sustain
Synonyms—support, maintain, keep going
Antonyms—quit, stop, give up, abandon

T

tame
Synonyms—domestic, friendly, docile (obedient)
Antonyms—wild, untamed, feral (not domesticated)

tardy
Synonyms—late, slow, delayed
Antonyms—prompt, punctual, timely

tedious
Synonyms—boring, dull, dreary, monotonous (boring)
Antonyms—interesting, motivating, fascinating

temperate
Synonyms—moderate, pleasant, mild
Antonyms—extreme, severe, intense

temperamental
Synonyms—unpredictable, moody, volatile (explosive)
Antonyms—reliable, dependable, even-tempered

tenacious
Synonyms—stubborn, persistent, determined
Antonyms—unsure, hesitant, irresolute (undecided)

tentative
Synonyms—cautious, hesitant, uncertain
Antonyms—sure, definite, secure

tenuous
Synonyms—weak, flimsy, fragile
Antonyms—strong, sound, robust (strong)

List of Synonyms and Antonyms

tense
Synonyms—worried, anxious, stressed, uptight
Antonyms—relaxed, calm, tranquil, peaceful

terminate
Synonyms—end, finish, conclude, cease
Antonyms—begin, commence, originate

terse
Synonyms—abrupt, brief, concise (to the point), brusque (abrupt)
Antonyms—rambling, long-winded, wordy

therapeutic
Synonyms—healing, beneficial, helpful
Antonyms—harmful, destructive, unsafe, detrimental (harmful)

tolerant
Synonyms—broadminded, understanding, forbearing (patient)
Antonyms—intolerant, unforgiving, rigid, impatient

toxic
Synonyms—poisonous, deadly, lethal (deadly)
Antonyms—harmless, safe

tranquil
Synonyms—peaceful, calm, relaxing, serene (peaceful)
Antonyms—noisy, chaotic, frenzied

transgression
Synonyms—wrongdoing, disobedience, offense
Antonyms—good deed, kindness, favor

transient
Synonyms—temporary, brief, fleeting, short-lived
Antonyms—permanent, lasting, eternal, enduring

translucent
Synonyms—clear, transparent, see-through
Antonyms—opaque, dense, thick

treacherous
Synonyms—unsafe, dangerous, hazardous, perilous (dangerous)
Antonyms—harmless, safe, risk-free

trepidation
Synonyms—fear, anxiety, apprehension (fear)
Antonyms—composure, level-headedness, equanimity (calmness)

trivial
Synonyms—minor, insignificant, petty, negligible (not important)
Antonyms—crucial, essential, important, necessary, vital

truncate
Synonyms—shorten, abbreviate, trim
Antonyms—lengthen, extend, elongate (to make longer)

turbulent
Synonyms—chaotic, confused, tumultuous (in turmoil)
Antonyms—orderly, calm

U

unheralded
Synonyms—unannounced, unpredicted, unexpected
Antonyms—forecasted, foretold, expected

uniform
Synonyms—unchanging, unvarying, standardized, homogeneous (the same)
Antonyms—different, dissimilar, unlike, diverse (different)

unpalatable
Synonyms—unpleasant, distasteful, disagreeable
Antonyms—enjoyable, pleasing, satisfying

unparalleled
Synonyms—matchless, unequaled, incomparable, supreme
Antonyms—common, ordinary, everyday, regular

unstinting
Synonyms—generous, giving
Antonyms—stingy, tightfisted

untenable
Synonyms—indefensible, unreasonable
Antonyms—justifiable, understandable

utilitarian
Synonyms—useful, practical, functional
Antonyms—ineffective, nonfunctional

utopian
Synonyms—perfect, ideal
Antonyms—problematic, flawed

V

vague
Synonyms—unclear, hazy, indistinct (not clear)
Antonyms—definite, distinct, evident (clear)

valid
Synonyms—legitimate, reasonable, sensible
Antonyms—invalid, illegitimate, unsound, fallacious (not true)

validate
Synonyms—confirm, approve, certify, authorize
Antonyms—invalidate, cancel, disapprove, deny

valid
Synonyms—authentic, legal, legitimate, official
Antonyms—invalid, worthless, void (not valid)

verdant
Synonyms—green, lush, luxuriant
Antonyms—bare, stripped, withered

List of Synonyms and Antonyms

versatile
Synonyms—adaptable, resourceful, multitalented
Antonyms—limited, narrow, restricted

vex
Synonyms—annoy, pester, irritate, exasperate (frustrate)
Antonyms—please, satisfy, calm

virtuoso
Synonyms—expert, master, ace, whiz
Antonyms—amateur, beginner, dabbler, hobbyist

viscous
Synonyms—thick, sticky, gluey
Antonyms—thin, runny

vitality
Synonyms—energy, liveliness, durability
Antonyms—weariness, sluggishness, lethargy (lack of energy)

vital
Synonyms—essential, fundamental, crucial
Antonyms—unimportant, insignificant, trivial

vivacious
Synonyms—lively, cheerful, spirited
Antonyms—slow, languid (lacking energy), lethargic (slow)

vivid
Synonyms—bright, vibrant, colorful
Antonyms—dull, dreary, faded, lackluster (dull)

volatile
Synonyms—explosive, unpredictable, unstable
Antonyms—calm, placid (calm), inert (inactive)

voluntary
Synonyms—unpaid, honorary, pro bono (done without pay)
Antonyms—paid, compensated, remunerated (paid)

vulnerable
Synonyms—unprotected, in danger, at risk
Antonyms—secure, protected

W

wane
Synonyms—diminish, decline, fade
Antonyms—increase, develop, wax (to fade or decline)

waver
Synonyms—hesitate, fluctuate, vacillate (to be indecisive)
Antonyms—decide, resolve, choose

whimsical
Synonyms—fanciful, quirky, eccentric (unusual)
Antonyms—normal, regular, ordinary

wordy
Synonyms—rambling, long-winded, verbose (full of words)
Antonyms—concise (brief), taciturn (quiet), reticent (quiet)

Y

youthful
Synonyms—young, vigorous, vital
Antonyms—aged, decrepit (old), infirm (ill)

Z

zealous
Synonyms—eager, passionate, fervent (full of passion)
Antonyms— bored, lethargic (slow), listless (lacking energy)

zeal
Synonyms—enthusiasm, passion, eagerness
Antonyms—disinterest, indifference, apathy (lack of interest)

Math Formulas for Memorization

Perimeter

Add the lengths of the sides.

Square

$P = 4s$

Rectangle

$P = 2l + 2w$

Triangle

$P = s_1 + s_2 + s_3$

Circle (circumference)

$C = \pi d$ or $2 \pi r$

Area

Always express volume in square units. Multiply the length by the width.

Square

$A = s^2$

Rectangle

$A = bh$

Triangle

To find the area, multiply the length by the width, and divide by 2.

$A = \frac{1}{2} bh$

Circle

$A = \pi r^2$

Math and Geometry Formulas

Volume

Always express volume in cubic units.

Cube

$V = s^3$

Rectangle

$V = lwh$

Cylinder

$V = \pi r^2 h$

Angles

Straight line = 180°

Triangle = 180°

Rectangle = 360°

Square = 360°

Circle = 360°

Polygon = $(n-2)180°$ where n = # of sides

Pythagorean Theorem

$a^2 + b^2 = c^2$

Percent Change

$$\frac{\% \text{ change}}{100} = \frac{\text{difference}}{\text{original \#}}$$

Percent to Decimal

$25\% = \frac{25}{100} = 0.25$

Reverse for Decimal to Percent

Percent to Fraction

$25\% = \frac{25}{100} = \frac{1}{4}$

Reverse for Fraction to Percent

Distance/Rate/Time

To find distance, use $D = RT$ (Distance = Rate × Time)

To find rate, use $R = \frac{D}{T}$ (Rate = Distance ÷ Time)

To find time, use $T = \frac{D}{R}$ (Time = Distance ÷ Rate)